BLOOM'S PERIOD STUDIES

BLOOM'S PERIOD STUDIES

The Italian Renaissance

Edited and with an introduction by
Harold Bloom
Sterling Professor of the Humanities
Yale University

CHELSEA HOUSE
PUBLISHERS
A Haights Cross Communications Company
Philadelphia

WALLINGFORD PUBLIC LIBRARY
WITHDRAWN
200 NORTH MAIN ST
WALLINGFORD, CT 06492

YA
945.05
ITA

©2004 by Chelsea House Publishers, a subsidiary of
Haights Cross Communications.

A Haights Cross Communications ✦ Company

Introduction © 2004 by Harold Bloom.

All rights reserved. No part of this publication may be
reproduced or transmitted in any form or by any means
without the written permission of the publisher.

Printed and bound in the United States of America.
10 9 8 7 6 5 4 3 2 1

Library of Congress Cataloging-in-Publication Data

The Italian Renaissance / Harold Bloom.
      p. cm. — (Bloom's period studies)
   Includes bibliographical references.
   ISBN 0-7910-7895-7
   1. Italy—Civilization—1268-1559—Juvenile literature. 2.
Renaissance—Italy—Juvenile literature. I. Bloom, Harold. II. Series.
   DG445.I765 2004
   945'.05—dc22

                                                    2004003797

Contributing Editor: Brett Foster

Cover designed by Keith Trego

Layout by EJB Publishing Services

Contents

Editor's Note

My Introduction meditates upon Petrarch, whose lyric achievement can be judged to be the starting-point of Italian Renaissance literature. Petrarch's swerve from Dante to erotic "idolatry" inaugurates something of a secular spurt in what was to follow him.

The culture of Renaissance Florence is seen by Gene A. Brucker as a movement from the communal to the private sphere, while J.G.A. Pocock finds in Republican Venice an involuntary apotheosis of Machiavellianism.

Eugenio Garin sets the interpretive frame for Petrarch's humanism, after which the great scholar Paul Oskar Kristeller charts the transition away from Scholasticism.

A movement towards the reduction of women into aesthetic objects is argued by Joan Kelly, while a pluralism of male worldviews is sketched by Peter Burke.

The underlying growth of a sense of Italian unity in the Renaissance is intuited by Denys Hay, after which Carla Freccero examines the political aesthetic of Castiglione's *Courtier*.

Machiavelli's *Prince*, with its ironical allegory, is analyzed by Victoria Kahn, while Brian Richardson recounts the effects of printing upon the writers.

Francis Ames-Lewis defines some relations of text to image in early Renaissance Art, and John M. Najemy returns us to the complexities of politics in Florence.

Tasso's poetic greatness is splendidly illuminated by David Quint, after which the equal eminence of Ariosto is slyly demonstrated by Alberto Casadei.

HAROLD BLOOM

Introduction

Idolatry, however repugnant to an Augustinian moralist, is at the linguistic level the essence of poetic autonomy. Because language and desire are indistinguishable in a literary text, we may say that by accusing his persona of an idolatrous passion Petrarch was affirming his own autonomy as a poetic creator.　　　　　　　　—JOHN FRECCERO

The anguish of contamination (or anxiety of influence) no longer seems to me a particularly modern (or Romantic) malady. Jeremiah the prophet shadows the poet of the Book of Job, Jesus Ben Sirach in his Ecclesiasticus is haunted by Ecclesiastes (Koheleth), and Aristophanes savagely mauls Euripides for his misprisions of Aeschylus. If we add Plato's agon with Homer, and the Gnostics' sense of belatedness in regard both to Plato and the Hebrew Bible, then we have a considerable catalog of ancient literary sorrows.

Petrarch's relation to Dante is enormously complex and difficult to judge, partly because Petrarch's own influence upon poetry after him was so great that it veils everything that is problematical in Petrarch's over-whelming originality. Each strong poet strives to make himself seem more different from his central precursor than he actually is, and Petrarch's strong misreading of Dante, implicit in Petrarch's own poetry, has affected us more than we can know, particularly in helping to present some among us with a Dante wholly given over to the allegory of the theologians, and so apparently altogether free of idolatrous or Petrarchan passion, at least in the *Commedia*. Here Robert M. Durling returns us to the deep affinities between Dante's *rime petrose* and Petrarch's *rime sparse*:

1

To see one's experience in terms of myth is to see in the myth the possibility of the kind of allegorical meaning that was called tropological. Petrarch knew and used freely the traditional allegorical interpretations of the Ovidian myths. But he dissociated them from clear-cut moral judgments, and in this he was closer to the Dante of the *petrose* than of the *Commedia*. To say that falling in love and becoming a love poet is a transformation into a laurel tree involves the sense that the channeling of the vital energy of frustrated love into the sublimated, eternizing mode of poetry has consequences not fully subject to conscious choice or to moral judgment. For Petrarch the perfection of literary form, which exists polished and unchanging on the page in a kind of eternity, is achieved only at the cost of the poet's natural life. His vitality must be metamorphosed into words, and this process is profoundly ambiguous. If on the one hand Petrarch subscribes to—even in a sense almost single-handedly founds—the humanistic cult of literary immortality and glory, on the other hand he has an acute awareness that writing poetry involves a kind of death. This recognition has something very modern about it; it gives a measure of the distance that separates Petrarch from Dante, who gambled recklessly on the authority his poem would have as a total integration. Petrarch is always calling attention to the psychologically relative, even suspect, origin of individual poems and thus of writing itself. His hope is that ultimately the great theme of praise will redeem even the egotism of the celebrant.

It is fascinating to me that one could substitute Rilke's name for Petrarch's here, and still retain coherence, particularly if one also substituted Goethe for Dante. What Freccero calls an idolatrous passion (for Laura, for poetry, for literary immortality and glory), Durling calls a kind of death. Both critics are true to Petrarch, and to Rilke, or Yeats, or Wallace Stevens, all of them in a profound sense still Petrarchans. Or perhaps we could say that all of them, like Petrarch himself, come out of the strongest of Dante's stony lyrics, the great sestina "To the Dim Light and the Large Circle of Shade." I give it here in Dante Gabriel Rossetti's piercing version, the best poem that Rossetti ever wrote:

To the dim light and the large circle of shade
I have clomb, and to the whitening of the hills,

There where we see no colour in the grass.
Natheless my longing loses not its green,
It has so taken root in the hard stone
Which talks and hears as though it were a lady.

Utterly frozen is this youthful lady,
Even as the snow that lies within the shade;
For she is no more moved than is the stone
By the sweet season which makes warm the hills
And alters them afresh from white to green,
Covering their sides again with flowers and grass.

When on her hair she sets a crown of grass
The thought has no more room for other lady,
Because she weaves the yellow with the green
So well that Love sits down there in the shade,—
Love who has shut me in among low hills
Faster than between walls of granite-stone.

She is more bright than is a precious stone;
The wound she gives may not be healed with grass:
I therefore have fled far o'er plains and hills
For refuge from so dangerous a lady;
But from her sunshine nothing can give shade,—
Not any hill, nor wall, nor summer-green.

A while ago, I saw her dressed in green,—
So fair, she might have wakened in a stone
This love which I do feel even for her shade;
And therefore, as one woos a graceful lady,
I wooed her in a field that was all grass
Girdled about with very lofty hills.

Yet shall the streams turn back and climb the hills
Before Love's flame in this damp wood and green
Burn, as it burns within a youthful lady,
For my sake, who would sleep away in stone
My life, or feed like beasts upon the grass,
Only to see her garments cast a shade.

How dark soe'er the hills throw out their shade,
Under her summer-green the beautiful lady
Covers it, like a stone covered in grass.

The Lady Pietra degli Scrovigni, sublimely hard-hearted, takes her place with Shakespeare's Dark Lady of the Sonnets as a muse stimulating one of the two greatest Western poets since Homer and the Bible to unprecedented depths of imaginative degradation. Dante, already quester if not yet pilgrim, climbs the high hills, presumably at twilight, or on a winter day, in search of fulfillment, only to find that he is in love with a Medusa. Petrarch's Laura, in one of her aspects, is also a Medusa who transforms her poet into a stone man. Freccero and Durling agree that Petrarch is properly ambivalent about being the object of such a transformation. The ironies of Dante doubtless transcend those of his son Petrarch, but all the ironies of Dante's sestina seem directed against the poet himself, and not against the superbly cruel Pietra, who reduces her lover to the condition of Nebuchadnezzar, feeding like beasts upon the grass. Troubadour love, culminating in the poetry of Arnaut Daniel, emphasized the oxymoronic destructiveness of the obsessive image of the beloved that the poet carried in his head. This is the disaster of a particular moment, the precise time when the poet falls in love, akin to falling in battle. A purely secularized moment so intense is bound to become a confrontation with the Medusa. Here is Poem 30 of the *rime sparse*, a sestina in which Petrarch has the courage to confront Dante's stony sestina:

A youthful lady under a green laurel
I saw, whiter and colder than snow
not touched by the sun many and many years,
and her speech and her lovely face and her locks
pleased me so that I have her before my eyes
and shall always have wherever I am, on slope or shore.

Then my thoughts will have come to shore
when green leaves are not to be found on a laurel;
when I have a quiet heart and dry eyes
we shall see the fire freeze, and burning snow;
I have not so many hairs in these locks
as I would be willing, in order to see that day, to wait years.

But because time flies and the years flee
and one arrives quickly at death

either with dark or with white locks,
I shall follow the shadow of that sweet laurel
in the most ardent sun or through the snow,
until the last day closes these eyes.

There never have been seen such lovely eyes,
either in our age or in the first years;
they melt me as the sun does the snow:
whence there comes forth a river of tears
that Love leads to the foot of the harsh laurel
that has branches of diamond and golden locks.

I fear I shall change my face and my locks
before she with true pity will show me her eyes,
my idol carved in living laurel;
for, if I do not err, today it is seven years
that I go sighing from shore to shore
night and day, in heat and in snow.

Inwardly fire, though outwardly white snow,
alone with these thoughts, with changed locks,
always weeping I shall go along every shore,
to make pity perhaps come into the eyes
of someone who will be born a thousand years from now—
if a well-tended laurel can live so long.

Gold and topaz in the sun above the snow
are vanquished by the golden locks next to those eyes
that lead my years so quickly to shore.

Durling's translation is prose, and attempts to be literal; Rossetti breaks through his own rhetorical sublimations and repressions in the impassioned verse of his Dante translations. Yet, without prejudice to Petrarch (or to Durling), a contrast of Dante's and Petrarch's Italian texts seems to me productive of results remarkably similar to a juxtaposition of Rossetti and Durling. I cannot conceive of a lyric poet more gifted at what I call "poetic misprision" than Petrarch; his sestina is a beautiful evasion of Dante's, yet an evasion whose gestures depend upon the stony sestina of the great precursor. The unifying element in those gestures is their striking and indeed audaciously deliberate idolatry, cunningly analyzed both by Durling and by

Freccero. I wish to add to Durling and Freccero only the speculation that Petrarch's idolatrous gestures, here and elsewhere, are revisionary tropes, figures or ratios intended to widen the distance between Dante and Petrarch. In order to clear a space for his own art, Petrarch overtly takes the spiritual (and aesthetic) risk of substituting idolatry for typology, Laura for Beatrice.

Dante's sestina, if judged by the moral code of the *Commedia*, would condemn its poet to the Inferno, but then that is an overt power of the poem: this is the deep degradation of Dante before his conversion, before his turn (or return) to Beatrice. Still, poetically his degradation is Sublime, and can be said to mark a limit for the erotic Sublime. The obsessive force of his sestina is unmatched and is still productive in our century in poems like the sleepwalker's ballad of Lorca and the laments for barren passion of Yeats. Dante's sestina spares neither the Lady Pietra nor himself. She is stone, not flesh, and utterly frozen, as much a victim of the Medusa as the Medusa herself. You cannot flee from Pietra; her icy sunshine penetrates every covert place, and so allows no shade. She will not take fire for Dante as other ladies do, despite his hyperbolical devotion (or because of it?) and her lovely green is profoundly sinister, because it is the color of Dante's desire, and not nature's green at all. In some dark sense the Lady Pietra is antithetical to Beatrice, so that Dante's passion for her is decidedly idolatrous, anti-Augustinian, and a triumph for the allegory of the poets over the allegory of the theologians.

Petrarch memorializes the seventh anniversary of his falling in love with Laura, which he celebrates as a falling into idolatry, since it is also a falling into poetic strength. Fire indeed will freeze, snow burn, before Petrarch gives up poetry, since poetry alone allows him "to make pity perhaps come into the eyes / of someone who will be born a thousand years from now," a prophecy now two-thirds accomplished in time. All that is idolatrous enough, but Petrarch superbly culminates his sestina by giving scandal, by subverting Psalm 119, which in the Vulgate reads, "I have loved Your commandments above gold and topaz," to which Petrarch replies:

> Gold and topaz in the sun above the snow
> are vanquished by the golden locks next to those eyes
> that lead my years so quickly to shore.

The golden locks of Laura have replaced God's commandments, in a remarkable turn upon Dante's Pietra, whose "curling yellow mingles with the green / so beautifully that Love comes to stay in the shade there." Petrarch has won a victory over Dante's trope, but at the high cost of an idolatry beyond nearly all measure. Dante's response to Petrarch's sestina can be heard proleptically throughout the *Commedia*, which teaches us that what we behold must be the truth, since great or small we gaze into that mirror in which, before we think, we behold our thought. What Petrarch beholds is at once poetry, fame, and death; he does not behold a transcendental truth, or for that matter a demonic one. He asserts a limited authority, because after Dante's extraordinary authority no other sort could be persuasive or authentic. Dante, like Milton, casts a shadow of belatedness over those who come after. Petrarch, whose genius had to flourish just one generation later and whose own father had been a friend of Dante's, exiled from Florence with Dante, chose a gorgeous solipsism as his poetic stance. Call that solipsism idolatry or what you will; Petrarch urges you to do so. As a wager with mortality, such a stance invented lyric poetry as we continue to know it today.

GENE A. BRUCKER

Culture

FOUNDATIONS AND PREMISES

For two centuries, from the age of Dante and Giotto to that of Machiavelli and Michelangelo, Florence was one of Latin Europe's most dynamic and creative centers of intellectual and artistic activity. This chapter will attempt to define the nature of that cultural achievement, and to relate it to the city's institutions and values, and to her experience. Perhaps no problem of historical analysis is so challenging and provocative, and so beset with pitfalls, as the attempt to explain the relationship between social and cultural phenomena. Every student of Florentine history is confronted by these questions: Why was this society so creative, and so receptive to change and innovation? Of all the major Italian cities, why did Florence—and not Milan or Genoa or Venice—achieve the greatest distinction in art and learning during these centuries?

The Florentine contribution to Renaissance culture was not limited to a few specialized areas; it encompassed many fields and disciplines. In painting, sculpture, and architecture, the city's achievement was spectacular. Florentine artisans excelled in a variety of craft activities, from terracotta and metal casting to the weaving of silk brocades. A long tradition of technological skill and innovation lay behind the work of the architect Brunelleschi and the inventor Leonardo da Vinci. In classical studies and in

From *Renaissance Florence.* © 1969 by John Wiley & Sons, Inc. Supplements © 1983 by the Regents of the University of California.

those disciplines—history, poetry, moral philosophy—stimulated by the renewed interest in antiquity, Florentines were preeminent. The city's jurists, physicians, and theologians made significant contributions to their disciplines. The catalogues of the *Biblioteca Nazionale* describe thousands of manuscripts that indicate the broad range of Florentine cultural interests. These include copies of the Villani chronicles and Boccaccio's *Decameron*; French chivalric romances translated into the Italian vernacular; saints' lives and moral tracts; books on medicine and cuisine; Latin classics in the original and in translation. The list of works composed or copied by Florentine hands would be even longer and more diverse if certain categories—for example, heretical literature and occult writings—had not been systematically destroyed.

The ingredients which were fused together into Florence's cultural matrix derived from two distinct sources: the Graeco-Roman-Christian tradition, universal in scope, hierarchical and authoritarian in structure; and the vernacular tradition, which gave expression to the particular attitudes and values of this Tuscan community. The classic-Christian tradition was based upon the Latin language, upon the principles of Roman law, and upon certain philosophical concepts derived from Greek antiquity and reformulated in European monasteries, cathedral schools, and universities during the medieval centuries. This tradition was professional in its orientation; it trained—and imposed its values upon—theologians, lawyers, notaries, rhetoricians. Its educational organs were the grammar schools, the *studia* in the Florentine monasteries, and the universities. The vernacular tradition, on the other hand, was quite flexible and unstructured. Its modes of communication were largely oral and visual; its written form was not yet bound by rules of grammar and orthography. Both of these major traditions were divided into segments or disciplines, each with its educational method, its subject matter, and its professional concerns. From antiquity and the Christian tradition came the legal culture of Florence's lawyers and notaries, the classical culture of her humanists and certain of her artists, and the scholastic culture of her learned priests and monks. The vernacular tradition embraced the mercantile culture of the city's business community, the chivalric culture of her nobility and pseudo-nobility, and a cluster of more obscure subcultures: those of the streets and slums, of the popular heresies (most notably the Fraticelli), and of the occult.

The most distinctive feature of Florentine intellectual life was not its variety and complexity—which was matched, to some degree, by Milan, Venice, and Naples—but rather the unusually close rapport between these cultural traditions. Contributing to this atmosphere of free communication was the social structure, perhaps the most flexible of any major Italian city. But another important factor was the towering figure of Dante Alighieri. The poet represented a crucial stage in the fusion of the universalist, hierarchical ideals of the classic-Christian tradition with the parochial values and interests of the local milieu. In the Florentine schools and *studia* (and perhaps also at the University of Bologna), Dante had absorbed those universal ideals which had been summarized so brilliantly by Thomas Aquinas. The poet wrote scholastic treatises, and he also composed essays praising the Christian virtues. His political ideas, his veneration for the Empire and the values of ancient Rome, were likewise universal and hierarchical. Yet his *Divine Comedy* was written in the local Tuscan dialect, not in Latin. And although this work contains the universal concepts of the classical and Christian traditions, it is also a Florentine poem, replete with the particular values, emotions, and concerns of that community. The poet did not succeed in reconciling all of the contradictions between the two traditions, but his genius enabled him to surmount these discordant elements, and to create a magnificent synthesis combining ideal and reality, the universal and the particular. He also established a lofty standard of excellence, to serve as challenge and inspiration for later generations of Florentine intellectuals.

In the realm of the visual arts, Giotto di Bondone (d. 1337) filled a role similar to Dante's in literature. Giotto's subject matter was traditionally Christian; he learned to paint in the Byzantine style of the thirteenth century. His great contribution to fresco painting was to humanize the wooden, stylized figures of Byzantine art, to create scenes that were naturalistic and lifelike but also grandiose and monumental. His fresco cycle in Padua of Christ's life and the scenes in S. Croce from the life of St. Francis are supreme statements of these qualities in Giotto's art, worthy of comparison with the *Divine Comedy*. Certain attempts have been made to identify the sources of Giotto's inspiration and genius, for example, in the Franciscan emphasis upon Christ's humanity, and the striving for a more intense religious experience. Rather less persuasive is that interpretation which depicts him as a representative of the Florentine bourgeoisie, whose monumental human figures reflect the self-confidence of a rising social class, emancipating itself from subjection to the church and the feudal nobility. Giotto's fame during his lifetime was enormous, although his reputation declined during the second half of the fourteenth century. But his frescoes made a profound impact upon the revolutionary generation of Florentine artists in the early Quattrocento, who recovered Giotto's sense of the monumental, which had disappeared from the Florentine art of the preceding age.

Complexity of social structure, variety of intellectual interests, a history of fruitful intercourse between different traditions—these are some factors which fostered cultural vitality and innovation in Florence. The aristocracy did not merely patronize art and learning; it was actively involved in the city's cultural life. Nearly every prominent family counted a lawyer and a cleric among its number; and by the middle of the fifteenth century, many houses—Strozzi, Corbinelli, Rossi, Medici, Davanzati, Alessandri—could also boast of a humanist scholar. The intellectual interests of many Florentines cut across cultural and disciplinary barriers. Cosimo de' Medici is a good example: banker, statesman, scholar, a friend and patron of humanists (Bruni, Niccoli, Marsuppini, Poggio), artists (Donatello, Brunelleschi, Michelozzo), and learned clerics (Ambrogio Traversari, Pope Nicholas V). The library of a wealthy merchant, Piero di Duccio Alberti, was inventoried in 1400; it contained a large number of business papers and ledgers, a book of hours, several Latin grammars and works by the classical authors Aesop, Cicero, Seneca, Eutropius, and Vigentius. A notary, Ser Matteo Gherardi, died in 1390, leaving a collection of legal treatises (decretals, commentaries, works on canon law), but also a nucleus of religious works (a book of homilies, a psalter, a prayer collection, and a Bible), and the writings of Aesop and Boethius. Lapo Mazzei's letters to Francesco Datini contain references to the Bible and to Christian authors (St. Augustine, St. Bernard, St. Francis, St. Thomas Aquinas), to ancient writers (Cicero, Seneca, Sallust, Horace, Livy, Vergil, Valerius Maximus, Boethius), and to the vernacular works of Dante, Jacopone da Todi, and the Vallombrosan hermit Giovanni dalle Celle. In a treatise on the subject of fortune written about 1460, Giovanni Rucellai incorporated citations from an unusually wide range of classical, Christian, and Italian authors. Aristotle, Epictetus, Sallust, Cicero, Seneca, St. Bernard, Dante, Petrarch, and a Florentine theologian, Leonardo Dati.

Communication between merchants, politicians, artists, and scholars was also facilitated by certain attitudes and conventions, to some degree institutionalized, of this society. Wealthy bankers and poor artisans sat together as equals in the Signoria, a political tradition which must have facilitated intellectual discourse between aristocratic patrons and the sculptors, painters and other craftsmen they employed to build their palaces and decorate their chapels. The open and candid discussions about the problems of cathedral construction (in which bankers, lawyers, friars, and craftsmen participated) also cut across social and professional barriers. Among the citizens invited to counsel the Signoria were men representing all of the major professions and occupations (with the sole exception of theology). These included the lawyers Filippo Corsini, Lorenzo Ridolfi, and Giuliano Davanzati; the physician Cristofano di Giorgio; the humanists Leonardo Bruni, Palla Strozzi, and Agnolo Pandolfini, who were thus provided with an arena for voicing their political opinions and for publicizing ideas and perspectives derived from their disciplines. This forum may have stimulated interest in classical antiquity, and thus contributed to Florence's precocious adoption of humanism as a moral and educational system.

Another device for promoting communication between men of diverse disciplines and cultural interests was the Florentine version of the salon. One of these meetings was described in the *Paradiso degli Alberti* by Giovanni da Prato; other groups gathered around the Augustinian friar Luigi Marsili, the humanist chancellor Coluccio Salutati, and the Camaldolese prior of S. Maria degli Angeli, Ambrogio Traversari. Scholars have also discovered references to an informal gathering which met in the early 1400s under the Tettoio dei Pisani, a pavilion adjacent to the Piazza della Signoria, and another two decades later organized by the Augustinian scholars, Fra Evangelista of Pisa and Fra Girolamo of Naples.

Participants in these *convegni* came from every social class except the lowest, although the majority were either professional scholars and writers, or patricians with strong intellectual interests. Giovanni da Prato's assembly at the Villa Paradiso included himself, the son of a used-clothes dealer who had obtained a law degree at the University of Padua; Marsilio da S. Sophia, a distinguished professor of medicine; Guido, count of Poppi, scion of a noble family in the Casentino; several Florentine patricians—Alessandro Buondelmonti, Giovanni de' Ricci, and Guido del Palagio; and Luigi Marsili as the sole representative of the clergy. Only a few of the "most excellent and highly reputed men of this city" who frequented Marsili's discussions have been identified by name: Coluccio Salutati, Poggio Bracciolini, and three young Florentine patricians interested in classical studies: Niccolò Niccoli, Roberto de' Rossi, and Giovanni di Lorenzo. More patrician and secular in composition was the group of Greek enthusiasts who met with Ambrogio Traversari in the 1420s: Cosimo and Lorenzo de' Medici, Giannozzo Manetti, Leonardo Dati, Ugolino and Filippo Peruzzi, Franco Sacchetti, Bartolomeo Valori, and two friars, Fra Michele and Fra Jacopo Tornaquinci.

One important consequence of this intellectual cross-fertilization was the relatively open and tolerant cultural climate in Florence, in which no single tradition or professional caste became so powerful that it could dominate others. In some parts of Latin Europe (but not in Italy), the church had long maintained a cultural hegemony through its monopoly of education. In Florence and generally throughout the Italian peninsula, secular learning had flourished since the thirteenth century, thus providing an alternative to the schools and intellectual interests of the clergy. Theology was a respected discipline in Florence; it was taught both in the conventual *studia* and in the university. But its appeal was never strong, and it occupied a relatively low place in the hierarchy of Florentine intellectual concerns. Moreover, the church's role as cultural censor was quite firmly restricted by the state. The small number of heresy trials was due less to the orthodoxy of the populace than to the commune's restrictions upon the Inquisition. Supporters of the Fraticelli in the fourteenth century were rarely molested by the authorities, and the execution of a sorcerer condemned by the Inquisition in 1383 aroused widespread opposition. An anonymous chronicler remarked that "there was much discussion in the city, because no inquisitor in Florence had done anything similar for many years, and the bishop and the clergy and many doctors of canon law were opposed to this execution." A century later (1493), when a Franciscan preacher, Bernardino da Feltre, denounced the Florentine government for permitting the Jews to live in the city and engage in usury, he was expelled by the authorities.

In Italy, the most serious threat to cultural pluralism did not come from the church, but rather from the eminence which certain disciplines enjoyed in the universities, most notably in Bologna and Padua. Civil and canon lawyers dominated Bologna's intellectual life, while Padua was the preserve of the natural scientists, students of Aristotelean philosophy. Florence was saved from a similar fate by the chronic weakness of her university. The instruction in Greek offered by Manuel Chrysoloras in the 1390s did stimulate interest in classical studies and contributed to that wave of enthusiasm for the *studia humanitatis* in the Quattrocento. Yet, while humanism became the most potent intellectual force in Florence by the mid-fifteenth century, it did not oust the other disciplines. Nourished by their strong and viable traditions, and by their useful contributions to the community, they continued to thrive.

This analysis of the foundations of Florence's Renaissance culture has emphasized those social and institutional elements which promoted creativity and innovation. Another dimension of the problem is the identification of those particular qualities of mind and personality fostered by the Florentine historical experience. Throughout its history, this community had always existed precariously, and had engaged in perilous enterprises which made heavy demands upon its resources. Much of its wealth derived from participation in an international economy encompassing many markets and regions, and involving great risks. To protect itself, the city extended its control over much of Tuscany and thus aroused the enmity of its neighbors.

Survival in this hostile and dangerous milieu required intelligence, astuteness, and fortitude. Within Florence itself, the competitive atmosphere and the high degree of social and economic mobility also made heavy demands upon the inhabitants. In balance, these pressures were constructive; they induced Florentines to sharpen their wits and to expand their intellectual horizons. These stimuli may also have played a part in the development of particular mental attributes: a sense of quality, and particularly of esthetic quality; and sensitivity to the distinctive, the particular, the unique.

The Florentine sense of quality was a product of the city's craft tradition and the exceptional skills of her artisans. The industrial and craft guilds had developed a system of quality control to protect their trades; every Florentine realized that the maintenance of high standards benefited the city's economy. This appreciation of quality, and a corresponding disdain for the shoddy and the inferior, became a characteristic feature of the Florentine mentality and mode of perception. It is revealed in this letter written by a lawyer, Rosso Orlandi, to a friend in Venice, Piero Davanzati, about a very small problem, the purchase of a piece of cloth:

> I received your letter in which you instruct me to buy and send you twelve yards of good blue cloth. One of my neighbors is a good friend and a cloth expert. First we looked around in the cloth factories, where occasionally one may find some nice remnants at a discount, but we didn't see anything we liked. Then we visited all of the retail shops which sell for cash. It is not their custom to allow buyers to examine and compare the cloth of one shop with that of another. However, we did find a way to examine the finest and most beautiful cloth in each shop, and we also seized the opportunity to compare these pieces side by side. From them all, we chose a cloth from the shop of Zanobi di Ser Gino. There were none that were better woven or more beautifully dyed. Furthermore, the cloth was nearly a foot wider than the others, even after it had been washed and trimmed. Since the Florentine shearers do better work than those in Venice, I have had the cloth washed and trimmed here. When you see it, I believe that you will be pleased with it. You will like it even better after you have worn it for several months; for it is a cloth which will wear extremely well.

The Florentine esthetic sense was derived from this appreciation for quality; it is stamped upon the physical city and upon the rural landscape, fashioned by generations of men who prized beauty. It is revealed too in contemporary writing, for example, in a letter from a banker, Jacopo Pazzi, to his friend Filippo Strozzi in Naples (1464), thanking him for a consignment of gold coins: "They are so beautiful that they give me great pleasure, because I love coins which are well designed; and you know that the more beautiful things are, the more they are cherished." Writing in his diary in the 1460s, Giovanni Rucellai described "the most attractive and pleasing aspects" of his villa at Quarachi, a few miles west of Florence near the Arno. He mentioned the house, the garden planted with fruit trees, the fish pond surrounded by fir trees, and another wooded grove at the edge of the garden adjacent to the road. "This park is a source of great consolation," Rucellai wrote, "not only to ourselves and our neighbors, but also to strangers and travelers who pass by during the heat of summer ... who can refresh themselves with the clear and tasty water.... And no traveler passes who does not stop for a quarter of an hour to view the garden filled with beautiful plants. So I feel that the creation of this park ... was a very worthy enterprise." Also illustrating the Florentine concern for esthetic values is a document in the files of the republic's diplomatic correspondence. During a crucial period of the Milanese war (December 1400), the Signoria wrote to the general of the Camaldolese order concerning the sale of a grove of fir trees which were to be cut down, near the ancient monastery of Camaldoli in the Apennines. Expressing their shock and dismay at this vandalism, the priors reminded the general that the trees had been planted and nourished by his predecessors "for the consolation of the hermits and the admiration of the visitors." Four years later (September 1404) the commune again raised this issue urging the general to cease the despoliation of the monastic patrimony, whose beauty was as pleasing to God as to man.

Florentines were unusually sensitive to physical environment, and they possessed a rare talent for communicating their perceptions. They were also intensely aware of other men: their features and habits, their character, their virtues and vices. This curiosity led them ultimately to develop an introspective interest in themselves. Professor Kristeller has noted that humanist writing is characterized by "the tendency to express, and to consider worth expressing, the concrete uniqueness of one's feelings, opinions, experiences and surroundings...." These qualities are displayed in Latin treatises and letters, and also in the diaries and private correspondence of ordinary Florentines. Even such prosaic documents as tax declarations are frequently couched in very expressive language, as they describe the topography of a hill farm or the antipathetic character of a surly peasant. This appreciation of the concrete, the specific, and the unique was fostered not only by the literature of antiquity, but also by the social and intellectual climate of Renaissance Florence.

CULTURAL PATRONAGE IN RENAISSANCE FLORENCE: STRUCTURES, MOTIVATIONS, TRENDS

Renaissance culture, so the textbooks assert, was subsidized by a new social class, the urban bourgeoisie. Replacing the nobility and the clergy as the dominant group in society, the bourgeoisie also supplanted them in their traditional role as patrons of culture. With the wealth gained from their mercantile, banking, and industrial enterprises, they were able to hire the poets, scholars, and artists whose brilliant achievements brought fame and glory to them and their city. Through these intellectuals and artists, their employees and agents, the bourgeoisie were able to express their own ideals and values. Stated so simply and crudely, this analysis is valid, but it does require elaboration, qualification, and refinement. One must examine the methods and techniques by which this society encouraged and nourished—materially and psychologically—its intellectuals. How was talent recognized and merit rewarded? What were the peculiar and unique opportunities Florence offered for creative achievement? How effectively were the city's intellectual resources exploited, and how much talent was attracted from abroad? Finally, how were changes in the structure and values of the society reflected in different forms of patronage?

Intellectual activity in medieval and Renaissance Florence was predominantly—almost exclusively—functional; it was related to specific vocational and professional purposes, and directed toward the satisfaction of social needs. The educational system was organized to train some boys for mercantile careers and others for professional careers in law, the notarial discipline, medicine, and theology. In his statistical survey of Florence prior to the Black Death, Giovanni Villani cites some interesting figures on school enrollment. In a population of approximately 100,000, between 8000 and 10,000 youths were enrolled in the city's private schools. While the majority attended elementary schools, which taught the rudiments of the vernacular, 1000 advanced students went to special schools to learn the mathematics necessary for a business career, and another 500 enrolled in preprofessional academies which taught Latin grammar, rhetoric, and logic. Although these figures may be inflated, they do indicate the great value attached to education in Florence, and also the unusually high literacy rate, perhaps one-fourth or one-third of the male population. A basic knowledge of reading, writing, and arithmetic was an essential prerequisite for a business career, even in one of the artisan trades. An incident described in the protocols of the Merchants' Court illustrates this recognition of the value of education among the city's underprivileged. A young emigrant from the Perugian *contado*, Antonio di Manno, instituted a lawsuit for the recovery of a gold florin which he had paid in advance for some elementary instruction. Antonio worked as an apprentice in a shoemaker's shop where a fellow employee, Miniato, agreed to teach him reading and writing for a year, but then broke his promise when he left the shop.

The size and quality of Florence's educational system (which included conventual *studia* and a university as well as primary and secondary schools) was one factor in the city's ability to attract talent from abroad. Alongside the institutions which provided formal schooling were the guilds with their system of instruction for apprentices. Young artists like Giotto from the Mugello and Masaccio from S. Giovanni Valdarno came to Florence to study in the workshops of the great masters, to live and work in a stimulating intellectual environment, and to gain wealth and fame in a community which subsidized the arts. The city's attraction for men with professional training is documented by the unending flow of petitions from foreign lawyers, notaries, and physicians who sought Florentine citizenship. In 1381 a young physician, Ugolino of Montecatini, had just begun his professional career in Pisa, where he had a small practice and a lectureship in the university. He was then invited to become the town physician of Pescia in the Valdinievole. The most compelling reason for abandoning his teaching post at Pisa to accept this offer was the opportunity to pursue his medical studies in Florence, to take part in disputations, and to enlarge his experience. Ugolino admitted that the move to Pescia would not redound to his honor, but he believed that it would benefit his career. Apparently, his ultimate goal was to practice medicine in Florence and lecture in the university, but he was realistic about the difficulties confronting him. It required years to build a medical reputation, and then the physician had to endure the jealousy of his colleagues. But Ugolino was willing to accept the challenge of the metropolis, aware that "our profession is one of those influenced by fortune." In 1429, a young Lucchese lawyer, Filippo Balducci, was contemplating a move to Florence from Siena, where he taught and practiced law. To a Florentine acquaintance, he wrote: "Since I have always had a great affection for that magnificent and glorious city, which I consider one of the three [greatest] in the world, I would rather be there than here, even though I will earn less."

Public recognition of distinguished achievement in Florence took various forms. The most tangible mark of distinction was the bestowal of a public office, a university professorship, or an artistic commission upon the meritorious, and these were distributed quite generously to prominent scholars and artists. In 1375, Coluccio Salutati became the first humanist chancellor of the republic; his successors in that office were men of great learning and reputation: Leonardo Bruni, Poggio Bracciolini, Carlo Marsuppini. In 1300, the commune granted a tax exemption to the architect Arnolfo di Cambio, "since this master is the most renowned and the most expert in church construction of any other in these parts; and that through his industry, experience and genius, the Florentine commune ... from the magnificent beginning of this church ... hopes to have the most beautiful and the most honorable cathedral in Tuscany." A century and a half later, Leonardo Bruni and Poggio Bracciolini obtained similar exemptions; Poggio had claimed that "he cannot pay the assessments levied against citizens who have profited from trade and the emoluments of public service, since he plans to devote all of his energies to study...." Although Filippo Brunelleschi obtained no tax exemption from the state, he did receive a rare public acknowledgement of his talent. Described in a provision of June 1421 as a "man of the most perspicacious intelligence and admirable industry," he was granted a three-year patent on a boat he had invented, which apparently reduced the costs of transporting goods on the Arno. In reserving all benefits for this invention to Brunelleschi, the law stated that its objective was to prevent "the fruits of his talents and virtue from accruing to another," and also "to stimulate him to greater activity and even more subtle investigations...."

During his lifetime, Dante Alighieri received no accolades from his native city, but after the poet's death, the Florentines made some belated gestures of apology. Giovanni Villani wrote that "because of the virtues and knowledge and worthiness of this citizen, it seems proper to grant him perpetual memory in our chronicle, even though his own noble works, which he has left to us in writing, bear witness to him and bring renown to our city." Giovanni Boccaccio's appointment (1373) as the commune's official lecturer on the *Divine Comedy* was an unprecedented sign of Dante's exalted reputation. Twenty-three years later, the councils passed a law authorizing the officials in charge of the cathedral to arrange for the return of the bodies of five illustrious Florentines who had died and been buried abroad. Munificent tombs were planned for these men in the cathedral, where no other interments were to be permitted. Four of the charter members of this Pantheon—Dante, Petrarch, Boccaccio, and Zanobi da Strada—were literary men, and the fifth was a distinguished lawyer named Accursius (d. 1260?) who taught for many years in the University of Bologna. This project failed completely, for the guardians of these bodies refused to surrender them. In 1430, the Signoria again appealed to the lord of Ravenna for Dante's remains. "Our people," so the official letter read, "harbor a singular and particular affection for the glorious and undying memory of that most excellent and renowned poet, Dante Alighieri; the fame of this man is such that it redounds to the praise and splendor of our city...."

Not every distinguished citizen remained home to adorn his native city with his talents. Petrarch was never attracted to Florence, nor was Boccaccio an enthusiastic admirer of the city. After 1400, however, the pendulum swung quite decisively in Florence's favor, and during the first half of the Quattrocento, her cultural magnetism was particularly intense. Native artists and writers—Masaccio, Brunelleschi, Ghiberti, Manetti—stayed home and made only brief excursions abroad, while their ranks were supplemented by foreigners: Bruni, Poggio Bracciolini, Gentile da Fabriano. S. Croce, not the cathedral, became Florence's Pantheon, and the tombs in that Franciscan basilica are visual evidence of the magnitude of Florentine genius, and also of the city's inability to retain and exploit that genius fully. Dante, Petrarch, and Boccaccio are still missing, although Dante is commemorated by an ugly modern cenotaph. From an esthetic viewpoint, the two most noteworthy tombs are those of the humanists Bruni and Marsuppini, both of whom received imposing state funerals. Lorenzo Ghiberti, Niccolò Machiavelli, and Michelangelo are all buried in S. Croce, although Michelangelo died where he had lived and worked, in Rome. His body was spirited away to Florence by agents of Duke Cosimo I. Some distinguished Florentines of the Quattrocento are not interred in S. Croce. These include Palla Strozzi, who died in Padua while living in involuntary exile, Leon Battista Alberti, who died in Rome in 1472, and Leonardo da Vinci, who abandoned both Florence and Italy to spend his last years at the French court of Francis I.

The official recognition of intellectual and artistic distinction was one aspect of the collective, public nature of artistic and scholarly patronage in early Renaissance Florence. The great architectural monuments of the fourteenth and fifteenth centuries were supervised by commissions of *operai* selected by the guilds. In 1402, Lorenzo Ghiberti won a commission for the Baptistery doors in a public competition organized by the consuls of the Calimala guild, and judged by a special committee of thirty-four painters, sculptors, and goldsmiths. In the realm of letters and scholarship, official patronage was also important and useful, generally assuming the form of a communal office or a university professorship. The bestowal of the chancellor's office upon distinguished humanists like Salutati and Bruni was a reward for their fame and reputation, as well as payment for services rendered to the republic. By the middle of the fifteenth century, however, public subsidy of culture was declining, and the role of the private patron, and of culture created exclusively for private needs, now assumed greater importance than before. This trend can be charted in two quite different contexts: in the history of the Florentine Studio, and in Medicean patronage of the arts.

The fortunes of the city's major institution of higher learning provide a valuable corrective to the idealized picture of this society as totally committed to intellectual distinction, and willing to make heavy sacrifices to achieve and maintain excellence. From the beginning, Florence's efforts to create a university of the first rank met with very limited success. In 1321, a *studium generale* was established by the commune; it never flourished and ceased to function in the 1330s. But even before the Black Death had run its course, a courageous and imaginative Signoria enacted a decree (August 26, 1348) which authorized the reopening of the Studio, and bravely proclaimed that "from the study of the sciences, the city of Florence will receive an increase in honors and a full measure of wealth...." Although the circumstances of its foundation could not have been less promising, the university did survive and gradually developed a modest reputation. But its existence was never secure, and it limped along on the rather meager resources which the commune grudgingly provided. Records of the deliberations on the university's budget in the 1360s reveal that some citizens doubted whether the school was worth its cost. During its most flourishing Period, in the 1380s, the university operated with a substantial budget of 3000 florins, which paid for a staff of twenty-four Professors. But one consequence of the debilitating wars with Giangaleazzo Visconti was the closing of the university in 1406; it did not reopen again until 1413. Thereafter, its budget was repeatedly cut during the Milanese wars of the 1420s; it was finally reduced to 200 florins in 1426. Four years later, the Studio governors candidly admitted that the university was in a parlous state. "It grieves us sorely," they announced, "that this glorious republic, which has surpassed the rest of Italy and all previous centuries in beauty and splendor, should be surpassed in this one respect by some of our neighboring cities, which in every other way are inferior to us."

This failure of the university to achieve the distinction which its founders and supporters envisaged is perhaps the crucial factor in the reluctance of Florence's ruling class to provide adequate and sustained support. The solid reputations of Bologna and Padua were never really challenged by the Studio, and shrewd politicians may have realized that no amount of money would change that fact. Patrician interests were not affected adversely by the mediocre quality of Studio instruction; wealthy citizens could send their sons to other Italian universities, and particularly to Bologna, to acquire the skills and the degrees needed to further their professional careers. Also contributing to the declining importance of the university was the tendency, in Florence and elsewhere, for humanistic studies—rhetoric, moral philosophy, poetry—to flourish outside of the university. Although these subjects were offered regularly in the Studio, occasionally by such distinguished scholars as Chrysoloras, Filelfo and Marsuppini, most teaching in the humanities occurred in a private context: tutors instructing students in their homes, scholars assembling in monasteries or in private palaces to discuss classical texts. Like other facets of patrician life in Quattrocento Florence, learning and education were becoming more private, aristocratic, and exclusive.

The most renowned institution of higher learning in Florence in the second half of the fifteenth century was not the Studio, but the Platonic Academy, an informal coterie of scholars and students united by an interest in Platonic philosophy. Its leader was Marsilio Ficino, whose translations of Platonic writings were subsidized by the Medici. The Academy had a geographical focus in Ficino's villa at Careggi outside of Florence, but it possessed no formal organization, nor did it provide any regular instruction. Its only scheduled events were irregular lectures by Ficino and occasional banquets and symposia held infrequently at the Careggi villa. Ficino did provide loose and informal guidance to his disciples and to visiting scholars like Pico della Mirandola and Jacques Lefèvre d'Étaples. But the essential qualities of this community were privacy, intimacy, and learning pursued for its own sake, without any concern for vocational or practical benefits.

This shift in the form and object of patronage from the public-corporate to the private sphere also occurred in the plastic arts. Communal and guild patronage was at its height between 1375 and 1425, when the Loggia dei Lanzi and the cathedral dome were built, when guilds were commissioning Baptistery doors and statues for Orsanmichele and erecting new headquarters for themselves. In these decades, too, private subsidy of the arts was largely (although not exclusively) directed toward public enterprises. The first architectural projects financed by Cosimo de' Medici were reconstructions of churches and monasteries: S. Lorenzo, S. Marco, the Badia of Fiesole, and the church of S. Francesco in Bosco in the Mugello. This pattern was sanctioned by tradition, and so too was its collective form, since other families were involved in several of these projects. If only because of his superior resources, Cosimo's voice in these collective enterprises tended to predominate; S. Lorenzo, for example, was finally completed with

Medici money twenty years after the project had been initiated. Cosimo's reluctance to finish this work earlier was apparently due to his unwillingness to appear too bold and ambitious as a patron. His plan to rebuild S. Marco was thwarted when other families with burial rights in the convent refused to surrender them.

Despite these limitations imposed upon Cosimo's patronage by community sentiment and tradition, and by his own sense of propriety, his total contribution was impressive. His greatest achievement was, of course, the palace on the Via Larga, and it was within the confines of that structure that later Medici generations satisfied their esthetic needs. Lorenzo was recognized as the premier connoisseur of the arts in Italy, and his advice on painters and architects was sought by princes throughout the peninsula. As one dimension of his foreign policy, he sent Florentine artists to work for those rulers whose favor he desired. But Lorenzo's material subsidy of the arts in Florence was niggardly. Most of his money for this purpose was spent not on ecclesiastical or civic projects, but on his private collection of precious gems and antique art. This had been assembled for his enjoyment, and for that of close friends and visiting dignitaries, whose appreciation of the gesture might be politically advantageous as well as personally gratifying. Lorenzo's collection of *objets d'art* was the esthetic counterpart of the Platonic Academy.

FLORENTINE HUMANISM: ITS EVOLUTION AND SIGNIFICANCE

From 1380 to 1450, the central theme in Florentine cultural history is the emergence of classical antiquity as the major source, focus, and inspiration of intellectual life. These years witnessed the development of an educational curriculum founded upon the *studia humanitatis*, the subjects of grammar, rhetoric, poetry, history, and moral philosophy which had formed the basis of classical education, but which had been changed and modified— although never entirely rejected—by the different needs and interests of the medieval world. This phenomenon, usually described as the "rise of humanism," occurred in an atmosphere of great enthusiasm for classical literature, both Latin and Greek, similar in its intensity to the excitement created in twelfth-century France by the discovery of Aristotelian logic and its application to theological problems. Some manifestations of the rise of humanism are the striking increase in the number of students pursuing classical studies, the formation of groups linked by their common interest in the writings of antiquity, and the intensive search for unknown manuscripts of ancient authors. Progress in humanistic studies can also be measured by the perfection of techniques for the study of classical texts, and greater knowledge of the character of Greek and Roman civilization. Another dimension of Florentine humanism was the broadening of classical interests from purely literary sources to other disciplines: to architecture and sculpture, to music, to mathematics and the physical sciences. Its most controversial aspect, which has been much discussed and debated, concerns its influence upon contemporary values, and its role in stimulating the changes in the ways that Florentines viewed their world and themselves.

This interest in classical antiquity, and acquaintance with its literary heritage, was not a wholly new phenomenon; it had a long and continuous history extending back to classical times. Medieval Europe had never lost its fascination for ancient Rome, nor had it ever abandoned its study of Roman literature. Generations of students destined for ecclesiastical careers learned to read Latin by studying passages from Livy and Horace in medieval grammars. This sympathetic interest in the classical past was strongest in Italy, whose natives took pride in their descent from the ancient Romans. In their studies of Roman law, the beginnings of which can be traced back to Bologna in the eleventh century, Italian legal scholars became acquainted not only with the codes and digests, but also with the political and institutional history of republican and imperial Rome. And while the Bologna lawyers were immersing themselves in the intricacies of Justinian's Code, other young men were preparing for notarial careers, the basic discipline for which was rhetoric. These students read Cicero and Livy, and while their future professional activity was devoted to such prosaic tasks as the composition of wills, deeds of sale, and mercantile contracts, some continued their study of the classics as an avocation.

The foundations for a strong interest in the ancient world and its literature were thus well established in the fourteenth century, and it was upon these foundations that Petrarch fashioned his crusade for the "new learning." He was born in Arezzo in 1304, the son of an exiled Florentine notary who later found a position in the papal court at Avignon. Sent to Bologna to study law, Petrarch abandoned that discipline in favor of poetry; it was as a writer of verse in the Tuscan vernacular that he first gained an Italian reputation. His lyrics were enormously popular, and they exercised a profound and lasting influence upon the writing of poetry, not only in Italy, but also in France and England. Early in his student career, Petrarch had developed a strong enthusiasm for the works of Latin authors Cicero in particular, and he became the most influential spokesman for the new learning and its staunchest defender against critics. During his lifetime and largely as a result of his efforts, the study of the classics became a controversial issue in the Italian scholarly world. It also exhibited the characteristics of a cult, with disciples, a program, and a strong proselytizing impulse.

A crucial figure in Florence's development as a center of the new learning was Coluccio Salutati, a notary from the village of Stignano (in the Valdinievole between Lucca and Pistoia), who came to Florence in 1375 to accept the post of chancellor of the republic. He held that important office until his death in 1406, becoming a powerful and influential statesman and a respected member of the patriciate. Salutati's entrenched position in Florentine society was an important factor in his successful promotion of humanism. Although Petrarch achieved much greater fame as a writer, he never lived and worked in Florence, and so his influence there was limited. Less brilliant intellectually, and less renowned in the Italian literary world, Salutati was nevertheless able to achieve more for classical studies in Florence.

Salutati was a member of that group of scholars and citizen savants who met in the Augustinian convent of S. Spirito under the aegis of Luigi Marsili to discuss moral and philosophical issues. After Marsili's death in 1394, Salutati became the titular leader of this group, and the leading champion of the classics in Florence. His disciples includes some of the leading humanistic scholars of the next generation—Leonardo Bruni, Pietro Paul Vergerio, Poggio Bracciolini—and also a group of young Florentine patricians whom he encouraged to pursue classical studies and who regarded him as their patron and mentor: Niccolò Niccoli, Angelo Corbinelli, Roberto de' Rossi, Cino Rinuccini. For these men, Salutati was an example and a secure foundation upon which to build their scholarly and literary interests. Under his guidance and patronage, they met regularly to discuss their problems. They borrowed books from the chancellor's library, probably the best private collection of classical works in Florence, and widened their acquaintance with the literature of antiquity. The chancellor was the bridge between the world of learning and scholarship and the world of commerce and politics. Aspiring humanists could point to Salutati's fame and reputation, his political influence and social standing, in arguments with their elders who might question the value of classical studies. Vespasiano da Bisticci described one such skeptic, the merchant Andrea de' Pazzi who "knew little of learning, thought it to be of little value, and had no desire that his son [Piero] should spend time over it."

Through his professional career and his writings, Salutati endeavored to make classical studies relevant to the world in which he lived. His state letters, written in a style considered elegant and Ciceronian for the time, and replete with classical allusions, served as models for Italian chancery correspondence. According to a widely circulated story, Giangaleazzo Visconti once said that a Salutati letter was worth an army of 1000 lances. This hyperbolic statement does indicate the inflated importance which was attached to humanist talents employed for political purposes. In 1394, the Florentine Signoria requested the lord of Padua, Francesco da Carrara, to refrain from sending diplomatic notes in the vernacular, "for either through some stylistic flaw or a secretary's error, your letters might be misinterpreted...." The value of rhetorical training for members of an ambassadorial mission had long been recognized, and the commune paid increasing attention to this qualification in making ambassadorial appointments. The *Consulte e Pratiche* records provide further evidence of the impact of rhetoric upon political thinking and practice. The early volumes of this source, compiled in the middle decades of the Trecento, contain very short and pithy summaries of speeches, which suggests both oratorial brevity and the notary's reluctance or inability to write long and detailed summaries. Coinciding with Salutati's tenure as Florentine chancellor, the accounts of these speeches were greatly expanded, written in a more elegant style, and occasionally embellished by classical references and quotations. By the beginning of the fifteenth century, if not earlier, oral eloquence was a significant political asset, although it occasionally prompted some criticism, illustrated by Gino Capponi's caustic remark that a speech of Piero Baroncelli "was very pretty but lacking in substance."

Salutati's social and cultural values have been subjects of scholarly controversy. The difficulties arise primarily from certain contradictions in his writings, and other discrepancies between his words and his actions. In his defense of classical studies, he was quite consistent, repeating arguments which had been formulated earlier to justify the reading of pagan literature. He insisted that the concern of many classical authors with moral problems legitimized their study by Christian scholars. But on other issues, Salutati was ambiguous and contradictory. His chancery correspondence contained some very eloquent statements eulogizing political freedom and liberty, praising republican government in Florence and condemning the despotism of Milan. However, in his treatise *De tyranno*, he argued that monarchy is the best form of government, and he condoned the destruction of the Roman republic by Caesar. His essay, *De seculo et religione*, was a restatement of an old medieval theme, the superiority of the monastic life of solitude and prayer. Yet in private letters to friends, Salutati developed a coherent and persuasive justification for the "active life" which he led. In another letter,

Salutati was severely critical of a man who had abandoned his literary studies to pursue a notarial career to improve his economic circumstances. This letter idealized the figure of the indigent scholar intent only upon learning, and it contrasts sharply with Salutati's own professional career, which j brought him wealth and high social rank.

The inconsistencies and contradictions in Salutati's writings appear to reflect the doubts and confusions of his generation, searching for meaningful values. The most comprehensive analysis of this problem is Hans Baron's book, *The Crisis of the Early Italian Renaissance*. Baron argues that a new cultural phenomenon, civic humanism, came into being in Florence after 1400. Although its classical orientation was inherited from Trecento scholars, its outlook and values differed significantly from those espoused by Petrarch and Salutati. The origins of civic humanism are to be found in the Florentine political scene around 1400 and, more specifically, in the threat to the city's independence posed by Giangaleazzo Visconti. This crisis had a profound impact upon the Florentine mentality. It strengthened the citizenry's commitment to its republican government and to the ideals of liberty and freedom traditionally associated with that government. The humanists became the leading exponents of those political values, the most articulate propagandists for Florentine republicanism. They developed a new interpretation of Florentine history based upon the city's founding by Sulla when the Roman republic still flourished (and not by Caesar, who destroyed the republic). And in their writings and speeches, the humanists also formulated an ideology for the Florentine citizenry which, while derived from classical sources, was also firmly rooted in the realities of the city's experience. This ideology exalted the civic virtues of participation in public affairs, the concept of the "active life" pursued by merchants and statesmen, as opposed to the contemplative life of ascetics and scholars. Furthermore, it viewed the acquisition of wealth not as an impediment to knowledge and salvation, but instead as a resource to be used in the promotion of learning and morality.

This rough summary of the Baron thesis does not do justice to the richness and complexity of the author's analysis, nor to his vast erudition, which can only be appreciated by a careful reading of his works. The thesis rests upon certain premises and assumptions which are not clearly articulated in his writing or in much of the criticism which his arguments have stimulated. Perhaps the most striking feature of his interpretation is the sharpness of the distinction between the two stages of humanism. Separating Salutati, the spokesman for the older humanism dominated by medieval preoccupations and values, and Leonardo Bruni, the voice of the new civic humanism, is a generational gulf which forms the dividing line between medieval and Renaissance Florence. Baron is committed to a sociological view of culture, and he views intellectual innovation as a direct response to change in the material world. By dating, as precisely and accurately as possible, the writings of Florentine humanists around 1400, he has sought to demonstrate that the political crisis of 1402 had an immediate and profound impact upon their ideas. Also underlying Baron's interpretation of Florentine culture is the concept, which is clearly formulated in Von Martin's *Sociology of the Renaissance*, of a dominant social class which expresses the values and ideals of the whole society.

Criticism of Baron's interpretation has focused upon his concept of civic humanism, and his theory of intellectual change as a response to political crisis. A recent article by Jerrold Seigel (*Past and Present*, No. 34, July 1966) illustrates the direction and tone of this criticism and develops a very different theory about the historical development of Florentine humanism. Much of Seigel's argument is concerned with the chronology of Bruni's early writings; he believes that two important treatises, the *Laudatio Florentinae Urbis* and the *Dialogi ad Petrum Istrum*, were written prior to 1402 and thus were not influenced by the crisis of that year. Seigel concludes that Bruni's motives for composing these treatises were neither political nor ideological, but professional and practical. Bruni was exhibiting his rhetorical skills; he was demonstrating that he could develop eloquent and persuasive arguments on both sides of an issue, as he does in the *Dialogi*. By writing these laudatory treatises, Seigel further suggests, Bruni may have hoped to obtain a position in the Florentine chancery under Salutati. Seigel then surveys the development of Florentine humanism around 1400 and concludes that humanism was not affected significantly by social and political conditions. Changes which occurred in humanist thinking were internal, inspired by new attitudes and viewpoints arising from the rhetorical tradition, and not as a response to outside stimuli. Instead of viewing ideas as the product of specific historical events or circumstances, Seigel prefers to treat them as developing within a particular intellectual tradition or discipline. He emphasizes the occupational differences, the professional castes—lawyers, humanists, theologians—and suggests that men in these fields pursued their interests quite independently, as untouched by developments in other disciplines or professions as by social upheaval or political crisis.

The central issue in this debate is the nature of the relationship between ideas and experience. Although quite sympathetic to Baron's conception of this relationship, the author is not persuaded by every part of his analysis. One can accept his thesis that a fundamental change in humanist values and perception occurred in the early Quattrocento, and still be skeptical of his explanation for this intellectual revolution. Although the Milanese threat to Florentine independence was certainly a factor in this mental and psychological readjustment it was not the sole—or perhaps even the most important—stimulus. The *Consulte e Pratiche* protocols, those records of deliberations by the Florentine political class, furnish some clues to the state of the civic mind in the early Quattrocento. While not conclusive, the evidence from these protocols suggests that the most critical moments in these "crisis" years did not occur during the Milanese wars, but a decade later, during Florence's struggles with Genoa and King Ladislaus of Naples (1409–1414). A significant aspect of political discussion in these years is its critical and introspective quality, its harsh and bitter judgment of Florentine institutions, practices, and attitudes which—so the blunt and candid critics assert—were responsible for the city's perilous condition. In these deliberations, the traditional appeals to defend Florentine liberty and republican institutions were supplemented by a tough and realistic appraisal of the flaws in those institutions, and a demand for reform.

These protocols support the hypothesis that Florence's cultural revolution of the early Quattrocento was not simply a response to a particular moment of crisis, a specific catalytic event; it was a gradual process stimulated by several factors and circumstances, both internal and external, which impelled Florentines to examine themselves more objectively and realistically. The origins of this cultural revolution should not be sought in Florence's status as a beleaguered republican city, but in the particular character of this society and its political traditions, which facilitated communication between intellectuals, merchants, and statesmen, and which provided a unique forum for the spread of new ideas and opinions. From these institutions and circumstances, there developed that symbiotic bond, so peculiarly Florentine, between the worlds of thought and action. Unusually sensitive to their society and its needs, the humanists of Bruni's generation exploited the literary resources of their discipline to provide Florentines with the techniques and the materials for reexamining themselves, their values and goals.

One of the most important humanist tools was a new historical perspective which—as Hans Baron has shown—was developed by Leonardo Bruni. Whereas medieval historical thinking was universal in scope and teleological in character, concerned with tracing the implementation of the divine plan, Bruni's historical outlook was temporal, secular, and particular. In his judgment, the historical experience of Florence and republican Rome merited the highest praise, for these communities had created the optimum conditions for human existence, the pursuit of an active civic life. The temporal existence of these cities was justified not by any reference to a divine plan, but in terms of their secular achievements. Moreover, the historical record of that experience provided a model for emulation and a framework by which human actions could be comprehended and judged. The first documented utilization of this perspective in political deliberations occurred in the spring of 1413, during the war with Ladislaus. Messer Piero Beccanugi made this statement, the first of its kind recorded in the extant protocols: "To administer public affairs intelligently, it is essential to look to the past [for guidance] to provide for the present and the future." Thereafter, the appeal to historical example, as justification for a particular policy or viewpoint, became a standard feature of political discussion. Most commonly cited were events from the Florentine past, embracing not only recent occurrences familiar to every citizen, but others going back nearly a century: the dictatorship of the Duke of Athens in 1342–1343, the war with Pisa in the 1360s, Emperor Charles IV's invasion of Tuscany in 1368. It is perhaps significant that the protocols contain several references to Florence's wars with Giangaleazzo, but none that points specifically to the crisis of 1402. Speakers also utilized the sources of classical antiquity. Messer Filippo Corsini cited events from the Punic wars—the massacre of the Roman army at Cannae and the siege of Saguntum—to bolster his arguments concerning Florentine policy toward Ladislaus, Messer Rinaldo Gianfigliazzi quoted Seneca: "Only that which is honest is good," and the example of the Spartan king Lycurgus who "in promulgating laws stated that public affairs are properly directed by the few with the authority of the many."

Another example of humanist influence upon Florentine political thinking, and upon policy, was the radical transformation of the city's self-image in the early fifteenth century. Although Trecento Florence had many cosmopolitan features, its inhabitants were quite insular and parochial in their outlook: fearful of the outside world, suspicious of all foreigners, and of distinguished visitors in particular. From 1273 to 1419, no pope or emperor came to Florence; princes and prelates were frequently rebuffed wren they sought permission to visit the city. The first signs of a change in this defensive attitude are visible in the deliberations of 1407, in which a few speakers proposed Florence as the site for an ecumenical council designed to end the Schism which had divided Latin Christendom for thirty years. This idea disturbed many citizens, who did not enjoy the prospect of their city overrun by foreigners, and sheltering a large group of ecclesiastical and secular dignitaries. Advocates of the council argued that God would reward those devout Christians who had contributed to the healing of the Schism; they asserted, too, that Florence's reputation would be enhanced throughout Christendom. One speaker, Antonio Alessandri, claimed that nothing would gain greater merit in the eyes of God, and greater fame among men, than to assemble a council in Florence to restore church unity. This argument added a new dimension to the idea that civic fame could be achieved not only by the construction of magnificent cathedrals and palaces or through the exploits of famous sons, but also by creating a setting for a major historical event. Here in embryonic form is the vision of Florence described by many Quattrocento humanists: a city known and admired throughout the civilized world, an international city. Pisa, not Florence, was finally chosen as the site for the ill-fated council of 1409. But those Florentines who had developed this new and enlarged vision of their city were rewarded in 1438, when Pope Eugenius IV transferred the council, assembled to reunite the Greek and Latin churches, from Ferrara to Florence.

The records of the republic's deliberations thus provide some clues to the movement of new attitudes and values, new modes of perception, from the realm of ideas to the world of action, from the *vita contemplativa* to the *vita attiva*. As a result of fundamental changes in educational method and philosophy, these values became more firmly established in the city. Since Dante's time, classical studies had attracted a minority of Florentine students, but after 1400 the *studia humanitatis* became the core and foundation of the aristocracy's academic curriculum. In his biography of Filippo Brunelleschi, Antonio Manetti noted that when Filippo was a boy (he was born in 1377), "few persons among those who did not expect to become doctors, lawyers or priests were given literary training [i.e., instruction in Latin]." But in his memoirs written about 1420, the merchant Giovanni Morelli prescribed an academic program for his sons which contained such traditional features as reading, writing, mathematics, and the Bible, but also a surprising emphasis upon the classics:

> Every day for at least an hour, read Vergil, Boethius, Seneca and other authors.... Begin your study with Vergil.... Then spend some time with Boethius, with Dante and the other poets, with Tully [Cicero] who will teach you to speak perfectly, with Aristotle who will instruct you in philosophy.... Read and study the Bible; learn about the great and holy acts which our Lord God accomplished through the prophets; you will be fully instructed in the faith and in the coming of God's son. Your spirit will gain consolation and joy. You will be contemptuous of the world and you will have no concern for what may happen to you.

It is instructive to compare this passage with Leon Battista Alberti's views on education contained in his treatise on the family (1435). Alberti based his curriculum exclusively upon classical authors (Cicero, Livy, Sallust); he did not mention the Bible or any work by a Christian author. These Latin writers were the foundations of his own education, and during his lifetime (he died in 1466), they formed the essential academic diet for the children of the Florentine aristocracy.

THE ARTISTIC REVOLUTION

Coinciding with, and closely linked to the emergence of humanism as the premier intellectual concern in early Quattrocento Florence were developments in the plastic arts which marked the beginnings of a new style. A distinctive feature of this artistic revolution was the revived interest in ancient art, and the intensive study of those physical remnants of classical antiquity which had survived the ravages of time. From this investigation, Florentine artists rediscovered the formulas and principles that had guided the buildings and sculptors of the ancient world. And in painting, the medium for which no ancient examples had survived, the Florentines developed particular techniques to create a more realistic image of the physical world. As the humanists had discovered and exploited the dimension of time as an essential element in their mode of perception, so the artists used perspective and proportion to organize space in a manner which expressed their particular view of reality.

In contrast to the humanistic movement, which is amply documented, very little evidence concerning the artistic revolution has survived, either in written or plastic form. Art historians have been very diligent in combing archives and libraries for contemporary documents—letters, commissions, tax records—that throw light upon this development, and in analyzing the extant paintings, sculptures, and architectural monuments, many of which have been damaged by the elements and inept restorers. They have plotted the course of this revolution, identifying and dating the works which marked the significant advances in style and technique.

Quite as much controversy has developed over the origins of this artistic revolution, as has been generated by the concept of civic humanism. The central problem, the focus of much of the discussion, is the degree to which changes in the plastic arts have been influenced by a transformation of the intellectual milieu, or by a significant recasting of the political and social order. Many art historians, perhaps the majority, deny that this question is a legitimate concern of their discipline, which they define as the patient accumulation of data about artistic works and their creators and the close analysis of style. Their approach to their subject is similar to that of the intellectual historian who focuses his attention exclusively upon his texts, treating ideas as an independent and autonomous dimension of history. At the opposite pole of the spectrum is the Marxist scholar who views all cultural phenomena as mirroring the structure and values of the society that creates them. Significant changes in the arts are thus indices of alterations and readjustments of the social order and indeed can be utilized to show the direction and tempo of that transformation. When presented in its most dogmatic form—as for example, in Frederick Antal's *Florentine Painting and its Social Background*—the Marxist viewpoint has won few adherents or sympathizers. Between these poles, however, much significant work is being done by scholars who are examining the connections between Florentine society and its artistic achievement. They have studied the incomes of painters, sculptors, and goldsmiths; their relations with corporate and individual patrons; the social and political function of artistic works, as devices for advertising family power, prestige, and wealth; and their ideological function, as expressions of the values and ideals of the community and, particularly, its ruling elite.

Why did the new Renaissance style originate in Florence? The city was a likely site for this development, with its exceptional size and wealth, and its tradition of excellence in the crafts and plastic arts. The community of artists was large, active, and well patronized by clients, public and private, secular and ecclesiastical. Giotto's frescoes in S. Croce and Andrea Pisano's Baptistery doors lay conveniently at hand, to be admired, studied, and copied by young artists. These material factors may help to explain why the revolution occurred in Florence and not in Arezzo or Genoa; but they do not reveal why it occurred at a specific time—in the second decade of the fifteenth century—or why it assumed a particular form. Perhaps the most puzzling fact about the new style was the suddenness of its appearance, after three decades of artistic stagnation. No painter or sculptor of the first rank was active in Florence between 1370 and 1400. The recurring plagues of the late fourteenth century may have killed off many young and promising artists or disrupted the workshops that trained them. Perhaps the political and social disturbances of these years strengthened the conservative tendencies among artists and patrons. The distinctive features of "late Gothic," the dominant style of the period, were its linear and decorative qualities, its concern with detail and color. It was an attractive, charming, graceful style which made only a muted appeal to the emotions and none to the intellect.

Perhaps the limitations of this style and the mediocrity of its practitioners contributed to the artistic revolution, by inducing the leaders of the new generation—Brunelleschi, Donatello, Ghiberti, Masaccio—to search elsewhere for guidance and inspiration. With the exception of the painter Masaccio, these men all received their initial training in goldsmiths' shops, even though Brunelleschi specialized later in architecture, Ghiberti and Donatello in sculpture. In their chosen fields, therefore, they were largely autodidacts, free to develop their interests and techniques without the inhibiting hand of a master. These men were strong and independent personalities, endowed with a sense of their unique talents and capacities, an enormous curiosity, and a willingness to experiment. In his *Commentaries*, Lorenzo Ghiberti praised the great artists of the early fourteenth century— Giotto, Niccolò and Andrea Pisano—who influenced him, but he did not mention any of his own teachers. Nor does Brunelleschi's biographer, Antonio Manetti (who knew his subject personally), identify the masters who instructed the young sculptor and architect. Brunelleschi and Donatello journeyed to Rome to study classical ruins; this was not the only excursion into unfamiliar areas which these artists undertook to increase their knowledge and experience. Manetti is our source for the information that Brunelleschi learned some mathematics—so crucial for his discovery of perspective—from Paolo Toscanelli. He also noted that Filippo was very interested in theology and often frequented the disputations held by masters in that discipline.

The creators of the Renaissance style rejected their contemporaries and went back a century to the work of Giotto. The quality they most admired in this master was his ability to make dramatic and moving statements about the Christian tradition by creating realistic human forms. Giotto achieved this effect by focusing the viewer's attention upon a few monumental figures. Naturalism, the depiction of reality, was a central concern for these painters and sculptors, as it had been for Giotto. But this did not involve simply the faithful copying of nature, the creation of a mirrored image of the physical universe. Instead, these artists selected particular elements of the visible world and organized them rationally and scientifically to create the illusion of reality. For painting, Brunelleschi made the crucial contribution through his invention of perspective, the geometric device for depicting three-dimensional space upon a flat plane surface. The employment of this technique strengthened the impression of realism, enabling the artist to stimulate the viewer's emotions and sensibilities. With mathematical precision, objects could be fixed, and their relations to each other established, in this three-dimensional world. Discovery of the rules of proportion made it possible for Florentine painters to depict the human form realistically in this new spatial order. While mastering these new techniques, they also began to experiment with light and shadow to intensify the sense of reality, and to enlarge the dramatic possibilities of a scene.

This impulse toward a greater realism, a more accurate rendition of the visible world, was the most powerful current in the Florentine artistic revolution. But it was the blending of naturalism with classical forms which gave this movement its distinctive character and vitality. The process by which these two currents merged in this creative relationship defies easy description and analysis. The patriciate's enthusiasm for classical studies is not an adequate explanation. Florentine artists of the early Quattrocento were guild craftsmen, the social equals of stonemasons and retail merchants. Their education was not classical, but vocational and vernacular. Nor is there any concrete evidence to suggest that, in the early and crucial stages of this revolution, they were encouraged by aristocratic patrons to utilize antique forms. This classical interest developed among the artists themselves. Brunelleschi and Donatello were the first men of their generation to examine, thoroughly and systematically, the ruins of ancient Rome. They discovered the principles of classical building and—equally important—the qualities of mind and spirit of classical artists. Through his measurement of columns, pediments, and arches, Brunelleschi worked out the mathematical ratios used by Roman architects, and he also grasped the idea of space as the essential dimension in the visual arts. He spent the rest of his professional career working out the implications of this discovery.

The first creations of the new style were conceived and executed in the second and third decades of the fifteenth century. Donatello's statue of St. Mark (1411–1413), commissioned for Orsanmichele by the guild of linen makers and used clothes' dealers, is generally recognized as the first Renaissance monument. In the decade following the completion of this work Brunelleschi formulated, and began to implement, his plans for the cathedral dome and for the Foundling Hospital, the city's first classical building. Meanwhile, Donatello was pursuing his revolutionary course in sculpture, working both in marble and bronze. His statue of St. George (1420) was the first piece of free-standing sculpture to be carved since classical times, and his bronze panel for the baptismal font in the Sienese Baptistery (1427) opened up new and exciting vistas for artists in that medium. The youngest and most precocious member of this revolutionary cadre was the painter Masaccio, born in 1400 and dead by 1428. During his short but prolific career of six years (he entered the painters' guild in 1422), Masaccio revolutionized Florentine painting with such works as the *Trinity* in S. Maria Novella (1427) and his fresco cycle dedicated to the life of St. Peter which he and his partner,

Masolino da Panicale, painted in the Brancacci chapel of S. Maria del Carmine (1426–1427).

Masaccio's *Trinity* is a superb example of the new art; it illustrates many of its characteristic features, its ethos, and its purpose. This fresco, recently restored, is attached to the north wall of the nave in S. Maria Novella. In the center of the painting is the crucified Christ, above, the dove symbolizing the Holy Spirit, and in the background, the awe-inspiring figure of God the Father. Standing at the foot of the cross are the Virgin and St. John, while outside the scene are the donor and his wife kneeling in prayer. All of the new techniques invented and developed by Brunelleschi and Donatello are employed in this fresco to create a dramatic, realistic scene of great emotional intensity. Masaccio has utilized perspective brilliantly to create a sense of depth, of three dimensions. To strengthen the impression of space disciplined and organized, he placed his subject in a classical setting: an arched chapel, which might have been designed by Brunelleschi, framed by two classical pilasters and a pediment. Within this geometrically ordered space, the human figures are drawn to scale, and their relation to each other is accurately defined. Masaccio's treatment of space is absolutely novel, without precedent in the history of painting, but in his depiction of the human figure, he followed Giotto. His saints and donors are solid, massive, immobile, like pieces of statuary, and they contribute to the impression of gravity and monumentality, which are trademarks of the great Trecento master. Masaccio had also grasped Giotto's principle that the dramatic impact of a painting is weakened by irrelevant and extraneous detail. But in his portrayal of the nude form, the figure of the dead Christ, the young painter had progressed far beyond his mentor or, indeed, beyond any contemporary artist of his time.

This new style was developed by an artistic community which was experiencing a significant transformation of its structure, its relations with society, and also its self-awareness. These developments—stylistic, social, and psychological—all influenced each other. The fifteenth century witnessed the decline of the traditional view of the artist as craftsman, practicing his metier within a rigid guild structure. The artists who originated the Renaissance style were a special breed who did not function well in the old corporate system. In their intense dedication to their work, they correspond more closely to the modern idea of the artist than to the medieval craftsman. It is instructive to compare the career of Agnolo Gaddi (d. 1396), who, according to Vasari, "was more devoted to trading and commerce than the art of painting," with those of Brunelleschi and Donatello, who never married or devoted much thought to their material concerns. Vasari also relates the anecdote about Paolo Uccello (d. 1475), whose wife reported that "Paolo would remain the night long in his study to work out the lines of his perspective, and then when she called him to come to rest, he replied: 'Oh, what a sweet thing perspective is!'" With their strong personalities and their awareness of their creative talents, these artists chafed under discipline and preferred to work independently. Brunelleschi deliberately sabotaged the work on the cathedral dome until Ghiberti retired from the project and he was given a free hand to execute his plan. Ghiberti wrote in his *Commentaries* that the guild officials responsible for the construction of the Baptistery doors, the Gates of Paradise, "gave me permission to execute it in whatever way I believed would result in the greatest perfection, the most ornamentation and the greatest richness."

Public opinion responded quite slowly to this novel conception of the artist. Until quite late in the century, Florentine architects were still regarded as the passive agents of their patrons, and not the creators of the buildings which they designed. A letter of 1436 sent by the Signoria to the marquis of Ferrara expresses the traditional view of the artist and his vocation. The marquis had commissioned a painted wax image from a firm of Florentine craftsmen, but a quarrel had arisen over the price of the finished work. The priors vouched for the honesty of these men, describing them as "innocent, good and simple." Price was determined solely by the cost of material and labor. The tone of the letter suggested that the marquis should understand that disagreements often occurred in such matters involving ignorant artisans, but that justice required that they be adequately compensated for their labors. But the writings of Archbishop Antonino in mid-century suggest that these traditional attitudes were gradually disappearing. In a brief discussion of painting in his *Summa*, Antonino accepts the painters' claim to be paid "not only by the amount of work but more in proportion to their application and greater expertness in their trade." Implicit, too, in Antonino's discussion is the assumption that Florentine painters enjoyed considerable freedom in their treatment of subjects, in their selection of motifs.

Contributing to the emancipation of Quattrocento artists from their traditional craft milieu and mentality was the emergence of the idea that painting, sculpture, and architecture should be classified among the liberal arts, and were thus equal in status to poetry, rhetoric, and mathematics. This argument was first advanced in 1435 by Leon Battista Alberti in his treatise on painting, but it was not immediately accepted by Florence's scholarly community. Time was needed for old prejudices to dissolve, and for a tradition of communication and cooperation to develop between artists and humanists. With their extensive knowledge of classical architecture and sculpture,

Brunelleschi and Donatello may have stimulated some interest in humanist circles, but the sources are silent on this point. Lorenzo Ghiberti was the first artist to display an interest in classical literature and to be on friendly terms with Bruni, Traversari, and Niccoli. Scattered through his *Commentaries* are fragments of information about classical art which he had culled from Pliny and other ancient authors. Leonardo Bruni had submitted a design to Ghiberti for the second pair of Baptistery doors, the first documented example of humanist collaboration in an artistic enterprise. Although the sculptor did not use these plans, his execution of the Gates of Paradise was profoundly influenced by his contacts with the humanist milieu in Florence. From this source, so Professor Gombrich has argued persuasively, Ghiberti conceived the idea of progress in the arts, and of his mission to surpass all earlier works, including his own first set of Baptistery doors.

There is little concrete information about the public reaction to the new Renaissance style. Within artistic circles, there must have been lively discussion, and perhaps a sharp division be tween traditionalists and innovators, but no echoes of this controversy—if it arose—can be found in the sources. The old style did not lose favor with the public, but instead enjoyed a revival in the 1420s, when an Umbrian artist, Gentile da Fabriano, introduced the so-called International Gothic style into Florence. This style had its origins in Italian, and particularly Sienese painting of the Trecento; it was further developed and refined north of the Alps, in Avignon and at the Burgundian court. While possessing many of the characteristics of late Trecento Florentine painting, it also exhibited certain differences reflecting the Burgundian influence. Colors were richer; clothing and accoutrements were more elegant; and space was crammed with a plethora of figures, animal and human, which were depicted in very realistic detail. While Masaccio was working on the *Trinity* and the Brancacci frescoes, Gentile da Fabriano was painting his *Adoration of the Magi*, one of the most opulent and flamboyant works in this archaic style. This altarpiece was commissioned by the wealthy statesman and humanist Palla Strozzi, who paid Gentile 300 florins for the work. Apparently, Palla was more old-fashioned in art than in his literary interests. Cosimo de' Medici favored both styles. His palace on the Via Larga was built according to classical principles, but its chapel was decorated by Benozzo Gozzoli with a gaudy and ornate Magi scene strongly reminiscent of the secular, courtly art of the International Gothic.

The coexistence of these antithetical styles, and their persistent popularity throughout the fifteenth century, suggests that each appealed to certain qualities of the Florentine temperament. Those who favored the Renaissance style were attracted by the sense of order, coherence, and regularity, by relationships clearly defined according to mathematical laws. They conceived of space, and of the physical world, as phenomena which could be defined, measured, and controlled by the human mind. Such ideas have their obvious parallels in Florentine experience: in the precision and accuracy of mercantile account books and communal treasury records, in the trend toward systematic and centralized administration, in efforts to control economic and social activity, in the development of a sense of time in history. The qualities of simplicity, restraint, and austerity—all characteristics of the new art—likewise reflect typically Florentine modes of thought and action. With its penchant for opulence, color, and pageantry, the International Gothic style appealed to the aristocratic impulse which became so prominent in the Quattrocento. In contrast to the intellectuality and high seriousness of Renaissance art, Gothic art was light and decorative in tone and feeling. Its treatment of religious subjects was formal and stylized; it lacked the emotional intensity of a Masaccio Madonna or an Old Testament prophet carved by Donatello.

When viewed internally, this creative epoch in Florentine art is a history of discoveries and achievements by individual artists who work out their particular solutions to esthetic problems. These breakthroughs are copied and absorbed by other artists; what began as an individual statement becomes a trend, a movement, a new style. From another viewpoint, this is a history of artists and their public: the response of the patriciate to a new style, the degree to which this style defines the values of the patron class. From a third and still broader perspective, one may view this artistic development as a dimension of the collective experience of the community. Like learning and education, Florentine art was functional. It satisfied particular social needs and was influenced by changes in the nature and priority of those needs. Artists benefited from periods of prosperity and suffered in times of crisis; some metiers were active and productive when others languished. The patterns of such vicissitudes and oscillations in the fifteenth century give us some clues to the external pressures which influenced the artist and his work.

The first quarter of the fifteenth century was a period of exceptionally intense activity for sculptors and architects who were working on the large civic enterprises: the cathedral, the Foundling Hospital, the Baptistery doors, the Orsanmichele statues commissioned by the guilds, the sculptured figures of saints for the cathedral façade. These commissions were granted by guild officials; they were collective decisions, the result of lengthy deliberations and careful scrutiny of candidates. These guildsmen tended to choose "progressive" artists like Donatello and Brunelleschi to execute their commissions, with the result that their stylistic innovations were displayed publicly and were visible to the entire community. Painters did not enjoy this public and corporate patronage; they created altarpieces for parish and monastic churches and devotional images for private dwellings. It is possible but difficult to prove that the private and cloistered nature of this patronage was a factor in the conservatism of Florentine painters, in their dilatory response to the stylistic innovations of Donatello and Brunelleschi. Masaccio's revolutionary works of 1426–1427 were commissioned by two families, the Brancacci and the Lenzi, as funerary monuments; this was part of a vogue for monumental tombs which became quite strong in the 1420s, after a lapse of several decades, and which seems to have been a manifestation of the aristocratic spirit. But we can only speculate about the reasons for the selection of Masaccio to execute these frescoes. Had his patrons seen examples of his work, and were they aware of his unusual talents? Was he recommended to them by his friend Brunelleschi? Or was he selected because he was young and relatively unknown, and therefore inexpensive?

The 1420s were a period of astonishing creativity in the arts; by contrast, the succeeding decade was undistinguished. Time was required for the second generation to absorb and assimilate the revolutionary achievements of the past; some of the lesser artists never mastered the new concepts and techniques of Donatello and Masaccio. The arts also suffered from the effects of the Milanese wars, the fiscal crisis, and the political disturbances surrounding the Medici restoration in 1434. Public funds for civic monuments were eliminated or drastically curtailed, while private subsidy of the arts declined sharply. The establishment of the Medici regime marked the beginning of a more stable phase in Florentine history, but it also drove into exile a small contingent of wealthy citizens like Palla Strozzi, whose patronage was lost to the community. Not until after 1440, when Florentines enjoyed greater prosperity and security, did the arts experience a revival. This decade inaugurated the age of the great Renaissance palaces built by the Medici, Pitti, and Rucellai; these enterprises employed architects and painters, but not sculptors. Not even the great Donatello found adequate employment in Florence during his last years; he worked abroad, in Padua and Siena, and received some help from his friend Cosimo de' Medici. "In order that Donatello's chisel might not be idle," Vespasiano reported, "[Cosimo] commissioned him to make the pulpits of bronze in S. Lorenzo and the doors of the sacristy." One of the rare public commissions given to sculptors in the 1440's was Bernardino Rossellino's tomb of Leonardo Bruni (d. 1444). It is ironic that this monument to a distinguished humanist was created at a time when both civic humanism and civic art were in decline.

The artistic scene in mid-Quattrocento Florence is complex, although certain patterns and trends are visible. Most striking is the superiority of the painters: Fra Angelico, Fra Filippo Lippi, Domenico Veneziano, Andrea del Castagno, Uccello. These men were more original and creative than the architects and sculptors, who did not have many opportunities to display their talents, and who produced no worthy successors to Brunelleschi and Donatello. The old tensions and rivalries continue: between religious and secular art, between the austere, geometric Renaissance style and the colorful, graceful examples of International Gothic. The stylistic divisions are no longer neat and clear-cut, if indeed they ever were, and much of the painting of these middle decades displays ideas and motifs drawn from both traditions. Every Florentine painter of this generation had mastered perspective and proportion; but some of the greatest artists—Fra Angelico and Fra Filippo Lippi—used these techniques to paint scenes which were linear, delicate, decorative, sentimental, a sharp contrast to the austere creations of Paolo Uccello and Andrea del Castagno.

Whereas styles were mixed and confused in these years, the qualitative distinction between secular and religious art was very sharp and clear. The best art was religious painting, commissioned by ecclesiastical communities for their churches and monasteries. For their secular needs for busts and portraits, wedding chests, and coats of arms—the Florentines tended to employ second-rate artists. One of the busiest workshops was operated by two painters, Apollonio di Giovanni and Marco del Buono, who specialized in the decoration of *cassoni*, the wedding chests which held the trousseaux of Florentine brides. These chests were decorated with scenes from classical history and literature—incidents from Vergil's *Aeneid*, the assassination of Caesar—and occasionally a contemporary event, like the wedding scene which decorates the famous Adimari *cassone*, or a tournament held in the Piazza S. Croce. Between 1446 and 1463, over 300 of these *cassoni* were manufactured by this workshop and distributed to patrician households. Stylistically, these paintings were archaic and old-fashioned, a derivation of the International Gothic which did not lose its attraction for the Florentines. For their public buildings and their churches, they insisted upon the highest standards of quality. But in their domestic surroundings, they rejected the monumental style, with its austerity and rigor, in favor of decorative art, which was more conducive to pleasure and relaxation. In art as in other experiences of the mind and the senses, Florentines enjoyed a variety of styles and subjects, each in its proper context, each for its particular purpose.

Notes

The preeminent role of Florence in the culture of Renaissance Italy has focused attention upon her poets, humanists, and artists. Every general work on Renaissance culture devotes many pages to the Florentine achievement. Subjects which have been most thoroughly investigated are Dante and the literary culture of his time, the humanists, and the artists. Two lesser known aspects of Florentine culture, the legal and the mercantile, are the subjects of recent books: L. Martines, *Lawyers and Statecraft in Renaissance Florence* (Princeton, 1968) and C. Bee, *Les marchands écrivains à Florence 1375–1434* (Paris and The Hague, 1967).

My views about the relationship between Florentine culture and society owe much to D. Hay, *The Italian Renaissance in its Historical Background*.

Meetings of Florentine intellectuals are described by A. Della Torre, *Storia dell'Accademia platonica di Firenze* (Florence, 1902). The social status of humanists is described by L. Martines, *Social World of the Florentine Humanists*. The libraries of Piero Alberti and Ser Matteo Gherardi are inventoried in *Atti del Podestà*, 3784, fols. 29r–31v; and *Conventi Soppressi*, no. 83, vol. 102, part 9. Bee, *Les marchands écrivains*, 117, 307, comments on the reading of Lapo Mazzei and Giovanni Rucellai. The popular reaction to the sorcerer's conviction in 1383 is described in Brucker, "Sorcery in Early Renaissance Florence," *Studies in the Renaissance*, X (1963), 22–23.

In his article, "Florence, a City that Art Built," published in *History and the Social Web* (Minneapolis, 1955), 135–174, A. Krey emphasizes the role of the Florentine artisans and their skills in the development of a sense of quality and an appreciation of beauty. Rosso Orlandi's letter to Piero Davanzati concerning the purchase of cloth is in *Conventi Soppressi*, no. 78, vol. 315, no pag. Jacopo de' Pazzi's letter to Filippo Strozzi is in *Acquisti e Doni*, vol. 293, no pag. G. Rucellai describes his park in *Giovanni Rucellai ed il suo Zibaldone*, I, 20–21. The Signoria's letters to the Camaldoli are in *Missive*, 25, fol. 24r; 26, fol. 58r. Kristeller's comment on the quality of concreteness in humanist writing is in *Renaissance Thought* (New York, 1961), 20.

Giovanni Villani's statistics on Florentine school population are in his *Cronica*, XI, chap. 94. The sad tale of Antonio di Manno described in *Mercanzia*, 1179, fol. 233r. Filippo Balducci's letter eulogizing Florence is cited in L. Martines, *Lawyers and Statecraft*, 105–106. I thank my colleague, Randolph Starn, for transcribing the document. Ugolino of Montecatini's letter to Jacopo del Bene is in *Carte Del Bene*, 49, fol. 201r.

The eulogy to Arnolfo di Cambio is printed in Gaye, *Carteggio inedito d'artisti dei secoli XIV, XV, XVI* (Florence, 1839–1840), I, 445–446. Leonardo Bruni's tax exemption is noted in Martines, *Social World*, 168, 171; Poggio Bracciolini's petition is in *ASF, Balìe*, 25, fols. 45v–46r. Brunelleschi's patent is printed in Gaye, I, 547–549. Giovanni Villani's comments on Dante are recorded in his *Cronica*, IX, chap. 136. The plans to erect tombs for five distinguished Florentines are described in *Provvisioni*, 85, fols. 282r–283r.

The discussion of the Florentine Studio is a summary of my article, "Florence and its University, 1348–1434," in *Action and Conviction in Early Modern Europe*, eds. J. Seigel and T. Rabb (Princeton, 1969). The account of Medicean patronage is based upon E. Gombrich's article, "The Early Medici as Patrons of Art," in *Italian Renaissance Studies*, ed. E. F. Jacob (London, 1960).

The early history of Italian humanism is traced by P. Kristeller, "Humanism and Scholasticism in the Italian Renaissance," in his *Renaissance Thought*. Petrarch's career is summarized in E. H. Wilkins' *Life of Petrarch* (Chicago, 1961); and Salutati's in B. Ullman, *The Humanism of Coluccio Salutati* (Padua, 1963). A recent important book by J. Seigel,

Rhetoric and Philosophy in Renaissance Humanism (Princeton, 1968) was published after this chapter was written. Andrea de' Pazzi's derogatory reference to classical studies is in his son Piero's biography in Vespasiano da Bisticci, *The Vespasiano Memoirs* (London, 1926; Harper Torchbook edition, New York, 1963), 310. The Signoria's letter concerning the use of Latin in diplomatic correspondence is in *Missive*, 24, fol. 43r. Gino Capponi's remark about Piero Baroncelli's oratory is in *Consulte e Pratiche*, 39, fol. 117r.

Hans Baron's *chef d'oeuvre* is *The Crisis of the Early Italian Renaissance* (Princeton, 1955, revised 2nd ed., 1966). J. Seigel's article, "'Civic Humanism' or Ciceronian Rhetoric?," *Past and Present*, no. 34 (July, 1966), contains references to the scholarly judgments of Baron's interpretation. Baron's reply, "Leonardo Bruni: 'Professional Rhetorician' or 'Civic Humanist'?" is in no. 36 (April, 1967) of the same journal. For my understanding of the significance of historical perspective in Florentine thought, I am indebted to Baron's work, to M. Gilmore's article, "The Renaissance Conception of the Lessons of History," in *Humanists and Jurists* (Cambridge, Mass., 1963), chap. 1; to L. Green's article, "Historical Interpretation in fourteenth century Florentine Chronicles," *Journal of the History of Ideas*, XXVIII (1967), 161–178; and above all to the first chapter of W. Bouwsma's book, *Venice and the Defense of Republican Liberty* (Berkeley, 1968).

Volumes 35–42 of the *Consulte e Pratiche* contain the deliberations for the years 1401–1414. The records for the critical summer of 1402 are in vol. 35, fols. 127v–151r. The crisis in Florence's relations with Ladislaus begins in the spring of 1409 (*ibid.*, 39, fols. 135v–166v; 40, fols. 3r–25r). The most intense criticism of Florentine war policy was voiced between September 1412 and June 1413 (*ibid.*, 41, fols. 135r–190r; 42, fols. 1r–36v). Messer Piero Beccanugi's speech on the value of historical perspective is in *ibid.*, 42, fol. 21r. Other historical references during these months are in *ibid.*, 41, fol. 175r; 42, fols. 3r, 10r, 12v–14r, 16v, 24v, 26r, 36r. The earliest discussion of Florence as a possible council site occur in September 1407 (*ibid.*, 38, fols. 69r–82v). The debate continued in the early months of 1408 (*ibid.*, 39, fols. 5v–7r) and reached a climax in the summer and autumn of that year (*ibid.*, fols. 75v–88r). Forthcoming is an expanded, fully documented version of my arguments on changes in Florentine attitudes and perspectives, as revealed in these deliberations. In his *Lawyers and Statecraft*, 289–296, L. Martines discusses another aspect of changing views and policies in the early Quattrocento: the role of lawyers in Florence's withdrawal of obedience from Pope Gregory XII and the acceptance of the conciliar idea (1408–1409).

The selection from Manetti's biography of Brunelleschi is printed in E. Holt, *Documentary History of Art*, I (New York, 1957), 168. Giovanni Morelli's comments on education are in his *Ricordi*, 270–273; those of Alberti in *Opere volgari*, ed. C. Grayson, I (Bari, 1960), 68–72.

The literature on Florentine art in the fourteenth and fifteenth centuries is vast. I have found the following works of particular value: A. Blunt, *Artistic Theory in Italy* (Oxford, 1940), P. and L. Murray, *The Art of the Renaissance* (New York and Washington, 1963), P. Francastel, *Peinture et société* (Lyon, 1951), M. Meiss, *Painting in Florence and Siena after the Black Death*, H. Janson, *The Sculpture of Donatello* (Princeton, 1957), R. Krautheimer, *Lorenzo Ghiberti* (Princeton, 1956), M. Wackernagel, *Der Lebensraum des Künstlers in der florentinischen Renaissance* (Leipzig, 1938). For "materialist" interpretations of the artistic revolution, one may consult F. Antal, *Florentine Painting and its Social Background* (London, 1948), and A. Hauser, *The Social History of Art*, II (New York, 1952). Two perceptive discussions of art style are M. Shapiro, "Style," in A. Kroeber, ed., *Anthropology Today* (Chicago, 1953), and J. Ackerman, "A Theory of Style," *Journal of Aesthetics and Art Criticism*, XX (1962), 227–237.

The *Commentaries* of Lorenzo Ghiberti are edited by J. von Schlosser (Berlin, 1912); E. Holt has translated selections in her *Documentary History of Art*, I, 151–167. Antonio Manetti's *Vita di Filippo di ser Brunellesco* was edited by E. Toesca (Florence, 1927); a translated excerpt is in Holt, I, 167–179. A standard source for information on Florentine artists is G. Vasari's *Lives of the Painters, Sculptors and Architects* (several English editions).

The status of Florentine architects in the Quattrocento is discussed by E. Gombrich, "The Early Medici as Patrons of Art." The Signoria's letter to the marquis of Ferrara is in *Missive*, 34, fols. 123r–123v. Antonino's views on art have been analyzed by C. Gilbert, "The Archbishop on the Painters of Florence, 1450," *Art Bulletin*, XLI (1959), 75–85. Alberti's treatise, *On Painting*, has been translated by J. Spencer (New Haven, 1956). Ghiberti's classical interests are described by Krautheimer, *Ghiberti*, 306–314, and by E. Gombrich, "The Renaissance Conception of Artistic Progress," published in his *Norm and Form* (London, 1966), 5–8. The religious orientation of the Renaissance style, contrasted with the secular concern of International Gothic, is emphasized by Gilbert, *Art Bulletin*, XLI, 83. F. Hartt's article, "Freedom in Quattrocento Florence," *Essays in Memory of Karl Lehmann*, ed. L. Sandler (New York, 1964), 119, discusses the civic commissions of sculptors and architects, and the private and ecclesiastical commissions of painters. I have borrowed C. Gilbert's scheme of artistic cycles in Florence from his Antonino article, *Art Bulletin*, XLI, 85–88. The sudden popularity of monumental tombs in the 1420s is noted by J. Coolidge, "Further Observations on Masaccio's Trinity," *Art Bulletin*, XLVIII (1966), 382–384. The artistic scene in mid-fifteenth century Florence is succinctly analyzed in P. and L. Murray, *Art of the Renaissance*, 89–120. The information on the *cassone* workshop is derived from E. Gombrich's article, "Appollonio di Giovanni," *Norm and Form*, 11–28.

J.G.A. POCOCK

Giannotti and Contarini:
Venice as Concept and as Myth

[1]

Donato Giannotti (1492–1573) is known, if at all, to readers of English as
"the most excellent describer of the commonwealth of Venice" (the phrase is
Harrington's 1656)[1] and by less specific statements to the effect that he was
the intellectual heir of Machiavelli and the last major thinker in the
Florentine republican tradition. No detailed study of his thought has yet
been written in English,[2] but we have gone far enough in the present analysis
to have uncovered an anomaly in his received reputation: it is odd, on the
face of it, that the same man should have been at once an admirer of Venice
and an admirer of Machiavelli. And the oddity grows as we look deeper, for
Giannotti proves to have employed his detailed knowledge of Venetian
procedures to construct a model of Florentine government which was both
markedly popular and founded upon a citizen militia; both concepts very far
removed from the aristocratic *città disarmata* discerned by Machiavelli and
Guicciardini. The fact is, as already indicated, that his conception of Venice
is rather instrumental than ideal; he does not set up the *serenissima republica*
as a model to be imitated, but treats it as a source of conceptual and
constitutional machinery which can be adapted for use in the very difficult
circumstances of Florentine *popolare* politics. He is aided to do this by the fact
that the Aristotelian-Polybian model of mixed government, which Venice

From *The Machiavellian Moment*. © 1975 by Princeton University Press.

45

exemplifies, can be given either an aristocratic or a democratic bias without losing its essential shape. Giannotti, who specifically acknowledges his indebtedness to Aristotle and Polybius, as well as to Machiavelli, may be thought of, from our point of view, as a contributor of originality, if not of direct influence, to the theory of mixed government; he is the first author we shall meet of certain general assertions which were to recur in the history of this branch of republican thought. At the same time we may see him as continuing a tendency whereby Machiavelli's thought was reabsorbed into the tradition of Aristotelian republicanism and the edges of its drastic originality softened and blurred. On neither *innovazione*, *virtù*, nor even *milizia* is Giannotti's thinking as abrasive or as creative as that of his older friend. But the more we discount the legend of the "wicked Machiavel," the harder it becomes to see just how Machiavelli's true intentions were imparted to European tradition. As later Western republicanism grew, at all events, his image became progressively more orthodox and moral.

As already indicated by his habit of citing his authorities, Giannotti is a more formally academic thinker than either Machiavelli or Guicciardini; his political commitment is real, but his thought does not grow out of the tormenting experience of citizenship in the same way that theirs did. As a young man he frequented the Orti Oricellari and was friendly with Machiavelli while the latter was writing his history of Florence. From 1520 to 1525 he taught (and it is highly probable from the tone of his later writings that at some time he taught political theory) at the university of Pisa. In 1525–1527 he spent much of his time in Padua and Venice, and it was during this time that he wrote most of his *Libro della Repubblica de' Vineziani*, the work by which he is best known to posterity.[3] He returned to Florence after the fall of the Medici—he seems to have regarded his absence hitherto as an exile—and during the Great Siege of 1528–1530 held Machiavelli's old post as secretary to the Ten of War and like him was involved in the organization of a civic militia. Expelled from the city in 1530, he suffered the longevity of the exile; and his second major work, the *Della Repubblica Fiorentina*, is an expatriate's vision of a Florentine popular republic which was never to come into being. The work was not even printed until 1721, and though the study of Venice was published in 1540 and had an extensive reputation, we do not study Giannotti as one whose thought greatly affected the mind of his age. He was not a genius, as Machiavelli and Guicciardini both were; but his writings are those of a very intelligent man, in which we see what could be done with Aristotelian, humanist, Venetian, and Machiavellian concepts under significant and revealing circumstances. They further contain some new departures in thought concerning the politics of time.

Although Felix Gilbert has assembled evidence connecting Giannotti's composition of his work on Venice with the fall of the Medici in May 1527—which he and his friends eagerly anticipated while he was writing his first draft[4]—it would probably not be inappropriate to consider the *Repubblica de' Viniziani* as a fact-finding service which Giannotti intended to perform for his contemporaries. The Venetian model had been endlessly talked about since 1494; there existed a great deal of disseminated information about its workings; but the only written work of reference on the structure of Venetian government, that of Marcantonio Sabellico, was in Giannotti's view so unmethodical as to be uncritical. If the Medici regime were to fall, the *popolare* optimates among whom he moved must resume their struggle to erect a government in which their leadership would be combined with liberty, and Venice was paradigmatic for such a program. Giannotti therefore set out to inform them of the facts. He envisaged a tripartite study,[5] in which one book would outline the general governmental structure (*l'amministrazione universale*), a second would deal with the various magistracies in detail (*particolarmente*), and a third with *la forma e composizione di essa Repubblica*—a phrase suggesting theoretical analysis. But he had completed only the first section when revolution did break out at Florence and he returned, to serve under both the moderate regime of Niccolò Capponi and the much more radical government of the Siege, to experience (it may be) a greater degree of commitment to popular government than he anticipated in 1526–1527, and to suffer exile. Long afterwards, in 1538, he began preparing (but not revising) his incomplete work for the printer.[6] He may by then have completed the manuscript of his blueprint for a popular government at Florence, if so, it would be interesting to know why he did not publish the latter, but we should know why he did not complete the former. His theoretical work was done, and had been devoted to a different subject.

This being so, we are not to expect too much theoretical structure from the essentially incomplete *Repubblica de' Viniziani*. The first section is all that we have, and it suffers from almost the same inadequacies as those ascribed to Sabellico; for what his work lacked, we are told, was any account of *la forma, la composizione, il temperamento di questa Repubblica*[7]—precisely the themes which Giannotti himself was reserving for the third section which he never wrote. Even when it is laid down that the first section will deal with universal topics, leaving particulars to be treated later on, for the reason that universals are easier to understand, this does not mean that the essential principles of the republic's structure are to be expounded first and their specific applications followed up later; for the defense offered of this procedure is that painters begin by sketching in their outlines and sculptors by roughing out their marble, so that one can see what part of the block is going to be the head before the actual shape emerges. The *cose universali* are the general characteristics of the natural object which make it fit for the shape or form which it afterward assumes, and this is why the geographical site of Venice—itself, of course, an extraordinary phenomenon—is to be described before even the governmental structure.[8] In going from *universale* to *particolare*, then, we are not traveling from the principle to its application, so much as examining the matter before we study its form; and even then the scholastic image may be less appropriate than the artistic, for we are told that

> each republic is like a natural body, or rather it would be better to say that it is a body produced by nature in the first place and afterwards polished by art. When nature makes a man, she intends to make a universal whole, a communion. Since each republic is like a natural body, it must have its members; and since there is a proportion and relationship between the members of each body, who knows not this proportion and relationship knows not how the body is made. This is where Sabellico falls short.[9]

But if—to simplify the argument a little—nature supplies the matter of a republic and art the form, it follows that the principles of political harmony are not the work of nature and cannot be intuitively known; they can only be discovered once we see how the political artist has shaped his material. Sabellico merely described the various magistracies of Venice and did not consider the relationships between them which compose the form of the state. But this is all that Giannotti found time to do; Sabellico's deficiencies were to be made good only in the third section. We have not his theoretical analysis of Venetian government, and can only draw conclusions from the language of what we have, and its intimations, as to what that might have been. It is certainly significant, for instance, in the light of various doctrines which he was to develop in the book on Florentine government, that Sabellico should be blamed for failure to show how each magistracy is linked with and dependent upon every other, so that the *composizione* of the republic could be seen in its perfection.[10]

The *Repubblica de' Vineziani* would not have been a humanist work if it had not contained some consideration of the place of the individual in political time. The book is in dialogue form, and the principal speaker—the Venetian scholar Trifone Gabriello or Gabriele—is compared, in his leisurely retirement at Padua, with the Roman Pomponius Atticus. He acknowledges the compliment, but proceeds to draw a distinction. Pomponius Atticus lived when his republic was far gone in corruption, and withdrew into philosophic privacy because he could not save it and was unwilling to perish with it. But Venice is not corrupt, rather more perfect than ever before, and his retirement is that of a man free to choose between action and contemplation.[11] The tranquillity of Venice, favorably compared with the military glory of Rome,[12] is further contrasted with the present miserable state of Italy. Trifone says he does not know whether the present should be compared with the times when the Caesars were destroying Roman liberty, or with those when the barbarians were overrunning Italy; nor does it much matter, since the Caesars were the cause of the barbarian invasions and they in their turn the cause of the present calamities.[13] Giannotti's sense of history is notably causal and linear. Nevertheless it is the happiness of Venice to have escaped history, and this she has clearly done through her success in retaining inner stability and civic *virtù*. We look at this point for an account, Aristotelian or Polybian, of how stability may be retained through time by some harmony or mixture of the different elements composing a political society. The language is in many ways suggestive of such doctrine, and yet, as Gilbert has pointed out, the term "mixed government" and the apparatus of Polybian thought nowhere appear in the *Repubblica de' Vineziani*. They do appear in the *Repubblica Fiorentina*, and yet we cannot say for certain what principles of *composizione* and *proporzione* Giannotti would have educed from the functioning of Venetian magistracies if he had written his third section.

So far as our evidence goes, there is no indication that he would have presented Venice as a Polybian balance of monarchy, aristocracy, and democracy. Certainly we are told that the republic consists of a Consiglio Grande, a Consiglio de' Pregati, a Collegio, and a Doge; and of these the first, second, and fourth obviously correspond to the classical many, few, and one, while the Collegio is an executive presidium of serving magistrates which renders more efficient the aristocratic element of the *pregati*. But there is far less indication than there was in Guicciardini that the four members balance or check one another. We may suspect that Giannotti would in the end have put forward some such theory, but the fact remains that his study of the Venetian constitutional structure is developed in a double context, that of a historical account of how Venice came to be a closed aristocracy and that of a detailed investigation of Venetian voting procedures, neither of which has any obvious connection with the principles of Polybian balance.

When he wrote about Florentine politics, Giannotti as we shall see advocated a *vivere popolare*; he wished to extend membership in the Consiglio

Grande to all who paid taxes, not merely to those whose ancestry qualified them to hold magistracies. How far these sympathies were developed when he was writing about Venice in 1525–1527 is not quite clear,[14] but there is evidence that he was aware of the problem raised by the law of 1297, which had limited membership in the Venetian Consiglio to the descendants of those who sat in it at that date. In Florence the constitution of 1494, consciously modeled on that of Venice, was almost archetypically *the* popular constitution because it was based on a Consiglio Grande open to all qualified citizens; so long as there was no such provision as the Venetian law of 1297, there was bound to be tension within this image. Giannotti does not adopt Guicciardini's view that Florence is as aristocratic as Venice and Venice as democratic as Florence, since in either case there is a finite citizen body and the terms "aristocratic" and "democratic" have meaning only in relation to the distribution of power within that body. He points out, as he is to do again in the case of Florence, that in Venice there are poor, middling, and elite persons, *popolari*, *cittadini*, and *gentiluomini*. The first are those whose callings are too ignoble and whose poverty too great to qualify them for any kind of civic membership; the second are those whose descent and occupations give them standing and wealth enough to rank as sons of the *patria*; and the third are those who are truly of the city and the state.[15] When Giannotti writes as a Florentine advocating popular rule, he wishes to admit the second category to membership of the Consiglio, if not to magistracy itself;[16] but it is the characteristic of Venice that there is a Consiglio Grande, but that the law of 1297 limits it forever to persons in the last and highest grade. Once again, if we had Giannotti's final reflections upon the government of Venice, we might know how he thought this closed council contributed to Venetian stability; but it is noteworthy that in what we have, a first sketch in which the shape of the republic is roughed out (*dirozzato*),[17] the dialogue takes the form of a discussion of the history of the Venetian Consiglio and of the cause (*cagione*) and occasion (*occasione*)[18] of each form which it has assumed. It is noteworthy also that, though to a humanist writing history the cause of political innovation would normally be the perception by reforming legislators of some principle on which government should be modeled, Giannotti is unwilling to go too far in ascribing such perceptions to the ancestral Venetians; a caution which reveals a number of things about the problems which Venice presented to the political intellect.

In Venetian constitutional history he sees two critical moments: one occurring about 1170, when a Consiglio Grande was established, the other in 1297, when its membership was closed.[19] Both are moments in the institutionalization of a citizen body on a footing of proportionate equality among its increasingly finite membership. The Venetians constitute a civic aristocracy, and it is the characteristic of such an aristocracy—we know by now that it was hard to define the civic ethos in other than aristocratic terms—that its members pursue glory (Giannotti's term is *chiarezza*) in the public service. In this way individuals become renowned and their families preserve the memory of their deeds. This, Trifone explains, is why we know relatively little of Venetian history before 1170. Since there was no Consiglio, there was no institutionalized pursuit of *chiarezza*; there were no families constituted by the *chiarezza* of their ancestors and impelled to preserve records of past deeds and lineal continuities. The condition of Venice was not unlike that of Rome under the kings; in both cases only the advent of a civic aristocracy led to the institution of historic memory, and in the case of Venice it may be added that the term *gentiluomo*, before 1170, probably meant only what it means in other cities—an individual outstanding for his birth or for some other reason—and had not the precise civic and political significance it acquired with the development of the Consiglio.[20]

Giannotti is grappling with several problems in Venetian studies. One is the general paucity of historical information, and the circumstance that more is preserved in private archives than in public chronicles. Another is a problem of considerable importance in constitutional theory, already familiar to us from Machiavelli's *Discorsi*: since Venice claimed no hero-legislator and retained the memory of no great political crisis, it was difficult to explain how a citizen body could have perfected itself, especially since Giannotti does not spend much time on the possibility that the whole apparatus of perfection had existed since the beginning. When his interlocutors discuss the innovation of 1170, they face the question of how the Venetians could have thought of organizing themselves into a Consiglio Grande, seeing that no such institution existed anywhere in the world at that time. Very few men, they agree, are capable of political invention, and citizen bodies never approve proposals which have not been tested by experience, either their own or that of others. Innovation is almost always imitation; even Romulus is said to have borrowed from the Greeks, and Florence, after imitating the Venetian Consiglio in 1494 and the perpetual Dogeship in 1502, might have been saved from disaster if she had imitated what goes with them. It would therefore have been a miracle (*cosa miracolosa*) if the Venetians of 1170 had been able to excogitate the form of a Consiglio Grande without imitating it from somebody else, since it is this which has not only kept them free but raised them to unparalleled heights of grandeur. But we need not suppose that any such miracle occurred. Apart from a few hints in the scanty historical materials, it is reasonable to believe that some sort of Council was maintained by the Doges before 1170, so that those are right who maintain that the Council is of highest antiquity, so long as they do not mean the Consiglio Grande as established in that year.[21] In a passage faintly recalling Machiavelli's views on early Roman history, Giannotti suggests that reformers in 1170, wishing to strip the Doge of certain powers, resolved to transfer them to the Council, but realizing that there would be dangers and tensions if they were conferred upon a few, decided to transfer them to the citizens as a whole (while retaining a special degree of authority for themselves) and devised an annually elected Consiglio Grande to be truly representative of the whole.[22] No miraculous legislator is thus called for; Venetian history proceeds through pragmatic reflection on past experience and, far from hitting upon some miraculous recombination of elements, merely displays in 1170 a political sagacity exceeding that of the Roman patricians after the expulsion of the kings.

In the civic humanist perspective, a Consiglio Grande—whether Venetian or Florentine—was the foundation of all *libertà* in a *vivere civile*, because it brought together all citizens, on a footing of equality, in a competition for office and in *virtù*. Its appearance at Venice, then, could not as we have seen be left unexplained. But the closing of the Venetian Consiglio in 1297, so that membership became hereditary and new *gentiluomini* were next to never created, was a phenomenon of a different order. Giannotti writes that nothing can be learned of it from publicly commissioned histories, so that if one did not read the private records of noble houses one would remain almost wholly ignorant; and even in these sources nothing whatever is known about the *cagione* or the *occasione* of that law. From experience and history one recognizes that changes on this scale do not occur unless there has been some major emergency; but he has been unable to find out what this was, and he specifically says that he can see no imperfection in the Consiglio as established in 1170 which could have necessitated the *variazione* of 1297. It is possible, as he has earlier suggested, that all natives of good family were by now included in the Consiglio and that the closure was applied in order to keep out foreign merchants and preserve purity of lineage. But all this is mere conjecture, and nothing is known for certain.[23] It seems clear that Giannotti had encountered a double difficulty. He had really been unable to find any traditional or historical account of the closing of the Council; and, no less significantly, he could not deal with it by supposing that civic experience had led to the discovery of some political principle, because he could not imagine any principle which it exemplified. His attitude toward the closure is not free from ambiguity. When he first discusses it he asserts that Venetian *chiarezza* mounted higher than ever after 1297, and that few families of note already resident in Venice were excluded from power by the change; but in his subsequent treatment, while insisting that it was a change for the better, he concedes that some were excluded and embittered and allows the suggestion to be made that these declined in nobility and vanished from the historic record in consequence of their exclusion. Possibly the last word may be found in something that he writes in another context—admittedly with reference to a *particolarità* of much less importance than the great measure of 1297:

> You are to understand that in every republic there are many institutions (*costituzioni*) for which one can give no probable reason, let alone the true one. And this is to be found not only in those cities where the form of government has changed, but in those which have long been ruled and governed by the same laws. For although the usages have been kept up, their causes are none the less lost in antiquity.[24]

There are political phenomena which usage may justify, but cannot explain. If we know neither the occasion, the cause nor the principle on which the Council was closed in 1297, that measure is dangerously close to being one of them.

Giannotti's Venice, then, does not seem to have effected her escape from history through the divine intelligence of the legislator, or through achieving some Polybian or even Aristotelian combination of principles. If we now ask what are the salient features of Venetian government as he roughs them out in this initial sketch, the answer seems to emerge in two ways. In the first place there is what Giannotti's introductory remarks have prepared us to encounter: a description of the various councils and officers making up the Venetian pyramid, which ought at least to prepare the way for the never-written account of how they are linked together to compose *la forma di essa Repubblica*. It is a safe assumption that this account would have dealt both with the distribution of functions among the various magistracies and with the ways in which the Doge, the Collegio, and the Pregati came to be elected; for it was a characteristic of Aristotelian political science that the functions performed by public officials were not differentiated from the function of electing those officials, and that membership in the *ekklesia* or *consiglio* where magistrates were chosen was considered in itself a species of magistracy. This point is borne out when Giannotti, like Guicciardini a few years earlier, enumerates in more or less classic terms the principal powers of government. "It is said that there are four things which constitute the directive force (*il nervo*) of every republic: the creation of magistrates, the determination of peace and war, the making of laws and the hearing of appeals."[25]

Magistracies, or forms of power, are rendered interdependent by the ways in which they share these four modes of authority; but in that case the election of magistrates must itself be a kind of magistracy and enter into the complex distributions of authority. What rendered both Florence and Venice, in the eyes of both Giannotti and Guicciardini, governments of the *popolo* and of *libertà*, was the fact that in both (at least during Florence's republican interludes) there existed a Consiglio Grande in which all magistracies were distributed. The further problem, at least to minds trained on Aristotelian and humanist presumptions, was whether the Consiglio, as the assembly of all citizens, should have any other function than that of election. On the one hand it was possible, though as we know not very easy, to attribute to undifferentiated citizens species of intelligence which rendered them capable of other forms of decision. On the other it was possible to deny them any independent intelligence, to suppose that any specific type of decision needed a corresponding elite group or "few" to take it, and to reduce the role of the Consiglio Grande to that of ensuring that the election of these elite groups, which may now be termed "magistracies," took place under conditions of equality and impersonality. The latter we have seen to be the thrust of Guicciardini's argument; Giannotti, when writing some years later about Florentine government as one committed to some kind of popular supremacy, had to decide whether control of elections was a sufficient guarantee of this, or whether the Consiglio Grande must intervene also, to some degree, in the exercise of the other three powers making up the *nervo della repubblica*.

But when he wrote his description of Venice such problems did not demand his attention. The limited size of the Venetian citizen body precluded any division into *ottimati* and *popolo*, and he was able to ignore what would in a Florentine context have been the strongly elitist implications of the circumstance that the Consiglio discharged no functions other than the electoral, none at least that need detain his readers. In observing that new legislative proposals are dealt with by the Pregati, he remarks quite casually that some laws are also laid before the Consiglio Grande for its approval, if the initiating magistrate thinks they need the *maggior riputazione* which this brings.[26] Focussing his attention exclusively on the electoral organization of the Venetian Consiglio, he is able to deal at length[27] with a major constituent of the "myth of Venice" of which we have so far said little: the complex and fascinating routinization of nominating, voting and ballotting which visitors to the republic delighted to observe and describe. By a series of physical devices—the benches on which men took their seats at random, but rose up in a fixed order to cast their votes; the containers from which names and numbers were drawn at random, but in which positive or negative votes might be placed in secrecy—the Venetians were held, so to speak, to have mechanized *virtù*. That is, they had blended the elements of chance and choice in such a way as to present each voter with a clear set of alternatives, and to liberate him from every pressure and every temptation which might cause him to vote to please somebody else instead of stating his rational choice of the better candidate. If one thought of *virtù*, as one might, as the taking of decisions directed at the public good, and if one thought of the *sala del consiglio grande* as an enormous physical device for eliminating extraneous pressures and ensuring—almost enforcing—rationality in choosing for the public good, then one thought of Venetian government in a way for which such a phrase as "the mechanization of *virtù*," though anachronistic, is not inappropriate. No less than the image of a Polybian perfection of equilibrium, the belief that the Venetians had achieved this was a potent element of the *mito di Venezia*.

Giannotti's account of Venetian voting procedures was the first written and printed by a Florentine for Florentines, but their general nature had of course been known at Florence for a long time.[28] Guicciardini, we recall, did not believe in their efficacy; private interests and relationships could not be eliminated from what electors did in secret, and it would be better to have them declare their choices in public where their fellow-citizens could observe and respond to what they were doing. Mechanized secrecy of choice, in his view, was at once too oligarchic and not elitist enough. Guicciardini's criticism carries the very important implication that decision and *virtù*, in the last analysis, exist in the web of interactions between men; that what matters is less the rationality with which I choose what is for the public good than the concern for that good which I communicate to others in the act of choosing; and James Harrington, who admired the Venetian system, was to admit the force of the criticism that in these routinized and ritualized procedures, men did not learn to know each other.[29] In a secret ballot, each man chooses between alternatives that have been found for him and, even if his choice can be made perfectly rational, he does not have opportunity to declare his reasons to his fellows. If the Venetian Consiglio did nothing but choose magistrates and officers in this way, it would represent an extreme development of the principle that the many had no function but to ensure equality and impersonality in the choice of the governing elites. Giannotti does not comment on these problems, but it is possible to see from his subsequent writings that Venetian procedures reinforced in his mind the idea of a political activity which consisted purely in a silent and rational choice between alternatives found and presented by others. To understand the full range of his political thought, one must turn to those works in which he applied Venetian and other ideas to the problem of devising a popular government for Florence.

[11]

We have two short treatises which he wrote during the period of the last Florentine republic and the Great Siege (1527–1530). The first of these is a *discorso* on reordering the government, of familiar type, which, according to an appended letter of later date, Giannotti wrote at the request of the Gonfaloniere Niccolò Capponi, shortly before he fell from power and was replaced by a more radical ruling group. Assuming that this *Letter to Capponi*[30] retains the original text and was not revised in the light of later experience, Giannotti's thinking at this time (say late 1528) was so markedly aristocratic in character that it is hard to distinguish from that of Guicciardini's *Dialogo*, and Felix Gilbert has defined it as typical of the liberal *ottimati* who wanted to maintain elite rule within a popular system. Giannotti begins by laying down that the citizens of any republic are of diverse natures, and that the aspirations of all must be satisfied if the republic is to survive (an Aristotelian maxim). There are those who desire only liberty, and these are the many; there are those who seek that honor (*onore*) which is the reward of greater prudence (*prudenza*), and these are fewer; and there are those who seek the highest position of all, which can be enjoyed by only one man at a time. This variant of the traditional one-few-many differentiation was something of a Florentine cliché; Guicciardini, Machiavelli, and Lodovico Alamanni had used it already; but it was not a formula which had been found necessary by the student of Venetian affairs. There the citizen body was so homogeneous that it could be treated as consisting of equals; but in the sharply divided city of Florence, where an elite and a non-elite confronted each other (so it was thought) within the citizen body, it was far more necessary to categorize the different types of citizen and plan a mixed government as a combination of the one, few and many which the categories employed inevitably suggested. Though Giannotti does not use the language of *governo misto* when writing directly about Venice, the city begins to appear in that light as soon as its principles and methods are applied to the ordering of Florence.

The Consiglio Grande had been restored as soon as the Medici collapsed in 1527, and Gilbert presents Giannotti's *discorso* as one of a number of proposals to lessen its power in favor of the optimate *cerchio*.[31] So no doubt it is, but we should observe that Giannotti's criticisms of the existing system are directed at its over-narrow and over-restrictive character. The Gonfaloniere has too much influence over the Signoria; the Ten of War (to whom he was secretary) have too much power in matters of peace and war, and their procedure is so disorderly that decisions are often made by one or two men. All this is *strettissimo* and *violento*. Like the Guicciardini of the *Dialogo*, Giannotti argued that aristocratic leadership could function only on a footing of equality among aristocrats, and that this could be secured only by a regime of *libertà*, guaranteed by a Consiglio Grande. His threefold classification of citizens necessitated a four-step pyramid of government, exactly following that, he had observed in Venice. The many who desired liberty were to be represented (the term is in the original Italian) by a Consiglio Grande; the few who pursued *onore* by a senate elected for life. The role of the One was obviously to be played by a Gonfaloniere *a vita*, but since there would always be more than one seeking the supreme glory which could formally be vested in only one man at a time, he was to be assisted by a council of *procuratori*, like the *collegio* at Venice, consisting of the most experienced magistrates of all, sharing his preeminence and aspiring legitimately to his office should it fall vacant. Though election to the senate, the *procuratori* and the gonfalonierate was to be for life, the essence of *libertà* was to be retained by keeping all elections in the hands of the Consiglio. In this way, competition for elite membership was to be open, and men would owe their preeminence to public and not private favor. Giannotti no doubt assumed that there would be a sufficient turnover through death to satisfy the aspirations of the young to office.

It appears at this stage that the Consiglio Grande has been confined to the single function of preserving liberty through rendering public and political the emergence of elites. But Giannotti introduces the further principle that every public action is divisible into three phases, which he calls *consultazione*, *deliberazione*, and *esecuzione*.[32] If we place the first two beside Guicciardini's *deliberazione* and *approvazione*, some apparent confusion may arise; but the distinction being drawn in either case is that between the activity of proposing alternative courses of action and the activity of choosing between such alternatives. We know that it had already been used by Guicciardini, and it might have been suggested by many, though it corresponds exactly with none, of the distinctions between different modes of political activity drawn in Aristotle's *Politics*. In a Renaissance setting, it must necessarily have to do with the distinctions which the age observed between different modes of political understanding; and Giannotti proceeds to say that *consultazione* must be left to the few, since only a few possess the faculty of invention (*invenzione*) and these do not need the counsel of others[33] (though presumably they take counsel among themselves). To Florentines interested in Venetian procedures, the idea of a silent, routinized, rational choice implicit in the mechanisms of the ballot might well have heightened the sense of a distinction between invention and selection; but when Giannotti proceeds to lodge *deliberazione* in the many, it is characteristic of the way Florentine thought seems to have been developing that he says nothing about the intellectual or moral faculties which render the many capable of choosing where they cannot initiate. The reason why they should have this function is that if the few choose, or if *consultazione* and *deliberazione* are in the same hands, the temptations of power will pervert their reason; their choice will be determined by private ambitions, and in consequence *consultazione* will be exercised not by the few qualified, but by the even fewer ambitious. Here, once again, we are looking at the origins of the doctrine of the separation of powers, and it should be observed both how far these origins lay in the fear of corruption, and how little a role was played by any clear theory of a democratic mode of understanding.

If *consultazione* is left to the few, rationality is assured; if *deliberazione* is left to the many, "liberty will be secured, and those who have authority will have it by virtue (*virtù*) of the republic and not through their own presumption and importunity."[34] Execution may be left to the few, and it is not unfitting that those who proposed a policy should have responsibility for carrying it out. But as we examine what Giannotti is saying on these matters, we make two further discoveries. The first is that the composition of a public action by *consultazione*, *deliberazione* and *esecuzione* is depicted as occurring primarily within the senate, which is the organ of the few and *rappresenta lo stato degli ottimati*. When we read that *deliberazione* is carried out "by the many, that is, by the senate,"[35] we realize that the few in this case are the *procuratori* or the Ten of War, and that the numerical few–many distinction does not after all coincide with the qualitative distinction between the many who seek liberty through the Consiglio and the few who seek honor through the senate; it is internal to the latter. But we next discover a further reason for this. The analysis of action has so far been conducted solely with reference to the determination of questions of peace and war, which Giannotti like Guicciardini regarded as the most important single function of government once internal liberty was secured (if it was not more important even than that). These questions were to go no further than the senate. When he deals with the *procuratori* as initiators of new legislation,[36] however, Giannotti makes it clear that the final *deliberazione* must take place in the Consiglio Grande. He makes more specific provision for this than he had described as existing in Venice, and the reason may well have been the acute awareness possessed by Florentines that a new law could easily affect the distribution of political power—a thing assumed not to occur at Venice. But the legislative power ranks in importance after the power of peace and war, and the feeling that the latter was a matter of *prudenza*, and *prudenza* the characteristic of the few,[37] was to drag Giannotti's thought in an aristocratic direction even after he was much more openly committed to popular government than he was when he wrote the *Letter to Capponi*.

It was probably the siege of 1528–1530 that brought about an undeniable change in Giannotti's thinking. After the fall of Capponi he remained in Florence to the end and seems, not unlike Guicciardini, to have had ambivalent feelings toward the radical leaders, at once condemning their recklessness and admiring their courage. He had no good opinion of their Savonarolan religiosity or of the way they conducted the government of the city, but even before Capponi's removal from the scene, the defense of Florence was raising a political issue which may have formed the bridge between Giannotti's earlier philo-Venetian and his later *popolare* writings. This was the question of the militia. Machiavelli and Guicciardini had agreed in contrasting Venice, as an aristocratic *città disarmata*, with Rome as an armed, popular, turbulent, and expanding state; and in the *Repubblica de' Veneziani* Giannotti had allowed Trifone to contrast Roman military glory with Venetian peace and stability, to the latter's apparent advantage. Nevertheless, there was the militia tradition at Florence; there were Machiavelli's writings, with which Giannotti was acquainted; and before as well as after Capponi's overthrow, the republic set about organizing a militia which was held to have performed great deeds during the siege and became part of the legend cherished by Giannotti and other exiles in subsequent years. As secretary to the Ten, he was involved in organizing this force, and we have a *discorso* on the subject which is accepted as his work and seems to belong to the latter part of 1528.[38] It forms part of a substantial contemporary literature of the revived militia, with which it should be read; but in the context of Giannotti's own thinking, it can be seen working a change.

Giannotti opens by refuting various arguments against the establishment of a militia, the chief of which is that arms are contrary to the nature of the Florentines, since this has been so long formed by mercantile pursuits that it will be too difficult to accustom them to military exercises.[39]

His reply is an appeal from second to first nature: there is an absolute necessity for the city to be armed, since it is the nature of every creature to defend itself and a city must not lack the *virtù* which is given it in order to do so.[40] The fact that some men never develop their intellect does not alter the fact that men are endowed with intellect by nature; and as for the argument that the Florentines have grown used to other pursuits, this can be dealt with by saying that since use (*assuefazione*) is so mighty a power that it can operate even against nature, it can do even more when operating with nature on its side.[41] The revival of the militia, then, will restore the Florentines to what they are by the universal nature of all men, and this is a sufficient refutation of those who see it as somehow incompatible with civic life. If it is natural to men to bear arms, Giannotti means, and if it is natural to them to follow citizenship, there can be no incongruency between the two, and this is much more than a formal reconciliation: Giannotti goes on to argue that the militia is a powerful, indeed an indispensable, socializing, and politicizing agency. Military service makes men equal, in the sense that all who serve are equally subject to the public authority, and the private loyalties and affiliations which may disfigure and corrupt civic life have no place there and are eliminated.[42] Because men in arms defend the same things without distinction, they come to have the same values; because they are all disciplined to accept the same authority, they are all obedient to the *res publica*; because the public authority monopolizes force, there can be no subjection of one private citizen to another, so that liberty and authority are strengthened and guaranteed simultaneously.

But there is a dynamic involved in the view that the militia makes men citizens, as the military discipline imposed by Romulus made Romans out of a random collection of bandits;[43] it is that the more men we arm, the more citizens we must make. The inhabitants of Florence, Giannotti proceeds, are of three kinds: those capable of membership in the Consiglio, those capable only of paying taxes and those capable of neither. He now states the case for enrolling the second category in the militia as well as the first. The *beneficiati*—as in his later writings he calls the first class—are too few in numbers; the second class have the same material and emotional interests (fatherland, property, and families) as the first, and must be given the same opportunity to defend them. Once you give some men the right to defend their property with their own persons, to deny it to others who have the same property is to render them worse than slaves, the city would become a collection of masters and servants, and the latter would be lower than the dwellers in the subject cities and the countryside.[44] To leave them unarmed would divide the city, to arm them would unite it. Giannotti goes on from this point to state the case against excluding from the militia those suspected of collaboration with the Medici, and argues that to give them arms will be to reunite them with the city of which they are members. He does not put it into words at this stage, but it is clear that arms and a full equipment of civic rights are inseparable: on the one hand, to deny men arms which are allowed to others is an intolerable denial of freedom; on the other, those who bear arms in the militia become morally capable of a citizenship which it would be equally impossible to deny them. In the *Repubblica Fiorentina*, written a few years later, he followed a similar logic and contended that membership in the Consiglio Grande should be conceded to all who paid taxes, whether their ancestors had held magistracies or not.

We have returned to the point where it is seen that the armed state must be the popular state. Machiavelli had opted for Rome and against Venice on these grounds, and there is one moment in Giannotti's Venetian dialogue where the Florentine interlocutor asks how many men in Venice there are capable of bearing arms and how many *gentiluomini* enjoying the rights of citizenship.[45] The answer reveals a disproportion of 40,000 to 3,000, but no comment is made either on the meaning of this for Venetian political stability or on Venice's reliance on mercenary soldiers. In general, the case for the restricted size of the Venetian citizen body must rest on the assumption that those who are not *gentiluomini* are either resident aliens or plebeians of too base a calling to rank as political animals at all; neither claim could be made in the case of Florence. Even more than Machiavelli, Giannotti was driven by Florentine realities toward the ideal of the armed popular state, and he specifically applies the idea to Florentine conditions in a way that Machiavelli's *Discorsi* do not. We know from the *Repubblica Fiorentina* that he recognized Machiavelli as an authority on the military and civic role of the militia, but it should be observed that the theory set forth in the militia discourse of 1528 is much more overtly Aristotelian than is Machiavelli's. It is natural to man to defend his own, and it is natural to him to pursue common goods in citizenship. To restore him his power to do the former contributes to the restoration of his power to do the latter; both restorations constitute *riformazione* in the Aristotelian sense, the return of man to his prime nature. This is why militia service is an agency transforming men into citizens.

There was another dimension which thought on this subject could easily assume. In Giannotti's proposals for organizing the militia there is provision for a solemn ceremony on the feast-day of San Giovanni, at which the citizens in arms, mustered by their officers, shall hear mass, take an oath of obedience at the altar, and listen to an oration making clear the religious as well as civic meaning of their duties.[46] Such ceremonies were actually held, and we have the texts of several orations delivered to the militia by figures of the post-Capponi regime.[47] All of them strike a note essentially Savonarolan, in the sense that the Aristotelian idea of a *riformazione* of man as citizen is extended into the sphere of personal holiness and proclaimed with religious exaltation as a *rinnovazione*. Florence has been chosen by God to restore *libertà*,[48] and to exhibit men living socially according to the values of Christianity; "*vivere a popolo*," says one of them, "*non è altro the vivere da cristiano*."[49] Since militia service teaches men to be citizens,[50] it is part of this process of eschatological restoration; it is itself holy and miraculous, and arms are more than once spoken of as a "garment"—*sacratissima veste, incorruttibile veste dell' arme*.[51] The idea that the citizen-in-arms dedicates himself to the public good is of course dominant, and he is many times told why he should not fear death in doing so; but there is one significant passage in which the austerity and discipline of the soldier's life is equated with the Christian ideal of poverty, and we are told that poverty is the origin of every art, profession and study known to man, and that only the lovers of poverty have pursued liberty, founded republics and overthrown tyrants.[52] Poverty— we are looking here at the heritage of the radical Franciscans—is the ideal which impels the citizen to sacrifice his private satisfactions to the common good, and the warrior, the citizen, and the Christian have here become one; but as is usually the case in Christian thought, it is the will to sacrifice goods, not the nonpossession of goods, which is being praised. There is no contradiction between utterances such as these and those in which we are introduced once again to the Aristotelian doctrine that a city is supported by its *mediocri*—those who are neither too poor to be citizens nor so rich that they are tempted to self-regard.[53] Poverty is the virtue of the *mediocri* rather than the *poveri*.

Giannotti's thought nowhere follows this path, or extends Aristotelian citizenship into a realm of radical saintliness and eschatological vision, unless it be in the remark, made more than once in the *Repubblica Fiorentina* that the republic and the militia were restored and succeeded "contrary to the opinion of the wise"[54]—and Guicciardini, making the same point, had come close to equating faith with madness. But if he did not think with Savonarola that the citizen must be one in whom Christian ideals were realized, he did not think with Machiavelli that Christian and civic values were ultimately incompatible. His doctrine that military and civic life alike realized and "reformed" man's true nature precludes anything so radical as the latter; and in a sense it was his continued use of the Venetian model which indicated his separation from the former. If we think of the fall of Niccolò Capponi as the moment at which the radical Savonarolans broke finally with the liberal *ottimati* like Guicciardini, it would also be the moment at which the eschatological and "Venetian" projections of the republican image, introduced jointly by Savonarola and Paolantonio Soderini in 1494, split apart. Giannotti, a liberal optimate who remained with the republic to the end, had nothing of the Savonarolan about him, and was left by default to express the ideals of 1494 in Venetian terms.

It was not impossible to reconcile Venetian paradigms with the idea of the supreme importance of a Consiglio Grande; the significant tensions in Giannotti's thought lay elsewhere. The revival of the militia had convinced him of the need for *popolare* government; but the theory which asserted that such a form of rule must rest on a warrior citizenry, though it could be stated in Aristotelian and even Savonarolan terms, could not escape a strongly Machiavellian coloring in the mind of one who, like Giannotti, had read the *Arte della Guerra* and known its author. The whole tradition of debate in the Orti Oricellari, to which Machiavelli and Giannotti both belonged—and to which Guicciardini must in some way be related—posed an antithesis between Venice and armed popular government as typified in Rome. Machiavelli's treatment of *innovazione* and *virtù* contains a latent dynamism hard to reconcile with Aristotelian theory of the civic life as fulfilling a static human nature; yet the *Repubblica Fiorentina*, Machiavellian though it is at many points, explicitly declares its debt to Aristotle, "from whom, as from a superabundant spring that has spread through all the world overflowing streams of doctrine, I have taken all the fundamentals of my brief discourse,"[55] and this is in no way an empty compliment. When we add the variations that were beginning to appear within the Venetian model, between the idea of Polybian balance, the idea of a mechanized virtue, the idea of fundamental powers of government and the idea of differentiation between the component parts of a political act, and reflect that these concepts must now be applied to the theory of a government *popolare* in a sense in which that of Venice could never be defined, it becomes plain that the *Repubblica Fiorentina*, the wishful fantasy of an exile forever divorced from political action, is nevertheless a remarkable case study in the history of political conceptualization.

The aim of the work, we are told in language by now familiar, is to devise a durable if not a perpetual form of government for Florence.[56] No general theory of cities and their characteristics need be constructed, since the basic characteristics (*qualità*) of Florence have already been determined by those who live there. But the form of government is to the character of a city as the soul to the body, and if a human soul were to be placed in a bestial body, or vice versa, the two would corrupt and destroy one another—a use of the term *corruzione* differing somewhat from its technical employment. We must therefore consider what is the best form of government, but ask whether Florence has those characteristics which render a city capable of such a form, and how this can be imposed without altering Florentine manners and customs too greatly. Where the choice of a concrete and specific context drove Guicciardini to employ the analogy of the physician treating a sick man, Giannotti employs that of an architect rebuilding a house upon foundations already laid; the difference indicates the comparative radicalism and compulsive optimism of the refugee hoping to return.[57]

He proceeds to a theoretical disquisition purely Aristotelian and Polybian, in which the latter's Book VI is cited by name[58] for the first time among the writers we have studied. There are in principle three types of government, and which should obtain ought to be determined by the location of *virtù* in the one, the few, or the many. He does not specify what is meant by *virtù*, but the context shows it to have the standard ethical meanings, with the interesting, modification that the concentration of *virtù* in the many "is found in those cities which have military virtue, which is the property belonging to the multitude."[59]

If *virtù* in the one or the few means the ability to govern with regard to the good of all, it would be valuable to know if Giannotti shared Machiavelli's reasons for holding that this ability can only exist among the many if it takes a military form. However, he does not clarify his remark, but goes on to explain that each of the three types can exist only in ideality. There is no difference between the good and the bad form of each except the virtue or corruption of the ruling group; and it follows, first, that nothing prevents the degeneration of each type except the rulers' ability to escape the moral corruption which is rooted in their natures,[60] and second, that it would be morally impossible to establish any of the three pure types in the actual world, where we must presuppose that men are corrupt already.[61] Nothing is said about *fortuna*, and, despite his acknowledged debt to Polybius, Giannotti employs neither the idea of the cycle as a determinate order of succession of the forms nor the concept that each pure type is corrupted by the excessive power of its own special virtue; but we are clearly in that Christian world in which history is the dimension of the Fall of man, to which all these concepts history be rhetorically appropriate.

A theory of mixed government (*governo misto* or *stato misto*) now makes its appearance, in a form markedly more Aristotelian than Polybian, and Christian rather than Hellenic in the sense that it is intended for fallen and

imperfectly rational men. In every city there are different types of citizens
with different desires. There are the rich and great who desire to command;
these are necessarily few in number, and the differentiation of the "one" from
the "few" appears only because there are degrees of authority and
preeminence which only one man can enjoy at a time. There are the many
poor, who do not wish to command, or to be commanded by any authority
less universal than that of the laws; and there are the *mediocri*, who as well as
desiring *libertà* in the sense just defined have sufficient fortune to desire
onore—plainly meaning a share in command—in addition.[62] It is the latter
who fulfill Aristotle's definition of the citizen as one who rules and is ruled,
and if only for this reason it would be erroneous to assign them the role of
the "few." The *grandi* clearly possess many "oligarchical" characteristics, and
it emerges a little later, in the true Aristotelian tradition, that it is possible for
the *mediocri* to be so numerous that they absorb the category of the "many
poor" altogether; Giannotti's numerical and his qualitative categories do not,
as they need not, perfectly coincide. What is important at this stage is that
we are studying men's desires, not their virtues. These *desideri* are also called
umori, a term which carries nonrational connotations; they are irrational
because they are incompatible, there being no way of combining, without
modifying, the desire of some to command with the desire of others to be
commanded by none. Formally, it might seem, this could be done by
establishing a rule of laws, or by incorporating all citizens within the
category of *mediocri* who both command and are commanded; but whether as
a Christian, an Aristotelian, or a Machiavellian, it is important that Giannotti
was convinced that the *umori* could never wholly be abolished and
consequently that no mixed government could ever be a perfect blend.[63]

Governo misto is, initially at least, a beneficent deception practiced on
irrational men. It is possible to introduce a *modo di vivere*—in fact, if we look
closely, this is the only way in which a *modo di vivere* can be introduced—in
which men are given part of what they want, or are given it conditionally, in
such a shape that they believe they have been given the whole of it, or have
been given it absolutely.[64] The incompatibility of their desires is an
incompatibility arising from the nature of power; some men cannot
command all while others are free from command by any; and therefore the
beneficent deception consists in the fact that the former receive authority
and the latter liberty, in such a way that each party's enjoyment of its desire
is conditional upon the will of the other.

> In the form of government we are seeking it is necessary that
> one man be prince, but that his principate is not dependent on

himself alone, that the great command, but that their authority does not originate with themselves; that the multitude be free, but that their liberty involves some dependence; and finally that the *mediocri*, as well as being free, can attain to honours (*onori*— the word in the plural has the secondary meaning of "offices"), but in such a way as is not placed entirely at their will ...[65]

But the deception may lead men beyond the point of illusion. Assuming that it is the property of man as a rational political animal to rule with an eye to the common good, and assuming that this state of mutual political dependence will compel men so to rule whether they intend to or not, such a distribution of functions (Giannotti calls it *amministrazione*) will make men rational; *umori* will become *virtù*. But the agency precipitating them from unreason into reason is a structure of powers, arranged so that they depend upon and condition one another. Once these powers are exercised rationally, they become faculties in the individual whereby he acts rationally and politically and governs the actions of others (as they govern his) so that they act in the same way. That is, powers too have become *virtù*; and it is characteristic of the active connotations which this word always bore that Giannotti is able on occasion to use it interchangeably with terms like *forze* and *potestà*. The polity, once again, is a contrivance of human intelligence for the institutionalization Of *virtù*: for assigning men functions which will require them to act in such a way that their natures are reformed and are once again what they *are*, instead of what they *have become*.

Such a contrivance depends on the existence of *mediocri*, the only people capable of governing and being governed, and therefore of substituting rational behavior for the irrationalism of those who can only command or only obey. If there were a city consisting wholly of *mediocri*, it could be a democracy of the pure type—we know that the *virtù* of the *mediocri* would be military—but there is none.[66] Where the *mediocri* are stronger than, or equal to, the *grandi* and *poveri* in combination, or where they hold the balance of strength between the two, a *governo misto* is possible and indeed necessary, if the city is not to suffer that corruption which comes when the soul is disproportionate to the body. It remains to be shown that Florence satisfies these conditions and Giannotti proceeds to do so, in the form of a history of the city which indicates how his Aristotelian grounding had given him a more subtle and sanguine grasp of historical causation, and delivered him further from the grip of *fortuna*, than a merely Polybian theory of cycles could have done. His thought will also be found strikingly anticipatory of that of James Harrington in the next century.

Giannotti contends that Florence used to be a city of *grandi* and *poveri*, and has in the last century become increasingly one of *mediocri*. To understand this, he claims, is to understand Florentine history both before and after the Medicean regime of 1434–1494. Had he employed the scheme of Polybius's sixth book to this end, it would have suggested that rule by the few (*grandi*) had given place to rule by the many (*poveri*) and then to rule by a tyrant (Cosimo) and so round the clock again; each form would have existed in its purity, decayed through spontaneous inner degeneration and collapsed through some combination of circumstances precipitated by unpredictable *fortuna*. But such a scheme was unlikely to satisfy Florentines of the 1530s, whether historically or philosophically; they knew too much about the past by way of data, and demanded too much by way of explanation. Giannotti lays it down that in considering every event (*azione*), one must examine the general cause (*cagione*), the precipitating cause (*occasione*), and the immediate cause (*principio*). In the case of the fall of the Florentine republic in 1512, the *cagione* was the discontent of certain ambitious oligarchs with the form of government, the *occasione* was the war between Pope Julius and the king of France, and the *principio* was the attack of the Spanish army on Prato and Florence. *Cagione* is a disposition of things, which makes itself felt when *occasione* offers, and very frequently it is also the cause why *occasione* appears.[67]

In the case of Florentine politics in the thirteenth and fourteenth centuries, we are concerned with an unstable alternation between the *stati* of *grandi* and popolo—Giannotti is clearly not thinking of it as a cycle—and the *cagione* or *disposizione* was the rough equality between the forces (*forze*) of the two. The monopoly of *qualità* by the one was answered by the ascendancy of quantity in the other, so that neither could prevail or destroy its adversary— Giannotti would have agreed with Machiavelli's further contention that neither could devise a system of government acceptable to the other—and the victory of either party was the result of *occasione*, which might at some future date, and generally did, prove propitious to the other.[68] In this case *cagione* was all, and it is clearly of no importance what the various *occasioni* may have been. It is useful to contrast Machiavelli's use of *occasione* in *Il Principe*, where it signified the extreme irrationality and unpredictability of the particular event in a world of *fortuna*. Machiavelli knew far more about historical causation than that, but the contrast is still worth drawing. Giannotti's *occasione* is still the random unpredictable which turns the wheel and overthrows power systems; but the instability of politics is now caused rather than inherent. *Grandi* and *poveri*, quality and quantity, authority and liberty, constitute an unstable equilibrium from which most men cannot escape, being what they are; but one can see why their natures constitute instability, and consequently one can see how stability might replace it. *Fortuna* consequently plays little role in his system, and the word is hardly used. He relies instead on an Aristotelian theory of causation, and an Aristotelian theory of social forces.

Harrington, constructing in the next century an account of English history along comparable lines, ascribed to the king and barons of medieval England a role very like that of Giannotti's *grandi* and *poveri*; they were locked in an unstable equilibrium until the Tudors undermined baronial power by raising up a landowning people, whose advent proved no less ruinous to a monarchy that could no longer govern them.[69] A similar role is allotted by Giannotti to the Medici of the fifteenth century, who, by advancing poor men to office and depriving the aristocrats of any chance to display *generosità* and *grandezza* except at the nod of the ruling family, depressed some and exalted others to form a new and growing class of *mediocri*, who now hold the balance of power and make a stable *governo misto* possible in Florence.[70] Since 1530 the Medici have ruled with the support of a few *grandi* who owe them their advancement and a few more whom the excesses of the siege have *alienat[i] dal vivere universale e politico*, but their tyranny is self-abolishing; it deprives all men of what they desire and increases the number of *mediocri* whose presence alone can ensure that they achieve their various ends.[71] Like Harrington, Giannotti was a poor prophet but a successful enricher of the conceptual vocabulary; both men developed schemes of causation which wrongly predicted political stabilization and an end to historical turbulence, but increased the extent to which sequences of political change could be talked about in terms, concrete and social, which were not those of the irrational particularities of *fortuna*. One is tempted to say that both offered ways out of the Polybian cycle and into the rotating spheres of ordered government; but in fact their causal vocabularies were so rich that they never had recourse to the Polybian model at all. The vocabulary of Aristotle was less stilted, and it is this that Giannotti is using.

The apparatus of political analysis which it is possible to bring to bear on the city's problems continues to be a crucial question in Book II of the *Repubblica Fiorentina*, which is devoted to a criticism of the republican constitutions of 1494–1502–1512 and 1527–1530. Reforming legislators, Giannotti begins, like Numa and Lycurgus, have a harder task than those who found cities where none have existed before (we should remember that Machiavelli in the *Discorsi*, though not in *Il Principe*, had on the whole treated Lycurgus as belonging to this class). The latter have only to know what is good and may be fairly sure of the support of the unformed matter whom they lead and mold; but the former have to know what has been wrongly managed in previous constitutions, and there are familiar difficulties about this. In the first place there are always those who are used (*assuefatti*) to the previous order and will change only with difficulty; this is why Numa had to feign divine assistance and Lycurgus to use violence[72] (we recall the armed prophet of *Il Principe*). In the second place constitutional defects belong in the category of *cose particolari*, which are hard to understand by any means over and above mere experience; and in the third place no man is so free from human affections that he can always see clearly defects in which he has himself been involved.[73] Savonarola, both as a foreigner and as a friar, could hardly be expected to know much about the workings of Florentine institutions; nevertheless, the Consiglio Grande which he helped introduce would have reformed itself by degrees, if given time and if the treachery of certain *grandi* had not brought back the Medici.[74]

It is therefore of great importance to know if we can develop a political science by which the deficiencies of previous constitutions can be exposed and corrected. Giannotti proceeds to a critique of both republican constitutions, in which he argues that although the Consiglio Grande was nominally the foundation of the system, in practice the various magistracies—including the Ten and in some respects the Gonfaloniere—exercised so much irresponsible power that effective authority was in the hands of a few.[75] This disguised oligarchy should not be confused with a disguised aristocracy; Giannotti's links with the liberal *ottimati* are still strong enough to make him stress that this state of things alienated them from the government so much that their hostility grew worse under the gonfalonierate for life of 1502–1512, of which he otherwise approves, and that one's detestation of their treachery should not blind one to its causes (*cagioni*, not *occasioni*).[76] In these chapters he is essentially resuming and reworking the themes of the *Letter to Capponi*, and two lines of constitutional analysis are reappearing. In the first place it is evident that the irresponsibility of the various magistracies arose from a failure to separate powers: they could do as they liked because they had *deliberazione* as well as *consultazione*. When Giannotti reverts, as he does some chapters later, to the recommendation of Venetian voting procedures, it is because these decisively separate the function of resolving from the function of proposing. But in the second place—and this is less unambiguously Venetian—there is the thought that the irresponsibility of the magistrates meant that their power was not, as it should have been, dependent on the power of some authority outside themselves. The structure of mutual interdependence which was the essence of *governo misto* must at some stage be worked out in full. But at this moment

Giannotti strikes a new note, indicative of the movement of his ideas toward popular supremacy, by saying that the familiar four powers—election of magistrates, peace and war, hearing of appeals, and legislation—which constitute the *vigore* (formerly the *nervo*) of government, must be in the control of whoever is to be *signore* of the city. If the many are to rule they must possess the four powers, or such a city will not be truly free.[77] Clearly the problem is where the four powers are to be located in a *governo misto*, but all Giannotti has to say at the moment is that it was insufficient to vest the election of magistrates in the Consiglio Grande—even though in that respect the city might be termed free—if peace and war were to remain in the irresponsible control of the Ten.[78] This rendered the right of appeal against magistrates' decisions virtually meaningless; while as for legislation, though it was nominally determined by the Consiglio, it was for all practical purposes in the hands of a few men. That election of magistrates alone is insufficient is shown by the practice of the Medici, who always controlled the appointment of those who managed the three remaining powers and left the election of others entirely free. The master of the three, not the four, powers is master of all.[79]

Giannotti is on the point of breaking new ground, which will lead his thought away from a simple mixture of three elements or a simple institutionalization of *virtù*. But for the present he has finished his analysis of the remedial knowledge which a reforming legislator of Florence must possess, and has now to blend it with the universal principles on which such a figure must proceed. The aim of the legislator, we read at the beginning of Book III, is to erect a state which will last; states fall either through internal dissension or through external assault; a *buon governo* provides against the former danger, a *buona milizia* against the latter—though it may also be considered part of *buon governo* and functioning to the former end. We now enter upon the Machiavellian problem of deciding whether civil or military organization should come first, and the figure of Romulus makes his appearance. But whereas it was Lycurgus who attended to *governo* and *milizia* simultaneously, before Romulus gave a thought to either he devoted himself to acts of violence against his neighbors and to the aggrandizement of his people's empire. It might seem that this choice was conducive to, if not identical with, military organization; but it appears to have been the Rape of the Sabines that Giannotti had principally in mind, and he comments that behavior of this kind can only have originated in the lust for domination, since Romulus had enough men to make a city and there were, after all, other ways of procuring women for them.[80] A little later Romulus is stated to have attended to civil before military organization; so that the effect of Giannotti's analysis is to separate him sharply from Machiavelli's view that because Rome was from the beginning organized for expansion, she was developed along military and therefore along popular lines. This initial repudiation of the Roman model, to be carried further in later chapters, assists in the reintroduction of Venetian concepts; and it rests in part on the implication that the function of the militia is preservative rather than aggressive. Venice, preferring stability to empire, went so far as to have no civic militia at all, but Giannotti, with the experience of the Siege behind him, is clear that the function of the militia is defensive. Rome was held by Bruni and Machiavelli to have destroyed republican *virtù* in the rest of the world and to have lost her own in consequence; but a nonaggressive militia may remain a means of inculcating *virtù* in the citizens. Men defended the republic of 1527–1530 where that of 1512 fell without a struggle, and the main reason was that a citizen militia existed at the later date but not at the earlier (Machiavelli's had been a militia of *contadini* and Giannotti was aware of the theoretical difference). The ideal Florence is to be armed and popular like Rome, but stable and peaceable like Venice; and Giannotti has moved decisively away from the restless dynamism of Machiavelli. The militia in its politicizing aspects is only a part of the apparatus of *buon governo*, and he now gives the latter so great a priority that for the rest of the book he lays, on the whole, less stress on the militia's power to make men virtuous than he had in 1528.[81]

Since what he is designing for Florence is a *governo misto* and not a pure democracy, we have to understand the role in a *governo misto* both of a militia—we have been told that military virtue is a democratic characteristic—and of the four powers of government, since their location determines who shall be *signore* of a city and we do not yet know the place of such a *Signore* in a mixed government. Giannotti proceeds to develop a critical analysis of the idea of mixed government. This can mean, he says, either that the three parts (one, few, and many; *grandi, mediocri, popolari*) exercise powers equal to one another, or that some one of them exercises power (*forze, potenza*) greater than either of the other two; the aim in each case is to produce an equilibrium. If we think carefully, we shall see that the former is bound to be defective. The reason is that a mixture of political elements is not like a mixture of natural elements, in which each component (*semplice*) loses its distinctive *virtù* and the compound acquires a *virtù* of its own. A political mixture is made up of men, Of *grandi, mediocri* and *popolari*, each of whom remains after mixture what he was before (unless, presumably, all have become *mediocri*, in which case we are not constructing a mixed government at all). Each retains his distinctive characteristic, which Giannotti is now calling *virtù*, not *umore* or (as he might have done) *fantasia*;

and these *virtù* consist of desires and the power to pursue them, which we merely institutionalize in the construction of a polity. It is therefore impossible to "temper a state so perfectly that the *virtù*—let us call it power—of each part is not apparent," and if these are equal, then the oppositions and resistances between them will be equal, and the republic will be full of dissensions which will bring about its ruin.[82] Giannotti has analyzed the term *virtù* in such a way as to bring about the substitution of a mechanistic for a pseudo-organic model in political analogy; Guicciardini's cook, stirring a mound of pasta, has disappeared.

It further follows that Polybius was wrong in seeing the Roman republic as the model of mixed government. He declares that ambassadors to Rome, when dealing with the consuls, thought they were in a kingdom; when with the senate, in an aristocracy; when with the *populus*, in a democracy. But this indicates that the power of each was equal to and uncontrolled by that of each other, and if this was so it is small wonder that the republic was prey to civil dissensions. Had it been well-ordered, ambassadors would have sensed in dealing with the consuls their dependence on the senate and the people, with the senate their dependence on the consuls and the people, and with the people their dependence on the consuls and the senate; and the *virtù* of each would have been *temperata* by the others. This should have been attended to by Brutus and his colleagues at the expulsion of the kings, and it can be argued that they tried to vest superiority in the senate; but assuming that Polybius is right in his facts, the equality of power between the three organs of government exposed Rome to that instability and strife which destroyed her in the end.[83]

The repudiation of Polybius carries to a further stage Giannotti's repudiation of Machiavelli on the subject of Rome. He has already implicitly rejected Machiavelli's contention that the armed popular state must be one organized for expansion; he now rejects his contention that Roman civil strife was a sign of health because it led to the institution of the tribunate (of which Giannotti has very little to say). The more Rome is eliminated from paradigmatic stature, the more fascinating becomes his evident intention of employing Venetian forms and concepts for the organization of an armed popular state. The crucial point, however, is Giannotti's drastic remodeling of the concept of *governo misto*, not least because this anticipates so much in English and American constitutional thought during the seventeenth and eighteenth centuries. His contention at the moment is that you cannot construct a balance of equal and independent forces because the pressures and counterpressures between them will be equal and there will be no resolution of the contest. But we know that political authority is of so many kinds and can be distributed in so many combinations that it is possible to render three agents mutually dependent, and it may seem theoretically possible to erect a system of three equal yet interdependent parts. Giannotti does not examine this possibility; he assumes that interdependence requires inequality, to the extent that one part must enjoy a preponderance over the other two (*la repubblica deve inclinare in una parte*). A principal reason seems to be that one must institutionalize conflict; there will always be competition among the powers, and if all are theoretically equal a loser may blame a victor for his loss and pursue internecine strife instead of the common good, whereas if the loser's inferiority is built into the structure of the republic it will be accepted as legitimate. Giannotti stresses that he does not mean the preponderant part to enjoy an *imperio* from which the others are excluded, but merely that it shall be less dependent on them than they on it. He has yet to make clear what is the relevance to all this of his doctrine that the four powers of government must belong to the *signore* or *padrone*, and whether indeed such terms are applicable to that part to which *la repubblica inclina*.[84]

The next step is to consider whether the preponderant part should be the *grandi* or the *popolo* (that it might be the one on whom the few and the many depend he does not consider a contemporary possibility, though he holds that this provided a stable government in prerepublican Rome). Giannotti argues the case for the people at considerable length, much as Machiavelli had, and not all his arguments need detain us. The indictment of Roman institutions is resumed, but in a way revealing some significant tensions. We are told that if the people feel themselves oppressed by a particular individual, they rush to his house and revenge themselves by burning it down—such at least is the way of Florence—whereas if they feel that their wrongs are the result of the maldistribution of public authority they agitate for legal and institutional reforms which will assure them of greater justice and a greater share of power; and this explains why the struggle between the orders at Rome was relatively bloodless until the time of the Gracchi and brought the plebeians increasing participation in authority.[85] This point clearly owes much to Machiavelli's argument concerning the beneficent effects of strife at Rome, which Giannotti otherwise wished to reject. Elsewhere we read that if at the expulsion of the Tarquins the senate had been made dependent on the people instead of the reverse, the people would have been free from injuries and the senate weaker than the people, and Rome would as a result have been more tranquil and escaped the dissensions which ultimately destroyed her; the republic would have been eternal and her empire *stabilissimo*.[86] Rome, a popular state to Machiavelli, is to Giannotti as to Guicciardini a rather unstable optimacy.

There are some, he adds—though Machiavelli is plainly meant here—who argue that Rome could not have expanded (*crescesse*) without these civil dissensions, but that is true only of Rome as she was organized and it can be held that she would have expanded much more efficiently without them if organized on a popular basis.[87] But Giannotti has already indicated that imperial expansion is not a necessary mark of the armed popular state. One is left feeling that he had considerable difficulty in getting out of Machiavelli's shadow, if only because he aimed at establishing positions so like and yet unlike his—the armed popular state without Rome, Venice without her aristocracy or mercenaries.

He is happier developing Aristotelian and Machiavellian arguments for the superiority of the *popolo*. These are, in general,[88] that the few desire to command, an impulse easily destructive of the common good, where that *libertà* which the many desire to preserve—that condition in which each enjoys his own under law—is close to being the common good itself. Furthermore, the few command and the many obey—i.e., they obey the laws, rather than the few—and it is easier for one who knows how to obey the laws to learn how to give commands than for one whose aim is always to command to subject his will to law. The habit of obeying a wide variety of laws gives the many a certain prudence, which the few often lack since their passions know fewer restraints, practical experience and book-learning, the sources of prudence considered as information, are as accessible to *popolari* as to *grandi*;[89] and since the former outnumber the latter, "it can be said with probability that they make up a greater aggregate of prudence."[90]

Giannotti puts forward a democratic theory of *prudenza*. Instead of being the reward of the elite who thrust themselves into public service in pursuit of *onore*, it is the reward of those who obey the laws, pool their experience, suffer injuries rather than inflict them and react by the collective pursuit of public remedies rather than by the aristocratic pursuit of revenge on particular enemies. The many's interest in *libertà* means that they are better politicized, more apt to accept public authority as legitimate, than the ambitious few. Last and strongest argument of all, in a city where there are many *popolari* or *mediocri*, it would be *violenza* to subject them to the authority of the *grandi*.[91]

The rest of Book III is taken up with the anatomy of an ideal constitution. We know that this is to be a *governo misto*, owing much of its detail to Venice, and satisfying the aspirations, by combining the powers, of those who desire *grandezza*, *onore*, and *libertà*. The powers of each group are to be interdependent, but there is to be one—the power of those whose aim is *libertà*, namely the people—which preponderates, at least in the sense of being less dependent on the other two than they are on it; but there has also been mention of four powers or functions which constitute the *vigore* or *nervo* of government and belong to whatever individual or group is to be *signore*. To modern readers, this *signore* sounds very like a sovereign, and a sovereign does not seem to fit into the balanced distribution of powers which constitutes a *governo misto*, even of the weighted kind which Giannotti has in view. We have a problem, therefore, and perhaps Giannotti had too, in relating these concepts to one another.

Giannotti begins by declaring that the republic is to be composed of three principal members, but that, just as in Venice, there is to be a fourth, called the Collegio, to go between the senate and the *gonfaloniere* (or prince) and satisfy the aspirations of those who seek *grandezza* by associating them as closely as possible with the supreme authority which only one man can exercise.[92] The members of this Collegio are to be magistrates rather than counselors, in the sense that specialized functions in regard of war (the Ten), justice (the *procuratori*), and so on, are to be assigned to each of them; and it is assumed that they excel in respect not only of ambition, but also of intellectual qualities, perhaps including experience, but certainly extending to originality, initiative, and the ability to propose policies. If at this end of the scale there is to be overlap between the one and the few, between *grandezza* and *onore*, at the other end the Consiglio Grande, though its function is to preserve *libertà* and therefore to represent the *popolari* who look no higher, is to be open to all citizens, whether *grandi*, *mediocri*, or *popolari*, whether (we may add) they seek *grandezza*, *onore*, or *libertà*. It is in fact to be composed of citizens reckoned as equals and by number. Giannotti goes on to explain why there will be a category of *plebei* who find no place in the Consiglio because they are not members of the city; their trades are vile and they are foreigners with homes to go to (he may have in mind peasants from the surrounding villages). But he insists at some length that those who pay taxes, but are not eligible for magistracies, must be members of the Consiglio Grande.[93] Since it seems to have been the experience of the militia of 1528–1530 which convinced him of the need to treat these *non-beneficiati* as citizens, it is interesting, and possibly significant of the way his thought was turning, that the arguments he now deploys are stressed as being operative when the city is not armed, no less than when it is. If the *non-beneficiati*—he is now calling them *popolari*—are not admitted to *onori* (membership of the Consiglio is plainly an *onore*), they will not love the republic or voluntarily contribute to or defend it; they will be liable to follow particular leaders; and these dangers will be exacerbated in time of arms. Aristotle would certainly condemn both Venice and Florence for failure to mobilize this class in citizenship,[94] and Giannotti is plainly aware that not membership in the Consiglio alone, but all forms of magistracy and *onore*, should be open to them, though he concedes that this may not be practicable as things are. There is no one who is not ambitious of exaltation and glory, he says, unless repressed and debased as the French have been; and the arming of a city serves to bring this truth to the surface.[95] At this stage the class of those, once called *popolari*, who desire *libertà* alone would seem to have disappeared, but perhaps it would be truer to say that it has become open-ended: it is a category to which all men may, and to some extent do, belong, but this is in no way incompatible with the existence of a constant competition in *virtù*, from which governing elites emerge and in which all citizens may take part. Giannotti is as hostile as Guicciardini to the imposition of qualifications of wealth or birth for membership in the higher magistracies.

He now explicitly declares that the Consiglio Grande is to be *signore* of the city and consequently must exercise those "functions which are sovereign in the republic and embrace all the power of the state."[96] We ask ourselves how such a monopoly can be reconciled with a mere lessening of dependence in a structure of interdependence. The functions or powers in question, we recall, are the election of magistrates, the determination of peace and war, the hearing of appeals and the approval and promulgation of new laws. Giannotti is able to explain a modified version of Venetian procedure whereby the Consiglio elects all magistrates, from the senate up through the Collegio to the Gonfaloniere. The last is to be elected for life, but the senate, he decides after consideration—and contrary to his opinion in the *Letter to Capponi*—to be reelected every year, with no bar to the serving of successive terms; this will ensure a stable elite, in which it will however be possible to lose one's place.[97] But

> the determination of peace and war must terminate in the senate ... and though it cannot pass to the Consiglio, it will nevertheless depend upon the latter since this is where the senate in which it terminates is elected. It might perhaps be well, when a new war is proposed for the first time, to refer the decision to the Consiglio Grande, as did the Romans, who used to ask the people if it was their will and command that war be made on this or that prince or republic; but all consequent decisions (*accidenti*) must terminate in the senate.[98]

Similarly the power of hearing appeals must terminate in a specialized body of magistrates, imitated from the Venetians, called the Quarantie.

Giannotti subsequently remarks that the *signore* of a state or city, whose *proprietà* this power rightfully is, often finds that it takes up too much of his time to exercise it in person (one suspects that it was also the problem of time which made Giannotti withhold the *accidenti* of war from the Consiglio), and for this reason the Consiglio Grande which is *signore* of Venice has set up the Quarantie, and the king of France has deputed his judicial power to four *parlements*.[99] It is arguable, then, that the power of election safeguards the *dependenza* of the judicial as of the military power upon the Consiglio. The difficulty is the vigor with which Giannotti earlier contended that a city might be free—i.e., that its Consiglio might be supreme—in respect of the election of magistrates but unfree in respect of the way those magistrates exercised their power, and that it was precisely this, in relation to military and judicial matters, which had made the republics Of 1494 and 1527 violent and unfree governments. It was insufficient to keep—as Giannotti's plan continues to keep—the final approval of legislation in the power of the Consiglio, since legislation was not thought of as regulating the military and judicial functions.

It is possible to modify what seems a theoretical failure on Giannotti's part by pointing out that the former magistrates' irresponsibility had consisted in his view not only in their independence of control by the Consiglio Grande, but also in the fact that the same men proposed, resolved upon, and executed policies.[100] This alone had sufficed to make them closed cliques of the self-seeking, and he now takes up again his earlier proposals to separate *consultazione* and *deliberazione* and in this way to make men functionally responsible to each other. He effected this by detailing the relations between the senate and the various boards composing the Collegio, and he is able (as in the *Letter to Capponi*) to use the terms "few" to denote the body, e.g., the Ten, which exercises *consultazione*, and "many" to denote the senate which resolves on their proposals.[101] Yet as long as military and judicial matters do not reach the Consiglio, the term "many" cannot carry its usual meaning, and as long as the election of magistrates is thought of as one among four powers, and not as a prior and separate determinant of the other three, such a Consiglio cannot qualify as a *signore* exercising all four; but that is the only definition of *signore* which we have. It can of course be argued— and this is much more plausible—that if the Consiglio elects the senate, the Collegio, and the Gonfaloniere, it exercises indirect control over those two of the four powers which do not remain under its immediate authority, and is therefore very much less dependent on the one and the few than they are on it. But the problem throughout has been the relation between the concept of lesser *dependenza* and that of *signore*, and the two cannot be said to have been reconciled, much less identified. If we take Giannotti's theory of the *signore* and its four powers as a primitive attempt at a theory of sovereignty, we may add that the linguistic confusions which arose when one spoke of sovereignty in a context of mixed government, and vice versa, were to bedevil political discourse to the American Revolution and beyond.

Giannotti's mind was independent, forceful, and original, but lacked the unpredictable creativity of genius which we find in Machiavelli; and for this reason it may be taken as displaying in some detail the bent and the limitations of humanist political thought. His chief originality consists in his perception that *virtù* in a mixed government was a kind of power, and in his consequent attempt to define the four functions of government whose location determined the *signore*. But he failed to concentrate these functions and was obliged to distribute them instead; and the ultimate reason was that humanist political thought was overmasteringly concerned with the ideal of civic virtue as an attribute of the personality, and in the last resort always turned from the establishment of institutionalized authority to the establishment of conditions, termed *libertà*, in which virtue might have free play and escape corruption. Our analysis of the *Repubblica Fiorentina*, like that of the *Discorsi*, should close with its distinctive contribution to the theory of corruption: Giannotti condemns the way in which, under the Savonarolan regime of 1529–1530, the brethren of San Marco became involved in politics and ambitious politicians sought conspicuous association with them as a means to enhanced authority with the citizens. This, he says, was no less corruption than was the open bribery of voters at Rome—it was, so to speak, an attempt to buy authority with coin other than that existing for the purpose—and to make things worse, bribery was at least acknowledged to be an evil, whereas if you attacked hypocrisy you were taken for an enemy of Jesus Christ.[102] Humanist political thought excelled at this sort of analysis, and subordinated the consideration of power to it, liberty, virtue, and corruption, rather than the location of authority, were its prime concerns. It is not even certain that Machiavelli was an exception. As we complete this study of the last phase of Florentine political theory, the most vivid impression remaining should be that of the continuity of a basically Aristotelian republicanism from which Machiavelli did not seem to his friends (who were each other's enemies) to have greatly departed. Certainly we can discover areas of his thought where he seems to have radically departed from the medieval concept of a teleologically determined human nature, though equally there are moments at which he seems to be using, if he does not formally reason from, the idea that men are formed to be citizens and that the reformation of their natures in that direction may be corrupted but cannot be reversed; the prince cannot make them anything else. But it is of some significance that the revolutionary aspects of his thinking—those in which man appears most dynamic and least natural—did not arrest the attention of his friends. Guicciardini's concept of citizenship remains a concept of *virtù*, loaded in the midst of its realism with Aristotelian language and assumptions, and in Giannotti the principle that man's nature is that of a citizen is explicitly stated, explicitly Aristotelian, and stops short only of becoming Savonarolan. It was in the Aristotelian and civic humanist channel that the stream of republican tradition was to flow, and Machiavelli as a historical figure, to whom theorists like Harrington and Adams referred, was to swim quite successfully in that channel. And the tradition to which the Florentines belonged was to be supported rather than impeded by their tough-mindedness in retaining a basically moralist concern with liberty and corruption; it continued to present politics as the erection of conditions under which men might freely exercise active virtue.

Giannotti also reveals to us the high capacity of Aristotelian political science, as an analytical and explicatory system, to absorb theories put forward as variations on its basic ideas. The Polybian theory of cycles, Machiavelli's doctrine of the militia, the model (rather than the myth) of Venice—all these are alluded to, explored, but finally used rather than followed; and they are used in the service of a basically Aristotelian method of categorizing the elements composing a city and showing how their interactions lead to stability, instability, or change in the polity. The classical republicanism to which John Adams still adhered was basically a Renaissance rephrasing of the political science set forth in Aristotle's *Politics*, and it possessed a high degree of capacity for dealing with the social phenomena of the seventeenth and eighteenth centuries. For Giannotti, however, perhaps its main importance was its ability to provide causal explanations of particular happenings and particular characteristics of cities; the *Repubblica Fiorentina*, is after all, a partially successful attempt to show how Venetian procedures and their underlying principles can be used in devising a different style of government for the very different conditions obtaining at Florence; and we have seen how, using Aristotelian categories both of causation and political composition, he was able to construct historical explanations and predictions concerning Florentine conditions which may have been misleading, but nevertheless dispelled much of the sense of mystery surrounding the particular. He is less dependent on concepts of usage, providence, or *fortuna*, when it comes to explaining how Florence has come to be as she is or what she may expect in the future, than either Savonarola or Machiavelli; he does not expect a miracle, like the former or his epigoni in 1529–1530—he has seen what their faith could and could not do—and he has less than the latter's sense of the desperate difficulty of creative action in the face of *fortuna*, or the almost miraculous qualities required for its success. This no doubt has much to do with his choice of a rational Venice, rather than a dynamic Rome, as the source of his principles of organization.[103] His theory is highly articulated and he is relatively confident of its applicability in practice.

Guicciardini, had he ever read the *Repubblica Fiorentina*, would have acidly remarked that its author had never had to put his theories into effect, and certainly it is sad, as one reads Giannotti's demonstrations that the regime of the early 1530s cannot possibly last, to reflect that this intelligent man had forty more years of life in which to see himself proved wrong (Guicciardini was just as wrong about the same regime in his own way). But in the present study we are concerned less with the predictive capacity of ideas than with their capacity to enlarge the paradigmatic vocabulary of a civilization; in this sense, an unsuccessful prophecy can be reused. Giannotti found Aristotelian political analysis complex and plausible enough to give him confidence that he understood something of the way things happened in time, and for this reason his thought is not focused on apocalyptic expectation, like Savonarola's, or on *innovazione* and *occasione* like Machiavelli's. Time is not in the foreground. The work concludes—as do *Il Principe* and the *Dialogo del Reggimento di Firenze*—with what we can now see as an almost conventional section[104] on the problems of actualization. Like Machiavelli and Guicciardini, Giannotti reviews the occasions on which, and the personalities by whom, republics may be securely founded; but his thought is directed toward Florentine actuality, and the fact that he writes as an exile in time of tyranny leaves him, as he recognizes, very little to say. Only a liberator (like Andrea Doria at Genoa) can be legislator for Florence, and concerning a liberator we can say only that either he will come or he will not. Others—presumably including Machiavelli—have written so well on the theory of conjurations and conspiracies as to teach him all he can learn about the *occasione* of the overthrow of governments; our part is to study the theory of establishing them, since it is better that we should complain of Fortune that she never sent us a liberator, than she of us that we did not know what to do when he came.[105] In these concluding words of his treatise, Giannotti accepts the role of the theorist in exile, and indicates once more that his attitude to time and *fortuna* is realistic. He is not naive about the difficulties of action, neither does he think them capable only of a miraculous solution (Machiavelli, who has been accused of the former, is nearer to the latter position). When he acknowledges the primacy of *fortuna*, he means only that there are always things beyond our control.

If this is largely the reason why Giannotti prefers Venice to Rome, and does not adopt Machiavelli's concept of a dynamic *virtù*, it is also a reason why he does not present Venice as a miracle or a myth. The problem of time was not, to his mind, such that only a Venetian miracle could solve it. He accepted the view that the purpose of legislation—and of his own planning for Florence—was to found constitutions that would endure, and he profoundly admired Venice's success in achieving near-perpetual stability. But the components of the *mito di Venezia* were the belief that only miraculous wisdom could bring such stability, and the belief that Venice had achieved a miracle by the art and contrivance of many, and since Giannotti did not adopt the former position, he presented neither a Polybian balance nor the mysteries of Venetian electoral machinery as constituting a miraculous solution to the problem of duration. He was obliged to see Venice's success as the product of many causes, simply by the circumstance that he was applying Venetian paradigms to the problem of achieving the same success in the very different conditions of Florence, and his mainly Aristotelian vocabulary gave him so many ways of differentiating conditions and causes that he could not see the problem as apocalyptic or its solution as miraculous or simple. The problem of legislation for durability was capable of complex solutions, and these could be built up over time. In both Giannotti's major works, his account of Venetian history, while serving as a kind of antithesis to Machiavelli's history of Rome, is equally an account of a complex historical process.

But we have seen that republican theory is in essence Aristotelian political science, selectively simplified by a drastic emphasis on the problem of time. It was possible to move away from such an emphasis, into a conceptual world so rich in its vocabulary that the potentialities of action increased and the problem of time grew less. But it was equally possible to move in the reverse direction, toward a position where only divine grace, the heroic action of a Lycurgus, or the attainment of a miraculous equilibrium seemed to offer solutions to the problem. The Renaissance obsession with time and fortune ensured that, since Venice was the paradigm of the solution last mentioned, the *mito di Venezia* would endure, and if Giannotti's nonmythical account became one of the standard books in the literature of the *mito*, it is valuable to study the contemporary and no less widely read treatise of Gasparo Contarini, in which the mythical element is far more pronounced.

[III]

Contarini, a Venetian aristocrat and churchman, wrote his *De Magistratibus et Republica Venetorum* at an uncertain time[106] during the twenties and thirties of the sixteenth century, and it was printed only in 1543, after which it became a book of European reputation and was many times reprinted. Though its renown exceeded that of Giannotti's *Repubblica de' Veneziani*, it is a work of rather less intensive and technical character as far as its treatment of the Venetian magistracies and their history is concerned; but it is completed where Giannotti's treatise is incomplete, and Contarini has found space to state his philosophy of government as relevant to the Venetian theme. Since his book had a traceable impact in many countries, it is of some value to quote it in the English of its Elizabethan translation, the work of Lewes Lewkenor, which appeared in 1599.

Contarini's language is panegyrical from the start: he states that Venice appears, both physically and politically, "rather framed by the hands of the immortal Gods, than any way by the arte, industry or inuention of men."[107] But it is a crucial point with him that Venice is the work of human art and above all of human virtue. Following a line of thought opened up by the Florentines, but becoming usual with Venetian writers, he states that virtue may appear in either a civil or a military form, but that although the latter is glorious and necessary it must exist only for the sake of the former. He is in the mainstream of Aristotelian and Christian thought in insisting that the end of war must be peace, but as an Italian writing in the civic humanist tradition he has also to explain how it is that Venetian *virtù* involves the employment of mercenaries while the citizens remain unarmed themselves. To Lewkenor, who furnished his own commentary by way of introduction, this paradox—and it seemed one to him no less than to a Florentine—was part of the generally miraculous way in which Venetian political procedures controlled, both rationally and morally, all departments of civic life.

> Besides, what is there that can carrie a greater disproportion with common rules of experience, th? that unweaponed men in gownes should with such happinesse of successe give direction & law to many mightie and warlike armies ... and long robed citizens to bee serued, yea and sued unto for entertainment by the greatest princes and peers of *Italy*; amidst which infinit affluence of glorie, and unmeasurable mightinesse of power, of which there are in soueraignty partakers aboue 3000 gentlemen, yet is there not one among them to bee found that doth aspire to any greater appellation of honour....[108]

Contarini does not go quite as far as his translator, though he does explain later that, because the civil constitution of Venice grew up under conditions of separation from the *terra firma* and therefore from military life—like most writers on these questions, he does not regard maritime power as posing any problems for civil organization—when the city finally became a land power, it was thought better not to let citizens exercise military commands for fear that

> this their continual frequentation of the continent, and diuorcement as it were from the ciuile life, would without doubt haue brought forth a kinde of faction different and disioyned from the other peaceable Citizens, which parcialitie and dominion would in time have bred ciuile warres and dissentions within the City.... To exclude therefore out of our estate the danger or occasion of any such ambitious enterprises, our auncestors held it a better course to defend their dominions vppon the continent, with forreign mercenarie souldiers, than with their homeborn citizens, & to assigne them their pay & stipende out of the tributes and receipts of the Prouince, wherein they remayned....[109]

But he does not mean that military and civic virtue are necessarily incompatible, or that it is the mechanized routine of decision at Venice which keeps the former subordinate to the latter. This is the work of virtue, and of a virtue which Contarini depicts as inherent in the Venetian aristocracy as a whole. In a passage which a knowledge of Florentine thought greatly illuminates, he bases this assertion on the familiar themes that Venice has never had a legislator, that a legislator has a difficult task with those less virtuous than himself, and that there is little historical evidence preserved concerning the city's early history. Giannotti had been puzzled to account for the creation of stable orders by the early Venetians' unaided intelligence, but to Contarini the mystery is to be proudly affirmed rather than explained.

> There were in *Athens, Lacedaemon* and *Rome*, in sundry seasons sundry rare and vertuous men of excellent desert and singular pietie towards their country, but so fewe, that being ouerruled by the multitude they were not able much to profit the same. But our auncestors, from whome wee have receyued so flourishing a commonwealth, all in one did vnite themselues in a consenting desire to establish, honour and amplifie their country, without hauing in a manner any the least regarde of their owne priuate glorie or commodity. And this any man may easily coniecture ...

in regarde that there are in *Venice* to bee found none, or very few monuments of our auncestors, though both at home and abroad many things were by them gloriously atchieued, and they of passing and singular desert towards their countrie. There are no stately tombes erected, no military statues remaining, no stemmes of ships, no ensignes, no standards taken from their enemies, after the victory of many and mighty battailes....[110]

With this then exceeding vertue of mind did our auncestors plant and settle this such a commonwealth, that since the memory of man, whosoeuer shal go about to make compare between the same & the noblest of the ancients, shal scarcely find any such: but rather I dare affirme, that in the discourses of those great Philosophers, which fashioned and forged commonwealths according to the desires of the mind, there is not any to be founde so well fayned and framed....[111]

To Florentine theorists it was evident that ambition and the pursuit of *onore* and *chiarezza* motivated any civic aristocracy, and that a problem in government was to prevent this thirst from corrupting itself. Giannotti considered the need to give it the appearance of satisfaction, while rendering that satisfaction dependent on the concurrence of others, one of the necessities that kept *governo misto* a second best, appropriate to an imperfect world. But if Contarini is prepared to endow the Venetians with virtue in the full sense of a disregard of all except the public good, then the *governo misto* of Venice must be much less a contrivance against corruption, much more an expression of its absence. When he proceeds to state his philosophy of government, it involves the usual case against the simple rule of the one, the few or the many, but on grounds less close to Polybius than to the main lines of Christian Aristotelian politics. As beasts are governed by men, so should men be governed by that which is higher than man. God does not govern commonwealths directly, but there is in man an element of the divine, which is "the mind, pure and devoid of perturbation"; a long way from Giannotti's conception of *virtù*. Since there are also in man "inferior and brutish powers," we cannot ensure the rule of the mind by entrusting government to any man, group or combination of groups of men, but "by a certaine diuine counsell when by other meanes it might not, mankinde through the inuention of laues seemeth to have attained this point, that the office of gouerning assemblings of men should be giuen to the mind and reason onely...."[112]

If laws can attain the status of pure reason—the apocryphal authority of Aristotle is given for the view "that God was the same in the vniuersity of things, as an ancient lawe in a civill company"[113]—then laws must rule and not men; the participation of individuals and groups in government is subordinate to this. But the argument is in danger of becoming circular: laws ensure that reason rules and not particular passions, but they are invented and maintained by men and can prevail only when men are guided by reason to the public good and not by passion to private ends. The laws must maintain themselves, then, by regulating the behavior of the men who maintain them; and in "assemblings of men," in cities, that is to say, where men regularly meet face to face to enforce and make laws and to transact public business, the term "laws" must have the principal meaning of a set of orders and regulations for the conduct of assemblies and the framing of decisions. Such laws must have the effect of directing men's energies solely toward the public good, which is to say solely in the paths of pure reason. The *mito di Venezia* consists in the assertion that Venice possesses a set of regulations for decision-making which ensure the complete rationality of every decision and the complete virtue of every decision-maker. Venetians are not inherently more virtuous than other men, but they possess institutions which make them so.

An individual in whom pure mind always reigned, without the need for external controls or assistance, would as we know be an angel rather than a man. As Hobbes's Leviathan was an "artificial man" and a "mortal god," so Contarini's Venice, it may be suggested, was an artificial angel: men who were not wholly rational functioned as members of an institutional framework which was. Lewkenor seems to have sensed this:

> beholde their great Councell, consisting at the least of 3000 Gentlemen, whereupon the highest strength and mightinesse of the estate absolutely relyeth, notwithstanding which number all thinges are ordered with so diuine a peaceableness, and so without all tumult and confusion, that it rather seemeth to bee an assembly of Angels, then of men.
>
> ... their penall Lawes most unpardonably executed; their encouragements to vertue infinite; especially by their distribution of offices and dignities, which is ordered in such a secrete, straunge, and intricate sort, that it utterly ouerreacheth the subtiltie of all ambitious practises, neuer falling upon any but upon such as are by the whole assembly allowed for greatest wisedome, vertue and integritie of life.

... there are sundry other so maruellous and miraculous considerations, and in their owne exceeding singularitie, beyond all resemblance or comparison with any other Commonwealth so unspeakeablie straunge, that their wonderful) rarenesse being verified, maketh the straungest impossibilities not seeme altogether incredible....[114]

To an Elizabethan mind, Venice could appear a phenomenon of political science fiction: a series of marvelous devices for keeping men virtuous, where in other states this was left to individual reason or divine grace. Contarini, who was after all a churchman, does not press the language of mystery and miracle so far, but he has endowed his Venetians with exceptional virtue by whose means they have evolved political procedures which maintain it. Inevitably, the theoretical Language he adopts obliges him to present virtue as the maintenance of a balance between the one, the few, and the many; these are the categories into which persons fall and which must consequently be transcended if an impersonal government is to be maintained. But in his ideal constitution it is the laws which rule, and the distribution of authority between one, few, and many is a means of keeping all three subject to law and reason:

yet is the multitude of itselfe unapt to governe, unlesse the same be in some sort combined together; for there cannot bee a multitude without the same bee in some vnitie contayned, so that the ciuill society (which consisteth in a certain vnity) will bee dissolued, if the multitude become not one by some meane of reason....[115]

The language reveals that older philosophical traditions are directing and binding the simpler formulae of mixed government. We do indeed read, shortly after this, that Venice has combined the princely, noble, and popular forms of authority "so that the formes of them all seeme to be equally balanced, as it were with a paire of weights ...,"[116] but it is not a question of distinguishing political functions as distinct modes of power, and ascribing them to the one, few, and many so as to form a balance. This raised, as we have seen, the problem of explaining just how one mode of power could be said to "balance" another; Giannotti had decided that the question could not be resolved in those terms and would have to be rephrased (a task in which he had not been very successful), but Contarini, writing apparently without knowledge of the Florentine's work,[117] may be found at one point repudiating the very language in which Giannotti had restated it.

> there cannot happen to a commonwealth a more daungerous or pestilent contagion, then the ouerweighing of one parte or faction aboue the other: for where the ballance of iustice standeth not euen, it is vnpossible that there should bee a friendly societie and firme agreement among the citizens: which alwaies happeneth where many offices of the commonwealth meete together in one. For as every mixture dissolueth, if any one of the elementes (of which the mixed body consisteth) ouercome the other: and as in musicke the tune is marred where one string keepeth a greater noyse than hee should doe: so by the like reason, if you will haue your commonwealth perfect and enduring, let not one part bee mightier than the other, but let them all (in as much as may bee) have equal, share in the publique authoritie.[118]

Read in conjunction with Giannotti, this may seem a simple recession to the theory of Polybian balance; but there is rather more to it than that. The context in which it occurs is that of a provision which forbids more than three members of a family holding office in the senate at any one time, so that the "partes or factions" which must not overbalance one another are not merely the traditional Polybian three, but might include any grouping whatever into which the citizens might fall. Polybian theory, we remember yet again, was a paradigmatic simplification of Aristotelian political science, and Aristotle had known well enough that the one, few, and many were categories which it was convenient and necessary to employ. A durable constitution must satisfy all social groups; a one-few-many analysis was merely an operationally satisfactory means of ascertaining whether it was doing so.

But Contarini, far more than Giannotti, is self-consciously a philosopher in politics; and where the Florentine developed the concept of virtù in the direction of power, the Venetian retained it primarily with the connotation of rationality. Government was an act of wisdom directed at the common good, so that "equall share in the publique authoritie" meant, among other things, "equal share in the exercise of public intelligence." But a body politic in which every conceivable part or category exercised the mode of intelligence appropriate to it would be one whose rationality was perfect, and participation in its public intelligence would also be perfect. It is not insignificant that from the beginnings of the *mito*, Venetian mixed government had been idealized by equation less with Polybius's Book VI than with Plato's Laws.[119] The "artificial angel" was miraculously, because rationally, stable, perfect, and timeless, relatively free from the shadows of ambiguity and ultimate doom that overhung Polybius's Rome or Machiavelli's Florence. Where Giannotti, knowing that his own city's history was one of instability, had first asked questions about Venetian history which he left unanswered,[120] and had later felt obliged to devise means of analyzing instability and providing for stability that carried him away from all three of his masters—Aristotle, Polybius, and Machiavelli—Contarini needed to take neither of these steps. Nor did he follow Savonarola in presenting his republic as playing a messianic role at an apocalyptic moment.

Yet we must avoid dismissing Venetian republican thought as the mere projection into myth of a Platonic self-image. In a most magisterial treatment of the subject, William J. Bouwsma has shown that Venetian thought did not stand still with Contarini but developed during the next eighty years, first with Paruta and afterwards with Sarpi, a sense of the particularity and moral autonomy of history which was founded on a series of assertions of Venice's unique individuality against the universalist claims of the Counter-Reformation papacy.[121] And just as for Florence, the republican vision of history carried with it shadows as well as lights; Sarpi's *History of the Council of Trent* is as disenchanted a record of human failure and frailty as anything in Guicciardini.[122] The timeless myth and the history that lacked finality were, we must recollect, two responses to the same problem: the republic's struggle to attain self-sufficient virtue and stability in a context of particularity, time, and change. It might escape from history by a self-constituent act of timeless rationality; it might seek to tame history by combining in a grand synthesis all the elements of instability, identified and interwoven; or it might confess that the problem could not be solved and that the pitfalls of history remained forever open. Contarini is nearer to the first position than to the second; Machiavelli, Guicciardini, and Sarpi nearer to the third than to the second. Giannotti's significance lies in the originality of his contributions to the second, to the science that pursued stability.

He has appeared in these pages, it is true, as a thinker who to some extent sought to draw Machiavelli's fangs, reconciling Rome with Venice, transcending both models, and presenting the armed popular republic as devoted to its own virtue rather than to conquest and expansion—thus seeming to free it from the Ragnarok of the "universal wolf," partly because he was less interested in war than was Machiavelli, and more interested in the theory of constitutional equilibrium, he was able to carry the science of mixed government to points not reached by other Florentine analysts; but while on the one hand this means that fortune's role in his thought is restricted by the wealth of his explanatory devices, his failure to develop a theory of sovereignty resting on the legislative power meant that he had not escaped from the world in which Contarinian myth and Machiavellian or Guicciardinian realism were the confining alternatives, since a republic which could not legislate itself must be restricted to the struggle to maintain *prima forma*. It reverted to being the political form in which was attained the universal good, which meant that there was no political activity other than the maintenance of form. If Machiavelli and Guicciardini did not, with all their brilliance, succeed in seeing political activity as creative, but only in showing just how difficult, or impossible, the maintenance of republican order really was, we are obliged to think of *cinquecento* civic realism, even at its height, as a kind of negative capability of the Aristotelian mind. Its awareness of the qualitative character and even the irreversibility of historical change was arrived at by recombining the categories of Aristotelian thought, and its concern with *fortuna* varied inversely as these categories could suggest new conceptual means of controlling her. It can be suggested also that these limitations were in part imposed upon Machiavellian thought by its obstinately durable moralism.

Aristotelian republicanism was exclusively concerned with the citizen, and there was no need for Florentine and Venetian theorists to abandon it so long as they too were concerned only with him and his chances of escaping corruption; indeed, within its traditions they found it possible greatly to enlarge their vocabulary for discussing his problems. But for all the tough-mindedness of Machiavelli and Guicciardini, the fact remains that the weakness of the Aristotelian and humanist tradition was the insufficiency of its means for discussing the positive, as opposed to the preservative, exercise of power. We earlier considered the possibility that some political agency might acquire so developed a capacity for dealing with particular and changing problems as they arose that society's institutional means of dealing with such problems were in constant change and capable of changing themselves. It is evident that such an agency would be government in the modern sense, that it would be legislating in the modern sense, and that such a political society would be a modern administrative state possessed of a dimension of historical change and adaptation. But a body of political theory exclusively concerned with how the citizen is to develop his human capacities by participating in decisions aimed at the subjection of private to public goods is unlikely to develop a concern for, or a vocabulary for dealing with, government as a positive or creative activity. Under sixteenth-century conditions, it tended to reduce politics to the structure within which the individual asserted his moral autonomy, and legislation to the purely formal activity of establishing and restoring such a structure, so that any but a destructive innovation in time became virtually impossible. We have also seen that a view of politics which confined it to the assertion of values, or virtues, by individuals in public acts discouraged, every time that it encouraged, any attempt to treat it as the concurrent exercise of different kinds of power. Giannotti took a first step in that direction, but was unable to take a second; and the Polybian concept of a balance between different agencies exercising power seems so far to have been acutely self-limiting. We may say that all this reveals the deficiencies of Aristotelian theory, but it is possible also—though debatable—that power in a face-to-face polis must be so far dispersed and personal as to render difficult the growth of theory about the several specialized ways of exercising it. The next step will be to study the development of humanist and Machiavellian thought in a society made up of several institutionalized agencies exercising different kinds of power: post-Tudor England, with its king, its law, its parliament, and its church. But we shall find that each of these agencies secreted and disseminated its own ideology, its own modes of defining political society and the political individual; with the consequence that it was only with difficulty, and in a variety of very special senses, that the English realm could be defined as a civic community or republic, in which politicized individuals pursued a *vivere civile*. We shall have to study how it happened that Englishmen could begin to project an image of themselves and their society in Machiavellian terms; but we shall find that this process involved a restatement of civil history in terms both positive and negative, which defined government as modern in the act of rebelling against its modernity. Exported to the Atlantic's western shores, this contributed powerfully to the complexity of American values.

NOTES

1. At the beginning of the Preliminaries to *Oceana*; see Toland, ed., p. 35 (above, ch. 1, n. 28).

2. For his life and career, see Roberto Ridolfi, *Opuscoli di Storia Letteraria e di Erudizione* (Florence: Libr. Bibliopolis, 1942); Randolph Starns, *Donato Giannotti and his Epistolae* (Geneva: Libr. Droz, 1968); and the publication by Felix Gilbert described in the next note. R. von Albertini (*op. cit.*) devotes pp. 14–66 to a study of his thought, as does Starns in "*Ante Machiavel*: Machiavelli and Giannotti" (Gilmore, ed., *Studies on Machiavelli*) and there is a short account, which seeks to relate him to English thought of the Shakespearean age, in C. C. Huffman, *Coriolanus in Context* (Lewisburg: Bucknell University Press, 1972) pp. 17–20.

3. Felix Gilbert, "The Date of the Composition of Contarini's and Giannotti's Books

on Venice," in *Studies in the Renaissance*, xiv (New York: The Renaissance Society of America, 1967), pp. 172–84.

4. *Ibid.*, pp. 178–79.

5. Donato Giannotti, *Opere* (3 vols., ed. G. Rosini, Pisa, 1819), I, 9: "E perché nel primo ragionamento fu disputato dell'amministrazione universale della repubblica; nel secondo particolarmente di tutti i magistrati; nel terzo della forma e composizione di essa repubblica, noi dal primo penderemo il principio nostro, non solamente perché naturalmente le cose universali sono di piú facile intelligenza, ma perché ancora del primo ragionamento il secondo, il terzo dall'uno e dall'altro depende."

6. Gilbert, "Date and Composition," pp. 180–82.

7. *Opere*, I, 20.

8. *Opere*, I, 34–35: "I dipintori, e scultori, se drittamente riguardiamo, seguitano nello loro arti i precetti dei filosofi; perciocché ancora essi le loro opere dalle cose universali cominciano. I dipintori, prima che particolarmente alcuna imagine dipingano, tirano certe linee, per le quali essa figura universalmente si dimostra; dopo questo le danno la sua particolare perfezione. Gli scultori ancora osservano nelle loro statue il medesimo; tanto che chi vedesse alcuno dei loro marmi dirozzato, direbbe piú tosto questa parte debbe servire per la testa, questa per lo braccio, questa la gamba: tanto la natura ci costringe, non solamente nel conoscere ed intendere, ma eziandio nell'operare, a pigliar il principio dalle cose universali! Per questa cagione io incominciai dalla descrizione del sito di Venezia, come cosa piú che l'altre universale."

9. *Opere*, I, 21: "Perciocché ciascuna repubblica è simile ad un corpo naturale, anzi per meglio dire, è un corpo dalla natura principalmente prodotto, dopo questo dall'arte limato. Perciocché quando la natura fece l'uomo, ella intese fare una università, una comunione. Essendo adunque ciascuna repubblica come un'altro corpo naturale, dove ancora i suoi membri avere. E perché tra loro è sempre certa proporzione e convenienza, siccome tra i membri di ciascuno altro corpo, chi non conosce questa proporzione e convenienza, che è tra l'un membro e l'altro, non può come fatto sia quel corpo comprendere. Ora questo è quello dove manca il Sabellico."

10. *Ibid.*: "... non dichiara come l'uno sia collegato con l'altro, che dependenza abbia questo da quello, tal che perfettamente la composizione della repubblica raccoglier se ne possa."

11. *Opere*, I, 16–17: "... Pomponio considerando che la repubblica sua era corrottissima, e non conoscendo in sé facoltà di poterle la sanità restituire, si ritrasse da lei per non essere costretto con essa a rovinare. Perciocché la repubblica, quando è corrotta, è simile al mare agitato dalla tempesta, nel quale chi allora si mette, non si può a sua porta ritrarre. Io già non mi son ritratto dalle cure civili per questa cagione, perciocché la mia repubblica non è corrotta, anzi (se io non m'inganno) è piú perfetta ch'ella mai in alcun tempo fosse ..."

12. *Opere*, I, 17: "E quantunque i Romani possedessero tanto maggiore imperio quanto è noto a ciascuno, non però giudico la repubblica nostra meno beata e felice. Perciocché la felicità d'una repubblica non consiste nella grandezza dell'imperio, ma si ben nel vivere con tranquillità e pace universale. Nella qual cosa se io dicessi che la nostra repubblica fosse alla romana superiore, credo certo che niuno mi potrebbe giustamente riprendere."

13. *Opere*, I, 15: "... due tempi mi pare che tra gli altri siano da ricordare: Uno, nel quale fu il principio della ruina sua [i.e., Italy's] e dello imperio Romano, e questo fu quando Roma dalle armi Cesariane fu oppressa: l'altro, nel quale fu il colmo del male italiano; e questo fu quando l'Italia dagli Unni, Goti, Vandali, Longobardi fu discorse e saccheggiata. E se bene si considerano gli accidenti che da poco tempo in qua, cosi in Oriente come in Occidente, sono avvenuti, agevolmente si può vedere che a quelli che

oggi vivono in Italia soprasta uno di quelli due tempi. Ma quel di loro piú si debba avere in orrore non so io già discernere: perciocché dal primo si può dire nascesse il secondo, e dal secondo tutta quella variazione, che ha fatto pigliare al mondo quella faccia, che ancora gli veggiamo a' tempi nostri, e lasciar del tutto quella che al tempo de' Romani aveva ..."

14. But see I, 42: "... non è dubbio alcuno, che gli uomini, dove eglino non si trovano a trattar cose pubbliche, non solamente non accrescono la nobiltà loro, ma perdono ancora quella che hanno e divengono peggio che animali, essendo costretti viver senza alcun pensiero avere che in alto sia levato."

15. *Opere*, I, 35–36: "... per popolari io intendo quelli che altramente possiamo chiamare plebei. E son quelli, i quali esercitano arti vilissime per sostentare la vita loro, e nella città non hanno grado alcuno. Per cittadini, tutti quelli i quali per essere nati eglino, i padri e gli avoli loro nella città nostra, e per avere esercitate arti piú onorate, hanno acquistato qualche splendore, e sono saliti in grado tal che ancora essi si possono in un certo modo figliuoli di questa patria chiamare. I gentiluomini sono quelli che sono della città, e di tutto lo stato, di mare o di terra, padroni e signori."

16. See below, nn. 93–95; cf. Guicciardini in 1512, above, ch. v, n. 29.

17. E.g., p. 50.

18. E.g., p. 77.

19. *Opere*, I, 42-43.

20. *Opere*, I, 61–62, 63–64: "Ma poscia che il consiglio fu ordinato, e che l'autorità de' dogi fu co' magistrati e coi consigli temperata, allora i cittadini, adoperandosi nelle faccende, acquistarono gloria e riputazione. Ed è accaduto alla nostra città quel medesimo che avenne a Roma.... E da questo, credo, che nasca che noi non abbiamo molta notizia dell'antichità delle famiglie de' gentiluomini innanzi a Sebastiano Ziani ... e ... che in tutte le nostre memorie non trovo menzione alcuna di questo nome *gentiluomo*, eccetto che nella vita di Pietro Ziani doge XLII, figliuolo del sopradetto Sebastiano.

"... e non credo che questo nome *gentiluomo* significasse quello che oggi significa ... ma che ... s'intendesse quello che oggi nell'altre città significa, cioè chiunque o per antichità, o per ricchezze o per autorità piú che gli altri risplende."

21. *Opere*, I, 66–68: "Ma quello che piú mi stringe è che gran cosa saria stata, che i nostri maggiori senza esempio alcuno avessero trovato si bell'ordine, si bel modo di distribuire i carichi e le onoranze della città, cioè il gran consiglio. Perciocché egli non è dubbio alcuno che quando questo consiglio fu trovato, non era simile forma di vivere in luogo alcuno di mondo, di che s'abbia notizia. E le cose, le quali senza esempio alcuno s'hanno ad introdurre, hanno sempre tante difficoltà che come impossibile sono le piú volte abbandonate. Il che nasce perché gli uomini nel azioni umane non approvano quegli ordini, l'utilità de' quali non hanno né per la propria, né per l'altrui esperienza, conosciuta; e pochissimi sono sempre stati e sono quelli che sappiamo cose nuove trovare e persuaderle. E perciò nelle innovazioni degli ordini si vanno imitando i vecchi cosí proprii come gli altrui.... Saria stata adunque cosa miracolosa, che i nostri maggiori senza averne esempio alcuno, avessero, nel riordinare la nostra repubblica, saputo trovare ed introdurre sì bella, sì civile, sì utile ordinazione come è questa del gran consiglio, la quale senza dubbio è quella che non ha solamente mantenuto libera la nostra patria, ma eziandio, procedendo di bene in meglio, l'ha fatta salire in quella grandezza d'imperio e riputazione, alla quale voi essere pervenuta la vedete. è adunque credibile per le due dette ragioni, oltre a quelle poche memorie che ce ne sono, che innanzi a Sebastiano Ziani fosse qualche forma di consiglio.... Quegli adunque i quali dicono che il consiglio è antichissimo, se non intendo quel conglio che s'ordino per distribuire i magistrati, forse non s'ingannano; ma se intendono questo altro, senza dubbio sono in errore."

22. *Opere*, I, 72–74.

23. *Opere*, I, 77: "… dico che io nell'antiche nostre memorie non ho trovato mai che si fossa cagione di far serrare il consiglio; come voi dite, non par da credere che un ordine tanto nuovo potesse nascere senza qualche grande occasione. Di che noi potremmo addurre infiniti esempii, non solamente di quelle repubbliche che hanno variato in meglio, tra le quali è la nostra, siccome io stimo, ma di quelle che sono in peggio trascorse. Ma le variazioni della nostra repubblica medesima, se bene le considerate, vi possono dare di quello che diciamo certissima testimonianza. Nondimeno io non ho letto mai, né inteso, che cagione e che occasione facesse il consiglio serrare. Né da me stesso posso pensare che da quella forma del consiglio potesse nascere disordine alcuno, che avesse ad essere cagione della sua variazione; tanto che io credo che coloro che furono autori di tal mutazione … vedendo nella città nostra concorrere quantità grandissima di forestieri per conto di faccende mercantili…. Ma questa è tutta congettura; perciocché, come ho detto, non ne ho certezza alcuna."

24. *Opere*, I, 116: "Ed avete ad intendere che in ogni repubblica sono assai costituzioni, delle quali non si può assegnare alcuna probabile non che vera ragione. E questo non solamente avviene in quelle città che hanno il loro governo variato, ma in quelle ancora le quali con le medesime leggi si sono lungo tempo rette e governate. Perciocché quantunque l'usanze si siano mantenute, nondimeno le cagioni di quelle sono dall'antichità oscurate."

25. *Opere*, I, 51: "Dicono adunque che quattro sono le cose nelle quali consiste il nervo d'ogni repubblica. La creazione de' magistrati; le deliberazioni della pace e della guerra; le introduzione delle leggi; e le provocazioni." Cf. p. 86.

26. *Opere*, I, 125–26: "Usano ancora i nostri fare confermare alcune leggi non solamente nel consiglio dei pregati, ma ancora nel grande; la qual cosa, credo che sia in potestà di quel magistrato che principalmente le introduce. E credo che questo s'usi fare, acciochè a questo modo s'acquisti a quella legge maggior riputazione …"

27. *Opere*, I, 91–117.

28. Gilbert, "Venetian Constitution," pp. 463–500 (above, ch. iv, n. 26).

29. See the speech of Epimonus de Garrula in *Oceana* (*Works*, ed. Toland, 1771; p. 110): "The truth is, they have nothing to say to their acquaintance; or men that are in council sure would have tongues; for a council, and not a word spoken in it, is a contradiction…. But in the parliament of Oceana, you had no balls or dancing, but sober conversation; a man might know and be known, shows his parts and improve 'em."

30. *Discorso al … Gonfaloniere … Niccolò Capponi sopra i modi di ordinate la Repubblica Fiorentina*; *Opere*, III, 27–48.

31. Gilbert, "Venetian Constitution," p. 498 and n.

32. *Opere*, III, 32–33.

33. III, 32: "Tutti quelli che consigliano è necessario che sieno valenti, e di quel primo ordine, che scrive Esiodo, nel quale sono connumerati quelli che hanno invenzione per loro medesimi, e non hanno bisogno di consiglio d'altri."

34. III, 41: "Il consiglio saria in pochi, cioè nei valenti; la deliberazione in molti: e perciò la libertà saria sicura, e quelli che avrebbero la autorità, l'avrebbero per virtù della repubblica, e non per loro presunzione e importunità."

35. *Ibid.*: "… essendo le cose determinate da molti, cioè dal senato …"

36. *Opere*, III, 30: "Vorrei dare a costoro una cura speciale di considerar sempre le cose della città, e i primi pensieri d'introdurre nuove leggi e correggere le vecchie, secondo che ricerca la varietà de' tempi."

37. *Opere*, III, 28: the *ottimati* are "quelli che il piú delle volte hanno prudenza, il premio della quale pare che sia l'onore come testimonio d'essa."

38. *Archivio Storico Italiano* (hereafter A.S.I.), ser. 5, vol. 8 (1891), G. R. Sanesi (ed.), "Un discorso sconosciuto di Donato Giannotti intorno alla milizia," pp. 7–27.

39. *Ibid.*, p. 14: "... non tanto perché da natura non hanno questa inclinazione, quanto perché, essendo la città lungo tempo vivuta tra gli esercizii mercantili, difficilmente si potria assuefare a uno esercizio tanto diverso e contrario."

40. *Ibid.*: "... dico che assolutamente la città si debbe armare: perché lo essere disarmato repugnia alla natura, ed alla autorità di tutti quelli che hanno trattato delli governi delle città. Repugnia alla natura, perché noi vediamo in ogni uomo particulare, essere d'appetito naturale di potersi difendere; ed a qualunche non sopliscano le forze di poterlo fare, pare che sia imperfetto, per mancare di quella virtù: la quale è ordinata dalla natura per conservazione di sé stesso."

41. *Ibid.*, p. 16: "E chi dicie che lo essersi assuefatto ad altri esercizii impediscie tale ordinazione, si inganna interamente: perché, essendo di tanta forza la assuefazione, che ella puote operare contro alla natura, tanto piú facilmente potrà in una cosa che è secondo la natura, cioè l'esercizio delle armi."

42. *Ibid.*, p. 17: "Ma vuol dire regolare gli uomini, e rendergli atti al potere difendere la patria da gli assalti esterni e dalle alterazioni intrinseche, e porre freno a' licenziosi: li quali è necessario che ancora essi si regolino, vedendo per virtù della ordinanza ridotti gli uomini alla equalità, né essere autorità in persona, fuori che in quelli a chi è dato dalle leggi.... Non è adunque da omettere di introdurre tale ordinanza: la quale, oltre alle predette cose, toglie ogni autorità a chi per ambizione estraordinariamente cercassi riputazione; perché, sapiendo ciascuno chi egli abbia a ubbidire, non si può destinare alla ubbidientia di Persona."

43. *Ibid.*, p. 20: "... Romulo, il quale messe l'ordinanza in quella sua turba sciellerata ed assuefatta a ogni male: il che poi che ebbe fatto, tutti quelli uomini diventorno buoni; e quello furore che usavano nel male operare, lo convertirono in far bene." Note how arms serve to convert habit, and how virtù is a reversed furore.

44. *Ibid.*, p. 18: "Sono alcuni che dicono che le armi non si dovriano dare se non a quelli che sono abili al consiglio, dubitando se elle si dessino a quelli altri che sono a graveza, essendo maggior numero, non rovinassino lo stato. Chi seguitassi tale oppinione, primamente armerebbe poco numero di uomini, e lasciando gli altri, che sono a graveza, disarmati, saria necessario che restassino mal contenti, e conseguentemente nimici della repubblica; talché quelli pochi che sarebbono armati, a poco altro servirebbono che a guardia dello stato contro a quelli, che rimanessino disarmati.... A' quali se si togliessi anche il potere difendere le cose sue con la persona propria, sarebbano peggio che stiavi; di modo che la città sarebbe uno aggregato di padroni e servi; e sarebbano in peggiore grado, elle i sudditi e contadini."

45. *Opere*, I, 45–46.

46. *A.S.I.* (1891), pp. 26–27.

47. *A.S.I.*, vol. 15 (1851), "Documenti per servire alla storia della Milizia Italiana ... raccolti ... e preceduti da un discorso di Giuseppe Canestrini," pp. 342–76 (orations of Luigi Alamanni and Pier Filippo Pandolfini); R. von Albertini, *op. cit.*, pp. 404–11 (oration of Piero Vettori).

48. *A.S.I.* (1851), p. 355 (Pandolfini): "... questa libertà non è opera umana, tanti anno sono che la fu predetta, et vedesi nata et data a questo popolo miracolosamente ..."

49. *Ibid.*, p. 356.

50. *Ibid.*, p. 354: "Chi exaerita il corpo, lo dispone ad ubbidire al consiglio, e fa l'appetito obbediente alla ragione; et cosí l'uomo diventa facile a sopportare il dolore, et disporsi a disprezzare la morte. L'obbedienza è necessaria in ogni cosa, et maxime in

una republica. A buon cittadino niente piú si conviene, che sapere comandare et ubbidire."

51. *Ibid.*, p. 345 (Alamanni): "... et allor tutti insieme parimente si vestiron l'arme, et dieron forma a questa militar disciplina; alla quale oggi noi, dalla divina grazia illuminati, darem principio ..." p. 347: "Nessuno sia, non volendo offendere Dio, le leggi, la libertà et se medesimo, che si cinga questa sacratissima veste dell'arme con altra privata speranza che con quella di salvare la sua patria et i suoi cittadini." Albertini, p. 409: "... per salvatione et libertà di voi medesimi vi siate cinta questa incorruttibil veste dell'arme ..."

52. *Ibid.*, p. 344 (Alamanni): "Oh! se fusse, o popolo mio Fiorentino, ben conosciuta da te quello che ella vale, et quanto sia da essere onorata la povertà, come ti faresti lieto di ritrovarti al presente in questo stato! Quanti pensieri, quante fatiche, quanti affanni si prendon gli uomini indarno, che si lascerieno indietro! Guarda pure quale arte, quale esercizio, quale studio lodevole oggi o mai furono in terra, et gli vedrai fabbricati tutti et messi avanti dalla povertà, unica inventrice di tutti i beni."

53. *Ibid.*, pp. 358–59 (Pandolfini): "... la mediocrità et il mezzo sendo ottimi in ogni cosa, manifesta cosa è che la mediocre possessione della fortuna è ottima [note that fortune here can be possessed]; imperocché questi tali felicissimamente obbediscono alla ragione: ma se eccedono il modo in una o altra parte ... è difficile obbedischino alla ragione.... Cosí si fa una città di servi et padroni, non di uomini liberi.... Adunque la città vuol essere di pari et simili quanto piú si può, et da questi la città è ben governata, et questi si conservano nella città; perché non desiderano le cose d'altri, né i loro beni son desiderati da altri.... Per la qual cosa è manifesta che la società e ottima, che si mantiene per uomini mediocri; et quelle città son ben governate, nelle quali son molti mediocri et possono assai." Pandolfini's *discorso* throughout is an interesting document of revolutionary Aristotelianism.

54. Giannotti, *Opere*, II, 37, 46, 98, 141.

55. *Opere*, II, 12: "Aristotile, dal quale io come da uno abbondantissimo fonte, che ha sparso per tutto'l mondo abbondantissimi fiumi di dottrina, ho preso tutti i fondamenti di questo mio breve discorso ..."

56. *Opere*, II, 2: "... ho deliberato ragionare in che modo si possa in Firenze temperare un'amministrazione che non si possa alterare senza extrema forza estrinseca."

57. *Opere*, II, 9–10: "É adunque il subietto nostro la città di Firenze tale duale ella è, nella quale vogliamo introdurre una forma di repubblica conveniente alla sue qualità, perché non ogni forma conviene a ciascheduna città, ma solamente quella la quale puote in tal città lungo tempo durare. Perciocché siccone il corpo prende vita dall'anima, così la città dalla forma della repubblica, tal che se non è conveniente tra loro, è ragionevole che l'una e l'altra si corrompa e guasti, siccome avverrebbe se un'anima umana fusse con un corpo di bestia congiunta, o un'animo di bestia con un corpo umano; perche l'uno darebbe impedimento all'altro, di che seguirebbe la corruzione ... siccome anco fanno i prudenti architettori, i quali chiamati a disegnare un palazzo per edificare sopra i fondamenti gettati per l'addietro, non alterano in cosa alcuna i trovati fondamenti; ma secondo le qualità loro disegnano un edificio conveniente a quegli; e se hanno a racconciare una casa, non la rovinano tutta, ma solo quelle parti che hanno difetto; ed all'altre lassate intere si vanno accomodando."

58. *Opere*, II, 17.

59. *Opere*, II, 13–14: "Queste tre specie di reggimento nascono da questo, perché in ciascuna città o egli si trova uno che è virtuosissimo, o pochi o molti virtuosi.... Ma dove i molti sono di virtù ornati, quivi nasce quella terza specie di governo chiamata repubblica, la quale amministrazione si è trovato in quelle città, che hanno virtù militare, la quale è propria della moltitudine."

60. *Opere*, II, 16: "... bene è vero, che nelle tre rette, quelli che ubbidiscono stanno subietti volontariamente; nelle tre corrotte, stanno paziente per forza; e perciò si púo dire che le buone siano dalle corrotte in quello differenti.... Nondimeno a me pare ... che questa differenza non sia propria, ma piuttosta accidentale, perché può essere che i subietti nella tirannide volontariamente ubbidiscano, essendo corrotti dal tiranno con largizioni ed altre cose, che si fanno per tenere gli uomini tranquilli e riposati. Non essendo adunque altra differenza tra i buoni e tra i corrotti governi che quella che è generata dal fine da loro inteso e seguitato, seguita che i buoni senza alcuna difficoltà, cioè senza intrinseca o estrinseca alterazione, si possono corrompere e divenir malvagii."

61. *Opere*, II, 18: "... tale introduzione è impossibile, perché essendo gli uomini piú malvagii che buoni, e curandosi molto piú de' privati comodi che del pubblico, credo fermamente che nei tempi nostri non si trovi subietto che le possa ricevere, perché in ciascuna di quelle tre sorte si presuppongono gli uomini buoni: tal che avendo i subietti a ubbidire volontariamente a quello, se è uno, o a quelli, se son pochi o molti virtuosi, non saria mai possibile indurre a ciò gli uomini non buoni, i quali per natura loro sono invidiosi, rapaci e ambiziosi, e vogliono sempre piú che alle sua natura non conviene ... Per la qual cosa non si potendo le buone repubbliche, e le malvagie non essendo convenevole introdurre, è necessario trovare un modo e una forma di governo, che si possa o sia onesto introdurre: questo modo e questa forma per questa via, si potrà agevolmente trovare."

62. *Opere*, II, 18–19: "... i grandi, perché eccedono gli altri in nobiltà e ricchezze, vogliono cómandare non ciascuno da per sé, ma tutti insieme, perciò vorriano una forma di governo nella quale essi solo tenessero l'imperio; e tra loro ancora sempre alcuno si trova che aspira al principato e vorrebbe comandar solo. I poveri non si curano di comandare, ma temendo l'insolenza de' grandi, non vorriano ubbidire se non a chi senza distinzione a tutti comanda, cioè alle leggi, e però basta loro esser liberi, essendo quegli libero che solamente alle leggi ubbidisce. I mediocri hanno il medesimo desiderio de' poveri, perché ancora essi appetiscono la libertà; ma perché la fortuna loro è alquanto piú rilevata, perciò oltre alla libertà, desiderano ancora onore. Possiamo adunque dire che in ogni città sia chi desidera libertà, e chi oltre alla libertà onore, e chi grandezza, o solo o accompagnato."

63. *Opere*, II, 19–20: "A volere adunque istituire un governo in una città, dove siano tali umori, bisogna pensare di ordinarlo in modo che ciascuna di quelle parti ottenga il desiderio suo; e quelle repubbliche che sono cosí ordinate si può dire che sono perfette, perché, possedendo in esse gli uomini le cose desiderate, non hanno cagione di far tumulto, e perciò simili stati si possono quasi eterni reputare. A' desiderii di queste parti similmente non si può soddisfare, perché bisogneria introdurre in una città un regno, uno stato di pochi ed un governo di molti, il che non si può immaginare, non che mettere in atto, salvo che in Genova, dove innanzi che Messer Andrea Doria le avesse con grandissima sua gloria renduta la libertà, si vedeva una repubblica ed una tirannide."

64. *Opere*, II, 20: "Possonsi bene detti desiderii ingannare, cioè si può introdurre un modo di vivere nel quale a ciascuna di quelle parti paja ottenere il desiderio suo, quantunque pienamente non l'ottenga."

65. *Ibid*.: "Onde in questo governo che cerchiamo bisogna che uno sia principe, ma che il suo principato non dependa da lui; bisogna che i grandi comandino, ma che tale autorità non abbia origine da loro; bisogna che la moltitudine sia libera, ma che tal libertà abbia dependenza; e finalmente che i mediocri, oltre all'esser liberi, possano ottenere onori, ma che tal facoltà non sia nel loro arbitrio collocata ..."

66. *Opere*, II, 24.

67. *Opere*, II, 37–38: "Ed è da notare che in tutte le azioni sono da considerare tre cose,

la cagione, l'occasione e il principio. Sono molti che pigliano l'occasione per la cagione, e della cagione non fanno conto, come saria se alcuno (poniamo) dicesse che la cagione della rovina dello stato di Firenze nel MDXII fosse la differenza che nacque tra Papa Giulio ed il re di Francia, e l'aver perduto il re di Francia Milano; la qual cosa non fu la cagione, ma l'occasione, e la cagione fu la mala contentezza d'alcuni cittadini malvagii ed ambiziosi; il principio poi fu la venuta ed assalto degli Spagnuoli per rimettere i Medici. Non è adunque la cagione altro che una disposizione, la quale si risente qualche volta l'occasione si scopre, e molto spesso è tanto potente la cagione, che non aspetta, anzi fa nascere l'occasione."

68. *Opere*, II, 39: "... era necessario che le parti tumultuassero, e quando reggesse l'uno, e quando l'altro; e se alcuno domandasse qual sia stata l'occasione, perché i grandi non prevalessero mai tanto al popolo, né il popolo ai grandi, che l'una parte e l'altra potesse lo stato suo fermare, dico che la cagione di tal cosa era perché le forze del popolo e de' grandi erano uguali, e però l'una non poteva abbassare mai l'altra intieramente; e quando l'una prevaleva all'altra nasceva dall'occasioni, che erano ora a questa parte, ora a quell'altra conformi, e non era possibile, quando l'una prevaleva all'altra, che interamente si assicurasse ..." Cf. pp. 42–43 for the contrast benveen quantity in the popolo and qualità— "nobilità, ricchezze e favori, dignità, disciplina e simili cose ... reputazione, ricchezze, clientele, favori, cosí esterni come domestici"—in the *nobili*.

69. See below, pp. 388–89.

70. See, at length, *Opere*, II, 45–48.

71. *Opere*, II, 47–48: 'É succeduto poi il secondo ritorno de' Medici nel MDXXX con quella violenza che è nota a tutto'l mondo, e perché nella resistenza grande che s'é fatta loro, sono stati offesi molti cittadini di gran qualità, è necessario che abbiano l'animo alienato dal vivere universale e politico, parendo loro essere stati da quello maltrattati; la qual cosa pare che generi quella stessa difficultà all'introduzione d'un vivere civile che saria se la città, cosí come già era, fusse piena di grandi, e mancasse di mediocri, come di sopra discorremmo. Ma questa difficultà a poco a poco manca, per il violento modo di vivere che al presente si osserva, nel quale tutti i cittadini, di qualunque grado, appariscono concultati ed abbietti, senza onore, e senza reputazione, e senza autorità. Talché è necessario che ciascuno, deposti gli odii particolari ed unite le volontà, viva con desiderio grande di pacifico e quiete vivere, ed aspetti l'occasione di ricuperarlo."

72. *Opere*, II, 52–53.

73. *Opere*, II, 53: "A che si aggiugne che la considerazione de' difetti, nei quali hanno di bisogno di reformazione, è molto malagevole, non solamente perché in cose particolari consistono, le quali con difficoltà si possono altrimenti che per esperienza conoscere, ma perché ancora niuno mai si trovò che tanto fosse libero dalle umane affezioni che in ogni cosa il difetto e mancamento suo potesse vedere ..."

74. *Opere*, II, 54–55 "Non conobbe adunque Fra Girolamo questi particolari mancamenti, né è da maravigliarsene molto; perché essendo forestiero e religioso, non poteva trovarsi nelle pubbliche amministrazioni; talché veduti egli i modo del procedere in esse, avesse potuto far giudizio di quello che era bene o male ordinato ..."

75. *Opere*, II, 59: "In Firenze adunque nei due passati governi, la creazione de' magistrati senza dubbio era in potere degli assai, perché tutta la città dependeva dal gran consiglio, e però in questa parte la città era libera; la deliberazione della pace e guerra era in potere del magistrato dei dieci, i quali di quelle due cose, e conseguentemente di tutto lo stato della città potevano disponere; di che seguitava che i pochi e non gli assai fossero signori dello stato della città: e dove tal cosa avviene, quivi non può esser vera e sincera libertà."

76. *Opere*, II, 81–82: "... talché costretti da questa mala contentezza, consentirono alla

rovina di quello stato, ed a rimettere i Medici; benché questi tali non meritino laude alcuna, anzi biasimo e vituperio, non è però che quel modo di procedere sia da biasimere e da correggere, per tor via le cagioni di quelle male contentezze...."

77. The first occurrence of this thought is at *Opere*, II, 58–59: "Ma è da notare che quattro sono le cose nelle le quali consiste il vigore di tutta la repubblica; l'elezione de' magistrati; la deliberazione della pace e guerra; e provocazioni; e l'introduzione delle leggi; le quali quattro cose sempre devono essere in potere di chi è signore della città. Per la qual cosa in quei governi, dove gli assai reggono, è necessario che sieno in potestà degli assai, altrimenti in quella città, dove sieno tali ammfistrazioni, non sarebbe libertà."

78. Cf. the *Letter to Capponi*, above, and nn. 32, 75.

79. *Opere*, II, 59–60: "Veniva adunque la città quanto alla creazione de' magistrati ad esser libera, ma quanto all'altre tre cose, che non sono di minore importanza, non era libera ma all'arbitrio e podestà di pochi soggetta. Che le tre ultime cose non fossero di minor momento che la creazione de' magistrati è manifesto, se non per altra, perché chi è stato padrone delle tirannidi passato non si è curato dell'elezione de' magistrati, eccetto quelli ne' quali era posto l'autorità delle tre dette cose, parendo loro che chi è signore di quelle sia signore di tutto; e senza dubbio, chi può deliberare della pace e guerra, introdurre leggi ed ha il ricorso de' magistrati, è padrone d'ogni cosa."

80. *Opere*, II, 96–97: "Pensò adunque Romulo a fare violenza, e d'avere a vincere, e per conseguente al propagare l'imperio, e far grande la sua repubblica. La cagione ancora, che l'indusse a far tal violenza, non fu altro che la cupidità dell'imperio, perché se non voleva quello accrescere, non gli era necessario usare tal violenza; perciocché aveva tanti uomini, che facevano conveniente corpo d'una città non ambiziosa, la quale si voglia solamente mantenere, e non desideri accrescimento; e delle donne per gli uomini suoi avrebbe trovato in spazio di tempo, senza che quelle d'Alba non gli sariano mai mancate."

81. *Opere*, II, 98–99: "Ma se noi consideriamo bene, è di maggiore importanza introdurre una buona forma di repubblica, perché dietro a questa agevolmente s'introdurrà buona milizia: ma dove fosse la milizia introdotta, non saria forse cosí agevolmente introdurre buona ordinazione; perché naturalmente gli uomini militari sono meno che gli altri trattabile. E perciò Romulo primieramente introdusse gli ordini civili, e poi gli ordini militari; e potette costui in brevissimo tempo ogni cosa condurre, perché essendo principe assoluto non aveva che contradicesse.... In Firenze adunque, essendo di maggiore importanza introdurre un buon governo che una buona milizia (perché invero la città ne' tempi passati ha piuttosto patito per mancamento di governo che di milizia, forse per le qualità dell'armi e de' tempi) tratteremo prima di quella parte ..."

82. *Opere*, II, 99–100: "... il primo modo, secondo il quale le forze di ciascuna parte sono eguali a quelle dell'altra, senza dubbio è difettivo e non si debbe seguitare, perché non è possibile temperare uno stato tanto perfettamente che la virtù (vogliamo dire potestà di ciascuna parte) non apparisca; perciocché in tal mistione avviene il contrario che nella mistione delle cose naturali, nella quale le virtù particolari delle cose di che si fa mistione non rimangono nel misto apparenti, ma di tutte se ne fa una sole; la qual cosa non può nel temperare una repubblica avvenire; perché bisogneria pestare e tritare in modo gli uomini, che dei grandi, popolari e mediocri se ne facesse una sol cosa diversa in tutto da quelle tre fazioni; la qual cosa senza dubbio è impossibile. Rimanendo adunque le virtù di ciascuna parte apparenti nella mistione, è necessario che essendo l'opposizioni e resistenze eguali, non manchino le repubbliche in tal modo temperate di civili dissensioni, le quali aprano la via alla rovina loro."

83. *Opere*, II, 101–103.

84. *Opere*, II, 103: "... quella parte dove la repubblica inclina, viene ad esser più potente

che l'altra; e però facilmente può opprimere gli insulti che le fossero fatti; e perché quella potenza che ha nasce dalla forma della repubblica, però se la parte contraria si reputa ingiuriata, non l'imputa alla fazione avversa ma alla forma della repubblica. E perché la repubblica è temperata in modo che non vi è adito a rovinarla, però è necessato che viva quieta; onde in tale repubblica non può nascere alterazione alcuna. É ben da notare che quando io dico che la repubblica deve inclinare in una parte, non dico che quella parte abbia sola l'imperio, e l'altra sia esclusa dall'amministrazione, ma che l'una abbia poca dependenza e l'altra assai.... Concludendo adunque dico che è necessario che una repubblica inclina ad una parte, a volere che sia diuturna e viva sempre senza alterazioni civili."

85. *Opere*, II, 107–108: "... se possono apporre la cagione delle ingiurie ricevute a qualche particolare, subito li corrono a casa, e coli' armi e col fuoco si vendicano, siccome in Firenze molte volte si trova essere avvenuto. Ma se tali cagioni nascono dall'ordinazione della repubblica, talché a nessuno particolare si possano applicare, allora i popolari, non avendo contro a chi voltare l'ira sua, si separano da' grandi, e chieggono o legge o magistrato per lo quale si possano difendere ed ottenere la loro ragione; e questo fu grandissima cagione che ne' tumulti del popolo Romano contro al senato, non si venne mai al sangue de' cittadini, insino ai Gracchi; perché le ingiurie che pativano i popolari non da' privati cittadini, ma dalla forma della repubblica nascevano, e perciò l'ingiuriati non de' cittadini ma dell'ordine della repubblica si potevano lamentare; onde avveniva che nelle sovversioni non chiedeva altro che qualche legge o qualche magistrato, per virtù della quale si difendesse, e la potenza de' pochi si venisse ad abbassare, ed essi più della repubblica partecipassero."

86. *Opere*, II, 114–15.

87. *Opere*, II, 115–16.

88. *Opere*, II, 109–16.

89. *Opere*, II, 110: "Quanto al leggerle, cosí le può leggere un popolare come un grande; e la pratica non veggio maggiore nell'una parte che nell'altra ..."

90. *Opere*, II, 111: "... perché i popolari fanno molto maggiore numero che i grandi, si può probabilmente dire che facciano maggiore aggregato di prudenza ...

91. *Opere*, II, 116.

92. *Opere*, II, 117: "Per il consiglio adunque si soddisfa al desiderio della libertà; per il senato all'appetito dell'onore; per il principe al desiderio del principato. Resta di trovar modo di soddisfare a chi appetisce grandezza, non potendo più che uno ottenere il principato. Bisogna adunque collocare un membro tra il senato ed il principe, e questo sarà un aggregato d'alcuni magistrati, i quali col principe consiglieranno, ed eseguiranno le faccende grandi dello stato e della città ... e questo membro si può chiamare, se vogliamo imitare i Veneziani, il collegio."

93. *Opere*, II, 118: "Il consiglio grande essere un aggregato composto di quei tre membri, i quali noi di sopra descriveremmo, cioè grandi, mediocri e popolari; de' plebei non occorre far menzione, come ancora di sopra dicemmo, essendo gente forestiera che vengono alla città per valersi delle fatiche corporali, e ne vanno a casa loro, qualunque volta torna loro a proposito. Quelli che io chiamai popolari (cioè quelli che sono a gravezza, ma non sono abili a' magistrati) è necessario connumerare in detto consiglio, perché sono poco meno che principal membro della città per fare grandissimo numero, e per non potere la città senza quelli stare, e per mantenere la sua grandezza."

94. *Opere*, II, 119–20: "... di qui nasce che i popolari amano più molte volte un privato che la repubblica, e per lui prendere l'armi contro alla patria, sperando avere ad esse da quello arricchiti ed onorati.... Appresso, se Aristotile, il quale ha trattato con tanta dottrina

e sapienza de' governi di tutte le repubbliche, entrasse in Venezia o in Firenze, dove vedesse d'una gran moltitudine d'uomini non esser tenuto conto alcuno, salvo che ne' bisogni della città, senza dubbio si riderebbe di tali ordinazioni, avendo nel settimo libro della sua Politica distribuiti gli uffici della città convenienti a tutte le qualità degli abitanti della medesima."

95. *Opere*, II, 120–21: "E se alcuno dicesse che questi popolari non sono ambiziosi ... questo curarsi (poco?) de' magistrati non è naturale, ma accidente, perche non è uomo sì misero che non desideri essere esaltato. Ma perché questi popolari sono stati tenuti bassi dalla superbia dei grandi, perciò son divenuti non ambiziosi, siccome ancora ne' tempi nostri sono i Franzesi, i quali per essere stati sbattuti dalla nobiltà loro, sono divenuti vilissimi. Non essendo adunque naturale tal viltà di animo in questi popolari, non è da privarli de' magistrati, e massimamente perché armandosi la città, diverriano subito desiderosi di gloria come gli altri ..."

96. *Opere*, II, 122: "... azioni le quali sono principali nella repubblica ed abbracciano tutta la forza dello stato."

97. *Opere*, II, 129–30.

98. *Opere*, II, 123: "Le deliberazioni della pace e guerra abbiano a terminare nel senato ... e quantunque elle non passino nel consiglio, avranno pure da lui la dependenza, essendo da quello il senato, dove l'hanno a terminare, eletto ... Saria forse bene, quando si ha a muovere una guerra di nuovo, vincere questa prima deliberazione nel consiglio grande (siccome facevano i Romani, i quali domandavano il popolo, se volevano e comandavano che si movesse guerra a questo ed a quello altro principe o repubblica); dipoi tutti gli accidenti di essa avessero a terminare nel senato."

99. *Opere*, II, 157: "... è da notare che questo atto dell'ascoltare le provocazioni pare che sia proprietà di quello che è signore dello stato e della città: ma perché chi è signore, o egli non vuole, o egli non può se non con difficoltà tal cosa eseguire, perciò vediamo tale uffizio essere attribuito ad un altro giudizio dagli altri separato. Laonde perché in Francia il re non vuole, ed anco con difficoltà potrià occuparsi in tal faccenda, sono ordinati quattro parlamenti, i quali odono e giudicano le provocazioni di tutto il regno. In Venezia, perché il consiglio grande, che è signore di tutta la repubblica, non può fare tale effetto, perché bisogneria che stesse tutto l'anno occupato in tal materia (il che saria impossibile rispetto alle faccende private) sono ordinate tre quarantie ..."

100. See his criticisms of the arrangements made in 1502, 1512, and 1527 at pp. 140–41.

101. See generally pp. 139–47, and particularly 144–45.

102. *Opere*, II, 194–99; especially p. 196: "Questo modo di vivere che tengono questi che fanno professione di religione, conversando coi frati di San Marco e continuando simulatamente l'orazione e la comunione, senza dubbio è pessimo nella nostra città; perché egli fa il medesimo effetto che facevano in Roma le largizioni. Ma questi è ancora molto peggiore, perché dove le largizioni si potevano in qualche modo correggere, a questa cosí fatta vita con difficoltà si trova rimedio; perché chi ragionasse di proibire questi modi di vivere, parrebbe che volesse vietare agli uomini il bene operare, e sarebbe ributtato non altrimenti che un pessimo nemico nella fede di Cristo."

103. But cf. *Opere*, II, 255–56: "Conchiudendo adunque dico che tal forma di repubblica della nostra città non potrebbe patire alcuna intrinseca alterazione: e per virtù della milizia nel sopradetto modo ordinata, si difenderebbe dagli assalti esterni, e se la fortuna concedesse a questa repubblica colle sue armi armata una sola vittoria, acquisterebbe la nostra città sola tanta gloria e reputazione che toccherebbe il cielo; e non saria maraviglia alcuna se Firenze diventasse un'altra Roma, essendo il subbietto per la frequenza e natura

degli abitatori, e fortezza del sito, d'un imperio grandissimo capace." At this point Giannotti is drawing nearer to both the Savonarolan and the Machiavellian modes of thinking.

104. Book III, ch. 8 (the last); pp. 258–69.

105. *Opere*, II, 269: "Saria ben necessario esser accorto nel prender l'occasione; perché questa è quella che ha le bilance delle faccende umane e tutte quelli che in tal cosa non usano prudenza grandissima sono costretti a rovinare. Ma di questa materia non è da parlare, perché appartiene delle congiure, la quale è stata da altri prudentissimamente trattata.

"Conchiudendo adunque dico che questi sono i modi per i quali alcun cittadino potrià recare si gran benefizio alla nostra città; e benché la malignità della fortuna abbia oppressati quelli che hanno questi modi seguitati, non è però da disperare ... acciocché la città nostra s'abbia píú tosto a lamentare della fortuna per non avere mostrato mai alcuna intera occasione, che ella della città, per non v'essere stato chi l'abbia saputa conoscere e pigliare."

106. Perhaps 1522–25. See Gilbert, "Date of the Composition," *loc. cit.* (above, n. 3).

107. Lewkenor, *The Commonwealth and Government of Venice. Written by the Cardinall Gasper Contareno and translated out of Italian into English by Lewes Lewkenor* (London, 1599), p. 2. The Latin text runs (Contarini, *De Magistratibus et Republica Venetorum*, Paris, 1543, p. 1): "deorum immortalium potius quam hominum opus atque inuentü fuisse ...

108. Lewkenor, sig. A3.

109. Lewkenor, p. 130. Contarini, pp. 100–101: "Haec vero frequens consuetudo c?tinentis, ac inrermissio urbanae, faction? quandam ciuium paritura facile fuerat ab aleis ciuibus disiuncta: quapropter proculdubio res Venera breui ad factiones et ad bells ciuilia deducta fuisset.... Ne erge huiusmodi quispiam morbus in Venetam ciuitatem obreperet, satius esse maiores statuerunt, ut continentis imperium externo ac conducto milite quam Veneto defenderetur. Stipend?? uero illi statuit ex uectigalibus totius prouinciae. Aequ? enim erat eius regionis impensis militem uiuere, qui ad eam tuendam accersitus fuerat ..."

110. Lewkenor, p. 6. Contarini, pp. 5–6: "Fuere Athenis, Lacedaemone, ac Romae nonulli ciues uitae probitate, atq: in Rempub. pietate insignes uiri, sed adeo pauci, ut multitudine obruti, non multum patriae rei rofuerint. At maiores nostria, a quibus tam praeclaram Rempub. accepimus, omnes ad unum consensere in studio patriae rei firmandae et amplificandae, nulla prope priuati commodi et honoris habita ratione. Huiusce rei coniecturam facere quiuis facile poterit ... q: nulla, aut admod? paura antiquor? monum?ta Venetiis extent: alioquin domi forisq: praeclarissimorum homin?, et qui de Rep. bene meriti fuerint, non sepulchra, n? equestres aut pedestres statua, n? rostra naui?, aut uexila ab hostibus direpta, ingentibus praeliis superatis."

111. Lewkenor, p. 7, Contarini, p. 6: "Hac ergo incredibili uirtute animi maiores nostri hanc Remp, instituere, qual? post homin? memoriam nullam extitisse, si quis h?c nostram cum celeberrimis antiquorum c?ferar, meridiana luce clarius intuebitur. Quin adfirmare ausim, neq: monumentis insignium philosophorum, qui pro animi uoto Reip. formas effinxere, tam recte formatam atq: effictam ullam contineri."

112. Lewkenor, p. 11. Contarini, pp. 8–9: "... menti purae, ac motionum animi immuni id munus conferendum est. Quamobrem diuino quodam consilio, cum alia ratione id fieri non posset, inuentibus legibus hoc assecutum humanunn genus uidetur, ut menti tantum ac rationi nullis perturbantibus obnoxiae, hoc regendi hominum coetus officium demandatum sit..."

113. Lewkenor, p. 12. Contarini, pp. 9–10: "Aristoteles philosophorum facile princeps, in co libello qu? de mundo ad Alexandrum regem Macedonum scripsit, nihil aliud reperit

cui sirnilem deum optimum faceret, praeter antiquam regem in ciuitate recte instituta: ut id propemodum tam magni philosophi sententia sit deus in hac reium universitate, quod antiqua lex in ciuili societate."

114. Lewkenor, sig. A2v.-3.

115. Lewkenor, p. 13. Contarini, p. 11: "Ac equidem multitudo omnis est per se inepta gubernationi, nisi in unum quodammodo coalescat: quandoquidem neuue esse ulla multitudo queat, nisi unitate aliqua contineatur. Qua de re ciuilis quoque societas dissipabitur, quae unitate quadam c?stat, nisi quapiam ratione multitudo unum efficiatur."

116. Lewkenor, p. 15. Contarini, p. 13: "... adeo ut omnium formas pari quadam libram?to commiscuisse uideatur ..."

117. Gilbert, "Date of the Composition," pp. 172–74, 182.

118. Lewkenor, p. 67. Contarini, p. 53: "Nam nulla perniciosior pestis in Rempublicam obrepserit, q[uam] si quaepi? eius pars caeteris praeualuerit. Sic nanque (?) quoniam ius non seruatur, impossibile est societatem inter ciues consistere. Quod usu euenire solet ubicunque plura in unum conueniunt. Sic soluitur mixtum, si quodpi? elementor? ex quibus constat, alla superauerit. Sic omnis consonantia dissonans sit, si fidem seu uocem un? plus intenderis quam par sit. Non dispari ratione si ciuitatem aut Rempublicam constare uolueris, necesse est id in primis seruari, ne qua pars aliis efficiatur potentior, sed omnes, quoad fieri possit, participes fiat publicae potestatis."

119. Gilbert, "Venetian Constitution," pp. 468–70

120. Above, nn. 23, 24.

121. William J. Bouwsma, *Venice and the Defense of Republican Liberty: Renaissance Values in the Age of the Counter Reformation* (Berkeley and Los Angeles: University of California Press, 1968).

122. Bouwsma, ch. x.

EUGENIO GARIN

Interpretations of the Renaissance

There is today a lively interest in the problem of the Renaissance which impells many people to take another look at Renaissance Humanism. This new interest is not entirely due, it seems to me, to the fact that after so many attempts all purely historical interpretations of the Renaissance have been exhausted. There was a time when many of us were seduced by these historical interpretations. But now there is not a single such interpretation which satisfies our methodological demands. Too many new problems have come to our knowledge. They define and help us to understand a great many aspects and motifs which used to be either neglected or obscured by the purely historical approach. There can be little doubt that any purely historical interpretation of the Renaissance creates more problems than it solves. But in the last instance, the crisis through which all purely historical interpretations of the Renaissance are going results from our need to give an account of the essential and directive lines of thought in western civilisation. This need continuously turns us back upon what is, after all, a crucial period in the history of the west. The Renaissance was indeed a crucial period—not only in the history of philosophy in the narrow sense in which philosophy is a discipline concerned with the technical discussion of certain defined problems, but in the history of the view of the life of man. For it was precisely during this time that the horizons of the most serious of all researches began to alter. As a result there disappeared, even though many people were not fully aware of it at the time, a well-established and venerable

From *Science and Civic Life in the Italian Renaissance* trans. Peter Munz. © 1969 by Doubleday & Co.

form of philosophising. The truth is that at this time there emerged, once and for all, a new manner of seeing the world, and an ancient way of seeing it disappeared. True, the old manner of seeing it disappeared in a blaze of glory, for the old manner had aspects which gave rise to the new manner. But all in all it did amount to a solemn burial of a dead, if noble, interpretation of reality. The only thing is that that burial was not accomplished all at once. The knowledge that the old world was dying matured very slowly and agonisingly. And it is perhaps only today that we can fully understand the catastrophic conclusion of this process. The centre of interest was shifted from one method of research to another. A complete change in the relationships between man and the ultimate realities, between man and things, between man and human institutions took place. And all this bore witness to a total change in man's attitude. If one goes to the bottom of things, these changes indicate the end of a sense of security and the beginning of an age of torment. The direction the new search was to take was at first not clear, for the new conception of the "free" man was placed in the very margin of the destruction of all preconceived forms: "you, who are neither a citizen of heaven nor a citizen of the earth, neither mortal nor immortal, you are, by yourself almost free and a sovereign creator. You must shape and hew yourself in an image which you must choose for yourself."

There was a way of writing history which pictured this rebirth of the free man as something like a triumphal march of certainties and resounding achievements. But if one peruses the most important testimonies of that age, and I am thinking chiefly of the fifteenth century, one will all the time discover that people, instead of being conscious of a beginning, were dimly aware that something was ending. The ending they sensed, though glorious, was nevertheless an ending. True, there is no lack of reminders that something new was being constructed. And there were assurances that man is indeed capable of carrying out a reconstruction of the world and of himself. But there was also an awareness of the fact that the secure tranquillity of a homely and familiar universe, ordered and adjusted to our needs, was lost forever. Even where the most ancient themes lingered on, they changed in tone and flavour. Thus people kept believing that perhaps our illnesses are written in the stars. But in such cases they ceased to think of astral communications as the work of benevolent celestial deities and interpreted them as signs of man's sad enslavement to obscure and indifferent forces, beyond man's grasp. For this reason, people came to think of the liberation from astral destiny as a liberation from man's annihilation by things. To free man from the tyranny of the stars meant to free him from the anxiety of not being able to achieve anything or be anything.

Today we derive great pleasure from reading those new praises of nature and hymns to the infinite. But this is only because we somehow imagine that there was a tranquil confidence which kept shining through; or at least because we keep having a confident hope that the infinite which was promised was something positive. The sense of loss which ran through the whole of that civilisation thereby escapes us. For that civilisation, once it had smashed the ancient idols, was aware of the boundary it had reached, and knew of its own responsibility before unknown possibilities. A fine example of this is the spiritual itinerary of Ficino, who had come to the infinity of nature through Lucretius. In that infinite nature, man, because of his substance, has no prerogatives. Later he discovered that same loss and that same indifference to the meaning life once was supposed to have had in the immobile and timeless rigidity of the thought of Averroës and in the Aristotelianism of Alexander of Aphrodisia. It was then that he donned the garments of a priest and turned towards Plato and Plotinus in order to find someone who might transform into hope the restlessness that troubled him, and to assure him that the meaning which we are unable to discover here on earth, the positive certainty of things, is in reality up on high, where it will be revealed to us in the end. Both his Christianity and his Platonism helped him to keep alive at least one comforting doubt: "perhaps things as they appear to us are not true; perhaps, at present, we are asleep." Hence emerged the Ficino who was more sincere and more lively than the one who arranged everything in well-ordered and systematic concepts and substances which he could then place as a screen between himself and his bewilderment. His systematic universe was as fictitious as it was comforting. It was solidified in a reassuring hierarchy in which even the much celebrated dignity of man tended to vanish, for there was always the risk that the idea that man stood in the centre would reduce itself to the mere determination of a spatial locality.

There was another sense and another courage in the rich appeal to human virtue, to a virtue capable of overcoming destiny, capable of changing that destiny and constructing its own world and of giving a new shape to things with the help of that human artfulness which joins science and poetry. This, indeed, was the meaning of the civic humanism of Florence in the fifteenth century. This meaning inspired both Alberti and Pico when they transformed rhetorical and philological humanism into the metaphysics of man the creator. This metaphysics, I believe, was the most profound part of the whole of the Renaissance.

If we regard the ideas of Alberti as typical it would be wrong to see in his idea of virtue nothing more than the joyful certainty of a man confident of his actions and unaware that he is standing on the edge of an abyss. Just because Alberti is always a poet, and that means a creator, he was well aware of the risk involved in all creativity, in every construction which amounts to bringing about a fundamental change in what is given to us and indeed in the whole world. He was very aware of how unstable all constructions are and how in the very end all virtue will be vanquished. Campano wrote that there is no man whose virtue is not defeated in one last battle, be it only the one with death, for all human beings and all things are destined to perish.

One ought to remember that Alberti's sadness was not a well-articulated pessimism. It was simply nourished by the knowledge that everything must change. Alberti had experienced many economic and political changes in his own home and had watched a whole mode of life disappear before his eyes. All this made him extremely thoughtful about the insecurity of life. His beautiful dialogue *Fatum et Fortuna* is one of the most deeply serious works in our whole moral literature; it eliminates all chances of optimism. The man who wants to know too much is aware of the shadows that darken the tempestuous river of life, and they remind him how vain it is for beings who are allowed to know only through sense experience to seek to understand God. And just as there is a limit to knowledge, there is also a limit to action. One cannot escape the rapids and falls of the river *Bios*. They form stumbling-blocks and ambushes which will sooner or later break every ship, even when a calm and free mind, with the help of the arts, can maintain it within certain limits and guide its course safely for a certain distance. The ultimate truth is harsh: "I have understood that fate determines the course of everything in the life of man and that it runs its course according to its law ... I have also understood that for us, *Fortuna* is hard, if we have to be drowned in the river at the very moment when we ought to be fighting the violence of the wave with a strong arm: nevertheless we cannot ignore that in human affairs prudence and industry count for much."

These reservations insistently recall the obscurity of the foundations of life and its uncertainties. They are a reminder of the ineluctable limits set on all our efforts to determine our fate. Everything in this vision reminds one of the myth of Er in which the element of fortuity that is present at the launching of every fate is emphasised by the blindness that is at the very root of the human condition. The wise builder, the master of architecture was to tell us, constructs solid buildings, capable of withstanding the ravages of time. The many calculations by which he has dealt with even the most minute natural forces are hidden. For the artist's dreams are not dreamt in a state of intoxication. On the contrary, the artist builds on the basis of a detailed and prudent plan; and he builds things that will be fruitful and useful. He will always bear in mind his own interests and those of his friends. But in spite of everything, the edifice must one day fall to pieces. There can be no such thing as absolute stability. Everything decays: even the things that have taken their inspiration from absolute stability, stable goodness and stable truth, including those things which pretend to have been built according to absolute rules. And when they decay, they do not decay because of the malignity of men or because of the adversity of matter. They decay because in our world there is no such thing as a fixed rule and an absolute certainty. "There was a time ... when I was in the habit of basing my views on truth, my zeal on considerations of utility, my words and expressions on my innermost thoughts.... But I have learnt now to adapt my views to the prevailing superstitions, my zeal to caprices, and to frame all my words so as to be capable of deception." These myths console us and create the illusions and seductions of our daily life. They are like the many branches of the ivy into which Momo transformed himself so as to be able to embrace, possess, and corrupt the beautiful daughter of virtue.

One could say that Alberti's mood was no more than a pleasantry, a bitter way of telling a tale, an expression of contempt, perhaps a joke. But the very opposite is true. The full flavour of his *Momus* comes out in the way that gaiety is made to appear serious. The *Momus* is meant to demonstrate the validity of a caprice, the philosophy of a mere poet, the non-philosophy of the philosopher. In reality, the philosopher himself is an extraordinary myth-maker. He calls these myths "systems." As Telesio was to observe in all seriousness, these systems fashion whole worlds according to his arbitrary will in competition with God. The worst aspect of these philosophical constructions is that they are so often ugly, inconsistent, sterile, and serious to the point of boredom whereas the artist has at his disposal the imagination of very life itself, and he builds even as life builds and makes no claims for his creations over and above their own inherent value. The world of the artist is the world of living imagination just as the world of nature is the living imagination of God. The artist is a creator and his forms take shape, rejoice and appear among us, live with us and transform our lives as the fables of ancient superstition were wont to do. In the *Momus*, Charon says something which is on the face of it quite trivial but he gives it immediately a new subtle interpretation: "you, who know the course of the stars but are ignorant of human affairs, you are indeed a fine philosopher! I will not report the opinions of a philosopher—for all your science, you philosophers, is limited to verbal subtleties. I will relate instead what I have heard from a painter. That painter, when he observes the shapes of bodies, sees more things than all you philosophers together have ever seen in your efforts to measure and explore the skies." Charon then shows us what it is that the painter has seen when he prefers the loving observation of flowers to rational and speculative discourse. When he hears of subtle doctrines, he is stupefied and demands to know why "you neglect flowers when in a single flower all things combine into beauty and gracefulness ..." Alberti's main theme is life in its spontaneity. He talks about the function of artists and poets as it was to be understood later by Vico. Hence he finds nourishment for his disconcerting praise of the vagabond, of the man who breaks all bonds and restraints and who refuses to accept any position as absolute; of the man who is free and who is, in spite of his gay caprices, fundamentally serious—for he is aware of the non-value of all sacred values as well as of the value of what seems mere folly. Alberti's *Momus* is much less famous than Erasmus' *Praise of Folly*. But often enough it touches upon very profound matters. In the end, it furnishes a lavish proclamation of the importance of myth. It includes a critique of religious myths and recognises the validity of myth-making for the life of man. But in spite of all this not one of the venerable forms of the most authoritative traditions is salvaged—neither philosophy (except perhaps Socratic irony) nor religion, which is finally demolished by Charon: "If I were by myself I would just laugh at it. But among so many people I pretend to respect it." If *Momus* had continued his tales, the gods would have been dispersed in next,to no time. For this reason Alberti silenced him by a curious final reminder of the limit—a reminder which recalls his *Fatum et Fortuna*. Hence, Alberti's "dispersal," contained in this kind of irony and therefore essentially ambiguous, is very different from the enthusiastic and confident "dispersal" of Bruno. Bruno's "dispersal" came close to blasphemy but ended up by reassembling in its own way all the gods, all the laws, and all the old certainties—amounting, therefore, perhaps to no more than the rebellion of a penitent. Alberti's dispersal, in spite of its vague tone, is a very terrible one in that it reminds man of the full responsibility with which it is fraught. For after, the dispersal the consoling and well-systematised world of the metaphysicians, as well as the no less tranquil and reassuring world of the gods, is gone forever. Even if an infinitely far-away and unknowable absolute God were to be invoked or rejected, man's situation in the universe could never be changed again. Lefèvre d'Étaples was to give us a description of Pico della Mirandola. When he was carried away by the most powerful wave of Savonarolan faith, Pico intoned a moving prayer in the Lucretian manner and bemoaned the fact that God was so far-away.

Bruno was solidly confident that he would be able to open a passage through the shattered walls of the world and that that passage would lead towards the all embracing One, the absolute which was well worth one's infinite love and the truth of which was a guarantee of the positive sense of reality. Bruno, and Cusanus before him, supply good arguments against those who reason that the culture of the Renaissance was a continuation of traditional culture. Both thinkers were men who had undertaken the construction of a metaphysical system and had thus taken up the traditional themes inherent in the logic of every speculation. They had not succeeded in determining the structure of reality by fixing necessary and stable forms. A truly "humanistic" standpoint, rather, has to be a poetical one. It proceeds by ignoring scholastic philosophy, or at least by considering it as something foreign. It has to remain deaf to it. A humanistic approach has to refute scholasticism as something which exhausts itself in the elaboration of rational schemes and paradigms that not only fail to explain or unravel reality but also have absolutely nothing to do with it. It is for this reason that Alberti never speaks of the actual infinity of man or of his substantial dignity, either of which might serve to reassure man about his transcendental destiny. He always speaks instead of the infinite number of human possibilities which, in the manner of a good humanist, he emphasises. These possibilities are the many mundane possibilities of the architect, the poet, the builder and the administrator of the city, the merchant and the householder. In the last analysis we are to be consoled in our melancholy position by beautiful fables and myths. Every time we approach the Renaissance we sense that its truth is to be found in Valla, Alberti, and Poliziano, in its Masaccios, Brunelleschis, Leonardos, Michelangelos, and Galileos—that is, in the artists, poets, historians and philologists, scientists—and last but not least in politicians and historians like Guicciardini and Machiavelli as well as in a prophet and reformer like Savonarola. It is not that this period is without its philosophers and could not have made its contribution to philosophy or that if it did, it only impinged upon the most obstruse parts of metaphysics, ontology, and gnoseology. It is rather that the most conscious form of human speculation took place in the sphere of philology, history, and science, all of which were opposed to the traditional ways of philosophising, which were busy "competing with God" instead of seeking to understand the world in order to change it and subject it to human requirements. This was the manner in which Telesio, for one, defined the difference between the old and the new way. It was no accident that the historico-philological attitudes, in the widest meaning of the term, proved a critical consummation and consolidation of the ancient way of viewing the world. While the old Aristotelian physics, in one last and fatal crisis, was dying of exhaustion, there emerged into full daylight a body of magical and alchemical doctrines consisting of techniques which could change the world. And in their wake came the irreverent experimental arts designed to break all laws and subvert all order. They were destined to move the stars from their courses, to transform all living beings, and to bring the dead to life. Men like Francis Bacon, Giordano Bruno, and Tommaso Campanella were to be among those who were seduced by the fascination of the experimental arts. It is worth recalling that in this environment there was nourished the theory that truth is the daughter of time; for, as magicians and astrologers were only too quick to notice, the certainties of today can only be slowly built by conquering the errors of the past. This was not likely to be done by people who seek to deduce once and for all the rational order of the world *a priori* but only by people who are engaged in the laborious pursuit of experimentation.

Towards the end of the fifteenth century, in a work which could well be compared with the *Discourse on Method* and the *Novum Organum*, Giovanni Pico della Mirandola defined the implications of the new image of man with great precision. He considered that the essence of the new image was man's independence of every predetermined species of form, as if man were breaking the bounds of the world of forms, as if he were the lord not only of his own form but also, through magic, the lord of the whole world of forms which he might combine with one another, transform, or remake. At the same time, reinterpreting the very ancient doctrine that the universe was a grand book of great originality, he demonstrated how historico-philological research coincided with the investigation of nature and how the world of man coincided with the world of nature provided the latter was transfigured and humanised by the effort of man. On the other hand he tended to intrude a religious element into this vision of man. He managed to achieve this through his historical critique of astrology as an astral religion and through his attempt to explain the biblical narratives by precise methods. In this way humanism attempted to become aware of its own radically new implications. It laid down the precise limits of the validity of a philosophy which, in Italy, was to continue along the royal road of historico-philological research. On this road we find Galileo, Vico, Muratori, to mention only the greatest names. This refutes Spaventi's theory that after the Renaissance philosophy emigrated from Italy. The theory, with all due respect to the subtle philosopher that Spaventi was, was due to a failure to understand fully the meaning and the inheritance of the humanistic ideal of the Renaissance.

We are bound to misunderstand the genuine significance of the Renaissance if we do not appreciate the proper meaning of humanism and keep on seeking its secret in the writings of a belated grammarian or in an alleged continuity with the middle ages. At the same time, the humanistic praise of the dignity of man can easily lead to a facile rhetoric if one does not bear in mind the price which had to be paid for it. The price was indeed high: one had to pay for the freedom to fight in a world that was stubbornly opposed to any effort and in which progress was difficult by relinquishing the reassuring idea that a given order existed. One also had to abandon the belief in a justice which would always in the end, albeit sometimes by very obscure means, triumph. What emerged instead was a political life without illusions, in which people were buffeted by forces without pity and in which the vanquished were eliminated without compassion. Similarly, people began to sense that everything in the world was frail and that God, if a God remained, was terribly far-away and ineffable and likely to issue unintelligible decrees to punish the just and save the sinner—a God to Whom it was vain to address prayers. If it is necessary to mention names, one need only think of Machiavelli and Pomponazzi, of Luther and Calvin as well as of the faces sculpted by Michelangelo. And finally, with Copernicus, Bruno, and Galileo, there came the end of the homely and well-ordered Ptolemaic system.

Once this is understood, one can give proper emphasis to the question of what precisely was new in the thought of the Renaissance. From a number of different standpoints attempts have been made to push back the Renaissance to the twelfth century or even to the Carolingian age and even to deny that apart from literary and artistic development, there ever emerged, anything that was really new. It would be no exaggeration to say that much of modern historical writing about the origin of modern thought is devoted to the attempt to demolish the conventional view that there was anything like a break between one way of thinking about the universe and another way. Admittedly this reaction was encouraged by the fact that the upholders of this view used to take their stand on arguments which are only too easily discounted. It is perfectly true that such things as a love for pagan antiquity and the classical writers, a lack of piety or of religion, atheism, naturalism, and radical immanentism can without difficulty be traced back into the middle ages. In this sense it has actually been helpful to stress and illustrate the continuity between the middle ages and the world of humanism and, for that matter, between the ancient world and the middle ages. In this way it has been possible to document the fact that humanism did not amount to a rebirth of ancient culture because ancient culture had always been alive throughout the middle ages, at least since the twelfth century. This view, when all is said and done, was not even very new, for it had been a not infrequent habit among the writers of the fifteenth and sixteenth centuries to trace the Renaissance back to Dante, a position that was propounded with some solemnity in the *Commentari urbani* of Raffaele da Volterra. Similarly, the argument that the Renaissance goes back to the days of Charlemagne and Alcuin was not invented by modern French medievalists; it was put forward by Filippo de' Medici, Archbishop of Pisa and Florentine ambassador to Paris on the occasion of the coronation of Louis XI. He mentioned it in his official speech in 1461 and referred to an explicit statement in the Letter Dedicatory to the Sovereign of the *Vita di Carlo Magno*, presented as a formal gift by Donato Acciaiuoli.

However this may be, it is certainly one of the merits of modern historical research to have understood that the myth of rebirth, of the new light, and hence the corresponding conception of a preceding darkness was the result of the attacks made by the humanists themselves upon the culture of the preceding centuries. There can be no doubt that the writers of the fifteenth century insisted with exasperating repetitiveness of the fact that they had revolted against an age of barbarism in order to bring about an age of humaneness (*humanitas*). It is equally beyond doubt that in the preceding centuries the sense of rapid historical development had never been as lively. From every corner emerged the idea that an old world was on the wane, and wherever people looked they found confirmation of the view that an established vision of the world was being abandoned. The new discoveries broke the traditional image of the world, and the old conception of the universe was shaken long before Galileo. Ever since criticism had destroyed the psychological premisses of the Ptolemaic system, it had become necessary to face the consequences of the idea that the universe was infinite, that there were other inhabited worlds and that the earth was not in a privileged position. There is no need to enlarge upon the effects that ideas and observations of this kind had on theology. The curious thing is that modern historiography, in its attempt to grasp the idea the Renaissance had of itself, has managed to stand this idea on its head by denying that it included any element of newness. If it is true that the light–darkness opposition is very old and goes back to an ancient religious tradition, and if it is therefore true that the alleged contrast between the darkness of the middle ages and the consequent rebirth was nothing more than an occasion for a conventional controversy, then all insistence upon a break and the emergence of something new is of doubtful value. As a result of much critical work it has now been clearly established that much of what we believed to belong to the Renaissance goes back to the middle ages. People in the middle ages loved the classics no less than people in the Renaissance. Everybody knew their Aristotle in the middle ages—and perhaps they knew him better than the people of the fifteenth century. Even Plato was known in the middle ages and by no means only indirectly. Ancient poets, historians, and orators were known and appreciated. Bernardo Silvestre had written philosophical poems worthy of Bruno; Bernard of Chartres had been aware that truth was the daughter of time, and jurists had been busy reconstructing the whole essence of Roman wisdom. The revaluation of man had been more powerfully and profoundly conceived by St. Thomas than by Ficino. Furthermore, the naturalism and lack of piety of Machiavelli, Pomponazzi, and Bruno, even where they seemed most bold and most new, turned out to be quite old. In fact, these men were the heirs, more or less consciously so, of medieval Alexandrism (condemned as early as 1210) and of Averroism and, through Arabic science, of other Hellenistic currents.

In this way the recognition that both in content and in problems there was nothing very original in the Renaissance as far as the history of thought was concerned forced some people to regard humanism as an aspect of *studia humanitatis* understood in a narrow sense as grammatical studies. They alleged that such studies assumed in the fourteenth century a major importance. But not even here did these people allow that something really new had happened. At most, they assigned to the rhetorical arts a somewhat more dignified place than they had occupied before. One is tempted to say that with this conclusion the academic controversy resounded in favour of the grammarians. Grammarians, it was held, had simply continued their customary labours which they had never interrupted; but now they were translating more accurately and more widely—though even this is doubted by some. Thus they were said to have diffused a more solid knowledge of both Latin and Greek, but indirectly, with a consequence which was always purely marginal. It is curious that this argument completely obscured the importance of the Salutati, the Bruni, the Poggio, of men who had been the great exponents of the highest culture and of a grand epoch, of citizens, magistrates, thinkers, and all this in order to vindicate in a facile manner the continuity of the scholastic habits of a whole lot of second-rate compilers of knowledge. Looked at from this angle, even Valla's philology, instead of bearing the imprint of an era of rebellion, is reduced to a burnt-out case.

It was quite justifiable to make an attempt to understand the slow process by which a grand period of culture had blossomed and matured. But in the end this attempt misfired so completely that the preoccupation with minute forms crowded out all sense of proportion. The same error which had been at the basis of the old interpretations had proved fatal in this case. The old interpretations sought to discover what exactly was new in the Renaissance by comparison with the middle ages. It might have been useful to observe that there was a correspondence between the bodily gestures of a fifteenth-century Madonna and the astrological representation of the *facies* of the Virgin, but it would be absurd to claim that such a comparison could be elevated into a judgment about the meaning of a whole period. The glorious myth of a rebirth, of a light which shattered the darkness, of a return of the ancient world, has great polemical strength. But as such it is not essentially linked to any special content. It stresses the fact that there was a new soul, a new form, a new way of looking at things and, above all, it emphasises that this new birth made man conscious of himself in a new way. The ancient world, classical antiquity, which as a result of this new birth had come to be regarded with much nostalgia, came now to be loved and cherished in a completely new manner. There is no denying that the ancient world had been known and loved in the middle ages as well. The ancient gods peopled the dreams of the anchorites and appeared to them as tempters, and at times they turned up in the old places to demand solemn sacrifices from the people. We have all read about the rages of Gunzone and the dreams of Vilgardo da Ravenna. They are full of classical scenes and in some of them people are invited to nothing less than an apostasy of the Christian gods and a return to pagan rites. We know of countless verses that are full of a profound love for ancient Rome, and Dante allowed the ancient poets to intrude into the economy of sacred history. He even brought in the ancient gods, turned demons, and made them live in the caves of hell.

Humanism, however, though full of love for Vergil and Cicero, no longer accepted Vergil as a prophet, and if humanists had faith in him, it was a completely new kind of faith. They believed in him in the sense that one believes in every human being who partakes of the light of truth. In this sense, the humanists were very far from worshipping the ancient gods—so much so that at times they gave the impression of not even believing in the new ones. The humanist's passion for the ancient world was no longer based on a barbarous confusion of his own culture with that of the ancient world. On the contrary his attitude was one of critical detachment. He saw the ancient world in historical dimensions and contemplated it as something which was situated in the august temple of the past. The myth of Renaissance paganism may have a certain justification for the purposes of argument; perhaps it can even be supported by reference to one of the decadent writers. But only historians lacking in wisdom can uphold it. As soon as we start to study the profound seriousness of humanistic philology, the myth is exploded. Gentile well observed that philology was the essential feature of the culture of humanism. By philology is meant a study so rich and complex that it includes a complete critical survey of the totality of man. It was not a pseudo-philosophy put forward by people who were not philosophers to use in their fight against genuine philosophy. It was a true, new, and serious philosophy. It amounted to both a restoration and a discovery of antiquity. But for this very reason it implied that antiquity was taken as something other, as something completely distinct from the thought of the humanists who did the discovering. The discovery was the result of laborious reconstruction; and for this reason antiquity was no longer seen as part of contemporary life. Antiquity, therefore, came to be defined as something that confronted the humanists. Its discovery was the discovery of an object which had to be placed into a valid relationship with the people who discovered it. The humanists thus found themselves vis-à-vis a historical past that was very different from their own world. It was precisely in this field of philosophy that there took place the conscious detachment from the past of which the humanists were so proud. It was a critic's detachment. The humanist wanted to learn from the classics not because he imagined that he shared a world with them but in order to define his own position as distinct from theirs. For this reason there arose a veritable gulf between those people who had loved the ancients because they thought they shared a common culture with them and the people who now realised that antiquity was something that had to be restored. The former, to make their belief come true, had often been forced to do violence—loving violence—to antiquity; and the latter sought to restore it with a passion for accuracy which bordered on pedantry. Thus a whole world closed up; and it was rediscovered at the very point where it was most closed. The face of ancient culture could no longer be simply reinterpreted. It had become once and for all part of history. It had ceased to be part of people's lives and had to be contemplated instead as a historical truth. There was detachment; and as a result of this detachment a classical author ceased to be part of me and I began to define my own identity as something different from him. I found my own identity by discovering his. The Renaissance myth of ancient civilisation was based upon a definition of the character of that civilisation. And in defining that character the Renaissance reduced that civilisation to something dead. There was not much of a break between antiquity and the middle ages—certainly less of a break than there was between the middle ages and the Renaissance. For it was precisely the Renaissance, or better, humanistic philology which made people conscious of the fact that there had been a break. It was here that the most important requirement of our culture came to the fore. We had to define our own identity by defining the identity of another civilisation. Thus we had to acquire a sense of history and a sense of time. We had to learn to see both history and time as the dimensions proper to the life of man. We had to abandon for good the idea that the world was solid and fixed, that it exhibited a graduated order and a permanent hierarchy—in short, that it was something definitive. We had to give up the notion that the world was a cosmos which could be contemplated, indifferent to the passage of time, secure in eternity and forever rotating in continuing circles. This old reality had been supposed to be utterly solid and to have a timeless subsistence—so much so that its very solidity had crushed all prophets of man's liberation. It had led instead to the grand manner of medieval speculation and to the diabolical temptation to absorb the disquietening Christian message into the security of the Aristotelian world.

From Petrarch onwards, humanism took up an entirely different position. A genuinely fruitful renewal, it sought a way out of an insoluble problem, in the areas of poetry and philology, ethics and politics. In the end it even sought a new way in a field which might appear hostile to humanism but which was nevertheless intimately connected with it: the field of the arts which godlessly attempted to change and subvert the world. Philology and poetry, understood in the sense of Vico, gave birth to the new philosophy.

PAUL OSKAR KRISTELLER

Humanism and Scholasticism
in the Italian Renaissance

Ever since 1860, when Jacob Burckhardt first published his famous book on the civilization of the Renaissance in Italy,[1] there has been a controversy among historians as to the meaning and significance of the Italian Renaissance.[2] Almost every scholar who has taken part in the discussion felt it was his duty to advance a new and different theory. This variety of views was partly due to the emphasis given by individual scholars to different historical personalities or currents or to different aspects and developments of the Italian Renaissance. Yet the chief cause of the entire Renaissance controversy, at least in its more recent phases, has been the considerable progress made during the last few decades in the field of medieval studies. The Middle Ages are no longer considered as a period of darkness, and consequently many scholars do not see the need for such new light and revival as the very name of the Renaissance would seem to suggest. Thus certain medievalists have questioned the very existence of the Renaissance and would like to banish the term entirely from the vocabulary of historians.

In the face of this powerful attack, Renaissance scholars have assumed a new line of defense. They have shown that the notion embodied in the term "Renaissance" was not an invention of enthusiastic historians of the last century, but was commonly expressed in the literature of the period of the Renaissance itself. The humanists themselves speak continually of the revival or birth of the arts and of learning that was accomplished in their own time

From *Renaissance Thought and Its Sources* ed. Michael Mooney. © 1979 by Columbia University Press.

after a long period of decay.[3] It may be objected that occasional claims of an intellectual revival are also found in medieval literature.[4] Yet the fact remains that during the Renaissance scholars and writers talked of such a revival and rebirth more persistently than at any other period of European history. Even if we were convinced that it was an empty claim and that the humanists did not bring about a real Renaissance, we would still be forced to admit that the illusion itself was characteristic of that period and that the term Renaissance thus had at least a subjective meaning.

Without questioning the validity of this argument, I think that there are also some more objective reasons for defending the existence and the importance of the Renaissance. The concept of style as it has been so successfully applied by historians of art[5] might be more widely applied in other fields of intellectual history and might thus enable us to recognize the significant changes brought about by the Renaissance, without obliging us to despise the Middle Ages or to minimize the debt of the Renaissance to the medieval tradition.

Moreover, I should like to reexamine the relation between the Middle Ages and the Renaissance in the light of the following consideration. Scholars have become so accustomed to stress the universalism of the medieval church and of medieval culture and also to consider the Italian Renaissance as a European phenomenon that they are apt to forget that profound regional differences existed even during the Middle Ages. The center of medieval civilization was undoubtedly France, and all other countries of Western Europe followed the leadership of that country, from Carolingian times, down to the beginning of the fourteenth century.[6] Italy certainly was no exception to that rule; but whereas the other countries, especially England, Germany, and the Low Countries, took an active part in the major cultural pursuits of the period and followed the same general development, Italy occupied a somewhat peculiar position.[7] Prior to the thirteenth century, her active participation in many important aspects of medieval culture lagged far behind that of the other countries. This may be observed in architecture and music, in the religious drama as well as in Latin and vernacular poetry in general,[8] in scholastic philosophy and theology,[9] and even, contrary to common opinion, in classical studies.

On the other hand, Italy had a narrow but persistent tradition of her own which went back to ancient Roman times and which found its expression to certain branches of the arts and of poetry, in lay education and in legal customs, and in the study of grammar and of rhetoric.[10] Italy was more directly and more continually exposed to Byzantine influences than any other Western European country. Finally, after the eleventh century, Italy developed a new life of her own which found expression in her trade and economy, in the political institutions of her cities, in the study of civil and canon law and of medicine, and in the techniques of letter-writing and of secular eloquence.[11] Influences from France became more powerful only with the thirteenth century, when their traces appeared in architecture and music, in Latin and vernacular poetry, in philosophy and theology, and in the field of classical studies.[12] Many typical products of the Italian Renaissance may thus be understood as a result of belated medieval influences received from France, but grafted upon, and assimilated by, a more narrow, but stubborn and different native tradition. This may be said of Dante's *Divine Comedy*, of the religious drama which flourished in fifteenth century Florence, and of the chivalric poetry of Adosto and of Tasso.

A similar development may be noticed in the history of learning. The Italian Renaissance thus should be viewed not only in its contrast with the French Middle Ages, but also in its relation to the Italian Middle Ages. The rich civilization of Renaissance Italy did not spring directly from the equally rich civilization of medieval France, but from the much more modest traditions of medieval Italy. It is only about the beginning of the fourteenth century that Italy witnessed a tremendous increase in all her cultural activities, and this enabled her, for a certain period, to wrest from France her cultural leadership in Western Europe. Consequently, there can be no doubt that there was an Italian Renaissance, that is, a cultural Renaissance of Italy, not so much in contrast with the Middle Ages in general or with the French Middle Ages, but very definitely in contrast with the Italian Middle Ages. It appears from a letter of Boccaccio that this general development was well-understood by some Italians of that period,[13] and we should keep this development constantly in mind if we want to understand the history of learning during the Italian Renaissance.

The most characteristic and most pervasive aspect of the Italian Renaissance in the field of learning is the humanist movement. I need hardly say that the term "humanism," when applied to the Italian Renaissance, does not imply all the vague and confused notions that are now commonly associated with it. Only a few traces of these may be found in the Renaissance. By humanism we mean merely the general tendency of the age to attach the greatest importance to classical studies, and to consider classical antiquity as the common standard, and model by which to guide all cultural activities. It will be our task to understand the meaning and origin of this humanist movement which is commonly associated with the name of Petrarch.

Among modern historians we encounter mainly two interpretations of

Italian humanism. The first interpretation considers the humanist movement merely as the rise of classical scholarship accomplished during the period of the Renaissance. This view which has been held by most historians of classical scholarship is not very popular at present. The revival of classical studies certainly does not impress an age such as ours which has practically abandoned classical education, and it is easy to praise the classical learning of the Middle Ages in a time which, except for a tiny number of specialists, knows much less of classical antiquity than did the Middle Ages. Moreover, in a period such as the present, which has much less regard for learning than for practical achievements and for "creative" writing and "original" thinking, a mere change of orientation, or even an increase of knowledge, in the field of learning does not seem to possess any historical significance. However, the situation in the Renaissance was quite different, and the increase in, and emphasis on, classical learning had a tremendous importance.

There are indeed several historical facts which support the interpretation of the humanist movement as a rise in classical scholarship. The humanists were classical scholars and contributed to the rise of classical studies.[14] In the field of Latin studies, they rediscovered a number of important texts that had been hardly read during the Middle Ages.[15] Also in the case of Latin authors commonly known during the Middle Ages, the humanists made them better known, through their numerous manuscript copies[16] and printed editions, through their grammatical and antiquarian studies, through their commentaries, and through the development and application of philological and historical criticism.

Even more striking was the impulse given by the humanists to the study of Greek. In spite of the political, commercial, and ecclesiastic relations with the Byzantine Empire, during the Middle Ages the number of persons in Western Europe who knew the Greek language was comparatively small, and practically none of them was interested in, or familiar with, Greek classical literature. There was almost no teaching of Greek in Western schools and universities, and almost no Greek manuscripts in Western libraries.[17] In the twelfth and thirteenth centuries, a great number of Greek texts were translated into Latin, either directly or through intermediary Arabic translations, but this activity was almost entirely confined to the fields of mathematics, astronomy, astrology, medicine, and Aristotelian philosophy.[18]

During the Renaissance, this situation rapidly changed. The study of Greek classical literature which had been cultivated in the Byzantine Empire throughout the later Middle Ages, after the middle of the fourteenth century began to spread in the West, both through Byzantine scholars who went to

Western Europe for a temporary or permanent stay, and through Italian scholars who went to Constantinople in quest of Greek classical learning.[19] As a result, Greek language and literature acquired a recognized place in the curriculum of Western schools and universities, a place which they did not lose until the present century. A large number of Greek manuscripts was brought from the East to Western libraries, and these manuscripts have formed the basis of most of our editions of the Greek classics. At a later stage, the humanists published printed editions of Greek authors, wrote commentaries on them, and extended their antiquarian and grammatical studies as well as their methods of philological and historical criticism to Greek literature.

No less important, although now less appreciated, were the numerous Latin translations from the Greek due to the humanists of the Renaissance. Almost the whole of Greek poetry, oratory, historiography, theology, and non-Aristotelian philosophy was thus translated for the first time, whereas the medieval translations of Aristotle and of Greek scientific writers were replaced by new humanist translations. These Latin translations of the Renaissance were the basis for most of the vernacular translations of the Greek classics, and they were much more widely read than were the original Greek texts. For in spite of its remarkable increase, the study of Greek even in the Renaissance never attained the same general importance as did the study of Latin which was rooted in the medieval tradition of the West. Nevertheless, it remains a remarkable fact that the study of the Greek classics was taken over by the humanists of Western Europe at the very time when it was affected in the East by the decline and fall of the Byzantine Empire.

If we care to remember these impressive facts, we certainly cannot deny that the Italian humanists were the ancestors of modern philologists and historians. Even a historian of science can afford to despise them only if he chooses to remember that science is the subject of his study, but to forget that the method he is applying to this subject is that of history.

However, the activity of the Italian humanists was not limited to classical scholarship, and hence the theory which interprets the humanist movement merely as a rise in classical scholarship is not altogether satisfactory. This theory fails to explain the ideal of eloquence persistently set forth in the writings of the humanists, and it fails to account for the enormous literature of treatises, of letters, of speeches, and of poems produced by the humanists.[20] These writings are far more numerous than the contributions of the humanists to classical scholarship, and they cannot be explained as a necessary consequence of their classical studies. A modern classical scholar is not supposed to write a Latin poem in praise of his city, to welcome a distinguished foreign visitor with a Latin speech, or to write a political manifesto for his government. This aspect of the activity of the humanists is often dismissed with a slighting remark about their vanity or their fancy for speech-making. I do not deny that they were vain and loved to make speeches, but I am inclined to offer a different explanation for this side of their activity. The humanists were not classical scholars who for personal reasons had a craving for eloquence, but, vice versa, they were professional rhetoricians, heirs and successors of the medieval rhetoricians,[21] who developed the belief, then new and modern, that the best way to achieve eloquence was to imitate classical models, and who thus were driven to study the classics and to found classical philology. Their rhetorical ideals and achievements may not correspond to our taste, but they were the starting point and moving force of their activity, and their classical learning was incidental to it.

The other current interpretation of Italian humanism, which is prevalent among historians of philosophy and also accepted by many other scholars, is more ambitious, but in my opinion less sound. This interpretation considers humanism as the new philosophy of the Renaissance, which arose in opposition to scholasticism, the old philosophy of the Middle Ages.[22]

Of course, there is the well-known fact that several famous humanists, such as Petrarch, Valla, Erasmus, and Vives, were violent critics of medieval learning and tended to replace it by classical learning. Moreover, the humanists certainly had ideals of learning, education, and life that differed from medieval modes of thinking. They wrote treatises on moral, educational, political, and religious questions which in tone and content differ from the average medieval treatises on similar subjects.

Yet this interpretation of humanism as a new philosophy fails to account for a number of obvious facts. On one hand, we notice a stubborn survival of scholastic philosophy throughout the Italian Renaissance, an inconvenient fact that is usually explained by the intellectual inertia of the respective philosophers whom almost nobody has read for centuries and whose number, problems and literary production are entirely unknown to most historians. On the other, most of the works of the humanists have nothing to do with philosophy even in the vaguest possible sense of the term. Even their treatises on philosophical subjects, if we care to read them, appear in most cases rather superficial and inconclusive if compared with the works of ancient or medieval philosophers, a fact that may be indifferent to a general historian, but which cannot be overlooked by a historian of philosophy.

I think there has been a tendency, in the light of later developments, and under the influence of a modern aversion to scholasticism, to exaggerate the opposition of the humanists to scholasticism, and to assign to them an importance in the history of scientific and philosophical thought which they neither could nor did attain. The reaction against this tendency has been inevitable, but it has been equally wrong. Those scholars who read the treatises of the humanists and noticed their comparative emptiness of scientific and philosophical thought came to the conclusion that the humanists were bad scientists and philosophers who did not live up to their own claims or to those of their modern advocates. I should like to suggest that the Italian humanists on the whole were neither good nor bad philosophers, but no philosophers at all.[23]

The humanist movement did not originate in the field of philosophical or scientific studies, but it arose in that of grammatical and rhetorical studies.[24] The humanists continued the medieval tradition in these fields, as represented, for example, by the *ars dictaminis* and the *ars arengandi*, but they gave it a new direction toward classical standards and classical studies, possibly under the impact of influences received from France after the middle of the thirteenth century. This new development of the field was followed by an enormous growth, both in quantity and in quality, of its teaching and literary production. As a result of this growth, the claims of the humanists for their field of study also increased considerably. They claimed, and temporarily attained, a decided predominance of their field in elementary and secondary education, and a much larger share for it in professional and university education. This development in the field of grammatical and rhetorical studies finally affected the other branches of learning, but it did not displace them. After the middle of the fifteenth century, we find an increasing number of professional jurists, physicians, mathematicians, philosophers, and theologians who cultivated humanist studies along with their own particular fields of study. Consequently, a humanist influence began to appear in all these other sciences. It appears in the studied elegance of literary expression, in the increasing use made of classical source materials, in the greater knowledge of history and of critical methods, and also sometimes in an emphasis on new problems. This influence of humanism on the other sciences certainly was important, but it did not affect the content or substance of the medieval traditions in those sciences. For the humanists, being amateurs in those other fields, had nothing to offer that could replace their traditional content and subject matter.

The humanist criticism of medieval science is often sweeping, but it does not touch its specific problems and subject matter. Their main charges are against the bad Latin style of the medieval authors, against their ignorance of ancient history and literature, and against their concern for supposedly useless questions. On the other hand, even those professional scientists who were most profoundly influenced by humanism did not sacrifice the medieval tradition of their field. It is highly significant that Pico, a representative of humanist philosophy, and Alciato, a representative of humanist jurisprudence, found it necessary to defend their medieval predecessors against the criticism of humanist rhetoricians.[25]

Yet if the humanists were amateurs in jurisprudence, theology, medicine, and also in philosophy, they were themselves professionals in a number of other fields. Their domains were the fields of grammar, rhetoric, poetry, history, and the study of the Greek and Latin authors. They also expanded into the field of moral philosophy, and they made some attempts to invade the field of logic, which were chiefly attempts to reduce logic to rhetoric.[26]

Yet they did not make any direct contributions to the other branches of philosophy or of science. Moreover, much of the humanist polemic against medieval science was not even intended as a criticism of the contents or methods of that science, but merely represents a phase in the "battle of the arts," that is, a noisy advertisement for the field of learning advocated by the humanists, in order to neutralize and to overcome the claims of other, rivaling sciences.[27] Hence I am inclined to consider the humanists not as philosophers with a curious lack of philosophical ideas and a curious fancy for eloquence and for classical studies, but rather as professional rhetoricians with a new, classicist idea of culture, who tried to assert the importance of their field of learning and to impose their standards upon the other fields of learning and of science, including philosophy.

Let us try to illustrate this outline with a few more specific facts. When we inquire of the humanists, it is often asserted that they were free-lance writers who came to form an entirely new class in Renaissance society.[28] This statement is valid, although with some qualification, for a very small number of outstanding humanists like Petrarch, Boccaccio, and Erasmus. However, these are exceptions, and the vast majority of humanists exercised either of two professions, and sometimes both of them. They were either secretaries of princes or cities, or they were teachers of grammar and rhetoric at universities or secondary schools.[29] The opinion so often repeated by historians that the humanist movement originated outside the schools and universities is a myth which cannot be supported by factual evidence. Moreover, as chancellors and as teachers, the humanists, far from representing a new class, were the professional heirs and successors of the medieval rhetoricians, the so-called *dictatores*, who also made their career exactly in these same two professions. The humanist Coluccio Salutati occupied exactly the same place in the society and culture of his time as did the *dictator* Petrus de Vineis one hundred and fifty years before.[30] Nevertheless there was a significant difference between them. The style of writing used by Salutati is quite different from that of Petrus de Vineis or of Rolandinus Passagerii. Moreover, the study and imitation of the classics which was of little or no importance to the medieval *dictatores* has become the major concern for Salutati. Finally, whereas the medieval *dictatores* attained considerable importance in politics and in administration, the humanists, through their classical learning, acquired for their class a much greater cultural and social prestige. Thus the humanists did not invent a new field of learning or a new professional activity, but they introduced a new, classicist style into the traditions of medieval Italian rhetoric. To blame them for not having invented rhetorical studies would be like blaming Giotto for not having been the inventor of painting.

The same result is confirmed by an examination of the literary production of the humanists if we try to trace the medieval antecedents of the types of literature cultivated by the humanists.[31] If we leave aside the editions and translations of the humanists, their classical interests are chiefly represented by their numerous commentaries on ancient authors and by a number of antiquarian and miscellaneous treatises. Theoretical works on grammar and rhetoric, mostly composed for the school, are quite frequent, and even more numerous is the literature of humanist historiography. Dialogues and treatises on questions of moral philosophy, education, politics, and religion have attracted most of the attention of modern historians, but represent a comparatively small proportion of humanist literature. By far the largest part of that literature, although relatively neglected and partly unpublished, consists of the poems, the speeches, and the letters of the humanists.

If we look for the medieval antecedents of these various types of humanist literature, we are led back in many cases to the Italian grammarians and rhetoricians of the later Middle Ages. This is most obvious for the theoretical treatises on grammar and rhetoric.[32] Less generally recognized, but almost equally obvious is the link between humanist epistolography and medieval *ars dictaminis*. The style of writing is different, to be sure, and the medieval term *dictamen* was no longer used during the Renaissance, yet the literary and political function of the letter was basically the same, and the ability to write a correct and elegant Latin letter was still a major aim of school instruction in the Renaissance as it had been in the Middle Ages.[33]

The same link between humanists and medieval Italian rhetoricians which we notice in the field of epistolography may be found also in the field of oratory. Most historians of rhetoric give the impression that medieval rhetoric was exclusively concerned with letter-writing and preaching, represented by the *ars dictaminis* and the somewhat younger *ars praedicandi*, and that there was no secular eloquence in the Middle Ages.[34] On the other hand, most historians of Renaissance humanism believe that the large output of humanist oratory, although of a somewhat dubious value, was an innovation of the Renaissance due to the effort of the humanists to revive ancient oratory and also to their vain fancy for speech-making.[35] Only in recent years have a few scholars begun to realize that there was a considerable amount of secular eloquence in the Middle Ages, especially in Italy.[36] I do not hesitate to conclude that the eloquence of the humanists was the continuation of the medieval *ars arengandi* just as their epistolography continued the tradition of the *ars dictaminis*. It is true, in taking up a type of literary production developed by their medieval predecessors, the humanists modified its style according to their own taste and classicist standards. Yet the practice of speech-making was no invention of the humanists, of course, since it is hardly absent from any human society, and since in medieval Italy it can be traced back at least to the eleventh century.[37]

Even the theory of secular speech, represented by rules and instructions as well as by model speeches, appears in Italy at least as early as the thirteenth century. Indeed practically all types of humanist oratory have their antecedents in this medieval literature: wedding and funeral speeches, academic speeches, political speeches by officials or ambassadors, decorative speeches on solemn occasions, and finally judicial speeches.[38] Some of these types, to be sure, had their classical models, but others, for example, academic speeches delivered at the beginning of the year or of a particular course or upon conferring or receiving a degree, had no classical antecedents whatsoever, and all these types of oratory were rooted in very specific customs and institutions of medieval Italy. The humanists invented hardly any of these types of speech, but merely applied their standards of style and elegance to a previously existing form of literary expression and thus satisfied a demand, both practical and artistic, of the society of their time. Modern scholars are apt to speak contemptuously of this humanist oratory, denouncing its empty rhetoric and its lack of "deep thoughts." Yet the humanists merely intended to speak well, according to their taste and to the occasion, and it still remains to be seen whether they were less successful in that respect than their medieval predecessors or their modern successors. Being pieces of "empty rhetoric," their speeches provide us with an amazing amount of information about the personal and intellectual life of their time.

In their historiography, the humanists succeeded the medieval chroniclers, yet they differ from them both in their merits and in their deficiencies.[39] Humanist historiography is characterized by the rhetorical concern for elegant Latin and by the application of philological criticism to the source materials of history. In both respects, they are the predecessors of modern historians.[40] To combine the requirements of a good style and those of careful research was as rare and difficult then as it is at present. However, the link between history and rhetoric that seems to be so typical of the Renaissance was apparently a medieval heritage. Not only was the teaching of history in the medieval schools subordinate to that of grammar and rhetoric, but we also find quite a few medieval historiographers and chronists who were professional grammarians and rhetoricians.[41] Even the Renaissance custom of princes and cities appointing official historiographers to write their history seems to have had a few antecedents in medieval Italy.[42]

Most of the philosophical treatises and dialogues of the humanists are really nothing but moral tracts, and many of them deal with subject matters also treated in the moralistic literature of the Middle Ages. There are, to be sure, significant differences in style, treatment, sources, and solutions. However, the common features of the topics and literary patterns should not be overlooked either. A thorough comparative study of medieval and Renaissance moral treatises has not yet been made so far as I am aware, but in a few specific cases the connection has been pointed out.[43] Again it should be added that the very link between rhetoric and moral philosophy which became so apparent in the Renaissance had its antecedents in the Middle Ages. Medieval rhetoric, no less than ancient rhetoric, was continually quoting and inculcating moral sentences that interested the authors and their readers for their content as well as for their form. Moreover, there are at least a few cases in which medieval rhetoricians wrote treatises on topics of moral philosophy, or argued about the same moral questions that were to exercise the minds and pens of their successors, the Renaissance humanists.[44]

Less definite is the link between humanists and medieval Italian rhetoricians in the field of Latin poetry. On the basis of available evidence, it would seem that in the Italian schools up to the thirteenth century verse-making was less cultivated than in France. Throughout the earlier Middle Ages, historical and panegyric epics as well as verse epitaphs were composed abundantly in Italy, yet prior to the thirteenth century her share in rhythmical and didactic poetry seems to have been rather modest.[45] It is only after the middle of the thirteenth century that we notice a marked increase in the production of Latin poetry in Italy, and the appearance of the teaching of poetry in the schools and universities. This development coincides with the earliest traces of Italian humanism, and it is tempting to ascribe it to French influences.[46]

The same may be said with more confidence of the literature of commentaries on the Latin classics, which are the direct result of school teaching. It is often asserted that Italy throughout the Middle Ages was closer to the classical tradition than any other European country. Yet if we try to trace the type of the humanist commentary back into the Middle Ages, we find hardly any commentary on a Latin poet or prose writer composed in Italy prior to the second half of the thirteenth century, whereas we find many such commentaries, from the ninth century on, written in France and the other Western countries that followed the French development.[47] Only after 1300, that is, after the earliest phase of humanism, did Italy produce an increasing number of such commentaries. Also, there is very little evidence of antiquarian studies in Italy prior to the latter part of the thirteenth century.[48]

Whereas we have abundant information about the reading of the Latin poets and prose writers in the medieval schools of France and other Western countries, and whereas such centers as Chartres and Orléans in the twelfth and early thirteenth centuries owed much of their fame to the study of the Latin classics,[49] the sources for Italy are silent during the same period and begin to speak only after the middle of the thirteenth century.[50] It was only after the beginning of the fourteenth century that the teaching of poetry and the classical authors became firmly established in the Italian schools and universities, to continue without interruption throughout the Renaissance.[51] Italian libraries, with the one exception of Monte Cassino, were not so well furnished with Latin classical poets as were some French and German libraries, and it has been noticed that the humanists of the fifteenth century made most of their manuscript discoveries not in Italy but in other countries. The conclusion seems inevitable that the study of classical Latin authors was comparatively neglected in Italy during the earlier Middle Ages and was introduced from France after the middle of the thirteenth century.[52] The Italian humanists thus took up the work of their medieval French predecessors just about the time when classical studies began to decline in France, and whereas the classical scholarship of the earliest humanists in its range and method was still close to the medieval tradition, that of the later Renaissance developed far beyond anything attained during the Middle Ages. Consequently, if we consider the entire literary production of the Italian humanists we are led to the conclusion that the humanist movement seems to have originated from a fusion between the novel interest in classical studies imported from France toward the end of the thirteenth century and the much earlier traditions of medieval Italian rhetoric.

We have seen that the humanists did not live outside the schools and universities, but were closely connected with them. The chairs commonly held by the humanists were those of grammar and rhetoric,[53] that is, the same that had been occupied by their medieval predecessors, the *dictatores*. Thus it is in the history of the universities and schools and of their chairs that the connection of the humanists with medieval rhetoric becomes most apparent. However, under the influence of humanism, these chairs underwent a change which affected their name as well as their content and pretenses. About the beginning of the fourteenth century poetry appears as a special teaching subject at Italian universities. After that time, the teaching of grammar was considered primarily as the task of elementary instructors, whereas the humanists proper held the more advanced chairs of poetry and of eloquence. For eloquence was the equivalent of prose writing as well as of speech. The teaching of poetry and of eloquence was theoretical and practical at the same time, for the humanist professor instructed his pupils in verse-making and speech-making both through rules and through models. Since classical Latin authors were considered as the chief models for imitation, the reading of these authors was inseparably connected with the theoretical and practical teaching of poetry and of eloquence.

Thus we may understand why the humanists of the fourteenth and fifteenth centuries chose to call their field of study poetry and why they were often styled poets even though they composed no works that would qualify them as poets in the modern sense.[54] Also the coronation of poets in the Renaissance must be understood against this background.[55] It had been originally understood as a kind of academic degree, and it was granted not merely for original poetic compositions, but also for the competent study of classical poets.[56]

History was not taught as a separate subject, but formed a part of the study of rhetoric and poetry since the ancient historians were among the prose writers commonly studied in school. Moral philosophy was always the subject of a separate chair and was commonly studied from the *Ethics* and *Politics* of Aristotle. However, after the beginning of the fifteenth century, the chair of moral philosophy was often held by the humanists, usually in combination with that of rhetoric and poetry.[57] This combination reflects the expansion of humanist learning into the field of moral philosophy. The chairs of Greek language and literature which were an innovation of the fourteenth century were also commonly held by humanists. This teaching was not as closely tied up with the practical concern for writing verses, speeches, or letters as was the study of Latin, and it was therefore more strictly scholarly and philological. On the other hand, since the fifteenth century we find several cases where humanist teachers of Greek offered courses on Greek texts of philosophy and science and thus invaded the territory of rival fields.[58]

Later on, the fields of study cultivated by the humanists were given a new and more ambitious name. Taking up certain expressions found in Cicero and Gellius, the humanists as early as the fourteenth century began to call their field of learning the humane studies or the studies befitting a human being (*studia humanitatis, studia humaniora*).[59] The new name certainly implies a new claim and program, but it covered a content that had existed long before and that had been designated by the more modest names of grammar, rhetoric, and poetry. Although some modern scholars were not aware of this fact, the humanists certainly were, and we have several contemporary testimonies showing that the *studia humanitatis* were considered as the equivalent of grammar, rhetoric, poetry, history, and moral philosophy.[60]

These statements also prove another point that has been confused by most modern historians: the humanists, at least in Italy or before the sixteenth century, did not claim that they were substituting a new encyclopaedia of learning for the medieval one,[61] and they were aware of the fact that their field of study occupied a well defined and limited place within the system of contemporary learning.[62] To be sure, they tended to emphasize the importance of their field in comparison with the other sciences and to encroach upon the latter's territory, but on the whole they did not deny the existence or validity of these other sciences.

This well defined place of the *studia humanitatis* is reflected in the new term *humanista* which apparently was coined during the latter half of the fifteenth century and became increasingly popular during the sixteenth. The term seems to have originated in the slang of university students and gradually penetrated into official usage.[63] It was coined after the model of such medieval terms as *legista, jurista, canonista*, and *artista*, and it designated the professional teacher of the *studia humanitatis*. Thus the term *humanista* in this limited sense was coined during the Renaissance, whereas the term *humanism* was first used by nineteenth century historians.[64] If I am not mistaken, the new term *humanism* reflects the modern and false conception that Renaissance humanism was a basically new philosophical movement, and under the influence of this notion the old term humanist has also been misunderstood as designating the representative of a new *Weltanschauung*. The old term *humanista*, on the other hand, reflects the more modest, but correct, contemporary view that the humanists were the teachers and representatives of a certain branch of learning which at that time was expanding and in vogue, but well limited in its subject matter. Humanism thus did not represent the sum total of learning in the Italian Renaissance.

If we care to look beyond the field of the humanities into the other fields of learning as they were cultivated during the Italian Renaissance, that is, into jurisprudence, medicine, theology, mathematics, and natural philosophy, what we find is evidently a continuation of medieval learning and may hence very well be called scholasticism. Since the term has been subject to controversy, I should like to say that I do not attach any unfavorable connotation to the term scholasticism. As its characteristic, I do not consider any particular doctrine, but rather a specific method, that is, the type of logical argument represented by the form of the *Questio*.

It is well-known that the content of scholastic philosophy, since the thirteenth century, was largely based on the writings of Aristotle, and that the development of this philosophy, since the twelfth century, was closely connected with the schools and universities of France and England, especially with the universities of Paris and Oxford. The place of Italy, however, is less known in the history and development of scholastic philosophy. Several Italians are found among the most famous philosophers and theologians of the twelfth and thirteenth centuries, but practically all of them did their studying and teaching in France. Whereas Italy had flourishing schools of rhetoric, jurisprudence, and medicine during the twelfth and early thirteenth century, she had no native center of philosophical studies during the same period. After 1220 the new mendicant orders established schools of theology and philosophy in many Italian cities, but unlike those in France and England, these schools of the friars for a long time had no links with the Italian universities. Regular chairs of theology were not established at the Italian universities before the middle of the fourteenth century, and even after that period, the university teaching of theology continued to be spotty and irregular.

Aristotelian philosophy, although not entirely unknown at Salerno toward the end of the twelfth century, made its regular appearance at the Italian universities after the middle of the thirteenth century and in close connection with the teaching of medicine.[65] I think it is safe to assume that Aristotelian philosophy was imported at that time from France as were the study of classical authors and many other forms of intellectual activity.[66] After the beginning of the fourteenth century, this Italian Aristotelianism assumed a more definite shape.[67] The teaching of logic and natural philosophy became a well-established part of the university curriculum and even spread to some of the secondary schools. An increasing number of commentaries and questions on the works of Aristotle reflect this teaching tradition, and numerous systematic treatises on philosophical subjects show the same general trend and background. During the fourteenth and fifteenth centuries, further influences were received from Paris in the field of natural philosophy and from Oxford in the field of logic;[68] and from the latter part of the fourteenth century on we can trace an unbroken tradition of Italian Aristotelianism which continued through the fifteenth and sixteenth century and far into the seventeenth century.[69]

The common notion that scholasticism as an old philosophy was superseded by the new philosophy of humanism is thus again disproved by plain facts. For Italian scholasticism originated toward the end of the thirteenth century, that is, about the same time as did Italian humanism, and both traditions developed side by side throughout the period of the Renaissance and even thereafter.

However, the two traditions had their locus and center in two different sectors of learning: humanism in the field of grammar, rhetoric, and poetry and to some extent in moral philosophy, scholasticism in the fields of logic and natural philosophy. Everybody knows the eloquent attacks launched by Petrarch and Bruni against the logicians of their time, and it is generally believed that these attacks represent a vigorous new movement rebelling against an old entrenched habit of thought. Yet actually the English method of dialectic was quite as novel at the Italian schools of that time as were the humanist studies advocated by Petrarch and Bruni,[70] and the humanist attack was as much a matter of departmental rivalry as it was a clash of opposite ideas or philosophies. Bruni even hints at one point that he is not speaking quite in earnest.[71]

Such controversies, interesting as they are, were mere episodes in a long period of peaceful coexistence between humanism and scholasticism. Actually the humanists quarreled as much among each other as they did with the scholastics. Moreover, it would be quite wrong to consider these controversies as serious battles over basic principles whereas many of them were meant to be merely personal feuds, intellectual tournaments, or rhetorical exercises. Finally, any attempt to reduce these controversies to one issue must fail since the discussions were concerned with many diverse and overlapping issues.[72] Therefore, we should no longer be surprised that Italian Aristotelianism quietly and forcefully survived the attacks of Petrarch and his humanist successors.

But the Aristotelianism of the Renaissance did not remain untouched by the new influence of humanism. Philosophers began to make abundant use of the Greek text and the new Latin translations of Aristotle, his ancient commentators, and other Greek thinkers. The revival of ancient philosophies that came in the wake of the humanist movement, especially the revival of Platonism and of Stoicism, left a strong impact upon the Aristotelian philosophers of the Renaissance.[73] Yet in spite of these significant modifications, Renaissance Aristotelianism continued the medieval scholastic tradition without any visible break. It preserved a firm hold on the university chairs of logic, natural philosophy, and metaphysics, whereas even the humanist professors of moral philosophy continued to base their lectures on Aristotle. The literary activity of these Aristotelian philosophers is embodied in a large number of commentaries, questions, and treatises. This literature is difficult to access and arduous to read, but rich in philosophical problems and doctrines. It represents the bulk and kernel of the philosophical thought of the period, but it has been badly neglected by modern historians. Scholars hostile to the Middle Ages considered this literature an unfortunate survival of medieval traditions that may be safely disregarded, whereas the true modern spirit of the Renaissance is expressed in the literature of the humanists. Medievalists, on the other hand, have largely concentrated on the earlier phases of scholastic philosophy and gladly sacrificed the later scholastics to the criticism of the humanists and their modern followers, a tendency that has been further accentuated by the recent habit of identifying scholasticism with Thomism.

Consequently, most modern scholars have condemned the Aristotelian philosophers of the Renaissance without a hearing, labeling them as empty squibblers and as followers of a dead past who failed to understand the living problems of their new times. Recent works on the civilization of the Renaissance thus often repeat the charges made against the Aristotelian philosophers by the humanists of their time, and even give those attacks a much more extreme meaning than they were originally intended to have. Other scholars who are equally unfavorable to the humanists include both scholastics and humanists in a summary sentence that reflects the judgments of seventeenth-century scientists and philosophers. Only a few famous figures such as Pietro Pomponazzi seem to resist the general verdict.

There has been a tendency to present Pomponazzi and a few other thinkers as basically different from the other Aristotelians of their time and as closely related with the humanists or with the later scientists. This is merely an attempt to reconcile the respect for Pomponazzi with modern preconceptions against the Aristotelians of the Renaissance. Actually Pomponazzi does not belong to the humanists or to the later scientists, but to the tradition of medieval and Renaissance Aristotelianism. The number of modern scholars who have actually read some of the works of the Italian Aristotelians is comparatively small. The most influential comprehensive treatment of the group is found in Renan's book on Averroës and Averroism, a book which had considerable merits for its time, but which also contains several errors and confusions which have been repeated ever since.[74] If we want to judge the merits and limitations of Renaissance Aristotelianism we will have to proceed to a new direct investigation of the source materials, instead of repeating antiquated judgments. It will be necessary to study in detail the questions discussed by these thinkers, such as the doctrine of immortality and its demonstrability, the problem of the so-called double truth, and the method of scientific proof.[75] Due consideration should also be given to the contributions made by these Aristotelian philosophers to medicine and natural history, and to the influence they exercised upon such early scientists as Galilei and Harvey.[76] Current notions about the prevalence of Thomism among the Aristotelians, about the controversy of the Averroists and the Alexandrists, about the continuity and uniformity, of the school of Padua, and even the very concept of Averroism will have to be reexamined and possibly abandoned. Also the widespread belief that the Italian Aristotelians were atheists and free-thinkers who merely did not dare to say what they thought must be investigated in its origin and validity.[77]

Thus we may conclude that the humanism and the scholasticism of the Renaissance arose in medieval Italy about the same time, that is, about the end of the thirteenth century, and that they coexisted and developed all the way through and beyond the Renaissance period as different branches of learning. Their controversy, much less persistent and violent than usually represented, is merely a phase in the battle of the arts, not a struggle for existence. We may compare it to the debates of the arts in medieval literature, to the rivaling claims of medicine and law at the universities, or to the claims advanced by Leonardo in his *Paragone* for the superiority of painting over the other arts. Humanism certainly had a tendency to influence the other sciences and to expand at their expense, but all kinds of adjustments and combinations between humanism and scholasticism were possible and were successfully accomplished. It is only after the Renaissance, through the rise of modern science and modern philosophy, that Aristotelianism was gradually displaced, whereas humanism became gradually detached from its rhetorical background and evolved into modern philology and history.

Thus humanism and scholasticism both occupy an important place in the civilization of the Italian Renaissance, yet neither represents a unified picture, nor do both together constitute the whole of Renaissance civilization. Just as humanism and scholasticism coexisted as different branches of culture, there were besides them other important, and perhaps even more important branches. I am thinking of the developments in the fine arts, in vernacular literature, in the mathematical sciences, and in religion and theology. Many misunderstandings have resulted from the attempts to interpret or to criticize humanism and scholasticism in the light of these other developments. Too many historians have tried to play up the fine arts, or vernacular poetry, or science, or religion against the "learning of the schools." These attempts must be rejected. The religious and theological problems of the Protestant and Catholic Reformation were hardly related to the issues discussed in the philosophical literature of the same time, and supporters and enemies of humanistic learning and of Aristotelian philosophy were found among the followers of both religious parties. The development of vernacular poetry in Italy was not opposed or delayed by the humanists, as most historians of literature complain. Some humanists stressed the superiority of Latin, to be sure, but few if any of them seriously thought of abolishing the *volgare* in speech or writing. On the other hand, many humanists are found among the advocates of the *volgare*, and a great number of authors continued to write in both languages. Again, modern historians have tried to interpret as a struggle for existence what in fact was merely a rivalry between different forms of expression.[78]

The admirable development of the fine arts which is the chief glory of the Italian Renaissance did not spring from any exaggerated notions about the creative genius of the artist or about his role in society and culture. Such notions are the product of the Romantic movement and its eighteenth-century forerunners, and they were largely foreign to the Italian Renaissance.[79] Renaissance artists were primarily craftsmen, and they often became scientists, not because their superior genius anticipated the modern destinies of science, but because certain branches of scientific knowledge, such as anatomy, perspective, or mechanics were considered as a necessary requirement in the development of their craft. If some of these artist-scientists were able to make considerable contributions to science, this does not mean that they were completely independent or contemptuous of the science and learning available in their time.

Finally, mathematics and astronomy made remarkable progress during the sixteenth century and assumed increasing importance in their practical applications, in the literature of the time, and in the curriculum of the schools and universities. If this development did not immediately affect philosophy, this was due not to the stupidity or inertia of contemporary philosophers, but to the fact that physics or natural philosophy was considered as a part of philosophy and that there was almost no traditional link between the mathematical sciences and philosophy. Galileo was a professional student and teacher of mathematics and astronomy, not of philosophy. His claim that physics should be based on mathematics rather than on logic was not merely a novel idea as far as it went, but it revolutionized the very conceptions on which the curriculum of the schools and universities was based. It is hence quite understandable that he was opposed by the Aristotelian physicists of his time who considered his method as an invasion of their traditional domain by the mathematicians. On the other hand, there is no evidence that Galileo met with any serious resistance within his own field of mathematics and astronomy in which the main chairs were soon occupied by his pupils. If we want to understand and to judge these developments we must know the issues and the professional traditions of the later Middle Ages and of the Renaissance.

Modern scholarship has been far too much influenced by all kinds of prejudices, against the use of Latin, against scholasticism, against the medieval church, and also by the unwarranted effort to read later developments, such as the German Reformation, or French libertinism, or nineteenth-century liberalism or nationalism, back into the Renaissance. The only way to understand the Renaissance is a direct and, possibly, an objective study of the original sources. We have no real justification to take sides in the controversies of the Renaissance, and to play up humanism against scholasticism, or scholasticism against humanism, or modern science against both of them. Instead of trying to reduce everything to one or two issues, which is the privilege and curse of political controversy, we should try to develop a kind of historical pluralism. It is easy to praise everything in the past which happens to resemble certain favorite ideas of our own time, or to ridicule and minimize everything that disagrees with them. This method is neither fair nor helpful for an adequate understanding of the past. It is equally easy to indulge in a sort of worship of success, and to dismiss defeated and refuted ideas with a shrugging of the shoulders, but just as in political history, this method does justice neither to the vanquished nor to the victors. Instead of blaming each century for not having anticipated the achievements of the next, intellectual history must patiently register the errors of the past as well as its truths. Complete objectivity may be impossible to achieve, but it should remain the permanent aim and standard of the historian as well as of the philosopher and scientist.

NOTES

1. *Die Cultur der Renaissance in Italien* (Basel, 1860), trans. by S. G. C. Middlemore as *The Civilization of the Renaissance in Italy* (London, 1878), with many subsequent editions in both languages.

2. Hans Baron, "Renaissance in Italien," *Archiv für Kulturgeschichte* 17 (1927): 226–52

and 21 (1931): 95–119. Johan Huizinga, "Das Problem der Renaissance," *Wege der Kulturgeschichte*, trans. Werner Kaegi (Munich, 1930), pp. 89–139. See also the discussion in the *Journal of the History of Ideas* 4 (1943): 1–74. Wallace K. Ferguson, *The Renaissance in Historical Thought* (Boston, 1948). See Part 1, Introduction, note 1.

3. Konrad Burdach, *Reformation, Renaissance, Humanismus*, 2d ed. (Berlin-Leipzig, 1926). Wallace K. Ferguson, "Humanist Views of the Renaissance," *American Historical Review* 45 (1939–40): 1–28; *id.*, *The Renaissance in Historical Thought*, p. 1ff. See also, Herbert Weisinger, "The Self-Awareness of the Renaissance," *Papers of the Michigan Academy of Science, Arts, and Letters* 29 (1944): 561–67; *id.*, "Who Began the Revival of Learning," *ibid.*, 30 (1945), 625–38; *id.*, "Renaissance Accounts of the Revival of Learning," *Studies in Philology* 45 (1948): 105–18; *id.*, "The Renaissance Theory of the Reaction against the Middle Ages ...," *Speculum* 20 (1945): 461–67; *id.*, "Ideas of History during the Renaissance," *Journal of the History of Ideas* 6 (1945): 415–35. Franco Simone, *La coscienza della Rinascita negli Umanisti francesi* (Rome, 1949). Eugenio Garin, "Umanesimo e Rinascimento," in *Problemi ed orientamenti critici di lingua e di letteratura italiana*, ed. Attilio Momigliano, vol. 3: *Questioni e correnti di storia letteraria* (Milan, 1949), pp. 349–404. Most of the passages quoted by these scholars are later than the beginning of the fifteenth century. Yet Frate Guido da Pisa in his commentary on Dante wrote as early as 1330: "Per istum enim poetam resuscitata est mortua poesis.... Ipse vero poeticam scientiam suscitavit et antiquos poetas in mentibus nostris reviviscere fecit" (Orazio Bacci, *La Critica letteraria* [Milan, 1910], p. 163). "Ipse enim mortuam poesiam de tenebris reduxit ad lucem, et in hoc fuit imitatus Boetium, qui philosophiam mortuam suo tempore suscitavit" (Guido da Pisa, *Expositiones et glose super Comediam Dantis*, ed. Vincenzo Cioffari [Albany, N.Y., 1974], p. 4).

4. Burdach's attempts to derive the concept of the Renaissance from religious or mystical traditions no longer convince me. However, a Carolingian poet has the following line: "Aurea Roma iterum renovata renascitur orbi" (E. K. Rand, "Renaissance, why not?" *Renaissance* 1 [1943]: 34). Milo Crispinus says in his biography of Lanfranc: "quem Latinitas in antiquum scientiae statum ab eo restituta tota supremum debito cum amore agnoscit magistrum" (Migne, *P.L.*, CL, 29). For the political aspect of the concept, see P. E. Schramm, *Kaiser, Rom and Renovatio*, 2 vols. (Leipzig, 1929). See also Augustine's judgment on Ambrose (*Soliloquia*, II, 14, 26): "ille in quo ipsam eloquentiam quam mortuam dolebamus perfectam revixisse cognovimus."

5. Erwin Panofsky, *Renaissance and Renascences in Western Art* (Stockholm, 1960).

6. Étienne Gilson, "Humanisme médiéval et Renaissance," *Les Idées et les lettres* (Paris, 1932), pp. 171–96. E. R. Curtius, *Europäische Literatur and lateinisches Mittelalter* (Bern, 1948), pp. 41ff. and 387ff., trans. by Willard R. Trask as *European Literature and the Latin Middle Ages* (New York, 1953).

7. The isolation of Italy in the Middle Ages and the comparative scantiness of Italian antecedents for Dante has been noted by Karl Vossler, *Mediaeval Culture*, trans. W. C. Lawton, vol. 2 (New York, 1929, 1960), p. 4ff. Cf. Vossler, *Die göttliche Komödie*, vol. II, pt. I (Heidelberg, 1908), pp. 582ff.

8. There are notable exceptions, such as Guido of Arezzo, Alfanus of Salerno, and Henricus of Settimello, but they do not change the general picture. For the share of Italy in medieval Latin culture prior to the thirteenth century, see Francesco Novati and Angelo Monteverdi, *Le Origini* (Milan, 1926). Antonio Viscardi, *Le Origini* (Milan, 1939). Maximilian Manitius, *Geschichte der lateinischen Literatur des Mittelalters*, 3 vols. (Munich, 1911–31).

9. Although several of the most famous representatives of scholastic theology were

Italians, such as Lanfranc, Anselm, Peter Lombard, Thomas Aquinas, and Bonaventura, they did most of their studying and teaching in France. For Lanfranc, see Francesco Novati, "Rapports littéraires de l'Italie et de la France au XIe siècle," *Académie des Inscriptions et Belles-Lettres, Comptes Rendus des Séances de l'année 1910*, pp. 169–84. A typical representative of Italian theology in the eleventh century was Peter Damiani, and his background was juristic and rhetorical rather than philosophical; see J. A. Endres, *Petrus Damiani und die weltliche Wissenschaft* (Münster, 1910).

10. For the history of education in Italy, see Giuseppe Manacorda, *Storia della scuola in Italia*, 2 pts. (Milan, n.d.). Typical representatives of Italian rhetoric in the tenth and eleventh century are Gunzo of Novara and Anselm the Peripatetic. It should be noted that the library of Bobbio in the tenth century was rich in grammatical treatises, but possessed few classical poets (Gustav Becker, *Catalogi Bibliothecarum antiqui* [Bonn, 1885], p. 64ff).

11. Charles H. Haskins, *The Renaissance of the Twelfth Century* (Cambridge, Mass., 1927).

12. For French influences in the thirteenth century, see Giulio Bertoni, *Il Duecento*, 3d ed. (Milan, 1939). Many poems and prose works by Italian authors were written in French, and much of the early vernacular poetry and prose in Italian is derived from French models.

13. After having praised Dante and Petrarch as the restorers of poetry, Boccaccio continues: "inspice quo Romanum corruerit imperium ... quid insuper philosophorum celebres titulos et poetarum myrthea laureaque serta meditari ... quid in memoriam revocare militarem disciplinam ... quid legum auctoritatem ... quid morum conspicuum specimen. Haec omnia ... una cum Italia reliqua et libertate caelesti a maioribus nostris ... neglecta sunt et a nationibus exteris aut sublata aut turpi conquinata labe sordescunt ... et si omnia resarciri nequeant, hoc saltem poetici nominis fulgore ... inter barbaras nationes Roma saltem aliquid veteris maiestatis possit ostendere" (letter to Jacopo Pizzinghe in *Le Lettere edite e inedite di Messer Giovanni Boccaccio*, ed. Francesco Corazzini [Florence, 1877], p. 197). See Konrad Burdach, *Rienzo und die geistige Wandlung seiner Zeit* [*Vom Mittelalter zur Reformation*, vol. 2] (Berlin, 1913–28), p. 510ff. Also Salutati, in his letter to Peter of Mantua, after admitting that Rome now has lost her military power, says that there is no excuse for her being excelled by other nations in literary distinction. "Gaudebam igitur apud nos emergere qui barbaris illis quondam gentibus saltem in hoc palmam eriperet, qualem me tibi (read: te mihi) fama et multorum relatio promittit," alluding to the achievements of Peter of Mantua in the field of logic (*Epistolario di Coluccio Salutati*, ed. Francesco Novati, vol. 3 [Rome, 1896], p. 319ff).

14. For the classical studies of the humanists, see Georg Voigt, *Die Wiederbelebung des classischen Alterthums*, 3d ed., vol. 2 (Berlin, 1893), p. 373ff. Sir J. E. Sandys, *A History of Classical Scholarship*, vol. 2 (Cambridge, 1908), p. 1ff.

15. These discoveries included Lucretius, Tacitus, Manilius, several plays of Plautus, and several orations and rhetorical works of Cicero. See Remigio Sabbadini, *Le scoperte dei codici latini e greci ne' secoli XIV e XV*, 2 vols. (Florence, 1905–14). Maximilian Manitius, *Handschriften antiker Autoren in mittelalterlichen Bibliothekskatalogen* (Leipzig, 1935).

16. It is not generally realized that fifteenth-century manuscripts of the Latin classics are probably more numerous than those of all previous centuries taken together. These manuscripts are disregarded by most modern editors, and their value for establishing a critical text may be small. However, their existence is an important phenomenon since it reflects the wide diffusion of the classical authors during the Renaissance.

17. Louise R. Loomis, *Medieval Hellenism* (Lancaster, Pa., 1906).

18. For the translations of the twelfth century, see Charles H. Haskins, *Studies in the*

History of Mediaeval Science, 2d ed. (Cambridge, Mass., 1927). For the thirteenth century, see Maurice De Wulf, *Histoire de la philosophie médiévale*, 6th ed., vol. 2 (Louvain, 1936). A bibliography of Latin translations from the Greek is still a major desideratum, even though some partial contributions have been made recently. See esp. J. T. Muckle, "Greek Works translated directly into Latin before 1350," *Mediaeval Studies* 4 (1942): 33–42 and 5 (1943): 102–14. *Catalogus Translationum et Commentariorum*, ed. P. O. Kristeller and F. Edward Cranz, 3 vols. (Washington, D.C., 1960–76). For the study of Greek in the Middle Ages, see the articles by Roberto Weiss cited in essay 1, note 11.

19. For the study of Greek classical literature in medieval Constantinople, see Karl Krumbacher, *Geschichte der byzantinischen Literatur*, 2d ed. (Munich, 1897), p. 499ff. The direct influence of this Byzantine tradition on the Greek studies of the Italian humanists is beyond any question. There may also have been some indirect Byzantine influence on the Latin studies of the humanists. The range of interest of the humanists resembles that of many Byzantine scholars. See essay 7.

20. For the literary production of the humanists, see Voigt, *Die Wiederbelebung des classischen Alterthums*, vol. 2, p. 394ff. Vittorio Rossi, *Il Quattrocento*, 2d ed. (Milan, 1933).

21. The link between the humanists and the medieval rhetoricians has been recognized by only very few scholars, such as Francesco Novati, Helene Wieruszowski, and Ernst Kantorowicz. These scholars, however, chiefly noticed that the medieval rhetoricians show some of the personal characteristics commonly attributed to the humanists. I should like to go further and assume a direct professional and literary connection of which the personal similarities are merely a symptom. The common opinion is quite different, and most historians speak of the *ars dictaminis* as if there were no humanist rhetoric, and vice versa. See note 38 and essay 13.

22. For the contributions of the humanists to philosophy, see Friedrich Ueberweg, *Grundriss der Geschichte der Philosophie*, 12th ed. vol. 3 (Berlin, 1924), p. 6ff. Guido De Ruggiero, *Storia della filosofia*, pt. 3, 2d ed., 2 vols. (Bari, 1937). Giovanni Gentile, *Storia della filosofia italiana*, ed. Eugenio Garin, 2 vols. (Florence, 1969), 1: 111–216. Ernst Cassirer, *Individuum und Kosmos in der Philosophie der Renaissance* (Berlin-Leipzig, 1927). For further literature on the entire subject of Renaissance philosophy, see P. O. Kristeller and J. H. Randall Jr., "The Study of the Philosophies of the Renaissance," *Journal of the History of Ideas* 2 (1941): 449–96. Eugenio Garin, *La filosofia [Storia dei generi letterari italiani]*, vol. 1 (Milan, 1947), pp. 169–274; *id.*, *Der italienische Humanismus* (Bern, 1947); *id.*, *Filosofi italiani del Quattrocento* (Florence, 1942). Cleto Carbonara, *Il secolo XV* (Milan, 1943). Giuseppe Saitta, *Il pensiero italiano nell'umanesimo e nel rinascimento*, vol. 1: *L'Umanesimo* (Bologna, 1949). See also, Charles Trinkaus, *Adversity's Noblemen* (New York, 1940); *id.*, *In Our Image and Likeness*, 2 vols. (Chicago, 1970).

23. This statement does not mean, as Eugenio Garin implies (*Giornale critico* [1952], p. 99) that I deny the philosophical significance of the Renaissance period. See essay 1.

24. This point has been rightly indicated by Richard McKeon, "Renaissance and Method in Philosophy," *Studies in the History of Ideas* 3 (1935): 37–114: "That shift in the emphasis in the three arts, that subversion of dialectic to grammar, is in itself sufficient to account for the changes which the Renaissance is reputed to have made" (p. 87). I am not convinced by McKeon's attempt to distinguish within the Renaissance, as two separate trends, an emphasis on grammar represented by Erasmus, and one on rhetoric represented by Nizolius. The grammatical character of early Italian humanism and its rise before the time of Petrarch have been illustrated in the studies of Roberto Weiss, *The Dawn of Humanism in Italy* (London, 1947); *id.*, "Lineamenti per una storia del primo umanesimo fiorentino," *Rivista storica italiana* 60 (1948): 349–66; *id.*, *Il primo secolo dell'unnanesinno* (Rome, 1949).

25. For Pico's defense of the medieval philosophers against Ermolao Barbaro, see P. O. Kristeller, "Florentine Platonism and its Relations with Humanism and Scholasticism," *Church History* 8 (1939): 203ff. Quirinus Breen, "Giovanni Pico della Mirandola on the Conflict of Philosophy and Rhetoric," *Journal of the History of Ideas* 13 (1952): 384–426, reprinted in his *Christianity and Humanism* (Grand Rapids, Mich., 1968), pp. 1–92. For Alciato's defense of the medieval jurists against Valla, see Remigio Sabbadini, *Storia del ciceronianismo* (Turin, 1885), pp. 88–92. Biagio Brugi, *Per la storia della giurisprudenza e delle università italiane: Nuovi saggi* (Turin, 1921), p. 111ff.

26. This humanist logic is represented by Valla, Agricola, Nizolius, and Ramus. For Nizolius, see Richard McKeon, "Renaissance and Method in Philosophy," *Studies in the History of Ideas* 3 (1935): 105ff. Mario Nizolio, *De veris principiis*, ed. Quirinus Breen, 2 vols. (Rome, 1956). For Ramus, see Perry Miller, *The New England Mind* (New York, 1939), p. 154ff. Walter J. Ong, *Ramus, Method, and the Decay of Dialogue* (Cambridge, Mass., 1958).

27. For the battle of the arts, see *The Battle of the Seven Arts ... by Henri d'Andeli*, ed. L. J. Paetow (Berkeley, 1914). There was a rivalry between medicine and law, in which the humanists were not directly concerned. See Lynn Thorndike, "Medicine versus Law at Florence," *Science and Thought in the Fifteenth Century* (New York, 1929), pp. 24–58. Behind this kind of literature is the rivalry of the various faculties and sciences at the universities, a rivalry that found its expression in the opening lectures delivered every year by each professor in praise of his own field. One such lecture by the humanist Philippus Beroaldus the Elder, professor at Bologna, is entitled "Declamatio philosophi, medici et oratoris" (in his *Varia Opuscula* [Basel, 1513]). Of course, the prize is given to the orator. See also Coluccio Salutati, *De nobilitate legum et medicinae*, ed. Eugenio Garin (Florence, 1947), p. xlvi ff.; id., *La Disputa delle Arti nel Quattrocento* (Florence, 1947).

28. Jacob Burckhardt, *Die Kultur der Renaissance in Italien*, 13th ed. (Stuttgart, 1921), p. 151.

29. For the careers of the humanists, see Voigt, *Die Wiederbelebung des classischen Alterthums*, and Rossi, *Il Quattrocento*.

30. For the connection of Salutati with the medieval tradition of the *ars dictaminis* and *ars notaria*, see Francesco Novati, *La giovinézza di Coluccio Salutati* (Turin, 1888), p. 66ff. This chapter was reprinted with important omissions in his *Freschi e minii del Dugento* (Milan, 1908), pp. 299–328. There is at Naples a manuscript of the early fifteenth century transcribed for a young student of rhetoric, which contains the letters of Petrus de Vineis, together with those of Salutati, and of the latter's contemporary Pellegrino Zambeccari (Ludovico Frati, "L'epistolario inedito di Pellegrino Zambeccari," *Atti e Memorie delta R. Deputazione di Storia patria per le provincie di Romagna*, 4th ser., 13 [1923]: 169ff.). Another manuscript with the same content is in The Hague (*Epistolario di Pellegrino Zambeccari*, ed. Ludovico Frati [Rome, 1929], p. xvii ff.). I am indebted for this information to Ludwig Bertalot. Although Burdach's attempt to make Cola di Rienzo the central figure of the Italian Renaissance must be rejected, it should be noticed that Cola was a notary by profession and owed a good deal of his reputation to the style of his letters and speeches. Burdach, who emphasized the influence of Joachimite ideas on Cola, fails to meet the objection that Cola became familiar with these ideas only after his flight from Rome (*Rienzo und die geistige Wandlung seiner Zeit* [Berlin, 1923–28], p. 10).

31. For the literary production of the humanists, see Voigt, *Die Wiederbelebung des classischen Alterthums*, and Rossi, *Il Quattrocento*. For their historiography, see Eduard Fueter, *Geschichte der neueren Historiographie*, 3d ed. (Munich, 1936).

32. For the grammatical studies of the humanists in their relation to the Middle Ages, see Remigio Sabbadini, *La scuola e gli studi di Guarino Guarini Veronese* (Catania, 1896), p. 38ff.

33. There are many humanist treatises on epistolography, and many collections of "salutations" in humanist manuscripts. The letters of most major humanists were collected and reprinted primarily as models for literary imitation.

34. Charles S. Baldwin, *Medieval Rhetoric and Poetic* (New York, 1928), pp. 206ff. and 228ff., especially p. 230. Richard McKeon, "Rhetoric in the Middle Ages," *Speculum* 17 (1942): 27ff. For the *ars dictaminis* in Italy, especially during the twelfth century, see Charles H. Haskins, *Studies in Medieval Culture* (Oxford, 1929), pp. 170–92. See also Ernst Kantorowicz, "An 'Autobiography' of Guido Faba," *Medieval and Renaissance Studies* 1 (1943): 253–80; *id.*, "Anonymi 'Aurea Gemma,'" *Medievalia et Humanistica* 1 (1943): 41–57. Helene Wieruszowski, "*Ars dictaminis* in the time of Dante," *ibid.*, 95–108. For the *ars praedicandi*, see Harry Caplan, *Medieval Artes Praedicandi*, 2 vols. (Ithaca, N.Y., 1934–36). Thomas M. Charland, *Artes Praedicandi* (Paris-Ottawa, 1936). Italy's contribution to the literature on preaching seems to have been small and belated.

35. Voigt, *Die Wiederbelebung des classischen Alterthums*, p. 436ff. For a typical collection of humanist orations, see Ludwig Bertalot, "Eine Sammlung Paduaner Reden des XV. Jahrhunderts," *Quellen und Forschungen aus italienischen Archiven und Bibliotheken* 26 (1936): 245–67.

36. See the studies of Ernst Kantorowicz and Helene Wieruszowski, and especially Alfredo Galletti, *L'eloquenza dalle origini al XVI secolo* [*Scoria dei generi litterari italiani*] (Milan, 1904–38), p. 430ff.

37. Galletti, *L'eloquenza*.

38. Some of the rhetorical treatises and models of the thirteenth century are discussed by Galletti, *L'eloquenza*, p. 454ff. Guido Faba's *Parlamenti ed epistole*, ed. Augusto Gaudenzi, *I suoni, le forme e le parole dell'odierno dialetto della città di Bologna* (Turin, 1889), include several model speeches. Models for political and funeral speeches are inserted in the anonymous "Oculus Pastoralis" and in other treatises written for the instruction of city officials (Fritz Hertter, *Die Podestàliteratur Italiens im 12. and 13. Jahrhundert* [Leipzig-Berlin, 1910]). For an example of early academic oratory, see Hermann Kantorowicz, "The Poetical Sermon of a Mediaeval Jurist," *Journal of the Warburg Institute* 2 (1938–39): 22–41. For the speech of an ambassador, see G.L. Haskins and Ernst Kantorowicz, "A Diplomatic Mission of Francis Accursius and his Oration before Pope Nicholas III," *English Historical Review* 58 (1943): 424–47. The medieval legal background of the wedding speeches of the humanists has been studied by Francesco Brandileone, *Saggi sulla storia della celebrazione del matrimonio in Italia* (Milan, 1906), but he does not mention any pre-humanist wedding speeches. Rhetorical rules and samples are included in some of the early instructions for advocates; see M.A. von Bethmann-Hollweg, *Der Civilprozess des gemeinen Rechts in geschichtlicher Entwicklung*, vol. 6 (Bonn, 1874), pp. 148–59. Boncompagno's *Rhetorica Novissima* (ed. Augusto Gaudenzi, *Bibliotheca iuridica medii aevi: Scripta Anecdota glossatorum*, vol. 2 [Bologna, 1892]) is not a treatise on *dictamen*, as most scholars seem to assume, but a rhetorical instruction for advocates. Also the treatise of Jacques de Dinant, published by André Wilmart, *Analecta Reginensia* (Vatican City, 1933), pp. 113–51, covers judicial oratory.

It is often asserted that the humanists did not cultivate judicial oratory (Rossi, *Il Quattrocento*, p. 154), yet this is contradicted by a passage of Jovius (Burckhardt, *Die Kultur der Renaissance*, p. 176), and there are at least a few examples of judicial speeches composed by humanists (Leonardo Bruni Aretino, *Humanistisch-Philosophische Schriften*, ed. Hans Baron [Leipzig, 1928], p. 179; Jules Paquier, *De Philippi Beroaldi Junioris vita et scriptis* [Paris, 1900], pp. 96–113). A systematic investigation of the various types of humanist oratory and of their medieval antecedents has not yet been undertaken. It ought to include a study of the mutual relations between sacred and secular eloquence, and of possible Byzantine influences. See Krumbacher, *Die Geschichte den byzantinischen Literatur*, pp. 454ff. and 470ff. The legal background of the wedding orations appears sometimes in their titles, e.g., "contractus matrimonialis compillatus per Manfredum de Justis Veronensem" (cod. Laur. Ashb. 271; cf. Cesare Paoli, *I codici Ashburnhamiani della R. Biblioteca Mediceo-Laurenziana di Firenze* [Rome, 1887–1917], p. 296 n. 195); "contractus Guarivi Veronensis pro comite Jacopino" (Ricc, 421 f. 43). The title of another form speech shows that also Pico's famous oration belonged to an established formal type: "ad colligendos audientium animos in disputatione fienda" (Ricc, 421 f. 28).

39. Fueter fails to discuss the relations between medieval and humanist historiography.

40. I should like to mention Carolus Sigonius for his masterful discussion of the forged charter of Theodosius II for Bologna university (*Opera Omnia*, vol. 6 [Milan, 1787], p. 985ff.). His remark on the task of history, made in connection with the donation of Constantine, is a quotation from Cicero: "primam legem historiae esse ut ne quid falsi audeat, ne quid veri non audeat" (*ibid.*, p. 985; cf. *De Oratore*, II, 15, 62).

41. For example, Boncompagno of Signa (*Liber de obsidione Anconae*, ed. G.C. Zimolo [Bologna, 1937]) and Rolandinus of Padua (*Cronica*, ed. Antonio Bonardi [Città di Castello, 1905–8]).

42. Giulio Bertoni, *Il Duecento*, p. 263. Machiavelli was on the payroll of the university of Pisa for writing his Florentine history.

43. Allan H. Gilbert, *Machiavelli's Prince and Its Forerunners* (Durham, N.C., 1938). The question *De nobilitate*, dear to the humanists of the fifteenth century, was already discussed in the thirteenth (Giulio Bertoni, "Una lettera amatoria di Pier della Vigna," *Giornale storico della letteratura italiana* 58 [1911]: 33ff.). The humanist treatises on the dignity and happiness of man also continued medieval discussions (Giovanni Gentile, "Il concetto dell'uomo nel Rinascimento," *Il pensiero italiano del rinascimento*, 3d ed. [Florence, 1940], pp. 47–113).

44. Boncompagno of Signa wrote two moral treatises: *Amicitia*, ed. Sarina Nathan (Rome, 1909), and *De malo senectutis et senii*, ed. Francesco Novati, *Rendiconti della Reale Accademia dei Lincei, Classe di Scienze Morali, Storiche e Filologiche*, 5th ser., 1 (1892): 50–59.

45. Novati and Monteverdi, *Le Origini*. Francesco Novati, *L'influsso del pensiero latino sopra la civiltà italiana nel Medio Evo*, 2d ed. (Milan, 1899). Umberto Ronca, *Cultura medioevale e poesia latina d'Italia nei secoli XI e XII*, 2 vols. (Rome, 1892). F. J. E. Raby, *A History of Secular Latin: Poetry in the Middle Ages*, 2 vols. (Oxford, 1934).

46. The rise of Latin poetry in Italy begins with the Paduan group of "pre-humanists." See Bertoni, *Il Duecento*, p. 272ff. Natalino Sapegno, *Il Trecento* (Milan, 1934), p. 149ff.

47. A comprehensive study of the literature of medieval and Renaissance commentaries on the classical authors is a major desideratum. Much scattered information may be found concerning the commentaries on individual authors. The commentaries written before 1200 are listed in Manitius, *Geschichte den lateinischen Literatur des Mittelalters*. An interesting survey of such commentaries up to 1300, by B.H. (Hauréau), is hidden in the *Histoire littéraire de la France* 29 (1885): 568–83. Hauréau lists only one commentary which he believes to be from Italy. Of Italian origin are also certain legal glosses on Seneca, written in the twelfth century (Carlo Pascal, *Letteratura latina medievale* [Catania, 1909], pp. 150–54). There are also some Italian commentaries on Martianus Capella, but this refers to the teaching of the "artes" rather than that of the "authores." The Paduans began to study Seneca's tragedies, and after the end of the thirteenth century, the number of classical commentaries begins to increase. That these early Italian commentators were acquainted with the work of their French predecessors has been shown in the case of Giovanni del

Virgilio by Fausto Ghisalberti ("Giovanni del Virgilio espositore delle 'Metamorfosi,'" *Giornale Dantesco* 34 [1933]: 31ff.). Relations between medieval and humanistic commentaries are also noticed by Eva M. Sanford ("The Manuscripts of Lucan: Accessus and Marginalia," *Speculum* 9 [1934]: 278–95). For the history and form of medieval commentaries, see E.A. Quain, "The Medieval Accessus ad auctores," *Traditio* 3 (1945): 215–64. R.W. Hunt, "The Introductions to the 'Artes' in the Twelfth Century," *Studia Mediaevalia in honorem admodum Reverendi Patris Raymundi Josephi Martin* (Brugis, c. 1949), pp. 85–112. R.B.C. Huygens, "Accessus ad Auctores," *Latomus* 12 (1953): 296–311, 460–84. Cf. also Ludwig Bertalot, *Deutsche Literaturzeitung* 32 (1911): 3166–69.

An important exception which seems to deserve further study is the manuscript 404 of the Pierpont Morgan Library in New York which was written in Italy in the twelfth century and contains the complete works of Horace with early glosses (Meta Harrsen and George K. Boyce, *Italian Manuscripts in the Pierpont Morgan Library* [New York, 1953], p. 6, no. 7). The dating of the manuscript has been confirmed to me by Luisa Banti. See also *Catalogus Translationum et Commentariorum*, ed. P.O. Kristeller and F. Edward Cranz, 3 vols. (Washington, D.C., 1960–76). *Der Kommentar in der Renaissance*, ed. August Buck and Otto Herding (Boppard, 1975).

48. See Sabbadini, *Le scoperie*.

49. Jules Alexandre Clerval, *Les écoles de Chartres au moyen âge* (Paris, 1895). Leopold Delisle, "Les écoles d'Orléans au douzième et au treizième siècle," *Annuaire-Bulletin de la Société de l'histoire de France* 7 (1869): 139–54. See also *The Battle of the Seven Arts*, ed. Paetow. For the contrast of "artes" and "authores," see Eduard Norden, *Die antike Kunstprosa*, vol. 2 (Leipzig, 1898), pp. 688ff. and 724ff. To the well-known material on the study of the "authores" in medieval France, I should like to add the following passage from the chronist Landulphus Junior; which seems to have remained unnoticed: "revocare Yordanum de Clivi a provincia que dicitur Sancti Egidii in qua ipse Yordanus legebat lectionem auctorum non divinorum sed paganorum" (*Historia Mediolanensis*, ed. Carlo Castiglioni [Bologna, 1934], p. 18). The event must be dated shortly after A.D. 1100.

50. Perhaps the earliest dated evidence of the reading of classical authors in an Italian school of the Middle Ages is the criminal record of the theft of "three books of Ovid" from a teacher of grammar in Bologna (1294), see O. Mazzoni Toselli, *Racconti storici estratti dall'archivio criminale di Bologna*, vol. 3 (Bologna, 1870), p. 39ff.

51. In 1321, Giovanni del Virgilio was appointed to lecture at Bologna on versification and on Vergil, Statius, Lucan, and Ovid (Ghisalberti, "Giovanni del Virgilio," p. 4ff.). L.J. Paetow comments on this document as follows: "This was a good beginning ... but the fair promise had no fulfillment" (*The Arts Course at Medieval Universities* [Urbana-Champaign, 1910], p. 60). Actually, the promise did find its fulfillment in the development of Italian humanism. The teaching of classical-authors never ceased in Italy after that memorable date which coincides with the approximate time when Petrarch was a student at Bologna.

52. For French influences on Italian humanism in the fourteenth century, see also B.L. Ullman, "Some Aspects of the Origin of Italian Humanism," *Philological Quarterly* 20 (1941): 20–31. Even earlier (1277) is the correspondence between two notaries concerning the loan of a manuscript of Ovid's *Metamorphoses* (*Il Notariato a Perugia*, ed. Roberto Abbondanza [Rome, 1973], pp. 252–54, no. 199).

53. Burckhardt, *Die Kultur der Renaissance in Italien*, p. 154.

54. Karl Vossler, *Poetische Theorien in der italienischen Frührenaissance* (Berlin, 1900). August Buck, *Italienische Dichtungslehren vom Mittelalter bis zum Ausgang der Renaissance* (Tübingen, 1958).

55. The work by Vincenzo Lancetti, *Memorie intorno ai poeti laureati d'ogni tempo e d'ogni nazione* (Milan, 1839), is antiquated, but has not been replaced. Important contributions were made by Francesco Novati, "La suprema aspirazione di Dante," *Indagini e postille dantesche* (Bologna, 1899), p. 83ff., and by E. H. Wilkins, "The Coronation of Petrarch," *Speculum* 18 (1943): 155–97. I believe that the coronation ceremony developed from the public recitals and approbations of books at the medieval universities (on such approbations, see Lynn Thorndike, "Public Readings of New Works in Mediaeval Universities," *Speculum* 1 [1926]: 101–3, and the additional notes by Haskins and Thorndike, *ibid.*, pp. 221 and 445ff.). The intermediary link is the coronation of the approved book, as in the case of Boncompagno at Bologna 1215 (Novati, *Indagini*, p. 86f.). There is definite evidence that Mussato was crowned not only for his tragedy *Eccerinis*, but also for his historical work on Henry VII. Also the diploma of Petrarch's coronation refers to him repeatedly as a poet and historian (*Opera Omnia* [Basel, 1581], IV, pp. 6–7), and there are later cases of persons crowned as poets and orators.

56. Petrarch was examined by King Robert of Naples and took the king's testimonial letters to Rome, that is, followed much of the procedure that was used for academic degrees in the kingdom of Naples. His diploma resembles doctoral diplomas and grants him the authorization "tam in dicta arte poetica quam in dicta historica arte ... legendi, disputandi atque interpretandi veterum scriptural et novas (read: novos) a seipso ... libros et poemata componendi...." (*Opera Omnia*, IV, 6–7).

57. The chair of moral philosophy was held, for example, by Barzizza and by Filelfo.

58. Lectures on the Greek or Latin text of Aristotle and other philosophical authors were given at Florence by Marsuppini, Argyropulos, Politian, at Bologna by Codrus Urceus, and at Padua by Leonicus Thomaeus.

59. On *humanitas* in Roman antiquity, see Werner Jaeger, *Humanism and Theology* (Milwaukee, 1943), pp. 20ff. and 72f. Max Schneidewin, *Die antike Humanität* (Berlin, 1897), p. 31ff. Richard Reitzenstein, *Werden und Wesen der Humanität im Altertum* (Strassburg, 1907). I. Heinemann, "Humanitas," in Pauly-Wissowa, *Real-Encyclopädie der classischen Alterturnswissenschaft, Supplementband* 5 (Stuttgart, 1931), col. 282–310. Joseph Niedermann, *Kultur* (Florence, 1941), p. 29ff.

60. The clearest statement is found in the famous library canon composed by Nicholas V in his youth for Cosimo de' Medici. After having listed many books on theology, then the works of Aristotle in *logicis*, in *physicis*, in *metaphysica*, and in *moralibus*, the Arabic and Greek commentators on Aristotle, other philosophical works translated from the Greek, and works on mathematics, he continued as follows: "de studiis autem humanitatis quantum ad grammaticam, rhetoricam, historicam et poeticam spectat ac moralem ..." (Giovanni Sforza, "La patria, la famiglia ed i parenti di papa Niccolò V," *Atti della Reale Accademia Lucchese di Scienze, Lettere ed Arti* 23 [1884]: 1–400, at 380).

An educational charter of the Jesuits of 1591 speaks of "studia humanitatis, hoc est grammaticae, historiae, poeticae et rhetoricae" (quoted by Karl Borinski, *Die Antike in Poetik und Kunsttheorie*, vol. 2 [Leipzig, 1924], p. 327). Pierre Bersuire calls Petrarch "poetam utique et oratorem egregium in omni morali philosophia nec non et historica et poetica disciplina eruditum" (Fausto Ghisalberti, "L'Ovidius moralizatus di Pierre Bersuire," *Studi Romanzi* 23 [1933]: 90). After Leonardo Bruni's death, according to his epitaph in S. Croce, "historia luget, eloquentia muta est, ferturque Musas tum Graecas tum Latinas lacrimas tenere non potuisse." Peter Luder announced at Heidelberg in 1456 public courses on "studia humanitatis id est poetarum oratorem ac hystoriographorum libros," and at Leipzig in 1462 on "studia humanitatis, hystoriographos, oratores scilicet et poetas" (Ludwig Bertalot, "Humanistische Vorlesungsankündigungen in Deutschland im

15. Jahrhundert," *Zeitschrift für Geschichte der Erziehung and des Unterrichts* 5 [1915]: 3–4). Giovanni Sforza's manuscript source for the "Inventarium Nicolai pape V quod ipse composuit ad instantiam Cosme de Medicis ut ab ipso Cosma audivi die XII novembr. 1463 ego frater Leonardus Ser Uberti de Florentia O.P. presente R. o patre fratre Sante de Florentia priore Sancti Marci Flor(entini) eiusdem ord(inis)" is cod. Conv. Soppressi J VII 30 (S. Marco) of the Biblioteca Nazionale in Florence, f. 180–185v (the reference given by Sforza, "La patria, ...," p. 359, is misleading). Characteristic is also the title of one of Filelfo's orations: "oratio de laudibus historie poetice philosophie et que hasce complectitur eloquentie" (cod. Vallicell. F 20 f. 213v). Charles Trinkaus, "A Humanist's Image of Humanism: The Inaugural Orations of Bartolommeo della Fonte," *Studies in the Renaissance* 7 (1960): 90–147.

61. This was attempted, however, in the sixteenth century by Vives in his work *De tradendis disciplinis*.

62. The humanist Leonardo Bruni, when comparing Dante and Petrarch, attributes greater knowledge in philosophy and mathematics to Dante, "perocché nella scienza delle lettere e nella cognizione della lingua latina Dante fu molto inferiore al Petrarca" (*Le Vite di Dante, Petrarca et Boccaccio*, ed. Angelo Solerti [Milan, n.d.], p. 292ff.). For Bruni, the learning of Petrarch is not universal and does not include philosophy. In his early letter to Antonio da S. Miniato, Ficino proposes to abandon his previous rhetorical style and to speak instead as a philosopher ("deinceps philosophorum more loquamur verba ubique contempnentes et gravissimas in medium sententias adducentes," Forlì, Biblioteca Comunale, Autografo Piancastelli no. 907: see P.O. Kristeller, *Studies in Renaissance Thought and Letters* [Rome, 1956], p. 146).

In the preface of his *De regimine sanitatis*, Antonio Benivieni relates that he turned from "oratorie artis studia" to philosophy and medicine (ed. Luigi Belloni [Turin, 1951], p. 19). Alamanno Rinuccini, in the letter to his son Filippo, which is a tract on education, insists that it is necessary to proceed from the study of grammar and rhetoric ("ubi nostrorum hominum plerique gradum sistere consueverunt") to that of philosophy (*Lettere ed Orazioni*, ed. Vito R. Giustiniani [Florence, 1953], p. 97). Pontanus in his dialogue *Aegidius* speaks of the decline of eloquence after the end of the Roman Empire, "cum tamen disciplinae ipsae in honore essent habitae, id quod physicorum theologorumque multitudo quae post Boetium extitit plane declarat, tum in Hispania, tum in Galliis Britaniisque ipsaque in Germania" (*I dialoghi*, ed. Carmelo Previtera [Florence, 1943], p. 259).

63. Rossi, *Il Quattrocento*, pp. 6 and 15, cites a poem of Ariosto (1523) for the earliest appearance of the term *umanista* in Italian, and an epigram of the late fifteenth century for the earliest appearance of the term *humanista* in Latin. I have not been able to verify the latter passage, but I found the following passage in a vernacular letter written in 1490 by the rector of Pisa university to the officials in Florence: "avendo le S. V. condocto quello Humanista the non è venuto," this will be a disappointment for many foreign students who have come "per udire humanità" (Angelus Fabronius, *Historia Academiae Pisane*, I [Pisa, 1791], pp. 369f.). The original letter (Archivio di Stato, Florence, *Studio Fiorentino e Pisano*, XI, f. 14) was sent by Andreas dal Campo notarius studii to the Officiali dello Studio on December 4, 1490. The original has "non essendo venuto" and some other variants not relevant to our discussion.

During the sixteenth century, the Latin term *humanista* appears in the university documents of Bologna and Ferrara. John Florio in his Italian–English dictionary has the following entry: "Humanista, a humanist or professor of humanitie" (*A Worlde of Wordes* [London, 1598], p. 164). Other examples of this usage are given by Augusto Campana ("The Origin of the Word 'Humanist,'" *Journal of the Warburg and Courtauld Institutes* 9

[1946]: 60–73) who arrives at the same conclusion as to the origin and meaning of the term. The term occurs repeatedly in the *Epistolae obscurorum viorum* (Karl Brandi, *Das Werden der Renaissance* [Göttingen, 1908], p. 23). The original meaning was still alive in the eighteenth century. Salvino Salvini (*Fasti Consolari dell'Accademia Fiorentina* [Florence, 1717], p. xiv) mentions Francesco da Buti as a "dottore in grammatica, come allora si dicevano gli Umanisti"; and Leibniz states of Valla, "qu'il n'étoit pas moins Philosophe, qu'Humaniste" (*Essais de Théodicée*, sec. 405). As a Spanish example of the late sixteenth or early seventeenth century, I noted the following title: "Discurso de las letras humanas llamado el humanista, compuesto por el maestro Francisco Cespedes, Cathedratico de prima de Rethorica en la Universidad de Salamanca" (Pedro Roca, *Catálogo de los manuscritos que pertenecierón a D. Pascual de Gayangos existentes hoy en la Biblioteca Nacional* [Madrid, 1904] p. 227, no. 643; this is now cod. 17736, as I was informed by Ramón Paz).

64. Apparently the term *Humanismus* was coined in 1808 by F. J. Niethammer to denote the educational theory that tried to defend the traditional place of classical studies in the school curriculum (Walter Rüegg, *Cicero and der Humanismus* [Zürich, 1946], p. 2ff.). Goethe (*Dichtung und Wahrheit*, bk. XIII, published 1814) uses the term in the sense of humanitarianism (my attention was called to this passage by Dino Bigongiari).

65. For the relation between theology, medicine, and philosophy in Italy, see Hastings Rashdall, *The Universities of Europe in the Middle Ages*, 2d ed., ed. F.M. Powicke and A.B. Emden, vol. 1 (Oxford, 1936), p. 261ff. There is some Aristotelianism in the writings of Urso and other Salerno masters (cf. Kristeller, *Studies in Renaissance Thought and Letters*, pp. 517–19), and there was a group of theologians and canonists at Bologna in the twelfth century who were influenced by Abelard. Yet the regular connection between medicine and Aristotelian philosophy, which was to become characteristic of Italian science, appears for the first time in the writings of Taddeo of Florence (late thirteenth century). See Bruno Nardi, "L'averroismo bolognese nel secolo XIII e Taddeo Alderotto," *Rivista di Storia della Filosofia* 4 (1949): 11–22.

66. The influence of the school of Paris upon the earliest Italian Aristotelians ought to be investigated further. The earliest tangible fact seems to be the notice that Gentile da Cingoli, who became a teacher of logic and philosophy at Bologna around 1300, attended a course on Aristotle by Johannes Vate who appears at Paris around 1290 (Martin Grabmann, *Mittelalterliches Geistesleben*, vol. 2 [Munich, 1936], p. 265ff.). It is well-known that Peter of Abano, the supposed founder of the school of Padua, studied at Paris and was in personal relations with Jean de Jandun. As late as 1340 the physician Gentile da Foligno is reported to have advised the ruler of Padua to send twelve youths to Paris to study the arts and medicine (Heinrich Denifle and Émile Chatelain, *Chartularium Universitatis Parisiensis*, II [Paris, 1891]), p. 558).

67. Martin Grabmann, "Studien über den Averroisten Taddeo da Parma," *Mittelalterliches Geistesleben*, vol. 2, pp. 239–60; *id.*, "Der Bologneser Averroist Angelo d'Arezzo," *ibid.*, pp. 261–71. Peter of Abano and Gentile da Cingoli belong to the same period. Urbano of Bologna would seem to belong to the second half of the fourteenth century. Anneliese Maier, "Eine italienische Averroistenschule aus der ersten Hälfte des 14. Jahrhunderts," *Die Vorläufer Galileis im 14. Jahrhundert* (Rome, 1949), pp. 251–78; Martin Grabmann, "Gentile da Cingoli, ein italienischer Aristoteleserklärer aus der Zeit Dantes," *Sitzungsberichte der bayerischen Akademie der Wissenschaften, Philosophisch-Historische Abteilung*, Jahrgang 1940, Heft 9 (published 1941). P.O. Kristeller, "A Philosophical Treatise from Bologna Dedicated to Guido Cavalcanti," in *Medioevo e Rinascimento: Studi in Onore di Bruno Nardi*, vol. 1 (Florence, 1955), pp. 425–63. See also, Zdzislaw Kuksewicz; *Averroïsme Bolonais au XIVe siècle* (Wroclaw, 1965); *id.*, *De Siger de Brabant à Jacques de Plaisance* (Wroclaw, 1968).

68. Pierre Duhem, "La tradition de Buridan et la science italienne au XVIe siècle," *Etudes sur Léonard de Vinci*, vol. 3 (Paris, 1913), pp. 113–259; *id.*, "La dialectique d'Oxford et la scolastique italienne," *Bulletin Italien* 12 (1912) and 13 (1913). Marshall Clagett, *Giovanni Marliani and Late Medieval Physics* (New York, 1941). Curtis Wilson, *William Heytesbury* (Madison, Wis., 1956). Theodore E. James, "De primo et ultimo instanti Petri Alboini Mantuani" (Ph.D. diss., Columbia University, 1968).

69. For this Italian Aristotelianism, see Friedrich Ueberweg, *Grundriss der Geschichte der Philosophie*, 12th ed., vol. 3 (Berlin, 1924), p. 22ff. Jakob Brucker, *Historia critica philosophiae*, vol. 4, pt. 1 (Leipzig, 1743), p. 148ff. Carl von Prantl, *Geschichte der Logik im Abendlande*, vol. 4 (Leipzig, 1870), pp. 118ff., 176ff., 232ff. Ernest Renan, *Averroës et l'averroïsme* (Paris, 1852; rev. ed., 1861). Clagett, *Giovanni Marliani*. Eugenio Garin, *La filosofia* (Milan, 1947), vol. 1, pp. 338–52 and vol. 2, pp. 1–65. Bruno Nardi, *Sigieri di Brabante nel pensiero del Rinascimento italiano* (Rome, 1945). P.O. Kristeller, "Renaissance Aristotelianism," *Greek, Roman and Byzantine Studies* 6 (1965): 157–74. Charles B. Schmitt, *A Critical Survey and Bibliography of Studies on Renaissance Aristotelianism* (Padua, 1971).

70. Usually the introduction of English dialectic in Italy is attributed to Paul of Venice at Padua after 1400. Yet Peter of Mantua, whom Prantl and Duhem treat as an author of the fifteenth century because of the publication date of his treatises, lived during the fourteenth century and probably died in A.D. 1400. He taught at Bologna and may have been the first Italian follower of the Oxford School. See the letter addressed to him by Salutati (note 13), and Novati's footnote which gives several biographical data and references to manuscripts, all unknown to historians of philosophy. A manuscript with logical works of Peter is in the Columbia University Libraries. The text of the "loyca Ferebrigh" appears in the library of the Franciscans in Assisi as early as 1381 (cf. Giuseppe Manacorda, *Storia della scuola in Italia* [Milan, n.d.], pt. 2, p. 361). However it is known that Peter of Mantua studied at Padua before beginning to teach at Bologna in 1392. See Roberto Cessi, *Athenaeum* 1 (1913): 130–31. A. Segarizzi, *Atti della I. R. Accademia di Scienze, Lettere ed Arti degli Agiati in Rovereto*, 3d ser., 13 (1970): 219–48. Cesare Vasoli, "Pietro degli Alboini da Mantova 'scolastico' della fine del Trecento e un'Epistola di Coluccio Salutati," *Rinascimento* 14 [n.s. 3] (1963): 3–21. James, "De primo et ultimo instanti Petri Alboini Mantuani."

71. After having joked about the Barbaric names of the English logicians, Bruni continues: "Et quid Colucci ut haec ioca omittam quid est inquam in dialectica quod non Britannicis sophismatibus conturbatum sit?" (*Leonardi Bruni Aretini Dialogus de tribus vatibus Florentinis*, ed. Karl Wotke [Vienna, 1889], p. 16).

72. For some of the humanist controversies see Remigio Sabbadini, *Storia del ciceronianismo* (Turin, 1885).

73. For Stoic elements in Pomponazzi, see Léontine Zanta, *La renaissance du Stoicisme au XVIe siècle* (Paris, 1914). For Platonic elements in Pomponazzi see essay 2.

74. Ernest Renan, *Averroës et l'averroïsme*, 2d ed. (Paris, 1861). Renan's work has been superseded for the thirteenth century by Pierre Mandonnet, *Siger de Brabant et l'averroïsme latin au XIIIe siècle*, 2d ed., 2 vols. (Louvain, 1908–11). There is a widespread belief that Renan has been entirely superseded by Mandonnet, but this is obviously not true for the fourteenth and later centuries. The more recent article by M.M. Gorce, "Averroïsme," *Dictionnaire d'Histoire et de Géographie Ecclésiastique* 5 (1931): 1032–92, does not supersede Renan either, although it supplements him in a few details. Gorce largely follows Renan for the later period and does not correct any of his major mistakes. There is a fairly large literature on Pomponazzi, and a monograph on Cesare Cremonini by Léopold Mabilleau, *Étude historique sur la philosophie de la Renaissance en Italie* (Paris, 1881). See also Bruno

Nardi, *Saggi sull'Aristotelismo padovano dal secolo XIV al XVI* (Florence, 1958). M. A. Del Torre, *Studi su Cesare Cremonini* (Padua, 1968).

75. An important contribution to the latter problem has been published by J. H. Randall, Jr., "The Development of Scientific Method in the School of Padua," *Journal of the History of Ideas* 1 (1940): 177–206, reprinted in his *The School of Padua and the Emergence of Modern Science* (Padua, 1961), pp. 13–68. Giovanni di Napoli, *L'immortalità dell'anima nel Rinascimento* (Turin, 1963); Martin Pine, "Pietro Pomponazzi and the Immortality Controversy" (Ph.D. diss., Columbia University, 1965).

76. For the contributions of the Aristotelians to sixteenth-century science, see Lynn Thorndike, *A History of Magic and Experimental Science*, vols. 5–6 (New York, 1941). For Galilei's connection with Italian Aristotelianism, see Randall, "The Development of Scientific Method in the School of Padua." I should like to add the following detail: Everybody knows Galilei's statement that the nobility of a science depends on the certainty of its method rather than on the dignity of its subject matter (*Opere*, Edizione Nazionale, vol. 6 [1896], p. 237 and vol. 7 [1897], p. 246). Remembering this statement, I was surprised to find among Pomponazzi's Questions on the first book of Aristotle's *de anima* the following one: "Nobilitas scientiae a quo sumatur. Quaestio est a quo sumatur magis nobilitas scientiae, an a nobilitate subiecti an a certitudine demonstrationis vel aequaliter ab ambobus" (Luigi Ferri, "Intorno alle dottrine psicologiche di Pietro Pomponazzi," *Atti della Reale Accademia dei Lincei*, 2d ser., 3 [1875–76], pt. 3, p. 423). Pomponazzi does not give a clear answer as does Galilei, but it is obvious that Galilei's statement is not an isolated aphorism, but a conscious answer given to a traditional question debated in the Aristotelian schools of philosophy. See Eugenio Garin, *La Disputa delle Arti nel Quattrocento* (Florence, 1947), p. xiii ff.

77. Most of these notions go back to Renan and have been repeated ever since, especially by French scholars. As I hope to have shown elsewhere, there is no evidence for the existence of an Alexandrist school in the sixteenth century; there is hardly a uniform Averroist tradition, especially not in the sense used by Renan, who fails to distinguish between the use made of Averroës as a commentator and the adherence to specific Averroist doctrines such as the unity of the intellect; there was no distinctive school of Padua, especially not in the fourteenth century, but merely a broad movement of Italian Aristotelianism in which the university of Padua came to play a leading role during the sixteenth century. Many philosophers listed by Renan as representatives of the Paduan school actually never lived in that city; the tradition that the Paduan Aristotelians were atheists and freethinkers is mainly based on unverified anecdotes and insinuations that developed in France during the seventeenth and eighteenth centuries when the freethinkers of that period were looking for forerunners and their orthodox opponents had no reason to defend the memory of thinkers who had tried to compromise between reason and faith in a way that was no longer considered permissible or possible by either side. P. O. Kristeller, "Petrarch's 'Averroisms,'" *Bibliothèque d'Humanisme et Renaissance* 14 [*Mélanges Augustin Renaudet*] (1952): 59–65; *id.*, "The Myth of Renaissance Atheism and the French Tradition of Free Thought," *Journal of the History of Philosophy* 6 (1968): 233–43; *id.*, "Paduan Averroism and Alexandrism in the Light of Recent Studies," in *Aristotelismo Padovano e Filosofia Aristotelica: Atti del XII Congresso Internazionale di Filosofia* 9 (Florence, 1960): 147–55.

78. On the question of Latin and *volgare* as discussed by the humanists, see Remigio Sabbadini, *Storia del ciceronianismo*, pp. 127–36. I do not agree with his presentation of the problem. The orations of Romolo Amaseo, and the similar one of Sigonius, were primarily defenses of Latin as a field of study, without any intention to abolish the *volgare*. We still

need a history of the Italian literary language that would show its gradual expansion, at the expense of Latin and also of local dialects, according to the various regions of Italy as well as to the various branches of literary expression. The problem was formulated by Burckhardt, *Die Kultur der Renaissance*, p. 418. See Kristeller, *Studies in Renaissance Thought and Letters*, pp. 473–93.

79. P.O. Kristeller, "The Modern System of the Arts," *Journal of the History of Ideas* 12 (1951): 496–527 and 13 (1952): 17–46, reprinted in *Renaissance Thought II: Papers in Humanism and the Arts* (New York, 1965), pp. 163–227.

JOAN KELLY

Did Women Have a Renaissance?

One of the tasks of women's history is to call into question accepted schemes of periodization. To take the emancipation of women as a vantage point is to discover that events that further the historical development of men, liberating them from natural, social, or ideological constraints, have quite different, even opposite, effects upon women. The Renaissance is a good case in point. Italy was well in advance of the rest of Europe from roughly 1350 to 1530 because of its early consolidation of genuine states, the mercantile and manufacturing economy that supported them, and its working out of postfeudal and even postguild social relations. These developments reorganized Italian society along modern lines and opened the possibilities for the social and cultural expression for which the age is known. Yet precisely these developments affected women adversely, so much so that there was no renaissance for women—at least, not during the Renaissance. The state, early capitalism, and the social relations formed by them impinged on the lives of Renaissance women in different ways according to their different positions in society. But the startling fact is that women as a group, especially among the classes that dominated Italian urban life, experienced a contraction of social and personal options that men of their classes either did not, as was the case with the bourgeoisie, or did not experience as markedly, as was the case with the nobility.

Before demonstrating this point, which contradicts the widely held

From *Becoming Visible: Women in History* eds. Renate Bridenthal and Claudia Koonz. © 1977 by Houghton Mifflin Company.

notion of the equality of Renaissance women with men,[1] we need to consider how to establish, let alone measure, loss or gain with respect to the liberty of women. I found the following criteria most useful for gauging the relative contraction (or expansion) of the powers of Renaissance women and for determining the quality of their historical experience: 1) the regulation of *female sexuality* as compared with male sexuality; 2) women's *economic and political roles*, i.e., the kind of work they performed as compared with men, and their access to property, political power, and the education or training necessary for work, property, and power; 3) the *cultural roles* of women in shaping the outlook of their society, and access to the education and/or institutions necessary for this; 4) *ideology* about women, in particular the sex-role system displayed or advocated in the symbolic products of the society, its art, literature, and philosophy. Two points should be made about this ideological index. One is its rich inferential value. The literature, art, and philosophy of a society, which give us direct knowledge of the attitudes of the dominant sector of that society toward women, also yield indirect knowledge about our other criteria: namely, the sexual, economic, political, and cultural activities of women. Insofar as images of women relate to what really goes on, we can infer from them something about that social reality. But, second, the relations between the ideology of sex roles and the reality we want to get at are complex and difficult to establish. Such views may be prescriptive rather than descriptive; they may describe a situation that no longer prevails; or they may use the relation of the sexes symbolically and not refer primarily to women and sex roles at all. Hence, to assess the historical significance of changes in sex-role conception, we must bring such changes into connection with all we know about general developments in the society at large.

This essay examines changes in sex-role conception, particularly with respect to sexuality, for what they tell us about Renaissance society and women's place in it. At first glance, Renaissance thought presents a problem in this regard because it cannot be simply categorized. Ideas about the relation of the sexes range from a relatively complementary sense of sex roles in literature dealing with courtly manners, love, and education, to patriarchal conceptions in writings on marriage and the family, to a fairly equal presentation of sex roles in early Utopian social theory. Such diversity need not baffle the attempt to reconstruct a history of sex-role conceptions, however, and to relate its course to the actual situation of women. Toward this end, one needs to sort out this material in terms of the social groups to which it responds: to courtly society in the first case, the nobility of the petty despotic states of Italy; to the patrician bourgeoisie in the second, particularly of republics such as Florence. In the third case, the relatively equal position accorded women in Utopian thought (and in those lower-class movements of the radical Reformation analogous to it) results from a larger critique of early modern society and all the relations of domination that flow from private ownership and control of property. Once distinguished, each of these groups of sources tells the same story. Each discloses in its own way certain new constraints suffered by Renaissance women as the family and political life were restructured in the great transition from medieval feudal society to the early modern state. The sources that represent the interests of the nobility and the bourgeoisie point to this fact by a telling, double index. Almost all such works—with certain notable exceptions, such as Boccaccio and Ariosto—establish chastity as the female norm and restructure the relation of the sexes to one of female dependency and male domination.

The bourgeois writings on education, domestic life, and society constitute the extreme in this denial of women's independence. Suffice it to say that they sharply distinguish an inferior domestic realm of women from the superior public realm of men, achieving a veritable "renaissance" of the outlook and practices of classical Athens, with its domestic imprisonment of citizen wives.[2] The courtly Renaissance literature we will consider was more gracious. But even here, by analyzing a few of the representative works of this genre, we find a new repression of the noblewoman's affective experience, in contrast to the latitude afforded her by medieval literature, and some of the social and cultural reasons for it. Dante and Castiglione, who continued a literary tradition that began with the courtly love literature of eleventh- and twelfth-century Provence, transformed medieval conceptions of love and nobility. In the love ideal they formed, we can discern the inferior position the Renaissance noblewoman held in the relation of the sexes by comparison with her male counterpart and with her medieval predecessor as well.

LOVE AND THE MEDIEVAL LADY

Medieval courtly love, closely bound to the dominant values of feudalism and the church, allowed in a special way for the expression of sexual love by women. Of course, only aristocratic women gained their sexual and affective rights thereby. If a knight wanted a peasant girl, the twelfth-century theorist of *The Art of Courtly Love*, Andreas Capellanus, encouraged him "not [to] hesitate to take what you seek and to embrace her by force."[3] Toward the lady, however, "a true lover considers nothing good except what he thinks will please his beloved"; for if courtly love were to define itself as a noble phenomenon, it had to attribute an essential freedom to the relation between lovers. Hence, it metaphorically extended the social relation of vassalage to the love relationship, a "conceit" that Maurice Valency rightly called "the shaping principle of the whole design" of courtly love.[4]

Of the two dominant sets of dependent social relations formed by feudalism—*les liens de dépendence*, as Marc Bloch called them—vassalage, the military relation of knight to lord, distinguished itself (in its early days) by being freely entered into. At a time when everyone was somebody's "man," the right to freely enter a relation of service characterized aristocratic bonds, whereas hereditability marked the servile work relation of serf to lord. Thus, in medieval romances, a parley typically followed a declaration of love until love freely proffered was freely returned. A kiss (like the kiss of homage) sealed the pledge, rings were exchanged, and the knight entered the love service of his lady. Representing love along the lines of vassalage had several liberating implications for aristocratic women. Most fundamental, ideas of homage and mutuality entered the notion of heterosexual relations along with the idea of freedom. As symbolized on shields and other illustrations that place the knight in the ritual attitude of commendation, kneeling before his lady with his hands folded between hers, homage signified male service, not domination or subordination of the lady, and it signified fidelity, constancy, in that service. "A lady must honor her lover as a friend, not as a master," wrote Marie de Ventadour, a female troubadour or *trobairitz*.[5] At the same time, homage entailed a reciprocity of rights and obligations, a service on the lady's part as well. In one of Marie de France's romances, a knight is about to be judged by the barons of King Arthur's court when his lady rides to the castle to give him "succor" and pleads successfully for him, as any overlord might.[6] Mutuality, or complementarity, marks the relation the lady entered into with her *ami* (the favored name for "lover" and, significantly, a synonym for "vassal").

This relation between knight and lady was very much at variance with the patriarchal family relations obtaining in that same level of society. Aware of its incompatibility with prevailing family and marital relations, the celebrants of courtly love kept love detached from marriage. "We dare not oppose the opinion of the Countess of Champagne who rules that love can exert no power between husband and wife," Andreas wrote (p. 175). But in opting for a free and reciprocal heterosexual relation outside marriage, the poets and theorists of courtly love ignored the almost universal demand of patriarchal society for female chastity, in the sense of the woman's strict bondage to the marital bed. The reasons why they did so, and even the fact that they did so, have long been disputed, but the ideas and values that justify this kind of adulterous love are plain. Marriage, as a relation arranged by others, carried the taint of social necessity for the aristocracy. And if the feudality denigrated marriage by disdaining obligatory service, the church did so by regarding it not as a "religious" state, but an inferior one that responded to natural necessity. Moreover, Christianity positively fostered the ideal of courtly love at a deep level of feeling. The courtly relation between lovers took vassalage as its structural model, but its passion was nourished by Christianity's exaltation of love.

Christianity had accomplished its elevation of love by purging it of sexuality, and in this respect, by recombining the two, courtly love clearly departed from Christian teaching. The toleration of adultery it fostered thereby was in itself not so grievous. The feudality disregarded any number of church rulings that affected their interests, such as prohibitions of tournaments and repudiation of spouses (divorce) and remarriage. Moreover, adultery hardly needed the sanction of courtly love, which, if anything, acted rather as a restraining force by binding sexuality (except in marriage) to love. Lancelot, in Chrétien de Troyes's twelfth-century romance, lies in bed with a lovely woman because of a promise he has made, but "not once does he look at her, nor show her any courtesy. Why not? Because his heart does not go out to her.... The knight has only one heart, and this one is no longer really his, but has been entrusted to someone else, so that he cannot bestow it elsewhere."[7] Actually, Lancelot's chastity represented more of a threat to Christian doctrine than the fact that his passion (for Guinevere) was adulterous, because his attitudes justified sexual love. Sexuality could only be "mere sexuality" for the medieval church, to be consecrated and directed toward procreation by Christian marriage. Love, on the other hand, defined as passion for the good, perfects the individual; hence love, according to Thomas Aquinas, properly directs itself toward God.[8] Like the churchman, Lancelot spurned mere sexuality—but for the sake of sexual love. He defied Christian *teaching* by reattaching love to sex; and experiencing his love as a devout vocation, as a passion, he found himself in utter accord with Christian *feeling*. His love, as Chrétien's story makes clear, is sacramental as well as sexual:

> ... then he comes to the bed of the Queen, whom he adores and before whom he kneels, holding her more dear than the relic of any saint. And the Queen extends her arms to him and, embracing him, presses him tightly against her bosom, drawing him into the bed beside her and showing him every possible satisfaction.... Now Lancelot possesses all he wants.... It cost him

such pain to leave her that he suffered a real martyr's agony....
When he leaves the room, he bows and acts precisely as if he were
before a shrine. (p. 329)

It is difficult to assess Christianity's role in this acceptance of feeling and this
attentiveness to inner states that characterize medieval lyric and romance,
although the weeping and wringing of hands, the inner troubles and turmoil
of the love genre, were to disappear with the restoration of classical attitudes
of restraint in the Renaissance. What certainly bound courtly love to
Christianity, however, aside from its positive attitude toward feeling, was the
cultivation of decidedly "romantic" states of feeling. In Christian Europe,
passion acquired a positive, spiritual meaning that classical ethics and classical
erotic feeling alike denied it. Religious love and courtly love were both
suffered as a destiny, were both submitted to and not denied. Converted by
a passion that henceforth directed and dominated them and for which all
manner of suffering could be borne, the courtly lovers, like the religious,
sought a higher emotional state, than ordinary life provided. They sought
ecstasy; and this required of them a heroic discipline, an ascetic fortitude, and
single-mindedness. Love and its ordeals alike removed them from the daily,
the customary, the routine, setting them apart as an elite superior to the
conventions of marriage and society.

Religious feeling and feudal values thus both fed into a conception of
passionate love that, because of its mutuality, required that women, too,
partake of that passion, of that adulterous sexual love. The lady of medieval
romance also suffered. She suffered "more pain for love than ever a woman
suffered" in another of Marie de France's romances. As the jealously guarded
wife of an old man, ravished by the beauty of her knight when she first saw
him, she could not rest for love of him, and *"franc et noble"* (i.e., free) as she
was, she granted him her kiss and her love upon the declaration of his—"and
many other caresses which lovers know well" during the time she hid him in
her castle.[9] So common is this sexual mutuality to the literature of courtly
love that one cannot take seriously the view of it as a form of Madonna
worship in which a remote and virginal lady spurns consummation. That
stage came later, as courtly love underwent its late medieval and Renaissance
transformation. But for the twelfth century, typical concerns of Provençal
iocs-partitz, those poetic "questions" on love posed at court (and reflecting
the social reality of mock courts of love played out as a diversion) were:
"Must a lady do for her lover as much as he for her?"; or, "A husband learns
that his wife has a lover. The wife and the lover perceive it—which of the
three is in the greatest strait?"[10] In the same vein, Andreas Capellanus

perceived differences between so-called "pure" and "mixed" love as accidental, not substantial. Both came from the same feeling of the heart and one could readily turn into the other, as circumstances dictated. Adultery, after all, required certain precautions; but that did not alter the essentially erotic nature even of "pure" love, which went "as far as the kiss and the embrace and the modest contact with the nude lover, omitting the final solace" (p. 122).

The sexual nature of courtly love, considered together with its voluntary character and the nonpatriarchal structure of its relations, makes us question what it signifies for the actual condition of feudal women. For clearly it represents an ideological liberation of their sexual and affective powers that must have some social reference. This is not to raise the fruitless question of whether such love relationships actually existed or if they were mere literary conventions. The real issue regarding ideology is, rather, what kind of society could posit *as a social ideal* a love relation outside of marriage, one that women freely entered and that, despite its reciprocity, made women the gift givers while men did the service. What were the social conditions that fostered these particular conventions rather than the more common ones of female chastity and/or dependence?

No one doubts that courtly love spread widely as a convention. All ranks and both sexes of the aristocracy wrote troubadour poetry and courtly romances and heard them sung and recited in courtly gatherings throughout most of medieval Europe. But this could happen only if such ideas supported the male-dominated social order rather than subverted it. The love motif could, and with Gottfried of Strasbourg's *Tristan* (c. 1210) did, stand as an ideal radically opposed to the institutions of the church and emerging feudal kingship. But in its beginnings, and generally, courtly love no more threatened Christian feeling or feudalism than did chivalry, which brought a certain "sacramental" moral value and restraint to the profession of warfare. While courtly love celebrated sexuality, it enriched and deepened it by means of the Christian notion of passion. While the knight often betrayed his lord to serve his lord's lady, he transferred to that relationship the feudal ideal of freely committed, mutual service. And while passionate love led to adultery, by that very fact it reinforced, as its necessary premise, the practice of political marriage. The literature of courtly love suppressed rather than exaggerated tensions between it and other social values, and the reason for this lies deeper than literature. It lies at the institutional level, where there was real agreement, or at least no contradiction, between the sexual and affective needs of women and the interests of the aristocratic family, which the feudality and church alike regarded as fundamental to the social order.

The factors to consider here are property and power on the one hand, and illegitimacy on the other. Feudalism, as a system of private jurisdictions, bound power to landed property; and it permitted both inheritance and administration of feudal property by women.[11] Inheritance by women often suited the needs of the great landholding families, as their unremitting efforts to secure such rights for their female members attest. The authority of feudal women owes little to any gallantry on the part of feudal society. But the fact that women could hold both ordinary fiefs and vast collections of counties—and exercise in their own right the seigniorial powers that went with them—certainly fostered a gallant attitude. Eleanor of Aquitaine's adultery as wife of the king of France could have had dire consequences in another place at another time, say in the England of Henry VIII. In her case, she moved on to a new marriage with the future Henry II of England or, to be more exact, a new alliance connecting his Plantagenet interests with her vast domains centering on Provence. Women also exercised power during the absence of warrior husbands. The lady presided over the court at such times, administered the estates, took charge of the vassal services due the lord. She was the lord—albeit in his name rather than her own—unless widowed and without male children. In the religious realm, abbesses exercised analogous temporal as well as spiritual jurisdiction over great territories, and always in their own right, in virtue of their office.

This social reality accounts for the retention of matronymics in medieval society, that is, a common use of the maternal name, which reflects the position of women as landowners and managers of great estates, particularly during the crusading period.[12] It also accounts for the husband's toleration of his wife's diversions, if discreetly pursued. His primary aim to get and maintain a fief required her support, perhaps even her inheritance. As Emily James Putnam put it, "It would, perhaps, be paradoxical to say that a baron would prefer to be sure that his tenure was secure than that his son was legitimate, but it is certain that the relative value of the two things had shifted."[13] Courtly literature, indeed, reveals a marked lack of concern about illegitimacy. Although the ladies of the romances are almost all married, they seldom appear with children, let alone appear to have their lives and loves complicated by them. Much as the tenet that love thrives only in adultery reflected and reinforced the stability of arranged marriage, so the political role of women, and the indivisibility of the fief, probably underlies this indifference to illegitimacy. Especially as forms of inheritance favoring the eldest son took hold in the course of the twelfth century to preserve the great houses, the claims of younger sons and daughters posed no threat to family estates. Moreover, the expansive, exploitative aristocratic families of the eleventh and twelfth centuries could well afford illegitimate members. For the feudality, they were no drain as kin but rather a source of strength in marital alliances and as warriors.

For all these reasons, feudal Christian society could promote the ideal of courtly love. We could probably maintain of any ideology that tolerates sexual parity that: 1) it can threaten no major institution of the patriarchal society from which it emerges; and 2) men, the rulers within the ruling order, must benefit by it. Courtly love surely fit these requirements. That such an ideology did actually develop, however, is due to another feature of medieval society, namely, the cultural activity of feudal women. For responsive as courtly love might seem to men of the feudality whose erotic needs it objectified and refined, as well as objectifying their consciousness of the social self (as noble), it did this and more for women. It gave women lovers, peers rather than masters; and it gave them a justifying ideology for adultery which, as the more customary double standard indicates, men in patriarchal society seldom require. Hence, we should expect what we indeed find: women actively shaping these ideas and values that corresponded so well to their particular interests.

In the first place, women participated in creating the literature of courtly love, a major literature of their era. This role they had not been able to assume in the culture of classical Greece or Rome. The notable exception of Sappho only proves the point: it took women to give poetic voice and status to female sexual love, and only medieval Europe accepted that voice as integral to its cultural expression. The twenty or more known Provençal trobairitz, of whom the Countess Beatrice of Die is the most renowned, celebrated as fully and freely as any man the love of the troubadour tradition:

> Handsome friend, charming and kind,
> when shall I have you in my power?
> If only I could lie beside you for an hour
> and embrace you lovingly—
> know this, that I'd give almost anything
> to see you in my husband's place,
> but only under the condition
> that you swear to do my bidding.[14]

Marie de France voiced similar erotic sentiments in her *lais*. Her short tales of romance, often adulterous and always sexual, have caused her to be ranked by Friedrich Heer as one of the "three poets of genius" (along with Chrétien de Troyes and Gautier d'Arras) who created the *roman courtois* of the twelfth century.[15] These two genres, the romance and the lyric, to which women made such significant contributions, make up the corpus of courtly love literature.

In addition to direct literary expression, women promoted the ideas of courtly love by way of patronage and the diversions of their courts. They supported and/or participated in the recitation and singing of poems and romances, and they played out those mock suits, usually presided over by "queens," that settled questions of love. This holds for lesser aristocratic women as well as the great. But great noblewomen, such as Eleanor of Aquitaine and Marie of Champagne, Eleanor's daughter by her first marriage to Louis VII of France, could make their courts major cultural and social centers and play thereby a dominant role in forming the outlook and mores of their class. Eleanor, herself granddaughter of William of Aquitaine, known as the first troubadour, supported the poets and sentiments of Provence at her court in Anjou. When she became Henry II's queen, she brought the literature and manners of courtly love to England. When living apart from Henry at her court in Poitiers, she and her daughter, Marie, taught the arts of courtesy to a number of young women and men who later dispersed to various parts of France, England, Sicily, and Spain, where they constituted the ruling nobility. Some of the most notable authors of the literature of courtly love belonged to these circles. Bernard of Ventadour, one of the outstanding troubadours, sang his poems to none other than the lady Eleanor. Marie de France had connections with the English court of Eleanor and Henry II. Eleanor's daughter, Marie of Champagne, was patron both of Andreas Capellanus, her chaplain, and Chrétien de Troyes, and she may well be responsible for much of the adulterous, frankly sexual behavior the ladies enjoy in the famous works of both. Chrétien claimed he owed to his "lady of Champagne" both "the material and treatment" of Lancelot, which differs considerably in precisely this regard from his earlier and later romances. And Andreas's *De remedio*, the baffling final section of his work that repudiates sexual love and women, may represent not merely a rhetorical tribute to Ovid but a reaction to the pressure of Marie's patronage.[16]

At their courts as in their literature, it would seem that feudal women consciously exerted pressure in shaping the courtly love ideal and making it prevail. But they could do so only because they had actual power to exert. The women who assumed cultural roles as artists and patrons of courtly love had already been assigned political roles that assured them some measure of independence and power. They could and did exercise authority, not merely over the subject laboring population of their lands, but over their own and/or their husbands' vassals. Courtly love, which flourished outside the institution of patriarchal marriage, owed its possibility as well as its model to the dominant political institution of feudal Europe that permitted actual vassal homage to be paid to women.

THE RENAISSANCE LADY: POLITICS AND CULTURE

The kind of economic and political power that supported the cultural activity of feudal noblewomen in the eleventh and twelfth centuries had no counterpart in Renaissance Italy. By the fourteenth century the political units of Italy were mostly sovereign states that regardless of legal claims, recognized no overlords and supported no feudatories. Their nobility held property but no seigniorial power, estates but not jurisdiction. Indeed, in northern and central Italy, a nobility in the European sense hardly existed at all. Down to the coronation of Charles V as Holy Roman Emperor in 1530, there was no Italian king to safeguard the interests of (and thereby limit and control) a "legitimate" nobility that maintained by inheritance traditional prerogatives. Hence, where the urban bourgeoisie did not overthrow the claims of nobility, a despot did, usually in the name of nobility but always for himself. These *signorie*, unlike the bourgeois republics, continued to maintain a landed, military "class" with noble pretensions, but its members increasingly became merely the warriors and ornaments of a court. Hence, the Renaissance aristocrat, who enjoyed neither the independent political powers of feudal jurisdiction nor legally guaranteed status in the ruling estate, either served a despot or became one.

In this sociopolitical context, the exercise of political power by women was far more rare than under feudalism or even under the traditional kind of monarchical state that developed out of feudalism. The two Giovannas of Naples, both queens in their own right, exemplify this latter type of rule. The first, who began her reign in 1343 over Naples and Provence, became in 1356 queen of Sicily as well. Her grandfather, King Robert of Naples—of the same house of Anjou and Provence that hearkens back to Eleanor and to Henry Plantagenet—could and did designate Giovanna as his heir. Similarly, in 1414, Giovanna II became queen of Naples upon the death of her brother. In Naples, in short, women of the ruling house could assume power, not because of their abilities alone, but because the principle of legitimacy continued in force along with the feudal tradition of inheritance by women.

In northern Italy, by contrast, Caterina Sforza ruled her petty principality in typical Renaissance fashion, supported only by the Machiavellian principles of *fortuna* and *virtù* (historical situation and will). Her career, like that of her family, follows the Renaissance pattern of personal and political illegitimacy. Born in 1462, she was an illegitimate daughter of Galeazzo Maria Sforza, heir to the Duchy of Milan. The ducal power of the Sforzas was very recent, dating only from 1450, when Francesco Sforza, illegitimate son of a condottiere and a great condottiere himself, assumed control of the duchy. When his son and heir, Caterina's father, was assassinated after ten years of tyrannous rule, another son, Lodovico, took control of the duchy, first as regent for his nephew (Caterina's half brother), then as outright usurper. Lodovico promoted Caterina's interests for the sake of his own. He married her off at fifteen to a nephew of Pope Sixtus IV, thereby strengthening the alliance between the Sforzas and the Riario family, who now controlled the papacy. The pope carved a state out of papal domains for Caterina's husband, making him Count of Forlì as well as the Lord of Imola, which Caterina brought to the marriage. But the pope died in 1484, her husband died by assassination four years later—and Caterina made the choice to defy the peculiar obstacles posed by Renaissance Italy to a woman's assumption of power.

Once before, with her husband seriously ill at Imola, she had ridden hard to Forlì to quell an incipient coup a day before giving birth. Now at twenty-six, after the assassination of her husband, she and a loyal castellan held the citadel at Forlì against her enemies until Lodovico sent her aid from Milan. Caterina won; she faced down her opponents, who held her six children hostage, then took command as regent for her young son. But her title to rule as regent was inconsequential. Caterina ruled because she mustered superior force and exercised it personally, and to the end she had to exert repeatedly the skill, forcefulness, and ruthless ambition that brought her to power. However, even her martial spirit did not suffice. In the despotisms of Renaissance Italy, where assassinations, coups, and invasions were the order of the day, power stayed closely bound to military force. In 1500, deprived of Milan's support by her uncle Lodovico's deposition, Caterina succumbed to the overwhelming forces of Cesare Borgia and was divested of power after a heroic defense of Forlì.

Because of this political situation, at once statist and unstable, the daughters of the Este, Gonzaga, and Montefeltro families represent women of their class much more than Caterina Sforza did. Their access to power was indirect and provisional, and was expected to be so. In his handbook for the nobility, Baldassare Castiglione's description of the lady of the court makes this difference in sex roles quite clear. On the one hand, the Renaissance lady appears as the equivalent of the courtier. She has the same virtues of mind as he and her education is symmetrical with his. She learns everything—well, almost everything—he does: "knowledge of letters, of music, of painting, and

... how to dance and how to be festive."[17] Culture is an accomplishment for noblewoman and man alike, used to charm others as much as to develop the self. But for the woman, charm had become the primary occupation and aim. Whereas the courtier's chief task is defined as the profession of arms, "in a Lady who lives at court a certain pleasing affability is becoming above all else, whereby she will be able to entertain graciously jovery kind of plan" (p. 207).

One notable consequence of the Renaissance lady's need to charm is that Castiglione called upon her to give up certain "unbecoming" physical activities such as riding and handling weapons. Granted, he concerned himself with the court lady, as he says, not a queen who may be called upon to rule. But his aestheticizing of the lady's role, his conception of her femaleness as centered in charm, meant that activities such as riding and skill in weaponry would seem unbecoming to women of the ruling families, too. Elisabetta Gonzaga, the idealized duchess of Castiglione's *Courtier*, came close in real life to his normative portrayal of her type. Riding and skill in weaponry had, in fact, no significance for her. The heir to her Duchy of Urbino was decided upon during the lifetime of her husband, and it was this adoptive heir—not the widow of thirty-seven with no children to compete for her care and attention—who assumed power in 1508. Removed from any direct exercise of power, Elisabetta also disregarded the pursuits and pleasures associated with it. Her letters express none of the sense of freedom and daring Caterina Sforza and Beatrice d'Este experienced in riding and the hunt.[18] Altogether, she lacks spirit. Her correspondence shows her to be as docile in adulthood as her early teachers trained her to be. She met adversity, marital and political, with fortitude but never opposed it. She placated father, brother, and husband, and even in Castiglione's depiction of her court, she complied with rather than shaped its conventions.

The differences between Elisabetta Gonzaga and Caterina Sforza are great, yet both personalities were responding to the Renaissance situation of emerging statehood and social mobility. Elisabetta, neither personally illegitimate nor springing from a freebooting condottiere family, was schooled, as Castiglione would have it, away from the martial attitudes and skills requisite for despotic rule. She would not be a prince, she would marry one. Hence, her education, like that of most of the daughters of the ruling families, directed her toward the cultural and social functions of the court. The lady who married a Renaissance prince became a patron. She commissioned works of art and gave gifts for literary works dedicated to her; she drew to her artists and literati. But the court they came to ornament was her husband's, and the culture they represented magnified his princely being, especially when his origins could not. Thus, the Renaissance lady may play an aesthetically significant role in Castiglione's idealized Court of Urbino of 1508, but even he clearly removed her from that equal, to say nothing of superior, position in social discourse that medieval courtly literature had granted her. To the fifteen or so male members of the court whose names he carefully listed, Castiglione admitted only four women to the evening conversations that were the second major occupation at court (the profession of arms, from which he completely excluded women, being the first). Of the four, he distinguished only two women as participants. The Duchess Elisabetta and her companion, Emilia Pia, at least speak, whereas the other two only do a dance. Yet they speak in order to moderate and "direct" discussion by proposing questions and games. They do not themselves contribute to the discussions, and at one point Castiglione relieves them even of their negligible role:

> When signor Gasparo had spoken thus, signora Emilia made a sign to madam Costanza Fregosa, as she sat next in order, that she should speak; and she was making ready to do so, when suddenly the Duchess said: "Since signora Emilia does not choose to go to the trouble of devising a game, it would be quite right for the other ladies to share in this ease, and thus be exempt from such a burden this evening, especially since there are so many men here that we risk no lack of games." (pp. 19–20)

The men, in short, do all the talking; and the ensuing dialogue on manners and love, as we might expect, is not only developed by men but directed toward their interests.

The contradiction, between the professed parity of noblewomen and men in *The Courtier* and the merely decorative role Castiglione unwittingly assigned the lady proclaims an important educational and cultural change as well as a political one. Not only did a male ruler preside over the courts of Renaissance Italy, but the court no longer served as arbiter of the cultural functions it did retain. Although restricted to a cultural and social role, she lost dominance in that role as secular education came to require special skills which were claimed as the prerogative of a class of professional teachers. The sons of the Renaissance nobility still pursued their military and diplomatic training in the service of some great lord, but as youths, they transferred their nonmilitary training from the lady to the humanistic tutor or boarding school. In a sense, humanism represented an advance for women as well as for the culture at large. It brought Latin literacy and classical learning to daughters as well as sons of the nobility. But this very development, usually taken as an index of the equality of Renaissance (noble) women with men,[19] spelled a further decline in the lady's influence over courtly society. It placed her as well as her brothers under male cultural authority. The girl of the medieval aristocracy, although unschooled, was brought up at the court of some great lady. Now her brothers' tutors shaped her outlook, male educators who, as humanists, suppressed romance and chivalry to further classical, culture, with all its patriarchal and misogynous bias.

The humanistic education of the Renaissance noblewoman helps explain why she cannot compare with her medieval predecessors in shaping a culture responsive to her own interests. In accordance with the new cultural values, the patronage of the Este, Sforza, Gonzaga, and Montefeltro women extended far beyond the literature and art of love and manners, but the works they commissioned, bought, or had dedicated to them do not show any consistent correspondence to their concerns as women. They did not even give noticeable support to women's education, with the single important exception of Battista da Montefeltro, to whom one of the few treatises advocating a humanistic education for women was dedicated. Adopting the universalistic outlook of their humanist teachers, the noblewomen of Renaissance Italy seem to have lost all consciousness of their particular interests as women, while male authors such as Castiglione, who articulated the mores of the Renaissance aristocracy, wrote their works for men. Cultural and political dependency thus combined in Italy to reverse the roles of women and men in developing the new noble code. Medieval courtesy, as set forth in the earliest etiquette books, romances, and rules of love, shaped the man primarily to please the lady. In the thirteenth and fourteenth centuries, rules for women, and strongly patriarchal ones at that, entered French and Italian etiquette books, but not until the Renaissance reformulation of courtly manners and love is it evident how the ways of the lady came to be determined by men in the context of the early modern state. The relation of the sexes here assumed its modern form, and nowhere is this made more visible than in the love relation.

THE RENAISSANCE OF CHASTITY

As soon as the literature and values of courtly love made their way into Italy, they were modified in the direction of asexuality. Dante typifies this initial reception of courtly love. His *Vita Nuova*, written in the "sweet new style" (*dolce stil nuovo*) of late-thirteenth-century Tuscany, still celebrates love and the noble heart: "*Amore e 'l cor gentil sono una cosa.*" Love still appears as homage and the lady as someone else's wife. But the lover of Dante's poems is curiously arrested. He frustrates his own desire by rejecting even the aim of union with his beloved. "What is the point of your love for your lady since you are unable to endure her presence?" a lady asks of Dante. "Tell us, for surely the aim of such love must be unique [*novissimo*]!"[20] And novel it is, for Dante confesses that the joy he once took in his beloved's greeting he shall henceforth seek in himself, "in words which praise my lady." Even this understates the case, since Dante's words neither conjure up Beatrice nor seek to melt her. She remains shadowy and remote, for the focus of his poetry has shifted entirely to the subjective pole of love. It is the inner life, *his* inner life, that Dante objectifies. His love poems present a spiritual contest, which he will soon ontologize in the *Divine Comedy*, among competing states of the lover poet's soul.

This dream-world quality expresses in its way a general change that came over the literature of love as its social foundations crumbled. In the north, as the *Romance of the Rose* reminds us, the tradition began to run dry in the late-thirteenth-century period of feudal disintegration—or transformation by the bourgeois economy of the towns and the emergence of the state. And in Provence, after the Albigensian Crusade and the subjection of the Midi to church and crown, Guiraut Riquier significantly called himself the last troubadour. Complaining that "no craft is less esteemed at court than the beautiful mastery of song," he renounced sexual for celestial love and claimed to enter the service of the Virgin Mary.[21] The reception and reworking of the troubadour tradition in Florence of the late 1200s consequently appears somewhat archaic. A conservative, aristocratic nostalgia clings to Dante's love poetry as it does to his political ideas. But if the new social life of the bourgeois commune found little positive representation in his poetry, Florence did drain from his poems the social content of feudal experience. The lover as knight or trobairitz thus gave way to a poet scholar. The experience of a wandering, questing life gave way to scholastic interests, to distinguishing and classifying states of feeling. And the courtly celebration of romance, modeled upon vassalage and enjoyed in secret meetings, became a private circulation of poems analyzing the spiritual effects of unrequited love.

The actual disappearance of the social world of the court and its presiding lady underlies the disappearance of sex and the physical evaporation of the woman in these poems. The ladies of the romances and troubadour poetry maybe stereotypically blond, candid, and fair, but their authors meant them to be taken as physically and socially "real." In the love poetry of Dante, and of Petrarch and Vittoria Colonna, who continue his tradition, the beloved may just as well be dead—and, indeed, all three authors made them so. They have no meaningful, objective existence, and not merely because their affective experience lacks a voice. This would hold for troubadour poetry too, since the lyric, unlike the romance, articulates only the feelings of the lover. The unreality of the Renaissance beloved has rather to do with the *quality* of the Renaissance lover's feelings. As former social relations that sustained mutuality and interaction among lovers vanished, the lover fell back on a narcissistic experience. The Dantesque beloved merely inspires feeling's that have no outer, physical aim; or, they have a transcendent aim that the beloved merely mediates. In either case, love casts off sexuality. Indeed, the role of the beloved as mediator is asexual in a double sense, as the *Divine Comedy* shows. Not only does the beloved never respond sexually to the lover, but the feelings she arouses in him turn into a spiritual love that makes of their entire relationship a mere symbol or allegory.

Interest even in this shadowy kind of romance dropped off markedly as the work of Dante, Petrarch, and Boccaccio led into the fifteenth-century renaissance of Graeco-Roman art and letters. The Florentine humanists in particular appropriated only the classical side of their predecessors' thought, the side that served public concerns. They rejected the dominance of love in human life, along with the inwardness and seclusion of the religious, the scholar, and the lovesick poet. Dante, for example, figured primarily as a citizen to his biographer, Lionardo Bruni, who, as humanist chancellor of Florence, made him. out as a modern Socrates, at once a political figure, a family man, and a rhetor: an exemplar for the new polis.[22] Only in relation to the institution of the family did Florentine civic humanism take up questions of love and sexuality. In this context, they developed the bourgeois sex-role system, placing man in the public sphere and the patrician woman in the home, requiring social virtues from him and chastity and motherhood from her. In bourgeois Florence, the humanists would have nothing to do with the old aristocratic tradition of relative social and sexual parity. In the petty Italian despotisms, however, and even in Florence under the princely Lorenzo de' Medici late in the fifteenth century, the traditions and culture of the nobility remained meaningful.[23] Castiglione's *Courtier*, and the corpus of Renaissance works it heads, took up the themes of love and courtesy for this courtly society, adapting them to contemporary social and cultural needs. Yet in this milieu, too, within the very tradition of courtly literature, new constraints upon female sexuality emerged. Castiglione, the single most important spokesman of Renaissance love and manners, retained in his love theory Dante's two basic features: the detachment of love from sexuality and the allegorization of the love theme. Moreover, he introduced into the aristocratic conception of sex roles some of the patriarchal notions of women's confinement to the family that bourgeois humanists had been restoring.

Overtly, as we saw, Castiglione and his class supported a complementary conception of sex roles, in part because a nobility that did no work at all gave little thought to a sexual division of labor. He could thus take up the late medieval *querelle des femmes* set off by the *Romance of the Rose* and debate the question of women's dignity much to their favor. Castiglione places Aristotle's (and Aquinas's) notion of woman as a defective man in the mouth of an aggrieved misogynist, Gasparo; he criticizes Plato's low regard for women, even though he did permit them to govern in *The Republic*; he rejects Ovid's theory of love as not "gentle" enough. Most significantly, he opposes Gasparo's bourgeois notion of women's exclusively domestic role. Yet for all this, Castiglione established in *The Courtier* a fateful bond between love and marriage. One index of a heightened patriarchal outlook among the Renaissance nobility is that love in the usual emotional and sexual sense must lead to marriage and be confined to it—for women, that is.

The issue gets couched, like all others in the book, in the form of a debate. There are pros and cons; but the prevailing view is unmistakable. If the ideal court lady loves, she should love someone whom she can marry. If married, and the mishap befalls her "that her husband's hate or another's love should bring her to love, I would have her give her lover a spiritual love only; nor must she ever give him any sure sign of her love, either by word or gesture or by other means that can make him certain of it" (p. 263). *The Courtier* thus takes a strange, transitional position on the relations among love, sex, and marriage, which bourgeois Europe would later fuse into one familial whole. Responding to a situation of general female dependency among the nobility, and to the restoration of patriarchal family values, at once classical and bourgeois, Castiglione, like Renaissance love theorists in general, connected love and marriage. But facing the same realities of political marriage and clerical celibacy that beset the medieval aristocracy, he still focused upon the love that takes place outside it. On this point, too, however, he broke with the courtly love tradition. He proposed on the one hand a Neo-Platonic notion of spiritual love, and on the other, the double standard.[24]

Castiglione's image of the lover is interesting in this regard. Did he think his suppression of female sexual love would be more justifiable if he had a churchman, Pietro Bembo (elevated to cardinal in 1539), enunciate the new theory and had him discourse upon the love of an aging courtier rather than that of a young knight? In any case, adopting the Platonic definition of love as desire to enjoy beauty, Bembo located this lover in a metaphysical and physical hierarchy between sense ("below") and intellect ("above"). As reason mediates between the physical and the spiritual, so man, aroused by the visible beauty of his beloved, may direct his desire beyond her to the true, intelligible source of her beauty. He may, however, also turn toward sense. Young men fall into this error, and we should expect it of them, Bembo explains in the Neo-Platonic language of the Florentine philosopher Marsilio Ficino. "For finding itself deep in an earthly prison, and deprived of spiritual contemplation in exercising its office of governing the body, the soul of itself cannot clearly perceive the truth; wherefore, in order to have knowledge, it is obliged to turn to the senses ... and so it believes them ... and lets itself be guided by them, especially when they have so much vigor that they almost force it" (pp. 338–339). A misdirection of the soul leads to sexual union (though obviously not with the court lady). The preferred kind of union, achieved by way of ascent, uses love of the lady as a step toward love of universal beauty. The lover here ascends from awareness of his own human spirit, which responds to beauty, to awareness of that universal intellect that comprehends universal beauty. Then, "transformed into an angel," his soul finds supreme happiness in divine love. Love may hereby soar to an ontologically noble end, and the beauty of the woman who inspires such ascent may acquire metaphysical status and dignity. But Love, Beauty, Woman, aestheticized as Botticelli's Venus and given cosmic import, were in effect denatured, robbed of body, sex, and passion by this elevation. The simple kiss of love-service became a rarefied kiss of the soul: "A man delights in joining his mouth to that of his beloved in a kiss, not in order to bring himself to any unseemly desire, but because he feels that that bond is the opening of mutual access to their souls" (pp. 349–350). And instead of initiating love, the kiss now terminated physical contact, at least for the churchman and/or aging courtier who sought an ennobling experience—and for the woman obliged to play her role as lady.

Responsive as he still was to medieval views of love, Castiglione at least debated the issue of the double standard. His spokesmen point out that men make the rules permitting themselves and not women sexual freedom, and that concern for legitimacy does not justify this inequality. Since these same men claim to be more virtuous than women, they could more easily restrain themselves. In that case, "there would be neither more nor less certainty about offspring, for even if women were unchaste, they could in no way bear children of themselves ... Provided men were continent and did not take part in the unchastity of women" (pp. 240–241). But for all this, the book supplies an excess of hortatory tales about female chastity, and in the section of the dialogue granting young men indulgence in sensual love, no one speaks for young women, who ought to be doubly "prone," as youths and as women, according to the views of the time.

This is theory, of course. But one thinks of the examples: Eleanor of Aquitaine changing bedmates in the midst of a crusade; Elisabetta Gonzaga, so constrained by the conventions of her own court that she would not take a lover even though her husband was impotent. She, needless to say, figures as Castiglione's prime exemplar: "Our Duchess who has lived with her husband for fifteen years like a widow" (p. 253). Bembo, on the other hand, in the years before he became cardinal, lived with and had three children by Donna Morosina. But however they actually lived, in the new ideology a spiritualized noble love *supplemented* the experience of men while it *defined* extramarital experience for the lady. For women, chastity had become the convention of the Renaissance courts, signaling the twofold fact that the dominant institutions of sixteenth-century Italian society would not support the adulterous sexuality of courtly love, and that women, suffering a relative loss of power within these institutions, could not at first make them responsive to their needs. Legitimacy is a significant factor here. Even courtly love had paid some deference to it (and to the desire of women to avoid conception) by restraining intercourse while promoting romantic and sexual play. But now, with cultural and political power held almost entirely by men, the norm of female chastity came to express the concerns of Renaissance noblemen as they moved into a new situation as a hereditary, dependent class.

This changed situation of the aristocracy accounts both for Castiglione's widespread appeal and for his telling transformation of the love relation. Because *The Courtier* created a mannered way of life that could give to a dependent nobility a sense of self-sufficiency, of inner power and control, which they had lost in a real economic and political sense, the book's popularity spread from Italy through Europe at large in the sixteenth and seventeenth centuries. Although set in the Urbino court of 1508, it was actually begun some ten years after that and published in 1528—after the sack of Rome, and at a time when the princely states of Italy and Europe were coming to resemble each other more closely than they had in the fourteenth and fifteenth centuries. The monarchs of Europe, consolidating and centralizing their states, were at once protecting the privileges of their nobility and suppressing feudal power.[25] Likewise in Italy, as the entire country fell under the hegemony of Charles V, the nobility began to be stabilized. Throughout sixteenth-century Italy, new laws began to limit and regulate membership in a hereditary aristocratic class, prompting a new concern with legitimacy and purity of the blood. Castiglione's demand for female chastity in part responds to this particular concern. His theory of love as a whole responds to the general situation of the Renaissance nobility. In the discourse on love for which he made Bembo the spokesman, he brought to the love relation the same psychic attitudes with which he confronted the political situation. Indeed, he used the love relation as a symbol to convey his sense of political relations.

The changed times to which Castiglione refers in his introduction he experienced as a condition of servitude. The dominant problem of the sixteenth-century Italian nobility, like that of the English nobility under the Tudors, had become one of obedience. As one of Castiglione's courtiers expressed it, God had better grant them "good masters, for, once we have them, we have to endure them as they are" (p. 116). It is this transformation of aristocratic service to statism, which gave rise to Castiglione's leading idea of nobility as courtiers, that shaped his theory of love as well. Bembo's aging courtier, passionless in his rational love, sums up the theme of the entire book: how to maintain by detachment the sense of self now threatened by the loss of independent power. The soul in its earthly prison, the courtier in his social one, renounce the power of self-determination that has in fact been denied them. They renounce *wanting* such power; "If the flame is extinguished, the danger is also extinguished" (p. 347): In love, as in service, the courtier preserves independence by avoiding desire for real love, real power. He does not touch or allow himself to be touched by either. "To enjoy beauty without suffering, the Courtier, aided by reason, must turn his desire entirely away from the body and to beauty alone, [to] contemplate it in its simple and pure self" (p. 351). He may gaze at the object of his love-service, he may listen, but there he reaches the limits of the actual physical relation and transforms her beauty, or the prince's power, into a pure idea. "Spared the bitterness and calamities" of thwarted passion thereby, he loves and serves an image only. The courtier gives obeisance, but only to a reality of his own making: "for he will always carry his precious treasury with him, shut up in his heart, and will also, by the force of his own imagination, make her beauty [or the prince's power] much more beautiful than in reality it is" (p. 352).

Thus, the courtier can serve and not serve, love and not love. He can even attain the relief of surrender by making use of this inner love-service "as a step" to mount to a more sublime sense of service. Contemplation of the Idea the courtier has discovered within his own soul excites a purified desire to love, to serve, to unite with intellectual beauty (or power). Just as love guided his soul from the particular beauty of his beloved to the universal concept, love of that intelligible beauty (or power) glimpsed within transports the soul from the self, the particular intellect, to the universal intellect. Aflame with an utterly spiritual love (or a spiritualized sense of service), the soul then "understands all things intelligible, and without any veil or cloud views the wide sea of pure divine beauty, and receives it into itself, enjoying that supreme happiness of which the senses are incapable" (p. 354). What does this semimystical discourse teach but that by "true" service, the courtier may break out of his citadel of independence, his inner aloofness, to rise and surrender to the pure idea of Power? What does his service become but a freely chosen Obedience, which he can construe as the supreme virtue? In both its sublimated acceptance or resignation and its inner detachment from the actual, Bembo's discourse on love exemplifies the relation between subject and state, obedience and power, that runs through the entire book. Indeed, Castiglione regarded the monarch's power exactly as he had Bembo present the lady's beauty, as symbolic of God: "As in the heavens the sun and the moon and the other stars exhibit to the world a certain likeness of God, so on earth a much liker image of God is seen in ... princes." Clearly, if "men have been put by God under princes" (p. 307), if they have been placed under princes as under His image, what end can be higher than service in virtue, than the purified experience of Service?

The likeness of the lady to the prince in this theory, her elevation to the pedestal of Neo-Platonic love, both masks and expresses the new dependency of the Renaissance noblewoman. In a structured hierarchy of superior and inferior, she seems to be served by the courtier. But this love theory really made her serve—and stand as a symbol of how the relation of domination may be reversed, so that the prince could be made to serve the interests of the courtier. The Renaissance lady is not desired, not loved for herself. Rendered passive and chaste, she merely mediates the courtier's safe transcendence of an otherwise demeaning necessity. On the plane of symbolism, Castiglione thus had the courtier dominate both her and the prince; and on the plane of reality, he indirectly acknowledged the courtier's actual domination of the lady by having him adopt "woman's ways" in his relations to the prince. Castiglione had to defend against effeminacy in the courtier, both the charge of it (p. 92) and the actuality of faces "soft and feminine as many attempt to have who not only curl their hair and pluck their eyebrows, but preen themselves ... and appear so tender and languid ... and utter their words so limply" (p. 36). Yet the close-fitting costume of the Renaissance nobleman displayed the courtier exactly as Castiglione would have him, "well built and shapely of limb" (p. 36). His clothes set off his grace, as did his nonchalant ease, the new manner of those "who seem in words, laughter, in posture not to care" (p. 44). To be attractive, accomplished, and seem not to care; to charm and do so coolly—how concerned with impression, how masked the true self. And how manipulative: petitioning his lord, the courtier knows to be "discreet in choosing the occasion, and will ask things that are proper and reasonable; and he will so frame his request, omitting those parts that he knows can cause displeasure, and will skillfully make easy the difficult points so that his lord will always grant it" (p. 111). In short, how like a woman—or a dependent, for that is the root of the simile.

The accommodation of the sixteenth- and seventeenth-century courtier to the ways and dress of women in no way bespeaks a greater parity between them. It reflects, rather, that general restructuring of social relations that entailed for the Renaissance noblewoman a greater dependency upon men as feudal independence and reciprocity yielded to the state. In this new situation, the entire nobility suffered a loss. Hence, the courtier's posture of dependency, his concern with the pleasing impression; his resolve "to perceive what his prince likes, and ... to bend himself to this" (pp. 110–111). But as the state overrode aristocratic power, the lady suffered a double loss. Deprived of the possibility of independent power that the combined interests of kinship and feudalism guaranteed some women in the Middle Ages, and that the states of early modern Europe would preserve in part, the Italian noblewoman in particular entered a relation of almost universal dependence upon her family and her husband. And she experienced this dependency at the same time as she lost her commanding position with respect to the secular culture of her society.

Hence, the love theory of the Italian courts developed in ways as indifferent to the interests of women as the courtier, in his self-sufficiency, was indifferent as a lover. It accepted, as medieval courtly love did not, the double standard. It bound the lady to chastity, to the merely procreative sex of political marriage, just as her weighty and costly costume came to conceal and constrain her body while it displayed her husband's noble rank. Indeed, the person of the woman became so inconsequential to this love relation that one doubted whether she could love at all. The question that emerges at the end of *The Courtier* as to "whether or not women are as capable of divine love as men" (p. 350) belongs to a love theory structured by mediation rather than mutuality. Woman's beauty inspired love but the lover, the agent, was man. And the question stands unresolved at the end of *The Courtier*—because at heart the spokesmen for Renaissance love were not really concerned about women or love at all.

Where courtly love had used the social relation of vassalage to work out a genuine concern with sexual love, Castiglione's thought moved in exactly the opposite direction. He allegorized love as fully as Dante did, using the relation of the sexes to symbolize the new political order. In this, his love theory reflects the social realities of the Renaissance. The denial of the right and power of women to love, the transformation of women into passive "others" who serve, fits the self-image of the courtier, the one Castiglione sought to remedy. The symbolic relation of the sexes thus mirrors the new social relations of the state, much as courtly love displayed the feudal relations of reciprocal personal dependence. But Renaissance love reflects, as well, the actual condition of dependency suffered by noblewomen as the state arose. If the courtier who charms the prince bears the same relation to him as the lady bears to the courtier, it is because Castiglione understood the relation of the sexes in the same terms that he used to describe the political relation: i.e., as a relation between servant and lord. The nobleman suffered this relation in the public domain only. The lady, denied access to a freely chosen, mutually satisfying love relation, suffered it in the personal domain as well. Moreover, Castiglione's theory, unlike the courtly love it superseded, subordinated love itself to the public concerns of the Renaissance nobleman. He set forth the relation of the sexes as one of dependency and domination, but he did so in order to express and deal with the political relation and its problems. The personal values of love, which the entire feudality once prized, were henceforth increasingly left to the lady. The courtier formed his primary bond with the modern prince.

In sum, a new division between personal and public life made itself felt as the state came to organize Renaissance society, and with that division the modern relation of the sexes made its appearance,[26] even among the Renaissance nobility. Noblewomen, too, were increasingly removed from public concerns—economic, political, and cultural—and although they did not disappear into a private realm of family and domestic concerns as fully as their sisters in the patrician bourgeoisie, their loss of public power made itself felt in new constraints placed upon their personal as well as their social lives. Renaissance ideas on love and manners, more classical than medieval, and almost exclusively a male product, expressed this new subordination of women to the interests of husbands and male-dominated kin groups and served to justify the removal of women from an "un-ladylike" position of power and erotic independence. All the advances of Renaissance Italy, its protocapitalist economy, its states, and its humanistic culture, worked to mold the noblewoman into an aesthetic object: decorous, chaste, and doubly "dependent—on her husband as well as the prince.

NOTES

I first worked out these ideas in 1972–1973 in a course at Sarah Lawrence College entitled "Women: Myth and Reality" and am very much indebted to students in that course and my colleagues Eva Kollisch, Gerda Lerner, and Sherry Ortner. I thank Eve Fleisher, Martin Fleisher, Renate Bridenthal, and Claudia Koonz for their valuable criticism of an earlier version of this paper.

1. The traditional view of the equality of Renaissance women with men goes back to Jacob Burckhardt's classic, *The Civilization of the Renaissance in Italy* (1860). It has found its way into most general histories of women, such as Mary Beard's *Women as Force in History* (1946), Simone de Beauvoir's *The Second Sex* (1949), and Emily James Putnam's *The Lady* (1910), although the latter is a sensitive and sophisticated treatment. It also dominates most histories of Renaissance women, the best of which is E. Rodocanachi, *La femme italienne avant, pendant et après la Renaissance*, Hachette, Paris, 1922. A notable exception is Ruth Kelso, *Doctrine for the Lady of the Renaissance*, University of Illinois Press, Urbana, 1956, who discovered there was no such parity.

2. The major Renaissance statement of the bourgeois domestication of women was made by Leon Battista Alberti in Book 3 of *Della Famiglia* (c. 1435), which is a free adaptation of the Athenian situation described by Xenophon in the *Oeconmicus*.

3. Andreas Capellanus, *The Art of Courtly Love*, trans. John J. Parry, Columbia University Press, New York, 1941, pp. 150–151.

4. Maurice Valency, *In Praise of Love: An Introduction to the Love-Poetry of the Renaissance*, Macmillan, New York, 1961, p. 146.

5. "*E il dompna deu a son drut far honor / Cum ad amic, mas non cum a seignor.*" Ibid., p. 64.

6. Lanval (Sir Launfal), *Les lais de Marie de France*, ed. Paul Tuffrau, L'Edition d'Art H. Piazza, Paris, n.d., p. 41. English ed., *Lays of Marie de France*, J.M. Dent and E.P. Dutton, London and New York, 1911.

7. Excellent trans. and ed. by W. W. Comfort, *Arthurian Romances*, Dent and Dutton Everyman's Library, London and New York, 1970, p. 286.

8. Thomas Aquinas, *Summa Theologiae*, pt. 1–2, q. 28, art. 5.

9. Lanval, *Les lais*, p. 10.

10. Thomas Frederick Crane, *Italian Social Customs of the Sixteenth Century*, Yale University Press, New Haven, 1920, pp. 10–11.

11. As Marc Bloch pointed out, the great French principalities that no longer required personal military service on the part of their holders were among the first to be passed on to women when male heirs were wanting. *Feudal Society*, trans. L.A. Manyon, University of Chicago Press, Chicago, 1964, p. 201.

12. David Herlihy, "Land, Family and Women in Continental Europe, 701–1200," *Traditio*, 18 (1962), 89–120. Also, "Women in Medieval Society," *The Smith History Lecture*, University of St. Thomas, Texas, 1971. For a fine new work on abbesses, see Joan Morris, *The Lady Was a Bishop*, Collier and Macmillan, New York and London, 1973. Marie de France may have been an abbess of Shaftesbury.

13. Emily James Putnam, *The Lady*, University of Chicago Press, Chicago and London, 1970, p. 118. See also the chapter on the abbess in the same book.

14. From *The Women Troubadours*, trans. and ed. by Meg Bogin, Paddington Press, New York/London, 1976.

15. Friedrich Heer, *The Medieval World: Europe 1100–1350*, Mentor Books, New York, 1963, pp. 167, 178–179.

16. This was Amy Kelly's surmise in "Eleanor of Aquitaine and Her Courts of Love," *Speculum*, 12 (January 1937), 3–19.

17. From *The Book of the Courtier*, by Baldesar Castiglione, a new translation by Charles S. Singleton (New York: Doubleday, 1959), p. 20. Copyright © 1959 by Charles S. Singleton and Edgar de N. Mayhew. This and other quotations throughout the chapter are reprinted by permission of Doubleday & Co., Inc.

18. Selections from the correspondence of Renaissance noblewomen can be found in the biographies listed in the bibliography.

19. An interesting exception is W. Ong's "Latin Language Study as a Renaissance Puberty Rite," *Studies in Philology*, 56 (1959), 103–124; also Margaret Leah King's "The Religious Retreat of Isotta Nogarola (1418–1466)," *Signs*, Summer 1978.

20. Dante Alighieri, *La Vita Nuova*, trans. Barbara Reynolds, Penguin Books, Middlesex, England and Baltimore, 1971, poem 18.

21. Frederick Goldin, trans., *Lyrics of the Troubadours and Trouvères*, Doubleday, New York, 1973, p. 325.

22. David Thompson and Alan F. Nagel, eds. and trans., *The Three Crowns of Florence: Humanist Assessments of Dante, Petrarca, and Boccaccio*, Harper & Row, New York, 1972.

23. For Renaissance humanistic and courtly literature, Vittorio Rossi, *Il quattrocento*, F. Vallardi, Milan, 1933; Ruth Kelso, *Doctrine for the Lady of the Renaissance*, University of Illinois Press, Urbana, 1956. On erotic life, interesting remarks by David Herlihy, "Some Psychological and Social Roots of Violence in the Tuscan Cities," *Violence and Civil Disorder in Italian Cities, 1200–1500*, ed. Lauro Martines, University of California Press, Berkeley, 1972, pp. 129–154.

24. For historical context, Keith Thomas, "The Double Standard," *Journal of the History of Ideas*, 20 (1959), 195–216; N.J. Perella, *The Kiss Sacred and Profane: An Interpretive History of Kiss Symbolism*, University of California Press, Berkeley, 1969; Morton Hunt, *The Natural History of Love*, Funk & Wagnalls, New York, 1967.

25. Fernand Braudel, *The Mediterranean World*, Routledge & Kegan Paul, London, 1973; A. Ventura, *Nobiltà e popolo nella società Veneta*, Laterza, Bari, 1964; Lawrence Stone, *The Crisis of the Aristocracy, 1558–1641*, Clarendon Press, Oxford, 1965.

26. The status of women as related to the distinction of public and private spheres of activity in various societies is a key idea in most of the anthropological studies in *Women, Culture, and Society*, eds. Michelle Zimbalist Rosaldo and Louise Lamphere, Stanford University Press, Stanford, 1974.

PETER BURKE

Worldviews: Some Dominant Traits

A social group, large or small, tends to share certain attitudes—views of God and the cosmos, of nature and human nature, of life and death, space and time, the good and the beautiful. These attitudes may be conscious or unconscious. In a period of controversy people may be extremely conscious of their attitudes to religion or the state, while remaining virtually unaware that they hold a particular conception of space or time, reason or necessity.

It is not easy to write the history of these attitudes. Historians have stalked their quarry from different directions. One group, the Marxists, have concerned themselves with 'ideologies'. Aware of the need to explain as well as to describe ideas, they have sometimes ended by reducing them to weapons in the class struggle.[1] Another group, the French historians of 'collective mentalities', study assumptions and feelings as well as conscious thoughts, but find it difficult to decide where one mentality ends and another begins.[2] In this chapter I shall employ the somewhat more neutral term of 'worldview', while attempting to include what Raymond Williams calls 'structures of feeling' (1961, pp. 64–88), and to avoid the risk inherent in this third approach of providing description without analysis, or remaining at the level of consciously formulated opinions.[3]

In this chapter an attempt is made to move from the immediate environment of the art and literature of the Renaissance to the study of the surrounding society. The assumption behind it is that the relation between

From *The Italian Renaissance: Culture and Society in Italy*, second edition. © 1986, 1999 by Peter Burke.

art and society is not direct but mediated through worldviews. More precisely, there are two assumptions behind the chapter, two hypotheses which need to be tested. In the first place, that worldviews exist, in other words that particular attitudes are associated with particular times, places and social groups, so that it is not misleading to refer to 'Renaissance attitudes', for example, 'Florentine attitudes' or 'clerical attitudes'. In the second place, that these worldviews find their most elaborate expression in art and literature.

These hypotheses are not easy to verify. The sources, which are predominantly literary, are richer for the sixteenth century than for the fifteenth, much richer for Tuscany than for other regions, and in the overwhelming majority of cases the views they express are those of men of what we would call the upper or upper-middle class (the social structure of the period will be discussed below). As in the case of the study of aesthetic taste, it pays to look not only at relatively formal literary works, but also at documents produced in the course of daily life, such as official reports and private letters. To uncover unconscious attitudes the historian has to attempt to read between the lines, using changes in the frequency of certain keywords as evidence of a shift in values.[4]

This account will begin with a summary of some typical views of the cosmos, society and human nature (needless to say, it will be extremely selective). It will end with an attempt to examine general features of the belief system, and signs of change. The quotations will usually come from well-known writers of the period, but the passages have been chosen to illustrate attitudes they shared with their contemporaries.

VIEWS OF THE COSMOS

Views of time and space are especially revealing of the dominant attitudes of a particular culture, precisely because they are rarely conscious and because they are expressed in practice more often than in texts. In his famous study of the religion of Rabelais, the French historian Lucien Febvre emphasized the vague, task-oriented conceptions of time and space in sixteenth-century France, such as the habit of counting in 'Aves', in other words the amount of time it takes to say a 'Hail Mary' (Febvre, 1942, part 2, book 2, ch. 3). Febvre made the French appear, in these respects at least, almost as exotic as the Nuer of the Sudan, who were described at much the same time in an equally classic work by the British anthropologist E. E. Evans-Pritchard (1940, ch. 3).[5] Whatever may have been the assumptions of the Italian peasants of this period, the evidence from the towns suggests that much more precise attitudes to time were widespread, like the mechanical clocks which both expressed these new attitudes and encouraged them. From the late fourteenth century, mechanical clocks came into use; a famous one was constructed at Padua to the design of Giovanni Dondi, a physician-astronomer who was a friend of Petrarch, and completed in 1364. About 1450, a clock was made for the town hall at Bologna; in 1478, another for the Castello Sforzesco in Milan; in 1499; another for Piazza San Marco in Venice, and so on. By the late fifteenth century, portable clocks were coming in. In Filarete's utopia, the schools for boys and girls had an alarm clock (*svegliatoio*) in each dormitory. This idea at least was not purely utopian, for in Milan in 1463 the astrologer Giacomo da Piacenza had an alarm clock by his bed (Cipolla, 1967; Wendorff, 1980, pp. 151f; Landes, 1983, pp. 53f).

There is an obvious parallel between the new conception of time and the new conception of space; both came to be seen as precisely measurable. Mechanical clocks and pictorial perspective were developed in the same culture, and Brunelleschi was interested in both. The paintings of Uccello and Piero della Francesca (who wrote a treatise on mathematics) are the work of men interested in precise measurement working for a public with similar interests. Fifteenth-century narrative paintings are located in a more precise space and time than their medieval analogues.[6]

Changing views of time and space seem to have coexisted with a traditional view of the cosmos. This view, memorably expressed in Dante's *Divine Comedy*, was shared in essentials by his sixteenth-century commentators, who drew on the same classical tradition, especially the writings of two Greeks, the astronomer-geographer Ptolemy and the philosopher Aristotle. According to this tradition, the fundamental distinction was that between Heaven and Earth.

'Heaven' should really be in the plural. In the centre of the universe was the earth, surrounded by seven 'spheres' or 'heavens', in each of which moved a planet: Moon, Mercury, Venus, Sun, Mars, Jupiter and Saturn. The planets were each moved by an 'intelligence', a celestial driver often equated with the appropriate classical god or goddess. This fusion of planets and deities had permitted the survival of the pagan gods into the Middle Ages (Seznec, 1940).

The importance of the planets resided in their 'influences'. As they sang in a Carnival song by Lorenzo de'Medici, 'from us come all good and evil things'. Different professions, psychological types, parts of the body and even days of the week were influenced by different planets (Sunday by the Sun, Monday by the Moon, and so on). Vasari offered an astrological explanation of artistic creativity in his life of Leonardo, remarking that 'The

greatest gifts may be seen raining on human bodies from celestial influences.'
To explain the past or discover what the future has in store, it was normal to
consult specialists who calculated the configuration of the heavens at a
particular time. The humanist physician Girolamo Fracastoro gave an
account of the outbreak of syphilis in Europe in terms of a conjunction of the
planets Saturn, Jupiter and Mars in the sign of Cancer. The philosopher
Marsilio Ficino believed that the 'spirit' of each planet could be captured by
means of appropriate music or voices ('martial' voices for Mars and so on),
and by making an appropriate 'talisman' (an image engraved on a precious
stone under a favourable constellation) (Walker, 1958, p. 17).

These beliefs had considerable 'influence' on the arts. Aby Warburg's
iconographical analysis of frescos in the Palazzo Schifanoia in Ferrara
showed that they represented the signs of the zodiac and their divisions into
thirty-six 'decans' (Warburg, 1932, 1966). The Florentine patrician Filippo
Strozzi consulted 'a man learned in astrology' to ensure a good constellation
before having the foundations of the Palazzo Strozzi laid on 6 August 1489,
just as the treatises of Alberti and Filarete recommended (Goldthwaite, 1980,
pp. 84–5). When a Florentine committee was discussing where to place
Michelangelo's *David*, one speaker suggested that it should replace
Donatello's *Judith*, which was 'erected under an evil star' (Gaye, 1839–40,
vol. 2, p. 456; Klein and Zerner, 1966, p. 41). Raphael's patron, the papal
banker Agostino Chigi, was interested in astrology and some of the paintings
he commissioned refer to his horoscope (Saxl, 1934).

Astrology was permitted by the Church; it was not considered
incompatible with Christianity. As Lorenzo de'Medici put it, 'Jupiter is a
planet which moves only its own sphere, but there is a higher power which
moves Jupiter' (D'Ancona, 1872, p. 264). The twelve signs of the zodiac were
associated with the twelve apostles. A number of popes took an interest in the
stars. Paul III, for example, summoned to Rome the astrologer who had
predicted his election (Luca Gaurico, whose brother Pomponio's treatise on
sculpture has already been quoted), and gave him a bishopric. Yet there was
a sense in which theology and astrology formed two systems which in
practice competed with each other. The saints presided over certain days; so
did the planets. People might take their problems to a priest or to an
astrologer. It was largely on religious grounds that some leading figures of
the period rejected astrology, notably Pico della Mirandola (who declared
that 'astrology offers no help in discovering what a man should do and what
avoid'), and fra Girolamo Savonarola.[7]

Above the seven heavens and beyond the sphere of the 'fixed stars',
God was to be found. In the writing of the period, God was indeed almost

everywhere. Even commercial documents might begin with the monogram YHS, standing for 'Jesus the Saviour of Mankind' (*Jesus Hominum Salvator*). When disaster struck, it was commonly interpreted as a sign of God's anger. 'It pleased God to chastise us' is how the Florentine apothecary Luca Landucci comments on the plague. When the French invasion of 1494 left Florence virtually unharmed, Landucci wrote that 'God never removed His hand from off our head.'[8] The name of God constantly recurs in private letters, like those of the Florentine lady Alessandra Macinghi degli Strozzi: 'Please God free everything from this plague ... it is necessary to accept with patience whatever God wants ... God give them a safe journey', and so on. Even Machiavelli ends a letter to his family 'Christ keep you all.'[9]

Of all the ways in which Christians have imagined God, two seem particularly characteristic of the period. The emphasis on the sweetness of God and the 'pathetic tenderness' of attitudes to Christ, which the great Dutch historian Johan Huizinga (1919, ch. 14) noted in France and The Netherlands in the fifteenth century, can be found in Italy as well. Savonarola, for example, addresses Christ with endearments such as 'my dear Lord [*signor mio caro*]', or even 'sweet spouse [*dolce sposo*]'. Christocentric devotion seems to have been spread by the friars, not only the Dominican Savonarola but the Franciscans Bernardino da Siena, who encouraged the cult of the name of Jesus, and Bernardino da Feltre, who was responsible for the foundation of a number of fraternities dedicated to Corpus Christi, the body of Christ. The *Meditations on the Passion* attributed to the Franciscan saint Bonaventura were something of a bestseller in fifteenth-century Italy, and so was the *Imitation of Christ*, a devotional text from the fourteenth-century Netherlands.[10]

This image of a sweet and human saviour coexisted with a more detached view of God as the creator of the universe, its 'most beautiful architect [*bellissimo architetto*]' as Lorenzo de'Medici once called him, or the head of the firm (D'Ancona, 1872, p. 267). Leonardo da Vinci addressed God as you who 'sell us every good thing for the price of labour'. Giannozzo Manetti, a Florentine merchant and scholar, liked to compare God to 'the master of a business who gives money to his treasurer and requires him to render an account as to how it may have been spent'.[11] He has transposed the Gospel parable of the talents from its original setting, that of a landlord and his steward, to a more commercial environment. Thus Renaissance Italians projected their own concerns on to the supernatural world.

The lower, 'sublunary' world on which man lived was believed to be composed of four elements—earth, water, air and fire—as illustrated in Vasari's *Room of the Elements* in the Palazzo Vecchio in Florence. The elements were themselves composed of the four 'contraries'—hot, cold, moist and dry.

There were also four levels of earthly existence—human, animal, vegetable and mineral. This is what has been called the 'great chain of being' (Lovejoy, 1936). The 'ladder' of being might be a better term because it makes the underlying hierarchy more evident. Stones were at the bottom of the ladder because they lacked souls. Then came plants, which had what Aristotle called 'vegetative souls', animals, which had 'sensitive souls' (that is, the capacity to receive sensations), and at the top humans, with 'intellectual souls' (in other words, the power of understanding). Animals, vegetables and minerals were arranged in hierarchies; the precious stones were higher than the semi-precious ones, the lion was regarded as the king of beasts, and so on.

More difficult to place on the ladder are the nymphs who wander or flee through the poems of the period; or the wood spirits who lived in lonely places and would eat boys (as the grandmother of the poet Poliziano used to tell him when he was small); or the 'demons' who lived midway between the earth and the moon and could be contacted by magical means (Ficino was one of those who tried). The philosopher Pietro Pomponazzi doubted whether demons existed at all.[12] It seems, however, that he was expressing a minority view. When reading the poems of the period or looking at Botticelli's *Primavera*, it is worth bearing in mind that the supernatural figures represented in them were viewed as part of the population of the universe and not mere figments of the artist's imagination.

The status of another earthly power is even more doubtful. Two common images of Fortune associated it, or rather her, with the winds and with a wheel. The wind image seems to be distinctively Italian. The phrase 'fortune of the sea' (*fortuna di mare*) meant a tempest, a vivid example of a change in affairs which is both sudden and uncontrollable. The Rucellai family, Florentine patricians, used the device of a sail, still to be seen on the façade of their church of Santa Maria Novella in Florence; here the wind represents Fortune and the sail, the power of the individual to adapt to circumstances and to manage them (Warburg, 1966, pp. 213–46; Gilbert, 1949). The second image of Fortune was the well-known classical one of the goddess with a forelock which must be seized quickly, because she is bald behind. In the twenty-fifth chapter of his *Prince*, Machiavelli recommended impetuosity on the grounds that Fortune is a woman, 'and to keep her under it is necessary to strike her and beat her [*è necessario volendola tenere sotto, batterla e urtarla*]', while his friend the historian Francesco Guicciardini suggested that it is dangerous to try to make conspiracies foolproof because 'Fortune, who plays such a large part in all matters, becomes angry with those who try to limit her dominion.' It is hard for a modern reader to tell in these instances whether the goddess has been introduced simply to make more memorable conclusions arrived at by other means, or whether she has taken over the argument; whether she is a literary device, or a serious (or at any rate a half-serious) way of describing whatever lies outside human control.[13]

To understand and manipulate the world of earth, several techniques were available, including alchemy, magic and witchcraft. Their intellectual presuppositions need to be discussed.

Alchemy depended on the idea that there is a hierarchy of metals, with gold as the noblest, and also that the 'social mobility' of metals is possible. It was related to astrology because each of the seven metals was associated with one of the planets: gold with the Sun, silver with the Moon, mercury with Mercury, iron with Mars, lead with Saturn, tin with Jupiter and copper with Venus. It was also related to medicine because the 'philosopher's stone' which the alchemists were looking for was also the cure for all illnesses, the 'universal panacea'.

Jacob Burckhardt (1944, p. 334) believed that alchemy 'played only a very subordinate part' in Italy in the fifteenth and sixteenth centuries. It is dangerous to make general assertions about the popularity of such a deliberately esoteric subject as alchemy, but the odds are that he was wrong. The Venetian Council of Ten took it more seriously when they issued a decree against it in 1488. Several Italian treatises on the subject from the later part of our period have survived. The most famous is a Latin poem, published in 1515 and dedicated to Leo X, Giovanni Augurello's *Chrysopoeia*; there is a story that the pope rewarded the poet with an empty purse. A certain 'J. A. Pantheus', priest of Venice, also dedicated an alchemical work to Leo before inventing a new subject, 'cabala of metals', which he carefully distinguished from alchemy, perhaps because the Council of Ten were still hostile. On the other hand, some people treated the claims of the alchemists with scepticism. St Antonino, the fifteenth-century archbishop of Florence, held that the transmutation of metals was beyond human power, while the Sienese metallurgist Vannoccio Biringuccio suggested that it was 'a vain wish and fanciful dream' and that the adepts of alchemy, 'more inflamed than the very coals in their furnaces' with the desire to create gold, ought to go mining instead as he did.[14]

There are only a few tantalizing indications of the possible relation between alchemy and art and literature. Alchemy had its own symbolic system, possibly adopted as a kind of code, in which, for example, a fountain stood for the purification of metals, Christ for the philosopher's stone, marriage for the union of sulphur and mercury, a dragon for fire. To complicate matters, some writers used alchemical imagery as symbols of something else (religious truths, for example). The *Dream of Polyphilus*, an anonymous esoteric romance published in Venice in 1499, makes use of a number of these symbols, and it is possible that this love story has an alchemical level of meaning. Vasari tells us that Parmigianino gave up painting for the study of alchemy, and it has been suggested that his paintings make use of alchemical symbolism (Fagioli Dell'Arco, 1970). Unfortunately, the fact that alchemists used a number of common symbols (while giving them uncommon interpretations) makes the suggestion impossible to verify.

Magic was discussed more openly than alchemy, at least in its white form; for, as Pico della Mirandola put it:

> Magic has two forms, one of which depends entirely on the work and authority of demons, a thing to be abhorred, so help me the god of truth, and a monstrous thing. The other, when it is rightly pursued, is nothing else than the utter perfection of natural philosophy ... as the former makes man the bound slave of wicked powers, so does the latter make him their ruler and lord. (Cassirer et al., 1948, pp. 246f)

It should be noted that Pico believed in the efficacy of the black magic he condemns.

From a comparative point of view it might be useful to define magic, cross-culturally, as the attempt to produce material changes in the world as the result of performing certain rituals and writing or uttering certain verbal formulas ('spells', 'charms' or 'incantations') requesting or demanding that these changes take place. It would follow from this definition that the most influential group of magicians in Renaissance Italy were the Catholic clergy, since they claimed in this period that their rituals, images and prayers could cure the sick, avert storms and so on.[15]

From the point of view of contemporaries, however, the distinction between religion and magic was an important one. The Church—or, to be more sociologically exact, the more highly educated clergy—generally regarded magic with suspicion. Books of spells were burned in public by San Bernardino of Siena and also by Savonarola. It would be too cynical to explain this opposition to magic (and in some cases, as we have seen, to astrology) merely in terms of rivalry and competition. There were other grounds for clerical suspicion. Magic could be black for two reasons. First, it could be destructive as well as productive or protective.

Secondly, the magician might employ the services of evil spirits. Thus Giovanni Fontana, a fifteenth-century Venetian who made a number of mechanical devices to produce spectacular effects, gained the reputation of a necromancer who received assistance from spirits from hell, just as John Dee gained a sinister reputation in sixteenth-century Cambridge as a result of the too successful 'effects' he contrived for a performance of Aristophanes. No doubt many of their contemporaries viewed Brunelleschi and Leonardo in a similar light. At a more learned level, the philosopher Agostino Nifo argued that the marvels of magic showed that—contrary to Aristotle's belief—demons really existed.

The literature of the period is steeped in magic. Romances of chivalry, for example, are full of sorcerers and of objects with magical powers. In Ariosto's *Orlando Furioso*, the magician Merlino and the enchantress Alcina play an important part. Angelica has a magic ring; Astolfo is turned into a tree; Atlante's castle is the home of enchantment, and so on. We should imagine the book's first readers as people who, if they did not always take magic too seriously, did not take it too lightly either. They believed in its possibility. In the same milieu as Ariosto, at the court of Ferrara, Dosso Dossi painted a picture of Circe, the enchantress of the *Odyssey*, who attracted much interest in Renaissance Italy.

One reason for this interest in Circe is that she was taken to be a witch, notably by Gianfrancesco Pico della Mirandola (the nephew of the universal man), who published a dialogue on witchcraft in 1523 in which he made considerable use of the testimony of ancient writers such as Homer and Virgil.[16] Witchcraft was the poor man's magic, or rather the poor woman's; that is, a considerable proportion of the elite of educated men distinguished magic from witchcraft and associated the latter with poor women who were supposed to have made a pact with the devil, to have been given the power to do harm by supernatural means but without study, to fly through the air and to attend nocturnal orgies called 'sabbaths'.[17] Particularly vulnerable to these accusations were those villagers, male and female, who were called in by their neighbours to find lost objects by supernatural means or to heal sick people and animals. 'Who knows how to cure illness knows how to cause it [*Qui scit sanare scit destruere*]' went a proverb current at the time.[18] It is more difficult to say whether the neighbours thought that these powers were or were not diabolical, and hardest of all to reconstruct what the accused thought she or he was doing. In Rome in 1427, two women confessed that they turned into cats, murdered children and sucked their blood; but the record does not tell us, in this case as in the majority of trials, what pressure had been brought to bear on the accused beforehand.

An illuminating exception is the case of a certain Chiara Signorini, a peasant woman from the Modena area, accused of witchcraft in 1520. She and her husband had been expelled from their holding, whereupon the lady who owned the land had fallen ill. Chiara offered to cure her on condition that the couple were allowed to return. A witness claimed to have seen Chiara place at the door of the victim's house 'fragments of an olive tree in the form of a cross ... a fragment of the bone of a dead man ... and an alb of silk, believed to have been dipped in chrism'. When Chiara was interrogated, she described visions of the Blessed Virgin, which her interrogator attempted to interpret as a diabolical figure. After torture, Chiara agreed that the devil had appeared to her, but she would not admit to having attended a 'sabbath'. The use of the cross and the holy oil, like the vision of the Blessed Virgin, may well be significant. Some of the 'spells' which inquisitors confiscated took the form of prayers. What one group views as witchcraft, another may take to be religion. In this conflict of interpretations, it was the interrogator, backed by his instruments of torture, who had the last word (Ginzburg, 1961).

Nevertheless, a few writers did express scepticism about the efficacy of magic and witchcraft. The humanist lawyer Andrea Alciato, for example, suggested (as Montaigne was to do) that so-called witches suffered from hallucinations of night flight and so on and deserved medicine rather than punishment (Hansen, 1901, pp. 310f). The physician Girolamo Cardano pointed out that the accused confessed to whatever the interrogators suggested to them, simply in order to bring their tortures to an end.[19] Pietro Pomponazzi, who taught the philosophy of Aristotle at the University of Padua, argued in his book *On Incantations* that the common people simply attributed to demons actions which they did not understand. He offered naturalistic explanations of apparently supernatural phenomena such as the extraction of arrows by means of incantations and the cure of the skin disease called 'the king's evil' by virtue of the royal touch. Pomponazzi held similar views about some of the miracles recorded in the Bible and about cures by means of relics, arguing that the cures may have been due to the faith of the patients, and that dogs' bones would have done just as well as the bones of the saints. It is not surprising to find that this book, which undermined the Church's distinction between religion and magic, was not published in the philosopher's lifetime.[20]

VIEWS OF SOCIETY

The first thing to say about 'society' in Renaissance Italy is that the concept did not yet exist. It was not until the later seventeenth century that a general term began to be used (in Italian as in English, French and German) to describe the whole social system. A good deal was said and written, however, about various forms of government and social groups, and about the differences between the present and the past.[21]

In Italy as in other parts of Europe, a recurrent image, which goes back to Plato and Aristotle, was that of the 'body politic' (*corpo politico*). It was more than a metaphor. The analogy between the human body and the political body was taken seriously by many people and it underlay many more specific arguments. Thus a character in Castiglione's *Courtier* could defend monarchy as a 'more natural form of government' because 'in our body, all the members obey the rule of the heart'.[22] The ruler was often described as the 'physician' of this body politic, a commonplace which sometimes makes its appearance even in a writer as original and as deliberately shocking as Machiavelli, who wrote in the third chapter of *The Prince* that political disorders begin by being difficult to diagnose but easy to cure, and end up easy to diagnose and difficult to cure.

However, in Italy this 'natural' or 'organic' language of politics was less dominant than elsewhere. A rival concept to the 'body politic', that of 'the state' (*lo stato*) was developing, with a range of reference which included public welfare, the constitution and the power structure. One character in Alberti's dialogue on the family declares that 'I do not want to consider the state as if it were my own property, to think of it as my shop [*ascrivermi to stato quasi per mia ricchezza, riputarlo mia bottega*].'[23] 'If I let a mere subject marry my daughter', says the emperor Constantine in a play written by Lorenzo de'Medici, *Saints John and Paul*, 'I will put the state into great danger [*in gran pericolo metto / Lo stato*].' Machiavelli uses the term 115 times in his *Prince* (and only in five cases in the traditional sense of the 'state of affairs') (D'Ancona, 1872, p. 244; Hexter, 1973, ch. 3; Rubinstein, 1971).

The existence within the peninsula of both republics and principalities made people unusually aware that the political system (*governo, reggimento*) was not god-given but man-made and that it could be changed. In a famous passage of his *History of Italy*, Francesco Guicciardini reports the discussions which took place in Florence after the flight of the Medici in 1494 about the relative merits of oligarchy (*governo ristretto*), democracy (*governo universale*) or a compromise between the two.[24] This awareness of the malleability of institutions is central to the contemporary literature on the ideal city-state. The treatises on architecture by Alberti and Filarete sketch social as well as architectural utopias. Leonardo's designs for an imaginary city express the same awareness that it is possible for social life to be planned (Garin, 1963; Bauer, 1965). Machiavelli offers a quite explicit discussion of political innovation (*innovazione*). In Florence between 1494 and 1530 the many reports and discussions of political problems which have survived show that the new language of politics, and the awareness of alternatives it implied, was not confined to Machiavelli and Guicciardini but was much more widespread. It was this awareness which Jacob Burckhardt emphasized and discussed in his *Civilization of the Renaissance in Italy*, in his chapter on 'The State as a Work of Art [*Der Staat als Kunstwerk*]'.[25]

Awareness of differences in social status seems also to have been unusually acute in Italy; at least, the vocabulary for describing these differences was unusually elaborate. The medieval view of society as consisting of three groups—those who pray, those who fight and those who work the soil—was not one which appealed to the inhabitants of Italian cities, most of whom performed none of these functions (Duby, 1978; Niccoli, 1979). Their model of society was differentiated not by functions but by grades (*generazioni*) and it probably developed out of the classification of citizens for tax purposes into rich, middling and poor. The phrases 'fat people' (*popolo grasso*) and 'little people' (*popolo minuto*) were commonly used, especially in Florence, and it is not difficult to find instances of a term like 'middle class' (*mediocri*).[26] However, contemporaries did not think exclusively in terms of income groups. They differentiated families and individuals according to whether they were or were not noble (*nobili*, *gentilhuomini*); whether or not they were citizens (*cittadini*), in possession of political rights; and whether they were members of the greater or lesser guilds. One of the most important but also one of the most elusive items in their social vocabulary was *popolare*, because it varied in significance according to the speaker. If he came from the upper levels of society, he was likely to use it as a pejorative term to denote all ordinary people. At the middle level, on the other hand, a greater effort was made to distinguish the popolo, who enjoyed political rights, from the *plebe*, which did not. The point of view of these 'plebs' has gone unrecorded (F. Gilbert, 1965, pp. 19f; cf. Cohn, 1980, ch. 3).

Awareness of the structure of society and of potentially different structures is also revealed in discussions of the definition of nobility, whether based on birth or individual worth, which are relatively frequent in the period, from the treatise of the Florentine jurist Lapo da Castiglionchio (written before 1381) and Poggio Bracciolini's dialogue *On True Nobility* to the debate in Castiglione's *Courtier*. This discussion needs to be placed in the context of political and social conflict in Florence and elsewhere, but it is also related to contemporary concern with the value of the individual (below, p. 197).

Renaissance Italy was also remarkable for a view of the past taken by some artists and humanists, a view which was possibly more widespread. With the idea of the malleability of institutions, already discussed, went an awareness of change over time, a sense of anachronism. The term 'anachronism' is literally speaking an anachronism because the word did not yet exist, but in his famous critique of the authenticity of the document known as the *Donation of Constantine*, the humanist Lorenzo Valla did point out that the text contained expressions from a later period. He was well aware that 'modes of speech' (*stilus loquendi*) were subject to change, that language had a history.[27] Another fifteenth-century humanist, Flavio Biondo, argued that Italian and other romance languages had developed out of Latin. Biondo also wrote a book called *Rome Restored*, in which he tried to reconstruct classical Rome on the basis of literary evidence as well as the surviving remains. In another book he discussed the private life of the Romans, the clothes they wore and the way in which they brought up their children (Weiss, 1969).

By the later fifteenth century, this antiquarian sensibility had become fashionable and had begun to affect the arts. In the *Dream of Polyphilus*, the Venetian romance already mentioned, the lover searches for his beloved in a landscape of temples, tombs and obelisks and even the language is a consciously archaic Latinate Italian (Mitchell, 1960). Among the artists whose work illustrates the growing interest in antiquarianism are Mantegna and Giulio Romano. Like his master and father-in-law Jacopo Bellini, Mantegna was extremely interested in copying ancient coins and inscriptions. He was a friend of humanists such as Felice Feliciano of Verona. His reconstructions of ancient Rome in the *Triumphs of Caesar* or the painting of Scipio introducing the cult of the Cybele are the pictorial equivalents of Biondo's patient work of historical reconstruction (Saxl, 1957, pp. 150–60). As for Giulio Romano, his painting of Constantine in battle draws heavily on the evidence of Trajan's Column, as Vasari pointed out in his life of the artist, 'for the costumes of the soldiers, the armour, ensigns, bastions, stockades, battering rams and all the other instruments of war'.

Vasari himself shared this sense of the past. His *Lives* are organized around the idea of development in time, from Cimabue to Michelangelo. He believed in progress in the arts, at least up to a point, but he also believed that individual artists ought to be judged by the standards of their own day, and he explained that 'my intention has always been to praise not absolutely but, as the saying goes, relatively [*non semplicemente ma, come s'usa dire, secondo che*], having regard to place, time, and other similar circumstances' (Panofsky, 1955, pp. 169–225).

Another material sign of the awareness of the past is the fake antique, which seems to have been a fifteenth-century innovation. The young Michelangelo made a faun, a Cupid and a Bacchus in the classical style. He was essentially competing with antiquity, but by the early sixteenth century the faking of classical sculptures and Roman coins was a flourishing industry in Venice and Padua. This response to two new trends, the fashion for ancient Rome and the rise of the art market, depended—like the detecting of the fakes—on a sense of period style (Kurz, 1967).

This new sense of the past is one of the most distinctive but also one of the most paradoxical features of the period. Classical antiquity was studied in order to imitate it more faithfully, but the closer it was studied, the less imitation seemed either possible or desirable. 'How mistaken are those', wrote Francesco Guicciardini, 'who quote the Romans at every step. One would have to have a city with exactly the same conditions as theirs and then act according to their example. That model is as unsuitable for those lacking the right qualities as it would be useless to expect an ass to run like a horse.'[28] However, many people did quote the Romans at every step; Guicciardini's friend Machiavelli was one of them.

Another paradox was that at a time when Italian culture was strongly marked by the propensity to innovate, innovation was generally considered a bad thing. In political debates in Florence, it was taken for granted that 'new ways' (*modi nuovi*) were undesirable, and that 'every change takes reputation from the city' (Gilbert, 1957). In Guicciardini's *History of Italy*, the term 'change' (*mutazione*) seems to be used in a pejorative sense, and when a man is described, like Pope Julius II, as 'desirous of new things [*desideroso di cose nuove*]' the overtones of disapproval are distinctly audible. Innovation in the arts was doubtless less dangerous, but it was rarely admitted to be innovation. It was generally perceived as a return to the past. When Filarete praises Renaissance architecture and condemns the Gothic, it is the latter which he calls 'modern [*moderno*]'. It is only at the end of the period that one can find someone (Vasari, for example), cheerfully admitting to being *moderno* himself (above p. 15).

VIEWS OF MAN

Classical views of the physical constitution of man, and the distinction between four personality types (choleric, sanguine, phlegmatic and melancholy), were taken seriously by writers in this period, which was an important one in the history of medicine (Park, 1985; Siraisi, 1997). These views are not without relevance to the arts. Ficino, for example, joined the suggestion (which comes from a text attributed to Aristotle) that all great men are melancholics to Plato's concept of inspiration as divine frenzy, and argued that creative people (*ingeniosi*) were melancholic and even 'frantic' (*furiosi*). He was thinking of poets in particular, but Vasari applied his doctrine to artists and so helped create the modern myth of the bohemian (Klibansky et al., 1964; cf. p. 84 above).

However, the major theme of this section is inevitably one which contemporaries did not discuss in treatises but which was discovered (or, as some critics would say, invented) by Jacob Burckhardt: Renaissance individualism. 'In the Middle Ages,' wrote Burckhardt (1944, p. 81), in one of the most frequently quoted passages of his essay, '... Man was conscious of himself only as a member of a race, people, party, family or corporation, only through some general category. In Italy this veil first melted into air ... man became a spiritual *individual*, and recognized himself as such.' He went on to discuss the passion for fame and its corrective, the new sense of ridicule, all under the general rubric of 'the development of the individual'. For the use of this 'blanket term', he has been severely criticized (Nelson, 1933). As it happens, Burckhardt came to be rather sceptical about the interpretation he had launched, and towards the end of his life he confessed to an acquaintance that 'You know, so far as individualism is concerned, I hardly believe in it any more, but I don't say so; it gives people so much pleasure.'[29]

The objections are difficult to gainsay, since urban Italians of this period were very much conscious of themselves as members of families or corporations (Weissman, 1985; Burke, 1992b). And yet we need the idea of individualism, or something like it. The idea of the self, as the anthropologist Marcel Mauss pointed out more than half a century ago, is not natural. It is a social construct, and it has a social history.[30] Indeed, the concept of person current (indeed, taken for granted) in a particular culture needs to be understood if we are to comprehend that culture, and as another anthropologist, Clifford Geertz, has suggested, it is a good way into that culture for an outsider (Geertz, 1983, pp. 59–70; cf. Carrithers et al., 1985, Burke, 1992b).

If we ask about the concept of person current—among elites, at least—in Renaissance Italy, we may find it useful to distinguish the self-consciousness with which Burckhardt was particularly concerned from self-assertiveness, and both from the idea of the unique individual.[31]

The idea of the uniqueness of the individual goes with that of a personal style in painting or writing, an idea which has been discussed already (p. 23). At the court of Urbino, the poet Bernardo Accolti went by the nickname *L'unico Aretino*. The poet Vittoria Colonna described

Michelangelo as *unico*. An anonymous Milanese poem declares that just as there is only one God in Heaven, so there is only one 'Moro' (Lodovico Sforza) on earth. In his biographies, the bookseller Vespasiano da Bisticci often refers to men as 'singular' (*singolare*).

There is rather more to say about self-assertion. Burckhardt (1944, pp. 87f) argued that the craving for fame was a new phenomenon in the Renaissance. The Dutch historian Huizinga (1919, ch. 4) retorted that on the contrary, it was 'essentially the same as the chivalrous ambition of earlier times'. The romances of chivalry do indeed suggest that the desire for fame was one of the leading motives of medieval knights, so what Burckhardt noticed may have been no more than the demilitarization of glory. However, it is remarkable quite how often self-assertion words occur in the Italian literature of this period. Among them we find 'competition' (*concertazione*, *concorrenza*); 'emulation' (*emulazione*); 'glory' (*gloria*); 'envy' (*invidia*); 'honour' (*onore*); 'shame' (*vergogna*); 'valour' (*valore*); and, hardest of all to translate, a concept of great importance in the period referring to personal worth, which we have already met when discussing its complementary opposite, fortune: *virtù* (see Gilbert, 1951). Psychologists would say that if words of this kind occur with unusual frequency in a particular text, as they do, for example, in the dialogue on the family by the humanist Leon Battista Alberti, then its author is likely to have had an above-average achievement drive, which in Alberti's case his career does nothing to refute. That the Florentines in general were unusually concerned with achievement is suggested by the *novelle* of the period, which often deal with the humiliation of a rival (see Rotunda, 1942); by the institutionalization of competitions between artists; by the sharp tongues and the envy in the artistic community, as recorded by Vasari, notably in his life of Castagno; and, not least, by the remarkable creative record of that city.

At any rate self-assertion was an important part of the Tuscan image of man. The humanists Bruni and Alberti both described life as a race. Bruni wrote that some 'do not run in the race, or when they start, become tired and give up half way'; Alberti, that life was a regatta in which there were only a few prizes: 'Thus in the race and competition for honour and glory in the life of man it seems to me very useful to provide oneself with a good ship and to give an opportunity to one's powers and ability [*alle forze e ingegno tuo*], and with this to sweat to be the first.'[32] Leonardo da Vinci recommended artists to draw in company because 'a sound envy' would act as a stimulus to do better.[33] For a hostile account of the same kind of struggle, we may turn to the Sienese pope, Pius II (who was not exactly backward in the race to the top), and his complaint that 'In the courts of princes the greatest effort is devoted to pushing others down and climbing up oneself.'[34]

It is not unreasonable to suggest that competition encourages self-consciousness, and it is interesting to discover that the Tuscan evidence for this kind of individualism is once again richer than anything to be found elsewhere. The classic phrase of the Delphic oracle, 'know thyself', quoted by Marsilio Ficino among others, was taken seriously in the period, although it was sometimes given a more worldly interpretation than was originally intended.

The most direct evidence of self-awareness is that of autobiographies, or more exactly (since the modern term 'autobiography' encourages an anachronistic view of the genre) of diaries and journals written in the first person, of which there are about 100 surviving from Florence alone (Bec, 1967; Brucker, 1967; Guglielminetti, 1977; Anselmi et al., 1980). The local name for this kind of literature was *ricordanze*, which might be translated 'memoranda', a suitably vague word for a genre which had something of the account book in it, and something of the city chronicle, and was focused on the family, but none the less reveals something about the individual who wrote it: the apothecary Luca Landucci, for example, who has been quoted more than once in these pages, or Machiavelli's father Bernardo, or the Florentine patrician Giovanni Rucellai, who left a notebook dealing with a variety of subjects, a 'mixed salad' as he called it.[35] Even if these memoranda were not intended to express self-awareness, they may have helped to create it. Rather more personal in style are the autobiographies of Pope Pius II (written, like Caesar's, in the third person, but none the less self-assertive for that), of Guicciardini (a brief but revealing memoir), of the physician Girolamo Cardano (a Lombard, for once, not a Florentine) and of the goldsmith Benvenuto Cellini.

Autobiographies are not the only evidence for the self-consciousness of Renaissance Italians. There are also paintings. Portraits were often hung in family groups and commissioned for family reasons, but self-portraits are another matter. Most of them are not pictures in their own right but representations of the artist in the corner of a painting devoted to something else, like the figure of Benozzo Gozzoli in his fresco of the procession of the Magi, Pinturicchio in the background to his *Annunciation*, or Raphael in his *School of Athens*. In the course of the sixteenth century, however, we find self-portraits in the strict sense by Parmigianino, for example, and Vasari, and more than one by Titian. They remind us of the importance of the mirrors manufactured in this period, in Venice in particular. Mirrors may well have encouraged self-awareness. As the Florentine writer Giambattista Gelli put it in a Carnival song he wrote for the mirror-makers of Florence, 'A mirror allows one to see one's own defects, which are not as easy to see as those of others' (Singleton, 1936, pp. 357f).

Evidence of self-awareness is also provided by the conduct books, of which the most famous are Castiglione's *Courtier* (1528), Giovanni Della Casa's *Galateo* (1558) and the *Civil Conversation* of Stefano Guazzo (1574). All three are manuals for the 'presentation of self in everyday life' as the sociologist Erving Goffman (1959) puts it—instructions in the art of playing one's social role gracefully in public. They inculcate conformity to a code of good manners rather than the expression of a personal style of behaviour, but they are nothing if not self-conscious themselves and they encourage self-consciousness in the reader. Castiglione recommends a certain 'negligence [*sprezzatura*]', to show that 'whatever is said or done has been done without pains and virtually without thought', but he admits that this kind of spontaneity has to be rehearsed. It is the art which conceals art and he goes on to compare the courtier to a painter. The 'grace' (*grazia*) with which he was so much concerned was, as we have seen, a central concept in the art criticism of his time. It is hard to decide whether to call Castiglione a painter among courtiers or his friend Raphael a courtier among painters, but the connections between their two domains are clear enough. The parallel was clear to Giovanni Pico della Mirandola in his famous *Oration on the Dignity of Man*, in which he has God say to man that 'as though the maker or moulder of thyself, thou mayest fashion thyself in whatever shape thou shalt prefer' (Cassirer et al., 1948, p. 225).

The dignity of man was a favourite topic for writers on the 'human condition' (the phrase is theirs, *humana conditio*). It is tempting to take Pico's treatise on the dignity of man to symbolize the Renaissance, and to contrast it with Pope Innocent III's treatise on the misery of man as a symbol of the Middle Ages. However, both the dignity and the misery of man were recognized by writers in both Middle Ages and Renaissance. Many of the arguments for the dignity of man (the beauty of the human body, its upright posture and so on) are commonplaces of the medieval as well as the classical and Renaissance traditions. The themes of dignity and misery were considered as complementary rather than contradictory (Trinkaus, 1970; Craven, 1981). All the same, there does appear to have been a change of emphasis revealing an increasing confidence in man in intellectual circles in the period. Lorenzo Valla, with characteristic boldness, called the soul the 'man-God [*homo deus*]', and wrote of the soul's ascent to heaven in the language of a Roman triumph. Pietro Pomponazzi declared that those (few) men who had managed to achieve almost complete rationality deserved to be numbered among the gods. Adjectives such as 'divine' and 'heroic' were increasingly used to describe painters, princes and other mortals. Alberti had called the ancients 'divine' and Poliziano had coupled Lorenzo de'Medici with Giovanni Pico as 'heroes rather than men', but it is only in the sixteenth century that this heroic language became commonplace. Vasari, for example, described Raphael as a 'mortal god' and wrote of the 'heroes' of the house of Medici. Matteo Bandello referred to the 'heroic house of Gonzaga' and to the 'glorious heroine' Isabella d'Este. Aretino, typically, called himself 'divine'. The famous references to the 'divine Michelangelo' were in danger of devaluation by this inflation of the language of praise (Weise, 1961–5, vol. 1, pp. 79–119).

These ideas of the dignity (indeed divinity) of man had their effect on the arts. Where Pope Innocent III, for example, found the human body disgusting, Renaissance writers admired it, and the humanist Agostino Nifo went so far as to defend the proposition that 'nothing ought to be called beautiful except man'. By 'man' he meant woman, and in particular Jeanne of Aragon. One might have expected paintings of the idealized human body in a society where such views were expressed. The derivation of architectural proportions from the human body (again, idealized) also depended on the assumption of human dignity. Again, at the same time that the term 'heroic' was being overworked in literature, we find the so-called 'grand manner' dominant in art. If we wish to explain changes in artistic taste, we need to look at wider changes in worldviews.

Another image of man, common in the literature of the time, is that of a rational, calculating, prudent animal. 'Reason' (*ragione*) and 'reasonable' (*ragionevole*) are terms which recur, usually with overtones of approval. They are terms with a wide variety of meanings, but the idea of rationality is central. The verb *ragionare* meant 'to talk', but then speech was a sign of rationality which showed man's superiority to animals. One meaning of *ragione* is 'accounts': merchants called their account books *libri della ragione*. Another meaning is 'justice': the Palazzo della Ragione in Padua was not so much the 'Palace of Reason' as the court of law. Justice involved calculation, as the classical and Renaissance image of the scales should remind us. *Ragione* also means 'proportion' or 'ratio'. A famous early definition of perspective, in the life of Brunelleschi attributed to Manetti, called it the science which sets down the differences of size in objects near and far *con ragione*, a phrase which can be (and has been) translated either as 'rationally' or 'in proportion'.

The habit of calculation was central to Italian urban life. Numeracy was relatively widespread, taught at special 'abacus schools' in Florence and elsewhere. A fascination with precise figures is revealed in some thirteenth-century texts, notably the chronicle of fra Salimbene of Parma and Bonvesino della Riva's treatise on 'The Big Things of Milan', which lists the city's fountains, shops and shrines and calculates the number of tons of corn the inhabitants of Milan demolished every day.[36] The evidence for this numerate mentality is even richer in the fourteenth century, as the statistics in Giovanni Villani's chronicle of Florence bear eloquent witness, and richer still in the fifteenth and sixteenth centuries. In Florence and Venice in particular, an interest was taken in statistics of imports and exports, population and prices. Double-entry bookkeeping was widespread. The great *catasto* of 1427, a household-to-household survey of a quarter of a million Tuscans who were then living under Florentine rule, both expressed and encouraged the rise of the numerate mentality (Herlihy and Klapisch-Zuber, 1985). Time was seen as something 'Precious', which must be 'spent' carefully and not 'wasted'; all these terms come from the third book of Alberti's dialogue on the family. In similar fashion, Giovanni Rucellai advised his family to 'be thrifty with time, for it is the most precious thing we have'.[37] Time could be the object of rational planning. The humanist schoolmaster Vittorino da Feltre drew up a timetable for the students. The sculptor Pomponio Gaurico boasted that since he was a boy he had planned his life so as not to waste it in idleness.

With this emphasis on reason, thrift (*masserizia*) and calculation went the regular use of such words as 'prudent' (*prudente*), 'carefully' (*pensatamente*) and 'to foresee' (*antevedere*). The reasonable is often identified with the useful, and a utilitarian approach is characteristic of a number of writers in this period. In Valla's dialogue *On pleasure*, for example, one of the speakers, the humanist Panormita, defends an ethic of utility (*utilitas*). All action—writes this fifteenth-century Jeremy Bentham—is based on calculations of pain and pleasure. Panormita may not represent the author's point of view. What is relevant here, however, is what was thinkable in the period, rather than who exactly thought it. This emphasis on the useful can be found again and again in texts of the period, from Alberti's book on the family to Machiavelli's *Prince*, with its references to the 'utility of the subjects [*utilità de'sudditi*]', and the need to make 'good use' of liberality, compassion and even cruelty. Again, Filarete created in his ideal city of Sforzinda a utilitarian utopia which Bentham would have appreciated, in which the death penalty has been abolished because criminals are more useful to the community if they do hard labour for life, in conditions exactly harsh enough for this punishment to act as an adequate deterrent.[38]

Calculation affected human relationships. The account-book view of man is particularly clear in the reflections of Guicciardini. He advised his family:

Be careful not to do anyone the sort, of favour that cannot be done without at the same time displeasing others. For injured men do not forget offences; in fact, they exaggerate them. Whereas the favoured party will either forget or will deem the favour smaller than it was. Therefore, other things being equal, you lose a great deal more than you gain.[39]

Italians (adult males of the upper classes, at any rate) admitted a concern (unusual for other parts of Europe in the period, whatever may be true of the 'age of capitalism') with controlling themselves and manipulating others. In Alberti's dialogue on the family, the humanist Lionardo suggests that it is good 'to rule and control the passions of the soul', while Guicciardini declared that there is greater pleasure in controlling one's desires (*tenersi le voglie oneste*) than in satisfying them. If self-control is civilization, as the sociologist Norbert Elias suggests in his famous book on *The Civilizing Process*, then even without their art and literature, the Italians of the Renaissance would still have a good claim to be described as the most civilized people in Europe.[40]

TOWARDS THE MECHANIZATION OF THE WORLD PICTURE

It is time to end this necessarily incomplete catalogue of the beliefs of Renaissance Italians, and to try to see their worldview as a whole. One striking feature of this view is the coexistence of many traditional attitudes with others which would seem to be incompatible with them.

Generally speaking, Renaissance Italians, including the elites who dominate this book, lived in a mental universe which was, like that of their medieval ancestors, animate rather than mechanical, moralized rather than neutral and organized in terms of correspondences rather than causes.

A common phrase of the period was that the world is 'an animal'. Leonardo developed this idea in a traditional way when he wrote that 'We can say that the earth has a vegetative soul, and that its flesh is the land, its bones are the structure of the rocks ... its blood is the pools of water ... its breathing and its pulses are the ebb and flow of the sea.'[41] The operations of the universe were personified. Dante's phrase about 'the love that moves the sun and the other stars' was still taken literally. Magnetism was described in similar terms. In the *Dialogues on Love* (1535) of the Jewish physician Leone Ebreo, a work in the neoplatonic tradition of Ficino, one speaker explains that 'the magnet is loved so greatly by the iron, that notwithstanding the size and weight of the iron, it moves and goes to find it'.[42] The discussions of the 'body politic' (above p. 192) fit into this general picture. 'Every republic is like a natural body' as the Florentine theorist Donato Giannotti put it. Writers on architecture draw similar analogies between buildings and animate beings, analogies which are now generally misread as metaphors. Alberti wrote that a building is 'like an animal', and Filarete that 'A building ... wants to be nourished and looked after, and through lack of this it sickens and dies like a man.' Michelangelo went so far as to say that whoever 'is not a good master of the figure and likewise of anatomy' cannot understand anything of architecture because the different parts of a building 'derive from human members'.[43] Not even Frank Lloyd Wright in our own century could match this organic theory of architecture.

The universe was 'moralized' in the sense that its different characteristics were not treated as neutral in the manner of modern scientists. Warmth, for example, was considered to be better in itself than cold, because the warm is 'active and productive'. It was better to be unchangeable (like the heavens) than mutable (like the earth); better to be at rest than to move; better to be a tree than a stone. Another way of making some of these points is to say that the universe was seen to be organized in a hierarchical manner, thus resembling (and also justifying or 'legitimating') the social structure. Filarete compared three social groups—the nobles, the citizens and the peasants—to three kinds of stone, precious, semi-precious and common. In this hierarchical universe it is hardly surprising to find that genres of writing and painting were also graded, with epics and 'histories' at the top and comedies and landscapes towards the bottom. However, more than hierarchy was involved on occasion. 'Prodigies' or 'monsters', in other words extraordinary phenomena, from the birth of deformed children to the appearance of comets in the sky, were interpreted as 'portents', as signs of coming disaster.[44]

The different parts of the universe were related to one another not so much causally, as in the modern world picture, as symbolically, according to what were called 'correspondences'. The most famous of these correspondences was between the 'macrocosm', the universe in general, and the 'microcosm', the little world of man. Astrological medicine depended on these correspondences, between the right eye and the sun, the left eye and the moon, and so on. Numerology played a great part here. The fact that there were seven planets, seven metals and seven days of the week was taken to prove correspondences between them. This elaborate system of correspondences had great advantages for artists and writers. It meant that images and symbols were not 'mere' images and symbols but expressions of the language of the universe and of God its creator. Historical events or individuals might also correspond to one another, since the historical process was often believed to move in cycles rather than to 'progress' steadily in one direction. Charles VIII of France was viewed by Savonarola as a 'Second Charlemagne' and as a 'New Cyrus'; more than the equivalent, almost the reincarnation of the great ruler of Persia (Weinstein, 1970, pp. 145, 166–7). The emperor Charles V was also hailed as the 'Second Charlemagne'. The Florentine poets who wrote of the return of the golden age under Medici rule may well have been doing something more than turning a decoratively flattering or flatteringly decorative phrase. The idea of the Renaissance itself depends on the assumption that history moves in cycles and employs the organic language of 'birth'.

This 'organic mentality' as we may call it, so pervasive was it, met a direct challenge only in the seventeenth century from Descartes, Galileo, Newton and other 'natural philosophers'. The organic model of the cosmos remained dominant in the fifteenth and sixteenth centuries. All the same, a few individuals, at least on occasion, did make use of an alternative model, the mechanical one, which is hardly surprising in a culture which produced engineers such as Mariano Taccola, Francesco di Giorgio Martini and, of course, Leonardo (Gille, 1964). Giovanni Fontana, who wrote on water-clocks among other subjects, once referred to the universe as this 'noble clock', an image which was to become commonplace in the seventeenth and eighteenth centuries. Leonardo da Vinci, whose comparison of the microcosm and the macrocosm has already been quoted, makes regular use of the mechanical model. He described the tendons of the human body as 'mechanical instruments' and the heart too as a 'marvellous instrument'. He also wrote that 'the bird is an instrument operating by mathematical law', a principle underlying his attempts to construct flying-machines.[45] Machiavelli and Guicciardini saw politics in terms of the balance of power. In the twentieth chapter of *The Prince* Machiavelli refers to the time when Italy was 'in a way in equilibrium [*in un certo modo bilanciata*]', while Guicciardini makes the same point at the beginning of his *History of Italy*, observing that at the death of Lorenzo de'Medici, 'Italian affairs were in a sort of equilibrium [*le cose d'Italia in modo bilanciate si mantenessino*]'. The widespread concern with the precise measurement of time and space, discussed earlier in this chapter, fits in better with this mechanical worldview than with the traditional organic one. The mechanization of the world picture was really the work of the seventeenth century, but in Italy at least, the process had begun.[46]

There would seem to be a case for talking about the pluralism of worldviews in Renaissance Italy, a pluralism which may well have been a stimulus to intellectual innovation. Such a coexistence of competing views naturally raises the question of their association with different social groups. The mechanical world picture has sometimes been described as 'bourgeois' (Borkenau, 1934). Was it in fact associated with the bourgeoisie? It will be easier to answer this question after discussing what the bourgeoisie were, and the general shape of the social structure in Renaissance Italy. This is the task of the following chapter.

NOTES

1. Famous examples which are not reductionist are Borkenau (1934) and Mannheim (1952).

2. For an extended discussion of the strengths and weaknesses of this approach, see Burke (1986). F. Gilbert (1957) offers a study of 'Florentine political assumptions' in more or less the French style.

3. The original models for this chapter were Tillyard (1943) and Lewis (1964), modified so as to allow analysis of the kind practised by historians of mentalities and ideologies.

4. A pioneer in the study of what he called 'fashion-words' (*Modewörter*) was Weise (1950, 1961:5).

5. The studies were independent, but both men owed a considerable debt to the ideas of Émile Durkheim.

6. On Piero and the gauging of barrels, see Baxandall (1972), pp. 86f. On space–time in narrative painting, see Francastel (1965).

7. Landucci (1883).

8. A good discussion of astrology can be found in Garin (1976).

9. Strozzi, *Lettere* (1877); Machiavelli, letter of 11 April 1527.

10. Bonaventura went through at least twenty-six editions, and the *Imitation* nine, see Schutte (1980), pp. 18–19.

11. Vespasiano da Bisticci, *Vite di huomini illustri*, p. 375.

12. On demons, see Walker (1958), pp. 45f, and Clark (1997).

13. Guicciardini, *Ricordi*, no. 20; and see Doren (1922). Pitkin (1984) has devoted an entire monograph to Machiavelli's phrase.

14. See Thorndike (1930–58), vol. 4; Biringuccio, *Pirotechnia* (1540), pp. 35f.

15. This argument is developed for England in Thomas (1971), ch. 1. On the use of images, see above pp. 125f.

16. On Pico and the intellectual and social context of his dialogue, see Burke (1977).

17. Fifteenth-century Italian treatises on witchcraft are conveniently collected in Hansen (1901), pp. 17f. Bonomo (1959), although outdated in some respects, remains a useful survey of witch-hunting in Italy.

18. So said a woman at a trial at Modena in 1499, quoted in Ginzburg (1966b), ch. 3. The Latin is, of course, that of the court, not the speaker.

19. Cardano, *De rerum varietate* (1557), p. 567.

20. Pomponazzi, *De incantationibus* (written *c.* 1520; posthumously published 1556).

21. Since this book was first published, two major studies of Renaissance political thought have appeared: Pocock (1975) and Skinner (1978).

22. Castiglione, *Il cortegiano* (1528), book 4, ch. 19. On the body politic in general, see Archambault (1967).

23. Alberti, *I libri della famiglia*, book 3, p. 221.

24. Guicciardini, *Ricordi*, book 1.

25. This point emerges clearly from the major—and somewhat neglected—study by von Albertini (1955).

26. Difficulties in the interpretation of the term *popolo minuto* and its synonyms are discussed by Cohn (1980), p. 69n.

27. For general surveys see Burke (1969, 1994) and Weiss (1969). On Valla, Kelley (1970), ch. 1.

28. Guicciardini, *Ricordi*, no. 110.

29. Burckhardt's Swiss German, not often recorded, is worth repeating. 'Ach wisse Si, mit den Individualismus, i glaub ganz nimmi dra, aber i sag nit; si ban gar a Fraid' (from Werner Kaegi's introduction, to Walser (1932), xxxvii).

30. His lecture of 1938 is reprinted with a valuable commentary in Carrithers et al. (1985) ch. 1–2.

31. Nelson (1933) distinguishes five elements in individualism. Cf. Batkin (1989), Burke (1995).

32. Bruni, *Epistolae*, vol. 1, p. 137; Alberti, *I libri della famiglia*, p. 139.

33. Leonardo da Vinci, *Literary Works*, ed. J. P. Richter. Oxford, 1939, p. 307.

34. Pius II, *De curialium miseriis epistola*, p. 32.

35. Rucellai, *Il zibaldone*.

36. See Murray (1978), pp. 182f, which discusses the 'arithmetical mentality'.

37. Rucellai, *Il zibaldone*, p. 8.

38. Filarete, *Treatise on Architecture*, book 20, pp. 282f.

39. Guicciardini, *Ricordi*, no. 25.

40. See Elias (1939), a book which does not place enough emphasis on the role of the Italians in the process of change he describes and analyses so well.

41. Leonardo da Vinci, *Literary Works*, ed. J. P. Richter. Oxford, 1939, no. 1000.

42. Leone Ebreo, *Dialoghi d'amore*, second dialogue, part 1.

43. Filarete, *Treatise on Architecture* (1965), book 1, pp. 8f; letter of Michelangelo quoted in Ackerman (1970), p. 37.

44. The discussion of 'the prose of the world' in Foucault (1966), ch. 2, has become a classic. For a more thorough analysis, see Ceard (1977).

45. On the coexistence of organic and mechanical modes of thought in Leonardo, see Dijksterhuis (1961), pp. 253–64.

46. Cf. Delumeau (1967), who stresses progress in the capacity for abstraction.

DENYS HAY

The Italian View of Renaissance Italy

A me piace abitar la mia contrada,
Visto ho Toscana, Lombardia, Romagna,
Quel monte che divide e quel che serra
Italia, e un mare e l'altro che la bagna.
Ariosto, *Satira*, III, 57–60

I must begin this brief essay with an apology for a title which may mislead. 'Renaissance,' as here used, is intended to cover a particular period of time— roughly the period between 1300 and 1550. In what follows I shall not be much concerned with the Italian awareness of the cultural innovations which took place in Italy at this time, a subject which has often been discussed and which forms a significant element of such fundamental books as *The Renaissance in Historical Thought*. My theme is different. I propose to examine the way in which some Italians looked at the geographical area in which they lived, at their *patria* in the largest sense of that term.

For most Italians, *patria* meant, not the entire peninsula, but those narrower localities with which they had immediate sentimental and political ties. Yet, however oblivious in practice to the demands of larger loyalties, literate Italians were forever referring to the land as a whole. It is hard to find a poet or historian, or writer of any kind, who does not offer observations or reflections which might be used to illustrate a view of Italy. During the

From *Renaissance Essays*. © 1988 by Denys Hay.

Risorgimento the scholars who promoted unification ransacked earlier literature to demonstrate that there had always been an Italy. And in the Renaissance they found much material. It was, of course, particularly noticeable in the sources for the late fifteenth and early sixteenth centuries, the years of the French invasion of 1494 and the subsequent Italian wars when 'liberty' was destroyed in Italy and many Italians were conscious of this. There is much recent work on this period, and on the reactions of (for example) Machiavelli and Guicciardini to the tortured choices before them, the safety of Florence against the safety of Italy, and how the individual could survive to influence events in those cruel days.[1] But the contemporary material is nearly all polemical. From Petrarch, in *Italia mia*, to the anguished writers who witnessed the campaigns of Charles VIII, Francis I, and Charles V, the picture of Italy as struggling against barbarism is distorted by immediate political purposes, which in the event were to be frustrated. What I intend to present in the following pages are the opinions of a few Italians who considered the land with no such urgency, who were anxious to display Italy without political overtones, Italy as such and not as an ideal or as a programme. I shall summon three witnesses: Dante (writing in the early fourteenth century), Flavio Biondo (mid-fifteenth), Leandro Alberti (mid-sixteenth). I shall indicate summarily their varying approaches and then attempt a few conclusions.

By way of preface we should recall the main features of the public scene in Italy during the two hundred and fifty years spanned by the lives of these men. At the beginning of the period, Italy was emerging from the chaos which had engulfed her with the fall of the Hohenstaufen in 1250; at the end, the country was entering the exhausted peace which followed the domination of the peninsula by Spanish armies. In the interval the emperors had lost all effective power and—after residence at Avignon, after the schism, the councils and Luther—so had the popes, save precariously in the states of the Church where they reigned like princes. From a peak of commercial wealth attained in Dante's day, Italian prosperity had generally and steadily declined until in 1550 it was a shadow of what it had been. But these too are the centuries of the Renaissance in Italy, one aspect of which was a heightened understanding of *Italianità*, of the uniqueness and value of Italy. The authors discussed below were not directly concerned to promote such an understanding but their works contributed to its development and reflect changes in cultural emphasis.

The work of Dante is rich in Italian reflections, not least in the *La divina commedia*, where there are many glancing references to the land, both affectionate and contemptuous. In one of his Latin works, the *De vulgari eloquentia* (c. 1305), he deliberately surveyed the scene in a dispassionate fashion, giving us a personal view of the map of Italy.[2] This work was, of course, intended not as a geographical or chorographical manual, but as a survey of the Romance languages and a guide to writers in 'il bel paese là dove il sì suono.' In the course of his remarkable analysis, the earliest and for ages the only scientific treatise on linguistics, Dante made several observations which reveal his way of apprehending Italy. In reading these portions of the *De vulgari eloquentia* it is important to remember that the author had before him, perhaps literally but most certainly in his mind, a map of the kind associated with Pietro Vesconte.[3] This displayed the peninsula as part of a circular world-map, with Jerusalem in the centre and Asia in the top half. Europe was depicted in the lower quarter on the left, separated by the Mediterranean from Africa in the lower quarter on the right. This arrangement—deriving from ancient sources and reflected in the medieval 'T & O' diagrams—meant that Italy was drawn with the Alps at the bottom left and the toe at the upper right. Dante's references to left and right are accordingly the reverse of later practice.

In discussing the Italian language Dante touches twice on the peninsula as a whole, in chapters ix and x of book I. To illustrate the linguistic variations of Italy he compares:

> the speech of the right side of Italy with that of the left: the Paduans talk differently from the Pisans. Neighbours have different speech: the Milanese differ from the Veronese, the Romans from the Florentines. Even peoples who are of one race are disparate: the Neapolitans and the men of Gaeta, for instance, or the people of Ravenna and those of Faenza.[4]

In a later passage he surveys the peninsula more systematically:

> Italy is divided into two parts, a right side and a left. If you ask about the dividing line I will briefly reply that this is the range of the Appenines, which, like the sloping ridge of a roof,[5] divides the waters running down, channelling them now to one shore and now to the other, as Lucan describes in the second book [of the *Pharsalia*]. The right side drains into the Tyrrhenian sea, the left into the Adriatic. The regions of the right are: Apulia (though not all of it), Rome, the duchy of Spoleto, Tuscany, the March of Genoa. Those of the left are: part of Apulia, the March of Ancona, Romagna, Lombardy, the March of Treviso with Venice.

Friuli and Istria thus have to belong to the left of Italy and the
Tyrrhenian islands, Sicily and Sardinia, belong to or rather are
naturally to be associated with the right of Italy.[6]

Dante goes on to point out that each of these regions had a distinct language;
there were at least fourteen. But, in addition to that in Tuscany, men from
Siena spoke differently from those of Arezzo; in Lombardy, the men of
Ferrara and those of Piacenza had their own languages. And he refers to an
earlier passage in which he had shown that even in a single town there could
be more than one vernacular. In Bologna the men of Borgo San Felice, just
outside the wall, had a tongue differing from that of the inhabitants of the
centre, of 'strada maggiore.'[7] All in all, Dante concludes, 'if one wanted to
count the main and the secondary vernaculars of Italy, together with their
further divisions, in this small corner of the world the number of linguistic
varieties would reach not merely a thousand but even more.'[8]

For centuries no subsequent writer looked at Italy so coolly as Dante
did in this extraordinary book. But the realities pointed to in the *De vulgari
eloquentia*, like the book itself, were to be ignored. The book, which
remained half-finished, was not influential. An Italian translation appeared in
1529 but the Latin original was not published until 1577 when, amid the
growing assertiveness of Tuscan, it was felt that Dante's strictures on that
species of the vernacular betrayed the cause; it was even argued that the work
was not an authentic writing of the poet.[9] Yet Dante's aim had been to
advocate a 'courtly' Italian which would unify the land and encourage the
fundamental cultural unity he discerned behind all the divisions.

No such ambition lay behind Flavio Biondo's *Italia illustrata*. Biondo,
in the papal secretariate from 1434, came from Forlì in the Romagna, and is
best known for his *Historiarum ab inclinatione Romanorum imperii decades*, a
history of Europe from the fall of Rome to his own day. He also wrote two
archaeological works, the *Roma instaurata* and the *Roma triumphans*. The
Italia illustrata was composed between 1448 and 1453, but it is likely that the
author had been collecting materials for some time earlier. It is not a long
book, but it is an important one. Dante's description was incidental to his
linguistic purposes; Biondo's was the first work expressly devoted to Italy as
a whole. It was published (in October 1453) before it was completed, in order
to frustrate the circulation of unauthorized copies, and Biondo tinkered with
it thereafter almost till his death (in 1463).[10] What was Biondo's purpose in
writing this unusual work? The inspiration for it came, it seems, from
Alfonso V who asked for a 'description of Italy in which the ancient names
were to be related to their modern equivalents.'[11] And this is what Biondo

set out to do, basing his account as far as possible on classical authorities, but adding details of men famous for valour and letters so that (in his own words) he provided 'not just a description of Italy ... but a sort of summary of Italian history.'[12]

The book begins with a general discussion of Italy, eschewing praises of the land—which have been sufficiently provided by Vergil, Pliny, and Petrarch—but giving its overall dimensions. Biondo then writes:

> Italy has a backbone, the sort we see in fish, and this is the Appenines, a mountain range which begins at the end of the Alps nearest the Tyrrhenian sea, goes straight down towards Ancona and seems about to end there; but it starts off again and goes through the middle of Italy, ending in Calabria ... Having displayed the site and the size of Italy, we must now divide up the land and describe in detail the places in it.[13]

He bemoans the difficulties of this task. Places have changed their names and Roman Italy is no more. Where of old there were seven hundred cities the Roman curia now counts only two hundred and sixty-four with bishoprics. Of the ancient regions only one has not significantly changed: ancient Etruria had the same boundaries as modern Tuscany; the other ancient regions have changed their names and limits several times. He accordingly divides his survey into eighteen regions (not including the islands), making use in general of those names best known in his own day. His regions are: Liguria or the Genoese (p. 295); Etruria (p. 299); Latium or the Campagna and Maritima of Rome (p. 313); Umbria or the duchy of Spoleto (p. 328); Picenum or the March of Ancona (p. 334); Romagna, or Flaminia and Emilia (p. 342); Gallia Cisalpina or Lombardy (p. 356); the Veneto (p. 369); Italia Transpadana or the March of Treviso (p. 374); Aquileia or Forum Julii (p. 384); Istria (p. 386); Samnium or the Abbruzzi (p. 389); Old Campania or Terra di Lavoro (p. 406); Lucania; Apulia (p. 421); Salentini or Terra d'Otranto; Calabria; Brutii.[14] These divisions Biondo derived ultimately from Pliny;[15] they bore little relation to the political facts of his day, save that Venice—by the mid-fifteenth century a major territorial power in Italy—was recognized as a separate region, and the existence of the *Regno*, conquered by his patron Alfonso V, was accepted by Biondo, in grouping at the end the provinces south of Rome. In fact, not only did Biondo omit the islands, he also omitted the last four regions, having been disappointed of help from Neapolitan scholars,[16] so that his survey is very defective.

Biondo begins each description of a region by listing its boundaries, and then proceeds to deal seriatim with towns, castles, rivers. In all this he follows wherever possible the ancient authorities, and never forgets that his aim is to relate ancient names with modern. But he regularly intersperses brief indications of scenery and notes the occasions when small places have momentarily had historical importance. When he discusses larger towns a succinct account is given of origins, of subsequent history, of the current situation, including the names of celebrated writers, and of families who have produced popes. All in all the work is an impressive attempt to come to terms with the history, geography, and monuments of divided Italy.

Yet the book is very unbalanced. Apart from the defective treatment of the south of the peninsula and the omission of the islands, the amount of space allocated to the regions of central and northern Italy is hardly what one would expect. The account of the Romagna is the most glaring example of this. It is as long as the sections on Tuscany or Rome and twice as long as the section on the Veneto. But then the Romagna was Biondo's native land. It was the home of the revival of letters and the birthplace of the Italian general Alberigo da Barbiano, whose indigenous militarism seemed to Biondo to point to a happier political future.[17]

The *Italia illustrata* was the first of the chorographical works of the Renaissance, and it deservedly attracted attention.[18] It circulated widely in manuscript form. It was printed at Rome in 1474 and (with other works) by Froben at Basle in 1531. In 1548 Lucio Fauno (who had earlier translated Pius II's abbreviation of the *Decades*) issued an Italian version of the *Roma triumphans* and of the *Italia illustrate* at Venice. This vernacular recension might well have been much to the taste of the public but, in the event, it was to be overtaken by another similar but more elaborate survey, the *Descrittione* of Leandro Alberti.

Leandro Alberti is much less well known than Dante or Biondo. He was born in 1479 and died probably in 1552. He came from Bologna and, though as a Dominican friar and provincial he travelled extensively in Italy, he spent much of his time in his native town. He wrote the history of the town and made a *tavola* of its leading families and he wrote of the great men of the Dominican order.[19] His chief claim to fame, however, was his *Descrittione di tutta Italia*, first printed at Bologna in 1550.[20]

The handsomely printed volume was five times longer than Biondo's but had the same general aim; in the author's words it was 'a work of a geographer, a topographer, and an historian all together.'[21] He began by cataloguing all other descriptions of the peninsula and explained that for moderns it resembled a human leg, beginning with the thickness of the thigh and descending down to the extremity of the foot. 'In fact,' he wrote, 'this seems to me a very helpful concept,' and he or his printer put in the margin at this point. 'Bella simiglianza.'[22] Then he explained that he planned to describe the boundaries of each region, to give the ancient and modern names not only of the regions but of towns, castles, mountains, rivers, lakes, and springs, narrating the marvels of nature, celebrating the famous deeds of those associated with these places; 'in a word I promise to record (as far as I may) the notable and commemorable things of this our Italy.'[23] And then (like Biondo) he urged the difficulties.

Biondo was his immediate model. The eighteen regions of the *Italia illustrata* were broadly followed, though Alberti sometimes defined their boundaries differently and, in all, identified nineteen regions. For the rest his book is more elaborate partly because he could not resist catalogues of ancient authorities. Where Biondo was content with one name, Alberti puts in half a dozen. It was, of course, the case that by the mid-sixteenth century a good many towns and localities had been written about by humanist scholars and topography, particularly in relation to ancient survivals, was establishing itself as a genre. Biondo had pioneered such studies and Alberti was able to make use of a wide range of secondary material which had not existed a century earlier.[24] The larger scale of the work also encouraged more detailed descriptions. These are sometimes extensive and evocative: for example, Lodi, which was discussed in a few lines by Biondo, occupies three pages or so of Alberti and we are told not only of its history but of the cheeses in the market and the irrigation of the countryside.[25] In general a great deal of geographical detail is provided. The *Descrittione* is also easier to follow because, unlike Biondo, Alberti moves systematically down one side of the peninsula and up the other.

There is, however, the same lack of proportion that we have noticed in Biondo though not to so marked an extent. This time the south is fairly discussed but Alberti, like his predecessor, came from Romagna and that province is given elaborate attention; it occupies, in fact, more space than the Campagna. Although under Rome are listed all the emperors and all the popes as well as the main monuments and a potted history, under Bologna there are catalogues of saints, prelates, professors, artists, and so on, in addition to a description of events and buildings.[26] The islands do not figure in the first edition though Alberti explained that he had written about them and if his work was well received, he would add them subsequently.[27] And not all of the recent authorities to which Alberti turned were reliable. He was a victim of the forgeries of his fellow Dominican Annius (Nanni) of Viterbo who died in 1502 and his pages contain many references to the (spurious) writings of Berosus the Chaldaean.

The elaboration and the completeness of the *Descrittione* nevertheless command respect and this was immediately recognized. In 1551 a second edition appeared at Venice[28] and down to 1631 there were a further nine Venetian editions. The promised additional section on the islands appeared in 1561 and in the edition of 1568 each island was accompanied by a map. Two editions of a Latin translation were issued at Cologne in 1566 and 1567, curious tribute to the European appeal of a book which was being used as the *vade mecum* of the northern visitor to Italy. Montaigne apparently had it with him on his celebrated journey,[29] but so had many other travellers down to the eighteenth century, as one can see from the inscriptions in the surviving copies.[30] Alberti's work is, in fact, a step towards the later guide book, destined to be made otiose only as and when that new type of travel literature made its appearance with the *Itinerarium Italiae* of François Schott (1600), another work which in various forms was to have a long life.[31] But this, as they say, is another story.

What small sustenance can one derive from these sketchy indications? Obviously the map of Italy has been turned the right way up, at least for those of us accustomed to having the north at the top. Dante's cartography was necessarily schematic and literary. Biondo and Alberti were looking at the country much as we look at it: the *portolano* had done its work and by Alberti's day Italy was rapidly moving into the first great age of systematic cartography. There can be no doubt that Alberti used maps and that the cartographers of his day and later used his book in making theirs.[32] The geographical unity of Italy is pronounced and through the centuries this is reflected in descriptive works.

Yet there are some curious discrepancies. All our witnesses testify to the Alps being the northern boundary: they had no geographical or historical alternative. Yet, in practice, they neglect the northern fringe of Italy. Dante said that Trent and Turin were on the frontier but, more surprisingly, also says this of Alessandria.[33] Biondo's discussion of the northern fringe of Lombardy is very scant and, by the time of Alberti, Piedmont, as he noted, was ruled by the king of France, Henry II, to whom (with his consort Catherine de' Medici) the *Descrittione* was dedicated.[34] Even odder is the neglect of the islands. Dante greatly admired the dialect of the Sicilian nobles of an earlier day, and admitted that Sicily and Sardinia were part of Italy; but in his survey he was contemptuous of Sardinian speech and did not mention Corsica.[35] In the *Italia illustrata* Biondo has no place at all for the islands, and no explanation for their absence. The work is admittedly defective in its discussion of the southern portions of the peninsula; it is hard to see how the author could have avoided Sicily if he had dealt at all adequately with the provinces comprised in the *Regno*, though in his request for information in December 1450 he does not mention the island from which Alfonso V had conquered the mainland.[36] There are fleeting references to Corsica and Sardinia in connection with Genoese activity overseas, almost as though they were simple colonies.[37] Alberti's approach to this matter is thus a marked change, for he firmly states in his introduction[38] that Corsica and Sardinia are part of Italy and from the start he had included the islands in his survey, although (as we have observed) these sections did not appear in the earlier editions.

What of the images which the three authors invoke to convey a picture of the peninsula? For Dante (and Lucan) the Appenines are, in a curious way, a unifying element in divided Italy. The rain rattles on the tiles and runs off east and west, but one roof shelters the chattering and quarrelling peoples. Biondo likens the structure of the land to a fish with a long spine and Alberti admires this: 'Veramente pare questo Monte un dorso ò sia schiena d'Italia.'[39] But his own preference, as we have seen, is for Italy as a leg; he elaborates the anatomical correspondence at wearisome length.[40] To some degree these inventions reflect the increasing precision of the maps which were available. It was only when representations of the peninsula became fairly accurate that the resemblance to a leg was evident. Alberti's 'bella simiglianza' also suggests the personified maps of Europe which were shortly to be made, such as that in Sebastian Münster's *Cosmographia* (1588).[41]

In more general terms the three texts adduced in these pages underline the peculiar provincialism of Italy. And by 'provincialism' I do not mean the 'Italic' provinces or regions into which the country was divided;[42] I mean those urban units to which real attachment was felt. Dante's analysis is town-based, though sometimes he was thinking also of the *contado*.[43] Biondo, like Alberti, measures the prosperity of the land by the number of its towns. In ancient times, Biondo pointed out, there were 700; Alberti increases this number to 1,166. In Biondo's day there were only 264 and Alberti could count only 300. The view which emerges is one of small urban units, town-based governments, overlaid from time to time (especially in Alberti's discussion) by larger but somehow irrelevant controls.

This impression is encouraged by the arbitrary names of provinces which Biondo adopted and which were carried on and elaborated by Alberti. True, these ancient names were to the taste of classically educated readers, and they had, like the bishoprics of Italy which had boundaries which often still fitted neatly into the old provinces,[44] a kind of permanence amid the perpetual fluctuations of the Italian political scene. Originally, after all, they had to some extent reflected permanent geographical features, not least the Appenines. Yet certain broad political entities were firmly established by the fourteenth century, not least the states of the Church and the kingdom of Sicily. By Biondo's day a large hereditary duchy of Milan might reasonably have figured as a permanent part of his world, though he was writing just after the attempt to establish the Ambrosian republic had failed. And Venice was likewise mistress of the northeastern provinces. It is not that Biondo or Alberti entirely ignore these features. Biondo (for instance) mentions that the Genoese have really dominated most of Liguria[45] and Alberti writes of the 'great empire and lordship which the gentlemen of Venice have had and still have both by sea and on *terra ferma*.'[46] But they did not see the country organized in such units; they avoided the basic issues of their day. No one concerned with the urgent pressures of politics could have afforded to do this. It is salutary to compare with Biondo his contemporary Pius II who was under no illusions about the state of Italy. This might be illustrated from many of his writings, and not least from the *Commentarii*, but it is displayed most succinctly in his section on the *novitates Italiae* in *De Europa*,[47] written when he was Cardinal Aeneas Sylvius Piccolomini. His chapters are devoted to Genoa, 'mistress and queen of the Ligurians,' Milan, Venice, Mantua, Ferrara, Bologna, Florence, Siena, Rome, Umbria, and the kingdom of Naples—this the longest section in the book.[48] Here again we are presented with towns: but it is those towns which were of general significance in mid-fifteenth century Italian politics. For the foreigners, looking at Italy from outside, the bigger units naturally obtruded; this is evident enough in diplomatic sources, but may be even more tellingly seen in the History of Italy compiled by the relatively unenlightened Welsh visitor, William Thomas.[49] Thomas certainly gives the old names of the provinces (he had beside him the *Italia illustrate* of Biondo), but he places them under their present rulers.[50] After reading Alberti it is refreshing to begin Thomas' book with: 'The greatest prince of dominion there at this present time is Charles the Fifth, Emperor of Almain, who for his part hath the realm of Naples and the duchy of Milan.'[51]

Dante's linguistic treatise was designed to promote Italian unity. It is clear also from his other writings, and especially from the *Monarchia*, that this was his aim. However, he accepted political diversities and had no desire that the emperor should obliterate the liberties of Italy. Biondo's *Italia illustrata* is a political morass, perhaps a reflection of the atmosphere of the curia in his day. For Alberti, division has come to stay—or so one feels. His artificial provinces dominate even the index to his work. Each letter of the alphabet is subdivided into nineteen sections, corresponding to each of the *regioni* of the *Descrittione*—a nightmare indeed for the user who did not know which of the ancient territories contained the place about which he sought information. Despite the general confusion Biondo is optimistic; a new day has dawned. This is far from being the sentiment to be distilled from Alberti. In the detailed descriptions of a good many places in the *Descrittione* cheerfulness and pride are evident, but in the introductory section on Italy as a whole he is gloomy enough. 'Evil, envy and unrestrained appetite for power are dominant in Italy and have led her to such misery that from being a lady and a queen she has become worse than a slave girl. One cannot think of this without great grief.'[52] Yet a curious absence of resentment is found in Alberti: he does not revile the French and Spanish barbarians. Biondo had been bitterly critical of the foreign mercenaries of trecento Italy.[53] Alberti accepts a situation which, at the price of foreign occupation, was to give the urban units of the peninsula a peace such as they had not known for three centuries.

Finally one must recognize a steady decline in the originality of the scholarship of the books we have glanced at. Perhaps it is unfair to compare Dante's *De vulgari eloquentia* with the others, for it was a work of rare genius which had few competitors and was, in any case, intended to explore problems to which the geography and history of Italy were in a sense peripheral. Yet his firm and angular Latin, precise and economical, compares favourably with the smooth Latin prose of Biondo, himself no stylist. In turn Biondo's style strikes one as clear and well-structured compared with the flaccid Italian of Alberti, whose sentences limp along with a mixture of Latinizing and vernacular phrases; reading him is a somewhat laborious business. With Alberti one is conscious too that the outpouring of the classical scholarship of the Renaissance can have a stultifying effect. He is besotted with his authorities, and his exposition becomes muscle-bound through over-exercise in name-dropping.

Yet Alberti in Italian was to reach a public infinitely wider than Biondo in Latin. This public was at first largely composed of his own countrymen but, as we have seen, soon the regular visitors to Italy from beyond the Alps were to find him a useful companion. The *Descrittione* overtook the *Italia illustrata*, even in Fauno's Italian version. The *Descrittione* itself, by the end of the sixteenth century, was gradually to be replaced by guide books on the one hand and by more scholarly works on individual towns on the other, a process with which successive publishers of the book strove to cope by revision.[54] Works of this kind, unlike the pilgrim literature of an earlier day, were in constant need of *aggiornamento*, were constantly in danger of becoming obsolete.

In their attempts to convey a total picture of Italy, Biondo and Alberti were thus bound to become outmoded. But one may suspect that in their quiet fashion they (and the men who in different ways were to succeed them—men like Ludovico Guicciardini, Ughelli, Muratori) were to do more by patient description and collection of materials than were the wilder enthusiasts from Dante down to Machiavelli. Biondo and Alberti were also to transmit to the rest of Europe the ambition to describe countries exactly, and to relate the ancient places to the modern names. Both the *Italia illustrata* and the *Descrittione di tutta Italia* have been undeservedly neglected. They expressed an important Italian mood and helped to construct a permanent awareness, at levels deeper than politics and war, of the underlying unity of Italy. They conveyed such an appreciation of Italy among foreign visitors. And they precipitated similar national self-consciousness elsewhere.

NOTES

1. A useful recent survey is provided by V. Illardi, 'Italianità,' *Traditio* XII (1956), 339–67.

2. I am grateful to Mr Colin Hardie for a note on the date of the work.

3. See *De vulgari eloquentia* (hereafter DVE), ed. A. Marigo (Florence 1938), pp. 47 and 82, notes: cf. P. Revelli, *L'Italia nella Divina Commedia* (Milan 1922), esp. pp. 59–73 on the 'confini e regioni d'Italia.' For a recent discussion of Dante's geography, see G. Vinay, 'Ricerche sul *De vulgari eloquentia*: iii Apenini devexione clauduntur,' *Giornale storico della litteratura italiana*, CXXXVI (1959), 367–82. I have to thank Professor Cecil Grayson for this reference.

4. DVE, I,ix,4–5 (Marigo, p. 66).

5. Cf. 'Si come neve tra le vive travi / per lo dosso d'Italia si congela ...' *Purg.* XXX. 85–6.

6. DVE, I,x,6.7 (Marigo, pp. 80–6).

7. DVE, I,ix,4 (Marigo, p. 66).

8. DVE, I,x,9 (Marigo, p. 88). It is difficult to put neatly into English the phrase 'primal et secundarias et subsecundarias vulgaris Ytalie variationes.'

9. See Marigo's introduction, pp. xliii–xlviii.

10. See the account by B. Nogara, *Scritti inediti e rari di Biondo Flavio, Studi e Testi*, 48 (Rome 1927), pp. cxxi–cxxvi; the editor prints, pp. 215–39, some of the later additions. A critical study of the *Italia illustrata*, and an authoritative text, would be welcome.

11. Nogara, *Scritti inediti*, pp. 163–4.

12. I quote from the Basel edition of 1531, p. 295.

13. *Italia illustrata*, p. 294.

14. The places are listed as on p. 293 of *Italia illustrata*, the page references are to the beginnings of the completed sections.

15. *Historia Naturalis*, III,v,45–III,,xx. Pliny's description is based on the eleven regions of Augustus. For these, and later modification, see R. Thomsen, *The Italic Regions* (Copenhagen 1947).

16. Nogara, *Scritti inediti*, cxxiv.

17. *Italia illustrata*, p. 350. Cf. D. Hay, 'Flavio Biondo and the Middle Ages,' above, chapter 3, pp. 35–66.

18. R. Weiss, 'Lineamenti per una storia degli studi antiquari in Italia,' *Rinascimento*, IX (1960 for 1958), 141–201.
Since my essay was written the late Roberto Weiss' *The Renaissance Discovery of Classical Antiquity* has appeared (Oxford 1969).

19. A brief life and bibliography by A.L. Redigonda is found in *Dizionario biografico degli italiani*, I (1950) (DBI). A study of Alberti and his *Descrittione* has been undertaken as a doctoral dissertation at Edinburgh by Miss Rosemary Austin, to whom I am obliged for checking the above account. I am also grateful to Dr Esmond de Beer for allowing me to consult his collection of editions of the *Descrittione*.

20. There are two versions of the first pages of the *editio princeps*, one with and one without the engraved portrait of Alberti.

21. Quoted Redigonda, DBI.

22. *Descrittione*, p. iii^V.

23. *Descrittione*, pp. vi–vii.

24. R. Weiss, '*Lineamenti*'.

25. *Italia illustrata*, p. 362; *Descrittione*, pp. 370–3.

26. *Descrittione*, pp. 96–141, 263–316.

27. *Ibid.*, p. 469. Venice is listed as an island (p. vii^V) but is in fact dealt with in the first edition, pp. 450^V–67^V, as are the 'Isole intorno Vinegia,' pp. 467^V–9.

28. This includes in the preliminaries the portrait of Alberti which is found in some issues of the first edition but which was omitted in later reprints. In some of the latter a certain amount of additional material is provided in the text.

29. E.S. de Beer, 'The Development of the Guide-book until the early Nineteenth Century,' *Journal of the British Architectural Association*, 3rd ser., XV (1952), 36n. Dr de Beer has kindly indicated to me a number of parallel passages which are conclusive. Alberti is not referred to by C. Dédéyan, *Essai sur le Journal de Voyage de Montaigne* (Paris, n.d.), whose discussion of 'les sources livresques,' pp. 155–9, is, however, perfunctory.

30. In 1778 W. Minto had a copy of the Venice edition of 1553 with him in Rome. A few years later he urged his executors to give it to the university library at Edinburgh when he died, writing in it: 'This valuable work is very scarce. It is the best Classical Description of Italy. Addison has taken a great many things from it.'

31. See E.S. de Beer, 'François Schott's *Itinerario d'Italia*,' *Library*, 4th ser., XXIII (1942), 57–83.

32. R. Almagià, *L'Italia di G.A. Magnini e la cartografia dell' Italia nei secoli* XVI e XVII (Naples 1922).

33. DVE, I,xv,8 (Marigo, p. 132); for the limits of the area of 'si' in Dante, see Vinay's article, note 3 above.

34. *Descrittione*, sig.* ij and p. 408.

35. DVE, I,xi,7; I,xxii,2,4 (Marigo, pp. 94, 96–8).

36. Nogara, *Scritti inediti*, p. 163: '... ea Italiae pars, quam regnum Siciliae appellamus, in aliquot divisa regiones, Campaniam scilicet veterem, Samnium ... Aprutium, Apuliam, Lucaniam, Calabros, Bruttios et Salentinos.'

37. *Italia illustrata*, p. 298, and Nogara, *Scritti inediti*, p. 229

38. *Descrittione*, p. vi^V.

39. *Descrittione*, p. iii; earlier classical 'figures' are listed.

40. *Descrittione*, pp. iii^V–iv.

41. Reproduced in my *Europe: the Emergence of an Idea* (rev. ed., Edinburgh 1968), frontispiece. But in this Italy appears as an arm, not a leg.

42. In fact, *provincia* is normally used by these writers to mean Italy itself, *regio* or *regione* its larger parts.

43. Cf. Marigo, p. 132n.

44. Thomsen, *The Italic Regions*, p. 316; cf. the areas of the *Rationes decimarum* (thirteenth and fourteenth centuries) used in papal taxation in Italy; cf. Revelli, *L'Italia*, p. 73.

45. *Italia illustrata*, p. 298.

46. *Descrittione*, p. 452[v].

47. *Opera Omnia* (Basle 1551), pp. 445–71.

48. As it was to prove to be one of the biggest problems of his pontificate. There are a few briefer chapters in the book, which is composed of collections intended to be used in a later expanded form.

49. William Thomas, *The History of Italy* (1549), ed. George B. Parkes (Ithaca, 1963).

50. *Ibid.*, pp. 16–19.

51. *Ibid.*, p. 16.

52. *Descrittione*, p. vi.

53. *Italia illustrata*, p. 349.

54. This is an aspect of the later editions of the *Descrittione* which merits study, though revision does not seem to have been very thorough-going. In the 1558 Venice edition of Fauno's translation of Biondo's work there are 'Annotationi,' sig. HH6–II 3[v].

CARLA FRECCERO

Politics and Aesthetics in Castiglione's *Il Cortegiano*: Book III and the Discourse on Women

When Kenneth Burke's *Rhetoric of Motives* appeared in 1969, there had been relatively little discussion of the political motives of Castiglione's aestheticization of the courtier.[1] Critics concentrated primarily on the ludic aspects of the text and on Castiglione's construction of the representative Renaissance self as a work of art.[2] Since that time, scholarship has drawn attention to the political context of early modern courtly literature in general and to manuals of courtesy in particular as documents of class struggle, both in sixteenth-century Italy and in Elizabethan England; Castiglione scholars in particular have concentrated on the rise of the absolutist state and the demise of feudalism in Italy as the motivating politics of the work.[3] Dain Trafton, for example, argues that "the Courtier and the Prince might be considered the fundamental political testaments of the sixteenth century."[4] Yet, although in its early reception, particularly in England, the political instrumentality of Castiglione's text may have been assumed, the history of *Il Cortegiano*'s modern reception indicates that it enjoys greater success as a literary achievement than as a political treatise, especially when compared to Machiavelli's *Principe*, a text that still claims a place in the curriculum of political philosophy.

Burke's reading of Castiglione, as a "series of formal operations for the dialectical purifying of a rhetorical motive" (221), indicates in part why this might be so. One of the accomplishments of *Il Cortegiano* is precisely to have

From *Creative Imitation: New Essays on Renaissance Literature In Honor of Thomas M. Greene*. eds. David Quint, Mararet W. Ferguson, G.W. Pigman III, and Wayne A. Rebhorn. © 1992 by the Center for Medieval and Early Renaissance Studies, State University of New York at Binghamton.

mystified, through a rhetoric of transcendence, the social relations it describes. Daniel Javitch has argued that such mystification is a pragmatic response to the "constraints of despotism," and that Castiglione's political contribution is to have "set forth an art of conduct tailored to the social and political exigencies of Renaissance despotism."[5] Elsewhere he argues that

> [1] The exigencies of the royal establishment, while depriving men of free political expression and participation, could serve to redirect eloquence into less socially immediate but more esthetic modes of expression; [2] Admirable esthetic achievements can be the product of social and political conditions we may consider detestable; and [3] the loss of political freedom, especially the loss of free speech, may be in certain cases a gain for poetic art.[6]

Javitch thus sets up an opposition between politics and aesthetics that privileges "poetic art" over political participation and suggests the class interests at stake both in Castiglione's mystification of the courtier and in the modern aestheticizing approach to Castiglione's text. Indeed, Ullrich Langer's work, which examines the contradictory contemporary models of condign and congruous "merit" that structure Castiglione's mystifications, suggests that modern readings of the text may inherit unproblematically the (mystified) notion of a meritocracy that Castiglione labors to construct.[7]

The "ultimate" ordering principle Burke sees as governing *Il Cortegiano*'s suasive strategy is a theological one, where God is, as Langer points out, "the paradigm of secular power."[8] In this order, social relations figure, and thus prefigure, the ultimate relationship between human and divine:

> The hierarchic principle of courtship sets a pattern of communication between "lower" and "higher" classes (or kinds). This can be universalized in terms of a climbing from body to soul, from senses through reason to understanding, from worldly to the angelic to God, from woman to beauty in general to transcendent desire for Absolute union.[9]

Thus the political can be conceived of as a stage in a process that finds its ultimate endpoint and ethical justification in a mystical spiritual fulfillment. For Langer, these rhetorics are "conceptual homologies," "channels of thought through which early modern society conceived of arbitrary or at least unconstrained power in ethical and esthetic realms of culture" (*Divine and Poetic Freedom*, 52–53). Burke however, suggests that there are strategic and motivated dimensions of the analogies between secular and sacred power and, he notes, the process is also reversible; the ultimate divine hierarchy may in turn be seen as the rhetorically "purified" figure for social hierarchies.

Thomas Greene has argued that *Il Cortegiano* enacts a "drama of containment," thus suggesting one way in which the political can be said to make its appearance in this text, as a threat to be contained.[10] I propose to examine the ways in which Castiglione's work addresses its political subject and how *Il Cortegiano* subverts the power structure that suppresses it by means of a "hypocritical" rhetoric of self-censorship that locates a transgression (or breach) and pretends to silence it. At the same time, I would like to point to the ways the text takes its own failure as a political treatise into account, the way in which it opens up the possibility for its own "retreat" into art for art's sake. For unlike Machiavelli, who demystifies his prince, Castiglione constructs an idealized courtier whose contradictions can be revealed only at the cost of a loss of class (or caste) identity.[11] In this view, *Il Cortegiano* is simultaneously an anachronistic, nostalgic text and a pragmatic attempt to accommodate to a set of political circumstances exerting its pressure on a class of men. It is a utopian projection, both reactionary and forward-looking in its attempt to address a political constraint. Finally, the complex tension *Il Cortegiano* enacts between mystification and demystification produces through displacement its most political result, a new category of mystified identity in the "donna di Palazzo" or court lady, whose creation in book III both exposes and conceals one of the dominant political problems of the courtier, his dependency on an (arbitrary) ruler.[12]

The frame narrative sets up an initial contradiction in the work. There are indications in the text that it represents an actual historical "reality," while at the same time another discourse works to deny the factual nature of what it is presenting. This is a familiar strategy of utopian discourse; Boccaccio and More use it and so does Rabelais in his "Abbaye de Thélème." In Castiglione's books, the process creates two worlds, similar to what Harry Berger calls "second world" and "green world."

> The second world is the playground, laboratory, theater or battlefield of the mind, a model or construct which the mind creates, a time or place which it clears, in order to withdraw from the actual environment. It may be the world of play or poem or treatise, the world inside a picture frame, the world of pastoral simplification, the controlled conditions of scientific experiment. Its essential quality is that it is an explicitly fictional, artificial, or

hypothetical world. It presents itself to us as a game which, like all games, is to be taken with dead seriousness while it is going on. In pointing to itself as serious play, it affirms both its limits and its power in a single gesture. Separating itself from the casual and confused region of everyday existence, it promises a clarified image of the world it replaces.[13]

The "green world," particularly in this case, is the ideal world (Urbino) placed within the fiction. Berger suggests that the author frames his world, puts boundaries around it (the boundary that is the book itself) in order to conduct a controlled experiment; a distancing takes place in order to address the world outside of the text.

The problem Berger poses in relation to such fiction is that of the desire to escape versus a will to power, a mastery over a reality that cannot be directly controlled. Castiglione's text includes both these movements. By recreating an idyllic (and, by the time the book was written, non-existent) Urbino with an appearance of leisurely game-playing by courtly aristocrats (all of whom had, in actuality, either died or become papal employees at the time the book was written) in order to discuss a privileged caste threatened with extinction, he withdraws into a golden age exempt from the relentless passing of time.

At the same time, however, Castiglione makes a claim to historical accuracy. He explicitly purports to be recording actual conversation: first, in an elaborate figure:

> Mandovi questo libro come un ritratto di pittura della corte d'Urbino, non di mano di Rafaello o Michel Angelo, ma di pittor ignobile e che solamente sappia tirare le linee principali, senza adornar la verità de vaghi colori o far parer per arte di prospettiva quello che non è.[14]

> I send you this book as a portrait of the Court of Urbino, not by the hand of Raphael or Michelangelo, but by that of a lowly painter and one who only knows how to draw the main lines, without adorning the truth with pretty colors or making, by perspective art, that which is not seem to be. (3)

Then, lest this be construed rhetorically as feigned modesty, in a more literal description of the process:

rinovando una grata memoria, recitaremo alcuni ragionamenti, i quali già passarono tra omini singularissimi a tale proposito; e benchè io non v'intervenissi presenzialmente per ritrovarmi, allor che furon detti, in Inghilterra, avendogli poco appresso il mio ritorno intesi da persona che fidelmente me gli narrò, sforzerommi a punto, per quanto la memoria mi comporterà, ricordarli, acciò che noto vi sia quello che abbiamo giudicato e creduto di questa materia omini degni di somma laude e al cui giudicio in ogni cosa prestar si potea indubitata fede. (I.i.81)

to revive a pleasant memory, we shall rehearse some discussions which took place among men singularly qualified in such matters. And even though I was not present and did not take part in them, being in England at the time when they occurred, I learned of them shortly thereafter from a person who gave me a faithful report of them; and I shall attempt to recall them accurately, in so far as my memory permits, so that you may know what was judged and thought in this manner by men worthy of the highest praise, and in whose judgment on all things one may have unquestioned faith. (12–13)

Other factors contribute to the illusion of reality in the text: the dialogic structure, the historic reality of the characters, and the near-total effacement of the author-narrator. This strategy, the claim to representational accuracy, seeks to "refashion" reality, to cope with, perhaps resolve, the political tensions of the context.

Whereas on the level of the "green world," *Il Cortegiano* is a fiction, a fantasy, taking the form of a *memento mori* or a nostalgic ode, in another dimension it represents the contemporary world of the courtier, Castiglione himself and his entire class. This is a world of political struggle, for courtiership, whether military, advisory, or ornamental is defined in relation to the Prince and the court, the geographical center of power within the society. Together, these levels constitute a rhetoric of negation (escape to an Arcadian past) and of subversion, an attempt to assert control in the present. Frank Whigham has argued that this literary construct results from the constraints upon the "advice to princes" genre in the context of despotic rule. Unable directly to provide the prince with counsel and thus fulfil the role of humanist educators, intellectuals resorted to describing life at court within an explicitly fictional framework. "This fictional fictiveness," Whigham writes, "allowed the would-be social servant to avoid culpable reference to the real actions of real rulers, while still employing the powers his education had taught him to see as his defining capacities. He had to work through techniques of sublimation and indirection. If his patrons regarded such fictions as entertainment rather than counsel, he was at least not silenced ..." (*Ambition and Privilege*, 14). Langer notes that Castiglione's nostalgia corresponds to this shift as well: "Condign merit [degna di laude] is clearly not within the reach of actual courtiers; it is an unrealized project in an irretrievable past, although during their lifetimes other courtiers at Urbino did achieve fame and fortune."[15]

Politics is the context within which the courtier performs his essential roles. This is true both of the man and the text; Castiglione defines the courtier in terms of the central authority figure ("gentilomo che viva in corte de principi," I.i.79), and *Il Cortegiano* as belonging to a tradition of political treatises:

> mi contenterò aver errato con Platone, Senofonte, e Marco Tullio, lassando il disputare del mondo intelligibile e delle idee; tra le quali, sì come, secondo quella opinione, è la idea della perfetta republica e del perfetto re e del perfetto oratore, così è ancora quella del perfetto Cortegiano. (I.iii.76)

> I am content to have erred with Plato, Xenophon, and Marcus Tullius; and just as, according to these authors, there is the idea of the perfect Republic, the perfect King, and the perfect Orator, so likewise there is that of the perfect Courtier. (7)

The references to classical political treatises both distance the work from its political context and bring that context more sharply into focus. Cicero, for example, composed *De oratore* when his great career as an orator had already begun to wane. In 58 BC he had been exiled and, although recalled in 57, he was, in 55 when the work was written, forced to remain outside the sphere of public action.[16] He laments his fate in the introductory letter to his brother Quintus:

> This hope, which was present in all my thoughts and purposes, was disappointed by a combination of disastrous political events and various domestic misfortunes.... (173)

Castiglione too, by the time he finished *Il Cortegiano*, had suffered the vicissitudes of political misfortune: he witnessed the fall of the court of

Milan, was banished from the court of Mantua, and saw the papacy put an end to the court of Urbino. He was, by that time, no longer a courtier as such but a papal nuncio, having foregone his allegiances to Urbino in the process.[17] His own introductory letter abstracts the causes of his misfortune, attributing them to *fortuna*

> Ma la fortuna già molt'anni m'ha sempre tenuto oppresso in così continui travagli, che io non ho mai potuto pigliar spazio di ridurgli a termine, che il mio debil giudicio ne restasse contento. (1168)[18]

> But Fortune for many years now has kept me ever oppressed by such constant travail that I could never find the leisure to bring these books to a point where my weak judgment was satisfied with them. (1)

The characters in *De oratore* are all dead at the time the dialogue is being narrated, and at least two of them, Marcus Antonius and Publius Sulpicius, were killed for political reasons. They are orators reduced to political impotence, just as Castiglione's characters (although he does not mention it) are courtiers deprived, in the context of despotic and distant rule, of their roles as counsellor to the prince. The explicitly political context of *De oratore* resembles the undiscussed situation of Castiglione's courtiers, as aristocrats whose class status is threatened by the changing political circumstances of the Italian peninsula:

> We must go back to the time when the Consul Philippus was making a fierce attack on the policy of the leading nobility, and when the tribunician power of Drusus, whose object was to maintain the authority of the senate, was beginning to lose its influence and stability. (180)

Thus, while the imitation of ancient texts separates the work from its immediate context, it also, at least in the case of *De oratore*, tacitly reinforces *Il Cortegiano*'s political dimension.

§

Book III enacts the transition between worldly and celestial courtship, according to Burke, in its passage through the discourse on love and the court lady. The book as a whole is introduced as an illustration of the superiority of the games that were played at the court of Urbino, with an allusion to the "facende più ardue" (III.i.336) from which these games are a diversion. Thus, from the outset, the subject matter of book III is marked as diversionary, marginal with regard to what is central in the activities of the court. Yet, as Dain Trafton notes, it is "the most truly political of the *Courtier*'s four books" in addressing the question of the courtier's relation to tyranny by means of a discourse on domination, not of the courtier by the prince, but of women by men.[19] In this book, the discourse on the court lady and love deflects political discourse, insofar as erotic courtship (and eventually, in Bembo's speech, theological courtship) sublimates the aggression that is alluded to in the playful "battle between the sexes" and in the examples, where rape is the predominant theme. Yet the very slippage between the specific caste description of the "donna di palazzo" (court lady) and the discussion of "donne" (women) in general in the examples destabilizes the distinction between erotics and aggression. There is, furthermore, an identification and a rivalry between the courtier and the "donna di palazzo," reinforced by the setting, which absents the infirm and impotent duke and installs the duchess in his stead.[20]

Freud, discussing authorial self-censorship, makes the following observation:

> A ... difficulty confronts the political writer who has disagreeable truths to tell to those in authority. If he presents them undisguised, the authorities will suppress his words—after they have been spoken, if his pronouncement was an oral one, but beforehand, if he had intended to make it in print. A writer must beware of the censorship, and on its account he must soften and distort the expression of his opinion. According to the strength and sensitiveness of the censorship he finds himself compelled either merely to refrain from certain forms of attack, or to speak in allusions in place of direct references, or he must conceal his objectionable pronouncement beneath some apparently innocent disguise: ... The stricter the censorship, the more far-reaching will be the disguise and the more ingenious too may be the means employed for putting the reader on the scent of the true meaning.[21]

Freud suggests here that the allegories generated by the political writer in his self-censorship are a conscious act; Burke's corrective to this notion of rhetoric is to argue that for "such aspects of persuasion as are found in 'mystification,' courtship, and the 'magic' of class relationships, ... the classical notion of clear persuasive intent is not an accurate fit, for describing the ways in which the members of a group promote social cohesion by acting rhetorically upon themselves and one another." Instead he suggests that rhetoric is involved as much with identification as with persuasion, and that identification is also (self-)mystificatory:

> There is an intermediate area of expression that is not wholly deliberate, yet not wholly unconscious. It lies midway between aimless utterance and speech directly purposive. For instance, a man who identifies his private ambitions with the good of the community may be partly justified, partly unjustified. He may be using mere pretext to gain individual advantage at the public expense; yet he may be quite sincere, or even may willingly make sacrifices in behalf of such an identification. Here is a rhetorical area not analyzable either as sheer design or as sheer simplicity.[22]

The allegory of woman in book III is such an intermediate area. It is at once a veil for "political" discourse, a persuasive analogy, and a discursive identification. It is, in other words, both mystifying and mystified. The very instability of the discourse makes this book the most political in its discussion of domination and submission, and the most politically mystifying in its sublimation of the relations of power.

What begins as a discussion of the court lady quickly moves to a philosophical argument about the comparative natures of women and men. Gasparo, anticipating Freud, argues that women desire to be men because all creatures naturally desire their own perfection, whereupon Giuliano objects, rejecting "instinto di natura" [natural instinct] in favor of political desire:

> Rispose sùbito il Magnifico Iuliano:—Le meschine non desiderano l'esser omo per farsi più perfette, ma per aver libertà e fuggir quel dominio che gli omini si hanno vendicato sopra esse per sua propria autorità. (III.xvi.357)

> The Magnifico Giuliano replied immediately: "The poor creatures do not desire to be men in order to become more perfect, but in order to gain freedom and to escape that rule over them which man has arrogated to himself by his own authority." (217)

Giuliano redefines the relationship between women and men as constructed rather than natural and as explicitly political. Here he anticipates the analogous relationship between courtier and prince, sublimated as educational exemplarity, that Ottaviano will propose in book IV. If the relationship between courtier and prince can be conceived as that of humanist educator to pupil, then the courtier can be, if not superior, then at least a peer. As Joan Kelly points out, "If the courtier who charms the prince bears the same relation to him as the lady bears to the courtier, it is because Castiglione understood the relation of the sexes in the same terms that he used to describe the political relation: i.e., as a relation between servant and lord."[23]

The examples reinforce the analogy between "women" and the courtier, and function as both an enactment of and a breach in the drama of containment. As anecdotal illustrations, they are contained within the dialogue and have no direct bearing on the fictive speaking situation. Yet, as argument, they bring into the discourse the erotic aggression this closed-door conversation otherwise willfully excludes. The "hypocritical" rhetoric of self-censorship in the dialogue dramatizes this containment and its transgression. "Non uscite dei termini, Signore magnifico, ma attendere all'ordine dato," ("Do not exceed bounds, signor Magnifico, but hold to the order given," 205) warns the duchess at the beginning of book III (iv, 341), yet transgressions of these very boundaries occur and are emphasized by the prohibitive gestures made in response to them.

Two revealing moments in this respect occur when the text "erupts," and the initial discourse triggers a change of tone, after which the original discussion is resumed. The first passage involves an attack on the secular authority of the ecclesiastical order. The dialogue preceding the attack builds to a theological climax as the interlocutors discuss the relative evil and holiness of Eve and the Virgin. Giuliano enters the defense on religious terms reluctantly: "Poichè nella sacrestia ancor vi giova d'entrare" (III.xix.362) ("Since you wish to take refuge in the sacristy," 220) and signora Emilia censures the diatribe after it takes place. The rhetoric of self-censorship frames the soliloquy, focusing attention on and emphasizing the importance of the attack:

> Così, con un velo di santità e con questa secretezza, spesso tutti i
> for pensieri volgono a contaminare il casto animo di qualche
> donna; spesso a seminare odii tra fratelli, a governar stati,
> estollere l'uno e deprimer l'altro, far decapitare, incarcerare e
> proscrivere omini, esser ministri delle scelerità e quasi depositari
> delle rubbarie che fanno molti principi. (III.xx.364)

Thus, under a veil of sanctity and in secret they frequently devote all their thoughts to corrupting the pure mind of some woman; sowing hatred between brothers; governing states; raising up one and putting down another; getting men beheaded, imprisoned, and proscribed; serving as instruments of crime and, as it were, repositories of the thefts that many princes commit. (222)

Giuliano moves easily from the subject of women to friars. It is a common literary topos to engage in anti-clerical banter. However, he quickly expands from an enumeration of petty vices (defaming female honor, for example) to a list of prerogatives reserved only for heads of state.[24]

The "censored" political referent of the courtiers aggression in this text is the papacy, as the centralized and distant authority most closely resembling the new statist government that will replace a (real or imagined) feudal past.[25] It constituted the principal threat to the court of Urbino in 1516 and became, as well, the principal employer for most of the prominent courtiers in the text, including Castiglione himself. José Guidi also notes that the curia was the only Italian power effectively equipped to negotiate with the national monarchies during the invasions. With the centralization of power, both in Italy and abroad, came a breakdown in the notion of feudal ties binding courtiers and individual princes in a relationship of mutual obligation. The bureaucratic structures that replaced these ties produced career diplomats subject to the perceived arbitrariness of the sovereign's pleasure and led to the kind of tensions Langer sees as informing the courtier's double bind of merit. In a text where courtiership and its concomitant feudal values are presented as ideal, such a situation would inevitably be repressed. Yet through the discourse on women, book III attacks both the papacy and the courtier's "new" position.

After the enumeration of violent accusations against the pope, the discourse retreats once again to the level of petty offenses. But the breach is noticed, called attention to, and condemned. Signora Emilia immediately censures Giuliano for his attack, but the interlocutors' attention, in the rapid exchange that follows, focuses on the act of "non parlare" [not speaking]:

Allora la Signora Emilia:—Tanto piacer,—disse,—avete di dir mal de' frati, che for d'ogni proposito siete entrato in questo ragionamento ... Rise allora il Magnifico Iuliano e disse:—Come avete voi, Signora, così ben indovinato ch'io parlava de' frati, non avendo io loro fatto il nome? ...—Or non parlare de' frati,—rispose la Signora Emilia; ... (XXI)—Son contento,—disse il

Magnifico Iuliano,—non parlare più di questo. (III.xx–xxi. 364–65)

Then signora Emilia said: "It gives you so much pleasure to speak ill of friars that you have strayed quite from the purpose in this.... Then the Magnifico Giuliano laughed and said: "How, Madam, have you guessed so well that I was speaking of friars when I did not name them? ... "Now do not speak of friars," replied signora Emilia.... [21] "I am willing to speak no more of this," said the Magnifico Giuliano. (222)

Thus the anti-clerical attack makes itself visible on the surface of the text which denies it permission to speak.

The second passage invokes the contingent situations of courtiers, among them Castiglione himself, who changed princely allegiances several times in his life. The outburst is charged with guilt:

Se ben considerate, non è ròcca tanto inespugnabile né così ben diffesa, che essendo combattuta con la millesima parte delle machine ed insidie, che per espugnar il constante animo d'una donna s'adoprano, non si rendesse al primo assalto. Quanti creati da signori, e da essi fatti ricchi e posti in grandissima esumazione, avendo nelle mani le for fortezze e ròcche, onde dependeva tutto 'l stato e la vita ed ogni ben loro, senza vergogna o cura d'esser chiamati traditori, le hanno perfidamente per avarizia date a chi non doveano? E Dio volesse che a' dì nostri di questi tali fosse tanta carestia, che non avessino molto maggior fatica a ritrovar qualcuno che in tal caso abbia fatto quello che dovea, che nominar quelli che hanno mancato. Non vedemo noi tant'altri che vanno ogni dì ammazzando omini per le selve e scorrendo per mare, solamente per rubar denari? Quanti prelati vendono le cose della chiesa di Dio? quanti iurisconsulti falsificano testamenti? quanti periuri fanno? quanti falsi testimoni, solamente per aver denari? quanti medici avvelenano gl'infermi per tal causa? quanti poi per paura della morte fanno cose vilissime? E pur a tutte queste così efficaci e dure battaglie spesso resiste una tenera e delicata giovane; chè molte sono si trovate, le quali hanno eletto la morte più presto che perder l'onestà. (III.xlvi.403)

If you will consider well, there is no fortress so unassailable that, were it attacked with a thousandth part of the weapons and wiles as are used to overcome the constancy of a woman, it would not surrender at the first assault. How many retainers of princes, made rich by them and held in the greatest esteem, who were in command of fortresses and strongholds on which that princes state and life and every good depended, without shame or any fear of being called traitors, have perfidiously and for gain surrendered those to persons who were not to have them? And would to God there were such a dearth of this kind of men in our day that we might not have a much harder time finding a man who had done his duty in such instances than we do in naming those who have failed in theirs! Do we not see many indeed who go about killing men in the forests, and who sail the seas for no other purpose than to steal money? How many prelates sell the things of God's church! How many lawyers forge wills, how many perjurers bear false witness solely to gain money! How many doctors poison their patients for the same motive! And again how many do the vilest things from fear of death! And yet a tender and delicate girl often resists all these fierce and strong assaults, for many have been known who chose to die rather than lose their chastity. (250)

What begins as a defense of women's "continence" turns into a diatribe against masculine professional class corruption. The comparison is logically inappropriate since, in the woman's case, the "rocca" which is at stake is her own. She would, therefore, be expected to defend more arduously against attack than the courtier who is asked to protect that which is not his. She has everything to lose and nothing to gain by capitulation, whereas the retainer, if he is successful, has a real opportunity for self-advancement. Such comparisons, of course, presuppose a difference between (weak) women and (powerful) men in order to invert the difference and thus "shame" the men into resuming their place in the hierarchy.[26] Cesare's discourse, which has received critical praise for its enlightened defense of women turns out, in this case, not to be making a point about women at all, but about the men of "courtier" standing. And his appeal is to feudal values of fidelity and honor that in this context seem outmoded, since he presents a choice between death and gain and compares it to a choice between death and a capitulation that would also result in total loss. Gasparo, though specifically referring to women, alludes to the anachronism in his reply: "Queste,—disse,—messer Cesare, credo che non siano al mondo oggidì" (xlvii.403) ("Messer Cesare, I do not believe that such women exist in the world today," 250).

The politics invoked by the examples of virtuous women expose a contradiction in the discourse on the courtier, illustrated by this appeal to an untenable ideal of conduct for retainers of princes. For, while absolute resistance may be the duty of common women who wish to be considered "oneste," it is not the code of conduct prescribed for the court lady, who is subject to the double bind of chastity and erotic engagement typical of masculine recommendations for female conduct in the treatises of this period.[27] By displacing the double bind onto the court lady, to be both amenable to erotic intercourse and chaste in her dealings with courtiers, Castiglione displaces the courtiers own aggressive double bind with regard to his prince, which in turn erupts "safely" within the examples. It is not surprising therefore that a reference, in the first redaction of *Il Cortegiano*, to the more pragmatic counterpart of the courtier, "la cortigiana," comes to be suppressed.[28]

Giuseppa Battisti, in her brilliant study of women in *Il Cortegiano*, points out that the "donna di palazzo" seems to be a late addition to Castiglione's (and other treatise writers') caste categories; she suggests that the reasons for this have yet to be explored.[29] It would seem from book III, however, that the court lady provides a counterpart in sublimation to the courtier that the examples of "donne" could not. "Woman" in Castiglione's text is a politicized category, inscribed in relations of domination and subordination, defined in the examples by resistance to male violence. It is also non-specific. By comparing courtiers to women, and by placing all women in the generic category of "donne," Castiglione risks diminishing the caste specificity of the courtiers themselves, thus undermining the exclusionary function of courtly literature outlined by Whigham. The comparison also threatens to expose the contingent political motivations of the courtier, which his discourse must both conceal and mystify, or, in Burke's terms, render "ultimate." The creation of the ideal court lady, like the creation of the ideal courtier, allows instead for the containment of violence and its erotic sublimation into "love."

In the course of the discussion about the court lady's involvement in love, Cesare argues for the benefits of loves sublimating power, first by reminding the company that Petrarch, "il qual così divinamente scrisse in questa nostra lingua gli amor suoi" (III.lii.413) ("who wrote of his loves so divinely in this language of ours," 258), did so because of his love for Laura, then by invoking the *Song of Solomon*:

Vedete che Salomone, volendo scrivere misticamente cose altissime e divine, per coprirle d'un grazioso velo finse un ardente ed affettuoso dialogo d'uno innamorato con la sua donna, parendogli non poter trovar qua giù tra noi similitudine alcuna più conveniente e conforme alle cose divine, che l'amor verso le donne. (III.lii.413)

Consider that Solomon, wishing to write mystically of very lofty and divine things, in order to cover them with a fair veil, imagined an ardent and tender dialogue between lover and lady, thinking that here below among us he could find no similitude more apt and suited to things divine than love of woman. (258)

Loves terms can be divinely translated, the political hierarchy converted into a celestial order that transcends (and mystifies) social relations, which otherwise potentially mobilize aggression. The "ultimate" appeal ultimately contains this violence, and gives rise to the "mythic" sacrificial role realized in Ottaviano's model of the courtier as Socratic educator for the prince. At the same time, "woman" becomes "mere" metaphor, detached from the political embodiment she represented earlier in the dialogue, while the creation of the courtier's ornamental or cosmetic counterpart, the court lady, frees the courtier to assume the loftier, and ultimately more mystified, identities of educator and mystic.[30]

In the preface to the last book of *Il Cortegiano*, Castiglione expresses a hope:

Però parmi che quella causa, o sia per ventura o per favore delle stelle, che ha così lungamente concesso ottimi signori ad Urbino, pur ancora duri e produca i medesimi effetti; e però sperar si po che ancor la bona fortuna debba secondar tanto queste opere virtuose, che la felicità della casa e dello stato non solamente non sia per mancare, ma più presto di giorno in giorno per accrescersi. (IV.ii.447)

It seems to me, however, that the cause, whether through chance or favor of the stars, that has for so long given excellent lords to Urbino, continues still to produce the same effects; and hence we may hope that good fortune will so continue to favor these virtuous achievements that the blessings of the court and the state shall not only not decline but rather increase at a more rapid pace from day to day. (287)

In the face of what is known about the political developments in sixteenth-century Italy and Castiglione's own role in these developments, the statement seems willfully utopian. Book IV of *Il Cortegiano* does, in fact, move into the realm of the hypothetical, first in a discussion of an "ideal" politics then in a metaphysical meditation on transcendence. Both moves attempt to offer solutions to the transitional realm in which the class of courtiers finds itself, one by fashioning an idealized educator, the other by offering a contemplative solution in mystical detachment. Both are individualistic solutions—presented as monologues rather than dialogues—and both retreat into the "green world" of a golden age.

Il Cortegiano thus fashions reified social identities from a set of political relations that then come to be detached from any aggression or will to power implied by those relations. The comparison, in book III, between courtiers and "donne," which identifies hierarchy with domination, produces instead another idealized social category, the "donna di palazzo." The image of the world turned upside down, where women govern cities, make laws, and lead armies while men cook or sew (III.x.349) threatens to expose, as did Machiavelli, the arbitrariness of hierarchies, and suggests that "any man" could be prince, and any man could be a courtier. Frank Whigham has argued that precisely such a message was conveyed to class aspirants by courtesy literature in this period, in spite of the exclusionary motives of its production. Perhaps it could be argued instead that the excluded other was not, in fact, the "sciocchi" [fools] to whom Federico Fregoso refers (I.xii.100) but women, as Joan Kelly has asserted. The failure of the courtesan to achieve similar respectability by negotiating the courtiers double bind and the loss of power by aristocratic women during this period suggest that this was indeed the case. Thus, if *Il Cortegiano's* exclusionary intent was "self-undercutting" in relation to other classes of men, it seems to have enjoyed success in its elimination of intra-class competition from women.

There is much to be said for the political effectiveness of Castiglione's "ultimate" hierarchic ordering for those who stand to benefit most from the established social order, though Lauro Martines argues for the cost to Italian political unity of the courtiers caste isolationism.[31] Modern claims for the greater inherent value of aesthetic categories "purified" of political content would seem to indicate that this strategy of class consolidation is still in effect. *Il Cortegiano's* greatest political achievement may then have been its strategic mystification of the politics of aesthetics; the loss of political power that necessarily makes a virtue of "poetic art" for the courtier now makes of "art" an inherent virtue.

NOTES

1. Kenneth Burke, *A Rhetoric of Motives* (Berkeley: Univ. of California Press, 1969). Since then several books have appeared focusing on the politics of Castiglione's *Il Cortegiano*; see Carlo Ossola, ed., *La Corte e il "Cortegiano": La scena del testo* (Rome: Bulzoni, 1980) and Adriano Prosperi, ed., *La Corte e il "Cortegiano": Un modello europeo* (Rome: Bulzoni, 1980); Robert Hanning and David Rosand, eds., *Castiglione: The Ideal and the Real in Renaissance Culture* (New Haven: Yale Univ. Press, 1983), in particular the essays by Daniel Javitch, Dain Trafton, and J. R. Hale.

2. See, in particular, Giuseppe Toffanin, *"Il Cortegiano" nella trattatistica del Rinascimento* (Naples: Libreria scientifica editrice, 1961); Wayne Rebhorn, "Ottaviano's Interruption: Book IV and the Problem of Unity in *Il Libro del Cortegiano*," *MLN* 87 (1972): 37–59, and his book, *Courtly Performances: Masking and Festivity in Castiglione's "Book of the Courtier"* (Detroit: Wayne State Univ. Press, 1978); and, to a lesser extent Richard Lanham, *The Motives of Eloquence: Literary Rhetoric in the Renaissance* (New Haven: Yale Univ. Press, 1976).

3. See Frank Whigham's work on courtesy literature and its reception in Elizabethan England, *Ambition and Privilege: The Social Tropes of Elizabethan Courtesy Theory* (Berkeley: Univ. of California Press, 1984). Joan Kelly's essay, "Did Women Have a Renaissance?" is still one of the best (and least cited) historical sketches of the political context of *Il Cortegiano* and its consequences for the ideology of aristocratic womanhood; see *Women, History, and Theory: The Essays of Joan Kelly* (Chicago: The Univ. of Chicago Press, 1984). Finally, there is Ullrich Langer's brilliant treatment of the theological question of merit in Castiglione's work and its relation to the problem of the absolute ruler; see *Divine and Poetic Freedom in the Renaissance: Nominalist Theology and Literature in France and Italy* (Princeton: Princeton Univ. Press, 1990).

4. Dain Trafton, "Politics and the Praise of Women: Political Doctrine in the *Courtier*'s Third Book" in Hanning and Rosand, eds., *Castiglione*, 30.

5. Daniel Javitch, "*Il Cortegiano* and the Constraints of Despotism" in Hanning and Rosand, eds., *Castiglione*, 17.

6. *Poetry and Courtliness in Renaissance England* (Princeton: Princeton Univ. Press, 1978), 14–15.

7. *Divine and Poetic Freedom in the Renaissance*, esp. 51–66. Langer argues that Castiglione articulates a tension between two kinds of merit: condign or commensurate merit, and congruous merit whereby reward depends upon the initial generosity of the sovereign power. "In the move from a contractual situation defined by the commensurability of the partners to a situation defined by the powerful sovereign's or God's generosity," he writes, "we see sketched out the transition from a feudal-contractual relationship between the king and his vassals to the preabsolutist court, where the courtiers are made to depend entirely on the favor of the prince" (55). Castiglione thus labors to construct a meritocracy that would confer inherent value on the perfect courtier while simultaneously recognizing and concealing the arbitrariness of the system of rewards. Modern critics tend to "believe" Castiglione's ascription of merit to the courtier as self-evident rather than as the product of the tensions Langer describes. Similarly they do not take into account Whigham's point that the ascription of inherent value to the courtier's function was in part designed to serve the purpose of excluding others from the Profession; see *Ambition and Privilege*, 18.

8. *Divine and Poetic Freedom*, 66.

9. *A Rhetoric of Motives*, 231–32.

10. Thomas Greene, "The Choice of a Game" in Hanning and Rosand, eds., *Castiglione*, 8: "It is healthy doubtless for a community to confront itself, but when the community rests upon unsteady political and ethical props, too much illumination can be destructive as well as enlightening.... We can follow the progress of the game in terms of the potentially threatening or divisive issues it raises, in terms of the doubts it flirts with, the embarrassments it skirts, the social and political and moral abysses it almost stumbles into, the dark underside of the authorized truth it sometimes seems about to reveal."

11. On *Il Cortegiano* as a work of class consolidation, see José Guidi, "Baldassar Castiglione et le pouvoir politique: du gentilhomme de cour au nonce pontifical," in *Les Ecrivains et le pouvoir en Italie à l'époque de la Renaissance*, Centre de recherche sur la Renaissance italienne (Paris: Université de la Sorbonne nouvelle, 1973), 243–78. Lanham also briefly discusses this aspect of Castiglione's work in *Motives of Eloquence*. Whigham, in *Ambition and Privilege*, discusses the motives of courtesy literature in general as attempts to preserve an exclusive sense of aristocratic identity during a time of extreme class mobility: "First promulgated by the elite in a gesture of exclusion, the theory was then read, rewritten, and reemployed by mobile base readers to serve their own social aggressions" (5–6).

12. Joan Kelly, *Women, History, and Theory*, 43: "The changed times to which Castiglione refers in his introduction he experienced as a condition of servitude. The dominant problem of the sixteenth-century Italian nobility, like that of the English nobility under the Tudors, had become one of obedience.... Bembo's aging courtier, passionless in his rational love, sums up the theme of the entire book: how to maintain by detachment the sense of self now threatened by the loss of independent power."

13. *Second World and Green World: Studies in Renaissance Fiction-Making* (Berkeley: Univ. of California Press, 1988), 11–12.

14. Bruno Maier, ed., *"Il libro del Cortegiano" con una scelta delle Opere minori* (Torino: UTET, 1964), Letter to De Silva I.i.71. All subsequent references are to this edition. English translations are taken from *The Book of the Courtier*, trans. Charles S. Singleton (Garden City, N.Y.: Doubleday, 1959).

15. *Divine and Poetic Freedom*, 60; see page 56: "The progressive supplanting of feudal relations between king and vassals by relations between sovereign and courtiers, or at least their increasing conflict, implies an esthetic cleavage: on the one hand, courtly literature is determined by the nostalgic desire for harmony between the inherent value of the courtier as artifact and his effect on the prince; on the other hand, the absolute priority of the princes favor corresponds to a grace that is not inherent but fitting.... The emphasis on relational qualities is precisely a consequence of the prior arbitrariness perceived in courtly merit."

16. Moses Hadas, ed., *The Basic Works of Cicero* (New York: The Modern Library, 1951), 171. All subsequent references to *De oratore* are taken from this edition.

17. José Guidi, "Baldassar Castiglione et le pouvoir politique," 269: "Non seulement Castiglione ne fera rien pour aider son maitre à reconquérir par les armes, en 1517, son ancien duché, mais, peu soucieux de partager son infortune, et au mépris de tout principe chevaleresque de fidélité, il s'empresse de s'en détacher." Castiglione failed to prevent Leo X from replacing Francesco Maria della Rovere with Lorenzo de Medici. After Francesco Maria della Revere's ouster in 1516, Castiglione returned to the Gonzaga court in Mantua. Shortly thereafter he became the representative of the Gonzaga court in Rome and, in 1521, definitively severed his ties with della Rovere to acquire clerical status and receive the tonsure. See J.R. Hale, "Castiglione's Military Career," 156.

18. Langer argues that Fortune is a figure for the arbitrariness of the sovereign's

actions; *Divine and Poetic Freedom*, 62: "The initial arbitrariness of the princes favor or disfavor is often presented by Castiglione through the figure of Fortune, which determines the unpredictable whims of the sovereign. Fortune, however, is only an element in the functioning of despotic power; in fact, obversely, Fortune is a *product* of despotism."

19. "Politics and the Praise of Women," 31. Trafton's interpretation of how the discourse on women is political differs considerably from my own. He says, "I shall try to demonstrate that the Courtier does in fact supply practical political instruction aimed at preparing courtiers who must guide princes. I intend to assert Castiglione's claim as a serious writer of political doctrine" (30).

20. The instances of identification and rivalry are too numerous to list in their entirety; I will only mention a few. At the end of book II the duchess specifically assigns to the company the task of forming the court lady, as perfect in every way as the courtier (II.xcix.332). The duchess also suggests the possibility of rivalry between the two (III.ii.337). Gasparo wants to return to a discussion of the courtier, and asserts that the court lady and the courtier ought to follow the same rules (III.iii.339). Il Magnifico suggests that the lady will "perhaps" be considered the courtier's equal (III.vi.346), while Gasparo's perception of their equality leads him to envision a world turned upside down (III.x.349). Emilia announces a playful challenge to Gasparo when he suggests that their court lady is so perfect that she does not exist: "'Io m'obligo trovarla, sempre che voi trovarete il cortegiano'" (III.lviii.421). Finally, at the end of book III, Ottaviano, in preparation for his speech, suggests that altogether too much time has been spent talking about women, and that it has distracted them from their true purpose, talking about the courtier (III.lxxvii.443). Kelly also discusses this aspect of the relation between the courtier and the court lady in *Women, History, and Theory*, 44–47.

21. Sigmund Freud, *The Interpretation of Dreams*, trans. James Strachey (New York: Avon Books, 1965), 175–76.

22. Kenneth Burke, *A Rhetoric of Motives*, xiv. Whigham, *Ambition and Privilege*, also focuses on this aspect of rhetoric in his Afterword, 185–87.

23 *Women, History, and Theory*, 46.

24. The use of bureaucratic language in this passage, such as "ministri delle scelerità" and "depositari delle rubbarie," reinforces the sense that the remarks are directed at the statist papacy rather than constituting merely anti-clerical banter. The passage also prefigures the outrage Castiglione suffered under Clement VII as a result of the sack of Rome: "De n'avoir su prévoir, et moins encore conjurer, en mai 1527, la mise à sac de Rome, lui vaudra par la suite des accusations les plus variées, dont la principale et la plus grave, celle de s'être laissé corrompre par l'or imperial ..." (Guidi, "Baldassar Castiglione et le pouvoir politique," 274).

25. "Baldassar Castiglione et le pouvoir politique," 262–65. See also Lauro Martines, "The Gentleman in Renaissance Italy: Strains of Isolation in the Body Politic" in Robert S. Kinsman, ed., *The Darker Vision of the Renaissance: Beyond the Fields of Reason* (Berkeley: Univ. of California Press, 1974), 77–93. Kelly, *Women History, and Theory*; and Langer, *Divine and Poetic Freedom* also discuss the historically transitional situation of the courtier in *Il Cortegiano*.

26. Cesare draws attention to this strategy when he says, "ma dico, signor Gaspar, che se esse sono, come voi dite, più inclinate agli appetiti che gli omini, il quale voi stesso consentite, sono tanto più degne di laude, quanto il sesso loro è men forte per resistere agli appetiti naturali" (III.xl.394). ("But I say, signor Gaspar, that if they are, as you say, more inclined to yield to their appetites than men, and if, for all that, they abstain therefrom more than men do [which you admit], they are the more worthy of Praise in that their sex

has less strength to resist natural appetites," 243.) Joan Kelly also makes the point in *Women, History, and Theory*, 19–50.

27. See the survey provided by Ann Jones, "Nets and Bridles: Early Modern Conduct Books and Sixteenth-Century Women's Lyrics" in Nancy Armstrong and Leonard Tennenhouse, eds., *The Ideology of Conduct: Essays on Literature and the History of Sexuality* (London: Methuen, 1987), 39–72. See also Giuseppa Saccaro Battisti, "La Donna, le donne nel *Cortegiano*" in Carlo Ossola, ed., *La Corte e il "Cortegiano": la scena del testo* (Rome: Bulzoni, 1980), 219–49; esp. 230–31.

28. Ann Jones, "Nets and Bridles," 44; and Battisti, "La Donna, le donne," 249. For a discussion of the earlier versions of *Il Cortegiano* see Chino Ghinassi, "Fasi dell'elaborazione del *Cortegiano*" in *Studi di Filologia Italiana* 25 (1967), 155–96. Tita Rosenthal's work on Veronica Franco (Univ. of Chicago Press, forthcoming) and the Venetian courtesans explores the identifications and rivalries between courtier poets and courtesans. She makes the point that male poets often displaced their own experiences of dependency and servitude through their poetic attacks on the courtesans, while simultaneously using such attacks to gain poetic fame at the expense of their female would-be rivals.

29. "La Donna, le donne nel *Cortegiano*," 231, n. 13. For a study of sixteenth-century Italian women's social realities as they relate to Castiglione 's portrait, see Adriana Chemello, "Donna di palazzo, moglie, cortigiana: ruoli e funzioni sociali della donna in alcuni trattati del Cinquecento" in Adriano Prosperi, ed., *La Corte e il "Cortegiano": un modello europeo* (Rome: Bulzoni, 1980), 113–32. Recent feminist work on Renaissance praises of women provides further support for the problematic I discuss here. See, in particular, Juliana Schiesari, "In Praise of Virtuous Women? For a Genealogy of Gender Morals in Renaissance Italy" in *Annali D'Italianistica* 7 (1989), "Women's Voices in Italian Literature," ed. Rebecca West and Dino Cervigni, 66–87; see also Constance Jordan, *Renaissance Feminism: Literary Texts and Political Models* (Ithaca: Cornell Univ. Press, 1990).

30. Kenneth Burke, *A Rhetoric of Motives*, 230–31. See also Kelly, *Women, History, and Theory*, 45–47.

31. "The Gentleman in Renaissance Italy," 91–92: "The peninsula was kept divided and exposed to invasion by Italian princes and oligarchies, all mutually suspicious and keenly jealous.... Oligarchies drew in on themselves and became more castelike. In territories under princely rule, recruitment for regional administrative bodies depended increasingly on birth and blood."

VICTORIA KAHN

Virtù and the Example of Agathocles in Machiavelli's *Prince*

> Only at a remove from life can the mental life exist, and truly engage the empirical. While thought relates to facts and moves by criticizing them, its movement depends no less on the maintenance of distance. It expresses exactly what is, precisely because what is is never quite as thought expresses it. Essential to it is an element of exaggeration, of over-shooting the object, of self-detachment from the weight of the factual, so that instead of merely reproducing being it can, at once rigorous and free, determine it.
>
> —*Theodor Adorno*

> What gods will be able to save us from all these ironies?
>
> —*Friedrich Schlegel*

Machiavelli's innovation in the history of political thought, it is often argued, lies in his revision not only of Scholastic but also of humanist notions of imitation and representation, a revision that is reflected in his own representation of the realm of politics. When humanism and Scholasticism alike are seen as proposing an idealist or an a priori notion of truth, this case is easily made. As many critics of *The Prince* have remarked, Machiavelli scandalizes his readers not because he advises the prince to act in ways previously unheard of, but because he refuses to cloak his advice in the pieties

From *Representations* 13 (Winter 1986). © 1986 by The Regants of the University of California.

of Scholastic or Christian humanist idealism. Instead, he insists that the prince acts in a world in which there are "no prefigured meanings, no implicit teleology,"[1] in which order and legibility are the products of human action rather than the a priori objects of human cognition. To recognize this, he argues, is to acknowledge the reality or truth of power, over against an idealist notion of truth conceived in terms of representation, as correspondence to some a priori standard of judgment or, more specifically, to some a priori moral ideal. Machiavelli accordingly declares his divergence from the idealist tradition of reflection on political affairs in the famous opening to chapter 15:

> Since I intend to write something useful [*utile*] to an understanding reader, it seemed better to go after the real truth [*la verità effettuale*] of the matter than to repeat what people have imagined. A great many men have imagined states and princedoms such as nobody ever saw or knew in the real world, for there's such a difference between the way we really live and the way we ought to live that the man who neglects the real to study the ideal will learn how to accomplish his ruin, not his preservation.[2]

It is important to see, however, that although Machiavelli criticizes the Stoic and idealist moral philosophy of some humanists, he borrows from the more flexible pragmatism of others, according to whom truth is governed by an intrinsically ethical standard of decorum and consensus. Only when we recognize Machiavelli's imitation of and final divergence from this humanist tradition of pragmatism (and it is in this sense that the term *humanist* will most often be used in the following pages), will we be able to chart his innovation in political thought with any precision. I will argue that Machiavelli moves beyond the constraints of previous humanist reflection on the pragmatic nature of truth—which from his perspective offers yet another version of a mimetic, correspondence, or idealist theory—to a conception of truth as power, in which the pragmatic humanist version of truth itself becomes one weapon among others in the prince's strategic arsenal.

Imitation and Representation

From the very beginning of *The Prince* it is clear that Machiavelli is drawing on the resources of humanism, in particular its notion of imitation.[3] Like the humanists, he wants to educate his reader's practical judgment, the faculty of deliberation that allows for effective action within the contingent realm of fortune, and like them he recognizes that such education must therefore focus on particular examples rather than on the general precepts appropriate to theoretical reason. Furthermore, Machiavelli is concerned, as the humanists were, with criticizing an unreflective relation to past examples that would take the form of slavish imitation, simple representation, or a one-to-one correspondence. In fact, it is precisely in the absence of correspondence, of a mirror reflection of the exemplar, that the humanist prince or poet finds both the room to exercise his own will and the measure of his own achievement. Correct imitation accordingly involves imitating and realizing a flexible principle of prudential judgment or decorum. And this in turn gives rise to texts designed to dramatize and inculcate such judgment, whose rhetoric is, therefore, not ornamental but strategic.

Thus, in the prefatory letter to *The Prince*, Machiavelli justifies his gift of a text to Lorenzo de' Medici by suggesting that the latter will be a more effective ruler if he learns to imitate the double perspective, the reflective distance, offered in *The Prince*: "To know the people well one must be a prince, and to know princes well one must be, oneself, of the people" (3 [14]). And in chapter 14, "Military Duties of the Prince," Machiavelli makes the humanist claim for textual imitation even more forcefully by comparing skill in government to skill in reading, by making the ruler's landscape into a text and the text into a realm of forces. The prince is advised to learn to read the terrain ("imparare la natura de' siti") and to "read history and reflect on the actions of great men." Here, to imitate great men means to imitate imitation, that is, to "take as a model of [one's] conduct some great historical figure who achieved the highest praise and glory by constantly holding before himself the deeds and achievements of a predecessor" (43 [64]).

Machiavelli's defining truth pragmatically (*la verità effettuale*), rather than ontologically or epistemologically as correspondence to a fixed or absolute origin, would also seem to be consonant with humanism. And yet, if Machiavelli's notion of imitation appears to be essentially humanist, his own pragmatic definition of truth is not; for Machiavelli preserves the humanists' strategic sense of rhetoric only to separate it from its presumed origin in (the author's) and goal of (the reader's) intrinsically ethical practices of imitation. In rejecting the Ciceronian and humanist equation between *honestas* and *utilitas*, the faith that practical reason or prudence is inseparable from moral virtue, Machiavelli thus turns prudence into what the humanists (and their detractors) always feared it would become—the amoral skill of *versutia* or mere cleverness, which in turn implies the ethically unrestrained use of force—in short, *virtù*. He thus opens up a gap between the political agent and the political actor—or rather he makes the agent an actor who is capable of (mis)representation: the prince must appear to be good, virtuous, and so on in order to satisfy his people and thus to maintain his power (chapter 15).[4]

This redefinition of representation as ruse and thus of mimesis as power is the aim of *The Prince* as a whole,[5] but it finds a particularly forceful articulation in chapter 18. Machiavelli begins this chapter by distinguishing between human law and bestial force, but he then abandons the first pole of his binary opposition and proceeds to locate the range of political invention within the single second term of bestiality. Imitation may be a specifically human quality requiring the exercise of judgment, but the objects of imitation are bestial craft and force. Furthermore, the imitation of (bestial) nature has as its goal not correspondence to some fixed, determinate reality but the appearance of (what is conventionally accepted as) truth.

Here illusion is being turned against itself in order to present a truth to the people that will at the same time be effective for the prince. If, in the age-old debate between rhetoric and philosophy, the humanists want a rhetoric that is grounded in the truth and also effective, Machiavelli takes the further radical step not of subordinating or compromising truth in the interests of power, as he has sometimes been charged with doing, but of mutually implicating representation and force. Representation no longer involves even the correspondence to a practical standard of truth but has instead become theatrical. Correct or successful imitation no longer demands the exercise of self-knowledge and moral discretion but has itself become a rhetorical topic of invention to be manipulated in the interests of power.[6] Conversely, power becomes in part, if not entirely, an effect of the representational illusion of truth.

Machiavelli thus borrows—or imitates—the humanists' rhetorical strategies in order to educate his reader to an antihumanist conception of imitation and practice. My aim in the following pages is to clarify Machiavelli's similarity with and divergence from the humanists by taking a close look at what we might call, for heuristic purposes, the repertoire of figures in Machiavelli's strategic rhetoric. These heuristic figures should also help us to discover how Machiavelli's revision of the humanist notion of practical reason is at one and the same time the condition of *virtù* and the potential obstacle to its realization. As we will see, although Machiavelli's realistic analysis of the realm of politics avoids the ethical domestication of *virtù*, it threatens to allegorize, reify, or demonize *virtù*, thus finally undermining the flexible political skill that the strategic rhetoric of *The Prince* was designed to encourage.

Irony and Hyperbole

For hyperbole is a virtue [*virtus*], when the magnitude of the facts passes all words, and in such circumstances our language will be more effective if it goes beyond the truth than if it falls short of it.

—*Quintilian*

Machiavelli's criticism of the humanist version of pragmatism follows from his recognition of the intrinsic irony of politics, or of action within the contingent realm of human affairs: "If you look at matters carefully, you will see that something resembling virtue, if you follow it, may be your ruin, while something resembling vice will lead, if you follow it, to your security and well-being" (45 [66]).[7] But this formulation also allows us to see that Machiavelli wants to control this irony, or rather that he conceives of the man of *virtù* as someone who can *use* the ironies of political action to achieve political stability. (The refusal to *act* in the face of such ironies Machiavelli called literature; see *Florentine Histories*, book 5, chapter 1.)[8] This recognition of the irony of politics leads in turn to a revision of humanist argument in *utramque partem* (on both sides of a question). The humanists, following Aristotle, believed that it is necessary to be able to argue on both sides of a question, not so that one might actually defend a false position but so that one can anticipate and thereby more effectively rebut an opponent's arguments.[9] Machiavelli, however, argues that the prince will actually have to oppose what may appear to be good at a given moment. In fact, in Machiavelli's view, it is the humanists who are guilty of trying to accommodate at a single moment contrary qualities or arguments (e.g., in chapters 16 and 17) when they claim that the good and the useful are always compatible. Knowledge in *utramque partem* is necessary according to Machiavelli because "the conditions of human life simply do not allow" one "to have and exercise" only morally good qualities (45 [65]; cf. chapter 18, 50 [73]).

It is precisely this intrinsic irony of politics—the gap or lack of a mimetic relation between intention and result—that both allows for and requires solutions that seem extreme from the perspective of the humanist ideal of *mediocritas* (the "middle way").[10] Hence the place of hyperbole and exaggeration in Machiavelli's rhetoric. On the one hand, the examples of great men will always seem hyperbolic or excessive to—beyond the reach of—the imitator. On the other hand, Machiavelli argues, this hyperbole has a rhetorical and pedagogical function.

Men almost always prefer to walk in paths marked out by others and pattern their actions through imitation. Even if he cannot follow other people's paths in every respect, or attain to the *virtù* of his originals, a prudent man should always follow the footsteps of the great and imitate those who have been supreme. His own *virtù* may not come up to theirs, but at least it will have a sniff of it. Thus he will resemble skilled archers who, seeing how far away the target lies, and knowing the *virtù* of their bow, aim much higher than the real target, not because they expect the arrow to fly that far, but to accomplish their real end by aiming beyond it. (16 [30])

In this view, hyperbolic examples do not correspond to things as they are but to what they might be; they are figures of action rather than perception, of desire rather than cognition or representation. Hyperbole as a mode of speech or behavior is thus the proper response to the irony of politics: it is predicated on a recognition of one's distance both from the situation as it stands and from the situation one would like to create, but it also involves the recognition that such distance—as in the epigraph from Adorno—is itself a precondition of considered action. Finally, hyperbolic action is often ironic according to the classical definition of irony (Quintilian *Institutio oratoria* 8.6.54; 9.2.44–47) because it involves saying or doing one thing in order to arrive at its opposite. In short, the world of Machiavellian politics is intrinsically ironic, and the most effective mode of behavior in such a world is theatrical and hyperbolic. An analysis of the example of Agathocles in chapter 8 will serve to illustrate this point. At the same time, it should also help us to see how Machiavelli's strategic practice as a writer imitates that of his ideal prince.

STRATEGIC STYLE: THE EXAMPLE OF AGATHOCLES

In a world where a flexible faculty of judgment is constitutive of *virtù*, it is not surprising that Machiavelli should offer us no substantive definition of his terms. This is not simply a failing of analytical skill, as Sydney Anglo has complained,[11] but a sophisticated rhetorical strategy, the aim of which is to destabilize or dehypostatize our conception of political virtue, for only a destabilized *virtù* can be effective in the destabilized world of political reality.[12] In this context, the most effective critique of an idealist or mimetic notion of truth and of representation will be one that stages or dramatizes this lack of conceptual stability, rather than simply stating it as a fact. This rhetorical indirection would not in itself differentiate Machiavelli from the humanists. What is important to see, however, is that Machiavelli uses humanist rhetoric theatrically for antihumanist purposes. Chapter 8 on Agathocles the Sicilian is an exemplary instance of how the Machiavellian critique of representation implicates the humanists' ethical pragmatism as well.

In chapter 8, Machiavelli presents Agathocles as an example of someone who rises to power not by *virtù* or fortune but by crime. Readers of *The Prince* have tended to interpret this example in one of two ways. In this narrative, some argue, Machiavelli registers his own discomfort with the notion of *virtù* that he has been elaborating: it does violence to his sense of morality as well as to that of the reader. J.H. Whitfield speaks of Machiavelli's condemnation of Agathocles, and Claude Lefort remarks on the "réserve troublante" that qualifies Machiavelli's admiration of this figure.[13] Others see the story as an illustration of a cruel but effective use of violence. The interpreters who fall into this camp then differ as to whether this use of violence is immoral or amoral.[14] But in neither case is Machiavelli's own interpretation of Agathocles as one who rose to power by means of crime subject to scrutiny.[15] Thus, although the proponents of the first interpretation make note of Machiavelli's qualifications of Agathocles' actions ("Non si può ancora chiamare virtù ammazzare li sua cittadini"; 42), they read this qualification as a simple pun ("It certainly cannot be called 'virtue' to murder his fellow citizens"; 26) and so save Machiavelli from the charge of failing to make moral distinctions. The second group of interpreters, in accepting the story of Agathocles as an illustration of the uses of crime rather than of *virtù*, make an analogous moral distinction between the excessive cruelty of Agathocles and the politic restraint of the man of *virtù*. In both cases one would argue that this making of distinctions was precisely Machiavelli's intention. Following from the story of Cesare Borgia in chapter 7, the next chapter would serve, in these readings, to correct the reader who had begun to think *virtù* identical with crime. In chapter 8 Machiavelli would then reassure the reader by acknowledging that there is a difference between the two.

In fact, however, there is hardly a less reassuring experience of reading in *The Prince* than that of chapter 8. And it is a chapter whose disturbing quality increases as we read further in the work: in chapter 6 Machiavelli describes the relation of *virtù* and *fortuna* as a dialectical one, but he goes further in chapter 25 when he claims that *fortuna* and *virtù* divide the world of events between them. How then, we wonder, could crime be a third term in Machiavelli's analysis of the way princes rise to power?

In spite of the title and the first paragraph of chapter 8, Machiavelli's introductory remarks about Agathocles seem to confirm the polar opposition of chapter 25. He tells us that Agathocles "joined to his villainies such *virtù* of mind and body that after enlisting in the army he rose through the ranks to become military governor of Syracuse" (25 [41]). And a little further on he reiterates that Agathocles' success was due to *virtù*: "Considering the deeds and *virtù* of this man, one finds little or nothing that can be attributed to fortune" (26 [41]). But, then, anticipating his reader's objections, he quickly adds:

> Yet it certainly cannot be called *virtù* to murder his fellow citizens, betray his friends, to be devoid of truth, pity, or religion; a man may get power by means like these, but not glory. If we consider simply the *virtù* of Agathocles in facing and escaping from dangers, and the greatness of his soul in sustaining and overcoming adversity, it is hard to see why he should be considered inferior to the greatest of captains. Nonetheless, his fearful cruelty and inhumanity, along with his innumerable crimes, prevent us from placing him among the really excellent men. For we can scarcely attribute to either fortune or *virtù* a conquest which he owed to neither. (26 [42])

How are we to make sense of the vertiginous distinctions in this paragraph? Russell Price has suggested that Machiavelli is differentiating in this passage between the military *virtù* and glory ["gloria"] that apply to captains and the political *virtù* and glory that apply to "the really excellent men."[16] Of the former he writes: "It seems that [Agathocles] ... deserves credit for his martial spirit and deeds (that is, as a *capitano*) after he became ruler; what blackens his reputation is how he became ruler, because he treacherously slaughtered his friends and fellow citizens. Trickery and violence are to be condemned in a ruler or an aspiring ruler.... The stain he incurred by the way he seized power is indelible like original sin" (611). Apart from the dubious appropriateness of an analogy with original sin for a writer of such rabid anti-Christian sentiment, this analysis fails to take account of the fact that Borgia also used trickery and violence to secure his power but is nevertheless not being offered as an example of one who rose to power by crime. Furthermore, although Borgia is not condemned by Machiavelli, neither is he called one of the really excellent men, a phrase that, as J.G.A. Pocock reminds us, refers to legislators rather than new princes.[17]

A more sophisticated version of Price's analysis is presented by Claude Lefort, who argues that the introduction of the theme of *gloria* in chapter 8 signals a turning point in the argument of *The Prince*. Whereas the earlier chapters were concerned with the necessary exercise of violence in the acquisition of power, the example of Agathocles introduces the necessity of *representing* oneself to the people in a certain way in order to hold on to the power one has acquired. Machiavelli had previously emphasized the self-sufficiency of the prince; he now places the action of the prince in a social context in which it acquires its real significance (380–81). In this way, *virtù* itself is neither identical with nor exclusive of crime, but it does require glory, and it is this concern for glory that will induce the prince to moderate his violent behavior and take greater interest in the welfare of his people. According to this reading, in the sentence that begins "Yet it certainly cannot be called *virtù* to murder his fellow citizens," it is *called* that should be stressed: *virtù* is not equal to crime, though even a "virtuous" man (Borgia, for example) may find it necessary on occasion to act criminally. Yet if Lefort is not as reassuring as those readers who claim that Machiavelli is asserting a clear-cut distinction between military and political (moral) *virtù*, he nevertheless claims that there is a distinction between Borgia and Agathocles, one that does not lie in the nature of their deeds, since both were guilty of criminal behavior, but rather in the fact that the deeds of the latter "were committed without justification, or without a pretext [*sans masque*], by a man whom nothing, except his ambition, destined to reign ... a man—Machiavelli took the trouble to make clear—*di infima e abjetta fortuna*, the simple son of a potter" (380; my translation).

It is not so much the crimes of Agathocles that constitute his original sin, according to Lefort, as his lowly birth. But this interpretation trivializes both the notion of representation and that of fortune in *The Prince*, neither of which, as Lefort elsewhere recognizes, is a static concept involving a one-to-one correspondence, according to which the bad fortune of lowly birth would forever restrict Agathocles' possibilities for representing himself in a favorable light. In fact, by the end of the chapter Agathocles is offered as an example of someone who used cruelty well rather than badly, and who was consequently "able to reassure people, and win them over to his side with benefits" (28 [44]). It would seem, then, that far from excluding Agathocles from the category of "representative men," Machiavelli goes out of his way to stress his inclusion.

As we have seen, most readings of chapter 8 respond to the pressure to make distinctions that is implicit in the apparently contradictory reiteration of *virtù*. But it is important to see that clear-cut or permanent distinctions are finally what cannot be made. Throughout *The Prince* Machiavelli sets concepts in polar opposition to each other and then shows how the opposition is contained within each term so that the whole notion of opposition must be redefined.[18] Thus he begins chapter 25 by telling the reader that "fortune governs one half of our actions, but that even so she leaves the other half more or less in our power to control." Fortune is then presented as a natural force, a torrential stream against which men can take countermeasures "while the weather is still fine." But this opposition is a generalization that undergoes startling revision when we come to "the particulars." For a man's ability to take countermeasures—his *virtù*—turns out to be a fact of (his) nature and thus a potential natural disaster over which he has no control:

> If a prince conducts himself with patience and caution, and the times and circumstances are favorable to those qualities, he will flourish; but if times and circumstances change, he will come to ruin unless he changes his method of proceeding. No man, however prudent, can adjust to such radical changes, not only because we cannot go against the inclination of nature, but also because when one has always prospered by following a particular course, he cannot be persuaded to leave it. (71 [100])

In this more particular view, human nature is itself a torrential stream that cannot redirect its course with dikes and restraining dams; the favorable constraints are instead introduced by fortune. The purely formal *virtù* that is the ability to "adjust one's behavior to the temper of the times"—and that is precisely not constancy of character—is not a quality that can be attributed once and for all; it is rather a generalization that designates only the, fortunate coincidence of "nature's livery and fortune's star." Or, as Machiavelli writes of men of *virtù* in chapter 6: "Without the opportunity their *virtù* of mind would have been in vain, and without that *virtù* the opportunity would have been lost" (17 [31]).

If we now return to chapter 8, we can begin to see why Machiavelli cannot call Agathocles' crimes virtuous. In the light of chapter 25, it seems that we should place an even stronger emphasis on called: in the case of neither Borgia nor Agathocles can crime be called *virtù*, because *virtù* cannot be *called* any one thing. In short, once the temporal dimension of circumstance is introduced, the fact that crime cannot necessarily be called *virtù* means also that it can be called *virtù*. The danger of chapter 7 is not only that we might identify Borgia's murder and treachery with *virtù* but also that we would identify *virtù* with any particular act—criminal or not. The aim of the passage, in short, is to dehypostatize *virtù*, to empty it of any specific meaning. For *virtù* is not a general rule of behavior that can be applied to a specific situation but is rather, like prudence, a faculty of deliberation about particulars.

On one level, then, the conclusion of the paragraph concerning Agathocles' *virtù* ("for we can scarcely attribute to either fortune or *virtù* a conquest which he owed to neither") seems to reinforce the distinctions between *virtù*, fortune, and crime with which the chapter began—perhaps as an ironic concession to the reader's moral sensibility. On another level, it simply points up the incommensurability between the generalizations of *fortuna* and *virtù* and the specific instances that cannot be usefully subordinated to any (conceptual) generalization. How else is it possible to explain the end of chapter 8, where Machiavelli makes a distinction between two sorts of cruelty—cruelty used well and used badly—thereby placing the distinction between *fortuna* and *virtù* within cruelty itself: "Cruelty can be described as well used (if it's permissible to speak well about something that is evil in itself) when it is performed all at once, for reasons of self-preservation" (27–28 [44]). Once again the emphasis is on *chiamare* ("Bene usate si possono chiamare quelle [se del male è licito dire bene]"), but here the temporal dimension is explicit, as is the consequent and necessary making of distinctions within "cruelty." And once again, in the parenthetical remark, Machiavelli speaks to the reader's moral sensibility but he has answered the implied question even before it has been posed. Cruelty *can* be called "well used" because Machiavelli has just done so in the preceding clause. The adverbial *bene* then takes on some of the paronomastic color of the earlier paragraph on *virtù*. The reader wonders if it is permissible to speak good (*bene*) words about evil, whereas Machiavelli replies by speaking well (*bene*).[19]

These lines are important because they contain in little Machiavelli's critique of humanism. The humanist's assumption that *honestas* is compatible with *utilitas*, reflected in the maxim that the good orator is necessarily a good man, is politically useless to Machiavelli, however it is interpreted. When the goodness of the orator is interpreted to mean in conformity with ethical goodness (*honestas*; see Cicero *De officiis* 3.3.11, 3.11.49), then the maxim is a stoic tautology and the question of the orator's effectiveness (*utilitas*) need not enter in. When the orator's goodness is interpreted to mean persuasiveness as well as moral rectitude, then the claim that the orator is a good man is a synthetic judgment that is also idealistic and unfounded. One has only to look to experience to recall that many morally good men have been politically ineffective. Here the criterion of correct action is not moral goodness or the intrinsically moral judgment of prudence but the functional excellence or effectiveness of *virtù*: a *virtù* we might say, parodying Aristotle, that demonstrates its own excellence by being effective.[20] In speaking well rather than speaking good words, Machiavelli both dramatizes and thematizes this functional virtuosity. He shows that *virtù* is not a substance but a mode of action (not a noun, but an adverb) by speaking well about acting well.

The linguistic play of this paragraph and the earlier one on *virtù* are thus part of a rhetorical strategy to engage the reader in a critical activity that will allow him to discover not the content of "what should be" but the formality of what in any particular situation "can be."[21] Here, if the reader's "natural" disposition to make moral distinctions ("everyone agrees") may be compared to the natural force of the river in chapter 25, which serves as a metaphor for Fortune, Machiavelli's prose is the countermeasure that attempts to channel or redirect this course by introducing the element of reflection. In the rewriting of a metaphor from Quintilian (*Institutio oratoria* 9.4.7). Machiavelli proposes a style that is powerful precisely because it is rough and broken. He thus duplicates on the poetic level the practical problem of judgment that the prince will have to face—that of applying the rule of *virtù* to the particular situation at hand. Or, as Roland Barthes has written of Machiavelli's work, "The structure of the discourse attempts to reproduce the structure of the dilemmas actually faced by the protagonists. In this case reasoned argument predominates and the history [or discourse] is of a reflexive—one might say strategic—style."[22]

THEATRICALITY

The suggestion that Machiavelli's style is strategic means not only that the prince may learn something about strategy by reflecting on Machiavelli's prose (the structure and vocabulary of his examples) but also that the actual strategies he recounts may tell us something about Machiavelli's strategy as a writer. And this reciprocity in turn allows us to read the example of Agathocles in the light of Machiavelli's earlier remarks on Borgia. As a number of critics have remarked, Machiavelli's position as counselor is in some ways analogous to that of the new prince. Both are "student[s] of delegitimized politics,"[23] and for both the problem is how to impose a new form not only on matter but on already informed matter. But Machiavelli's *virtù* as a writer is not simply, as some readers have suggested, to dramatize in the writing of *The Prince* the resourcefulness and inventiveness of the effective ruler but also to manipulate his audience in much the same way that the prince must manipulate his subjects. In the first case, imitation involves the cultivation of a purely formal flexibility of judgment or *disponibilità*; in the second, that judgment is tested by the appearances of the text itself. Thus in chapter 7 Machiavelli proposes Borgia's behavior in the Romagna as an example worthy of imitation, and in chapter 8 he imitates it in order to test whether the reader has learned the lessons of chapter 7. In short, there are striking analogies not only between the careers of Borgia and Agathocles but also between the effect of Borgia's behavior on his subjects in the Romagna and Machiavelli's effect on the reader in chapter 8.

When Borgia took over the Romagna, he discovered that "the whole province was full of robbers, feuds, and lawlessness of every description" (22 [37]). His way of "establish[ing] peace and reduc[ing] the land to obedience" was to counter lawlessness with lawlessness: "He named Messer Remirro de Orco, a cruel and vigorous man, to whom he gave absolute powers. In short order this man pacified and unified the whole district, winning great renown" (22 [37]). But like Agathocles, Borgia knew that excessive authority can become odious,

> so he set up a civil court in the middle of the province, with an excellent judge and a representative from each city. And because he knew that the recent harshness had generated some hatred, in order to clear the minds of the people and gain them over to his cause completely, he determined to make plain that whatever cruelty had occurred had come, not from him, but from the brutal character of the minister. Taking a proper occasion, therefore, he had him placed on the public square of Cesena one morning, in two pieces, with a piece of wood beside him and a bloody knife. The ferocity of this scene left the people at once stunned and satisfied. (22 [37])

This story provides us with two examples of cruelty well used. The first is de Orco's, the second Borgia's. The function of the first is primarily destructive and repressive: to pacify his subjects. The function of the second is theatrical and cathartic; this too pacifies the subjects but by the theatrical display of violence rather than its direct application to the audience. The first example reestablishes justice from the perspective of the ruler; the second stages this reestablishment from the perspective of and for the ruled. As this theatrical display suggests, the story also provides us with two examples of representation well used. In the first, there is an element of representation insofar as Borgia delegates his power, but this delegation is ultimately a way of concealing the fact of representation (i.e., representation has become ruse) so that he can deny responsibility for de Orco's cruelty—as he does so effectively by means of (and this is the second example) his theatrical representation in the public square of Cesena.

The example of Agathocles in chapter 8 is just such a theatrical display on the part of Machiavelli. Like Borgia, Machiavelli is concerned with making a distinction between *virtù* and crime—not because they are mutually exclusive but because they are not identical. And like Borgia, he sets up a court with the reader as judge. "He determined to make plain that whatever cruelty had occurred [in the example of Agathocles] had come, not from him, but from the brutal character of the minister" (i.e., of his example). The reader is morally satisfied or reassured by Machiavelli's supposed condemnation of Agathocles, just as the people of the Romagna were by the dramatic and brutal disavowal of Remirro's brutality. But the reader who is taken in by this excuse is in the position of a subject rather than of a prince— for Machiavelli has not presented the example of Agathocles in order to pacify his readers but rather to try them. In short, Agathocles is proposed as an example for the prince who might have need to follow him, and the ability to determine that necessity is also the *virtuous* ability to make discriminations about what constitutes *virtù* with respect to any given situation. The example of Agathocles is a test of *virtù*.

THE AVOIDANCE OF TAUTOLOGY

When we turn from the examples of Borgia and Agathocles to the rest of *The Prince*, we see that this work is filled with examples of such extreme, ironic, or hyperbolic situations and actions. The most extreme example is perhaps Machiavelli's advice that the best way to keep a city is to destroy it (see chapter 5, 14 [28]; see also *The Discourses*, book 2, chapter 23; book 3, chapter 40). Many readers have thought that Machiavelli here and elsewhere could not possibly mean what he says, that he is ironic in the sense of unserious.[24] But the example of Agathocles has shown that what is mere exaggeration from the perspective of the conventional virtues may be simple pragmatic advice for the student of *virtù*. This advice will seem hyperbolic because it is beyond good and evil, because it involves the transgression of the conventional philosophical constraints on knowledge (knowledge as cognition of the truth) in the direction of knowledge defined as power.[25] But here precisely lies the problem. Although Machiavelli argues in chapter 15 that *virtù* involves knowledge that is useful or effective, he does not want to claim that *virtù* guarantees success. To make this claim would be to fall into a version of the tautology of *honestas* and *utilitas* that he condemns in the same chapter. If there were such a skill as a *virtù* that always yields success, then there would be no fortune or contingency; but contingency is precisely what makes room for *virtù*—indeed, what makes *virtù* necessary in Machiavelli's eyes. Still, a *virtù* that never resulted in success would be patently absurd. Thus Machiavelli claims early in *The Prince* that if we follow the examples of *virtù* that he presents, success will *usually* or most often result (11 [12]).

These ambiguities concerning the relation of *virtù* to success are reflected in Machiavelli's claim to be guided by the *verità effettuale della cosa*. On the one hand, he means that he will approach politics realistically, rather than idealistically, by beginning with things as they are. In this view, as Felix Gilbert has argued, "the measure of worth of a political figure [is] ... formed by his capacity to use the possibilities inherent in the political situations; politics [has] its own criteria to be derived from existing political opportunities."[26] On the other hand, implicit in the claim to be guided by the *verità effettuale* is the assumption that such an approach will prove to be *effective*: in short, that one does not simply imitate necessity but that one can manipulate it—effect it—to one's own advantage.

Machiavelli's vacillation is apparent throughout *The Prince*. Sometimes he equates *virtù* with successful political action; at other times he insists on distinguishing between the two.[27] In the first case, *virtù* becomes the goal of technical deliberation, and Machiavelli sounds like a dispassionate political analyst, subordinating means to ends. (The danger here, of course, is to assume that anyone who succeeds demonstrates *virtù*, when in fact success might be due to chance rather than to the activity of the individual.) In the second case, *virtù* is a practical skill that may be an end in itself, and thus structurally (although not ethically) similar to the classical notion of prudence.[28] In this way Machiavelli's vacillation simply conflates in a single term, *virtù*, an amoral version of the structural problem inherent in the classical and humanist concept of prudence—the problem of the relation of means to ends, of prudential deliberation to virtue or, in Machiavelli's case, to *virtù*.

This ambiguity or uncertainty about the status of deliberative skill and its relation to success is also reflected in the nature and function of examples in Machiavelli's texts. As I have suggested, a teacher who subordinates practical judgment to theoretical reason has only to present the student with general precepts and the logical rules of deduction, but a teacher whose theory of action equates judgment with the exercise of practical reason or the observance of decorum will have to educate such judgment through examples. Such examples will not have the status of mere illustrations of theory, as they would if they were subordinated to or subsumed under universally applicable abstract principles. They will not be expendable but necessary, since every judgment of decorum is a judgment of, and must conform to the exigencies of, a particular situation. If such judgment *merely* conformed to the particular, however, it would cancel itself out as a judgment, since it would involve no reference to a standard other than faithful representation (imitation) of the particular case. Judgment requires distance, and examples that educate such judgment must contain within themselves or dramatize this distance. Thus examples in humanist texts are to a certain extent problematizing since they are designed to provoke reflection. But their pedagogical aim also demands a limit to such problematizing: for if excessive identification with the particular leads to the collapse of judgment, excessive difference (the reflection on and putting in question of all possible standards of judgment—whether the standard of virtue or of *virtù*) does as well. Although Machiavelli lacked the humanists' faith in the ethical criterion of practical reason, he was not usually skeptical about the possibility of deliberation and action. Indeed, he insisted that such possibility could be realized only in a world purged of idealism. Machiavelli thus shares with the humanists a rhetoric of problematizing examples, and like the humanists he needs to limit such problematizing.[29]

The dilemma that Machiavelli faces is thus intrinsic to the problematic of imitation, but it is also tinged with a peculiarly Machiavellian irony insofar as the ethical claims for humanist imitation are a rhetorical topic contained within and thus ultimately undermined by the Machiavellian strategy of imitation. In this context, Agathocles' "over-shooting" of morality is exemplary because, in both Machiavelli's strategy as author and Agathocles' as agent, it dramatizes and encourages the distanced reflection and thus the reflective imitation necessary for, if not sufficient for, success.

IRONY AND ALLEGORY

> Irony descends from the low mimetic: it begins in realism and dispassionate observation. But as it does so, it moves steadily towards myth, and dim outlines of sacrificial rituals and dying gods begin to reappear in it.
> —*Northrop Frye*

As I have argued in the preceding pages, Machiavelli's reflection on the political uses of representation is tied to his revision of the humanist concept of prudential action. The prince is powerful to the extent that he diverges from a naive or moral concept of prudence, but he also maintains his power by "naively" imitating—or representing himself as faithfully reproducing—the conventional virtues. As in chapter 18, power is in part, if not entirely, the effect of the representational illusion of truth. But, as the case of Agathocles demonstrates, the exigency of representation, if representation is conceived of now as the means or the ability to generate the consensus and support of the people (chapter 8, 24 [44]); chapter 18, 51 [74]; *The Discourses*, book 2, chapter 23; book 3, chapter 19–23), also finally proves to be a forceful constraint on the abuse of power. Cruelty will be well used if "it is performed all at once, for reasons of self-preservation; and when the acts are not repeated after that, but rather turned as much as possible to the advantage of the subjects" (chapter 8, 27–28 [44]). The prince must in the long run please his audience if he is to maintain his rule. In the end, the rhetorical topic of truth proves to involve an ironic version of the ethical constraint that the humanists located in custom and consensus. This constraint also helps us to see how the analysis of power in *The Prince* logically gives way to that in *The Discourses*: the prince, to be successful in the long run, must found a republic because republics are capable of greater longevity and *virtù* than principalities. The "understanding reader" will see that when representation and force are mutually implicated, when representation becomes a means of power, and thus finally when power is mitigated by the exigencies of persuasion, the short-lived individual self-aggrandizement gives way to communal glory, and the prince must of necessity become a fellow citizen.[30]

This is the optimistic way to read the self-destructing rhetoric of *The Prince*. But, as most readers have noted, there is a more radical way in which the analysis of *virtù* undermines itself and Machiavelli's pedagogy in this text. As Machiavelli tells us over and over again, there are no general rules for virtuous behavior (e.g., chapter 20, 59 [85]), and there is no guarantee that the skill one practices in the interpretation of particular examples will enable one to respond appropriately in the next situation. This is, of course, as it should be. As Machiavelli writes in chapter 21, "No leader should ever suppose he can invariably take the safe course, since all choice involves risks. In the nature of things [*nell'ordine delle cose*], you can never try to escape one danger without encountering another; but prudence consists in knowing how to recognize the nature of the different dangers and in accepting the least bad as good" (65 [92]). But the essential emptiness of the concept of *virtù* receives a rather different and finally devastating articulation in chapter 25, where the role of fortune in the individual's ability to act virtuously finally seems to deprive the individual of any initiative whatsoever. As we saw, Machiavelli begins this chapter by discussing the relation of fortune and *virtù* in general terms. On this level he gives fortune a certain allegorical stability, as though fortune were something external to *virtù* that the latter had only to resist. When he descends to particulars, however, fortune has no stability whatsoever. The irony of politics and human action becomes so great—the possibility of action (as opposed to mere passivity) so compromised—that the distance constitutive of reflection finally collapses altogether. To recognize which situations require which kinds of imitation finally necessitates that the prince imitate the absolute flexibility of fortune itself. But one's ability to learn is itself, finally, a function of the *fortune* of one's natural disposition, and is necessarily limited by it. In thus conflating the realm of necessity or nature with the agent of *virtù*, Machiavelli runs the risk of reducing *virtù* to the mere repetition—that is, the willed acceptance—of necessity: the mimetic representation of nature.[31] In so doing, he finally does substitute for the tautology of *honestas* and *utilitas* the tautology of *virtù* and success. It is not surprising, then, that Machiavelli should at this moment invoke the personified figure of Fortune (*Fortuna*) as a woman in a desperate, inconsequential attempt to redeem the possibility of action by relocating it in an interpersonal context.[32]

A few remarks about the allegorical tendency of *The Prince* may help to clarify this point. According to Angus Fletcher, the allegorical hero confronts a world of contingency, a world in which the individual has very little control over the consequences of his actions, and in which there often seems to be little causal connection between events.[33] Narrative sequence is threatened by parataxis but restored on the level of cosmic, often magical necessity.[34] As a result, the hero also seems to be not simply at the mercy of external events but in the control of some external power. In fact, the allegorical hero could be said to operate in a world of demonic powers, a world in which functions have been compartmentalized, personified. The result is that the hero himself becomes depersonalized; he is not a person but rather a personification of a function. In a world of *Fortuna*, in short, the hero becomes of necessity the embodiment of *Virtù*.

In such a world, then, the virtues no longer seem to be attributes of individual agents; rather, they recover their original sense of powers or forces, of *virtù*. As Fletcher remarks, "Like a Machiavellian prince, the allegorical hero can act free of the usual moral restraints, even when he is acting morally, since he is moral only in the interests of his power over other men" (68). To redefine virtue as *virtù* is thus "to rediscover a sense of the morally ambivalent power in action" (an advance, one might say, in the direction of "realism"), but it is also, ironically, to run the risk of doing away with free will. Although the intention behind Machiavelli's various *exempla* of *virtù* is to help the reader understand the formal, innovative character of this faculty, and the role of free will in determining what constitutes *virtù* in any particular situation, the quasi-allegorical status of the man of *virtù*, or of the prince as a *personification* of *Virtù*, suggests that the individual is not at all in control of his behavior—a suggestion that, as we have seen, becomes explicit in chapter 25. The way Machiavelli chooses to combat this demonization or personification of the person is to repersonalize what was becoming an increasingly abstract and *unmanageable* concept of fortune by introducing the figure of Fortune as a woman. In a kind of parody of humanist rhetoric *in utramque partem*, allegory is used to fight the allegorization or reification of the prince's *virtù*.

In light of these remarks, one can also see that the allegorical tendency of Machiavelli's "realism" is manifest in the sublime rhetoric of his concluding chapter.[35] Fletcher calls our attention to the structural similarity between allegory and the sublime. Simply stated, the experience of the sublime involves the inability of the imagination to comprehend sensuous experience, which leads to an awareness of the higher faculty of reason and to "reflection on man's higher destiny" (249). This discrepancy between sensuous experience and the higher claims of reason is analogous to the separation of sensuous representation and allegorical signified in the allegorical text. Furthermore, as Longinus reminds us, allegory is not only analogous to the sublime but can itself have a sublime effect, an ideological (249) or epideictic force when it "incites to action" (246). But, Northrop Frye, in the epigraph to this section, suggests, the structural incommensurability in the allegorical sublime can also have an ironic effect, by implying that the principle of authority or meaning (reason, God) is infinitely removed from the world of sensuous immediacy.[36]

Machiavelli obviously intends the sublime or divine rhetoric of his concluding chapter to function as the best of all hyperboles: to incite the Medici to action. Consider the following claim:

> There is no figure presently in sight to whom she [Italy] can better trust than your illustrious house, which, with its fortune and its *virtù*, favored by God and the Church of which it is now the head, can take the lead in this process of redemption. (73 [102])

In these lines, Machiavelli conflates the fortune of the Medici with divine providence and the Church, and thus simultaneously debases religion and confers a certain grandeur upon the rulers of Florence.[37] In this light necessity, too, takes on a different and more positive appearance; it is no longer the necessity of fortune or of contingency or of (one's own) nature that resists *virtù* (as in chapter 25); rather, necessity is now the "providential necessity" that justifies the actions of the Medici. Describing men of *virtù*, he writes: "Their cause was no more just than the present one, nor any easier, and God was no more favorable to them than to you. Your cause is just: 'for war is justified when it is necessary, and arms are pious when without them there would be no hope at all'" (73 [103]). In its divine justification of the Medici as the redeemers of Italy, chapter 26 would be the final, brilliant example of Machiavelli's theatrical overshooting of the mark, of a rhetoric of representation that is neither constrained by logic to represent the truth nor guided by practical reason in its achievement of decorum, but that aims rather to produce the effect of truth—or to effect it. Yet the obvious alternative reading of the lines just quoted is that providential justification is conflated with the material realm of necessity. In this way, the collapse of the distance and difference necessary for action in chapter 25 turns out to anticipate the rhetoric of chapter 26, a rhetoric that, paradoxically, seems designed precisely to recoup the losses of the preceding chapter. In the end, exaggeration cannot free itself "from the weight of the factual, so that instead of merely reproducing being it can, at once rigorous and free, determine it" (Adorno; see the epigraph). In a final ironic twist, Machiavelli's providential rhetoric can then be seen to suggest that, to answer Schlegel's question, only (the hyperbolic figure of) God can save us from such ironies.

NOTES

I am grateful to Charles Trinkaus for his helpful criticism of an earlier draft of this essay. The epigraphs are from Theodor Adorno, *Minima moralia*, trans. E.F.N. Jephcott (London, 1978), 126–27; and from Friedrich Schlegel, "Über die Unverständlichkeit," *Kritische Schriften* (Munich, 1964), 538 (my translation).

1. Sheldon Wolin, *Politics and Vision* (Boston, 1960), 224.

2. Niccolò Machiavelli, *The Prince*, trans. and ed. Robert M. Adams (New York, 1997), 44. Throughout, I have substituted *virtù* for the various English translations Adams provides. References to the Italian text are taken from Machiavelli, *Il Principe e Discorsi*, ed. Sergio Bertelli (Milan, 1960), and are given in the text in brackets following English-text references; e.g., (44 [65]).

3. Recent interpretations of *The Prince* in the context of the humanist notion of imitation include Mark Hulliung, *Citizen Machiavelli* (Princeton, N.J., 1983), esp. 130–67; Hanna Fenichel Pitkin, *Fortune Is a Woman: Gender and Politics in the Thought of Niccolò Machiavelli* (Berkeley, Calif., 1983), 268ff.; and Thomas M. Greene, "The End of Discourse in Machiavelli's *Prince*," in *Literary Theory/Renaissance Texts*, ed. Patricia Parker and David Quint (Baltimore, 1986), 63–77. Gennaro Sasso also discusses Machiavelli's

notion of imitation in *Niccolò Machiavelli: Storia del suo pensiero politico* (Naples, 1958), 381–89. For earlier treatments of Machiavelli in the context of humanism, see Felix Gilbert, *Machiavelli and Guicciardini: Politics and History in Sixteenth-Century Florence* (Princeton, N.J., 1965); and his "The Humanist Concept of the Prince and the *Prince* of Machiavelli, *The Journal of Modern History* 11 (1939) 449–83; as well as Allan H. Gilbert, *Machiavelli's Prince and Its Forerunners: The Prince as a Typical Book De Regimine Principum* (Durham, NC; 1938) In considering Machiavelli's rhetoric, I have also benefited from Eugene Carver, "Machiavelli's *The Prince*: A Neglected Rhetorical Classic," *Philosophy and Rhetoric* 13 (1980): 99–120; from his *Machiavelli and the History of Prudence* (Madison, Wis., 1987); and from Nancy Struever's chapter on Machiavelli in her *Theory as Practice: Ethical Inquiry in the Renaissance* (Chicago, 1992).

4. Machiavelli's separation of the political agent from the political actor anticipates Hobbes in chap. 16 of *Leviathan*. On the distinction between cleverness or versutia and prudence, see Aristotle, *Nicomachean Ethics*, trans. Martin Ostwald (New York, 1962), 1144a.25–1144b (hereafter cited as *NE*).

5. See the discussion by Pierre Manent, *Naissances de la politique moderne: Machiavel, Hobbes, Rousseau* (Paris, 1977), 19: "If ruse is, in Machiavelli's eyes, the principal resource of political action, that is because ruse responds to the essence of the political Situation" (my translation).

6. Thomas M. Greene, *The Light in Troy: Imitation and Discovery in Renaissance Poetry* (New Haven, Conn., 1982), 142, 172, 184.

7. Wolin discusses Machiavelli's view of the intrinsic irony of politics in *Politics and Vision*, 227.

8. Cited by Hulliung, *Citizen Machiavelli*, 137.

9. Aristotle *Rhetoric* 1355a.20–1355b.5.

10. As Hulliung (*Citizen Machiavelli*, 158–59) and Sydney Anglo (*Machiavelli* [New York, 1969], 244–49) have remarked, Machiavelli's rejection of mediocritas is also reflected in his antithetical, either/or style of arguing.

11. Anglo, *Machiavelli*, 209.

12. Nancy Struever has an interesting discussion of the dereification of *virtù* in *Theory as Practice*, 157.

13. J. H. Whitfield, *Machiavelli* (Oxford, 1947), 80 and 108; Claude Lefort, *Le travail de l'oeuvre Machiavel* (Paris, 1972), 376. See later in this essay for further discussion of Lefort's position. Another representative of Whitfield's position is Jerrold Seigel, "*Virtù* in and since the Renaissance," in *Dictionary of the History of Ideas* (New York, 1968), 4:476–86.

14. For the first position, see Gennaro Sasso, *Niccolò Machiavelli*, 296ff.; Gabriele Pepe, *La politica dei Borgia* (Naples, 1945), 281–82; and Ugo Dotti, *Niccolò Machiavelli: La fenomenologia del potere* (Milan, 1979), 179ff.; for the second, see J.G.A. Pocock, *The Machiavellian Moment: Florentine Political Thought and The Atlantic Republican Tradition* (Princeton, N.J., 1975), 152 and 167.

15. Greene, in "The End of Discourse," notes the tenuousness of the distinction between Borgia and Agathocles (70), but sees this as evidence of a breakdown in the concept of *virtù* rather than a deliberate strategy on the part of Machiavelli. Manent, *Naissances* (16), however, sees the distinction as deliberately false.

16. Russell Price, "The Theme of *Gloria* in Machiavelli," *Renaissance Quarterly* 30 (1977): 588–631.

17. Pocock, *The Machiavellian Moment*, 168.

18. See *The Prince*, chap. 12, on the pseudodistinction between laws and arms, as well as chap. 19 on arms and friends.

19. Struever also discusses the general conflation of the ethical good and the amoral well in *The Prince* in *Theory as Practice*, 157.

20. Aristotle writes: "It is this kind of deliberation which is good deliberation, a correctness that attains what is good" (*NE*, 3141b.20). My definition of *virtù* as functional excellence is taken from Hulliung's discussion of the similarity between *virtù* and *aretê*: "Since the Latin word *virtus* meant almost exactly what *aretê* had meant in popular Greek usage, simply to use the Latin language as it had always been used had the effect, whether intended or unintended, of undoing the Platonic and Aristotelian effort of reworking and philosophizing pagan values. Once again, 'excellence' was synonymous with all that is heroic, noble, warlike, great"; *Citizen Machiavelli*, 136–37. See also 194–98, 212–17 and 253 on Machiavelli's critique of stoicism.

21. This phrase is taken from Whitfield, *Machiavelli*, 117.

22. Roland Barthes, "Le discours de l'histoire," *Social Science Information* 6 (1967): 72. Michael McCanles, in a book that came to my attention after the completion of this essay (*The Discourse of "Il Principe*," vol. 8 of *Humana Civilitas*, Studies and Sources Relating to the Middle Ages and Renaissance [Malibu, Calif., 1983]), proposes a reading of chap. 8. similar to the one I am offering here. He tends, however, to maintain a strict opposition between Christian virtue and *virtù*, even as he denies any substantive definition of the latter. That is, although he argues throughout his book for the dialectical understanding of *virtù* as necessarily including its opposite, he suggests here that what is evil from a Christian point of view will necessarily be good from a political point of view and vice versa (see 63). He also does not discuss Agathocles' conversion to representation at the end of chap. 8 (see 59–65).

23. Pocock, *The Machiavellian Moment*, 163.

24. See Adams's remarks on this example in his edition of *The Prince*, 14. See also Leo Strauss, *Thoughts on Machiavelli* (Chicago, 1958), 82; and Felix Gilbert, *Machiavelli and Guicciardini*, 165–66.

25. On Machiavelli's anticipation of Nietzsche, see Hulliung, *Citizen Machiavelli*, 30.

26. Felix Gilbert, *Machiavelli and Guicciardini*, 120.

27. *Virtù* is equated with success in chap. 8 (28 [44]), 19 (59 [84]), and perhaps chap. 25 (71 [100]), where Machiavelli equates the good with what is effective; cf. the end of chap. 25. where failure is equated with inaction. *Virtù* is differentiated from success in chap. 4 (14 [28]), chap. 6 (16 [30]), and chap. 7 (20 [34–35]). In *The Discourses* (bk. 3, chap. 35), Machiavelli remarks on the superficiality of judging by the result, as he does in the *Florentine Histories*, bk. 4, chap. 7; and bk. 8, chap. 22. On this problem of the relation of *virtù* to success, see Alkis Kontos, "Success and Knowledge in Machiavelli," in *The Political Calculus: Essays on Machiavelli's Philosophy*, ed. Anthony Parel (Toronto, 1972), 83–100.

28. I borrow the distinction between technical and prudential from Aristotle (*NE*), who argues that *technê* is concerned with production (the end results), whereas prudential deliberation is a process, and an end in itself. The many critics who argue that *virtù* is technical skill are right if they mean that the prince is concerned with results, but wrong if they equate *virtù* with the result rather than with deliberative skill and energy in action. *Virtù* is not completely technical because technical skill must result in a product (however much that product may reflect a compromise with one's original conception of the object), whereas *virtù* does not have to produce something else in order to be *virtù*. Or, as Ostwald observes (*NE*, 154, n. 20), "Practical wisdom is itself a complete virtue or excellence while the excellence of art depends on the goodness or badness of the product." Again, I am arguing only for the structural identity or homology of *virtù* and prudence or practical reason.

29. On problematizing examples, see Karlheinz Stierle, "L'exemple comme histoire, l'histoire comme exemple," *Poétique* 10 (1972): 176–98. Although Machiavelli was capable of using the same examples to illustrate different points (e.g., Giacomini's loss of favor in *The Discourses*; bk. 1, chap. 53; and bk. 3, chap. 16; cited in Felix Gilbert, *Machiavelli and Guicciardini*, 167), he needed, if his work was to have any practical effect, to stop short of the radical skepticism of a Montaigne, for whom examples could be used to illustrate almost anything. For if they are so used, then one has departed from the realm of *verità effettuale* and entered the realm of the unconstrained imagination, the realm of fiction.

30. Hulliung makes this point in *Citizen Machiavelli*, 56, 82, 231. See also Strauss, *Thoughts on Machiavelli*, 288–89; Manent, *Naissances*, 19–25; and *The Prince*, chap. 19, 53–54 [77–78], for Machiavelli's remarks on the origin of the French parliament. Nancy Struever has some interesting remarks about constraint in *The Prince* in *Theory as Practice*, 165–75.

31. See Manent, *Naissances*, 9–10, 35–39, for a more positive reading of the willing of necessity in *The Prince*.

32. Pitkin makes this point in *Fortune Is a Woman*, 292.

33. See Angus Fletcher, *Allegory: The Theory of a Symbolic Mode* (Ithaca, N.Y., 1964). All page references are given in the text of my essay.

34. On parataxis in *The Prince*, see Fredi Chiappelli, *Studi sul linguaggio del Machiavelli* (Florence, 1952), 40–42 (cited by McCanles, *The Discourse of "Il Principe*," 13; see also 13–15).

35. For some provocative interpretations of this concluding chapter, see Greene, "The End of Discourse"; and Sasso, *Niccolò Machiavelli*, 278–80.

36. Frye, *Anatomy of Criticism* (Princeton, N.J., 1957), 42. Fletcher is quoting Schiller: "For the sublime, in the strict sense of the word, cannot be contained in any sensuous form, but rather concerns ideas of reason, which, although no adequate representation of them is possible, may be excited and called into the mind by that very inadequacy itself which does admit of sensuous presentation"; *Allegory*, 251–52. See also Immanuel Kant, *Critique of Judgment*, trans. J. H. Bernard (New York, 1951), 88, 101 (pars. 25 and 28).

37. Pocock makes a similar point in *The Machiavellian Moment*, 171: "We must not say that divine inspiration is being lowered to the level of realpolitik without adding that realpolitik is being raised to the level of divine inspiration."

BRIAN RICHARDSON

From Pen to Print:
Writers and Their Use of the Press

In the preceding chapter we looked at the procedures which writers could
use in order to control and take advantage of the publication of their works
in print, in so far as it was possible to do so. We can now move on from these
mechanisms to focus on the writers themselves and their use of print as
opposed to the pen. After considering what attitudes, positive or negative,
they showed towards the publication of their works in the new medium, we
will go on to examine the ways in which print was used by a number of
authors. On the basis of this evidence, we can then reach some general
conclusions on the extent to which print proved important in the contexts of
the aspirations and work of Italian writers in the Renaissance.

1 THE ATTITUDES OF WRITERS TOWARDS PRINT PUBLICATION

Old habits died hard. It took some time for writers to adjust their mentality
to publishing their works in print and to working with the professionals who
created and sold the printed text. Indeed, in certain respects manuscript
publication could still seem a preferable option. There were two reasons to
avoid print which may be termed practical. We have seen that writers might
have to take on the burden and risk of providing an initial capital outlay if
they wished to see their work through the press. Then there was the question
of loss of control over the text itself. Although scribes were of course prone

From *Printing, Writers and Readers in Renaissance Italy.* © 1999 by Brian Richardson.

to alter, voluntarily or involuntarily, what they copied, transmission of a text in print was by no means more reliable. Writers could justifiably fear that a process which was overhasty, as was noted in chapter 1, and always to some extent profit-driven, would drag their texts inexorably away from their original. Editors, compositors and pressmen might all introduce deviations from the copy-text, and these would not necessarily be corrected at the proof stage. An example of the irritation which an author could express at the damage inflicted on his work by print publication is the lament which the humanist Marcantonio Sabellico addressed to Girolamo Donato about his *De Venetae urbis situ libri* (The site of Venice): 'I can scarcely say how much the carelessness, or rather the idleness of [the printers] has taken away from the true reading.'[1] Nor were scholars the only ones who saw themselves as victims, as one can see from the anger expressed by the poet Cassio da Narni in a stanza inserted at the end of his popular romance *La morte del Danese*, printed in Ferrara in 1521 by Lorenzo Rossi:

> Impressori ignoranti de più sorte
> han fatto errori, che più fiate mi hanno
> sdegnato sì che bramato ho la morte,
> per uscir for de sì strano affanno
> che mal da supportar più grave e forte
> credo non sia, né che faccia più danno,
> quanto veder lacerar gli suoi versi
> dagl'impressori in la ignorantia imersi.

(Ignorant printers of various sorts have several times made me so angry with their errors that I have longed for death, as a relief from an anxiety so strange that I believe there is no evil more heavy and hard to bear, nor one which does more harm, than to see one's verses torn to shreds by printers steeped in ignorance.)

Cassio's fury would have been all the greater because it was he who had paid for printing (see chapter 9, section 2). Even errors which he had corrected, presumably in proofs, were, he claimed, overlooked.[2] It was all too easy to use such accusations in order to counter possible criticisms of one's own shortcomings, but a cautious writer could well have considered that the risks of inaccurate diffusion in print outweighed any possible benefits. Further, at the end of chapter 2 we saw that writers in sixteenth-century Italy had increasingly to overcome problems of censorship before their works could be issued in approved form.

Writers might also be reluctant to go into print if they felt that a text was not yet in the finalized state which was required for reproduction on a wide scale. An author might judge that the matter or style of certain works made them more suitable for scribal publication. This might apply to works which commented on contemporary society and politics; examples are several texts by Niccolò Machiavelli. It might apply to some extent to the circulation of vernacular lyric poetry within a restricted circle, orally or in writing.[3] Theatrical texts, too, might be conceived solely for the audience before which they were performed. Ariosto, for instance, wrote his comedies for the court, not for the general public, and in the prologue of the verse reworking of *La Cassaria* (1529) he complained bitterly that the earlier prose version had been stolen and given as booty to 'greedy printers' who then sold it cheap 'in the shops and the public markets'. The performed text of a drama might well have differed from the author's written text, but for several decades authors do not seem to have tried to control, or at least seem not to have been successful in controlling, the diffusion of one or the other. Only from the 1530s did publication of plays in print begin to take precedence, from the authorial viewpoint, over performance or to involve authors in preparation of a version revised for the occasion (and here it was Pietro Aretino, to whom we shall be returning in section 2, who characteristically pointed the way). Growing confidence in the medium of print among authors in general must have played its part here, though it has also been suggested that an influential factor was the cultural penetration, from the 1530s and 40s of Aristotle's *Poetics*, which foregrounded the figure of the dramatist because of the importance given to tragedy.[4] For any type of work, a further consideration might be that, in order to be diffused in print, it needed a linguistic or stylistic revision which an author did not have the time or inclination to carry out. Thus in March 1532, during the very period when Ariosto was busily preparing for the printing of the third edition of his *Orlando furioso*, the poet took steps to prevent his four completed comedies from being printed because of 'the errors concerning language' which he recognized in them.[5]

A few writers may have been reluctant to contemplate using the press for publication because of moral or intellectual prejudice against it. Printing had been hailed by some on its arrival in Italy as a divine art, but, as can always happen with new media (one thinks of some reactions to television in the twentieth century), it was seen by others as an unwelcome intruder which could undermine the fabric of civilized society. At various moments in the Renaissance and beyond, printing was associated with a decline in standards of behaviour, of scholarship and of culture in general.[6] Some affected gentlemanly disdain for an activity which required mercantile resources and know-how and which, in an age when the term *meccanico* still had strongly negative connotations, involved a dirty and noisy manufacturing process, carried out in part by artisans with little or no education.[7] In higher social circles, the very idea of the diffusion of one's work to the masses might be looked at askance as indecorous. In Tudor England, print could be seen as having a stigma attached to it; a court poet of this period, it has been said, would have been 'embarrassed, if not insulted' if asked what he had published in print, for his purpose was 'the communication of experience within a limited group of intimate friends'.[8] The same was true of some Renaissance Italian intellectuals from similar backgrounds. The advice given in Castiglione's *Libro del cortegiano* was that the courtier should be skilled in writing both verse and prose, but that he should be circumspect about showing his work to an audience larger than just one trusted friend (I. 44).

There was also the possibility that a writer might not want his work published by any means. The Florentine historian Francesco Guicciardini ventured the opinion in the first redaction of his *Dialogo del reggimento di Firenze* (1521–5) that the time might come to publish this work before he grew old, but in the two subsequent redactions he stated simply that he was writing for 'recreation'. References to the reader in the texts of other writings of his, such as the *Ricordi* and his masterpiece, the *Storia d'Italia*, show they were not written for the author alone, but Guicciardini had no interest in their immediate diffusion, and nothing by him was printed in his lifetime.[9]

Yet from the point of view of writers, print publication had some potentially decisive advantages over scribal publication. It could establish their renown more firmly and spread it more widely and rapidly. Already in 1478 Bartolomeo della Fonte wrote that printers deserved praise because they conferred 'eternity' on writers both past and present, as well as serving scholars by providing quantities of books.[10] There was recognition, too, of the quality of permanence which printing bestowed on literary texts—it had rescued some classical works from the danger of oblivion—and of the uniformity which it could in theory bring to the circulation of a text. Another humanist, Bonaccorso, expressed in 1475 his appreciation of printed books not just for their lower price but also 'because when the impression and as it were the formation of such books is correct from the beginning, it runs through all the copies always in the same order, with scarcely the possibility of error—a thing which in manuscripts is apt to turn out very differently'.[11] Above all, as we saw in chapter 3, writers now had the possibility of profiting not only from the continuing system of patronage but also from the sale of their work to the public or even to a printer.

2 PRINT IN THE CAREERS OF WRITERS

Let us now look at some case studies of how, in practice, print was used in the context of the careers of writers. We can begin with some examples of fifteenth-century writers, most of them humanists, whose sociocultural status put them in a strong position to exploit the opportunities of the press. Of those working in Milan, the first to use print in order to enhance his own reputation was, perhaps surprisingly, the oldest of them all, Francesco Filelfo (1398–1481).[12] He did not write specifically for the new medium but exploited it to gain favour or publicity, sometimes in a rather underhand way. In 1475, it seems, he commissioned in Milan the printing of an earlier work of his but asked for the colophon to be postdated and to state that the edition had been printed in Rome, doubtless because he was due to take up a lectureship in that city and wanted some ostensibly local products to present or to sell more easily. He manipulated the evidence of a colophon again when his Latin translation of Xenophon's *Cyropaedia* (for which he had received 400 ducats in 1469, as a reward for dedicating it to Pope Paul II) was printed in Milan in 1471: some copies have a colophon which claims that they were printed in Rome, where Filelfo was planning to take up residence. Then, at the very end of Filelfo's life, both he and a former pupil, Giorgio Merula, used the press to publicize an exchange of abusive letters.[13]

In Florence, the first writer in the dominant literary circle of the Medici family to 'break the ice' (to use Ridolfi's image) by venturing into print was the philosopher Marsilio Ficino (1433–99).[14] Of the thirteen works of his which were printed during his lifetime, only two were published apparently without the author's knowledge and outside Florence or Venice. In other cases, the pattern of publication in print was very similar to that of publication in manuscript. Ficino would revise a work carefully and either prepare or arrange for the preparation of the 'archetype'—in the contemporary sense explained in chapter 3, section 1—which was to be reproduced by scribe or printer. In the case of at least two printed editions, though, it seems he did not correct proofs, since he complained about their inaccuracy. Just as rich friends of Ficino's paid the expenses of dedication manuscripts, so his supporters would act as intermediaries between him and the printing industry, footing the bill for paper and labour.[15] At least six of the early editions of his works were financed by men such as Francesco Berlinghieri, Filippo Valori, Lorenzo de' Medici, Piero del Nero and Girolamo Biondo. Biondo was very probably also the financer of the Aldine edition of Ficino's translations from Iamblichus and others (1497).[16] But Ficino was always allowed to insert his own dedications, and in at least one case (his translation of Plotinus, 1492) he was provided with a vellum copy to present to Cardinal Giovanni de' Medici.[17] It is possible that the same pattern of financing applied to most other Florentine first editions of Ficino's works between 1475 and 1496. Only one was definitely printed at the expense of a press, and that was a practical work, the *Consiglio contro la pestilenza*, probably compiled by someone else and brought out by the Ripoli press in 1481.[18]

Another member of the Medicean circle who took the opportunity to have his works published in print, both in Florence and elsewhere, was the leading scholar of the age, Angelo Poliziano (1454–94). We do not know how his scholarly works printed in Florence from 1482 onwards were financed, but his first work to be printed, an account of the unsuccessful conspiracy of the Pazzi family against the Medici in 1478, was part of a publicity campaign in print which was orchestrated by Lorenzo himself in order to counter the pope's own use of the press for propaganda.[19] No manuscript earlier than the first edition is known, and it is therefore likely that the author's 'archetype' was delivered direct to the printing house and was discarded there. Then, between 1480 and 1482, Poliziano prepared a revised edition for printing in Rome.[20] His first *Miscellanea*, a discussion of one hundred questions of classical scholarship, was most probably also conceived for the press, since no manuscript evidence earlier than the first edition of 1489 survives. At the very end of Poliziano's life, from June 1491 onwards, a number of his works were printed in Bologna with the assistance of an opportunist editorial collaborator, Alessandro Sarti. Most of these editions must have come out without Poliziano's knowledge or consent. However, he certainly authorized Sarti's edition of his Latin translation of Herodian. In the summer of 1494, he was planning the printing of his collection of Latin letters and perhaps other works, probably again through the agency of Sarti, and a book of Greek and Latin epigrams. The project for the volume of letters went ahead even after the scholar's untimely death in September of that year, but had to be abandoned when its Bolognese printer died in 1496.[21]

But the author most often printed by Florentine presses in the Quattrocento came from Ferrara: the Dominican friar and preacher Girolamo Savonarola. Over one hundred incunables, more than 14 per cent of the surviving output of Florence, contain works written by him or sermons copied down by others while he delivered them. Between 1495 and the friar's execution in 1498, editions of his works came out at the average rate of one every fortnight. The use of the press by Savonarola and his supporters was an integral part of the campaign to diffuse his message, a necessary corollary to his use of the pulpit. In a sermon of 1496 he urged the printing of an earlier sermon: 'Start to get that book on the art of a good death printed, and make sure you include those illustrations' ('Comincia a porre a stampa quello libro dell'arte del ben morire, fa' che tu ne abbi uno che vi sia di quelle figure').[22] He referred in his *Apologia dei Frati di San Marco* (printed in about 1497) to a forthcoming edition of 'our book on the Triumph of the Cross'. In at least some cases, the friar did not use the press directly: he needed the help of others who would mediate with the printers on his behalf by acting as patron-publishers. One of these was a faithful follower, the notary Lorenzo Violi, who took down some of Savonarola's sermons and paid for their printing from 1496 until well after the friar's death.[23] The printing of four of the friar's works in 1496 (one of them both in Latin and in the vernacular) was commissioned by the bookseller and publisher Piero Pacini, and, given this concentration of editions, Pacini's motives could have been religious as well as, or rather than, purely commercial.[24]

In late Quattrocento Venice, the foremost manipulator of the power of print publication among writers was Marcantonio Sabellico (c. 1436–1506). He, it has been suggested, 'probably deserves the title usually reserved for Erasmus—that of being the first writer to make a career from the new medium'.[25] When he came to have his twelve books of letters printed, he professed a lack of enthusiasm about releasing what he termed these base slaves from his house.[26] Yet the academic success which he enjoyed in Venice owed much to the ways in which he took advantage of the press.[27] Not only did he ensure publicity for his works through their circulation in print (even though he had cause to complain about printers' carelessness), but he seized the chance to improve his prospects of patronage and advancement by studding his printed texts with references to powerful families, by accompanying them with poems or letters which placed the works within an impressive network of patrician or academic contacts, and by sending gift copies of works such as the first part of his *Enneades*, a voluminous history of the world, to Italian princes and cardinals.[28] Sabellico appears to have funded the *Enneades* by himself (his privilege application of 1497 states that he 'had it printed'), but at least one recipient of a copy, Lodovico Sforza, rewarded him generously with fifty gold coins. On other occasions he may have been fortunate enough to find financial backing through the agency of middlemen such as the Brescian bookseller—publisher Antonio Moreto.[29]

The Cinquecento did not bring major changes in the underlying economic relationship between writers and printers, but it did increase the confidence with which writers used print. At the start of the century there could be a conflict between a writer's awareness of the benefits of print and an inhibiting feeling that it was somehow indecorous to demonstrate this awareness too openly. Thus Pietro Bembo, we saw in chapter 3, preferred in public to keep up the fiction that he was a gentleman amateur and that others were the publishers of his works. Yet it was he who commissioned the Aldine Petrarch of 1501, edited by himself, and he may have formed a joint company for the occasion with Aldo.[30] It was Bembo, too, who ordered his *Prose della volgar lingua* to be printed by Giovanni Tacuino in 1525, arranged for the supply of suitable paper, asked for intermediaries to obtain privileges in other states, and used all his influence to ensure that the perpetrator of a Venetian pirate edition was suitably punished. Tacuino was apparently unwilling to take on the work unless Bembo obtained privileges to prevent plagiarism in other states, and this might mean that author and printer had entered into a partnership.[31] In 1530, when he may have been in partnership with Nicolò Zoppino, Bembo took steps to ensure that copies of editions of his works were distributed to booksellers in Rome.[32] The existence of a pirated edition of the *Prose* suggests that Bembo was not acting as his own publisher out of necessity, at least on this occasion; he evidently preferred self-publication in order to retain control over the accuracy and physical appearance of the end product, as well as over profits.

Only three of the works of Niccolò Machiavelli (1469–1527) were published through the medium of print during his lifetime. The first was the *Decennale*, a historical narrative in *terza rima*, first published in manuscript in 1504 with a dedication to Alamanno Salviati and then printed, without that dedication, in 1506 at the expense of the author's colleague in the Florentine chancery, Agostino Vespucci. The second was his classicizing comedy *Mandragola*, printed in about 1518, but—typically for a theatrical work in these years—with no sign that Machiavelli was the author or in any way involved in the edition. The third, in 1521, was his dialogue *Arte della guerra* (Art of war), dedicated to Lorenzo Strozzi, a man whose generosity is praised by Machiavelli and who may well, like Vespucci earlier, have acted as his patron-publisher. Machiavelli sent gift copies of the *Decennale* and the *Arte della guerra* to at least one influential figure in each case, Ercole Bentivoglio and Cardinal Giovanni Salviati.[33] He was thus happy to use print publication on occasion. However, his other major prose works, *Il principe*, the *Discorsi su Tito Livio*, and the *Istorie fiorentine*, remained in manuscript until after his death. Machiavelli did not intend to keep them to himself or even within a closed circle of readers but can clearly be said to have 'published' them; even though he did not do so in the 'strong' sense, as defined by Harold Love, of providing large numbers of copies, he certainly did so in the 'weak' sense that he surrendered control over the future use of the manuscript supplied by him and that there was 'some practical likelihood of the text entering public channels of communication'.[34] The second and third of these works were in effect published when presented to their dedicatees, and *Il principe* was first published when the author made it available in such a way that it could reach a network of people with shared interests both within and outside the Florentine state. In the case of *Il principe*, we know that this 'author publication' was followed by the two other main modes of scribal publication defined by Love: entrepreneurial publication, or copying for sale by people other than the author (including at least the scribes Biagio Buonaccorsi, a close friend and former colleague of Machiavelli's, and Genesius de la Barrera), and user publication, or non-commercial replication for private use.[35] Why, then, did Machiavelli use print publication so selectively? The answer is probably not that the author had problems of funding (he seems to have been able to find resourceful patrons when he wished to do so) but because he, and no doubt others too, felt that, in Florence at least, circulation in manuscript was more appropriate for works of a controversial, anti-establishment nature. In the particular case of *Il principe*, it could well be that Machiavelli simply felt that the work would not achieve its purposes if he wrote it for the press. First of all, we know, from the reactions of the people who read it in the twenty years before it was printed, that its teachings could be admired and imitated in private, manuscript writings but were rejected in the more public context of print. Secondly, if the work had been printed, Machiavelli would have felt obliged to adopt a more stiffly formal style, as he did later in the *Arte della guerra*; but part of his strategy in *Il principe*, it seems, was precisely to use a deliberately informal, unadorned style, in order to shock his readers into realizing that the advice contained in *this* treatise on princes was closer to everyday reality than that of earlier treatises, whose statecraft was based on an imaginary world.[36]

While the example of Machiavelli demonstrates the continuing importance, in certain circumstances, of scribal publication, that of Ludovico Ariosto (1474–1533) and his continuation of Boiardo's chivalric epic, the *Orlando furioso*, underlines the growing importance which print publication was acquiring for writers. When he came to have the first version printed, he showed great resourcefulness in organizing the whole operation by himself from start to finish, using a decidedly hands-on approach and showing no inhibition about revealing, for example in his Venetian privilege request, his desire to receive remuneration for his efforts.[37] In 1515 he organized the importing of two hundred reams of paper from Lake Garda; he applied successfully for privileges in various Italian states and in France; and no doubt he commissioned and oversaw the printing itself, carried out in Ferrara between October 1515 and April 1516. All this was done without

financial assistance from the court, even though Ariosto was at this time in
the service of Cardinal Ippolito d'Este, brother of Duke Alfonso. It is
significant that both the duke and the cardinal had to buy copies of the
completed edition for themselves. Once printing was complete, Ariosto
arranged for sales to the general public. In a letter of May 1516, Ippolito
Calandra recounts how Ariosto arrived in Mantua with a chest full of copies,
he presented three of them to the marquis, Francesco Gonzaga, and his
family, but he wanted to arrange for the others, still unbound, to be sold ('li
altri lui li vole fare vendere'). Ariosto himself pointed out to Equicola in 1520
that he had received less money than he had expected from sales in Mantua:
either the bookseller acting on his behalf had not sold all his stock or—more
probably, since the edition had, as far as he knew, sold out elsewhere in
Italy—the bookseller was keeping the takings for himself.[38] A plausible
estimate, based on the quantity of paper imported, is that 1,300 copies of the
1516 edition were printed, and we know that one copy cost 1 lira unbound
(binding put the price up by 40 per cent or more). Even if only 10 per cent
of the income from sales went into the poet's pocket, his profit would still
have been over half of his official annual court salary of 240 lire, and close to
the 150 lire which he claimed to receive in reality.[39]

Encouraged by the commercial and critical success of this first edition,
Ariosto organized a second, including some linguistic revisions.[40] Needing
cash to finance at least part of the operation, he borrowed 100 lire in
November 1520 from a widow, Antonia del Panza. Printing was completed
rapidly (and hence with more errors than usual) by the following February.
Ariosto sold 100 copies for 60 lire, or 12 soldi each, to a local stationer who
undertook to sell them at no more than 16 soldi each (20 per cent cheaper
than the 1516 edition) and to buy any further copies from the author at the
same price. We know too that Ariosto got a nobleman to oversee sales in
Genoa, and he is likely to have organized sales in other cities through a
combination of personal contacts and booksellers. Again, business was brisk,
and he was able to pay off his loan, with 12 per cent interest, in March 1523.

Production and distribution of the third edition of the *Furioso*, now
expanded from forty to forty-six canti, were organized along the same
lines.[41] Ariosto protected his investment by obtaining several privileges. In
early 1532 he set about purchasing a supply of paper; this time he arranged
for the transport of no fewer than four hundred reams, which (if they were
all used) would have led to a print run of around 2,750 copies, a bold
investment on the poet's part. He met the bill of 300 lire from his paper
supplier by transferring to him an advance payment of his court salary,
equivalent to one and a quarter years. He was involved in correcting proofs

and continued to introduce changes during this opportunity for surveillance of which his fellow-courtier and imitator Cassio da Narri had failed to take advantage.[42] Printing was completed at the beginning of October. As before, Ariosto took charge of sales. He also arranged for the printing of some copies on vellum which he sent to influential figures such as Duke Alfonso, Federico Gonzaga and Isabella d'Este.

This gift-giving to the powerful was evidently an important part of Ariosto's strategy in making use of his creation. Yet, as far as one can judge, he was also unprecedentedly determined to use publication through print in order to obtain direct pecuniary reward for his talent by circulating his work among a wider public. To what extent, then, one might ask, is this new attitude to publication reflected in his writings? In the first place, it may help to explain a feature of the narrative technique of the *Furioso* on which critics have commented: the decreased use, in comparison with other authors of romances, of the fiction that the poet is reciting his work to a specific audience.[43] Boiardo had begun his *Orlando innamorato* with an appeal for quiet addressed in the second person plural to a supposed gathering of 'lords and knights'. Ariosto, in contrast, starts by setting out his central subject matter (the war between Charlemagne and Agramante, the madness of Orlando), before turning to his master, Cardinal Ippolito, and gratefully offering as a gift his 'opera d'inchiostro' (work of ink), which will include the story of the Estense ancestor Ruggiero. One is, of course, intended to take this ink to be that used in the original act of composition, as later references to Ariosto's pen make clear (XIV. 108, XV. 9, XXIX. 2), but the author always intended the diffusion of the complete work, both to the Estensi and to the general public, to depend on printer's ink.[44] Another aspect of Ariosto's technique which shows the writer adapting to a situation in which his poem would be read by all, rather than heard by a few, is his use of canto divisions. He follows tradition in using the ending of the canto, originally representing a unit of oral performance, in order to create cliff hanging suspense. But, as Peter Brand has pointed out, the suspension of excitement would have little significance for a reader who had only to turn the page; and so Ariosto uses the opening stanzas of the next canto to force the reader's attention away from the narrative, stepping outside the framework of the poem and commenting on its implications.[45]

In the second place, the fact that Ariosto devoted so much time and money to the publication of his poem can only have heightened his strong sense of resentment at the lack of esteem which his masters showed for his gifts as a writer. Although Ippolito is portrayed at the end of the *Furioso* as surrounded by philosophers, poets and musicians, elsewhere Ariosto puts more emphasis on the other side of the coin of patronage. Princes are seen to be courted by those who wish to win their favour, but they have neither the ability to discern true poets nor the generosity to reward them. Among the objects lost on earth which Astolfo sees stored on the moon, a pile of hooks of gold and silver represents the gifts which are given to miserly masters in the hope of reward, nooses hidden in garlands are acts of flattery, and the verses written in praise of lords are now seen to be cicadas which have swollen and burst with the sheer effort of singing too hard (XXXIV. 77). When the figure of Time empties names into the river Lethe at the start of canto XXXV, croaking crows and vultures, representing flattering courtiers, gather up some of the names but soon drop them again. Two white swans alone manage to carry some to the temple of Immortality; they are the true poets, but they are few, partly because their talent is rare, partly through the miserliness of lords (XXXV. 23). In print, but outside the text of the poem, Ariosto gave further prominence to the theme of ingratitude by using as his motto the biblical phrase 'Pro bono malum' (Evil in return for good), accompanied in the first two editions by an emblem of bees being smoked out of a log, and by including in some copies of the 1532 edition a woodcut of a ewe suckling a wolf cub.[46] In contrast with Lodovici's practice in 1535, then, Ariosto used woodcuts to refer to the frustrations rather than to the benefits of patronage. In 1517, immediately after the publication of the first edition of the *Furioso*, a crisis in Ariosto's life seemed to justify his sense of being unappreciated. When he preferred not to accompany Ippolito to Hungary, he was dismissed from the cardinal's service and lost his court salary. He gave vent in his first *Satira* (especially lines 88–108, 139–44) to his bitterness over his treatment at court: if he had received any reward, it was not because of his poetry, and Ippolito considered relatively unimportant the praise for him which it contained.

Through this satire runs the theme of the loss of liberty which a courtier's life implies (I. 115–20, 262–5), and in other satires Ariosto reveals his desire for enough wealth to flee the cage-like servitude of the court (III. 31–42, VII. 37–42). Print must have represented his main hope of escape: he was the first Italian writer openly to take advantage of the diffusion of his work through the hands of printers and booksellers to a genuinely appreciative wider public in order to achieve, if not a means of independence, then at least a source of income which would make him less dependent on the whims of his superiors. He must have placed particular hopes in the 1532 edition, because of its large print run. Unfortunately, the ill health which led to his death in July 1533 prevented him from deriving any benefits from it. As his brother Galasso wrote to Bembo soon afterwards, 'because of his illness three-quarters of the books have remained in the hands of his heirs, since they have not been sold'.[47]

In contrast with Ariosto, who had no hesitation over the publication of the *Furioso*, Baldesar Castiglione (1478–1529) claimed at first to be somewhat uncertain whether his *Libro del cortegiano* was ready to be released beyond a close circle of friends.[48] In the dedication of the first edition, completed in Venice in April 1528, he insisted that he had not had time to revise his dialogue to his satisfaction but had been practically forced into issuing it in print. He had given a manuscript to a friend, Vittoria Colonna; she, breaking a promise, had had a large part of the work copied, and this part had fallen into the hands of some people in Naples who wanted to have it printed. Castiglione preferred, he said, to revise the book hastily with the intention of publishing it ('publicarlo') himself, considering this the lesser of two evils. He had, in fact, considered 'letting it go' as early as September 1518: the question in his mind seems to have been not whether to publish the work but when it would be ready to be issued, and it is difficult to suppose that he was not contemplating having it printed. By early 1525 he had practically made up his mind. He was then in Madrid as papal nuncio, and from there he wrote in April to tell a friend in Italy that he was more eager than ever to 'let the *Cortegiano* go'. At this point he could still envisage having copies transcribed for friends, as he did when writing to a countess in June 1525. Between March and April 1527 he sent his manuscript to be printed in Venice by the Aldine press, the most prestigious in the city. Printing began in late November 1527, and privilege requests were granted in February and March 1528. The papal privilege referred to Castiglione's receiving 'the fruits of his labours' and stated that he would receive half of the 500-ducat fine to be imposed on offenders.

Castiglione's original intentions for the execution of the work, as he summarized them in a letter to his agent dated 9 April 1527, were to have 1,030 copies printed. He would pay the cost of half of the first 1,000, and also of 30 to be printed on royal paper. Of his 530 copies, 130 were to be used as gifts and 400 to be sold through a bookseller in order to cover expenses or to make a profit if possible. His agent reported on the following 21 November that the printers recommended a run of 2,000 and that they proposed to produce 130 for Castiglione at his own expense and the rest at theirs. Further, they wished the text to be revised and punctuated by Giovan Francesco Valerio, a friend of Bembo's: by now printers evidently linked the commercial success of an edition with linguistic correctness of the sort which Ariosto was soon to impose on the 1532 *Furioso*.[49] The outcome of the negotiations with the press is uncertain. An account probably written in 1528 suggests that the result may have been a compromise with the author's original proposal: Castiglione purchased the paper for 500 copies and received only 150. However, he was certainly thinking at some point about the costs and potential profits if he were to take a half share in a print run of 2,000, since he noted that paper would cost 140 ducats and printing as much again, and he estimated the amounts that could be earned from selling 1,000 copies at prices from 6 marcelli each, which would have brought in a profitable 480 ducats, down to 2 marcelli each, which would have earned a loss-making 160 ducats.[50]

It is not known whether Castiglione or his printers decided on the appearance of the work, an imposing folio with roman type, in the tradition of the Aldine editions of the 1490s rather than of the Cinquecento, but it would not be surprising if this was Castiglione's choice. Making a good first impression was, after all, one of his main recommendations to the courtier (II. 32–6). He certainly attached great importance to the production and distribution of gift copies, and on this he sent more detailed instructions to his agent in April 1528. Of the hundred copies which he now reckoned were to be his, thirty were to be on royal paper and one on vellum. This last copy was to receive the finest possible binding, Castiglione insisted, and was to be sent to Spain—no doubt it was intended for the emperor Charles V— together with others. Of the copies remaining in Italy, he specified that some were to be bound and presented to figures such as the marquis and marchioness of Mantua and the duchess of Urbino. Castiglione thus took a very close interest in every aspect of the publication of the *Libro del Cortegiano*, even though he was in Spain. He made every effort to exploit his investment of time and money: he would have liked to cover his costs, at the very least, and he also wished to use the time-honoured strategy of presenting copies to those in power and to friends in order to further his personal relationships and his standing. The *Cortegiano* proved, like the *Orlando furioso*, to be one of the best-sellers of the century; however, Castiglione's death in February 1529 prevented him too from reaping the full rewards of his dealings with the printing industry.

The background of Pietro Aretino (1492–1556) provides a strong contrast with that of Castiglione. He was of obscure birth, the son of a cobbler, and, though he too came to converse with great figures such as Charles V, he based his career on his skill with words rather than on success in the world of courts. He achieved his early success mainly through the sharpness of his wit, in conversation as well as with his pen. Ariosto famously characterized him in the *Furioso* of 1532 through the fear which he could arouse in the great, calling him 'the scourge of princes' (XLVI. 14). But

Aretino also used praise of the powerful as a means of self-advancement, and in 1524–5 the fashionable Roman press of Ludovico degli Arrighi brought out two editions of poems by him in praise of Pope Clement VII and his datary, Gian Matteo Giberti. In 1527 Aretino moved away from court circles to Venice. His first major literary project there was, ironically, in the courtly tradition, a continuation of Ariosto's *Furioso* called the *Marfisa*, begun for Federico Gonzaga. The long-suffering marquis's patronage came to an end in 1531, however, and despite Aretino's claims to be enjoying a rich style of life thanks to the generosity of rulers, he was in fact in some financial difficulties. In 1533–4 came a marked change of tactics. Previously, most of Aretino's writings had been circulated through scribal publication, but from this moment on he began to take full advantage of the resources of the Venetian presses in order to earn his living.[51]

Even for someone in his lowly social position, Aretino was daringly innovative in flaunting the income that he earned in one way or another from his publications. At the end of the dream of Parnassus which he describes in a letter of 1537, he is offered various poetic crowns but refuses them all in favour of 'a privilege by virtue of which I can sell or pawn the talent which the heavens have showered upon me'.[52] Publication was his means of survival. Francesco Marcolini brought out Aretino's first two books of letters, but because the printer was absent from Venice, Aretino had to turn elsewhere for the printing of the third book, explaining that he 'could not live without eating'.[53] Yet his pride led him to insist that his rewards were not tarnished by commerce. Earlier, on 22 June 1537, Aretino had declined to take any direct profit from Marcolini for the sales of his first book of letters. To have the books which one derives from one's imagination printed at one's own expense and to have them sold on one's behalf was, he wrote, like eating one's own limbs or prostituting one's art. His aim, rather, was to use his printed works to seek patronage. 'With God's help', he said, 'I want the courtesy of princes to pay for the labours of my writing, and not the poverty of those who buy them ... If someone wants to make profits, let him learn to be a merchant; he can become a bookseller and give up the name of poet.'[54] In 1538 he repeated to Bembo that his method of winning 'corone d'auro e non di lauro' (crowns of gold and not of laurel) was 'to foster the pride of the great with great praise, holding them ever aloft with the wings of hyperbole'.[55]

As a man who had risen from obscurity, then, Aretino could afford to be disarmingly frank about his desire to earn gold from his writings, but he was shrewd enough to counterbalance this openness with a paradoxically conservative contempt for mercantile profits. His technique was to use and develop indirect means of benefiting from publication. Two of these devices were the traditional, respectable ones of presentation and dedication. As soon as his three *canzoni* on papal politics were printed in Rome between late 1524 and early 1525, he promised a copy to Federico Gonzaga and linked his gift with a request for shirts embroidered with gold and silk and for gold bonnets; he was greatly annoyed that the nuns who made them did not deliver them until March.[56] Like Ariosto and Castiglione, he took great care over the preparation of dedication copies: for instance, he had a copy of his *Stanze in lode de la Sirena*, for presentation to the empress Isabella, decorated by the miniaturist Iacopo del Giallo; in return he received a gift of 300 scudi.[57] Dedications could lead to gifts such as a gold chain and a silk robe.[58] Aretino liked to stress his own largesse, portraying it even as prodigality, and so he could himself show generosity by using a dedication as a thank offering for a gift, as he did with his first book of letters (1538).[59] Gaining in impudence, in 1546 he successfully asked a secretary of Cosimo de' Medici's to beg the duke not to delay in rewarding him for the dedication of his third book of letters, suggesting with tongue in cheek that he could reasonably hope for the sum of 100 scudi annually.[60] In the same year, he was guilty of some dedicatory double-dealing. He offered his tragedy *Orazia* to Pier Luigi Farnese, duke of Parma and Piacenza, in order to encourage him to send a promised gift of 150 scudi; once he had received this sum, he promptly switched the dedication to Pier Luigi's father, Pope Paul III.[61]

Aretino's other and more innovative technique, linked to that of using dedications but partly independent of it, was to insert in his printed works open references to the giving or withholding of gifts to himself. The kind of transaction which was previously carried out behind the scenes was now spotlighted for the public gaze. He inserted expressions of gratitude to his patrons in two comedies, *Il Marescalco* (v. 3) and *La Cortigiana* (prologue), when they were revised for printing in 1533–4. But the main vehicles for his manipulation of the powerful were the six books of letters printed between 1538 and 1557. Here he would give ostentatious thanks for gifts actually received, carefully specifying the sum of money or the exact nature of the gift. He boasted in 1541 that he received 600 scudi a year in pensions and another 1,000 from his writing, in January 1544 that the alchemy of his pen had extracted over 25,000 scudi from princes since his arrival in Venice, and in September 1544 that he had already received 1,700 scudi in that year alone.[62] In return, his benefactors received wide publicity for their generosity, something which had not normally happened in the previous dealings of patrons with writers. On the other hand, Aretino could also use his letters to hint at miserliness on his patrons' part. Several letters, for example, refer to difficulties in obtaining the annual pensions which he was supposed to receive from the emperor, the king of France and the prince of Salerno. To arouse fear of losing face, whether in a bullying or a wheedling manner, was thus another weapon in his armoury, and he openly acknowledged that he forced the princes of his day to treat him favourably with continual tributes of gold.[63] Ariosto, we saw, felt that rulers had too little awareness of the power of the pen to immortalize, but Aretino had the utmost confidence that his militia of inks was mightier than any sword: whether the powerful liked the fact or not, his pen paid others in the coinage of honour or shame.[64] He believed this outspokenness had wrought a transformation in the status accorded not only to himself but to all who lived by artistic skill. 'Before I began to attack the reputation [of lords]', he wrote in 1537, 'men of talent had to beg for the basic necessities of life'; now, thanks to hire alone, talent wears brocade, drinks in gold cups, has necklaces and money, rides like a queen, is served as an empress and revered as a goddess.[65]

Aretino focused his readers' attention on his use of the printed word to prise open the purses of the rich; but who subsidized the printing of his works in the first place? A letter of his to an Aretine friend and possibly former teacher, Giovanni Lappoli, states as a general rule that no author's works are accepted by printers free of charge and that he will receive no satisfaction from them unless he pays what they demand.[66] Aretino was prepared to do this with his own works. He apparently expected to make a profitable investment in the printing of his epic *Marfisa*: in 1529 he asked for ten-year privileges for the work from the pope and the emperor, saying that 'I have hopes that the printing will reward me', and, when putting on a brave face after his requests were refused, he conceded that this setback might deprive him of 'the profit of some scudi'.[67] He made several Venetian privilege requests in his own name.[68] However, in writing to Lappoli he was trying to pour cold water on a mediocre poet's aspirations, and he omitted to mention the possibility, on which he seems to have been able to count at times, that printing costs might be met by others, who might or might not be professionally linked with the book trade. The letter of 22 June 1537 to Marcolini, already quoted, has to be treated with caution, because it was part of Aretino's campaign to create an image of himself as aloof from the commercial aspects of publication, and because in any case the letter was withdrawn five years later, which suggests that he may have decided to derive profits from sales after all; but his opening reference to giving Marcolini his first book of letters, as he had previously done with his other works, does suggest that Marcolini financed (and hence probably benefited from) the printing of a series of works by Aretino, some printed by Giovanni Antonio Nicolini da Sabbio at Marcolini's expense, others printed by Marcolini himself.[69] Marcolini requested Venetian privileges for various works of Aretino's in 1534 and again in 1541–2.[70] At least two other publishers commissioned editions of the first book of letters in 1539—Federico Torresani and Venturino Ruffinelli—but they may have been acting without the author's approval. On the other hand, Aretino may have sanctioned the publishing of two of his works in 1543 by the perfumer Biagio Perugino or Biagio Paternostraio, since Biagio made privilege requests for them and Aretino addressed friendly letters to him.[71] During and after Marcolini's absence from Venice in 1545–9, Aretino looked to other professional publishers, Melchior Sessa and Andrea Arrivabene.[72] But an important part was also played by patrons who either paid printing costs or gave Aretino money in order to help him prepare works destined for the press. In the former category comes Bernardo Valdaura, dedicatee of the *Dialogo ... nel quale la Nanna ... insegna a la Pippa*, who evidently gave Aretino 40 scudi to pay Marcolini to print the work in 1536 and in return kept the copies in order to sell them himself.[73] When Aretino had three of his religious works reprinted in 1551, costs were paid by Guidobaldo II della Rovere, duke of Urbino. But the production of this edition and of a companion edition of 1552 was also facilitated by a gift of money from Baldovino del Monte, brother of the dedicatee, Pope Julius III. Aretino presented copies to Duke Cosimo de' Medici, predictably demanding a gift in return.[74] Similarly, the first edition of his life of Saint Catherine of Alexandria, brought out by an unknown printer in 1540, had been promoted by the commissioning of the work by Alfonso d'Avalos. To mark the fulfilment of this commission, Aretino sent to his patron a printed text, not a manuscript. However, even though the commission was apparently formalized by a contract, payment of Aretino's fee was withheld in 1542 with the excuse that he was taking too long to complete his life of Saint Thomas Aquinas.[75]

Aretino was unique in his ability to use his writings in order to exert leverage on patrons, but his literary and social success played a leading part in promoting new opportunities for other Italian writers from the 1530s onwards. In an Italy whose social foundations had been shaken by over three decades of political upheaval, he showed that a writer without advantages of birth, and working outside, though still in contact with, the social framework of the court, could make opportunistic use of the press as an instant medium of diffusion for a range of works, from ribald dialogue to biographies of saints, which were destined to satisfy the appetites of quite different publics, and he flaunted the fact that this activity could be a powerful, if indirect, means of profit. His rise to fame was an incentive to other outspoken authors such as Franco, Doni and Lando.[76] Outside Venice, too, there was a widening of the social circles from which successful authors might emerge, as in the case of the self-educated Florentine cobbler Giovan Battista Gelli.

At the same time as Aretino's career was blossoming, a younger member of his circle, Lodovico Dolce (1508–68), an ordinary citizen of Venice and not a patrician, was showing that Venetian presses now offered other means for writers to make a name and earn some income. As with Aretino, Dolce's first works to be printed (from 1532 onwards) were verse compositions, and he continued to produce works in his own name throughout his life. But from 1535 he developed a parallel career as an editor of vernacular texts by earlier or living authors, from Dante to Aretino himself, and as a translator or adapter of texts by classical authors. In 1542 he began a long collaboration with the dominant printer of mid-Cinquecento Venice, Gabriele Giolito, at whose expense Dolce was stated to be living in 1553. The example set by Dolce, in conjunction with the printers who employed him, was soon followed by others who based their careers largely on regular collaboration with the Venetian press as editors, translators and anthologizers: men such as Antonio Brucioli, Lodovico Domenichi, Girolamo Ruscelli and Francesco Sansovino. The links between the presses and these *poligrafi*, as they are generally known because of their versatility, were so strong that Doni and Sansovino came to run their own printing houses in Florence and Venice respectively. As we shall see in chapter 6, section 2, from a reader's point of view the importance of their contribution lay first in the guidance which they offered to the less experienced in understanding and imitating vernacular classics. They helped to further the transition from what Petrucci has termed the 'author's book' evolved during the late Middle Ages to the 'publisher's book' ('libro d'editore' or 'libro editoriale') typical of the sixteenth century, often containing a wealth (not to say a surfeit) of extratextual material provided by people other than the author.[77] They also made available a range of classical works in vernacular translation, though the quality of their work in this area could be compromised by their limitations as scholars or by the sheer pressure of trying to meet printers' deadlines.[78]

One of the contemporary authors edited by Dolce was Bernardo Tasso (1493–1569). In 1554–5 his first four books of *Rime* were brought out by Gabriele Giolito, apparently at the printer's expense, since all that Bernardo asked of him, through Dolce, was that the few copies due to him for presentation should be printed on paper of special quality, for which he was willing to pay himself.[79] Bernardo was disappointed with Dolce's editorial work, but the Venetian was nevertheless one of those to whom the poet turned for support when he came to publish his epic *Amadigi*.[80] This poem had been begun in 1542–3, when Bernardo was in the service of Ferrante Sanseverino, prince of Salerno, and the complex process of composition and publication was bound up with the consequences of the prince's defection from the Spanish to the French cause in 1552. Bernardo followed Sanseverino, giving up his property in Naples and his wife Porzia's as yet unpaid dowry, but in 1556–8, after Porzia's death, he joined the court of Urbino, which was allied to Spain. He resolved to publish the *Amadigi*, its pro-French references now removed, and dedicate it to the Spanish king, Philip II, in the hope that this would be of advantage to himself and his family. In June 1557 he wrote that he was planning to have the poem produced at his own expense so as to derive profit and benefit ('utile, e beneficio') for his innocent son Torquato.[81] He was invited in the following January to have it printed at the expense of the newly formed Accademia Veneziana, but he replied that, precisely because he was poor, he preferred to publish it himself, sparing no expense on illustration, paper and so on, 'having, as a prudent father, to think of my offspring's benefit'.[82] Bernardo obtained a set of privileges himself. However, when he realized that printing costs might be as high as 275 ducats, he made a five-year agreement with Gabriele Giolito according to which printer and author were to share both the costs (Bernardo's contribution came to 150 ducats) and the profits from a print run of 1,200 copies. Bernardo was, then, planning for income from sales, but his main expectation of benefit lay in the bounty of King Philip.[83] In July 1559 his faith in the power of dedication was high: he had heard a rumour that the king was only waiting for the *Amadigi* in order to restore Porzia's dowry, probably so that he would not have to make a further gift on receiving the poem.[84] Bernardo also expected benefit from a third source, presentation copies. He had the paper for these made specially and was very upset in November 1559 when floods near Lake Garda carried it and the fulling mills away, so that printing had to be postponed until spring.[85] Of the 600 copies due to him, he had 154 bound for presentation at an extra cost of go ducats; no doubt many of the recipients were among the contemporaries whose names be had woven into the narrative and who included knights, rulers, cardinals, noble men and women, writers, scholars, and (perhaps with an eye on their purses) merchants and bankers.

Yet Bernardo Tasso complained that he got little tangible benefit from his investment of time and money in the *Amadigi*. He sold off some of his remaining 446 copies to Giolito at less than their price of i ducat each. In return for his presentation copies, he received little more than polite thanks.

The copy sent to King Philip was lost on its way to Spain. In 1562 Bernardo was heavily in debt. In summary, the publication of the *Amadigi* showed that there could still be a gulf between an author's expectations of reward from printing and the reality, in which an author was not only vulnerable to acts of God but still dependent to a large extent on another uncontrollable factor, the generosity of patrons.

When Bernardo's son Torquato Tasso (1544–95) was only eighteen years old, in 1562, he obtained his father's rather reluctant permission to have his chivalric romance *Rinaldo* printed in Venice. Torquato, no doubt advised by Bernardo, put himself in a position of firm control of publication by obtaining privileges from Venice and other states.[86] He went on to become one of the most often printed authors of the second half of the Cinquecento; yet he never succeeded in exercising the same degree of control over subsequent editions of his works. In 1575 he had high hopes of earning 400 scudi from a. combination of the gifts received after a recent performance of his pastoral play *Aminta* and the profits expected from the planned printing of his masterpiece, the epic *Gerusalemme liberata*. With these resources he felt he would be able to escape from the court of Ferrara and live in Rome, at least until his capital was used up.[87] He obtained a twenty-year privilege for the *Liberata* from Florence early in 1576.[88] However, Torquato was still dissatisfied with the poem, and for the time being nothing came of his plans. It was only after he had been confined in 1579 to the hospital of Sant'Anna in Ferrara, where he remained for seven years, that editions of the epic began to appear. The earliest did not have his approval, and he was to regret the association with a young Ferrarese courtier, Febo Bonnà, which led to two editions in June and July 1581. Torquato said that he had made a written agreement ('poliza') with Bonnà, but Bonnà obtained privileges in his own name, and there was always a danger of the poet losing control because of his confinement. Two years later Torquato complained that Bonnà was enjoying himself in Parisian society, having printed and sold the books as he, Torquato, had intended to do, but having failed to hand over any of the money specified in their agreement.[89] Torquato remained bitterly disappointed that he never received from the publication of the *Liberata* the profits which were certainly his due, though his fevered imagination may have led him to exaggerate his claims that he was offered 'many hundreds of scudi' to have it printed, or (in 1589) that others had milked 'over 9,000 ducats' out of it and that as many more could still be earned, while he had received nothing either in cash or in gifts.[90]

Torquato fared no better with editions of his other works. The *Aminta* was first printed in Venice by Aldo Manuzio the younger, protected by a privilege in favour of Aldo and with a dedication signed, much to Torquato's annoyance, by the printer rather than the author.[91] In 1587 he fell victim to the unscrupulous Giovan Battista Licino, who arranged for the printing of the *Discorsi dell'arte poetica* but failed to make any significant payments to him as author.[92] On the other hand, Torquato could not afford to publish his own works. In 1589 he tried to borrow 100 scudi in the hope of earning much more from a revised edition of his works. He complained in the same year that he was too short of cash to have his lyric poems printed with a commentary.[93] Duke Vincenzo Gonzaga had to finance the printing of the first part of a new Mantuan edition of the *Rime* in 1591, after inquiries had been made to see whether a Venetian printer would undertake the edition at his own expense or even give the poet some reward. A discouraging response had been received from Venice: the printers wanted first to know exactly what the contents were and whether they were saleable; in any case, Torquato's reward would have been only some fifty copies or 'a few scudi'.[94] Print thus helped to bring Torquato fame, but it also brought much frustration over the lack of tangible benefits which he felt were due to him. To some extent he may have been overoptimistic: book publishing had not even reached the point where a generous contract could be offered to the greatest living Italian poet. But he was also the victim of the lack of scruple of the cut-throat world of print. As he wrote in 1586, it was all very well for him to be known as 'good Tasso, dear Tasso', but he was also 'the Tasso who has been assassinated, especially by booksellers and printers'.[95]

3 CONCLUSIONS: PRINT PUBLICATION, WRITERS AND WRITING

A survey carried out by Christian Bec on the century from 1450 to 1550, the period during which printing was introduced, suggests that, in respect of their professional background, the condition of writers underwent only gradual and limited change.[96] He studied the careers of 210 writers with regard to their place of work and to whether they belonged to one of five categories: teachers, courtiers, lawyers, merchants (including men who had a private source of income) and clerics (including those who were also teachers or courtiers). As regards the geography of literature, a significant trend during these years is the rise of Venice, to the same levels as Florence and Rome, as a centre in which writers resided for longer periods (fifteen years on average). Among the professions, that of courtier dominates overall, rising from 23 per cent in the first third of the period to 44 per cent in the second. In the final third, though, courts provide somewhat fewer writers (39 per cent), while more writers are teachers, merchants or lawyers. An interesting novelty is the growth in the proportion of writers outside the five main categories, from about 13 per cent in the first third of the period to about 26 per cent in the last. The largest group among these writers is that that of printer-publishers: their proportion rises to nearly 13 per cent by 1550. There is also a significant rise in the proportion of women writers, from about 4 per cent to about 9 per cent. A broad underlying explanation for these trends must lie in the political upheavals of the period, which undermined the traditional social order and made the court an unstable institution. But it is probable that the rise of the printing industry also played some part: the presses, and those of Venice in particular, offered alternative opportunities which enabled writers who came from a variety of social and geographical backgrounds, and who lacked the humanist training that until about 1530 was an essential passport to success in literary society, to establish a reputation outside the milieu of the court.[97] During the sixteenth century, print acted more and more as an incentive to write; without it, one can imagine, several authors would have written less or not at all.

We have seen, though, that it was not easy for writers to improve their financial status with the help of the printing press, either indirectly, in other words through patronage, or directly, from sales or other payments. Print, because of its public-relations potential, seems to have stimulated writers to exploit their work even more than previously as a means of obtaining patronage. As the case of the publication of Ammirato's *Istorie fiorentine* shows, the possibility of dedicating printed books and of using them as gifts remained crucial to writers to the very end of the sixteenth century; the negotiations between Ammirato and his printer aimed at combining the former's need for patronage with the latter's commercial interests.[98] Yet just at the moment when competition for the largesse of patrons was growing, the wellsprings of patronage were drying up as regimes tottered and resources had to be diverted away from culture. Writers have always tended to complain of penury, but there may well have been some truth in Paolo Giovio's remark of 1548 to Cosimo de' Medici that 'these most turbulent times have castrated patrons, and hence crippled the right hand of authors'.[99] Indeed, Cosimo himself acknowledged, when writing to Aretino in 1552, that princes were being forced to spend their resources on warfare, neglecting rewards to those outside the military profession.[100] On the other hand, it was too early for writers to look to contracts with printers or publishers as a significant source of income. The possibility of such income was real, but as yet it too was limited. Among those writers who worked professionally for Venetian presses in the sixteenth century, even many years of activity seem to have brought little or no improvement in financial status.[101] In Britain it was only in the eighteenth century that the levels of production and consumption of printed material became high enough for authors to become professionals. A recent study has emphasized that even in the early 1700s 'authors primary economic relations were still typically with patrons rather than with booksellers', and that only by the middle of the eighteenth century was 'professional authorship ... becoming both economically feasible and socially acceptable'.[102]

The introduction of printing, then, led to no dramatic, sweeping changes in the professional status of writers. However, print publication undoubtedly enhanced the general recognition of the identity of the author as the creator and owner of the text. This recognition is reflected in the practice (which has been dated from 1479) of including, on the title page or elsewhere, portraits of the author which became increasingly true to life.[103] Print empowered writers through its ability to diffuse their works and through the operation of contracts, privileges and laws which protected their interests. Once texts had entered the legal system, they became, more clearly than before, commodities which belonged to authors and their families, had a negotiable value both within and outside the network of patronage, and were subject to the same kinds of protection as other property. By the end of the sixteenth century, the idea of profiting directly from writing was widely accepted as perfectly natural and respectable, as one can see from the confident way in which writers such as Salviati and Ammirato negotiated with their printers. Thus, important though patronage, in the traditional sense, remained to writers in this century, print determined the start of an underlying shift away from it. On the one hand, authors themselves began to emerge as masters of the destiny of their works. Fratta, in his dialogue on dedications, refers to what he calls the author's *padronia* or ownership of his works, his right to correct, print or reprint them as he wishes (f. B3v). On the other hand, the growing reading public was beginning to take over the determining role of the patron. What Arthur Marotti has written of Renaissance England is also true of Renaissance Italy: 'Within the literary institution developing in the context of print culture ... another set of social relations was emerging in which the patron was ultimately eclipsed by the increasing sociocultural authority of authors as well as by the economic and interpretive importance of the reader, the patron of the work as buyer and consumer in the modern sense of the term patronage.'[104] Even if the traditional patronage system still dominated the lives of writers to such an extent that none could afford to live outside its constraints, men such as Ariosto, Castiglione, Aretino, Bernardo and Torquato Tasso all sensed that the publishing of their works in print could make a difference to their careers and sought through the press, in different ways and with varying success, to achieve greater financial independence.

Just as the relationship between writers and the broadening reading public began to eclipse traditional patronage, so in some respects it affected the aims and practices of their writing. It has been suggested that in Renaissance England the main element which distinguished attitudes towards literature from modern ones is that it was 'aimed at a particular audience' and 'designed to achieve particular effects'. Whereas writers today do not usually direct their works principally at a constituency of people known to them, literature then had a 'public relations' function. It was a means of seeking from others what one wanted, whether this was financial support, protection, or professional or social advancement; in short, it was 'the instrument of a social transaction'.[105] The same undoubtedly holds true of much Italian Renaissance literature. The public-relations function of literature was not new, of course, but the advent of print may well help to explain its prominence in this period, particularly in dialogues, epics, lyric poetry and collections of letters, all of which genres were used to allude to contemporary figures and acquaintances of the author, and in historiography, with its obvious potential for justifying a particular regime or cause.[106] Through the press, authors could broadcast their citations of others to a readership many times greater than if they were using manuscript publication. Yet at the same time print necessarily brought about a sense of a wider audience; and here lay a source of both tension and opportunity which led to gradual changes in ways of writing. Writers became ever more conscious that they were no longer addressing only actual or potential patrons, or a small circle of like-minded readers, or even an audience within their own state, but also a greater reading and book-buying public which was largely unknown and invisible to them as they wrote and which might be spread throughout Italy or sometimes beyond. They would have been especially aware of the need to satisfy the demands of this public if, as was often the case, they themselves were funding publication in whole or in part, or if they were working on commission for a printer or publisher. Writing for a wider public meant, among other things, covering new kinds of subject matter, or approaching subjects in new ways, and we shall return to this topic in chapter 6. But the sense of public scrutiny, together with the greater sense of permanency which print bestows, also meant that writers had to give more thought to fixedness and acceptability in literary form and in matters of linguistic form—punctuation, spelling, grammar, choice of lexis. The fixity associated with print, it has been plausibly argued, foregrounds style 'by locking the exact arrangement of words permanently into place, down to the smallest detail, thus encouraging the writer to shape his sentences with extraordinary care and the reader to consider and reconsider the finer points in a way that a listener never can'.[107] That is not to say that writers before print were not attentive to details of style (one need think only of the meticulous revisions of a poet such as Petrarch), but print can only have increased this attentiveness. If Ariosto had been publishing the *Orlando furioso* in manuscript alone, he would surely not have gone to such trouble in revising its language. Even Aretino, so boastful of the power of his fluent pen, felt the need for more polish in his printed letters and asked the less talented but more assiduous Dolce to revise their presentation.

Print in the Italian Renaissance thus brought about a series of changes which affected in two principal respects the broad context in which most writers worked. First, it altered the process of publication, making it more complex but also potentially giving writers more control over the diffusion of their works. As Roger Chartier has pointed out, 'authors do not write books: they write texts that become written objects', manufactured by others.[108] The metamorphosis of text into printed object could now involve writers in dealings with a number of other people: they might have to negotiate with paper manufacturers, printers, publishers, booksellers or editors, borrow or ask for money, request privileges, meet the deadlines of press operators, look for errors in proofs, or (especially in the second half of the Cinquecento) pass the scrutiny of censors. At the same time, print publication could bring obvious advantages to writers. It gave them much greater power to diffuse their works; it could give them more control over the accuracy and the appearance of the published text, as long as they were prepared to and able to scrutinize the printing process carefully; and it could provide a new source of remuneration. Second, print affected the conditions in which writers created their works. In the woodcut of Francesco de' Lodovici presenting his poem to his patron, the portrayal of one of the sun's rays infusing its power into the poet refers to the inspiration of Apollo and perhaps also, since its rays resemble tresses, of the woman whom he described in his *Antheo gigante* as his Muse; and it reminds us that the advent of print did not alter the writer's need for individual creativity. Nevertheless, writers create in what Chartier has called a 'state of dependence', even if they are thought of and think of themselves as demiurges. Among the rules on which the writer's condition depends are, Chartier observes, those of patronage, subsidy and the market.[109] Print publication tended in the long term to make writers less dependent on patronage; at the same time, the logic of the new medium gave more importance to the rules of the market, so that writers who used print publication were now more likely to pay heed to what was expected, in matters of content and style, by the wider reading public.

NOTES

1. Sabellico, *Opera*, f. b4r. The work had appeared in an edition dedicated to Donato.

2. Beer, *Romanzi di cavalleria*, pp. 159–60 (I have slightly modified punctuation in the quotation), 167.

3. See for instance Bullock, 'Some notes', and Balduino, 'Petrarchismo veneto'.

4. Andrews, 'Written texts' (p. 85 for the evidence on publication preceding performance, pp. 86–7 for Aretino); Riccò, 'Testo per la scena', pp. 210–26 (pp. 221–2 for the comment on Aristotle).

5. Ariosto, *Lettere*, nos. 198–9.

6. Richardson, 'The debates'.

7. On *meccanico*, see Altieri Biagi, '"Vile meccanico"', and Cox, *The Renaissance Dialogue*, p. 39.

8. Saunders, 'The stigma of print', pp. 139, 154. For English hostility to print up to the eighteenth century, see Kernan, *Printing Technology*, especially pp. 1–23, 41–4.

9. Fiorato, 'François Guichardin'.

10. Biagiarelli, 'Editori', P. 215 and n. 11.

11. From the preface to Ovid, *Metamorphoses* (Milan: Filippo Lavagna, 1475), quoted in Scholderer, 'Printers and readers', p. 210 n. 2.

12. Sheppard, 'A fifteenth-century humanist'.

13. Ibid. 17–18; BMC, VII, 1136–7. For the scholarly use made of the press by Bonaccorso of Pisa, a pupil of Filelfo's, and Alessandro Minuziano, a pupil of Merula's, see Rogledi Manni, *La tipografia a Milano*, pp. 39–40, 42–3, 55–6.

14. Ridolfi, *La stampa in Firenze*, p. 21; P.O. Kristeller, *Supplementum ficinianum*, I, lvii–clxxxi.

15. P. O. Kristeller, *Supplementum ficinianum*, I, clxviii–clxxxi; see too I, clxxv, for the financing of the printing of Pico della Mirandola's *Heptaplus* by Roberto Salviati in 1489.

16. Fulin, 'Documenti', pp. 113–14 (doc. 28) and 123 (doc. 48); P. O. Kristeller, *Supplementum ficinianum*, I, cvi–cvii. Biondo obtained other Venetian privileges in 1495 and 1498, published a work by F.M. Grapaldi in 1517, and was a commercial partner of the sons of Luc'Antonio Giunti (Pettas, *The Giunti*, p. 109).

17. D. Fava, 'Libri membranacei', pp. 58–60.

18. P.O. Kristeller, *Supplementum ficinianum*, I, clxxvi; BMC, VI, 623.

19. A. Brown, *Bartolomeo Scala*, p. 159 and n. 68, Trovato, 'Il libro toscano', p. 543.

20. Perosa in Poliziano, *Della congiura*, pp. v–xvii.

21. Perosa, 'Contributi', pp. 92–3; Hill Cotton, 'Alessandro Sarti'; Veneziani, 'Platone Benedetti'.

22. Ridolfi, *La stampa in Firenze*, p. 24.

23. Romano, 'Predicazioni'; Villari, *La storia*, II, xxix–xxxi.

24. Rhodes, *Gli annali*, nos. 608, 644, 654, 683, 684. On Pacini, see Biagiarelli, 'Editori',pp. 217–19.

25. Lowry, *The World of Aldus Manutius*, p. 28.

26. Sabellico, *Opera*, ff. a1v, K8v.

27. Chavasse, 'The first known author's copyright'.

28. For examples, see Sabellico, *Opera*, ff. g2v–g6v, iiv; Chavasse, 'The first known author's copyright', p. 34.

29. Sabellico, *Opera*, ff. f5v–f6r; for another possible case, see f. K8v. On Moreto, see Monfasani, 'The first call', pp. 14–22, 28–31.

30. Trovato, *Cozz ogni diligenza corretto*, pp. 159–60 nn. 7–12.

31. Fulin, 'Documenti', docs. 248, 250; Bembo, *Lettere*, II, nos. 543, 555, 571, 579, 637, 644; Cian, *Un decennio*, pp. 54–7; Tavoni, 'Scrivere la grammatica', pp. 784–90; Nuovo, *Il commercio libraria nell'Italia del Rinascimento*, pp. 214–17.

32. Bembo, *Lettere*, III, no. 1095; Trovato, 'Per la storia', p. 466.

33. Ridolfi, *Vita*, I, 131, 142–4; II, 461–2 (*Decennale*); II, 507 (*Mandragola*); I, 309; II, 522–3 (*Arte della guerra*). On the *Decennale*, see also Trovato, *Con ogni diligenza corretto*, pp. 35–6, and Scarpa, 'L'autografo'.

34. Love, *Scribal Publication*, pp. 35–46 (p. 40).

35. Ibid. pp. 46–54, 73–83. For the early manuscripts of *Il principe* (*De principatibus*), see Giorgio Inglese's introduction to his critical edition, especially pp. 10–18, 37–56, 155–6. One can perhaps distinguish between a 'strong' and 'weak' use of entrepreneurial publication by Buonaccorsi, who copied the work both for sale and for presentation to a friend and patron, Pandolfo Bellacci.

36. Richardson, *'The Prince* and its early Italian readers', pp. 22–3.

37. Ariosto, *Lettere*, no. 16; Catalano, *Vita*, I, 428–39, 530; Fahy, *L''Orlando furioso'*, pp. 97–101.

38. Ariosto, *Lettere*, no. 29.

39. Catalano, *Vita*, I, 206–7; II, 136.

40. Ibid. I, 530–2; Fahy, *L''Orlando furioso'*, pp. 101–2.

41. Catalano, *Trita*, I, 595–604; Fahy, *L''Orlando furioso'*, especially pp. 93–175.

42. Ariosto's concern with accuracy is also reflected in the creation of a group of copies, on better and slightly larger paper, intended to contain the fully corrected text: Fahy, *L''Orlando furioso'*, pp. 167–75. On Cassio, see section 1 above.

43. See for instance Durling, *The Figure of the Poet*, pp. 112–14; Larivaille, 'Poeta, principe, pubblico'.

44. In a letter of 14 July 1512, Ariosto offered to have a transcription made for Francesco Gonzaga, but he is referring only to a sample section of a work in progress.

45. Brand, *Ludovico Ariosto*, pp. 135–7.

46. Fahy, *L'orlando furioso'*, pp. 112–18.

47. Catalano, *Vita*, II, 344–5.

48. The fullest account is Bertolo, 'Nuovi documenti'.

49. The process of correction is studied in Ghinassi, 'L'ultimo revisore'.

50. In his note he made the error of writing 'duc.' for 'marzelli' in some cases.

51. On this change, see Larivaille, *Pietro Aretina*, pp. 87–104. On Aretino's works in print, see Quondam, 'Aretino e il libro'.

52. Aretino, *Lettere* (1960), p. 353.

53. Aretino, *Lettere* (1609), III, f. 194r-v.

54. Aretino, *Lettere* (1960), p. 429.

55. Ibid. p. 504.

56. Baschet, 'Documents inédits', pp. 119–25.

57. Aretino, *Lettere* (1960), pp. 163, 1019 (letter 91 n. 1); see too pp. 139–40, 398–9. See Bongi, *Annali*, I, 109, for a possible identification of the dedication copy of the third book of letters.

58. Aretino, *Lettere* (1960), p. 600; see too pp. 542–3, 582–4.

59. Ibid. pp. 194–5.

60. Bongi, *Annali*, I, 109–11.

61. Ibid. pp. 131–2.

62. Aretino, *Lettere* (1960), p. 768; *Lettere* (1609), III, ff. 61r, 70v.

63. Aretino, *Lettere* (1609), III, f. 19v.

64. Aretino, *Lettere* (1960), p. 178.

65. Ibid. p. 135.

66. Ibid. p. 203. On Lappoli (known as Pollio or Pollastra) and Aretino, and on the printing of Lappoli's play *Parthenio* in 1520 at the expense of the Sienese booksellerGiovanni Landi, see Clubb and Black, *Romance*, pp. 23–6, 29–31.

67. Luzio, *Pietro Aretino*, pp. 29–32, 85–7.

68.The records in the ASV, ST up to 1550 concern the *Stanze* to the empress Isabella, 1536 (reg. 29, f. 109r); the life of Our Lady, 1539 (reg. 30, f. 130r); the third book of letters, 1545 (reg. 34, f. 120v); the *Orazia*, 1546 (reg. 34, f. 186v); the fourth book of letters, 1549 (reg. 36, f. 139v).

69. Aquilecchia, 'Pietro Aretino', pp. 73, 80–5. Giovanni Giustiniani thought it possible in 1540 that Marcolini or another of what he termed 'Aretino's printers' would agree to pay the costs of printing Giustiniani's comedies (i.e. his translations of Terence?), 12,000 lines long, in quarto, and that he himself might also receive some payment: Landoni (ed.), *Lettere scritte a Pietro Aretino*, vol. I, part I, 253–4.

70. For the *Cortegiana*, *Parafrasi dei Sette Salmi* and *La passione di Gesù* in 1534(ASV, ST, reg. 28, ff. 78r, 101r); for the life of Saint Catherine, the second book of letters, *La Talanta*, the *Ipocrito* and the second edition of the first book of letters in 1541–2 (ASV, ST, reg. 31, f. 144r; reg. 32, ff. 40v, 90r).

71. EDIT16, A2177 (Torresani), A2178 (Ruffinelli), A2216, A2219 (Biagio; the request concerning the life of Saint Thomas Aquinas is in ASV, ST, reg. 33, f. 46r). Biagio also requested a privilege for the *Dialogo del gioco*: ASV, ST, reg. 32, f. 185r.

72. EDIT16, A2219, A2222.

73. Aretino, *Lettere* (1960), p. 220.

74. Aretino, *Lettere* (1609), III, ff 36v–37v, 68r v, 80v.

75. Aretino, *Lettere* (1960), pp. 632–3, 688–9, 698–9, 836–7. Here too gift copies were distributed: see pp. 715, 716–17, 861.

76. Grendler, *Critics*, pp. 7–10.

77.Petrucci, 'La scrittura del testo' and 'Storia e geografia', pp. 1264–75; see also *Writers and Readers*, pp. 145–68.

78. For an example of this pressure—Dolce hastening to complete a translation for Gabriele Giolito—see Bongi, *Annali*, I, 252–3. Accounts of the work of these men can be found in Di Filippo Bareggi, *Il mestiere*; Trovato, *Con ogni diligenza corretto*; Richardson, *Print Culture*; Bonora, *Ricerche*.

79. B. Tasso, *Lettere*, II, 145.

80. Foffano, 'L'"Amadigi"', pp. 266–70; Bongi, *Annali*, II, 97–109; Dionisotti, 'Amadigi'.

81. B. Tasso, *Lettere*, II, 275.

82. Ibid. pp. 358–61, 362–5.

83. For example, ibid. pp. 477–9, 491–3.

84. Ibid. III, 138.

85. Ibid. II, 477–9.

86. Solerti, *Vita*, I, 58–60; II, 3–4, 94–5.

87. T. Tasso, *Le lettere*, I, no. 22; Solerti, *Vita*, I, 204–5.

88. Solerti, *Vita*, I, 219–20; II, 108–10.

89. Ibid. I, 333–4, 339–40; II, 156–7, 162, 452; T. Tasso, *Le lettere*, II, no. 258.

90. T. Tasso, *Le lettere*, II, no. 151; IV, no. 1131.

91. Solerti, *Vita*, I, 343–4; II, 22–3; III, 48.

92. Ibid. I, 518–21.

93. T. Tasso, *Le lettere*, IV, nos. 1079, 1084, 1094.

94. Solerti, *Vita*, I, 677–8; II, 336–7.

95. T. Tasso, *Le lettere*, III, no. 633; for similar complaints, see II, no. 205; III, nos. 640, 707; V, 110. 1280.

96. Bee, 'Lo statuto'.

97. See especially the portrait of mid-Cinquecento literature offered in 'La letteratura italiana nell'età del concilio di Trento', in Dionisotti's *Geografia e storia*, pp. 183–204.

98. See chapter 3, section 2, and compare Chartier, *The Order of Books*, pp. 47–8, on the French situation.

99. Giovio, *Lettere*, II, 122.

100. Larivaille (ed.), *Lettere di ... Aretino*, p. 77.

101. Di Filippo Bareggi, *Il mestiere*, pp. 242–81. But Doni enjoyed at least temporary prosperity: Grendler, *Critics*, pp. 61–2.

102. Rose, *Authors and Owners*, pp. 3–4. On this period, see too Kernan, *Printing Technology*.

103. Barberi, *Il frontespizio*, I, 117–20; Mortimer, 'The author's image'.

104. Marotti, *Manuscript, Print*, p. 292.

105. Tompkins, 'The reader in history', pp. 206–11.

106. For the dialogue, see Cox, *The Renaissance Dialogue*, pp. 3946.

107. Kernan, *Painting Technology*, pp. 172–81 (pp. 173–4).

108. Chartier, *The Order of Books*, pp. 9–10.

109. Ibid. p. X.

FRANCIS AMES-LEWIS

Image and Text:
The Paragone

This chapter and the following three offer discussions of aspects of the relationships between early Renaissance images and art-theoretical and other texts. The principal issue that runs through these discussions is: in what ways did the Renaissance artist respond to written texts, or engage with theoretical or intellectual questions relevant to his art practice that were also discussed in writings of the time? Issues raised in early Renaissance art theory have been extensively discussed in the literature and do not need much rehearsal here. The focus of this chapter will be on artists' contributions to such debate both in their own writings but more pointedly in their painting and sculpture.

There is little evidence that artists themselves were much concerned about theoretical or intellectual issues during the first half of the fifteenth century. There are, for example, no surviving writings by artists, beyond the occasional letter, between Cennini's *Craftsman's Handbook* of the 1390s, which is in intention a primer in good practice for the painter, and Ghiberti's ground-breaking *Commentaries* (*c.* 1450). Although not of high literary merit, this is a remarkable text that combines the first coherent history of Italian art, the first artistic autobiography and the first attempt by an artist to discuss in words some of the intellectual and scientific principles of the visual arts, notably optics. A new theoretical grounding for the art of painting was provided in *On Painting* by Alberti, who had a university education and was

From *The Intellectual Life of the Early Renaissance Artist*. © 2000 by Francis Ames-Lewis.

skilled in a range of intellectual activities. Writings by humanists and others about art and artists sometimes show a recognition that painting and sculpture deserve the enhanced status of liberal arts. This acknowledgment was much encouraged by Alberti's treatise, especially its first version, *De pictura*, written in Latin in 1435 for an educated readership at the court of Mantua. In the late fifteenth century artists themselves occasionally took up the pen to write on the theory or the practice of their arts. They sometimes attempted to gain footholds on the intellectuals' territory by writing poetry, and in their practice they responded imaginatively to an increasing range of written texts, both classical and contemporary. These examples of artists' growing responsiveness to theoretical and intellectual questions increasingly interweave and overlap as the early Renaissance unfolds.

In the notes for his unwritten Treatise on Painting, Leonardo da Vinci makes the case for the superiority of painting over all other 'sciences' because it is inimitable:

> Those sciences that are imitable are of such a kind that through them the disciple can equal the master ... [these] are not of such excellence as those that cannot be passed down in this way as if they are heritable goods. Amongst these, painting has first place. It cannot be taught to someone not endowed with it by nature, as can be done with mathematics ... It cannot be copied as can writing, in which the copy has as much worth as the original. It cannot be reproduced as can sculpture, in which the cast shares with the original the essential merits of the piece. It cannot produce infinite offspring, like printed books. Painting alone retains its nobility, bringing honours singularly to its author and remaining precious and unique ... such singularity gives it greater excellence than those things that are spread abroad.[1]

The question of the *paragone* between painting and sculpture—which of the two was the superior art, and why—had become a formal debate by the middle of the sixteenth century. In 1546 the Florentine Benedetto Varchi attempted to settle the issue in his lectures on the *paragone*. His views were in part based on the responses he received to a letter he had circulated to a number of leading artists of his day, asking for their opinions on the matter. But various contributions had been made to the discussion by writers on the visual arts, and by some artists themselves through their works, over the 150 or so years before this time. Inevitably, there is classical authority for the discussion. Philostratus the Elder, for example, in the introduction to his

Imagines, written in the third century AD, claims that by exploiting colour, painting can achieve more than the three-dimensional medium of sculpture.[2] Quattrocento contributions suggest that the *paragone* had once again become an issue of some importance amongst intellectuals concerned with the visual arts. Moreover, the writings of artists themselves, and images recorded in their works, suggest that they understood it to be an issue that deserved artistic exploration.

The noteworthy early fifteenth-century developments that seem to have inspired Alberti to write *On Painting* took place in Florence, principally—and paradoxically—in sculpture. This is in a sense acknowledged by the list of artists cited by Alberti as Brunelleschi's co-dedicatees of the vernacular translation of his treatise, *Della pittura*, for it comprises three living sculptors and one dead painter. One of Alberti's main aims in *On Painting* was, therefore, to redress this imbalance by asserting the primacy of painting over sculpture. This he sought to accomplish by developing a theoretical and intellectual foundation on which painters could build. But painters depended on sculpture to provide models for their study of the human figure to a degree that sculptors seldom depended on paintings. The higher status that sculpture apparently enjoyed, however, stimulated and was offset by powerfully expressed and keenly argued views about the greater versatility and naturalism of painting as an art form. Some painters in particular were eager to claim the superiority of their art by demonstrating how it could imitate and indeed improve on qualities and effects special to sculpture.

Much of the debate on the *paragone* that survives from the early Renaissance was conducted by the painters and sculptors themselves, either in words or through their artistic works. An important contribution to the debate that comes in a text written by an eminent man of letters, Baldassare Castiglione, is therefore especially significant. *The Book of the Courtier* was not published until 1528, but Castiglione started to write it around 1508, purporting to record intellectual discussion at the Montefeltro court at Urbino in 1506. A section of the dialogue between Emilia Pia, Count Lodovico da Canossa and the Mantuan court sculptor Giancristoforo Romano revolves around the *paragone* between painting and sculpture. Count Lodovico raises the issue at the end of his discussion, of the respect in which painting and painters were held in ancient times:

> if the statues which have come down to us are inspired works of art we may readily believe that so, too, were the paintings of the ancient world; indeed, they may have been still more so, because they required greater artistry.[3]

This challenge is taken up by Giancristoforo Romano who maintains that sculpture requires more effort and skill than painting, produces a more faithful imitation of Nature because it is in three dimensions, and cannot be gone over again if a mistake is made in the carving process. Count Lodovico presents the arguments in favour of painting—that it is superior for decorative purposes since it includes light and shade, colour, atmosphere and expressive accents not available to the sculptor. Moreover, the painter has to exercise skill greater than the sculptor's in showing perspective and foreshortening, and in presenting convincingly on a flat surface a range of motifs not available to the sculptor—metallic gleam, the darkness of night, weather conditions, varied landscape forms and so on. Presumably these arguments confounded Giancristoforo Romano, for the discussion moves directly on to the importance for the courtier of a knowledge of painting without further contributions on the relative superiority of painting or sculpture as art forms.

The arguments offered on both sides of the case are familiar from earlier discussions of the *paragone* between sculpture and painting. At much the time that *The Book of the Courtier* was being drafted, painters themselves engaged with the question, seeking to demonstrate that their art could illusionistically achieve results proper to sculpture. Conversely, in their practice, too, some sculptors sought expressive effects more appropriate to paintings when generating examples of the superiority of sculpture. But more significant is that as well as being artistically problematical the *paragone* issue had evidently gained an intellectual respectability by the early sixteenth century. It had become a matter worthy of discussion by intellectuals and courtiers, and this paved the way for Benedetto Varchi's attempt several decades later to solve the issue by appeal to common consent.

'Is it not true that painting is the mistress of all the arts or their principal ornament?', Leon Battista Alberti had already written in *On Painting*:

> The stonemason, the sculptor and all the workshops and crafts of artificers are guided by the rule and art of the painter. Indeed, hardly any art, except the very meanest, can be found that does not somehow pertain to painting. So I would venture to assert that whatever beauty there is in things has been derived from painting.[4]

In Naples, twenty years later, Bartolomeo Fazio recapitulated Alberti's ideas when he in turn wrote: 'what is true of painting is also true of carved and cast sculpture and of Architecture, all of which crafts have their origins in painting; for no craftsman can be excellent in these branches of art if the science of painting is unknown to him'.[5] Alberti, of course, had a polemical purpose in advancing so strongly the cause of painting as his preferred rival to sculpture or the other arts. Speaking, as he says at several points in the treatise, 'as a painter', he was evidently not unprejudiced in his views. Ghiberti wrote that 'for the sculptor and the painter, drawing is the foundation and the theory of both arts',[6] but for Alberti both derive from the artist's 'genius': 'Painting and sculpture are cognate arts, nurtured by the same genius. But I shall always prefer the genius of the painter, as it attempts by far the most difficult task'.[7] Further emphasising the relative difficulty of painting, he added that when studying the practice of painting, 'it will probably help also to practise at sculpting rather than painting, for sculpture is easier and surer than painting. No one will ever be able to paint a thing correctly if he does not know its every relief, and relief is more easily found by sculpture than by painting'.[8]

In his treatise *On Sculpture* (*De statua*), written around 1450, Alberti advanced no comparable arguments in favour of the superiority in any respect of sculpture over painting. Perhaps surprisingly, nor did Ghiberti make any such claims in his *Commentaries*, although his remark at the very end of the autobiographical section that 'I have made many preparatory models of wax and clay, and drawn a great many things for painters'[9] may be understood as a gentle reminder of the sculptor's importance for the painter. But Ghiberti is also an important example of a relief sculptor who responded to the concern with the geometrical basis of picture-making that developed during the second and third decades of the fifteenth century, and which was later encoded in theory by Alberti in *On Painting*. The contrast between the traditional, essentially late Gothic system of construction used in the reliefs of his first doors for the Baptistery in Florence, and the frank pictorialism of the reliefs for his second doors—the so-called 'Gates of Paradise'—shows how much Ghiberti was affected by new principles of the art of painting then being developed in the circle of Brunelleschi, notably in the work of Masaccio. Indeed, his consciousness of these questions is indicated by his departure from the programme that had been proposed by the eminent humanist and Chancellor of Florence, Leonardo Bruni, in 1426.[10]

Bruni had provided a list of subjects for twenty narrative reliefs and eight figures of prophets. This shows that he was thinking in terms of a pair of doors that would follow the pattern established nearly a century earlier in Andrea Pisano's doors, and adopted for Ghiberti's first doors at the time of the competition in 1401. But in his *Commentaries* Ghiberti states that despite this programme, which Bruni presumably devised at the request of the Clothworkers' Guild (Arte di Calimala), the Baptistery patrons, he 'was given permission to carry it out in the way I thought would turn out most perfectly and most richly and most elaborately ... I tried in every way to be faithful in seeking to imitate nature as far as was possible to me'.[11] Clearly one way he did this was to suggest, anticipating Alberti, that the bronze panels were 'an open window through which the subject to be [represented] is seen'.[12] Rather than building up figures in high relief against a flat surface, which was essentially his practice in his first set of doors, Ghiberti set out to generate perspectively projected spaces for his figures in much the same way as Masaccio had done in his paintings of these same middle years of the 1420s. In generating this new type of pictorial relief, Ghiberti anticipated Leonardo da Vinci's comments on low relief sculpture, although he would hardly have agreed with Leonardo's opinion:

> The sculptor says that low relief is a form of painting. This may be in part conceded as far as drawing is concerned, because it participates in perspective. As far as light and shade are concerned low relief fails both as sculpture and as painting, because the shadows correspond to the low nature of the relief, as for example in the shadows of foreshortened objects, which will not exhibit the depth of those in painting or in sculpture in the round. Rather, the art of low relief is a mixture of painting and sculpture.[13]

Like Ghiberti, Donatello too was striving for pictorial effects in his relief sculpture of the 1420s. The *Feast of Herod* relief on the Siena Baptistery font, modelled at about the same time as Ghiberti was starting work on the designs for the reliefs of his second Baptistery doors, is an early manifesto of Brunelleschian perspective. Moreover, it shows in a masterly way how geometrical spatial construction can be exploited in the interests of pictorial narrative. In this respect, too, Donatello's treatment of relief anticipates both Ghiberti's narrative method and Alberti's evolved theory of picture-making in *On Painting*. Donatello developed a second technique, the so-called *rilievo schiacciato* ('squashed relief'), for making his sculptural reliefs more like monochrome paintings. Leonardo da Vinci later asserted that 'the perspective used by sculptors [in reliefs] never appears correct, whereas the painter can make a distance of one hundred miles appear in his work. Aerial perspective is absent from the sculptors' work'.[14] When writing this he clearly did not bring to mind Donatello's *Ascension and Giving of the Keys to St*

Peter, for here the sculptor had proleptically challenged Leonardo's view by creating a convincing, deep landscape recession through subtle grading of the depth of the relief which is used to suggest the tonal change of aerial perspective.

In this way Donatello showed that relief sculpture can suggest effects of landscape space and atmosphere. Ghiberti sought to achieve something similar in his 'Gates of Paradise' panels, grading spatial depth both through varying the height of relief and through proportional diminution—though this was possible only up to a point, beyond which the narrative meaning of subsidiary scenes would become invisible. But these two approaches to pictorial relief, and especially Donatello's highly subtle carving technique, made little impression on sculptural practice. Desiderio da Settignano carved a few *schiacciato* reliefs, but in general sculptors found, perhaps, that the result did not justify the time and effort involved—either artistically or commercially. *Rilievo schiacciato* may be a means to approach the painter's achievements in atmospheric landscape, but it still lacks the element of colour through which the painter can achieve infinitely subtle and expressive effects. Polychromy was seldom a viable option for the sculptor. Bright, colourful pigmentation of sculpture is acceptable for devotional madonnas in terracotta or stucco and could also be used to enhance the legibility of narrative reliefs located at a distance from the viewer, as in Donatello's roundels in the Old Sacristy of S. Lorenzo, Florence. But the application of gesso and pigment was not appropriate for finely carved marble (let alone for bronze) reliefs, because it has a coarsening effect on the surface. Much of the fine detail of the carefully graded relief of the *Ascension and Giving of the Keys to St Peter* would have been rendered redundant if it had been polychromed. Despite Donatello's masterly attempts, sculpture could not hope to rival the possibilities offered by painting in this field.

When in 1546 Benedetto Varchi issued his appeal to major artists of his day for evidence that might enable him finally to decide the *paragone* issue one way or the other, the debate had become rather stale through overwork. But in the hundred or so years after Alberti's initial statement of his preference in *On Painting*, it was an issue of some interest to artists and their patrons. It was pursued both in written form and in aspects of artistic practice in which both painters and sculptors sought to demonstrate the superiority of their art in rivalling the other on its own ground. This suggests that, although the debate may seem somewhat vacuous to us today, it did engage the intellectual energies of many Renaissance artists. The presentation of their arguments offered them opportunities to show their prowess in intellectual discourse, as well as in the practice of their art.

Faithful to his concern that he should be taken seriously as a writer and theoretician, Filarete contributed to the *paragone* debate in his *Treatise on Architecture* (*c*. 1460–64).[15] In the light of the intellectual complexity of the theoretical debate that developed later, however, much of his discussion and many of his arguments have a rather naîve quality. In a section of dialogue between the writer and the Duke of Milan, Filarete takes up the *paragone* theme by proposing further arguments to those that Alberti had advanced some twenty-five years earlier. Surprisingly, though, given that he was by training a bronze sculptor, Filarete does not seek to press the case for the superiority of sculpture. He puts these arguments into the duke's mouth, while himself responding at greater length in favour of painting. The duke declared that he was

> under the impression that drawing and carving in marble or bronze was much worthier than painting, since [if] someone carving a figure in marble might well happen to have a bit of the nose or some other element break off, as it can happen sometimes that a piece is knocked off, how can he repair the figure? But a painter can cover up with colours, and patch things up even if they were spoiled a thousand times ...

Without objecting disloyally to the duke's arguments, Filarete develops others as he replies:

> Your lordship speaks truth, for carving in marble is a matter of great mastery. In ... aiming to counterfeit those colours that nature makes, [paintings] are great things too. For however good they are, [sculptures] always seems to be of the material they really are, but what is painted seems to be the actual thing.

Citing well-known anecdotes, both classical and more recent ones, that describe the deceptiveness of paintings, Filarete concluded that 'this is based on the knowledge of applying colours in the right places, and such miracles are not seen in sculpture.' These two ideas—that unlike paintings carved sculpture cannot be corrected, and that painting is more deceptively realistic because of its coloration—fuelled the debate that Leonardo da Vinci conducted with himself in numerous notes and drafts for inclusion in the Treatise on Painting.

'Applying myself to sculpture no less than to painting, and practised in both to the same degree', Leonardo wrote, 'it seems to me that I am able to form a judgement about them with little prejudice, indicating which of these two is of greater insight, difficulty and perfection.'[16] His prejudice in favour of painting becomes very clear in the notes for the discussion that was to have followed this preamble. He advances too many arguments to be repeated here: a sample must suffice to suggest the intellectual force of Leonardo's case. Some of them are fairly banal: for example, painting demands more of the intellect if only because carving imposes physical demands on the sculptor. The latter 'undertakes his work with greater bodily exertion than the painter, and the painter undertakes his work with greater mental exertion'; and 'Sculpture is not a science but a very mechanical art, because it causes its executant sweat and bodily fatigue.' Most of Leonardo's arguments are, however, intellectually more considered than this. As elsewhere in his projected treatise, in this discussion (repetitive thought it is) he demonstrates his high level of articulacy on artistic matters. He also shows that he had an intellectually well-founded understanding of the theoretical and practical issues surrounding art production at the turn of the century. He repeats the Duke of Milan's argument in Filarete's *Treatise*, but unlike Filarete he has a riposte:

> The sculptor says that if he removes more marble than he should, he cannot rectify his error as can the painter. To this it is replied that someone who removes more than he should is not a master, because a master is required to understand the true science of his profession ... We well know that someone with practised skill will not make such errors. Rather, obeying good rules, he will proceed by removing so little at any time that he takes his work along smoothly.[17]

The intellectually most sophisticated part of the discussion revolves, however, around what each art can and cannot represent. Anticipating Count Lodovico's arguments in *The Book of the Courtier*, Leonardo points out:

> The art of painting embraces and contains within itself all visible things. It is the poverty of sculpture that it cannot do this; namely, show the colours of everything and their diminution with distance. Painting shows transparent objects, but the sculptor shows you the things of nature without the painter's artistry.[18]

Painters can show rain, cloudy mountains and valleys; rivers of greater or less transparency; the stars above us; and 'innumerable other effects to which the sculptor cannot aspire'. Sculptors, on the other hand, 'cannot depict transparent bodies, nor can they represent luminous sources, nor reflected rays, nor shiny bodies such as mirrors and similar lustrous things, nor mists, nor dreary weather—nor endless other things'.

Low-relief sculpture, Leonardo concedes, involves 'more intellectual considerations than sculpture in the round ... because it is indebted to perspective'. But figure sculpture does not require the understanding of geometry and perspective that most writers agreed was a primary need of the painter. It can therefore be learned more quickly by a painter than painting can by a sculptor. The figure sculptor, writes Leonardo,

> has to make each figure in the round with many contours so that the figure will look graceful from all viewpoints ... but in truth this requirement cannot be said to rebound to the credit of the sculptor, considering that he shares with the painter the need to pay attention to the contours of forms seen from every aspect. This consideration is implicit in painting just as it is in sculpture;

and further

> The sculptor ... cannot produce the required figure ... if he does not move around it, stooping or rising in such a way as to see the true elevations of the muscles and the true gaps between them ... In this is said to reside the mental effort of sculpture ... [the sculptor] does not need any measure of mental activity—or we may say judgement—unless in rectifying the profiles of the limbs when the muscles are too prominent.[19]

In this, of course, lies the principal challenge of sculpture to painting: as Giancristoforo Romano put it in *The Book of the Courtier*,

> I still do not understand how you can maintain that what is real and is Nature's own creation cannot be more faithfully copied in a bronze or marble figure, in which all the members are rounded, fashioned and proportioned just as Nature makes them, than in a picture, consisting of a flat surface and colours that deceive the eye.[20]

The challenge to the painter was to rival sculpture in its own field— that of generating three-dimensionality of form and plasticity of surface.

One way in which this might be achieved was in representing the relief surface with a full range of tonality. Sebastiano del Piombo worked to Michelangelo's drawings in the *Raising of Lazarus* (London, National Gallery) by exploiting the rich tonality of a Venetian palette. He was thereby able to put into practice the view that Michelangelo later expressed, that painting could be excellent only in so far as it approached the quality of sculpture by possessing *rilievo*. Raphael's response to Sebastiano's challenge in his *Transfiguration* (Vatican, Pinacoteca) was to take up and extrapolate from Leonardo's *sfumato* and his technique of working down to the depths of shadows, with the result that the overall tonality of his works was deepened.[21] In *The Book of the Courtier* Castiglione puts into Giancristoforo Romano's mouth the aphorism about Raphael that 'the excellence you perceive in his work as a painter is so supreme that it cannot be rivalled by any sculpture in marble',[22] although one may doubt if this view of the ultimate superiority of painting was indeed held by the sculptor. It turns on its head Michelangelo's view that painting could at best be only a partial, impoverished imitation of sculpture. Raphael's excellence was at least in part due to his adoption of Leonardo's *sfumato* and use of deeper tonalities. Castiglione also suggests that the painter shows his superiority by his knowledge and understanding of light and shade, and foreshortening. This idea perhaps followed Leonardo's lead, for the creation of relief using light and shade was for Leonardo one of the primary tasks of the painter. Later, Lomazzo suggested that it was through exploiting his 'dark manner' that Leonardo could 'do everything that nature herself can do'.[23] This, too, echoes Castiglione's discussion of the effects that can be achieved in painting but not in sculpture:

> Nature's colours can be reproduced in flesh-tints, in clothing and in all the other objects that are coloured in life ... still less can [the sculptor] depict the love-light in a person's eyes..., the colour of blond hair; the gleam of weapons; the darkness of night; a tempest at sea; thunder and lightning; a city in conflagration; or the break of rosy dawn with its rays of gold and red. In short, it is beyond his powers to depict sky, sea, land, mountains, woods, meadows, gardens, rivers, cities or houses; but not beyond the powers of the painter.[24]

It was not until the early sixteenth century that defenders of sculpture, stung perhaps by critical arguments such as those advanced by Leonardo da Vinci, began to promote those characteristics that make sculpture superior to painting. Benedetto Varchi's academic investigation was shortly followed by Vasari's careful compromise in the first edition of his *Lives* (1550), repeated almost verbatim in the edition of 1568. Vasari chose not to commit himself as to the relative superiority of the two arts, reverting to Ghiberti's view on the primacy of drawing when writing that 'Design [*disegno*] ... is the foundation of both these arts [i.e. sculpture and painting], or rather the animating principle of all creative processes'.[25] Perhaps the last recorded word on the *paragone* theme before this masterly balancing act was that of the Venetian sculptor Tullio Lombardo. In a letter of 18 June 1526 to Marco Casalini of Rovigo, Tullio wrote:

> painting is an ephemeral and unstable thing, while sculpture is much more incomparable and not to be compared in any way with painting, because the sculpture of the ancients can be seen up to our time, while of their painting there is really nothing to be seen.[26]

This echoes discussion in *The Book of the Courtier*, where the count suggests that 'if the statues which have come down to us are inspired works of art we may readily believe that so, too, were the paintings of the ancient world.'[27] But this is not intellectually a particularly powerful case in favour of sculpture. The need to cite it suggests that the arguments advanced by Leonardo in his observations, and by Raphael and others in practice, had prevailed. Indeed, Leonardo had considered and refuted this argument too, maintaining that the durability of sculpture derived merely from its material, not from the art that went into its carving.

During the fifteenth and early sixteenth centuries statements were made about the *paragone* between painting and sculpture not only in written form but also in artistic practice itself. Indeed, the theoretical concern with the issue can be partly associated with the growing use of sculptures as prototypes for painting both in workshop drawing practice and in finished works. Only a few of the arguments set down in words could be usefully applied in artistic practice. Nevertheless, they suggest that a number of artists besides Leonardo da Vinci grappled with theoretical questions raised by the *paragone* debate. Donatello's reliefs carved in his *schiacciato* technique were made to appear to be monochrome paintings. Mantegna conversely produced monochrome paintings that deliberately imitated relief sculpture. This practice doubtless developed in part through his preoccupation with classical sculpture, and perhaps also in part because of his excellence in depicting materials, which itself depended on his immaculate painting technique. Early examples of his growing skill in imitating relief sculpture come in the *Circumcision* (Florence, Uffizi) where overdoor lunettes on Old Testament themes appear to be bronze reliefs.[28] Later in his career Mantegna made a group of independent easel paintings that deliberately imitated bronze sculpture. His *bronzi finti* for Isabella d'Este, which must have closely resembled the pendants of *Judith* and *Dido*, and Antico's parcel-gilt bronzes, such as the later recast of Bishop Ludovico Gonzaga's small bronze Apollo *Belvedere*, must indeed have complemented each other in Isabella's *grotta*. There is here surely a deliberate *paragone*: using shell-gold over a brown underpaint to model his forms sculpturally, Mantegna emulated in painting very much the effects achieved by a bronze sculptor like Antico.[29]

Mantegna's painted bronze 'reliefs' extrapolate both from the 'reliefs' in the Uffizi *Circumcision* and, more generally, from his earlier interest in suggesting direct comparisons between his painted figures and classical marble statuary. In his Vienna *St Sebastian* Mantegna seems deliberately to compare the structure of the saint's anatomy with the torso and head fragments of classical sculpture prominently placed in the left foreground. The sharp angularity of the saint's face suggests that Mantegna might even have had in mind Alberti's comment, in his discussion of the 'reception of light', that 'In painting I would praise ... those faces which seem to stand out from the pictures as though they were sculpted ...'[30] An even more conscious and pointed comparison is in the Paris *St Sebastian*, where a classical fragment of a sandalled foot is conspicuously placed next to the saint's right foot. By pointing out the source for his forms Mantegna here acknowledged the debt he owed to the antique. At the same time, moreover, he demonstrated the superiority of painting in its ability to provide the sculptural form with colour and lifelikeness. Both this demonstrative exercise and his later grisaille paintings may have been responses by Mantegna to the criticism of his master Francesco Squarcione when, according to the sixteenth-century Paduan historian Scardeone (as reported by Vasari), he

> singled out for attack the paintings that Andrea had done in the [Ovetari] chapel, saying that they were inferior work since when he did them Andrea had imitated marble statues. Stone, said Squarcione, was essentially a hard substance and it could never convey the softness and tenderness of flesh and natural objects, with their various movements and folds. Andrea would have done far better, he suggested, if he had painted his figures not in various colours but just as if they were made of marble, seeing

that his pictures resembled ancient statues and suchlike things
rather than living creatures.[31]

In his *Cronaca rimata*, Giovanni Santi also commented, with however greater
appreciation, on Mantegna's representation of sculpture:

> Nor has he overlooked relief, with soft attractive
> Methods by which to show to sculpture too
> What heaven and good fortune gave to him ...[32]

Celebrated for his ability to imitate marble and other materials, Mantegna
perhaps predictably established a new genre of painted 'reliefs' that were
surely intended to be understood as recreated classical relief sculpture. In the
Introduction of the Cult of Cybele in Rome, painted in 1506 for the Venetian
patrician Francesco Cornaro and still in Mantegna's workshop at his death
later that year, grisaille figures set against a subtly varied background
apparently of brightly coloured marble dramatically act out the narrative.[33]
Conversely, Antonio Lombardo later introduced coloured stones into his
reliefs for the Camerino d'alabastro of Alfonso d'Este to reproduce in relief
something akin to the effects that Mantegna strove for. In the Forge of
Vulcan Lombardo inlaid areas such as the blue of the sky and the brown
chimney-breast with coloured stones.[34] Here too is the sculptor's answer to
the accusation that sculpture lacks colour: by this artificial and inevitably
unsubtle means he strove to challenge Leonardo's view that 'the sculptor is
not able to achieve diversity using the various types of colours'.

Another means by which painters sought to counter the apparent
superiority of sculpture in the round for showing relief was to study a figure
from different angles, so as to build up a composite impression of its three-
dimensional reality. That this practice was already in use in the mid-fifteenth-
century workshop is demonstrated especially in Antonio Pollaiuolo's exemplary
Battle of the Nudes engraving in which several figures are shown twice, pivoted
through 180 degrees; and the system was adopted by Dürer, amongst others. It
was also later exploited in reverse by Gianlorenzo Bernini, when he received
from Van Dyck the triple portrait of Charles I (Windsor Castle), on the basis of
which Bernini carved his marble bust of Charles I, destroyed in the Whitehall
Palace fire of 1698.[35] If we are to believe Vasari, Giorgione also explored the
question of angles of view in a practical contribution to discussion of the
paragone issue. His demonstration was in response to the arguments of sculptors
'who maintained that since a statue showed to anyone walking around it
different aspects and poses, sculpture was superior to painting, which could

represent only one aspect of any given subject'.³⁶ In order to prove 'that painting requires more skill and effort and can show in one scene more aspects of nature than is the case with sculpture', Giorgione

> offered to show in a single view of one picture the front, back and two profiles of a painted figure. After he had made those sculptors rack their brains, Giorgione solved the problem in this way. He painted a man in the nude with his back turned and, at his feet, a limpid stream of water bearing his reflection. To one side was a burnished cuirass that the man had taken off, and this reflected his left profile ...; on the other side was a mirror reflecting the other profile of the nude figure ...

Unfortunately, no visual evidence survives to support the reliability of Vasari's anecdote. It may be pure invention; but more probably it derives from Paolo Pino's description of a similar painting by Giorgione in his *Dialogue on Painting* (*Dialogo di pittura*):

> he painted a full length picture of St George in armour, leaning on the broken shaft of a spear, his feet just at the edge of a clear and limpid brook in which the whole figure had its foreshortened reflection up to the top of the head; then there was a mirror in which one could see entirely the other side of St George. He wanted to prove by this picture that a painter can show a figure entirely at one glance, which a sculptor is incapable of.³⁷

The *Dialogue* was published in Venice in 1548, two years after Varchi elicited responses to his questions about the relative superiority of painting and sculpture from Central Italian painters. Pino's description may well be a true record of an experiment by Giorgione. The painter may have been stimulated to undertake this type of conscious demonstration of artistic skill by the conspicuous use of reflections in some early Netherlandish paintings. About fifty years before Giorgione's lost painting was made, Bartolomeo Fazio had particularly noted in a painting by Jan van Eyck of 'women of uncommon beauty emerging from the bath' that 'in one of them he has shown only the face and breast but has then represented the hind parts of her body in a mirror painted on the wall opposite, so that you may see her back as well as her breast'.³⁸ The parallel between this praise and Antonio Pollaiuolo's interest in pivoted and mirror-image figures might readily have inspired experiments such as Giorgione's.

A further, and final, indication of the popularity of the *paragone* issue in early sixteenth-century Venice is provided by Titian's *La Schiavona*, a female portrait that dates from around 1511. Close observation indicates that at a late stage Titian enlarged the parapet on which the sitter lays her left hand. This was presumably to provide the space into which he could insert the sitter's profile portrait in the guise of a carved cameo-like relief. It may be presumed that this change was sanctioned by the sitter; but in Titian's hands the rich vitality of the frontally posed woman's face as she compellingly engages the observer's gaze could hardly contrast more deliberately with the formal, almost clinically cool idealism of the profile. This demonstrates more clearly than any words Titian's view as to the representational superiority of painting over relief sculpture.

By the time Castiglione wrote his *Book of the Courtier*, it had become intellectually respectable to discuss the question of the relative superiority of painting and sculpture. The extent to which the visual arts had come to form suitable subject matter for men of letters to discuss is particularly well demonstrated in Castiglione's dialogue. The *paragone* was an issue worth debating not merely for painters such as Leonardo da Vinci in his writings, and Mantegna in his practice, but also for the courtiers of Guidobaldo da Montefeltro, Duke of Urbino. Moreover, both texts and paintings show how Renaissance artists also took up the challenge of the theoretical issues involved, and entered into the dialogue on the *paragone* alongside intellectuals like Alberti and Castiglione.

Notes

1. Kemp and Walker (1989), 19.
2. Land (1994) 30.
3. Castiglione/Bull (1967), 97–8.
4. Alberti/Grayson (1972), 61, para. 2–6.
5. Baxandall (1971), 104.
6. Ghiberti/Morisani (1947) 3 [my translation].
7. Alberti/Grayson (1972), 65, para. 2–7.
8. Alberti/Grayson (1972), 101, para. 58.
9. Gilbert (1980), 88.
10. Chambers (1970), 47–8; Krautheimer and Krautheimer-Hess (1956), 169–73 and 372–3 document 52.
11. Gilbert (1980), 86.
12. Alberti/Grayson (1972), 55, para. 19.
13. Kemp and Walker (1989), 42.
14. Kemp and Walker (1989), 42.
15. Gilbert (1980), 89–90; Spencer (1965), 1, 309 (book 23, fol. 181r).
16. Kemp and Walker (1989), 38.

17. Kemp and Walker (1989), 44–5.

18. Kemp and Walker (1989), 40.

19. Kemp and Walker (1989), 39–40.

20. Castiglione/Bull (1967), 98.

21. Posner (1974), 11–15.

22. Castiglione/Bull (1967), 98.

23. Lomazzo/Klein (1974), 51.

24. Castiglione/Bull (1967), 99.

25. Vasari/Bull (1965–87), I, 25.

26. '... la pittura e cosa caduca et instabele, la scolture e molto piu senza comparatione, et non da paragonarsi con pittura per niun modo: perche degli anticui se ritrova fina alti nostri tempi delle sue scolture, et picture veramente nulla si poi vedere'; Luchs (1995), 157 n. 94; Puppi (1971).

27. Castiglione/Bull (1967), 97.

28. Greenstein (1992), 89–92; Jones (1987); Lightbown (1986), colour pl. VI.

29. Martineau ed. (1992), 394–9, and 411–12 cats. 133–4.

30. Alberti/Grayson (1972), 89, para. 46.

31. Vasari/Bull (1965–87), I, 242.

32. '... ha ancor cum dolci e grati / Modi il rilievo per che alla scultura / Mostrar quanto idea el cielo e i dolci fati ...'; for translation, see Gilbert (1980), 97.

33. Martineau ed. (1992), 411–16, cat. 135.

34. Martineau and Hope eds. (1983), 363 cat. s 7.

35. Avery (1997) 224–7.

36. Vasari/Bull (1965–87), I, 275–6.

37. Klein and Zerner (1966), 16; also Luchs (1995), 75.

38. Baxandall (1971), 103–9.

JOHN M. NAJEMY

Civic Humanism and Florentine Politics

For forty-five years now historians have debated the arguments advanced by
Hans Baron in *The Crisis of the Early Italian Renaissance*,[1] and elaborated in
many separate studies and essays,[2] according to which a tenacious defense of
republican liberty and an ethic of civic participation suddenly emerged
among early fifteenth-century Florentine citizens and humanists as a
consequence of Florence's struggle for survival against the expansionist
ambitions of the Visconti dukes of Milan. Baron's thesis has enjoyed (and
suffered) a degree of attention and controversy that has not abated even now,
a decade after his death and in a completely transformed world of
historiographical assumptions and practices.[3] One reason for this is certainly
the dramatic quality of Baron's thesis—its claim that big and lasting changes
in the intellectual history of the Renaissance occurred as a direct and
immediate response to what Baron saw as the Florentines' life-and-death
conflict with Milan. Other reasons for the continuing debates may be less
clear, less related to the merits and weaknesses of Baron's historical
arguments, and rooted, perhaps, in the political agendas and ideological
stakes that still surround modern versions of civic humanism.[4] Whatever the
reasons, the problem of when and why civic and republican attitudes
emerged in Renaissance Florence still generates a good deal of debate.

The question of Florentine civic humanism, as understood *both* by
Baron and most of his critics, has typically been framed around three points:

From *Renaissance Civic Humanism* ed. James Hankins. © 2000 by Cambridge University Press.

the genesis, the originality, and the accuracy of the civic humanist representation of republican politics in fifteenth-century Florence. Baron's answers to these questions are well known. For the origin or cause of the civic humanist ideas of republican liberty and the active life, he focused on the long wars with Milan. As for their originality, he argued that they represented a radical break with the more militantly classical and essentially apolitical humanism of the fourteenth century, and a significant departure as well from the earlier civic ethos of the medieval city-states that was—in his view—largely untouched by the focus on Roman history and culture that later became the trademark of humanism. And on the question of the accuracy of the civic humanist view of Florentine politics, Baron believed that its defense of liberty, equality, and citizen participation in government reflected the lived experience of Florentine citizens and the animating spirit of the republic's institutions.

Baron's critics have disagreed with him on all these points. About the birth of civic humanism, some have contended that the appearance of the crucial texts cannot be correlated with any foreign policy crisis,[5] while others have suggested that Baron focused on the wrong crisis.[6] About the originality of fifteenth-century civic humanism, some critics have asserted that most or even all of its chief ideas about liberty, law, and the pursuit of the "common good" can be found in the theorists of communal government as far back as the thirteenth and early fourteenth centuries;[7] others claim that the fundamental assumptions of civic humanism were not peculiar to republican Florence, but rather the common property of humanist circles throughout northern Italy.[8] And about the accuracy, or lack of it, of the civic humanist view of things, many historians have rightly insisted that the polity of early fifteenth-century Florence was something less than a paradise of citizen equality and participatory liberty, that the city was in fact governed by a restricted oligarchy, and that this self-proclaimed defender of republican liberty could be quite ruthless in subjugating its neighbors in Tuscany.[9]

Questions about the precise "cause" of civic humanism, of whether it was an original or derivative political philosophy, and of the extent to which it accurately represented Florentine political life may now have exhausted their usefulness, at least in the terms in which they have usually been posed. Few historians now accept that the military crisis of 1402 could have been the single decisive factor in the emergence of civic humanism, and the question that needs to be asked about Baron's argument is what *kind of role*, if any, foreign policy played in the development of Florentine political attitudes, and in, what relation to domestic politics. The issue of originality may never have had much usefulness. All political ideas build on preceding traditions of discourse, and in this sense there are probably no absolutely radical breaks in the history of political thought. On the other hand, claims that it had all been said before usually ignore the ways in which context and circumstance change the meaning and force of ideas. In any case, Baron's claim was not that civic ideals were unknown in Florence and the other city-states before the "crisis"; what was new, in his view, was the combination of these civic ideas with the humanist educational and moral program that began with Petrarch.

But it is the question of civic humanism's "truth"—its more or less faithful representation of the alleged realities of Florentine politics—that may be the trickiest point of all. Baron's critics are quite right to point out the gap separating Leonardo Bruni's laudatory accounts of Florentine liberty, civic equality, and participatory government from what the political historians have established about the oligarchic character of the republic in the early fifteenth century.[10] It is undeniably the case that the writings of the civic humanists did not accurately or objectively represent the realities of Florentine politics. This has led some critics, from Jerrold Seigel thirty years ago to James Hankins very recently, to explain the gap by asserting that the "civic humanists" were professional rhetoricians and not political philosophers.[11] In his important essay on Baron and Bruni studies, Hankins asks: "Were men such as Salutati and Bruni really as rooted in the values and attitudes of the Florentine ruling classes as they had seemed to Baron?"[12] His answer of course is that they were not: "if we admit that Bruni's *impostazione* is primarily that of a rhetorician, the problem [of his inconsistencies] disappears." Thus Hankins concludes that we ought to "do away with the anachronism that men like Bruni and Salutati were ideologues (in the sense of having an exclusive commitment to one political ideology such as republicanism) ... [and] admit that Florentine republicanism as presented by Salutati and Bruni was a rhetorical artifact not necessarily in keeping with either their private beliefs or the political realities of the time ... [Their] attitude was that of permanent under-secretaries, loyal to Florence rather than to the regime and carrying out to the best of their abilities the changing policies of successive political masters. They were also, undeniably, professional rhetoricians in the most basic sense of being paid salaries to produce propaganda for the state. They were made by their political masters to write letters and speeches that were sometimes inconsistent with or hostile to their own private convictions, but no one thought the worse of them for that."[13]

There is potentially much to agree with here, but there are also difficulties that stem, I think, from the way in which key terms are used.

About "rhetoric" and "professional rhetoricians," one can agree that Salutati, Bruni, and the other chancellors were indeed professional rhetoricians, and that they were paid to defend the policies of the governments they worked for. But Bruni was not yet chancellor when he wrote the *Laudatio* or when he drafted the most republican and anti-imperial portions of his *Histories of the Florentine People*.[14] And into what category should we place those writers, like Gregorio Dati and Matteo Palmieri, who were never chancellors and were never paid to write on behalf of the republic, but who nonetheless display many of the ideas and attitudes that one finds in Bruni? What about a much later figure like Alamanno Rinuccini, who was not only never chancellor but indeed recapitulated much of the civic humanist ethos in an angry denunciation of the Medici regime? Writers like Dati, Palmieri, and Rinuccini alert us to the fact that the civic and republican ideas that emerged from the rhetoric of the chancery were not limited to that context. One should not for a moment dismiss the importance of rhetoric in the formation and sense of intellectual vocation of the humanists, whether professional or citizen, civic or classical. But Renaissance rhetoric, with its commitment to education and moral philosophy, should itself not be reduced to the figure of the "professional rhetorician" who simply did the bidding of his employer. "Professional rhetoricians" certainly existed, but they do not account for the full range and popularity of civic humanist ideas.

It might also be possible to agree that "Florentine republicanism as presented by Salutati and Bruni was a rhetorical artifact not necessarily in keeping with either their private beliefs or the political realities of the time." But to argue that, if we "admit" this, "we can at least save them from some of the more serious charges against their moral character" implies that Bruni and Salutati ought otherwise to fall under some suspicion of moral failure because of the gap between the "rhetorical artifact" and the "private beliefs" and/or "political realities" to which their utterances should have been anchored, and that the "charges" against them can be reduced once we realize that the poor devils were beholden to "political masters" and merely trying to keep their jobs. The clear inference here is that we have morally acceptable thinkers when we can certify the authenticity or integrity of their utterances as faithful reflections of either consistent "private beliefs" or objectively verifiable "political realities." The problem with the first of these tests is that "private belief" is often mutable and almost never of a piece; and the problem with the second is that no political thinker of any conceivable interest could pass it.

But there is at least a third possibility: namely, that political thinkers and writers move within, and help both to constitute and to modify, social, historical, and political traditions of discourse whose "authenticity" is reducible neither to private belief nor to objectively verifiable truth. Such traditions might usefully be called myths, which for these purposes I define not as lies or pure inventions, but as powerful stories that organize experiences, aspirations, fears, and memories into more or less coherent accounts of how the world is perceived to be and how it ought to be—but usually *not* how it actually is. In fact, one of the most important things that myths of this kind do is to help people *not* to see aspects of their world that are incompatible with prized beliefs or ideals. Such myths can also be called ideologies—not in the sense of consistently held private convictions (which I would prefer to call philosophies), but in the sense of collective belief systems that are often inconsistent with the "facts," but no less powerful or historically significant for those inconsistencies. When the founders of the American republic, in justifying their rebellion against the authority they had previously recognized, appealed to the "self-evident" and thus common belief that "all men are created equal," and proceeded to create a polity in which only propertied white men enjoyed political rights, they were reasoning from within the parameters of such a myth or ideology: a body of beliefs that helped them not to see how the facts on the ground flagrantly violated the principles at the core of those same beliefs.

I argue that civic humanism was such an ideology, and that in this sense the civic humanists can be considered ideologues—self-conscious promoters of a particular vision of Florentine politics and society that they did not invent (but to which they contributed significantly), and which had the political and intellectual support of powerful elements in that society. This vision of things could never be a matter of merely private conviction; its expression was a social and even ritual process, a way of belonging to the consensus that, as we shall see, was the core of the ideology. And it was not, even in the intention of its promoters, a dispassionate analysis of political realities; it was a normative discourse that couched itself in hortatory and educational rhetoric, even when it "described" the institutions of the republic. One of the most important senses in which civic humanism deserves to be called an ideology is precisely its role in persuading people of truths that would not easily have withstood being tested against the political realities on the ground.

Florentine civic humanism may sometimes appear on the surface to be a straightforward defense of republicanism against monarchy, and from this impression has flowed much of the attention to the foreign-policy dimension of its origins and polemical aims. But the Florentines did not need civic humanism in order to defend the autonomy of their republican state against threats from differently constituted polities. They had been doing that for a long time. It was rather the transformation of domestic politics from the 1380s into the opening decades of the fifteenth century—the half-century from the collapse of the last guild-based popular government in 1382 through the decades that preceded the victory of the Medici faction in 1434—that generated the ideology of civic humanism. Two very different kinds of republicanism confronted each other in this period of transformation, and civic humanism was the intellectual expression and ideological product of the ascendancy and triumph of the newer form of Florentine republicanism. I contend that civic humanism's real antagonist— the enemy it sought to defeat—was less the duke of Milan than the popular, guild republicanism that had periodically surfaced to challenge the hegemony of the elite in the thirteenth and fourteenth centuries.

The confrontation of rival republicanisms in Florence developed from longstanding class antagonisms. From the early thirteenth century down to the 1370s and 1380s, the Florentine guild community regularly presented itself as an alternative to the oligarchical governments favored by the great families. The guild community's brand of republicanism made of the guilds the constituent parts of the republic and authorized their systematic representation in the offices and councils of the commune. The republicanism of the guilds envisioned a society of separate and not always compatible interests, in which difference and division were acknowledged as legitimate, and in which government emerged from the constitutionally ordained representation and confrontation of these differences. The guild republic was thus a federation of autonomously constituted parts, each with a voice of its own. The institution of the guild itself, as a legal corporation or *universitas*, served as the model for this popular republicanism. The members of a guild voluntarily constituted the authority to which they subjected themselves, and each guild developed structures of representation (often of its own internal subdivisions) and systems of delegation and accountability of power. With their regular emphasis on the participation of the members in various assemblies and councils, the guilds were in effect miniature republics from whose experience and example the communal popular governments of 1292–5, 1343–8, and 1378–82 drew direct inspiration.[15]

Guild republicanism was the creation of the broad middle ranks of communal society, the class that the Florentines called the *popolo*: the regional merchants, notaries, moneychangers, manufacturers of cloth for the local market, retail clothdealers, and other professional groups of the major guilds who did not belong to lineages of great wealth or social prestige; and the shopkeepers, providers of services, builders, and artisans of various sorts in the minor guilds. Popular governments were made possible by coalitions between these two groups—the nonelite major guildsmen and the minor guildsmen—against the elite families, who constituted a minority, albeit a politically and economically potent one, within the major guilds. Until the end of the fourteenth century, the nonelite members of the major guilds were the fulcrum of Florentine politics. When they allied themselves with their fellow major guildsmen from the elite families, they helped forge oligarchic governments that reduced the influence of the guilds in general and thereby diminished the role of the minor guildsmen in government. But when the nonelite major guildsmen became dissatisfied with the leadership of the great families (which could happen because of fiscal mismanagement, economic crisis, or foreign-policy disasters), they sometimes turned to the rest of the guild community and supported constitutional reforms according to which all the guilds shared, more or less equally, in the offices and committees of communal government. These regimes regularly insisted on the frequent consultation of the full guild community. As an advisory committee to the Signoria recommended during the popular movement of 1378, legislation can only be said to enjoy "the consent [or pleasure: *contentamento*] of the whole city" if and when all the guilds have been consulted and have had the chance to voice their opinions.[16]

Each popular government in Florence was more radical than its predecessor, bringing larger numbers of "new men" from further down the social hierarchy to some voice in government, either directly through election to communal offices or indirectly through systems that allowed for the representation of a greater number of guilds. This progressive radicalization of popular politics culminated in the explosive summer of 1378 when thousands of workers in the textile industries, previously denied any right of corporate association, organized themselves into three new guilds, which collectively claimed no less than a third of the posts in the governing committee of the Signoria (with another third going to the minor guilds). Although the largest of these new guilds was disbanded within a matter of weeks, the other two continued to exist as members of an expanded community of minor guilds for three and a half more years within a regime that gave the minor guilds exactly one-half of the seats in the Signoria. And the vast majority of the major guildsmen who held the other half of the seats during these years came from the ranks of the nonelite members of their guilds. The popular government of 1378–82, more than its predecessors of 1343–8 and 1292–5, nearly completely excluded the elite families of Florence from the political offices that these families considered their birthright. But it was not only the elite families that were fearful of the policies of this most radical of Florentine popular regimes. The nonelite major guildsmen could now see that the constitutional reforms they had supported at the beginning of the popular challenge to the elite had gone far beyond their intentions. Perhaps more than anything else, it was the spectacle of workers and artisans in the textile industries enjoying an autonomous corporate existence, and thus the right to bargain collectively with the cloth manufacturers of the wool guild, that made even the nonelite members of the major guilds realize the profound threat to their own interests of popular regimes that were willing to open the doors to new members of the guild federation from the working classes.

The fear and loathing that the popular regime of 1378–82 engendered in the Florentine upper classes became the stuff of legend. Such sentiments are alluded to in the famous dictum of Gino Capponi, who, by way of saying how unthinkable submission to foreign lords (in this case Ladislaus of Naples) would be for the Florentines, claimed that it would be "better to live under the government of the Ciompi than under the tyranny of that king."[17] Only the popular movement of 1378, in other words, could rival the loss of liberty to foreign tyrants as a source of terror for the Florentine upper classes. And about the entire regime of 1378–82, there is the testimony (reported by the historian Giovanni Cavalcanti) of Rinaldo degli Albizzi's emotional diatribe in 1426—nearly fifty years after the target of his denunciation—against "those forty damned months" when the guilds and their consuls "held this people in servitude....."[18] Patrician contempt for the working classes was of course nothing new, but one has only to go to the chronicle of Marchionne di Coppo Stefani to see the angry reactions against the regime of 1378–82 from the very nonelite elements of the major guilds that had once strongly promoted guild republicanism. Stefani, who in other moments was capable of being sternly critical of the arrogance of the Parte Guelfa and the elite families, denounced the unskilled wool-workers as the latter-day equivalent of Christ-killers, incapable of any rational political action, and easily seduced by demagogues.[19] But his anger was not limited to the Ciompi alone. Commenting on the economic policies of the guild regime of 1378–82, he wrote: "So great was the power of the [nonelite] guildsmen that in every matter under deliberation they achieved their aims in the legislative councils ... Thus whoever has more power gets what he wants, with little concern however for whether it is good or useful for the city; everyone seeks his own advantage as best he thinks he can: neither law nor statute counts for much in such matters."[20] Stefani's reaction to the independent guild of the dyers negotiating terms of labor and piece-rates with their former masters in the wool guild was an especially irate one. He again denounced the "soperchio homore che soprabbondava negli artefici" and the "insolence" and "arrogance" of the dyers who "had no concern for who they were" or for the fact that they "used to be governed by and subject to the cloth manufacturers from whom they had their laws and to whose statutes they were [previously] subject." Their requests were "so alien to the cloth manufacturers and so abominable to the citizens that it was beyond all measure."[21] It is worth underscoring that these denunciations of the guild regime came not from some reactionary *arciguelfo* in the elite of great families, but from a man of modest family whose father, Coppo di Stefano, had been a rank-and-file member and occasional office-holder in the not very elite major guild of Por Santa Maria.

A half-century later, Leonardo Bruni's *Histories of the Florentine People* would make clear how crucial the memory of the Ciompi and fear of social revolution were to civic humanism's view of the Florentine past. His account of the events of 1378 contains a memorable passage that simultaneously evokes the still vivid fears of the workers in the minds of the Florentine upper classes and denies any legitimacy to their political aims: "Every day new movements were born, because some people were eager to plunder the possessions of the rich, others to gain revenge against their enemies, and still others to make themselves powerful. This may stand as a lesson for all time [*perpetuum documentum*] to the distinguished men of the city: never to let political initiative or arms into the hands of the multitude, for once they have had a bite, they cannot be restrained and they think they can do as they please because there are so many of them." Well-meaning but misguided attempts at reform had resulted in "making poor guildsmen and men of base condition the rulers of the city" and in putting noble and distinguished families at the mercy of the "stupidity of the aroused multitude. For there was no end or order to the unleashed appetites of the poor and the criminals, who, once armed, lusted after the possessions of rich and honorable men, and who thought of nothing except robbing, killing, and exiling citizens."[22] A similar attitude toward the poor is evident in Giovanni Morelli's advice about hiding grain harvested from one's farm: "If a poor man sees that you have grain to sell and that you are holding on to it to increase its price, he will damn and curse and rob you and burn your house, if he has the power to do so, and he will make you hated by the entire lower class, which is a most dangerous thing. May God preserve our city from their rule [*Idio ne guardi la rostra città dalla loro signoria*]."[23]

As I have argued elsewhere,[24] Bruni's condemnation of the Ciompi revolution as an eruption of irrational and even criminal impulses latent in "poor guildsmen and men of base condition" heavily conditions his treatment of both the guilds and the social bases of Florentine politics in the *Histories.*[25] In a work that (beginning with book II) surveys the history of Florence from the middle of the thirteenth century to 1402—the century and a half in which the guilds were at the center of Florentine political and constitutional developments—the only context in which Bruni acknowledges their leading role is the revolution of 1378 that he presents as the most dangerous moment of the city's turbulent history. Otherwise he ignores them, even in discussing the events of the 1290s and 1340s in which they had a decisive part. His purpose in this strategy was, clearly, to dissociate the guilds and their propensity to challenge the authority of the elite from what he wished to represent as the mainstream tradition of respectable politics dominated by the upper-class families: a "tradition"—still quite precariously in the process of consolidation around 1400—of civic unity and social consensus, of deference toward the republic's "natural" leaders from those same upper-class families, and of a political morality in which a citizen's worthiness was a function of dutiful acceptance of this leadership, and not of the promotion of the interests or rights of any group. Bruni sought to delegitimate the older guild republican notion that accepted the existence of different and legitimately contrasting social, economic, or political interests. It was because the guilds had sustained such a conception of politics in Florence that they had to be written out of Florentine history.

Bruni's recasting of Florentine history no doubt reflected the attitudes of the elite families that loathed the memory of 1378. But it also served the more complex needs of the class of nonelite major guildsmen that had been frightened away, by the same memory of 1378, from its former attachment to guild republicanism into a posture of awkward submission to the very elite families that they (or their fathers and grandfathers) had tenaciously opposed for over a century. In the generation after the last guild government of 1378–82, these nonelite major guildsmen finally and definitively chose alliance with the elite as preferable to what they now saw as the unacceptable risks of further revivals of the guild republic in coalitions with minor guildsmen and with all those workers who still wanted guilds—and thus a voice—of their own. As the political reforms of the 1380s, 1390s, and beyond eliminated the artisan and working classes from any significant role in communal politics,[26] diminished the political clout of the guilds,[27] and consolidated the leadership of the elite families,[28] the nonelite major guildsmen were offered in effect an unofficial compact according to which they would be included, collectively, in larger numbers than ever before, in the ranks of communal office-holders in return for renouncing, once and for all, any temptation to ally with the rest of the guild community in movements of opposition to the elite. They thus accepted occasional election to prestigious offices as the reward—or consolation prize—for relinquishing any real share of power.[29]

Participation without power was the central feature of the compact that overturned traditional assumptions about the nature of political participation in Florence. It thus needed, and engendered, a justification and rationalization that in due course became the ideology of civic humanism. From this perspective, civic humanism did not originate in this or that text of Coluccio Salutati or Leonardo Bruni. It had its beginnings in the changing attitudes toward political participation in the class of nonelite major guildsmen, the class whose deferential acquiescence in the hegemony of the elite was the foundation of the new configuration of Florentine politics and society in the decades around 1400. The elite of course welcomed and applauded these attitudes, but the true believers in the civic humanist ethic of citizenship carne not so much from the ruling class as from the nonelite members of the office-holding class over several generations from the late fourteenth to the mid-fifteenth century: from men like Marchionne di Coppo Stefani (1336–85?), Gregorio Dati (1362–1435), and Giovanni di Pagolo Morelli (1371–1444), and later figures like Matteo Palmieri (1406–75) and Marco Parenti (1422–97). Although some (like Dati) were merchants who achieved an imposing level of wealth, these were *not* men from the elite of great families. But they did rub elbows with the elite in the same guilds, and occasionally in the same offices of the republic, and even now and then married into the elite (although it is worth noting that in two cases—Giovanni Morelli's marriage to Caterina Alberti and Marco Parenti's marriage to Caterina degli Strozzi—the alliances were with exiled families of the elite). The ethic of civic duty and republican liberty to which these men subscribed functioned as a consolation for what they and their class had lost, as a rationalization for their submission to the elite, and thus as a legitimation of the elite's hegemony.

It has not been sufficiently recognized that the ideal of the *vita activa civilis* that we find both in these writers and in Leonardo Bruni was at its core an ethic of dutiful passivity. Far from encouraging the active pursuit of glory or political ambition, the image of the good citizen that they created was of one who suppresses his own ambition, who steadfastly exhibits deference toward the *reggimento* (or, simply, those who govern), whose willingness to cooperate borders on unquestioning obedience, and who has no ideas or policies or interests to promote or defend in the civic arena. On the occasion of his selection for one of the executive committees of government in 1412, Gregorio Dati commented as follows in his diary: "I feel I have received a very great favor, and I would have been satisfied if by some arrangement I could have been certain of being elected just once to one of the executive committees. If I had been able to know this for certain, I would not have wished for anything more. Therefore, in order not to appear ungrateful, and not wishing to stimulate an insatiable ambition [*appetito*] which, the more it gets, only wants still more, I have decided and resolved that from now on I must never implore the favors of anyone to secure [any office] ... I will instead leave such matters to those who oversee them [*lasciare fare a chi fia sopracciò*], and let happen to me whatever may please God. Henceforth, whenever my name is drawn for any communal or guild office, I promise to obey and not to refuse the burden, and to do as well as I can and know how. In this way I will ward off the vice of ambition and presumption [*il vizio della ambizione e del presumere di me*], and I will live as a free man not bound by the necessity of seeking favors [*viverò libero e non servo per prieghi*]."³⁰

As Dati saw himself, it was the stifling of his own ambition that made him a worthy citizen and free man and legitimated his selection for high office. All that he could offer in politics was his personal worth and virtue—his gratitude, lack of presumption, willingness to serve—and, of course, his submission to the will of "those who oversee" matters like scrutinies and elections. He had no point of view on political issues or policies; he represented no constituency or group; he did not come to office to shape or change things. He knew that he could advance in political life only by securing the favors of powerful patrons of the sort that he could never be, and he even admitted that to do so would make him a slave of ambition, a "servo per prieghi." So he resolved to steer clear of the hunt for patrons and to remain "free"—by his own definition, on the margins of the only kind of politics available to men of his class. But when Dati added that "should it happen that I do otherwise, I must penalize myself each time in the amount of two gold florins to be given to the poor," he must have been anticipating the impossibility of observing his own resolution and of not being a "servo" to the upper-class political bosses who are never directly mentioned, but are nonetheless very prominent, in this revealing passage.

Giovanni Morelli's advice about politics turns entirely on the necessity of playing the game that Dati wished he could avoid. Whether through marriage alliances or friendship, he thought it essential to "lean on someone in the ruling group [*fa ... che tu t'appoggi a chi è nel reggimento*], some powerful Guelf who is well thought of and free of suspicion ... Make him your friend by speaking well of him, helping him wherever you can, by going up to meet him and offering your services." One should cultivate such powerful men by asking their advice and inviting them to one's home. "Beyond this, always stand by those who hold and possess the palace and the rule of our city [*tient sempre con chi tiene e possiede il palagio e la signoria*], and obey and follow their wishes and commands. Keep yourself from denouncing or speaking evil of their undertakings and actions, even if they are harmful. Stay silent, and depart from your silence only to praise them." Morelli thinks it advisable even to refuse to listen to anything spoken "contro a chi regge," and to avoid the company of anyone who is "male contento." One should immediately and without second thoughts report to the government authorities any words that one hears spoken against them.[31] His loyal support for the leadership of the "buoni uomini antichi di Firenze" was accompanied by an expression of frank dislike of "parvenus, guildsmen, and people of modest stature [*gente veniticcia, artefici e di piccolo affare*]," for whom he wished "wealth, peace, and happy concord," but whose "reggimento" he did not like—an allusion to the regime of 1378–82—"although having them to a certain degree mixed in is good for restraining excessively ambitious spirits."[32] After recounting the suppression of the anti-government conspiracy of 1400, Morelli adds: "I have recalled these events ... so that every descendant of ours may take this as an example and never do anything against any *istato o reggimento*, being happy instead to support the wishes of our rulers, and especially to place himself in the hands of men of worth from old Guelf families [*sendo nelle mani degli uomini da bene, antichi e guelfi*], for you see the harm and the shame that follow one who seeks to do otherwise."[33]

These are the very qualities that Bruni will associate with the ideal of virtuous citizenship in the *Life of Dante*—an ideal that even Bruni's Dante falls short of. According to Bruni, Dante "left aside nothing of cultural and civic affairs" and "was frequently employed in affairs of the Republic." He emphasizes in particular that Dante "fought valorously for his native land" at the battle of Campaldino, which Bruni initially presents as a struggle between Florentines and Aretines (until he has to admit that Ghibellines from both cities were fighting Guelfs from both cities). The effect is to make Dante a man of no faction or party. The only policy or opinion that Bruni attributes to him in the factional wars of 1300–1302 that led to Dante's exile is that the priors sought to defend themselves against the armed bands of both factions. Bruni suggests that Dante was trying to remain neutral between the parties, even as circumstances began to identify him more closely with the faction of the White Guelfs.

The account that Bruni gives of Dante's exile is especially telling. At first, here too he gives us Dante the model citizen, who was in Rome as an envoy to the pope "in order to offer the agreement and peace of his citizens," while back in Florence Black Guelf partisans were destroying his house and property. Then came the order of banishment, promulgated under "a perverse and iniquitous law." But in exile Dante began to engage in riskier kinds of conduct. Although "he tried with good works and good behavior to win the favor that would allow him to return to Florence [*cercando con buone opere e con buoni portamenti racquistar la grazia di poter tornare in Firenze*]," when the new emperor Henry VII came to Italy to restore imperial power, "Dante could not maintain his resolve to wait for favor, but rose up in his proud spirit and began to speak ill of those who were ruling the land [*cominciò a dir male di quei che reggevano la terra*], calling them villainous and evil and menacing them with their due punishment through the power of the emperor ... Then Henry died ... and Dante entirely lost all hope, since he himself had closed the way of a change of favor by having spoken and written against the citizens who were governing the Republic [perocchè di grazia lui medesimo s'aveva tolta la via per to sparlare e scrivere contro i cittadini, che governavano la repubblica], and there remained no force to support his desires."[34]

In this way Bruni makes Dante himself responsible, despite the injustice of the original decree of banishment, for the fact that the exile became permanent. The implicit assumption behind the judgment that his error consisted in having "spoken ill of those who were ruling the city" is that even in exile, even in an unjust exile, the citizen owed respect, deference, and obedience not only to his republic, but also to those who ruled it.[35] Here again the good citizen is passive, loyal even to the point of turning a blind eye to the injustices perpetrated against himself by those in power. Bruni's Dante failed to follow the advice of Giovanni Morelli and thus brought on himself the indefinite extension of his exile. Bruni seems to imply that the Florentine ruling class need not have felt any guilt over the fact that the city's greatest poet died in exile. The *Vita di Dante* dates from 1436, and the passage on Dante's exile may have been intended as a cautionary tale for the new generation of exiles created by the victory of the Medici faction in 1434. Palla Strozzi, one of the most notable of these exiles, became legendary for his absolute loyalty to the rulers of Florence and for his refusal to utter a harsh word against the government or the Medici in thirty years of patiently suffered injustice.[36]

The characteristic posture of civic humanism's dutiful and subservient citizen is one of respectful distance from those who exercise power—the factions, patrician families, and patrons—and of isolation from all the many others like himself who must try to win the favor of the powerful or at least minimize the capacity of the latter to inflict harm on him. The good citizen never belongs to, or represents, a group. He is sometimes figured as representing the entire community—as in the case of Dante in war or diplomacy—but never as a spokesman for others like himself. His claim to a role in politics comes therefore to rest entirely and exclusively on his personal worth—on his virtue—and not on the extent to which he represents the voices or interests of some constituency. The growing emphasis on the link between virtue and political participation—one of the central ideas of civic humanism and a crucial point of intersection between the civic traditions of the medieval communes and the *studia humanitatis* grounded in Roman moral philosophy—needs to be understood as a crucial substitution of the operative criteria for the distribution of honors and offices. In place of the older guild republican idea that citizens merited their offices because they were elected by their constituencies and because they represented the collective interests of the latter, civic humanism embraced the idea that citizens became worthy of election when they demonstrated a sufficient level of personal virtue. The importance of this for the class relations underlying the configuration of political power in Florence is clear: the ruling elite had recognized the necessity of expanding the ranks of the office-holders in order to broaden the consensus around their hegemony, but they were willing to do so only if the hundreds and eventually thousands of nonelite office-holders accepted their posts as a recognition of, and reward for, personal merit and thus loyalty to their patrons, and not as an opportunity to represent the interests of their class. The politics of virtue delegitimated and supplanted the politics of class and collective interests.

The connection between virtue and the taming of class antagonisms can be seen in a revealing passage in book 3 of Matteo Palmieri's *Vita civile*.[37] Palmieri defines his overall purpose as that of "showing the approved way of life of virtuous citizens [*monstrare l'approvata vita de' civili virtuosi*]."[38] In book 3, following several pages on the importance of civic unity and the evils of factional divisions, Palmieri's spokesman Agnolo Pandolfini begins a discussion of distributive justice. Among the tasks of this kind of justice, he says, the first is that of "equitably conferring offices in the public sphere [*Questa in publico prima gl'honori egualmente conferisce*] ... It is according to the dignity of each man that public honors should be distributed." Realizing perhaps that this needed more definition, Palmieri acknowledges that contrasting concepts of dignity have been held by different social groups. In language that evokes Florence's tumultuous political past, he writes that "It is a difficult thing in a republic to prove who has more dignity, since among the people there has been much disagreement on the matter. The nobles and the powerful say that dignity resides in great wealth and in ancient and magnanimous families. The *popolari* [say that it consists] in the civility and friendly sociability of free and peaceful life [in a community]. Wise men say it consists in active virtue. Let those whose responsibility it will be to distribute offices in the city follow the most approved advice and give these offices to the most virtuous persons. For ... nothing is more worthy among men than the virtue of those who work for the public good."[39] Palmieri is here clearly alluding to the long struggle between the elite families and the *popolo*. He quickly summarizes their contrasting views of the "dignity" that renders citizens worthy of high office: the patrician emphasis on wealth and ancient lineage, and the popular preference for the collective values of broadly shared sociability. But Palmieri decides for neither of these opinions; to do so would be to take sides in the greatest of the "civil discords" that had, as he believes, plagued Florence. Instead he opts for the third opinion represented by those "wise men" who claim that "virtue" ought to be the decisive criterion for identifying the sort of dignity that merits elevation to high office.

Palmieri's approach implies that a proper appreciation of virtue, and of the way it qualifies citizens for political office, can make the social conflicts of the past irrelevant. He takes a dim view of citizens from aristocratic families who claim a right to public honors on the basis of their ancestors' accomplishments. Although he allows that where "the claims of virtue are equal, the man from a distinguished family is to be preferred [*preponendo sempre la nobiltà, quando sono pari virtù*]," Palmieri insists that "the man who seeks glory through the virtues of his forebears denudes himself of any claim to honor, and the man who uses up the fame of his ancestors is certainly wretched. Let him who merits honor give proof of himself, not of his family members." But he devotes the next two pages to examples from Roman history of men, not from the nobility but from the lower ranks of society, who rose to positions of great power and won the respect and admiration of their social betters: "The very wise ancients, who extended their empires so greatly, raised foreigners, workers, and men of the lowest condition to the highest positions of rulership when they recognized in them noteworthy excellence in virtue ... Let no one disdain being governed by virtuous men from humble beginnings and unknown family origins ... It would take a long time to recount those in Rome who, although humbly born, through their virtue alone gained the most honored ranks and splendidly adorned the republic."[40] The special pleading offered on behalf of the lowborn who attained great heights makes it clear that, in the moral economy of political virtue, those who rose from humble origins to achieve political power and glory, even if there were many of them, were and always would be the noteworthy exceptions. Given the context of class antagonism with which

Palmieri introduces this subject, the force of the claim that virtue ought to be the defining element of eligibility to office, and that many lowborn men achieved prominence in Rome in this way, is that virtue is the only legitimate avenue to political participation for citizens of the popular classes. The lowborn gain office and honors exclusively through the recognition, by their "natural" superiors, of their exceptional personal qualities. Such a definition of the relationship of virtue to political participation fits the purposes of the Florentine ruling elite quite nicely, even as it was a consoling fiction that helped the nonelite office-holders *not* to see their own political emasculation. Bruni had written something very similar just a few years before in the *1428 Oration for the Funeral of Nanni Strozzi*: "The hope of attaining office and of raising oneself up is the same for all, provided only one put in effort and have talent and a sound and serious way of life. Virtue and probity are required of the citizens by our city [*Virtutem enim probitatemque in cive suo civitas nostra requirit*]. Anyone who has these two qualities is thought to be sufficiently well born to govern the republic."[41]

By the early fifteenth century both the elite and the *popolo* felt the need to deny the old history of their conflict: the elite, because they were winning the long struggle and needed the passive support—the consensus—of the nonelite to make their victory more secure; and the *popolo* because they had lost an old war and needed the favor of their new patrons in order to hold on to the consolation prize; and both, because they feared and loathed the working classes. The discourse of political virtue was a crucial element of this denial. Its purpose was to buttress the myth of civic unity, to promote the notion of the republic as a single harmonious entity, and thus to suppress the legitimacy of claims of separate collective interests—of class, difference, dissent, and political conflict. Everywhere in the civic humanist texts we find the insistence on the fundamental homogeneity and unity of the republic. Here too the roots are in the characteristic assumptions of the politics of the 1380s and 1390s: for example, in the declaration by the *balìa* of 1382—the plenipotentiary body that dismantled the popular regime of 1378–82—that "the things that need to be done can in no way be carried out without the full, total, and absolute power and authority of the whole Florentine people ... and that this authority cannot legally be obtained, nor the will of the people requested, especially given the custom observed by the Florentine people in the past, except by a *parlamento* and convocation to the same of the whole Florentine people and by a general assembly."[42] As I have noted elsewhere,[43] general assemblies of the "whole Florentine people" had not in fact been part of the popular movement's constitutional program, which was grounded instead in the corporate representation of the guilds. The emphasis on the wholeness and oneness of the people, which gained strength toward the end of the fourteenth century, aimed at undermining the popular vision of the republic as a federation of independent parts and separate collective voices.

The assumption of a fundamental unity among all Florentines was of course wishful thinking, but the kind of wishful thinking that powerfully affects political behavior. Commenting on the electoral scrutiny of 1404, Giovanni Morelli noted that the results of the balloting displeased some members of the ruling group, "because of the suspicions they had of many *popolani* whom they did not consider their friends." The suspect *popolani* to whom he refers may have included Morelli himself, who, after many years of being passed over in the scrutinies, was at long last approved for high office in the 1404 scrutiny, and subsequently drawn for the executive college of the Sixteen Gonfalonieri in 1409.[44] They "need not have such suspicions," Morelli continues, "because the only reason one becomes an enemy of, or dislikes, the ruling group is if one does not belong to that good that is [held in] common [or, that good that is the commune: *se non perché e' non fa parte di quello bene che è comune*]. I do not mean one who takes it [the office] for his own evil purposes, but one who has conducted and continues to conduct himself well [*chi ha fatto e fa buoni portamenti*]. Such a person should not be held in contempt nor deprived of his honor. If you do these things to him; he will have every reason to hate you."[45] Morelli refused to see his exclusion from office before 1409 as the result of larger political or social conflicts. He could not imagine himself as representing interests or ideas opposed to those of the oligarchy. He saw his misfortune as personal, as the result of a marriage alliance[46] that deprived him for a time of his part in "quello bene che è comune." In any case, he believed that his "buoni portamenti" had finally proven his worth and rewarded him with his small place in the political sun. The conclusion he drew from this experience was not about the abyss that separated him from the powerbrokers in the *reggimento*. It was rather about the importance of being a team player and the victories that the acceptance of such a role makes possible: "I have recalled this in order to inform you of the methods one should employ to acquire the honor that the commune accords its citizens: doing good, obeying the laws, paying honor to the officials of the commune, to particularly respected citizens, to men of ancient families, and to persons of worth. The good deeds of your ancestors will make you known to such persons, will recommend you to them, and will keep you in their memory."[47] This is the very stuff of the consensus politics at the center of civic humanism. Morelli wants to see only the harmonious whole, and his "good conduct"—his political quiescence, his willingness to pay honor to the very oligarchs who had kept him on the sidelines—proved to him that virtue would in the end merit honor.[48]

Such attitudes underlie civic humanism's horror of political conflict. The texts abound with denunciations of factionalism and praise of civil concord. In the *Vita civile* Palmieri says that a citizen elected to any office must know that he is no longer a "privata persona": he now "represents the universal person of the whole city and has become a living republic [*rapresentare l'universale persona di tutta la città, et essere facta animata republica*]." He must know that the "public dignity has been entrusted to him and the common good left to his good faith." He must imprint in his mind Plato's admonition, as reported by Cicero in the *De officiis*, to preserve the "whole body of the republic in such a way that, as he defends one part, he does not abandon the others ... The condition and stability of every republic rest in civic unity [*Lo stato e fermamento d'ogni republics è posto nella unione civile*]." And "anyone who departs from this [precept] and attends to the well-being of individual citizens, and abandons the rest, sows scandal and grievous conflicts in the city, from which, with the citizens often divided amongst themselves, strife and civil wars result ... The end brings exiles, insurrections, slavery, and final destruction." Palmieri cites examples of ancient states that came to ruin because of civil conflicts, and about Florence he says that, although "it would perhaps be better to pass over in silence rather than recount the afflictions and miseries that have accompanied our city because of civil conflicts and quarrels," it is in fact useful to recall such things in order to ward off similar evils in the future. The brief history he provides of Florentine partisan conflicts, from the Guelfs and Ghibellines in the thirteenth century to the Black and White Guelfs in the early fourteenth century, proves, he says, that internal conflict has too often led to appeals by one or the other party to foreign princes for protection and to the loss of "la libertà, lo stato, et publica maiestà." Thus, those who possess "la dolce libertà"—the independence of Florence from foreign control—should learn from the examples of states that have been ruined by internal conflicts to resist and repair their own.[49] Liberty, understood as independence from foreigners, is here invoked to strengthen the frequent warnings against class conflict and to make even more urgent the exhortations to social harmony and civic unity. The argument that class and factional conflicts at home made the republic more vulnerable to foreign tyrants underscored the virtues of civic unity and social consensus as the standards by which good citizens were identified and measured. Here indeed was one of the links between foreign policy and civic humanism.

Bruni similarly emphasized unity and consensus. We have already seen his ferocious denunciation in the *Histories* of the conflicts of 1378. Many years earlier in the *Laudatio*, he had acknowledged that even the best governed cities have some "evil men." But "the perversity and evil of a few ought not to deprive an entire nation of being praised for its virtuous deeds." He distinguishes between "public and private crimes": the latter result from the "intentions of the individual wrong-doer," the former from the "will of the entire city [*universe civitatis voluntas*]." Here again is the assumption that an entire city has a single will, which is found by "following what has been hallowed by law and tradition [*legibus ac moribus sancitum sit*]," and "usually the entire city follows what the majority of the citizen-body would like. While in other cities the majority often overturns the better part, in Florence it has always happened that the majority view has been identical with the best citizens [*Sed in aliis guidem populis maior pars sepe meliorem vincit, in hac autem civitate eadem semper videtur fuisse melior que maioe*]."[50] The force of Bruni's assertion that "the majority view" is "identical with [that of] the best citizens" is that the "best citizens," which he of course identifies with the ruling elite, are the ones responsible for shaping that view. Bruni merges the "single will" of the city with "what has been hallowed by law and tradition," and both of these with the views of the "melior pars" of leading citizens. His mistrust of the lower orders ("the good qualities of a few men cannot really free the foolish and perverse mob from its infamy"[51]) leads him to privilege the authority of the republic's "natural" leaders from good patrician families.

A similar fear of the lower classes had earlier led Stefani to idealize the order and rationality, and thus the inevitable leadership, of the elite families. His reaction against the unwelcome sight of organized workers led him, not only to deny that artisans and laborers were capable of any political order or rational decision-making, but also to praise the "wisdom, gentility, and order" of those he called the *grandi*. He particularly admired the way (he thought) they arrived at decisions among themselves: "it is easy to bring about agreement among the great families of wisdom, gentility, and order, who revere the wisest person of their line or, at the most, the wisest few [*li Grandi di senno, di gentilezza, d'ordine e le famiglie, che hanno sempre reverenza a uno il più savio del loro legnaggio, o a pochi, è poco accordare*]." Precisely because there were "fewer of them to be convened and consulted," they were able to discuss their affairs and bring into harmony "la volontà degli appetiti."[52] Upper-class lineages may not in reality have made their common decisions in quite so orderly and hierarchical a fashion,[53] but the importance of Stefani's opinion is that in it we see the beginnings of a tendency to idealize the patrician families of Florence as models on which citizens could construct an ideological image of the communal constitution. In the minds of nonelite members of the political class, like Stefani, the elite families began to represent even in their private behavior an alternative vision of the political community based on the assumption that power should be held by the experienced few and confirmed by the passive but willing consensus of those who recognize those few as benevolent fathers to the whole civic family. In civic humanist thought, the family replaces the guild, or corporation, as the conceptual model for the republic. The republic is no longer a fraternity of equals, whose task is to create authority out of equality. Increasingly the republic is now seen as a kind of family, even a lineage, in which authority naturally belongs to experienced elders, which is to say, to the fathers of the best families.

Again, Bruni appropriates these themes and transforms them from a set of political attitudes into a moral and educational program. In the *Laudatio* he writes of the Florentine constitution that "under these magistracies this city has been governed with such diligence and competence that one could not find better discipline even in a household ruled by a solicitous father [*Sub his igitur magistratibus ita diligens et preclara est huius urbis gubernatio ut nulla unquam domus sub frugi patre familias maiori disciplina fuerit instituta*]."[54] This family-like republic is to be judged by the standards of the kind of paternal discipline that one expects to find in the household of a "solicitous father." Bruni's republic is a family writ large, in which "discipline"—culture, learning, and education—serves the program of virtue by preparing the individual to assume his place as a citizen. But it also serves the needs of power by reinforcing the authority of fathers and patricians. As the son is formed in the image of the father, so the citizen is to be shaped in the mold of "what has been hallowed by law and tradition." Education, and thus citizenship, have become theaters of socialization in the consensus that sustains the hegemony of the ruling elite. In the *Life of Dante* Bruni underscores the social dimension of education. When Dante devoted himself to studies, he "left aside nothing of cultural and civil affairs. It is a marvelous thing that although he was studying continuously, yet it would never have seemed to anyone that he studied, because of his pleasant habits and youthful conversation." Bruni further insists that the "studious life" is also fully compatible with marriage and family, as are both with the responsibilities of citizenship. What particularly irritates Bruni is the suggestion that the life of study ought to be conducted in "solitude and leisure ... hidden away and removed from conversation with men."[55] It is not difficult to surmise that, for Bruni, the danger posed by such isolated intellects is that they will not be properly socialized into the cultural and political consensus that sustains the structures of power. There is a sense in which Bruni's main point in the *Life* is that exile eroded Dante's participation in the "discipline" and thus the consensus that his studies, his family life, and his political role had earlier inculcated into him. He then became a critic, a dissenter from the very traditions of both culture and power that had created him, and, as such, a threat to the polity.

The family was the obvious and ideal metaphor for a republic that assumed the natural and benevolent leadership of experienced fathers, tolerated no opposition from its citizen/ children, and conceived of citizenship in terms of training, education, and socialization into the virtues of the whole community as represented by its revered elders. Not for nothing, therefore, did Palmieri introduce his main speaker in the *Vita civile*, Agnolo Pandolfini, as an "older and well-educated citizen [*antico et bene admaestrato cittadino*]" who will hold forth on virtue and the civic life "quasi con dimestico ragionamento"[56]—which is to say, with an almost domestic, or family-like, kind of discourse or conversation. The elder Pandolfini answers the questions of two younger men. Seeking to inquire into the "arti" (skills) and "discipline" with which it is possible to secure the good life of "some fine republic," Palmieri proposes to collect from the literature of antiquity the "precepts appropriate for teaching [*precepti accommodati a admaestrare*] the best life of citizens."[57] The *Vita civile* is dedicated to Alessandro degli Alessandri, and at the end of the preface Palmieri explicitly weaves together citizenship, education, the moral authority of the paternal example, and the nobility and power of great families: "You [Alessandro] are born of noble stock, offspring of an excellent father, trained in the study of the good arts, adorned with good manners ... your good habits clearly show in you the firm intention to strive with merited praise to become an honored and excellent citizen."[58] Good son; good student; good citizen—the terms are almost interchangeable.

Bruni had already suggested in the *Laudatio* that the Florentines were both the sons of their city and of their Roman founders. The terms in which he does so point to certain anxieties embedded in the family romances (or dramas) into which the civic humanists were fond of inscribing their vision of Florence. "As we may see several sons with so great a resemblance to their parents [*lantani habere cum parentibus similitudinem*] that they show it obviously in their faces, so the Florentines are in such harmony with this very noble and outstanding city that it seems they could never have lived anywhere else. Nor could the city, so skillfully created, have had any other kind of inhabitants."[59] Cities do indeed shape their inhabitants, but this passage makes the Florentines sound like so many identical cookie-cutter citizen/children who could in no way have been different from one another or have been other than they were. Other anxieties emerge in passages that make the Florentines the sons of the Romans: "The fact that the Florentine race [*genus*] arose from the Roman people is of the utmost importance. What nation in the entire world was ever more distinguished, more powerful, more outstanding in every sort of excellence than the Roman people?" Such thoughts may indeed have stimulated a sense of pride, but what reaction could Florentines have had to Bruni's claim in the next sentence that the "deeds [of the Romans] are so illustrious that the greatest feats done by other men seem like child's play [*pueriles ludi*] when compared to the deeds of the Romans"? The civic humanist insistence on the Roman origins of Florentine republicanism (and in general on the Romans as the perfect model in all things for the Florentines) merges with the sense of the republic as a patrilineal family writ large in which the elders (or the elite) shape citizen/sons in their own image: "Now if the glory, nobility, virtue, grandeur, and magnificence of the parents can also make the sons outstanding, no people in the entire world can be as worthy of dignity as are the Florentines, for they are born from such parents who surpass by a long way all mortals in every sort of glory."[60] But how does one ever escape the tutelage of such perfect parents? And what if the sons do not measure up? Later in the text Bruni, perhaps not fully aware of just how much this vision of Roman fathers and Florentine sons exposes the element of oppressive patriarchy in the metaphor that made of the republic a patrilineal family, writes: "The same dignity and grandeur of the parent also illuminate its sons, since the offspring strive for their own virtue. And you may be sure that if the descendants had been cowardly or dissolute or had in any way fallen from virtue, the splendor of the ancestor would not so much have hidden their vices as it would have uncovered them. The light of parental glory leaves nothing unhidden; indeed, the expectation that the virtues of the parent will be reduplicated in the son focuses all eyes on the offspring."[61] Do such ideas unintentionally register the insecurities and anxieties of the politically infantilized nonelite members of the office-holding class who were, as I have suggested, the true believers of civic humanism?

Civic humanism was, I think, deeply conservative in its denial of the legitimacy of class interests and conflict and in its affirmation of a natural leadership of patrician fathers over their citizen/children. It may also have served as the intellectual foundation for a regime of conformity and surveillance[62] in which the individual was allowed the status of citizen only insofar as he suppressed dangerous tendencies toward dissent or critical views of the ideological consensus. My answer to the question about whether the ideas of the civic humanists were rooted in the realities of Florentine politics and society would therefore begin with the observation that civic humanism was *not* a restatement of the central values of the popular republicanism of the thirteenth and fourteenth centuries. It was a new ideology that provided cultural, educational, historical, and moral buttressing for both the newly established hegemony of Florence's elite families and for the subordinate political and social status to which the middle ranks of Florentine society were now relegated. In this vision of things the elite families produced the wise fathers of the republic, devoted guardians of the best interests of all; the irony of their fate is that, in trying to make themselves *patres conscripti*, they made a *pater patriae*, and ultimately a prince. The middle-rank Florentines became their client/children, deprived, as the recent and well-illuminated example of Marco Parenti shows was still the case in the middle of the fifteenth century,[63] of any political voice and able only to go on repeating the platitudes of civic humanism: the fate also illustrated for us by the character Microtoxus in Alamanno Rinuccini's *De libertate*.[64] Civic humanism was not merely professional rhetoric from the chancery. It was a whole complex of attitudes, assumptions, and values that, to be sure, did not simply mirror the "realities" of Florentine life. But it had a huge part in a profound transformation of Florentine politics and social relations from the late fourteenth century through the middle of the next century and beyond.

NOTES

1. Hans Baron, *The Crisis of the Early Italian Renaissance: Civic Humanism and Republican Liberty in an Age of Classicism and Tyranny,,* 2 vols. (Princeton: Princeton University Press, 1955); and the revised one-volume edition with an epilogue (Princeton: Princeton University Press, 1966).

2. Many of them collected in Hans Baron, *In Search of Florentine Civic Humanism: Essays on the Transition from Medieval to Modern Thought,* 2 vols. (Princeton: Princeton University Press, 1988).

3. Some recent essays on Baron and his thesis: Albert Rabil, Jr., "The Significance of 'Civic Humanism' in the Interpretation of the Italian Renaissance," in *Renaissance Humanism: Foundations, Forms, and Legacy,* 3 vols. (Philadelphia: University of Pennsylvania Press, 1988), I: 141–74; Riccardo Fubini, "Renaissance Historian: The Career of Hans Baron," *Journal of Modern History* 64 (1992): 541–74; James Hankins, "The 'Baron Thesis' after Forty Years and some Recent Studies of Leonardo Bruni," *Journal of the History of Ideas* 56 (1995): 309–38; and the papers by Ronald Witt, Craig Kallendorf, and myself, with a comment by Werner Gundersheimer, in the *AHR Forum* on Baron and the *Crisis* in the *American Historical Review* 101 (1996): 117–44.

4. The papers read in the lecture series on "Humanism and Public Life" at the University of Washington in 1988–9, and published in *Modern Language* Quarterly 51

(June 1990): 101–271, make only occasional reference to Baron, but the imprint of his work is unmistakable in the common aim of these essays to explore the connections between politics and humanism in a variety of medieval, Renaissance, and early modern contexts. Two of the essays are particularly relevant to the Italian context: Lauro Martines, "The Protean Face of Renaissance Humanism," 105–21; and Ronald G. Witt, "Civic Humanism and the Rebirth of the Ciceronian Oration," 167–84.

5. Dismantling Baron's key date of 1402 was one of the aims of Jerrold Seigel in "'Civic Humanism' or Ciceronian Rhetoric? The Culture of Petrarch and Bruni," *Past and Resent* 34 (1966): 3–48.

6. Gene Brucker has observed that "Not until a decade after [the Milanese duke] Giangaleazzo's death"—and in the aftermath of the war against Ladislaus of Naples—"do clear signs of what Baron calls 'the new politico-historical outlook' appear" in the records of the consultative assemblies convened by the Florentine government; *The Civic World of Early Renaissance Florence* (Princeton: Princeton University Press, 1977), 300.

7. See especially Quentin Skinner, *The Foundations of Modern Political Thought*, 2 vols (Cambridge: Cambridge University Press, 1978), I: 69–84; also Skinner's essay on "Machiavelli's *Discorsi* and the Pre-Humanist Origins of Republican Ideas," in *Machiavelli and Republicanism*, ed. G. Bock, Q. Skinner, and M. Viroli (Cambridge: Cambridge University Press, 1990), 121–41.

8. A suggestion made by James Hankins in "The 'Baron Thesis'," 327–30.

9. The classic statement of this assessment of the medieval Italian republics, including Florence, is by P. J. Jones, "Communes and Despots: The City-State in Late-Medieval Italy," *Transactions of the Royal Historical Society*, 5th ser, 15 (1965): 71–96. Tending more cautiously in the same direction, and with a sharper focus on the Florentine situation, is Nicolai Rubinstein, "Florentine Constitutionalism and Medici Ascendancy in the Fifteenth Century," in *Florentine Studies*, ed. N. Rubinstein (Evanston: Northwestern University Press, 1968), 442–62. For a recent restatement of this approach, see Hankins, "The 'Baron Thesis'," 316–17 and 321–3.

10. See especially Dale Kent, *The Rise of the Medici: Faction in Florence, 1426–1431* (Oxford: Oxford University Press, 1978); and Brucker, *Civic World*. Nicolai Rubinstein's study of *The Government of Florence Under the Medici (1434 to 1494)* (Oxford: Clarendon Press, 1966) is often, and rightly, cited in support of this gap, but it should not be overlooked that among Rubinstein's main arguments is that the Medici regime, at least in its early decades, adhered far more than is commonly supposed to the constitutional norms and restraints of republicanism.

11. Eugenio Garin has expressed some useful caution about the tendency to see "rhetoric" as the single key to understanding the political ideas of the humanists in his "Leonardo Bruni: politica e cultura," in *Leonardo Bruni cancelliere della repubblica di Firenze*, ed. Paolo Viti (Florence: Leo S. Olschki, 1990), 3–14. Nicolai Rubinstein explores Bruni's dependence on specific rhetorical models, as well as the political purposes to which he ut his rhetoric, in "Il Bruni a Firenze: retorica e politica," in ibid., 15–28.

12. Hankins, "The 'Baron Thesis'," 318.

13. Ibid., 325–6.

14. A recent study that emphasizes the continuity of Bruni's thought from the early *laudatio* through the chancery letters is by Paolo Viti, *Leonardo Bruni e Firenze: studi sulle lettere pubbliche e private* (Rome: Bulzoni, 1992), especially the first essay, "Il primato di Firenze," 3–91.

15. On the republicanism of the guilds and their contributions to the popular governments of the commune, see Brucker, *Civic World*, chap. 1, 14–59; my *Corporatism*

and Consensus in Florentine Electoral Politics, 1280–1400 (Chapel Hill: University of North Carolina Press, 1982), and my essays, "Guild Republicanism in Trecento Florence: The Successes and Ultimate Failure of Corporate Politics," *American Historical Review* 84 (1979): 53–71; "*Audiant Omnes Artes*: Corporate Origins of the Ciompi Revolution," in *Il Tumulto dei Ciompi: un momento di storia fiorentine ed europea* (Florence: Leo S. Olschki, 1981), 59–93; and "Stato, comune, e 'universitas,'" *Annali dell'Istituto Storico Italo-germanico in Trento* 20 (1994): 245–63.

16. Florence, Archivio di Stato, Capitoli, Protocolli, 7, f. 190v; quoted in my "Guild Republicanism," 66.

17. Brucker, *Civic World*, 388.

18. Giovanni Cavalcanti, *Istorie fiorentine*, 2 vols., ed. F. Polidori (Florence, 1838), I:82; Brucker, *Civic World*, 473

19. *Cronaca fiorentina di Marchionne di Coppo Stefani*, ed. N. Rodolico, in *Rerum italiacarum scriptores*, vol. XXX, part I (Città di Castello, 1903–1955), 194, 199.

20. Ibid., 382: "Ma tanto era la forza degli artefici, che in ogni cosa di diliberazione vinceano ne' consigli ciò che volieno ... E così va a chi più può, non guardando però s'è pene o utile della città, e ciascun tira acqua a suo mulino, come meglio vede potere; nè legge, nè statuto vale nelle cose."

21. Ibid., 386; see allo Brucker, *Civic World*, 52.

22. Leonardo Bruni Aretino, *Historiarum florentini populi libri XII*, ed. E. Santini, in *Rerum italiacarum scriptores*, vol. XIX, part III (Città di Castello, 1914–26), 224 (my translation).

23. Giovanni di Pagolo Morelli, *Ricordi*, ed. V. Branca (Florence: Felice Le Monnier, 1969), 256 (my translation).

24. John M. Najemy, "*Arti* and *Ordini* in Machiavelli's *Istorie fiorentine*," in *Essays Presented to Myron P. Gilmore*, vol. 1: *History*, ed. Sergio Bertelli and Gloria Ramakus (Florence: La Nuova Italia, 1978), 161–91.

25. On Bruni's *Histories* and their contribution to the formation of an ideology of state sovereignty, see Riccardo Fubini, "La rivendicazione di Firenze della sovranità statale e il contributo delle 'Historiae' di Leonardo Bruni," in *Leonardo Bruni cancelliere*, 29–62.

26. See Brucker, *Civic World*, chap. 2, 60–101.

27. See my *Corporatism and Consensus*, chap. 8, 263–300.

28. The best profile of this elite in the first and second decades of the fifteenth century is in Brucker, *Civic World*, chap. 5, 248–318. Dale Kent provides an analysis of comparable value for the 1420s and 1430s in "The Florentine *Reggimento* in the Fifteenth Century," *Renaissance Quarterly* 28 (1975): 575–638.

29. The numbers of citizens nominated for the Signoria rose from approximately 3,500 in the mid-fourteenth century to 5,350 in 1382, 6,310 in 1391, and 6,354 in 1433 (even though the city's population was significantly lower in the early fifteenth century than it had been in the second half of the fourteenth century). The results of the scrutiny process that approved candidates were an official secret, a feature of the system that allowed hundreds, perhaps thousands, of citizens to nourish the hope that they had been or would some day be approved. In fact, after a slight decline in the 1390s, the numbers of those approved in the scrutinies also rose dramatically in the early fifteenth century: approximately 875 in 1382; 677 in 1391; 619 in 1393; 1,069 in 1411; and 2,084 in 1433. But even before this explosion in the number of approved office-holders, the policy of a wide distribution of offices within the upper class is already apparent. Between March 1382 and the end of 1399 the 963 available posts in the Signoria (nine in each two-month term of office) were held by 898 individuals from 989 families. Eighty-four percent of the

posts were held by 822 individuals who made only one appearance in the Signoria in these eighteen years. Never before in any period of comparable length were the seats in this office so widely distributed. For these data and the electoral reforms that produced them, see my *Corporatism and Consensus*, chap. 8, 263–300.

30. Gregorio Dati, *Il libro segreto*, ed. Carlo Gargiolli (Bologna, 1869), 72–3. Although portions of Dati's diary, including this passage, are excellently translated by Julia Martines in The Memoirs of *Renaissance Florence: The Diaries of Buonaccorso Pitti and Gregorio Dati*, ed. Gene Brucker (New York: Harper and Row, 1967), I have here preferred to use my own translation. I have previously commented on Dati's reflections on his election to office in *Corporatism and Consensus*, 301–3. On Dati and his political ideas, see Claudio Varese, "Una 'Laudatio Florentinae Urbis': La 'Istoria di Firenze' di Goro Dati," in Varese's *Storia e politica nella prosa del Quattrocento* (Turin: Einaudi,1961), 65–91. And on Dati's *Istoria di Firenze*, which recounts the Florentine war with Milan in a very patriotic key, see Baron, *The Crisis* (1966), 167–88; Louis Green, *Chronicle into History: An Essay on the Interpretation of History in Fourteenth-Century Florentine Chronicles* (Cambridge: Cambridge University Press, 1972), 112–44; Andrew P. McCormick, "Toward a Reinterpretation of Goro Dati's *Storia di Firenze*," *Journal of Medieval and Renaissance Studies* 13 (1983): 227–50; and Antonio Lanza, *Firenze contro Milano* (1390–1440) (Anzio: De Rubeis, 1991), 86–96. Lanza very usefully reprints (ibid., 211–98), but with some changes, the text of Dati's *Istoria* from the older edition of L. Pratesi (Norcia, 1904).

31. Morelli, *Ricordi*, 274–6.

32. Ibid., 196: "ma non gli piacque in tutto il loro reggimento, ma sì in alcuna cosa mescolato, ch'è buono per raffrenare li animi troppo grandi."

33. Ibid., 377.

34. Text in Hans Baron, *Leonardo Bruni Aretino: Humanistisch-Philosophische Schriften* (Leipzig: Teubner, 1928), 50–69, and 57–8 for the passages on Dante's exile, translation by Alan F. Nagel in *The Humanism of Leonardo Bruni: Selected Texts*, ed. G. Griffiths, J. Hankins, and D. Thompson (Binghamton: Medieval and Renaissance Texts and Studies and the Renaissance Society of America, 1987), 85–95 and 90–1.

35. For an illuminating discussion of the development of Stoic attitudes of resignation in the "art of accepting exile," in the wider theater of fifteenth-century Italian politics, see Randolph Starn, *Contrary Commonwealth: The Theme of Exile in Medieval and Renaissance Italy* (Berkeley: University of California Press, 1982).

36. See the portrait of Palla in the *Vite* of Vespasiano da Bisticci, ed. A. Greco, 2 vols. (Florence: Istituto Nazionale di Studi sul Rinascimento, 1976), II: 139–69. Vespasiano recalls that when other Florentine rebels or exiles went to visit Palla, "he dismissed them, did not wish to speak with them, and wanted no one to speak of the city in his house except with respect [*et della sua città non voleva che se ne parlassi in casa sua, se non onoratamente*]." A Florentine ambassador who visited Palla in exile was astonished "at his courage and to see him in good spirits and never complaining about the exile or the misfortunes he had suffered. He hardly seemed a man exiled from his country [*de la sua constaidia di viderlo istare di bonissima voglia, et mai dolersi dello esilio né di cose avesse ch'egli avessi, ma pareva ch'egli non fuse quello exule della sua patria*]"; ibid., 161.

37. For an extensive and up-to-date bibliography on Palmieri, see Alessandra Mita Ferraro's introduction to her edition and translation of the *De captivitate Pisarum* in Matteo Palmieri, *La presa di Pisa* (Naples: Istituto Italiano per gli Studi Storici and the Società Editrice Il Mulino, 1995), vii–xxxiii. Mita Ferraro dates the composition of the *Vita civile* to the years 1434–7: ibid, xvii.

38. Matteo Palmieri, *Vita civile*, ed. G. Belloni (Florence: Sansoni, 1982), 7.

39. Ibid, 136: "Difficile cosa è in ella republica provare di cui [=chi] sia la degnità magiore, però che di quella infra il popolo variamente si dissente: e nobili et potenti dicono la degnità essere posta nelle abondanti facultà et nelle famiglie generose et antiche, i popolari nella humanità et benigna conversatione del libero et pacifico vivere, e savi dicono nella operativa virtù. Coloro che nella città aranno a distribuire gl'honori, seguitando il più approvato consiglio, quegli sempre ne' più virtuosi conferischino, però che ... niuna cosa sarà mai più degna fra gl'huomini che la virtù di chi per publica utilità se exercita."

40. Ibid., 137–8.

41. Translation by Gordon Griffiths in *The Humanism of Leonardo Bruni*, 124. The Latin original of this passage is provided by Baron, *Crisis* (1966), 556.

42. Florence, Archivio di Stato, *Balìe*, 17, f. 5: "et quod ea que expediunt nullo modo exequi valent sine plenaria, libera, totali et absoluta potestate et auctoritate totius populi florentini ... et quod huiusmodi auctoritas juridice haberi non valet net voluntatis exquisitio, maxime considerato more in populo florentino hactenus observato, nisi per viam parlamenti et convocationis ad Parlamentum totius populi florentini et per adunantiam generalem."

43. "The Dialogue of Power in Florentine Politics," in *City-States in Classical Antiquity and Medieval Italy*, ed. A. Molho, K. Raaflaub, and J. Emlen (Ann Arbor: University of Michigan Press, 1991), 279–80, n. 23.

44. On the 1404 scrutiny, see Renzo Ninci, "Lo 'Squittivo del Mangione': il consolidamento legale di un regime (1404)," *Bullettino dell'Istituto Storico Italiano per il Medio Evo e Archivio Muratoriano* 94 (1988): 155–250. Morelli records his election to the Sixteen in *Ricordi*, 532.

45. Morelli, *Ricordi*, 430

46. He married Caterina d'Alberto di Luigi Alberti in 1395, two years after the Alberti had suffered a major political defeat at the hands of the Albizzi faction. He comments: "I believe that this marriage alliance has deprived me of much honor which I might have had from the commune if I had married into another family as I could have [*Credo che 'l detto parentado m'abbia tolto assai onore per avventura arei avuto dal mio Comune, se avesse imparentato con altre famiglie, come arei potuto*]"; ibid., 341.

47. Ibid., 431: "Di questo ho fatto memoria none ad altra fine se non per informami de' modi si vogliono tenere 'acquistare l'onoranza dà il Comune a' suoi cittadini: cioè con fare bene, ubbidire alle leggi, rendere onore agli ufficiali del Comune, a' cittadini molto onorati, agli uomini antichi e alle persone da bene: e a loro ti dà a conoscere, a loro tiraccomanda e ricorda l'operazione buone de' tuoi passati."

48. On Morelli, see Claudio Varese's two essays, "I 'Ricordi' di Giovanni Morelli," I and II, in *Storia e Politica*, 37–64; Christian Bec, *Les marchands écrivains à Florence, 1375 1434* (Paris: Mouton, 1967), 53–75; and Richard C. Trexler, *Public Life in Renaissance Florence* (New York: Academic Press, 1980), 159–86.

49. Palmieri, *Vita civile*, 131–6.

50. *Laudatio Florintinae urbis*, in Hans Baron, *From Petrarch to Bruni* (Chicago: University of Chicago Press, 1968), 250; translation by B. G. Kohl in "Panegyric to the City of Florence," in *The Earthly Republic: Italian Humanists on Government and Society*, ed. B.G. Kohl and R.G. Witt (Philadelphia: University of Pennsylvania Press, 1978), 158.

51. *Laudatio*, in Baron, *From Petrarch to Bruni*, 250; "Panegyric," in *The Earthy Republic*, 158.

52. Stefani, *Cronaca*, 194.

53. At least not in the thirteenth century: see Carol Lansing, *The Florentine Magnates: Lineage and Faction in a Medieval Commune* (Princeton: Princeton University Press, 1991).

But F.W. Kent believes that in the fifteenth century some of the patrician families may have held frequent meetings to discuss matters of common interest; see his *Household and Lineage in Renaissance Florence* (Princeton: Princeton University Press, 1977), 238–46.

54. *Laudatio*, in Baron, *From Petrarch to Bruni*, 262; "Panegyric," in *The Earthly Republic*, 173.

55. Text in Baron, *Leonardo Bruni Aretino*; translation by Nagel in *The Humanism of Leonardo Bruni*, 87.

56. Palmieri, *Vita civile*, 7.

57. Ibid., 4–5.

58. Ibid., 9.

59. *Laudatio*, in Baron, *From Petrarch to Bruni*, 233; "Panegyric," in *The Earthly Republic*, 136.

60. *Laudatio*, in Baron, *From Petrarch to Bruni*, 244; "Panegyric," in *The Earthly Republic*, 149–50.

61. *Laudatio*, in Baron, *From Petrarch to Bruni*, 248; "Panegyric," in *The Earthy Republic*, 155.

62. This notion is explored by Andrea Zorzi and Michael Rocke in two intriguing treatments of the proliferation in the early fifteenth century of government agencies with the power to investigate the private life of Florentines; see Zorzi's *L'amministrazione della giustizia penale* (Florence: Olschki, 1988), and Rocke's *Forbidden Friendships: Homosexuality and Male Culture in Renaissance Florence* (Oxford: Oxford University Press, 1996). See also my forthcoming article, "The Politics of Sex in Civic Humanist Florence."

63. See Mark Phillips, *The Memoir of Marco Parenti: A Life in Medici Florence* (Princeton: Princeton University Press, 1987).

64. *Dialogus de libertate*, ed F. Adorno, in *Atli e memorie dell'Accademia toscana di scienze e lettere "La Colombaria"*, 22 (1957): 270–303. English translation by Renée N. Watkins, in her *Humanism and Liberty: Writings on Freedom from Fifteenth-Century Florence* (Columbia, S.C.: University of South Carolina Press, 1978), 193–224.

DAVID QUINT

The Debate Between Arms and Letters in the *Gerusalemme Liberata*

It is well known that Tasso suppressed an episode that would have appeared in Canto 8 of the *Gerusalemme liberata*.[1] The Danish soldier Carlo has brought to the camp of the crusader army the sword of his slain prince Sveno, its blade indelibly stained by the blood of the infidel enemy. The bloodstain is, in fact, a kind of test: it will only disappear when the sword is picked up by its rightful new owner, the destined avenger of Sveno. Goffredo, then Raimondo are the first to try their hands at this "ventura," but the sword does not come clean; they realize that it is reserved for another—"ch'altrui si riserbava." This someone else, Carlo surmises, is probably the absent Rinaldo, whom Sveno had himself emulated and at whose side he had wanted to fight.

> Ahi! qual stata saria la coppia ardita
> s'era d'amor tanta virtude unita?[2]

> Alas, what daring couple would they have made, had so much valor been united by love?

Tasso cut the episode of the sword from his epic, noting in a letter that "I fear that the adventure of the sword has the flavor of romance."[3] Indeed, the passage seems reminiscent of the sword-in-the-stone that declared the legitimacy of Arthur.

From *Sparks and Seeds: Medieval Literature and its Afterlife* eds. Donald Beecher, Massimo Ciavolella, and Robert Fedi. © 2000 by Brepols.

But Tasso had another reason to excise this story of warriors competing for the arms of a dead companion. He was removing from his poem a direct allusion to one of its controlling models—the debate between Ajax and Ulysses over who should inherit the arms of Achilles as it is recounted by Ovid in *Metamorphoses* 13.1–383. Tasso doubly covered his tracks by dismissing the classically inspired episode as savoring of romance.

The Ovidian text provides, as we shall see, a virtual outline for the *Gerusalemme liberata*. It well might, since in their respective speeches Ajax and Ulysses each recall episodes from the *Iliad* and the Trojan war, the larger epic story on which Tasso based his account of the siege and conquest of Jerusalem. Nonetheless, the debate between Ajax and Ulysses has a privileged status among the literary models of the *Liberata*. If Tasso's normal practice of imitation is to combine together, through the practice of *contaminatio*, a series of predecessor texts in order to construct an episode, a scene, even an individual octave, in this case Ovid's passage affords him a single overarching source for much of the narrative material of his poem. Moreover, the rivalry between the hero of intellect, Ulysses, and the hero of force, Ajax, provides the ideological model for Tasso's opposition of Goffredo and Rinaldo. At the heart of the *Liberata* is an uncertainty about which of these two heroes—and which of their respective kinds of heroism— is to be preferred, and this uncertainty, in turn, reflects a wide-ranging debate in sixteenth-century elite culture that was contained under the shorthand title of arms versus letters, a debate that had newly become topical in Tasso's Ferrara as the Estense Duchy sought to assert its precedence over Medicean Florence. If this essay starts by examining Tasso's imitations of Ovid, it will show how, through these imitations, the *Liberata* and its poet are drawn into the larger preoccupations of late Renaissance culture.

In the contention over the arms of Achilles in *Metamorphoses* 13, Ovid's Ajax considers himself the obvious heir: he is related by blood to Achilles (30–31), and he is acknowledged to be the second champion of the Greek army. Ulysses, however, wins the day through his eloquence—"the skilled speaker took the arms of the strong man" (*fortisque viri tulit arma disertus*, 383)—and the dismayed Ajax commits suicide.[4] Ulysses claims an equally noble family as that of Ajax, tracing his genealogy back to the gods (141–47). But he also argues that the deeds of one's ancestors do not belong to oneself, and he bases his claim solely on his own exploits (140–41; 159–61). He displays the wounds he has suffered during the war (262–65), and he lists the works and good offices he has done the Greek side. In the company of Diomede, he brought back the young disguised Achilles from the island of Scyros (162–80), he went out on the night-exploit, killed Dolon, and stole the horses of Rhesus (242–52), and, on another occasion, he stole the Palladium from Troy (336–49); in the company of Menelaus, he went as an ambassador to Troy (196–205; see *Iliad* 3.205–24). Each of these episodes has its imitation in the *Liberata*. The stealing of the Palladium has its counterpart in Canto 2 in the theft of the image of the Virgin Mary from the Jerusalem mosque, a theft for which first Sofronia and then her companion from the supposedly stronger sex, Olindo, claim responsibility (2.5–53). The embassy of Ulysses and Menelaus to Troy is parallelled by the visit of the ambassador Alete, accompanied by the warrior Argante, to Goffredo and the crusader camp in the same canto (57–97). The episode of the Doloneia is recalled in the night-exploit of Canto 12, where Clorinda, in the company of the same Argante, burns down the Crusader siege-towers (12.2–48).[5] The conveying of Achilles from Scyros, where the young hero has been disguised as a girl, has its corresponding episode in the rescue of Rinaldo from Armida's island by Ubaldo and Carlo, where Tasso closely follows the version of the story in the *Achilleid* of Statius.[6]

The Ulyssean model in Ovid's text explains why the characters in these episodes of the *Liberata* work in pairs. Either a woman—Sofronia or Clorinda—or a figure of Ulyssean guile and experience—the eloquent Alete, "a l'ingannare accorto" (2.58), or Ubaldo, whose pursuit of "virtute e senno" (14.28) invokes the Dantean Ulysses[7]—is paired with a man or warrior, Olindo, Argante, Carlo.

Sofronia–Olindo
Alete–Argante
Clorinda–Argante
Ubaldo–Carlo
Vafrino–Erminia

The first of this series of Ulyssean figures, Sofronia, is linked by her name (temperance, self-control) to the wily Alete and Ubaldo, and suggests that the heroism of intelligence is itself an attribute of the "men forte sesso" (2.42). Tasso adds one more figure to the series and goes beyond the list of exploits enumerated by Ovid's Ulysses. In Canto 19, Vafrino, the clever squire of Tancredi who has been sent to spy on the pagan camp is recognized through his disguise by Erminia (80f.); Erminia does not betray him and reveals that she has just designed the false insignia with which the pagan soldiers plan to disguise themselves and infiltrate the crusader ranks to kill Goffredo in the upcoming battle. The episode recalls the story that Helen tells in the *Odyssey* (4.235–64) of having recognized Ulysses without giving him away, when he came disguised as a beggar to spy on Troy.[8] Tasso's final version of the cunning Ulyssean figure—Vafrino's name means "tricky"—meets his match in an equally crafty woman.

Tasso's poem repeatedly pairs a figure of intellect and/or feminine guile wording together with a figure of masculine force—a Ulysses with a Diomede or a Menelaus—in order to comment on the central heroic pairing of the *Liberata*, the commander-in-chief Goffredo with his lead warrior Rinaldo.[9] The action of the epic requires the cooperation of the two heroes that is only achieved when Rinaldo returns from self-imposed exile and submits himself to the rule and direction of Goffredo: an obvious rewriting of the *Iliad* in which Rinaldo plays the role of an Achilles angry and then reconciled with Agamemnon. The proper relationship that is to obtain between the two is spelled out to the dreaming Goffredo by the divine mouthpiece Ugone: "tu sei capo, ei mano / di questo campo" (14.13.6–7); that is, the hero of intelligence should direct the actions of the hero of force. Rinaldo is similarly instructed to let his fighting ardor be guided by the "senno" of Goffredo (17.63.5–8).

This is the same relationship of dependence that Ovid's Ulysses argues that Ajax bears to him and that is the ground of his superiority to his rival:

> tibi dextera bello
> utilis, ingenium est, quod eget moderamine nostro;
> tu vires sine mente geris, mihi cura futuri;
> tu pugnare potes, pugnandi tempora mecum
> eligit Atrides; tu tantum corpore prodes,
> nos animo; quantoque ratem qui temperat, anteit
> remigis officium, quanto dux milite maior,
> tantum ego te supero....   (13.361–68)

> Your good right arm is useful in the battle; but when it comes to thinking you need my guidance. You have force without intelligence; while mine is the care for tomorrow. You are a good fighter; but it is I who help Atrides select the time of fighting. Your value is in your body only; mine in mind. And, as he who directs the ship surpasses him who only rows it, as much as the general excels the common soldier, so much greater am I than you.

Ulysses claims to be the master strategist of the Greek army and he virtually displaces Agamemnon as its general. Tasso makes Goffredo a combination of Agamemnon and Ulysses, but it is Ovid's Ulysses with whom he is identified from the third line of the *Liberata*—"Molto egli oprò co'l senno e con la mano" that recalls *Metamorphoses* 13 and Ulysses' vaunt of the deeds he has done "consilioque manuque" (205) for the Greek cause.[10] These deeds—his having fortified the Greek camp with trenches (*fossa munimina cingo*, 212), his having consoled his associates (consolor socios, 213), his having stopped the Greek rank and file from abandoning the war at Agamemnon's own ill-advised suggestion and his putting down of Thersites (216–36)—find their parallels in the actions of Goffredo who has trenches dug around the Crusader tents (le tende munite / e di fosse profonde e di trinciere, 3.66), delivers a version of the "O socii" speech of Aeneas (5.90–92) that consoles (consola, 5.92.2) his men,[11] and quells the popular rebellion of Argillano (8.76f.). Tasso gives Goffredo further Ulyssean traits both in his immunity to the charms of Armida, who employs the arts of Circe and the voice of a siren to seduce his soldiers (4.86), and in his building of the siege machines that resemble the arch-stratagem of Ulysses, the Trojan horse.[12] It is then possible to view the relationship that Goffredo bears to Rinaldo in the *Liberata* not simply in terms of the Iliadic conflict between Agamemnon and Achilles, for Agamemnon, as Homer and Ovid's Ulysses make fairly clear, was not very bright. Goffredo is the poem's central Ulysses figure, and his opposition to the Achillean Rinaldo repeats a heroic contrast that belongs to the Homeric origins of epic itself.

The Goffredo–Rinaldo relationship has a secondary version or reflection in the poem's association of Raimondo and Tancredi. Raimondo, the aging counselor figure who recalls Homer's Nestor,[13] is a kind of abstraction of the Ulyssean "senno" that Goffredo combines with martial prowess in his own person; Tancredi is second only to Rinaldo as military champion in the Crusader forces. The relationship of the four characters is summed up in a couplet spoken by Erminia about Goffredo in Canto 3.

> Sol Raimondo in consiglio, ed in battaglia
> sol Rinaldo e Tancredi a lui s'aguaglia.   (3.58.7–8)

> Only Raimondo in counsel, and in battle only Rinaldo and Tancredi are his equals.

The relationship of Raimondo and Tancredi—a relationship of intellect to force—is also governed by the model of *Metamorphoses* 13, this time by Ajax's speech and side of the argument. In his claim to his right to the disputed arms, Ajax lists two of his exploits among others. Chosen by lot, he met Hector on the battlefield after Hector had challenged the Greek side to send out a champion to fight him in single combat (87–90), a battle Ajax leaves his listeners to infer, that placed him on the same level as the Achilles who finally killed Hector. On another occasion, Ajax recalls, he had extended his great shield to protect none other than Ulysses himself when the latter found himself in distress on the battlefield (73–81; see *Iliad* 11.461f.). In the *Liberata*, Argante plays the role of Hector and issues a similar challenge to the Crusader army;[14] he is initially met by Tancredi in Canto 6 (13–55), but when Tancredi, now the prisoner of Armida, fails to show up for the continuation of their duel in Canto 7, it is Raimondo who steps in, chosen by lot, to take his place (63–113). But Raimondo, a "debil vecchio" as he acknowledges himself to be in his prayer for divine aid (78.7), is not equal to the task on his own; he is assisted by his excellent horse (75–77) and—in answer to his prayers—by his guardian angel who interposes an invisible divine shield that shatters Argante's sword (92–93).[15] It will, however, be Tancredi who finally resumes the duel with Argante and finishes it by killing his pagan adversary in Canto 19. In Canto 20, moreover, the unarmed Tancredi rises from the bed in Jerusalem where he is still recovering from his battle with Argante, takes up his great shield and covers the unprotected Raimondo, who had fallen during the fighting inside the city. Tancredi acts as Raimondo's new guardian angel, and his shield, "il qual di sette / dure cuoia di tauro era composto" (86.1–2), clearly recalls the "sevenfold-ox-hide terrible shield" that Ajax carries in the *Iliad* as his trademark (*Il.* 7.245, 266) and beneath which the Ajax of the *Metamorphoses* reminds the Greeks that he had once sheltered the cowering Ulysses.

The Raimondo–Tancredi complex is another illustration of the need for cooperation between the hero of intelligence and the hero of force. But here the relationship is viewed from the point of view of an Ajax or Tancredi, the warrior hero who is the only one who can fight the decisive duel and who is required physically to protect the Ulyssean strategist. The Raimondo–Tancredi subplot thus opposes the central plot of the *Liberata* where the irascible warrior Rinaldo appears to be subordinated to the direction and wisdom of his captain, Goffredo. But the nature of this relationship is also called into question in the action of the last cantos of the poem. If Rinaldo does not rescue Goffredo himself, he does come to the aid of Eustazio, Goffredo's brother, as the two of them assault the walls of Jerusalem on ladders in Canto 18.

> Ed egli stesso a l'ultimo germano
> del pio Buglion, ch'è di cadere in forse,
> stesa la vincitrice amica mano,
> di salime secondo aita porse.   (18.79)

And he himself, extending his victorious hand in fellowship to the youngest brother of pious Goffredo, who was in risk of falling, gave him help to climb up second.

We may see this Eustazio who comes in second behind Rinaldo as a kind of symbolic substitute for his brother; Rinaldo saves him from falling as Tancredi will later rescue Raimondo. Moreover, the assault that Rinaldo successfully leads on the city wall, improbably enough where it is highest and best fortified (più munito ed alto, 72.8), is taken entirely on his own initiative and is not part of the design of Goffredo, who enters Jerusalem only to find Rinaldo already there before him—consigning him, like Eustazio, to second place. Similarly, in the final battle outside the city in Canto 20, Rinaldo exceeds Goffredo's orders to launch an attack on the enemy's left flank and cuts through the entire pagan army, killing Adrasto (103), Solimano (107), and Tisaferno (120) on its right wing and winning the battle singlehandedly. To Goffredo is left the less glamorous task of vanquishing the opposing commander Emireno (139), just as the aged Raimondo, revived beneath Tancredi's shield, kills his even more decrepit counterpart Aladino (89).

When Tasso translated the debate over the arms of Achilles in the *Metamorphoses* into the action of the *Gerusalemme liberata*, he took a sufficiently ambivalent attitude toward the rivalry between the heroism of intelligence, the attribute of the commander-in-chief, and the heroism of force that belonged to the warrior. The official position of the *Liberata* notwithstanding that, like Ovid's poem, awards superiority to the Ulyssean, thinking man's hero, Goffredo, Tasso's sympathies may lie with the prowess of Rinaldo and Tancredi, the soldier heroes whose combats may still generate the highest drama of his epic. It may have been, in part, to conceal or play down those sympathies that Tasso cut his romance version of Ovid's debate— the contention over who should inherit Sveno's marvelous sword—out of his poem. For in this version it was *Rinaldo*, the poem's Achillean fighter, who was destined to capture the arms which both Goffredo and Raimondo had tried to win.[16]

The *Liberata* nonetheless restages the Ovidian debate between Ulysses and Ajax by repeatedly pairing and opposing two types of heroes and heroism. The central conflict of Goffredo and Rinaldo, which those other pairings mirror and comment upon, opposes intelligence and self-control on the one hand, force and ardor on the other. The opposition, as the Ovidian model suggests, is as old as the history of epic itself and goes back to the contrast of Ulysses and Achilles as heroes of their respective poems, even to the roles that each plays in the *Iliad* itself.[17] Ovid might be allegorizing in the

Metamorphoses how the sequel to the *Iliad* will not be a similar poem in which an Achillean Ajax would be the protagonist but a new poem with a new type of hero—the man of many turns rather than the more one-dimensional warrior—who will visit both Achilles and Ajax in an underworld that is also the realm of an already superseded literary past. Furthermore, Ovid updates the heroism of Ulysses to the practice of Roman warfare, which gave importance to the strategist-general rather than the individual fighting man. Tasso may similarly give centrality to the commander-in-chief—his poem was to have been titled *Il Goffredo*—in an epic written for an age of artillery and mass warfare.[18] His Goffredo is supposed to combine both intelligence and martial prowess, and the evident model for such a combination of Ulyssean and Achillean traits is Virgil's Aeneas, who is both leader and principal warrior. But by explicitly assigning the latter role to Rinaldo, Tasso reduces his Aeneas-like hero to his Ulyssean, prudential dimension; as a fighter, Goffredo probably imitates Aeneas most closely at the moment when he is wounded and sent out of battle in Canto 11 (54f.; see *Aeneid* 12.318–19, 384f.)[19]

There are, however, contemporary contexts in which to read the opposition, however traditional it may be, of a Ulyssean Goffredo to an Achillean Rinaldo. Goffredo the captain is also the figure of a divinely sanctioned authority to which Rinaldo, the mighty individual and independent soldier of fortune, must submit. This political scenario, as I have discussed elsewhere, primarily describes obedience to the Counter-reformation Church.[20] But it also suggests the curtailing of feudal prerogatives by the nascent modern state whose princes enjoy—or claim to enjoy—absolute power over their subjects; such a state, as Tasso's dialogue, *Il Forno ovvero de la nobiltà*, asserts, was Ferrara itself where the "podestà assoluta o quasi assoluta e simile a quella de' re"[21] of the Este Dukes required the unconditional obedience of their nobility, a nobility that could best show its noble character *through* its obedience.

> Talché niuno altro segno di nobiltà maggiore posson dimostrare che la servitù co' vostri principi e l'ubbedienza e la fedeltà dimostrata, per la quale sono stati degni di tutti que' gradi e di tutti que' titoli ch'a nobilissimi cavalieri son convenienti; e vivono con splendore e con ornamento eguale a quello de' baroni de' grandissimi regni. (4:507)

So that they can show no greater sign of nobility than the servitude, obedience and loyalty they have shown to your princes, for which they have been worthy of all those ranks and titles that belong to the most noble cavaliers; and they live with a splendor and magnificence equal to that of barons of the largest kingdoms.

In this social and political setting, where noble identity, with its titles and ranks, is conferred upon the nobleman by the prince in exchange for the nobleman's submission, the two types of heroism, intellectual and martial, of the *Liberata* acquire a particular resonance. For here they may correspond to two kinds of nobility, equally dependent on the prince. The speakers of *Il Forno* discuss how a new noble lineage may begin.

> A. B. E gli uomini famosi per valor di guerra o per lettere o per negozio ne le corti sono il più illustre principio che possa avere il nuovo legnaggio.
> A. F. Senza fallo.
> A. B. Il quale suole essere in minor pregio de l'antico, perché l'istesse cose più lontane che vicine sono degne di gloria: laonde i nobili sprezzano ne' vivi quegli onori medesimi per li quali i maggiori sono onorati. (4:520)

> A. B. And men famous for valor in war or for letters or for the affairs of the court are the most illustrious beginning that a new lineage may have.
> A. F. Without doubt.
> A. B. Which is wont to be of less esteem than an old lineage, because the same things more distant rather than nearer in the past are worthy of glory: whence nobles disdain in the living the same honors for which their ancestors are honored.

One may be ennobled either through arms or letters or through court business, and it is significant that Tasso, the *letterato*, tries to distinguish the latter two categories. For the two were generally linked together under the name of letters and helped to define the occupation of an emergent noble class of princely servants and bureaucrats often trained in the law—what in France would be the *noblesse de robe*—that was to be distinguished from an older martial aristocracy.[22] This traditional nobility of arms looked down upon the newcomers, both, as Tasso indicates here, because they were new and because they were the products of a court culture that was unwarlike and even effeminate. So Ottaviano Fregoso famously complains in the fourth book of *Il Cortegiano* of a courtiership that often does nothing but "make their spirits effeminate ... whence it comes about that there are few who dare, I will not say to die, but even to risk any danger" (4.4).[23] The debates betweens arms and letters encountered in the *Cortegiano* (see 1.45–46) and throughout the literature of the sixteenth century thus encode a rivalry between anew nobility rising at court through intellectual talents and an older aristocracy anxious about losing its position as a military caste; such anxiety was only increased by an emergent style of absolutism that divested the old magnates of their feudal autonomy and reduced them to princely servants and courtiers along with their new rivals, both dependent on the favor of the ruler.

The opposition in the *Gerusalemme liberata* between an Achillean heroism of martial prowess and the Ulyssean heroism of intelligence, was in fact a *topos* of this debate between arms and letters—and over the nature of nobility. In 1571, Girolamo Muzio, the former schoolteacher of the young Tasso at the court of Urbino, published *Il Gentilhuomo*, a work "divided into three dialogues," in which "is treated the matter of nobility." Its third book contains a typical debate on arms and letters. Muzio's speakers take up a *topos* of this debate that had already appeared in the *Cortegiano*: the question of who was greater, Achilles, the greatest man of arms, or Homer, the greatest poet.

> *Nobile*: Ed io ti dico che di tanto maggior honore è degno Homero di Achille, quanto piu stimar si dee il vero, che il sogno. Fu Homero uno scrittor veramente eccellentissimo: Et Achille fu una favola. Et in questa favola fu egli descritto per un giovine furioso, & bestiale. Molto fu piu honorato Ulisse da Homero, che Achille: che oltra l'havere scritto una opera del nome di lui intitolata, & tutta di lui, ad Ulisse diede nome di vincitor di citta, il che non disse mai di Achille. Et dovete essere Ulisse uno huomo letterario: che Ovidio recita una oratio sua piena di arte oratoria. *Eugenio*: Quella oratione stata sarà piu di Ovidio che di Ulisse. *Nobile*: Qui non ci accade disputa.[24]

> *Nobile*. And I say to you that Homer is worthy of so much more honor than Achilles as one should esteem reality more than a dream. Homer was truly a most excellent writer: and Achilles was a fable. And in this fable he was portrayed as a furious and bestial youth. Ulysses was much more honored by Homer than Achilles: for beyond having written a work that took its title from the name of Ulysses and was totally about him, he gave to Ulysses the name of conqueror of cities, which he never said about Achilles. And

Ulysses must have been a man of letters: for Ovid recites an oration of his full of oratorical art. *Eugenio*: That oration will have been more Ovid's than Ulysses'. *Nobile*: We have no argument on that point.

Homer, the man of letters, has made a man of letters, Ulysses, into a hero, and both are superior to the *furioso* Achilles. Ulysses is a sacker of cities, specifically, one may infer, of the Troy which fell by his cunning stratagem. The clincher to this argument is Ovid's portrait of Ulysses as a skilled orator, winning the debate for the arms of Achilles, over Ajax, another Achillean man of arms. Muzio has put the argument into the mouth of a character named Nobile in dialogue with another named Eugenio: their names may seem to be synonyms, but in fact, Eugenio is "well-born." The claim for letters over arms is advanced against the traditional aristocracy of lineage and blood: it is the claim of a new noble class.[25]

Tasso himself offers complicated commentary on Achilles and Ulysses in *Il Forno*. He brings up the case of Achilles shortly after his speakers have remarked on the noble subject's duty to obey his prince, an obedience that is defined as a kind of self-control and thus as a form of prudence. Achilles was both king of the Myrmidons and subject to Agamemnon:

> A. B. Era dunque in Achille la virtù regia, la quale era la sua prudenza; ma non era peraventura la prudenza eroica, perch'e-gli ad Agammenone non avrebbe dovuto ubbedire. Nondimeno da Pallade fu consegliato ch'egli cedesse, e da Nestore ripreso ch'egli contendesse.
>
> A. F. Non per mio giudizio.
>
> A. B. Ma la fortezza d'Achille fu eroica, come si dimostrò quando egli solo pose in fuga Ettore e spaventò il campo de' Troiani.
>
> A. F. Fu senza fallo.
>
> A. B. Dunque Achille aveva la fortezza eroica, ma non la prudenza: era dunque e non era eroe: come stanno queste cose che paiono contrarie? Ma peraventura non sono, perch'in Achille non era la virtù eroica perfettamente: perch'egli avrebbe avuto insieme la prudenza e la fortezza in somma perfezione; o s'ella v'era, la virtù eroica consiste principalmente ne la fortezza e ne la magnanimità.
>
> A. F. Così mi pare.   (4:511–12)

A. B. Achilles thus possessed royal virtue, which was his prudence; but it was not perhaps heroic prudence, because he would not have had to obey Agamemnon. Nonetheless he was counseled by Pallas to yield, and he was rebuked by Nestor for his contentiousness.

A. F. Not in my judgment.

A. B. But the fortitude of Achilles was heroic, as was demonstrated when he alone put Hector to flight and terrified the Trojan army.

A. F. It was without doubt.

A. B. Thus Achilles had fortitude that was heroic, but not prudence: thus he was and was not a hero: how may these two things exist that appear contrary? But perhaps they are not contrary, for Achilles did not have heroic virtue in a perfect manner: for he would have had to have had together prudence and fortitude in highest perfection; or if he had perfect heroic virtue, heroic virtue consists principally in fortitude and magnanimity.

A. F. So it seems to me.

The tortuous logic of this passage sees in Achilles' wrathful disobedience to Agamemnon a lack of prudence and thus of perfect heroism which is a combination of "la prudenza e la fortezza in somma perfezione." We can read the passage as a gloss on the heroes of the *Liberata*: like the similarly insubordinate Rinaldo, Achilles can singlehandedly win the field of battle, but both fall short of the ideal heroism of a Goffredo who possesses both prudence and martial prowess. Yet Tasso qualifies this scheme both through the demurral of Antonio del Forno (A. F.) and through the final concession of Agostino Bucci (A. B.) that perhaps heroism is largely a matter of fortitude and magnanimity, in which prudence plays little role. We may sense here not only an admiration for an old-style heroism, but, in the context of *Il Forno*, as nostalgia for a more traditional feudal idea of nobility whose highest expression would not lie in the nobleman's servitude and obedience to his prince but in his own hereditary claims—Achilles is a king in his own right—and deeds of arms.

A similar social conservatism colors Tasso's treatment of Ulysses in a passage that comes near the beginning of *Il Forno*. The Greek hero is here coupled with the ugly, plebeian Socrates as an orator, and both are contrasted to noble heroes who did not need words to manifest a nobility that was evident in the physical beauty of their faces.

A. F. Socrate nondimeno aveva il volto come quello che si dipinge ne' satiri e ne' sileni, e usava quelle parole che sono in bocca del calzolaio e del sartore, con le quali s'egli persuadesse Alcibiade o no, sasselo quella notte che ricoperse il for ragionamento; ma non persuase egli al popolo ateniese. E se la medesima maniera d'eloquenza che'egli usava fosse stata usata da Ulisse co' principi de la Grezia, non avrebbe conseguito il suo fine; ma il raccontar le cose prudentemente e con singolar fortezza in guerra adoperate, il mostrar le ferite del suo petto, il ridurre agli iddii non men la nobiltà paterna che la materna gli recarono la desiderata vittoria; ma non l'avrebbe già potuta aver al giudizio d'Elena, se con Paride avesse conteso; e se Circe avesse dopo lui veduto Aiace, così da quel novo amor sarebbe stata presa come fu poi Alcina da quel di Ruggiero. Ma io credo che Socrate e Ulisse non tanto per alcuna eloquenza persuadessero, quanto per alcuna arte incantassero, non ch'altri, l'incantatrici medesime. (4:435–36)

A. F. Socrates nonetheless had a face like those one depicts on satyrs and silenuses, and he used those words that are in mouths of cobblers and tailors, with which whether or not he persuaded Alcibiades is known only to that night that covered their conversation; but he didn't persuade the Athenian people. And if that same manner of eloquence that he used had been used by Ulysses with the princes of Greece, he would not have obtained his end; but the recounting of the deeds he prudently and with singular fortitude had performed in war, the showing of the wounds on his breast, the tracing back to the gods the nobility of the lineage not only of his father but of his mother as well, gave him the desired victory; but he would not have been able to obtain it in the judgment of Helen had he contended with Paris; and if Circe had seen Ajax after him, she would have been taken by that new love as Alcina later was by her love for Ruggiero. But I think that Socrates and Ulysses did not so much persuade by a kind of eloquence, as they enchanted by some magical art no others than the enchantresses themselves.

In this retelling of Ulysses' speech claiming the arms of Achilles, Tasso acknowledges that Ulysses combined prudence and fortitude—what will later be defined as a perfect heroism. But the phrase, "le cose prudentemente e con singolar fortezza in guerra adoperate," already seems to tip the scale in favor of fortitude, and it seems to be Ulysses' further confirmation of that fortitude in the display of his wounds and his declaration of his aristocratic blue blood that win the day for him; it is specifically *not* an eloquence that would have linked him with the philosopher Socrates, who speaks the language of artisans. Moreover, in a final distancing of heroism and nobility from intellect and letters, Ajax, the old-style military hero whom Ulysses defeated in their debate, is fancifully made a victor over Ulysses in the domain of the latter's own epic: Circe would have fallen for the mere sight of the soldier Ajax and discarded the orator Ulysses.

In his treatment of both Achilles and Ulysses, then, the Tasso of the *Forno* seems to betray a sympathy for a traditional aristocracy of arms over a new nobility of letters. And yet Tasso was, like Homer in Muzio's text, a poet and man of letters himself; and, again like Muzio's Homer, he created in the *Liberata* a Ulyssean hero Goffredo, a hero of prudence and intellect, whom the poem appears to exalt above its other Achillean hero Rinaldo. But the *Liberata*, too, we have seen, wavers in the precedence it gives the heroism of mind over the heroism of force, and its poet may be suspected of upholding the claims of the latter, when, in the poem's final cantos of battle, he brings back both Rinaldo and Tancredi to win the day for Goffredo and Raimondo. It is not surprising that the intellectual and writer Tasso should have chosen to identify as much, if not more, with a hereditary nobility and its martial traditions as with *letterati* who had newly risen through court service to nobility—the class to which he and his father more clearly belonged. He embraces the *sprezzatura* with which *Il Forno* describes the old nobility looking down on the recently ennobled, and this snobbery can be clearly perceived in his treatment of the various figures of Ulyssean intelligence in the *Liberata*.

If we turn away from Goffredo and Raimondo and look at the five other versions of the Ulysses figure that I have isolated—Alete, Sofronia, Clorinda, Ubaldo, and Vafrino—we find either men from lower social origins or women. The pagan ambassador Alete, the first in the series, is also the explicit representative of the new class of princely servants:

> Alete è l'un, che da principio indegno
> tra le brutture de la plebe è sorto;
> ma l'inalzaro a i primi onor del regno
> parlar facondo e lusinghiero e scorto,
> pieghevoli costumi e vario ingegno
> al finger pronto, a l'ingannare accorto: (2.58.1–6)

Alete is one who has risen from an unworthy beginning among the ugliness of the plebeian class; but he was raised to the first honors of the realm by eloquent and flattering and clever speech, by adaptable manners and a mind of various nature, quick to feign and skilled in deceit.

This disparaging portrait of the court careerist who has risen from humble origins has been taken to be a satirical barb at powerful courtiers in the service of Alfonso II, Tasso's rivals.[26] Risen from the "brutture de la plebe," the eloquent Alete can be compared to the ugly, artisan Socrates with whom Tasso coupled Ulysses in *Il Forno*. This formerly lower-class character from the beginning of the poem is matched towards its end by Vafrino, the squire of Tancredi, who recalls, among other literary predecessors, the crafty Brunello of Boiardo and Ariosto, the "ribaldello" (*Innamorato* 2.3.39.6), who rises through royal service to become vassal king, before he is finally hanged in the *Furioso* (32.8) for the lowlife thief that he is. The knight-adventurer Ubaldo does not initially appear to belong in the same declassé company as Alete and Vafrino, but Tasso's description of him, "come uom che virtute e senno merchi" (14.28.5) links him and his Ulyssean intelligence with mercantile rather than aristocratic, heroic pursuits, mercantile pursuits that Goffredo, the poem's central hero of "senno," pointedly rejects in the last words spoken in the poem: "guerreggio in Asia, e non vi cambio o merco" (20.142.8).[27] The capacity that both Alete and Vafrino share for fraud, which is perhaps a sign of their class origins, is also shared by Sofronia, whose claim to have stolen the image of the Virgin Mary is a "Magnanima menzogna," (2.3.22), but a lie nonetheless, by Clorinda who stages the nighttime sneak attack on the siege machines, and by the Helen-like Erminia with whom Vafrino is paired—even though she protests her unwillingness to be involved "in atto alcun di frodo" (19.89.8). Tasso remarks in *Il Forno* that the art of Ulysses seemed to match that of the Circean "incantatrici" who were his adversaries, and the assimilation of these Ulyssean characters of the *Liberata* with feminine guile suggests their resemblance to the poem's central version of Circe, the fraudulent and seductive Armida.[28] If lower-class associations cling to the Ulyssean figure of intelligence and prudence, who, as the figure of Alete makes clear, is linked to the new nobility of letters, so do associations of effeminacy—and the two may seem to be much the same from the point of view of a traditional military aristocracy that saw the lower classes as unfit for the manly pursuit of arms and regarded the lettered peacetime culture of the court as potentially effeminizing. It is these associations—and the social bias that lies behind them—that may help to account for Tasso's reservations about the preeminence he grants Goffredo as the Ulyssean hero of his poem.

These reservations would have been heightened by the ideological climate in Ferrara during Tasso's composition of the *Liberata*. The struggle for precedence that the Este waged with the Medici rulers of Florence—a struggle that only intensified after the apparent victory of the Medici, who were named Grand Dukes of Tuscany in 1569—was viewed by the apologists on both sides as a kind of large-scale debate between arms and letters.[29] Since the Medici banking family could not boast a long dynastic history, their defenders extolled the antiquity of Florence itself and praised a Florentine citizenry whose nobility did not i so much depend on lineage than on the virtue of its deeds—and these included intellectual achievements. The Este, to the contrary, based their claim to precedence on long-held feudal dominion and an equally long, if sometimes imaginary history of military feats; one version of this history is recounted on the shield portraying the deeds of Rinaldo's Este ancestors in the *Liberata* (17.64f.).

Tasso contributed further to this propaganda war between Ferrara and Florence. In *Il Nifo ovvero del piacere*, he included an insulting passage that implied that Florentines were all lowborn tradesmen, *sarti* and *pizzicaruoli*, who talked mostly about their goods.[30] *Il Forno* is itself a document of the precedence controversy: in it Tasso asserts that "antichissima oltre l'altre famiglie de' principi italiani è quella d'Este" (518), and the dialogue ends with the Este being declared to be worthy of the same title of "serenissimo," enjoyed by the Medici Grand Dukes (536).[31] The whole discussion of nobility in *Il Forno* may, in fact, find its *raison d'être* in the passage that immediately follows on the already cited exchange on the founding of new lineages and the disdain in which they are held by nobles of long standing:

> ... laonde i nobili sprezzano ne' vivi quegli onori medesimi per li quali i maggiori sono onorati.
>
> A. F. Sempre veramente le più antiche famiglie sogliono esser in maggior venerazione.
>
> A. B. E quando l'antichità s'aggiunge a la nobiltà reale, sono quasi adorate, come aviene de' principi d'Este, i quali conservano con gran riputazione quello stato che da' for maggiori fu acquistato con gran valore.
>
> A. F. L'acquisto fu nobilissimo e la conservazione è onoratissima.   (4:520)

... whence nobles disdain in the living the same honors for which their ancestors are honored.

A. F. The oldest families are always wont to be held in the greater admiration.

A. B. And when one adds regal nobility to antiquity, they are almost adored, as happens with the princes of Este, who conserve with great repute the state that their ancestors acquired with great valor.

A. F. The acquisition was most noble and the conservation most honorable.

The Este, who originally won their state through the valor of arms, are not only the oldest, but, the text lets us infer, the noblest of Italian families: they clearly merit precedence over their *parvenu* Medici rivals.

Tasso never published the dialogue he specifically addressed to the conflict between the Este and the Medici, *Della precedenza*, though it has survived in manuscript.[32] The dialogue features the same speakers as *Il Forno* and appears to have been intended as a sequel to it. Tasso defends the precedence of Ferrara and her Duke, Alfonso II d'Este, not only over Florence and the Medici Grand Duke Francesco I but also over the Republic of Venice and her Doge. Comparing Florence and Ferrara, his speakers are willing to concede a possible Florentine superiority only in letters.

> Solo forse Ferrara a Firenze la gloria della poesia può invidiare: perciò, che non ha chi opporre al Boccaccio e mal può l'Ariosto a Dante paragonare; né al Petrarca ha chi opporre, se ben al Casa potrebbe opporre il Guarino; né co'l Guicciardino forse o co'l Machiavelli alcun Ferrarese può contendere. (497)

> Perhaps Ferrara may envy Florence only for the glory of poetry: inasmuch as she has no one to hold up against Boccaccio and Ariosto can ill be compared to Dante; nor does she have anyone to counter Petrarch, although Guarino could counter della Casa; nor perhaps could any Ferrarese compete with Guicciardini or with Machiavelli.

Tasso leaves himself out of this *paragone* of Ferrarese and Florentine men of letters, because of modesty and perhaps because he was not himself a native of Ferrara. We may nevertheless feel that he is the poet to compete with and to overgo Dante and Petrarch. But if mercantile Florence is conceded an

advantage in letters, chivalric Ferrara, with its "principe eroico" (495) is a
city of arms: "Firenze così attende alla mercantia come Ferrara alla vita
cavalleresca e militare" (496). The Venetians, inhabitants of another
commercial city, are similarly praised for prudence and eloquence, but
disparaged as soldiers—"prudentissimi ed eloquentissimi ma poco
guerrrieri" (488). The Duke of Ferrara rules over a less populous city, but
one whose citizens are accustomed to nobility and to the exercise of arms:
"molto più essercitato in maneggiare le armi e molto ardito nelle zuffe di
particolari e nelle guerre e non senza molta cognizione delle cose di
cavalleria per la pratica che ha con la nobiltà che nell'arte cavalleresca è
ammaestratissima" (490).[33] In fact, Alfonso is willing to defend his
precedence in single combat:

> E se nelle precedenze è alcuna considerazione la virtù eroica
> dell'animo e del corpo, Alfonso non solo a Francesco, ma a molti
> principi di lui maggiori deve senza contesa essere anteposto; e se
> la lite s'avesse con contesa a terminare, egli volentieri al giudicio
> della spada se ne rimetterebbe. (499)

> And if any consideration is given in questions of precedence to
> the heroic valor of the mind and body, Alfonso should without
> any contest be placed before not only Francesco but many
> princes greater than him; and if the dispute should have to be
> decided with battle, he would willingly submit himself to the
> judgment of the sword.

Continuing the military practices of their supposedly glorious feudal past,
the Este surpass in nobility the rulers of Florence and Venice—with their
more peaceable, republican and mercantile traditions—to the extent that
arms are nobler than letters, that martial valor is nobler than the intellectual
virtues of prudence and eloquence. To the extent, one might add, that an
Achilles or Ajax is nobler than a Ulysses.

For the pro-Este propaganda to which Tasso the courtier lent his pen
must have posed a dilemma for Tasso the poet of the *Gerusalemme liberata*.
He had written an epic that based its models of heroism on the debate
between Ulysses and Ajax in Ovid's *Metamorphoses*, and, in the figure of
Goffredo, had chosen to make its central and apparently most important
hero a Ulyssean hero of intelligence. The Ulysses of Ovid's debate had
dismissed as irrelevant his ancestry—although he made sure to trace his
genealogy on both paternal and maternal sides back to the gods—and he had

based his claims to heroic preeminence solely on his deeds, primarily on deeds of intellect and prudence: he thus pointedly opposed the claims of Ajax that were based on lineage and sheer martial prowess. The Ulyssean nature of Goffredo's heroism in the *Liberata* thus went directly against the prevailing ideology of nobility in Este Ferrara, an ideology that had a particular application in the precedence controversy with Florence. To exalt Goffredo over Rinaldo might seem to recognize the claims of a new nobility—like the Medicean upstarts themselves—a socially mobile class that could rise from non-noble origins through its intellectual talents and letters and whose clear representative in the poem is the devious, unwarlike Alete. Tasso, of course, draws back from the recognition of such claims—which may be the claims he could make for himself as a writer—by the snobbery with which he satirizes Alete and by the frequent inclination of his sympathies to the fighting man Rinaldo, the Este avatar. His poem incorporates its own version of the precedence controversy in its uncertainty about which of its heroes is the noblest of them all.

The presence of the Ovidian model behind the ideas of heroism in the *Liberata*, behind its systematic pairing and opposition of Ulyssean heroes of intelligence with Achillean heroes of force, may shed some light on the problem of the prose allegory that Tasso attached to his poem. In it he asserts that Goffredo represents the intellect and Rinaldo the irascible part of the tripartite human soul, and he cites Goffredo's dream where Ugone calls him the head and Rinaldo the right hand of the Crusader cause. There has been considerable controversy among scholars as to whether this allegory was composed *post-facto* when the *Liberata* was already substantially completed and when Tasso, it is presumed, was trying to appease the censors of the Roman inquisition, or whether the poet genuinely constructed his poem along allegorical lines.[34] A document that has been subject to divergent interpretations is a passage in Tasso's letter of June 1576 to Luca Scalabrino:

> Ma certo, o l'affezione m'inganna, tutte le parti de l'allegoria son in guisa legate fra loro, ed in maniera corrispondono al senso litterale del poema, ed anco a' miei principii poetici, che nulla più; ond'io dubito talora che non sia vero, che quando cominciai il mio poema avessi questo pensiero.[35]

> But certainly, or else my affection deceives me, all the parts of the allegory are so linked together among themselves and correspond in such a manner to the literal sense of the poem and also to my

> poetic principles, that they could not do more; whence I
> sometimes wonder whether it is not true that I had this thought
> when I began my poem.

It is difficult to determine the tone of this passage: is Tasso discovering that
all along he had been writing a poem with allegorical consistency, or is he
making a joke? Perhaps he is doing both at once. For the Ovidian debate
between Ulysses and Ajax had structured the *Liberata* into an extended
meditation on the relationship between heroic intellect and heroic force—or
between letters and arms. Even as Tasso concealed his Ovidian model by
suppressing the episode of Sveno's bleeding sword, he was transforming it
into the allegorical master plan of his epic.

NOTES

1. The passage is reprinted by Lanfranco Caretti as an appendix to his edition of the
Gerusalemme liberata (Milan, Mondadori, 1979), 598–99. It is discussed by Riccardo
Bruscagli in *Stagioni della civiltà estense* (Pisa: Nistri-Lischi, 1983), 215–16; see also
Lawrence Rhu, "From Aristotle to Allegory: Young Tasso's Evolving Vision of the
Gerusalemme liberata," *Italica* 65 (1988): 111–30.

2. Caretti, 599.

3. "La ventura de la spada dubito che senta del romanzo." Letter to Luca Scalabrino,
May 24, 1575. Tasso, *Lettere poetiche*, ed. Carla Molinari (Parma: Guanda, 1995), 89–90.
See also *Le lettere di Torquato Tasso*, ed. Cesare Guasti, 5 vol. (Florence: Le Monnier,
1852–1855), 1:81.

4. Citations from the *Metamorphoses* are taken from the Loeb Classical Library
edition, translated by Frank Justus Miller (Cambridge, Massachusetts and London:
Harvard Univ. Press, 1968), 2 vols. Matteo Residori has pointed out to me that the poet Il
Coppetta (Francesco Beccuti, 1503–1552) translated the Ovidian debate between Ulysses
and Ajax into Italian octaves; see G. Guidiccioni, F. Coppetta Beccuti, *Rime*; ed. Ezio
Chiorboli (Bari: Laterza, 1912), 255–70. Tasso seems to have read Il Coppetta, as he
begins his dialogue, *La Cavaletta*, with a criticism of one of the latter's sonnets; see Tasso,
Opere, ed. Bruno Maier (Milan: Rizzoli, 1965), 5:90–93. All citations of the *Liberata* and
from Tasso's published dialogues are taken from Maier's text. That Tasso had an early
interest in the Ovidian episode is attested by a note, "La contentione d'Aiace e d'Ulisse,"
that he added into the margin of a copy of the *Commentarii in primum librum Aristotelis de
arte poetarum* (1560) of Pier Vettori. See Claudio Scarpati, "Tasso, Sigonio, Vettori," in
Studi sul Cinquecento italiano (Milan: Vita e Pensiero, 1982), 156–200, esp. 166 n. 26.
Scarpati suggests that these notes appear to be tied to the composition of the youthful
Rinaldo (1562) and to the elaboration of Tasso's epic project. I am again grateful to Matteo
Residori for this reference.

5. These episodes are, of course, contaminated by other epic models. The embassy
of Alete and Argante to the Crusader camp concludes (2.89–90) with an imitation of the
declaration of war by the Roman envoys, Publicola and Fabius, to the Carthaginian senate
in the *Punica* of Silius Italicus (2.380f.). The *Punica* also contains a night-exploit (9.66–177)
that is an important, if little-noted model, for the duel between Clorinda and Tancredi; in

the darkness, Solimus unwittingly kills his father Satricus, and then commits suicide in turn: so Tancredi unknowingly slays the woman he loves. The night-exploit has a long history in epic after the Doloneia: from the Nisus and Euryalus subplot of *Aeneid* 9 to the Cloridano and Medoro episode in the *Orlando furioso* (18.165f.); all of these episodes find echoes in Tasso's version. For a discussion of the epic night-exploit from Virgil to Ariosto, see Barbara Pavlock, *Eros, Imitation and the Epic Tradition* (Ithaca and London: Cornell Univ. Press, 1990).

6. The parallels to the *Achilleid* are discussed by Beatrice Corrigan in "The Opposing Mirrors," *Italica* 33 (1956): 165–79.

7. Dante's Ulysses tells his men to pursue "virtute e conoscenza" (*Inf.* 26. 120). On Ubaldo and Ulysses, see David Quint, *Epic and Empire* (Princeton: Princeton Univ. Press, 1993), 262; Matteo Residori, "Colombo e il *volo* di Ulisse: una nota sul XV della *Liberata*," *Annali della Scuola Normale Superiore di Pisa, Classe di Lettere e Filosofia* 22 (1992): 931–42.

8. In her exchange with Vafrino, Erminia once again takes up the epic role of Helen that she has earlier played in Canto 3, where she pointed out the leading Crusader soldiers to King Aladino (17–20; 37–40; 58–63) in a scene that recalls Helen's conversation with Priam about the Greek host, the *teichoskopia* of *Iliad* 3.161f. In her designing or making the false insignias, Erminia is also like the Helen who is first seen weaving a robe depicting the events of the Trojan War in *Iliad* 3.125f. and also like Helen's antithesis in the *Odyssey*, the weaving Penelope, who, for all of her faithfulness, nonetheless shares with Helen a feminine craftiness that matches the wits of her husband, Ulysses. On the scene in *Odyssey* 4 and Helen's duplicity, see William S. Anderson, "Calypso and Elysium," *Classical Journal* 54 (1958): 2–11; Mihoko Suzuki, *Metamorphoses of Helen* (Ithaca and London: Cornell Univ. Press, 1989), 67–70.

9. In his dialogue *Il Manso ovvero de l'amicizia*, Tasso offers a gloss on the relationship of Ulysses and Diomede that may also describe the heroic coupling of Goffredo and Rinaldo in his own epic: "... i poeti antichi congiunsero ne' pericoli Ulisse e Diomede affinché la prudenza de l'uno aiutasse l'altro e vicendevolmente ricevesse aiuto da la fortezza de l'altro" (Tasso, *Opere*, 5:358–369).

Dante had placed Diomede and Ulysses together in a single, though divided flame in Hell in *Inferno* 26; he gives precedence to Ulysses, the "maggior corno" (85), and makes Diomede the silent partner in the canto. The two are punished for the fraud of the Trojan horse, for returning Achilles from Scyros, and for the theft of the Palladium (58–63); these are all events whose versions in the *Liberata*—Goffredo's siege machines, Carlo and Ubaldo's rescue of Rinaldo from Armida's island, the theft of the image of the Virgin from the Mosque for which Sofronia claims credit—are praiseworthy: the first two are essential to the taking of Jerusalem. Tasso's poem aims to celebrate, particularly in its central hero Goffredo, a Ulyssean heroism of the intellect *in bono*.

For a classic critical discussion of Dante's Ulysses as hero, see John Freccero, "Dante's Ulysses: From Epic to Novel," in *Dante: The Poetics of Conversion* (Cambridge, Massachusetts and London: Harvard Univ. Press, 1986), 136–51.

10. See Maier's notes to this passage in his edition of the *Gerusalemme liberata* in *Opere* 3:9.

11. Goffredo's actions most clearly repeat those of *Aeneas* (*Aeneid* 7.157–59; 1.198–203), whom Ovid may recall as well in these words of his Ulysses. But the "O socii" speech of Virgil's hero itself imitates the speech of Homer's Ulysses to his men at *Odyssey* 12.209f.; in turn, Dante, who did not know the *Odyssey*, would imitate the speech of Aeneas in the "orazion piccola" that *his* Ulysses uses to spur his men on into unknown seas (*Inf.* 26.112f.). By Tasso's arrival in the literary tradition, the eloquent, prudential dimension of

Aeneas was thus easily recognized as Ulyssean: insofar as Goffredo is an Aeneas-like hero whose sphere of action is limited to that of commander and strategist he is also a kind of Ulysses; see below. On Dante's triangulation of Virgil and the Homer he could not read, see Freccero, *Dante: The Poetics of Conversion*, 140–45; David Thompson, *Dante's Epic Journeys* (Baltimore: The Johns Hopkins Univ. Press, 1974); Giuseppe Mazzotta, *Dante, Poet of the Desert* (Princeton: Princeton Univ, Press, 1979), 89–90, 100–102.

12. Compare the depiction of the siege machine at 18.45 and its model, the description by Virgil's Aeneas of the Trojan Horse at *Aeneid* 2.235f. At 2.46 and 2.237, Virgil himself describes the horse as a "machina."

13. The honey-tongued Nestor was traditionally paired with Ulysses on account of their eloquence. So Ovid's Ajax compares Ulysses to Nestor (13.63–65). See also Horace *Odes* 1.15.21–22; Quintilian, *Inst.* 12.10.64–65; and, for Renaissance examples, Poliziano, *Manto* 23–24, referring to the oratory of Cicero, "pyliae non mella senectae / Nec jam dulichias audet conferre procellas;" and Shakespeare's Gloucester, the future Richard III, speaking of himself in *Henry VI*, Part 3: "I'll play the orator as well as Nestor / Deceive more slyly than Ulysses could" (3.2.188–89). Ovid, *Ars Amatoria* 2.736, juxtaposes the wisdom of Nestor with the might of Achilles. Tasso assigns Nestor's trait of honeyed eloquence to the ambassador Alete (2.61.5–6).

14. In general, Argante plays out the role of Hector in he *Iliad*, while Solimano, the other male pagan champion, assumes that of Turnus in the *Aeneid*. Solimano the Turk, whose descendant will be Saladin—and perhaps will find another embodiment in Suleyman the Magnificent—has a historical dimension that Argante lacks and hence he is fitted out with a Virgilian typology as an enemy of Rome, modelled after Turnus and after the Hannibal of the *Punica* of Silius Italicus; on this latter point, see Quint, *Epic and Empire*, 112, 384 n. 22. Argante is a more purely literary figure; he is assimilated both to Hector—and in Tasso's revised epic, the *Gerusalemme conquistata*, he will even be given a wife and infant son to play Andromache and Astyanax (22.51f.)—and to Ariosto's Rodomonte. Argante's death (19.21f.), however, like Rodomonte's, is a rewriting of the death of Turnus at the end of the *Aeneid*; see Lauren Scancarelli Seem, "The Limits of Chivalry: Tasso and the end of the *Aeneid*," *Comparative Literature* 42 (1990): 116–25.

15. For an analysis of this episode, see Timothy Hampton, *Writing from History* (Ithaca and London: Cornell Univ. Press, 1990), 94–110. Hampton shows how Raimondo's hesitation to finish Argante off (7.94–95) parallels Goffredo's later mistake in Canto 11, where he attempts to take Jerusalem without armor and without Rinaldo. Thus Raimondo, no less than Goffredo—both of them figures of prudential wisdom in the epic—are subject to error. On the later episode see Riccardo Bruscagli, "L'errore di Goffredo (G. L. XI)," *Studi tassiani* 40–41 (1992–1993): 207–32.

16. Rhu, "From Aristotle to Allegory," 125, notes that the rivalry between Goffredo and Rinaldo over the sword of Sveno "threatens to undermine the allegorical hierarchy" of the *Liberata*.

17. Thomas Greene distinguishes "executive" and "deliberative" scenes and heroism in epic poetry in *The Descent from Heaven* (New Haven and London: Yale Univ. Press, 1963) 12–21; see also James Nohrnberg, *The Analogy of "The Faerie Queene"* (Princeton: Princeton Univ. Press, 1976), 58–65. In *The Best of the Achaeans* (Baltimore and London: The Johns Hopkins Univ. Press, 1979) Gregory Nagy takes as the starting point for his discussion of archaic Greek heroism the passage in Demodokos's song in the *Odyssey* (8.75–82) that describes a quarrel between Achilles and Ulysses; see especially pp. 42–58.

18. See Michael Murrin, *History and Warfare in Renaissance Epic* (Chicago and London: Univ. of Chicago Press, 1994), 179–96, for a discussion of how the methods and conduct

of early modern war changed the way in which epic poetry represented battle: the commanding officers achieved new prominence. For Tasso's Goffredo, see pp. 194–96.

19. See Bruscagli, "L'errore di Goffredo," 213, 223; Fredi Chiappelli, *Il conoscitore di caos* (Rome: Bulzoni, 1981), 110–15. For an early seventeenth-century analysis of Goffredo as a hero, who like Aeneas, combines the attributes of Achilles and Ulysses, see the *Comparazione di Omero, Virgilio, e Torquato* (1607) of Paulo Beni, reprinted in *Controversie sulla Gerusalemme liberata* (Pisa: Niccolò Capurro, 1828), 4:146f. I am grateful to Matteo Residori for this reference.

20. Quint, *Epic and Empire*, 213–47.

21. Tasso, *Opere*, 4:507.

22. In the *Discorsi* (1585) of Annibale Romei, written in Tasso's Ferrarese ambience, the seventh and final dialogue on the precedence of arms and letters eventually identifies the profession of letters—including philosophy, poetry, oratory—with the jurisconsult: the lawyer Cati who takes up this argument not only argues for the subordination of arms to the rule of law, and hence to princely or civic authority, but also, in a remarkable passage condemns war itself: "E io dirò all'incontro, che l'arme sono al mondo di maggior travaglio, che d'ornamento, sendo elle principio dell'occupar i beni altrui, e di metter le città libere in dura servitù, sforzando il più delle volte uomini savi obedir alla pazzia degli atrocissimi tiranni. Dirò ancora, che per abuso e ingiustamente si drizzano statue, si danno corone e i trionfi a' vincitori guerrieri; perché qual può esser maggior abuso e cosa più inumana, che cercar la grandezza e la gloria dalle uccisioni, dagli incendi, dagli stupri, dai sacrilegi, dalle rapine, e finalmente trionfare delle miserie umane?" (277). One feels here, as elsewhere in the *Discorsi* the presence of what Norbert Elias has called the "civilizing process" overtaking an aristocratic society that nonetheless liked to think of itself in feudal, chivalric terms. For the final verdict on the day's debate, although split, is delivered in favor of the profession of arms. Romei's text is reprinted by Angelo Solerti in *Ferrara e la corte estense nella seconda metà del secolo decimosesto* (Città di Castello: Lapi, 1900). For a discussion of Romei's work, see Stefano Prandi, *Il "Cortegiano ferrarese: i "Discorsi" di Annibale Romei e la cultura nobiliare nel cinquecento* (Florence, Leo S. Olschki, 1990); for the issue of arms and letters and the nature of nobility, see pp. 185–210.

23. *The Book of the Courtier*, trans. Charles S. Singleton (Garden City, New York: Anchor Books, 1959), 289.

24. *Il gentilhuomo* (Venice, 1575), 238.

25. *Il gentilhuomo*, 21: "Et per parlar della Eugenia, et della Nobiltà, dico che molto più honorevole è questo, che quel nome, che in quello antichità di sangue, & in questo chiarezza di virtù si comprende."

26. See Maier's notes, *Opere* 3:64, which suggest an identification of Alete with Giovani Battista Pigna or Antonio Montecatini.

27. On Ubaldo, Goffredo, and mercantile commerce, see Quint, *Epic and Empire*, 262–64. For the disdain towards such commerce in Este Ferrara see the report of the Florentine diplomat, Orazio dalla Rena, cited in Solerti, *Ferrara e la corte estense*, lix.

28. On the dissimulation that links Armida to Sofronia, Erminia, even Clorinda, and Alete, see the studies of Sergio Zatti, "Il linguaggio della dissimulazione nella *Gerusalemme liberata*," in *Forma e parola: studi in memoria di Fredi Chiappelli*, ed. Dennis Dutschke, et al. (Rome: Bulzoni, 1992), 423–47, and Francesco Erspamer, "Il 'pensiero debole' di Torquato Tasso," in *La Menzogna*, ed. Franco Cardini (Florence: Ponte alle Grazie, 1989), 120–36.

29. For a discussion of the arguments over nobility that were employed by the Ferrarese and Florentine adversaries in the precedence controversy see Robert Williams,

"The Façade of the *Palazzo dei 'Visacci,'*" *I Tatti Studies* 5 (1993): 209–44, esp. 231–38. See also Venceslao Santi, "La precedenza tra gli Estensi e i Medici e *l'Historia dei principi d'Este* di G. Battista Pigna," *Atti e memorie della R. Deputazione di Storia Patria Ferrarese* 9 (1897): 37–122.

30. Tasso, *Opere*, 4:585–86. Williams, 233–34 n. 71, notes that the Florentine Filippo Valori singled out this work as well as Muzio's *Il gentilhuomo* for their disparaging treatment of Florence. See the opening of Valori's *Termini di mezzo rilievo e d'intera dottrina tra gli archi di casa Valori* (1604), reprinted in Filippo Villano, *De Famosis civibus ...*, ed. G. C. Galletti (Florence, 1847), 251. The offending passage in *Il gentilhuomo* appears to have been the following anecdote, 115–16, mocking the Florentines' lack of nobility told by the wellborn Eugenio who is himself a Florentine: "Fra noi si recita, che passando per quà uno Ambasciatore del Re di Francia, il quale andava a Roma, & essendosi fermato per non so che poco male, che gli haveva in una natica, fatto forse cavalcando, fu medicato da un barbiere. Et guarito, havendo havuto commissione dal suo Re di trattare alcuna cosa con questa Republica, si abbattè ad andare alla Signoria, che quel suo barbiere era fatto de' Signori. & entrato nel luogo della udienza, & raffigurato colui seder pro tribunali, volte le spalle se ne uscì dicendo, Non voler far relatione delle ambasciate del Re al medico del suo culo. *Nobile.* Adunque colui non riconosceva per nobile, tutto che quivi sedesse come Signore."

31. On the disputed title of "serenissimo," in the precedence controversy, see Quint, *Epic and Empire*, 227, 400 n. 38. In the dedicatory letter of the *Forno* written to Scipione Gonzaga in 1586, Tasso says that he originally wrote the work in 1579 to celebrate the marriage of Margherita Gonzaga to Duke Alfonso II d'Este. Freed from the imprisonment in which the Este had kept him for seven years and outside of their jurisdiction in Mantua, he now revised the dialogue to honor the marriage of Cesare d'Este to Virginia de'Medici, an event that signaled an uneasy truce in the feud between the two families and their cities. Noting that he would not keep silent "quel che allora non mi fu conceduto scriver de la casa de' Medici" (4:428), Tasso included a fulsome encomium of the Medici noting that they could lay claim, to a valor as high as that possessed by "gli antichi eroi di cui si fa menzione in questi dialoghi, o ne' principi e cavalieri moderni." As a further diplomatic gesture (429–30), he argued that the highest nobility lies in the soul's conserving the image of the divine in itself, and it is the souls of the religious that do this best: there are none nobler than the late Cardinal Ippolito d'Este, Cardinal Ferdinando de' Medici (the future Duke), and, from his patron's own family, Cardinal Giovan Vincenzo Gonzaga. In God all are equally noble, though some are more equal than others. Scipione Gonzaga himself was an ecclesiastic who aimed at the cardinalship that he would receive a year later in 1587.

32. The text of *Della precedenza* is printed by Ezio Raimondi in his critical edition of Tasso's *Dialoghi* (Florence: Sansoni, 1968), 3:471–506.

33. What was the social reality behind this claim? The Ferrarese did at least affect chivalry and the way of life of a soldierly nobility. Della Rena, cited in Solerti, *Ferrara e la corte estense*, lix, takes the sardonic Florentine view that it was all a painted façade: "hanno assai amore in tener vita cavalleresca come principal loro professione, ma però non sono molto vaghi d'impiegarla in guerra; lor fine è di esser tenuti signori da splendore e gentiluomini di gran portata. Tengon quei che hanno il modo niente niente dei cavalli in stalla, e cavalcano e armeggiano bene. Universalmente tutti, piccoli e grandi, portan la spada a canto, infiniti più per ornamento della vita che per occasion di far del male, perché sono amici della pace e rare sono le questioni e rarissimi gli omicidi che ne seguono.

Cercan sempre tutte le strade di parer cavalieri, a che s'aiutano ancora col farsi dipinger tali; ché ho osservato in molte imagini di private e mediocri persone aver visto dal ritratto, che, se non mi fosse stato detto il nome, arei pensato esser l'imagine di un Achille o di un Ettore, cosí fregiate d'oro son le dipinte armature del Dosso...."

34. The argument that Tasso's allegory was built into the composition of the *Liberata* is advanced by Michael Murrin in *The Allegorical Epic* (Chicago and London, 1980), 87–127; see also Rhu, "From Aristotle to Allegory;" Lucia Olini, "Dalle direzioni di lettura alla revisione del testo: Tasso tra 'Allegoria del Poema' e *Giudizio*," *La rassegna della letteratura italiana* 7 (1985): 53–68. For a counter-argument, see Walter Stephens, "Metaphor, Sacrament and the Problem of Allegory in *Gerusalemme Liberata*," *I Tatti Studies* 4 (1991): 217–47. An earlier, related discussion is found in William Kennedy, "The Problem of Allegory in Tasso 's *Gerusalemme Liberata*," *Italian Quarterly* 15–16 (1972): 27–51.

35. *Le lettere di Torquato Tasso*, ed. Guasti, 1:185.

ALBERTO CASADEI

The History of the *Furioso*

1

The 1974 celebrations marking the five hundredth anniversary of Ariosto's birth also signified the beginning of a renewed and urgent interest in studying, independently of one another, the three versions of the *Furioso* (printed in 1516, 1521, and 1532). Before these celebrations, studies had been conducted on this crucial problem pertaining to the understanding of the poem, which were further justified by the release of a critical edition in 1960. However, many of these early studies attempted to demonstrate the superiority of the last version (1532) without offering an objective and systematic analysis of each of the first two against the final version. The emphasis of those investigations, instead, always dealt with the variations (that is, modifications) among the three versions, paying greatest attention to the final result, as opposed to the initial motivation for writing the poem.

Attempts at analysing the variations among the versions by commentators and scholars like Ludovico Dolce and Giovan Battista Nicolucci, who was nicknamed 'il Pigna,' were recorded as early as the sixteenth century. Nicolucci made a list of changes identified among the various versions of the *Furioso* in his *Scontri de' luoghi mutati dall'autore ...*, found in the third book of *I romanzi*, published in Venice in 1554, while Girolomo Ruscelli, in the preface to the *Furioso* which he edited (Venice,

From *Ariosto Today: Contemporary Perspectives*, eds. Donald Beecher, Massimo Ciavolella, and Roberto Fedi. © 2003 by the University of Toronto Press Incorporated.

1556), claimed among other things to have seen a copy of the poem dating back to 1532, corrected by Ariosto himself in anticipation of a fourth edition that was never completed due to Ariosto's death on 6 July 1533. Quite apart from the imprecision of many of these attempts to record and study the variations, they at least manifested an interest in matters linguistic and stylistic; their purpose in fact was to demonstrate the increased 'purity' of the language, or the improved rhetorical construction of the third edition. This manner of analysis was predictable during a period in which the rules of the classicists had already become very rigid.

Such comparisons were re-proposed frequently until the end of the nineteenth century, after which time the study of variations became much more systematic. It was at the beginning of the twentieth century that this approach to the study of the three editions attained interesting new dimensions with the volume *Le correzioni all' 'Orlando furioso'* written by Maria Diaz (even though errors were still present). Further importance was given to this type of research by the re-publication of the first two versions of the poem, edited by Filippo Ermini on behalf of the Roman Philological Society (1909–11), and above all by the publication, approximately twenty years later, of *I frammenti autografi dell' 'Orlando furioso,'* edited by Santorre Debenedetti (1937). Even though this latter work presented only variations among the manuscripts and the last printed version, this masterful edition gave rise to numerous studies. The first of these was the celebrated article by Gianfranco Contini, entitled 'Come lavorava l'Ariosto' (1937) [How Ariosto Worked], in which he presented certain fundamental principles regarding the methods to be adopted when examining the variations.

Contini's methodologies have been used subsequently in many studies concerned with both the stylistic and the structural aspects of the *Furioso*. During the 1960s, aside from the publication of the critical edition of the poem, many other contributions were made that, once again, turned the attention of scholars to the importance of a diachronic study of the three versions. In particular, two works by Carlo Dionisotti on the *Cinque canti* (an attempt at a continuation of the poem written by Ariosto probably between 1519 and 1521, though published posthumously: see section 4.2 below), demonstrated, among other things, that the many phases of the formulation of the *Furioso* could not be reduced to a progression towards perfection, and that the version of 1516, on its own, is 'un capolavoro assoluto' [an absolute masterpiece] (Dionisotti *Appunti* 375).

In the years leading up to the 500th anniversary of Ariosto's birth, various hypotheses pertaining to the interpretations of the three versions of the work were advanced. In 1974, in Ferrara, the distinguished scholar

Lanfranco Caretti, in a presentation later published with the title *Codicillo*, reversed his prior beliefs in the matter by asserting that the revisions to the third *Furioso* were made in response to the political chaos provoked by the battles between the French and the Imperialists in Italy, and were tantamount to a form of 'rinascimento letterario' [literary renaissance] (Caretti 107). The first *Furioso*, by contrast, came into being in a more tranquil historical era. Two years later, Cesare Segre affirmed instead that, notwithstanding the additions and the variations, the *Furioso* of 1532 remained, substantially, that of 1516, and that Ariosto did little more through his revisions than improve certain formal aspects of the poem (cf. 'Introduzione' to Ariosto, *Orlando furioso*, ed. C. Segre: xxviii–xxx).

These different points of view (the first predominantly historical-ideological, the second structural-formal) must be examined more closely to understand their respective motivations (see section 5). In the meantime, it is necessary to add that in 1974 an interpretation of the entire poem appeared that considered both the changes and the elements of continuity between the three versions. This study appears in the essay 'Il "soggetto" del *Furioso*' by Eduardo Saccone (in a volume with the same name, 201–7). This essay provided an innovative avenue of inquiry that was later developed predominantly in the United States.

Yet, despite his own work, Saccone remained of the conviction (see 'Le maniere' 95–111) that between 1970 and 1990 very little had been done to examine further the question of the relationship between the versions. Subsequently, in addition to the important 'Introduzione' by Emilio Bigi in his annotated edition of the *Furioso* (1982), an extensive profile of *Orlando furioso* edited by Corrado Bologna was published in 1993. Nevertheless, many problems that could only be resolved by specific research have long been postponed, and only recently have new contributions on the evolution of the poem been proposed (see Casadei, *Il percorso*, and the new annotated edition of the *Furioso* by Remo Ceserani and Sergio Zatti).

In order to pursue the issues briefly outlined above, our critical considerations (to be examined in sections 3 to 5) will include the following:

a) the structural features of the *Furioso* of 1516 and its relation to the chivalric genre
b) the structural features of the *Furioso* of 1521 and the function of the *Cinque canti*
c) changes made to the *Furioso* of 1532 and their effect on the original project

Before continuing with this discussion it is necessary to deal with the period of composition of the poem to better understand the factors that lead Ariosto to write a sequel to the *Orlando innamorato* (Orlando in Love) written by Boiardo.

2.1

In all probability Ariosto began working on the *Furioso* around 1504–5. It is commonly accepted that he narrated a fair bit of the poem to Isabella d'Este, wife of Francesco Gonzaga, during the first part of 1507. It is noted that on 3 February of that year Isabella wrote from Mantua to her brother Ippolito, to whom Ariosto had dedicated the poem, to let him know that the narration of the new episodes of Orlando and the Paladins had given her great pleasure. Other information about the composition of the *Furioso* is documented in subsequent years, up to September of 1515, when preparations had begun for the first publication of the *Furioso*—which was completed by 22 April 1516.

Even before he decided to undertake a sequel to the *Innamorato*, Ariosto had begun a composition in tercets (the metre of Dante's *Divine Comedy*), now identified by the title *Obizzeide* (in Ariosto *Opere minori* 164–71; cf. Casadei *Il percorso* 23–34). It was an incomplete text of 211 verses, in which homage was paid to a descendent of the Estes, the lords of Ferrara, under whose patronage the poet had perhaps just been enlisted and for whom this rough draft was written for purely encomiastic reasons. This text best qualifies under the heading historical epic, which, following the model set out by Virgil's *Aeneid*, sings the praises of a noble family. Among the recent poems in the genre was the *Borsias*, an important poem in Latin, well known to Ariosto, written near the end of the fifteenth century by another Estense courtier, Tito Vespasiano Strozzi. It is important to note that in the *Obizzeide* the epic material was fused with the earliest material from the Breton chivalric tradition ('Canterò l'armi, canterò gli affanni / d'amor ...' in which 'love and war' are spoken of, as they are in the *Innamorato* and the *Furioso*. Clearly, Ariosto had already chosen to deal with this topic from the outset of the sixteenth century, a task that risked appearing rather commonplace. During that period, in fact, the most innovative works, such as the *Arcadia* written by Jacopo Sannazaro and Pietro Bembo's *Asolani*, were very different from the poems of love and war, which reached their greatest success in the previous century. Why, then, did Ariosto decide to continue the *Innamorato*?

2.2

Boiardo's fame was still current, when, in 1505, the first sequel to the *Innamorato*, the *Quarto libro* by Niccolò degli Agostini, was published in Venice. It was, however, mainly a commercial undertaking directed at a large audience, one that no longer paid homage to the great House of Este. For this reason, a need was felt for a Ferrarese courtier to continue the adventures of Ruggiero, whom Boiardo had conceived as the founder of the Este dynasty.

In 1505 Ariosto had just begun his *Furioso*, an undertaking that was immediately acknowledged with great favour by the noble court. However, it must be noted that he chose to continue the *Innamorato* for other reasons too, for in that epic he saw a text with great potential, both in terms of its content as well as on a formal level. As many modern critics have pointed out, Ariosto was highly proficient at rewriting earlier literary works; in the *Innamorato* he found at his disposal all the material necessary for writing a piece in the chivalric tradition (cf. the article by Franceschetti in this volume), but more importantly he found many interrupted episodes that could not only be concluded but could also be reinterpreted. Thus, Ariosto was able to combine classical and modern models, and conclude episodes conceived by Boiardo by using perhaps Ovid or Virgil; at the same time, he could add touches of irony or parody, or introduce levels of allegory. Each of these processes has been studied in recent years (cf. Marinelli, Sangirardi), affirming that the *Furioso* maintains a very close relationship with the *Innamorato*, while it draws less on fifteenth-century poems of chivalry (the exception being the *Morgante* of Luigi Pulci). It is important to determine how Ariosto, beginning with the 1516 edition, distinguishes his epic from that written by Boiardo.

3.1

The first *Furioso* was divided into forty cantos instead of the forty-six found in the last version. In 1532, in fact, episodes dealing with Orlando and Olympia (cantos 9–11), with the Rocca of Tristano (32–3), with Marganorre (37), and with Ruggiero and Leone (44–6) were inserted into the structure of the poem, for a total of more than seven hundred stanzas (cf. 'Tavola comparativa,' in Ariosto *I frammenti* 157–60). The 1516 version was published by Giovanni Mazocco dal Bondeno, who had been an active printer for some time in Ferrara before the printing of the *Furioso*. The best paper was requested and the run was of approximately 1300 copies (cf. Fahy

97–101). Rather close attention was paid even to the format, which included some extremely innovative aspects for a chivalric poem, such as precise indications of the beginnings and endings of each canto. Furthermore, there appeared a xylograph (depicting bees being removed from a tree stump with fire) and various figurative elements linked to a motto ('Pro bono malum,' meaning 'Evil instead of good' or 'Evil in return for good'), which has given rise to many interpretations (Fahy 116–18).

Finally, as far as the language of the text is concerned, it can be said that the first version contains a fair number of dialectal traits, and specifically non-Tuscan traits (at the time of Ariosto, Tuscan was already the basis for Italian poetic language). Nonetheless, these dialectal forms are significantly less frequent than they are in the *Innamorato* or in the *Mambriano*, another Ferrarese poem of that period. Angelo Stella, one of the most important contemporary scholars of Ariostian stylistics, has noted that, notwithstanding certain variations, the 1516 version already shows marked differences from the more typical forms of the Padua area (cf. Stella 49–64). In short, Ariosto was seeking to distinguish himself from his predecessors in the first *Furioso* by directing his attention decisively toward the Tuscan language, even though he did not always make correct use of its forms—understandably so, given the lack of clear and unambiguous grammatical norms. It is also likely that some of the non-Tuscan vocabulary was used consciously for its particular expressive and comical value.

From a metric-syntactic perspective, at least three major differences with respect to the *Innamorato* are clearly evident. a rare use of hendecasyllables with accents on the fourth and seventh syllables, which give an unpleasant rhythm and stress; a syntactic division of the octave according to even measurements (in other words, phrases are developed respecting the couplets that make up the octave); and an abundant use of hypotaxis, that is, of subordination, which allows for the creation of syntactic periods of four and sometimes six verses. All this generates a noticeable change in the development of the narration, which results in a much more fluid and flowing verse with respect to Boiardo's original. With the use of enjambements, Ariosto proposed certain modifications to the successive versions (cf. section 4.1), as has been noted by the most authoritative scholars on metrical matters. Yet even in this case the differences with respect to his predecessors are stronger than those with respect to the second and third version of the *Furioso*.

Moreover, it should be noted that many fundamental rhetorical devices (for example, the use of diphthongs or enumeration) were in full evidence in the first edition as a result of the influence of Petrarch, whom Ariosto will utilize as a model with greater frequency (though often subjecting him to polite parody).

It is only through a careful analysis of the first *Furioso* that one may be able to further delineate these aspects. It is nonetheless possible to state that by 1516 the linguistic-rhetorical features of the poem were already well defined and were the results of choices that Ariosto never completely changed, even if he corrected them at various times (cf. section 5.1). It is necessary, now, to examine the entire structure of the text to see just how much the episodes added in 1532 changed it.

3.2

In effect, the structure of the first *Furioso* cannot be derived by simply removing the episodes mentioned above from the third version. Aside from the fact that there exist about ten stanzas that were eliminated primarily for political reasons (cf. Casadei *La strategia* 73–7) and a few other additions made in 1521 (cf. section 4.1), the insertion of the adventures of Ruggiero and Leone creates a distancing of parts of the text that are otherwise tightly linked. The 1516 edition concluded quite differently from that of 1532, as can be seen through a brief analysis of the episodes.

It was detected some time ago that the concluding section of the *Furioso* is of an epic nature, beginning at least from the battle of Lipadusa (41.68ff.) and extending to the final duel between Ruggiero and Rodomonte (46.101–40). However, in this section, as in the entire poem, one can distinguish an alternation of 'epic' episodes, involving widespread references to the *Aeneid* and to the *chansons de geste*, in which the narration of the adventures and quests of the Paladins prevails. This alternation assumes, in the end, a particular significance, because the episodes are extremely dense with allusive meaning.

In the first *Furioso* the long sequence in which Rinaldo is the protagonist (42.28ff.) was placed just before the last canto of the poem, and was presented as a sort of 'comment' on all the scenes, beginning with those linked by 'la pazzia d'amore,' the madness of love. Rinaldo, in fact, having freed himself from the rage caused by his jealousy of Angelica, faces various tests of his wisdom, from which he learns that 'there is little point in seeking what one does not wish to find' (cf. 43.6.3–4) ['non conviene cercare quello che non si vorrebbe trovare']. This is, clearly, an ironical formulation, with a Horatian flavour, which is still present in the 1532 version. However, in the first version of the *Furioso* these and other concluding considerations drawn by Rinaldo constitute a type of 'morality' (as in fairy tales) with an emblematic value, precisely because they almost directly precede the last canto of the poem (40).

In this last canto all the narrative plots left unresolved unravel themselves one after the other: the Paladins believe everyone to be in Paris; Astolfo frees the hippogryph; and the marriage of Ruggiero and Bradamante is finally celebrated with a great feast at the court of Charlemagne. The latter situation brings the entire story back to the beginning of the *Innamorato*, which opens with the king at a banquet with his Paladins—a sort of 'circular closing' of all the *romantic* episodes, which however constitutes only a momentary *happy ending*.

In fact, the return of Rodomonte and his subsequent duel with Ruggiero (of an epic nature, as it is modelled after the duel between Enea and Turno that concludes the *Aeneid*) causes a sharp rupture in the apparently tranquil concluding section. It is in this battle undertaken by Ruggiero against death that the first *Furioso* suddenly demonstrates all the anxiety and anguish that up to that point seemed to have been exorcised from the text. In the first version, this episode was substantially dominated by irony; the mixing of the epic and the 'romanzesco' of the comic and the tragic was always very clever and monitored. In the 1532 version the themes of tension increase throughout the progression of the text and the ending is profoundly modified (cf. section 5.2). However, before we can speak of the last version of the text, it is necessary to pause a moment to look at the text of 1521 and the *Cinque canti*.

4.1

The second version of the *Furioso* was published in Ferrara, on 13 February 1521, by the press of Giovanni Battista da la Pigna, a Milanese printer of whom there are no other known publications. This version was prepared in a great hurry, as we learn from a letter dated 8 November 1520 to Mario Equicola, a learned courtier from Mantua, to whom Ariosto writes that the first version had been sold out, though he does not speak of having prepared a new one. Thus this version was published in a few weeks, with very little revision of the proofs. For this reason, this edition appears to contain many more errors than the first, as is also demonstrated by a long *Errata-corrige* drawn up by Ariosto himself. This printing was somewhat limited: of the perhaps five hundred copies only three survive today, in comparison to the twelve copies of the first edition and the twenty–four or more of the final version (cf. Fahy 101-2).

To this edition Ariosto added eleven stanzas, while removing as many, and corrected 2912 of the 32,944 verses (cf. Ariosto, *Orlando furioso*, ed. Debenedetti, 3:397–405; also cf. Catalano 1:530 n. 27). In many cases these corrections were due to specific errors, that is, those located in a specific area of the text. Ariosto also conducted more general corrections, which will be briefly considered.

The second *Furioso* does not change significantly at the textual level. Nonetheless, from a linguistic perspective one notes the elimination of certain dialectal forms from the Po Valley, which were present in the edition of 1516, and also the elimination of numerous Latinisms, that is, forms derived directly from Latin that do not correspond to Tuscan forms. Furthermore, expressions that were considered too base, common, or comic (often taken from the *Innamorato*), were also eliminated. Evidently, these words were no longer considered dignified, hence were inappropriate for a refined audience. In effect, rules having to do with proper etiquette were becoming more rigid during this period, and for this reason many words that were considered far too explicit were eliminated from conversation and banned from use in poetry (Mazzacurati 15–64). Above all, between 1516 and 1521 Ariosto improved his knowledge of Tuscan by spending time in Florence and Siena (as he states in the Prologue to the play *Il negromante*, completed in 1520), and by further emulating literary models such as those he found in the works of Petrarch and Boccaccio.

From a metric-syntactic perspective, one encounters at least two important changes with respect to the first edition: the elimination of a fair number of enjambements, which created unpleasant rhythms, and the correction of several phrases that were unclear because they contained too many subordinate clauses. As far as the first phenomenon is concerned, one can observe that Ariosto became much more sensitive to the 'prosaic' effects of certain enjambements after having employed them in his *Satire* (written beginning 1517), specifically to obtain a colloquial tone nearly resembling everyday conversation. As far as the second phenomenon is concerned, Ariosto had, by 1516, attempted to distinguish his work from previous chivalric poems, which made frequent use of parataxis (the placing of related clauses in a series without connecting words), thus increasing the hypotaxis. This procedure sometimes produced an imbalance in the rhythm of the stanzas, and while, in 1521, Ariosto wanted to improve this aspect (as we have seen with respect to enjambements), he decided also to correct the syntax where necessary. The structural changes were, by contrast, very few. Often stanzas were added only to better explain certain particulars of the story that were unclear or incongruous. In one case, though, the inserted stanzas are of a particular interest: they are the ones that deal with the battle of Lipadusa (cf. 42.20–2), in which the narrator speaks directly to a real character, the noble Federico Fregoso, in response to an objection he had regarding the verisimilitude of the story. It is a meta-narrative response that befits the ironic mode of dealing with chivalric material, which has already been discussed in relation to the first *Furioso*.

In its totality, the appearance of the second version presented several 'linee correttorie' [corrective lines], corresponding to Ariosto's new linguistic and literary experiences, thereby making it clear that the *Furioso* was, in all of its phases, a 'work in progress.' In comparison to the version of 1516, the unmodified part of the 1521 text is far superior to the modified part. This second version was prepared in haste, and did not completely correspond to the project of expansion envisioned by its author. In effect, the second *Furioso* would have been quite different if the poet had completed an additional section, of which only the *Cinque canti* remain.

4.2

The fragment, composed of five cantos, was published posthumously for the first time in 1545, in the appendix of an edition of the *Furioso* released by the famous Venetian typographer Manuzio. A second publication, with the addition of several stanzas and various corrections, was printed in 1548 by another important Venetian publisher, Giolito. Apart from these two editions, the fragment itself was handed down from a manuscript belonging to one of Ariosto's relatives during the mid-sixteenth century, and it is currently preserved in the Public Library of Ferrara.

Cesare Segre, who is responsible for the preparation of the modern-day critical edition of the *Cinque canti* (see Ariosto *Opere minori* 583–754), was the first to attest to the authenticity of the fragment, which previously had been greatly debated (Segre *Studi* 150–1). As far as the date of composition is concerned, in 1960 Carlo Dionisotti (see 'Per la data' 1–40) maintained that the fragment was first conceived in 1519–21, even though Ariosto reworked and corrected it at least until 1526–8, as is demonstrated by the linguistic forms analysed by Segre (*Studi* 165–7).

The interpretation of these cantos depends, above all, on the use Ariosto wanted to make of them. According to some critics, they constitute a new poem, different from the *Furioso* (Beer 143–9), but in reality the links with the latter are very strong, so much so that one can show precise similarities between certain stanzas. It is one of these similarities that has allowed us recently to demonstrate that Ariosto intended to place these cantos after the last canto (40) of the 1516 version, thus expanding his poem

(Casadei *Il percorso* 13–127). This view corresponds entirely to what the poet himself had written in one of his letters to Mario Equicola, dated 15 October 1519, in which he speaks of 'un poco di giunta' [a brief addition] that he was composing for the *Furioso* (almost all present-day scholars refer to the *Cinque canti* using this expression).

This fragment narrates battles involving all of the principal Paladins, as well as the citizens and kings of all of Europe, battles caused by the intrigues woven by Gano Maganza (he who betrays Orlando) and by the sorceress Alkane. Ariosto was clearly proposing a theme common to chivalric poems of the fifteenth century, specifically that of the snares created by Gano to trap the Paladins, which had been given very little space in the *Furioso*. However, in the *Innamorato* Boiardo had written (3.i.3) that Ruggiero would be killed by Gano, and Ariosto reiterates this prophecy in his poem (41.61–2). In other words, in these cantos he was planning a continuation of the story he had found in the *Innamorato*, even though in all probability he would not have described Ruggiero's death, as many years would have had to pass before this occurrence (41.61.3–4).

Hence, this augmentation was authorized by Ariosto's original plan, 'nell'antico progetto complessivo' [in the old overall project], even though the tone of the fragment is very different from that of the *Furioso*. In fact, in addition to an increase of 'esperimenti canterini' [experiments in the style of the cantari] in the *Cinque canti* (typical of the chivalric compositions of common origin, called 'cantari'), the principal models are no longer Boiardo and Virgil, but rather Pulci in his *Morgante* and Lucan in his *Pharsalia*. There are several potential reasons why Ariosto consciously made his text more coarse and almost dissonant.

First of all, the *Cinque canti* were composed during a difficult phase in the poet's life, as attested by the *Satires*. In all likelihood, the intrigues of the Este court, in which Ariosto was personally involved, were one of the fundamental reasons for the fragment. Yet this alone is not sufficient to justify the darkened political vision that one can draw from these cantos, and which involves not only a single court (that of Charlemagne), but all the courts of Europe.

One does well to recall that this period saw the beginning of the struggles between Francis I of France and Emperor Charles V for the control of the Holy Roman Empire, as well as an increase in the schisms that brought about the separation of the Lutherans and the Calvinists from the Catholic church. In his new text, Ariosto speaks more or less directly about all of these historical occurrences, proposing his own personal, disenchanted interpretation of the political situation of that era (Zatti 30–40). The final stanzas, which speak of the serious defeat of Charlemagne, are by implication not ironic but tragic and pessimistic reflections of a political reality.

The *Cinque canti* have often been considered a monotonous text in comparison to the *Furioso*. These cantos, undoubtedly, present certain innovative traits (as seen in the Council of the demons which opens the narration) that in some cases are borrowed by Tasso in his *Gerusalemme liberata*. Furthermore, the tragic material permits the attainment of a grandiose tone in certain passages, as in the ending, which has been compared to the film *Alexander Nevsky* by the Russian director Sergei Eisenstein.

This project of augmentation would have greatly changed the appearance of the *Furioso*, because on the one hand it would have made it more similar to the style and themes of chivalric poetry of the fifteenth century (such as the *Morgante*), while on the other hand it would have rendered the episodes of Ruggiero and the other Paladins as a sort of allegory of the contemporary political situation. Ariosto did not add these cantos to the poem in 1521, because they had not been completed when he decided to quickly publish the new version. When, at the end of the 1520s, Ariosto attempted to reorganize these cantos in order to use them in the third version of the *Furioso*, he must have realized that they were no longer appropriate for his purposes. For this reason he abandoned them, but used brief segments of these cantos for the new episodes previously mentioned (section 3.1). During the 1520s, many things had changed, both on the historical-political and on the cultural and literary levels. These changes will be discussed in the following section.

5.1

In 1525 Emperor Charles V defeated Francis I of France in the battle of Pavia, and as a result got a foothold in Italy. After further conflicts, culminating in the siege of Rome in 1527, Charles V was crowned emperor in Bologna in 1530. These events, at once marvellous and tragic, left a profound mark on the Italian collective imagination, and are found, more or less explicitly, even in the additions to the third version of the *Furioso*. Ariosto realized that the chivalric world, still represented by the King of France and his court, had been replaced by an imperial world, endowed with a more difficult brand of symbolism, as discussed by many scholars beginning with Frances Yates.

In addition to the changes in the historical-political texture of the poem in the text of 1532 (Casadei *La strategia* 21–85), the *Furioso* abandoned the Ferrarese 'municipal' and 'courtly' dimension in which it was born, and moved decisively toward a 'national' and 'imperial' view. This does not imply that the references to the court of Ferrara were eliminated; they are almost all preserved, but stand side by side with numerous other references pertaining to Italian and European history.

In 1525, an important event in the literary field was recorded: the publication of Pietro Bembo's *Prose della volgar lingua*. These samples of prose were in part already known thanks to their circulation in manuscript form, but their official publication signalled definitively the advent of new and precise grammatical and stylistic rules, based on the models of Petrarch and Boccaccio, that would be responsible for directing Italian literature toward classicism. Ariosto adapted his works to these new rules, feeling compelled to correct many of his verses in light of them, even though he had already chosen Tuscan as the language of his *Furioso* (Segre *Storia* 35–7). This process implied a large number of changes which, however, did not drastically change the appearance of the *Furioso* of 1516 and that of 1521; from this point of view, the elements of continuity remain superior to those of change.

The *Prose* by Bembo also provoked a shift in the critical opinions about specific, even new, value judgments regarding literary genres. Because the chivalric poem, after 1516, was the domain of mediocre authors, its status fell to the level of the humble and vulgar. Ariosto found himself having to 'defend' his *Furioso*, which had already enjoyed a vast and undisputed success. He put together a magnificent edition (containing a xylography of his portrait, prepared by Tiziano Vecellio) and edited it with great care for the press of Francesco de' Rossi of Valenza. It was first released on 1 October 1532 (for its complete history see Fahy 102–75). As far as the text is concerned, he not only improved it from the point of view of language, but improved its overall tone by adopting in the new episodes a more elevated style and carefully selected classical models, eliminating almost completely its comic traits. Furthermore, in these episodes he presented adventures of a 'noble' nature; in some instances, for example, the reader is confronted with clashes between the forces of Good, depicted by the Paladins, and the forces of Evil, portrayed by new and terrible characters such as Cimosco or Marganorre.

5.2

Given these premises, it is interesting to note the change to the ending, which has already been discussed (section 3.2). The insertion of the episode of Ruggiero and Leone interrupts the concluding sequence of 1516–21, in which all the various plot lines were resolved. The new ending proves to be much more complex, because of the increase in the references to Virgil and other classical models and because of new romantic episodes involving the paladin, Ruggiero. In this addition, as in all the other ones to the 1532 version, there are no further traces of the irony that dominated the first two versions of the *Furioso* (cf. Casadei *Il percorso* 159–72).

The text of the last *Furioso* contains sections that are more dissonant and anguished by comparison with the 1516 and 1521 editions. These sections were not motivated by Ariosto's withdrawal into himself, that is, they are not due to a personal crisis. Rather, he observes the new historical situation and records the positive and great events as well as the tragic ones.

With the third *Furioso* one can say that Ariosto attempted to create a new type of romance, one that, without recanting completely the ironic form of 1516–21, would be more classical and more tied to the new imperial ideology. The relationship with the chivalric genre, without doubt, changed, just as his relationship with the Ferrarese court changed; still, Ariosto managed to make his poem 'classical' without turning it upside down. The third *Furioso* is grander and more disquieting with respect to the first and the second, but it is not entirely different. It mirrors its times just as the previous versions spoke of theirs (and as did the *Cinque canti*, to a certain degree). For this reason, by following the evolution of Ariosto's poem we can re-create the entire historical-cultural evolution of this most important period of the Italian Renaissance.

TRANSLATED BY CARMELA COLELLA

NOTE

The critical edition of the three versions of the poem is: Ludovico Ariosto, *Orlando Furioso, secondo l'edizione del 1532, con le varianti delle edizioni del 1516 e del 1521*, ed. Santorre Debenedetti and Cesare Segre (Bologna: Commissione per i testi di lingua, 1960). References made to this text, even though quotations, for the convenience of the reader, were taken from the third edition.

BIBLIOGRAPHY

Ariosto, Ludovico. *I frammenti autografi dell' 'Orlando furioso.'* Ed. Santorre Debenedetti. Turin: Chiantore, 1937.
——— *Opere minori*. Ed. Cesare Segre. Milan-Naples: Ricciardi, 1954.
——— *Orlando furioso*. Ed. Emilio Bigi. 2 vols. Milan: Rusconi, 1982.
——— *Orlando furioso*. Ed. Remo Ceserani and Sergio Zatti. Turin: UTET, 1997.

———— *Orlando furioso*. Ed. S. Debenedetti. 3 vols. Bari: Laterza, 1928.

———— *Orlando furioso*. Ed. Cesare Segre. Milan: Mondadori, 1976.

———— *Orlando furioso, secondo le stampe del 1516 e del 1521*. Ed. Fillipo Ermini. 2 vols. Rome: Società Filologica Romana, 1909–11.

Beer, Maria. *Romanzi di cavalleria*. Rome: Bulzoni, 1987.

Bologna, Corrado. '*Orlando furioso*.' In *Letteratura italiana. Le opere (II)*. Turin: Einaudi, 1993. 219–352 (with an extensive bibliography).

Caretti, Lanfranco. 'Codicillo' (to 'L'opera dell'Ariosto'). In L. Caretti, *Antichi e Moderni*. Turin: Einaudi, 1976. 103–8.

Casadei, Alberto. *Il percorso del 'Furioso.'* Bologna: Il Mulino, 1993.

———— *La strategia delle varianti*. Lucca: Pacini-Fazzi, 1988.

Catalano, Michele. *Vita di L. Ariosto*. 2 vols. Geneva: Olschki, 1930–1.

Contini, Gianfranco. 'Come lavorava l'Ariosto' (1937). In G. Contini, *Esercizi di lettura*. Turin: Einaudi, 1982 (first ed. 1974). 232–41.

Diaz, Maria. *Le correzioni all' 'Orlando furioso.'* Naples: Tip. Tessitore, 1900.

Dionisotti, Carlo. 'Per la data dei *Cinque canti*.' *Giornale storico della letteratura italiana* 137 (1960): 1–40.

———— 'Appunti *sui Cinque canti* e sugli studi ariosteschi.' In *Studi e problemi di critica testuale (Atti del convegno—Bologna, 7–9 aprile 1960)*. Bologna: Commissione per i testi di lingua, 1961. 369–82.

Fahy, Conor. *L''Orlando furioso' del 1532*. Milan: Vita e Pensiero, 1989.

Marinelli, Peter V. *Ariosto and Boiardo*. Columbia: Missouri University Press, 1987.

Mazzacurati, Giancarlo. *Il Rinascimento dei moderni*. Bologna: Il Mulino, 1985.

Quint, David. *Epic and Empire*. Princeton, NJ: Princeton University Press, 1993.

Saccone, Eduardo. 'Le maniere dell'ultimo Ariosto.' In E. Saccone, *Le buone e le cattive maniere*. Bologna: Il Mulino, 1992. 95–111.

———— *Il 'soggetlo' del 'Furioso.'* Naples: Liguori, 1974.

Sangirardi, Giuseppe. *Bioardismo ariostesco*. Lucca: Pacini-Fazzi, 1993 (with an extensive bibliography).

Segre, Cesare. 'Storia interna dell'*Orlando furioso*' (1961). In C. Segre, *Esperienze ariostesche*. Pisa: Nistri–Lischi, 1966. 29–41.

———— 'Studi sui *Cinque canti*' (1954). In Segre, *Esperienze ariostesche*. 121–77.

Stella, Angelo. 'Note sull'evoluzione linguisitica dell'Ariosto' (1974). In *L. Ariosto: Lingua, stile e tradizione*. Ed. C. Segre. Milan: Feltrinelli, 1976. 49–64.

Zatti, Sergio. 'I *Cinque canti*: La crisi dell'autorità.' *Studi italiani* 8 (1992): 23–40.

Chronology

1304	Fransesco Petrarca (Petrarch) is born.
1309–1377	Exile of the Papal Court from Rome to Avignon (often called the "Babylonian Captivity" of the Church).
1313	Giovanni Boccaccio is born.
1321	Death of Dante Alighieri.
1327	Petrarch sees the woman he later names Laura in a series of poems collected in *Canzoniere*.
1353	Boccaccio's *Decameron*.
1367	Pope Urban V attempts to move the Papacy back to Rome.
1369	Venice repels the Hungarian invasion.
1374	Petrarch dies in Arquà.
1375	Boccaccio dies in Certaldo.
1378–1417	Christendom divided by creation of popes and anti-popes, variously supported by Rome, Avignon, and Pisa.
1378	Ciompi riots in Florence;Sculptor Lorenzo Ghiberti is born.
1380	Humanist Gianfrancesco Poggio Bracciolini is born.
1386	Building of the Cathedral in Milan.
1387	Chaucer's *Canterbury Tales*.
1397	Medici bank founded in Florence.

c. 1400–	Florentine civic humanist writings by Bruni, Palmieri, and Salutati.
1404–05	Venice annexes Bassano, Belluno, Vicenza, Padua, and Verona.
1406	Florence captures Pisa.
1410–1425	Donatello's, Ghiberti's, and Orcagna's sculptures at Orsanmichele, Florence.
1412	Filippo Maria Visconti becomes Duke of Milan.
1414–18	The Council of Constance takes place; election of Martin V ends the Great Schism.
1419	Decoration of Great Council Hall, Venice.
1420	Papacy returns to Rome from Avignon.
1420–36	Brunelleschi's dome is built atop Florence's cathedral.
1424	Francesco Foscari begins the west wing of Doge's Palace, Venice.
1425–52	Ghiberti's "Gates of Paradise" for Baptistery doors, Florence.
1425–54	Wars in Lombardi; Venice expands territory.
1427–28	Masaccio, *Trinity*, S. Maria Novella, Florence.
1429	Matteo Palmieri, *Della Vita Civile*.
1430–35	Alberti's *On the Family*, *On Painting*.
1434	Cosimo de' Medici returns to Florence from exile; dominates until 1464.
1438–52	Fra Angelico's frescoes at San Marco, Florence.
1440	Lorenzo Valla's treatise against the Donation of Constantine, discrediting the papacy's political authority.
1442–	Federico da Montefeltro begins Palazzo Ducale in Urbino; Alfonso of Aragon becomes King of Naples.
1447–48	Pisanello's fresco decorations in Palazzo Ducale, Mantua.
1450	Jubilee in Rome; 200 pilgrims killed on the Ponte Sant'Angelo; Francesco Sforza gains power in Milan.
1451	Cappella dei Mascoli, San Marco, Venice.
1452	Leon Battista Alberti, *On the Art of Building*.
1453	Turks conquer Constantinople; Greek scholars migrate to Italy; Alberti begins facade of the Tempio Malatestiano, Rimini.

1453–58	Triumphal Arch of King Alfonso of Aragon, Castel Nuovo, Naples.
1454	Peace of Lodi—Italian states join against Turks; Piero della Francesca's Arezzo frescoes.
1459	Benozzo Gozzoli's *Journey of the Magi*, Palazzo Medici-Riccardi, Florence.
1460s	Ficino's translation of Platonic works in Florence.
1461–62	Filarete's *Treatise on Architecture*.
1465–74	Andrea Mantegna's *Camera Picta*, Palazzo Ducale, Mantua.
1469	Lorenzo de' Medici assumes family dominance in Florence.
1472	Piero della Francesca's diptych of Federico da Montefeltro and Battista Sforza.
1475	Sixtus IV founds the Vatican Library; Poliziano, *Le Stanze*.
1476	Duke Galeazzo Maria Sforza is assassinated on Christmas day; Bellini, *S. Giobbe Altarpiece*, Venice; Masuccio Salernitano, *Novellino*.
1478	Pazzi Conspiracy in Florence; Giuliano de' Medici is assassinated.
1479	Lodovico Sforza "Il Moro" becomes Duke of Milan.
1480–81	Melozzo da Forli's *Sixtus IV, His Nephews, and Platina*; Poliziano, *Orfeo*.
1481–82	Leonardo da Vinci leaves Florence for Milan.
c. 1482	Botticelli, *Primavera*.
1483	Luigi Pulci, *Morgante*.
1483–85	Da Vinci's *Lady with an Ermine*, for Lodovico Sforza.
1485–90	Giovanni Bellini's *Portrait of a Young Senator*, Venice.
1485–93	*Scala dei Giganti*, Doge's Palace, Venice.
1486-04	Jacopo Sannazaro, *Arcadia*.
1488–93	Fra Lippo Lippi's frescoes in S. Maria Sopra Minerva, Rome.
1490	Aldine Press is established in Venice.
1490–95	Facade of Scuola Grande di San Marco is finished, Venice.
1491	Facade of the Certosa, Pavia.
1492	Pinturicchio's frescoes for Borgia Apartment, Vatican palace.

1494	Charles VIII of France invades Italy; expulsion of Medici from Florence; completion of Alberti's nave and portico of San Andrea, Mantua; Boiardo, *Orlando Innamorato*.
1494–98	Savonarola assumes power in Florence.
1495	Carpaccio's *Dream of St. Ursula*, Venice.
1495–97	Leonardo's *Last Supper*, Santa Maria delle Grazie, Milan.
1497–1500	Michelangelo's *Pieta* for St. Peter's.
1499	*Torre dell'Orologio*, Piazza San Marco, Venice.
1501–04	Michelangelo's *David*, Florence.
1502–10	Bramante's *Tempietto*, San Pietro in Montorio, Rome.
1506	Witnessed by Erasmus, Julius II and papal army enters Bologna in triumph; cornerstone laid for new St. Peter's, Rome; *Christ in Majesty* (in Byzantine style), semi-dome of apse of San Marco, Venice; Lorenzo Lotto's *St. Jerome in the Wilderness*, Venice.
1508	Ariosto, *La Cassaria*.
c.1508–09	Sebastiano del Piombo's *Judgment of Solomon*, Venice.
1508–12	Michelangelo's ceiling frescoes for the Sistine Chapel.
1508–14	Raphael's frescoes for the Vatican *Stanze*.
1508–17	Wars of the League of Cambrai (Emperor, France, Spain vs. Venice).
1509	Papal, imperial, French, and Spanish forces defeat Venice at Battle of Agnadello.
1511	The War of the Holy League (Pope, Spain, Venice vs. France).
1512	Battle of Ravenna, pyrrhic victory for French; Medici restored to Florence.
1513–18	Machiavelli's *The Prince, The Discourses*, and *Mandragola*.
1514	Antonio da Sangallo the Younger begins Palazzo Farnese, Rome; Giovanni Bellini's *The Feast of the Gods*, for Duke Alfonso d'Este I of Ferrara.
1515	Francis I of France invades Italy.
1516	First edition of Ariosto's *Orlando Furioso;* Titian, *Assumption of the Virgin*.
1517	Luther's *Ninety-Five Theses* inaugurate Reformation; Venice regains Terraferma lands.
1517–20	Raphael's *Transfiguration*.

1519–34	Michelangelo, Medici Chapel, Florence.
1523	Titian's *Bacchus and Ariadne*.
1525	Battle of Pavia: Charles V defeats France; Pietro Bembo, *Prose della vulgar llingua*.
1526	League of Cognac (Pope, France, Florence, Venice, Milan) vs. Charles V.
1526-34	*Giulio Romano*, Palazzo del Te, Mantua.
1527	Sack of Rome by Imperial troops—some scholars consider this event to mark the end of the renaissance.
1527–32	*Sala di Psiche* and *Sala dei Giganti*, Palazzo del Te, Mantua.
1528	Castiglione, *The Book of the Courtier*.
1529	Treaty of Barcelona: Charles V dominates Italy.
1530	Pietro Bembo, *Rime*.
1531	Coreggio, *Danae*.
1532	Third edition of Ariosto's *Orlando Furioso*.
1533	Henry VIII becomes supreme head of English Church; excommunicated by Rome.
1534–41	Michelangelo's *Last Judgment* in the Sistine Chapel.
1535	Francesco Guicciardini, *The History of Italy*.
1536	Charles V's triumphal entry at Rome.
1536–45	Titian's portraits of *La Bella*, *The Vendramin Family*, and *Pietro Aretino*, Venice.
1537–57	Pietro Aretino, *Lettere*.
1537–66	Jacopo Sansovino's Logetta, Biblioteca Marciana, and Zecca in Venice.
1538	Treaty of Nice between Francis I and Charles V, overseen by Paul III; Colonna, *Rime*.
1540	Paul III approves Ignatius Loyola's founding of the Society of Jesus.
1546–	Titian, *Pope Paul III*, Michelangelo, St. Peters (–1564).
1542	Inquisition reestablished.
1547–65	Council of Trent opens (sessions in 1545–57, 1551–52, 1562–63).
1550	Giorgio Vasari, *Lives of the Most Excellent painters, Sculptors, and Architects*; Andrea Palladio, Villa Rotonda.
1551–52	War of Parma (France vs. papal and imperial forces).

1554	Bandello, *Novelle*; Palestrina, *First Book of Masses.*
1558	Della Casa, *Rime e prosa* (w/ *Galateo*), Benvenuto Cellini, *Vita* (–1564)
1559	Treaty of Cateau-Cambresis: Italian wars end, imperial forces dominate peninsula.
1562–63	Paolo Veronese's *Marriage Feast at Cana*, Venice.
1564	Oratory of S. Filippo Neri founded in Rome; Index of Proscribed Books published; Tintoretto, *Crucifixion*, Venice.
1568	La Chiesa del Gesu begun by Vignola and della Porta.
1571	Navy battle of Lepanto: Holy League (Spain, Venice, papacy) defeats the Turks.
1573	Tasso, *Aminta*; Veronese, *Feast in the House of Levi.*
1577	Venice's Great Council Hall destroyed by fire.
1579–1620	Doge's Palace redecorated by Veronese, Tintoretto, Bassano, and others.
1580	Jacopo and Domenico Tintoretto's *S. Guistina and the Treasures*, Venice.
1581	Tasso, *Gerusalemme liberata.*
1590	Guarini, *Il pastor fido.*
1598	Ferrara annexed to papacy.
1600	Caravaggio, *Conversion of St. Paul.*

Contributors

HAROLD BLOOM is Sterling Professor of the Humanities at Yale University. He is the author of over 20 books, including *Shelley's Mythmaking* (1959), *The Visionary Company* (1961), *Blake's Apocalypse* (1963), *Yeats* (1970), *A Map of Misreading* (1975), *Kabbalah and Criticism* (1975), *Agon: Toward a Theory of Revisionism* (1982), *The American Religion* (1992), *The Western Canon* (1994), and *Omens of Millennium: The Gnosis of Angels, Dreams, and Resurrection* (1996). *The Anxiety of Influence* (1973) sets forth Professor Bloom's provocative theory of the literary relationships between the great writers and their predecessors. His most recent books include *Shakespeare: The Invention of the Human* (1998), a 1998 National Book Award finalist, *How to Read and Why* (2000), *Genius: A Mosaic of One Hundred Exemplary Creative Minds* (2002), and *Hamlet: Poem Unlimited* (2003). In 1999, Professor Bloom received the prestigious American Academy of Arts and Letters Gold Medal for Criticism, and in 2002 he received the Catalonia International Prize.

GENE A. BRUCKER is Professor Emeritus of History at the University of California-Berkeley. He has written or edited several books on Florence, including *Florentine Politics and Society, 1343–1378*, *Renaissance Florence: Society, Culture, and Religion*, and *Two Memoirs of Renaissance Florence*.

J.G.A. POCOCK, Professor Emeritus in History at The Johns Hopkins University, is best known for his book, *The Machiavellian Moment: Florentine Political Thought and the Atlantic Republican Tradition*. He has also written *Politics, Language, and Time*; *Virtue, Commerce, and History*; and *Barbarism and*

Religion, as well as edited texts by Edmund Burke and James Harrington. He also founded the Folger Institute Center for the History of British Political Thought.

EUGENIO GARIN, a prominent and prolific scholar of the Italian Renaissance, is Professor Emeritus at Scuola Normale Superiore of Pisa. Of his many books on the subject, those translated into English include *Italian Humanism: Philosophy and Civic Life in the Renaissance, Portraits from the Quattrocento, Science and Civic Life in the Italian Renaissance*, and *Astrology in the Renaissance: the Zodiac of Life*. He is also a longtime editor of the journal *Rinascimento*.

PAUL OSKAR KRISTELLER, a highly influential scholar and teacher of Renaissance Italy, was the author of many books, including *Renaissance Thought and Its Sources* and *Renaissance Concepts of Man, and Other Essays*. A Professor of Philosophy at Columbia University, his tireless efforts during three decades led to a grand inventory of manuscripts in Italy, the *Iter Italicum*.

JOAN KELLY was the author of *Leon Battista Alberti: Universal Man of the Early Renaissance*. Her essay, "Did Women Have a Renaissance?", is considered a seminal example of feminist interpretations of Renaissance culture.

PETER BURKE'S several books, on a variety of Renaissance subjects, include *The Renaisance Sense of the Past, Fortunes of the Courtier*, and *Historical Anthropology of Early Modern Italy*. He is a Reader in Cultural History and a Fellow at Emmanuel College, Cambridge University.

DENYS HAY was the author of a popular introduction to the Italian Renaissance, as well as general editor of the Longman History of Italy series. A professor of medieval and Renaissance history at the University of Edinburgh, his other books include *Church in Italy in the Fifteenth Century* and *Polydore Vergil: Renaissance Historian and Man of Letters*.

CARLA FRECCERO is the author of *Father Figures: Genealogy and Narrative Structure in Rabelais* and, more recently, *Popular Culture: An Introduction*. A Professor of Literature and Women's Studies at University of California-Santa Cruz, she has also co-edited *Pre-Modern Sexualities*.

VICTORIA KAHN is an authority on rhetoric during the Renaissance, and her books include *Rhetoric, Prudence, and Skepticism in the Renaissance* and *Machiavellian Rhetoric: from the Counter-Reformation to Milton*. She is also co-editor of *Machiavelli and the Discourse of Literature* and *Rhetoric and Law in Early Modern Europe*. She is a Professor of Rhetoric and Comparative Literature at the University of California–Berkeley.

BRIAN RICHARDSON, Professor of Italian Studies at the University of Leeds, is the author of two studies of printing and its influence in the Renaissance—*Print Culture and Renaissance Italy: the Editor and the Vernacular Text, 1470–1600* and *Printing, Writers, and Readers in Renaissance Italy*. He was recently elected to the British Academy.

FRANCIS AMES-LEWIS is the author of several books on Italian Renaissance art, artists, and the social and cultural worlds in which they existed. These studies include *Draftsman Raphael, Intellectual Life of the Early Renaissance Artist*, and the recently revised *Drawing in Early Renaissance Italy*. She is also co-editor of *Reactions to the Master: Michelangelo's Effect on Art and Artists in the Sixteenth Century* and *Concepts of Beauty in Renaissance Art*.

JOHN M. NAJEMY, Professor of history at Cornell University, has written *Corporatism and Consensus in Florentine Electoral Politics, 1280–1400* and *Between Friends: Discourses of Power and Desire in the Machiavelli-Vetttori Letters of 1513–1515*, as well as numerous essays on Florentine political history.

DAVID QUINT is the George M. Bodman Professor of English and Comparative Literature at Yale University. His books include *Origin and Originality in Renaissance Literature* and *Epic and Empire*. He has also published a study of Montaigne and translations of Poliziano's *Stanze* and Ariosto's *Cinque Canti*. His latest book is a study of *Don Quixote*.

ALBERTO CASADEI, Associate Professor of Italian Literature at the University of Pisa, writes frequently on Ariosto, Machiavelli, and Tasso. His books include *La strategia delle varianti: Le correzioni storiche del terzo 'Furioso'*, *Il percorso del 'Furioso'*, and *La fine degli incanti: Vicende del poema epico-cavalleresco rinascimentale*.

Bibliography

PRIMARY TEXTS

Alberti, Leon Battista. *Dinner Pieces*. Trans. David Marsh. Binghamton: MRTS, 1987.

———. *The Family in Renaissance Florence*. Trans. Reneé Neu Watkins. Columbia: University of South Carolina Press, 1969.

———. *On Painting*. Trans. and ed. John R. Spencer. New Haven: Yale University Press, 1956.

———. *On the Art of Building in Ten Books*. Trans. Joseph Rykwert, with Neil Leach and Robert Tavernor. Cambridge: MIT Press, 1988.

Aretino, Pietro. *Aretino's Dialogues*. Trans. Raymond Rosenthal. New York: Marsilio, 1971.

———. *Selected Letters*. Trans. George Bull. Harmondsworth: Penguin, 1976.

Ariosto, Lodovico. *Orlando Furioso*. Trans. Guido Waldman. Oxford: Oxford University Press, 1974.

———. *The Satires of Ludovico Ariosto*. Trans. Peter DeSa Wiggins. Athens: Ohio University Press, 1976.

Boccaccio, Giovanni. *Boccaccio on Poetry*. Trans. and ed. Charles G. Osgood. Indianapolis: Bobbs-Merrill, 1956.

———. *The Decameron*. Trans. G.H. McWilliam. 2d ed. London: Penguin, 1995.

Boiardo, Matteo. *Orlando Innamorato*. Trans. Charles Stanley Ross. 1989. Oxford: Oxford University Press, 1995.

Bruno, Giordano. *The Ash Wednesday Supper*. Trans. and ed. Edward A. Gosselin and Lawrence S. Lerner. Toronto: University of Toronto Press, 1995.

———. *The Expulsion of the Triumphant Beast*. Trans. Arthur D. Imerti. Lincoln: University of Nebraska Press, 1992.

Campanella, Tommaso. *The City of the Sun: A Poetical Dialogue*. Trans. Daniel J. Donno. Berkeley: University of California Press, 1981.

Cardano, Girolamo. *The Book of My Life*. Trans. Jean Stoner. New York: New York Review Books, 2002.

Castiglione, Baldesar. *The Book of the Courtier*. Trans. Charles Singleton. New York: Anchor, 1959.

Cellini, Benevenuto. *My Life*. Trans. Julia Conaway Bondanella and Peter Bondanella. Oxford: Oxford University Press, 2002.

Colonna, Francesco. *Hypnerotomachia Poliphili: the Stife of Love in a Dream*. Trans. Joscelyn Godwin. New York: Thames & Hudson, 1999.

Ficino, Marsilio. *Meditations on the Soul: Selected Letters of Marsilio Ficino*. Rochester, VT: Inner Traditions International, 1997.

Ficino, Marsilio. *Three Books on Life*. Ed. and trans. Carol V. Kaske and John R. Clark. Binghamton: RTS, 1989.

Galilei, Galileo. *Discoveries and Opinions of Galileo*. Trans. Stillman Drake. New York: Anchor, 1957.

———. *Sidereus Nuncius or The Sidereal Messenger*. Trans. Albert van Helden. Chicago: University of Chicago Press, 1989.

Guarini, Battista. *Il Pastor Fido / The Faithfull Shepherd*. Trans. Richard Fanshawe. Ed. J.H. Whitfield. Austin: University of Texas Press, 1976.

Guicciardini, Francesco. *The History of Florence*. Trans. Mario Domandi. New York: Harper & Row, 1970.

———.*The History of Italy*. Trans. Sidney Alexander. New York: Macmillan, 1969.

———.*Maxims and Reflections (Ricordi)*. Trans. Mario Domandi. Philadelphia: University of Pennsylvania Press, 1972.

Kohl, B.G., and R.G. Witt, eds. *The Earthly Republic: Italian Humanists on Government and Society*. Philadelphia: University of Pennsylvania Press, 1978.

Macchiavelli, Niccolò. *The Comedies of Machiavelli*. Trans. and ed. David Sices and James B. Atkinson. Hanover: University Press of New England, 1985.

———. *The Discourses*. Trans. Leslie J. Walker. Ed. Bernard Crick. London: Penguin, 1970.

———. *The Letters of Machiavelli*. Trans. and ed. Allan Gilbert. Chicago: University of Chicago Press, 1961.

———. *The Prince*. Trans. and ed. David Wootton. Indianapolis: Hackett, 1995.

———. *Florentine Histories*. Trans. Laura F. Banfield and Harvey C. Mansfield, Jr. Princeton: Princeton University Press, 1988.

Mantuanus, Baptista. *Adulescentia: The Eclogues of Mantuan*. Trans. Lee Piepho. New York: Garland, 1989.

Medici, Lorenzo de'. *Selected Poems and Prose*. Trans. John Thiem et al. University Park: Pennylvania State University Press, 1991.

Michelangelo. *Life, Letters, and Poetry*. Trans. George Bull, with Peter Porter. Oxford: Oxford University Press, 1987.

———. *The Poetry of Michelangelo*. Trans. and ed. James M. Saslow. New Haven: Yale University Press, 1991.

Mirandola, Pico della. *Oration on the Dignity of Man*. Trans. Charles Glenn Wallis. Indianapolis: Bobbs-Merrill, 1965.

Palladio, Andrea. *Four Books of Architecture*. New York: Dover, 1965.

Petrarca, Francesco. *Petrarch's 'Africa.'* Trans. Thomas G. Bergin and Alice S. Wilson. New Haven: Yale University Press, 1977.

———. *Petrarch: An Anthology*. Ed. David Thompson. New York: Harper & Row, 1971.

———. *Petrarch's Lyric Poems: The* Rime Sparse *and Other Lyrics*. Trans. Robert M. Durling. Cambridge: Harvard University Press, 1976.

———. *Petrarch's Book Without a Name*. Trans. Norman P. Zacour. Toronto: Pontifical Institute of Medieval Studies, 1973.

———. *Rerum Familiarum Libri*. Trans. Aldo S. Bernardo. Albany: State University of New York Press, 1975.

Penman, Bruce, ed. *Five Italian Comedies*. London: Penguin, 1978.

Piccolomini, Aeneas Sylvius (Pius II). *Memoirs of a Renaissance Pope*. Trans. Florence A. Gragg. New York: Capricorn, 1962.

Poliziano, Angelo. *The* Stanze *of Angelo Poliziano*. Trans. David Quint. University Park: Pennsylvania State University Press, 1993.

Sannazaro, Jacopo. *Arcadia & Piscatorial Eclogues*. Trans. Ralph Nash. Detroit: Wayne State University Press, 1966.

Tasso, Torquato. *Aminta: A Pastoral Play*. Ed. and trans. Charles Jernigan and Marchegiani Jones. New York: Italica Press, 2000.

———. *Jerusalem Delivered*. Trans. Ralph Nash Detroit: Wayne State University Press, 1987.

———. *Tasso's Dialogues*. Trans. Carnes Lord and Dain A. Tafton. Berkeley: University of California Press, 1982.

Vasari, Giorgio. *Lives of the Artists*. Trans. George Bull. 2 vols. Rev. ed. London: Penguin, 1971.

Vespasiano. *Renaissance Princes, Popes & Prelates*. New York: Harper & Row, 1963.

Vico, Giambattista. *The New Science of Giambattista Vico*. Trans. Thomas G. Bergin and Max Fisch. Ithaca: Cornell University Press, 1970.

SECONDARY TEXTS:

Acton, Harold. *The Pazzi Conspiracy: The Plot Against the Medici*. London: Thames & Hudson, 1979.

Ames-Lewis, Francis. *Drawing in Renaissance Italy*. 1981. New Haven: Yale University Press, 2000.

———. *The Intellectual Life of the Early Renaissance Artist*. New Haven: Yale University Press, 2000.

———and Paul Joannides, eds. *Reactions to the Master: Michelangelo's Effect on Art and Artists in the Sixteenth Century*. Burlington: Ashgate, 2003.

Angelo, Sydney. *Machiavelli: A Dissection*. New York: Harcourt, Brace & World, 1969.

Avery, Charles. *Donatello: An Introduction*. New York: Icon Editions, 1994.

Barkan, Leonard. *Gods Made Flesh: Metamorphosis and the Pursuit of Paganism*. New Haven: Yale University Press, 1986.

———. *Unearthing the Past: Archaeology and Aesthetics in the Making of Renaissance Culture*. New Haven: Yale University Press, 1999.

Barolini, Helen. *Aldus and His Dream Book*. New York: Italica Press, 1992.

Baron, Hans. *The Crisis of the Early Italian Renaissance*. 2 vols. Princeton: Princeton University Press, 1955.

———. *In Search of Florentine Civic Humanism*. 2 vols. Princeton: Princeton University Press, 1988.

Baxandall, Michael. *Giotto and the Orators: Humanist Observers of Painting in*

Italy and the Discovery of Pictorial Composition, 1350–1450. Oxford: Clarendon Press, 1971.

———. *Painting and Experience in Fifteenth-Century Italy.* Oxford: Oxford University Press, 1972.

Bedini, Silvio A. *The Pope's Elephant.* New York: Penguin, 1997.

Biagioli, Mario. *Galileo, Courtier: The Practice of Science in the Culture of Absolutism.* Chicago: Univ. of Chicago Press, 1993.

Blunt, Anthony. *Artistic Theory in Italy 1450–1660.* Oxford: Clarendon Press, 1940.

Bock, Gisela, et al., eds. *Machiavelli and Republicanism.* Cambridge: Cambridge University Press, 1990.

Bouwsma, William J. *Venice and the Defense of Republican Liberty.* Berkeley: University of California Press, 1968.

Braden, Gordon. *Petrarchan Love and the Continental Renaissance.* New Haven: Yale University Press, 1999.

Branca, Vittore, ed. *Merchant Writers of the Renaissance.* Trans. Murtha Baca. New York: Marsilio, 1999.

Brand, Peter, and Lino Pertile. *The Cambridge History of Italian Literature.* 1996. Rev. ed. Cambridge: Cambridge Univ. Press, 1999.

Brown, Alison. "Jacob Burckhardt's Renaissance." *History Today* 38 (1988): 20–26.

———, ed. *Language and Images of Renaissance Italy.* Oxford: Clarendon Press, 1995.

Brucker, Gene A. *The Civic World of Early Renaissance Florence.* Princeton: Princeton University Press, 1977.

———. *Giovanni and Lusanna: Love and Marriage in Renaissance Florence.* Berkeley: University of California Press, 1986.

———. *Renaissance Florence.* 1969. Berkeley: University of California Press, 1983.

———, ed. *The Society of Renaissance Florence: A Documentary Study.* New York: Harper & Row, 1971.

———, ed.. *Two Memoirs of Renaissance Florence: The Diaries of Buonaccorso Pitti and Gregorio Dati.* Trans. Julia Martines. Prospect Heights: Waveland Press, 1991.

Burckhardt, Jacob. *The Civilization of the Renaissance in Italy.* Trans. S.G.C. Middlemore 1878. Harmondsworth: Penguin, 1990.

Burke, Peter. *Fortunes of the Courtier: the European Reception of Castiglione's Cortegiano.* Cambridge: Polity Press, 1995.

———. *Historical Anthropology of Early Modern Italy: Essays on Perception and Communication.* Cambridge: Cambridge University Press, 1987.

———. *The Italian Renaissance: Culture and Society in Italy.* 2d ed. Princeton: Princeton University Press, 1999.

———. *Renaissance Sense of the Past.* New York: St. Martin's Press, 1970.

Canaday, John. *Late Gothic to Renaissance Painters.* New York: W.W. Norton, 1969.

Casadei, Alberto. "The History of the *Furioso*." In *Ariosto Today: Contemporary Perspectives.* Ed. Donald Beecher, Massimo Ciavolella, and Roberto Fedi. Toronto: University of Toronto Press, 2003.

Cassirer, Ernst. *The Individual and the Cosmos in Renaissance Philosophy.* Oxford: Blackwell, 1963.

———, et al., eds. *The Renaissance Philosophy of Man.* Chicago: University of Chicago Press, 1948.

Chastel, André *Crisis in the Renaissance, 1520–1600.* Trans. Peter Price. Geneva: Skira, 1968.

———. *Flowering of the Italian Renaissance.* Trans. Jonathan Griffin. New York: Odyssey, 1965.

———, ed. *The Renaissance: Essays in Interpretation.* London: Methuen, 1982.

———. *Sack of Rome, 1527.* Trans. Beth Archer. Princeton: Princeton University Press, 1983.

Cheney, Liana di Girolami, ed. *Readings in Italian Mannerism.* New York: Peter Lang, 1997.

Clark, Kenneth. *Leon Battista Alberti on Painting.* London: G. Cumberledge, 1945.

Cleugh, James. *The Divine Aretino.* London: Anthony Blond, 1965.

Cochrane, Eric. *Historians and Historiography in the Italian Renaissance.* Chicago: University of Chicago Press, 1981.

———, ed. *The Late Italian Renaissance, 1525–1630.* London: Macmillan, 1970.

Cole, Alison. *Art of the Italian Renaissance Courts: Virtue and Magnificence.* London: Weidenfeld & Nicolson, 1995.

Copenhaver, Brian, and Charles Schmitt. *Renaissance Philosophy*. Oxford: Oxford University Press, 1992.

Cox, Virginia. *Renaissance Dialogue: Literary Dialogue in its Social and Political Contexts, Castiglione to Galileo*. Cambridge: Cambridge University Press, 1992.

D'Amico, John F. *Renaissance Humanism in Papal Rome*. Baltimore: Johns Hopkins University Press, 1983.

Dandelet, Thomas James. *Spanish Rome 1500–1700*. New Haven: Yale University Press, 2001.

De Grazia, Sebastian. *Machiavelli in Hell*. New York: Vintage, 1989.

De Sanctis, Francesco. *The History of Italian Literature*. 2 vols. New York: Basic Books, 1959.

Di Cesare, Mario A. *Vida's* Christiad *and Vergilian Epic*. New York: Columbia University Press, 1964.

Di Maria, Salvatore. *The Italian Tragedy in the Renaissance*. Lewisburg: Bucknell University Press, 2002.

Erlanger, Rachel. *The Unarmed Prophet: Savonarola in Florence*. New York: McGraw-Hill, 1988.

Finocchiaro, Maurice A., trans. and ed. *The Galileo Affair: A Documentary History*. Berkeley: University of California Press, 1989.

Finucci, Valerie, ed. *Renaissance Transactions: Ariosto and Tasso*. Durham: Duke University Press, 1999.

Fragnito, Gigliola, ed. *Church, Censorship and Culture in Early Modern Italy*. Trans. A. Belton. Cambridge: Cambridge University Press, 2001.

Freccero, Carla. "Politics and Aesthetics in Castiglione's *Il Cortegiano*: Book III and the Discourse on Women." In *Creative Imitation: New Essays on Renaissance Literature In Honor of Thomas M. Greene*. Ed. David Quint, et al. Binghamton: MRTS, 1992.

Freedberg, S.J. *Painting in Italy: 1500–1600*. New Haven: Yale University Press, 1993.

Fryde, E.B. "Lorenzo de Medici: High Finance and the Patronage of Art and Learning." *Courts of Princes*. Ed. A.G. Dickens. New York: McGraw-Hill, 1977.

Garin, Eugenio. *Astrology in the Renaissance: the Zodiac of Life*. Trans. Carolyn Jackson and June Allen. London: Routledge & Kegan Paul, 1983.

————. *Italian Humanism: Philosophy and Civic Life in the Renaissance*. Trans. Peter Munz. Oxford: Blackwell, 1965.

————. *Portraits from the Quattrocento.* Trans. Victor A. and Elizabeth Velen. New York: Harper & Row, 1972.

————, ed. *Renaissance Characters*. Trans. Lydia G. Cochrane. Chicago: University of Chicago Press, 1991.

————. *Science and Civic Life in the Italian Renaissance*. Trans. Peter Munz. Gloucester, Mass.: Peter Lang, 1978.

Gilbert, C.E., ed. *Italian Art 1400–1500, Sources and Documents*. Englewood Cliffs, N.J.: Prentice-Hall, 1980.

Gilbert, Felix. *Machiavelli and Guicciardini: Politics and History in Sixteenth Century Florence*. Princeton: Princeton University Press, 1965.

Gilmore, Myron P. *The World of Humanism 1453–1517*. New York: Harper & Row, 1952.

Ginzburg, Carlo. *The Cheese and the Worms: The Cosmos of a Sixteenth-Century Miller*. Trans. John and Anne Tedeschi. Baltimore: Johns Hopkins University Press, 1980.

Godman, Peter. *From Poliziano to Machiavelli: Florentine Humanism in the High Renaissance*. Princeton: Princeton University Press, 1998.

Gombrich, E.H. *New Light on Old Masters*. Chicago: University of Chicago Press, 1986.

————. *Symbolic Images: Studies in the Art of the Renaissance*. London: Phaidon, 1972.

Grafton, Anthony. *Commerce with the Classics: Ancient Books and Renaissance Readers*. Ann Arbor: University of Michigan, 1997.

————. *Leon Battista Alberti: Master Builder of the Italian Renaissance*. New York: Hill and Wang, 2000.

————, and Lisa Jardine. *From Humanism to the Humanities*. London: Duckworth, 1986.

Greene, Thomas M. *The Light in Troy*. New Haven: Yale University Press, 1982.

Grendler, Paul. *The Roman Inquisition and the Venetian Press*. Princeton: Princeton University Press, 1977.

Griffiths, Gordon, et al., eds. *The Humanism of Leonardo Bruni: Selected Texts*. Binghamton: MRTS, 1987.

Hampton, Timothy. *Writing from History: The Rhetoric of Exemplarity in the Renaissance*. Ithaca: Cornell University Press, 1999.

Hankins, James. *Plato in the Italian Renaissance*. Leiden: Brill, 1990.

———, ed. *Renaissance Civic Humanism: Reappraisals and Reflections*. Cambridge: Cambridge University Press, 2000.

Hay, Denys. *The Italian Renaissance in its Historical Background*. 2d ed. Cambridge: Cambridge University Press, 1976.

———. *Renaissance Essays*. London: Hambledon Press, 1988.

———, and John Law. *Italy in the Age of the Renaissance 1380-1530*. London: Longman, 1989.

Herrick, Marvin T. *Italian Comedy in the Renaissance*. Urbana: University of Illinois Press, 1960.

Hibbard, Howard. *Bernini*. London: Pelican, 1965.

———. *Michelangelo*. 2d ed. New York: Harper & Row, 1974.

Hibbert, Christopher. *The House of Medici: Its Rise and Fall*. New York: William Morrow, 1975.

Holt, Elizabeth Gilmore, ed. *A Documentary History of Art*. 2 vols. Princeton: Princeton University Press, 1982.

Hulliung, Mark. *Citizen Machiavelli*. Princeton: Princeton University Press, 1983.

Janson, H.W. *Brunelleschi in Perspective*. Englewood Cliffs: Prentice-Hall, 1974.

Jardine, Lisa. *Wordly Goods*. London: Macmillan, 1996.

Kahn, Victoria. "*Virtu* and the Example of Agathocles in Machiavelli's *Prince*." In *Machiavelli and the Discourse of Literature*. Eds. Victoria Kahn and Albert Russell Ascoli. Ithaca: Cornell University Press, 1993.

———. *Rhetoric, Prudence and Skepticism in the Renaissance*. Ithaca: Cornell University Press, 1985.

Kelly, Joan. "Did Women Have a Renaissance?" *Women, History & Theory*. Chicago: University of Chicago Press, 1984.

———. *Leon Battista Alberti: Universal Man of the Early Renaissance*. Chicago: University of Chicago Press, 1969.

Kennedy, William J. *Authorizing Petrarch*. Ithaca: Cornell University Press, 1994.

———. *Jacopo Sannazaro and the Uses of Pastoral*. Hanover: University of New England Press, 1983.

Kerrigan, William, and Gordon Braden. *The Idea of the Renaissance*. Baltimore: Johns Hopkins University Press, 1989.

Klein, Robert and Henri Zerner. *Italian Art 1500–1600: Sources and Documents*. Evanston: Northwestern University Press, 1966.

Kristeller, Paul Oskar. *Classics and Renaissance Thought*. Cambridge: Harvard University Press, 1955.

———. *Iter Italicum*. London: Warburg Institute, 1963-1997.

———. *Medieval Aspects of Renaissance Learning: Three Essays*. Durham: Duke University Press, 1974.

———. *Renaissance Thought and Its Sources*. Ed. Michael Mooney. New York: Columbia University Press, 1979.

———, and Philip P. Wiener, eds. *Renaissance Essays*. Rochester: University of Rochester Press, 1992.

Land, Norman. *The Viewer as Poet: The Renaissance Response to Art*. University Park: Pennsylvania State University Press, 1994.

Levey, Michael. *Early Renaissance*. Harmondsworth: Penguin, 1967.

Mallett, Michael. "Diplomacy and War in Later Fifteenth-Century Italy." In *Art and Politics in Renaissance Italy*. Ed. George Holmes. Oxford: Oxford University Press, 1993.

Marinelli, Peter V. *Ariosto & Boiardo: The Origins of* Orlando Furioso. Columbia: University of Missouri Press, 1987.

Marsh, David. *Lucian and the Latins: Humor and Humanism in the Early Renaissance*. Ann Arbor: University of Michigan Press, 1998.

———. *The Quattrocento Dialogue*. Cambridge: Harvard University Press, 1980.

Martin, John. *Venice's Hidden Enemies: Italian Heretics in a Renaissance City*. Berkeley: University of California Press, 1993.

Martines, Lauro. *Power and Imagination: City-States in Renaissance Italy*. New York: Knopf, 1979.

———. *Strong Words: Writing and Social Strain in the Italian Renaissance*. Baltimore: Johns Hopkins Press, 2001.

Mazzotta, Giuseppe. *Cosmopoiesis: The Renaissance Experiment*. Toronto: University of Toronto Press, 2001.

———. *The Worlds of Petrarch*. Durham: Duke University Press, 1993.

McGregor, James H. et al., eds. *Renaissance Naples: c. 1400–1600*. New York: Italica Press, 2001.

McLaughlin, Martin L. *Literary Imitation in the Italian Renaissance*. Oxford: Clarendon Press, 1995.

Mitchell, R.J. *The Laurels and the Tiara: Pope Pius II, 1458–1464*. London: Harvill Press, 1962.

Murray, Linda. *The Late Renaissance and Mannerism*. London: Thames & Hudson, 1967.

Murray, Peter. *The Architecture of the Italian Renaissance*. Rev. ed. New York: Schocken, 1986.

Murray, Peter and Linda. *The Art of the Renaissance*. New York: Thames & Hudson, 1963.

Najemy, John M. "Civic Humanism and Florentine Politics." In *Renaissance Civic Humanism: Reappraisals and Reflections*. Ed. James Hankins. Cambridge: Cambridge University Press, 2000.

Quint, David. "The Debate Between Arms and Letters in the *Gerusalemme Liberata*." In *Sparks and Seeds: Medieval Literature and its Afterlife. Essays in Honor of John Freccero*. Ed. Dana E. Stewart and Alison Cornish. Turnhout, Belgium: Brepols, 2000.

———. *Epic and Empire*. Princeton: Princeton University Press, 1993.

———. *Origin and Originality in Renaissance Literature*. New Haven: Yale University Press, 1983.

Panofsky, Erwin. *Renaissance and Renascences in Western Art*. Stockholm: Almqvist & Wilksell, 1960.

———. *Studies in Iconology: Humanistic Themes in the Art of the Renaissance*. 1939. New York: Icon Editions, 1972.

Parker, Deborah. *Commentary and Ideology: Dante in the Renaissance*. Durham: Duke University Press, 1993.

Payne, Alina. *The Renaissance Architectural Treatise in the Italian Renaissance*. Cambridge: Cambridge University Press, 1999.

Plumb, J.H. *The Italian Renaissance*. New York: Harper & Row, 1961.

Pocock, J.G.A. *The Machiavellian Moment*. Princeton: Princeton University Press, 1975.

Prezzolini, Giuseppe. *Machiavelli*. Trans. Gioconda Savini. New York: Farrar, Straus & Giroux, 1967.

Rabil, Albert, ed. *Renaissance Humanism: Foundations, Forms and Legacy*. 3 vols. Philadelphia: University of Pennsylvania Press, 1991.

Ramsey, P.A., ed. *Rome in the Renaissance: The City and the Myth*. Toronto: MRTS, 1982.

Rebhorn, Wayne A. *Courtly Performances: Masking and Festivity in Castiglione's Book of the Courtier*. Detroit: Wayne State University Press, 1978.

———. *The Emperor of Men's Minds: Literature and the Renaissance Discourse of Rhetoric*. Ithaca: Cornell University Press, 1995.

Richardson, Brian. *Printing, Writers and Readers in Renaissance Italy*. Cambridge: Cambridge University Press, 1999.

Rowland, Ingrid D. *The Culture of the High Renaissance: Ancients and Moderns in Sixteenth-Century Rome*. Cambridge: Cambridge University Press, 1998.

Rosenthal, Margaret F. *The Honest Courtesan: Veronica Franco, Citizen and Writer in Sixteenth-Century Venice*. Chicago: University of Chicago, 1992.

Rubinstein, Nicolai. *The Government of Florence Under the Medici (1434 to 1494)*. Rev. ed. Oxford: Clarendon Press, 1997.

Ruggiero, Guido. *The Boundaries of Eros: Sex Crime and Sexuality in Renaissance Venice*. Oxford: Oxford University Press, 1985.

Schevill, Ferdinand. *The Medici*. New York: Harper & Row, 1949.

Scott, Geoffrey. *The Architecture of Humanism*. New York: W.W. Norton, 1974.

Seigel, Jerrold. *Rhetoric and Philosophy in Renaissance Humanism: the Union of Eloquence and Wisdom, Petrarch to Valla*. Princeton: Princeton University Press 1968.

Shapiro, Marianne. *The Poetics of Ariosto*. Detroit: Wayne State University Press, 1988.

Shaw, Christine. *Julius II: The Warrior Pope*. Oxford: Blackwell, 1993.

Shearman, John. *Mannerism*. 1967. London: Penguin Books, 1990

Skinner, Quentin. *The Foundations of Modern Political Thought*. Vol. 1. Cambridge: Cambridge University Press, 1978.

———, and et al., *The Cambridge History of Renaissance Philosophy*. Cambridge: Cambridge University Press, 1988.

Smart, Alistair. *The Renaissance and Mannerism in Italy*. London: Thames & Hudson, 1971.

Speroni, Charles, ed. *Wit & Wisdom of the Italian Renaissance*. Berkeley: University of California Press, 1964.

Stephens, John. *The Italian Renaissance: The Origins of Intellectual and Artistic Change before the Reformation*. Harlow: Longman, 1990.

Stinger, Charles L. *The Renaissance in Rome*. Bloomington: Indiana University Press, 1998.

Symcox, Geoffrey, ed. *Italian Reports on America, 1493–1522: Letters, Dispatches, and Papal Bulls*. Turnhout, Belgium: Brepols, 2001.

Symonds, J.A. *Renaissance in Italy: The Revival of Learning*. 1877. London: John Murray, 1937.

Syson, Luke, and Dora Thornton. *Objects of Virtue: Art in Renaissance Italy*. Los Angeles: J. Paul Getty Museum, 2001.

Tafuri, Manfredo. Venice and the Renaissance. Trans. Jessica Levine. Cambridge: MIT Press, 1995.

Thompson, David, and Alan F. Nagel, eds. *The Three Crowns of Florence: Humanist Assessments of Dante, Petrarca, and Boccaccio*. New York: Harper & Row, 1972.

Trexler, Richard C. *Public Life in Renaissance Florence*. Ithaca: Cornell University Press, 1980.

Turner, Richard A. *The Vision of Landscape in Renaissance Italy*. Princeton: Princeton University Press, 1966.

Verdon, Timothy, and John Henderson, eds. *Christianity and the Renaissance*. Syracuse: Syracuse University Press, 1990.

Walker, D.P. *Spiritual and Demonic Magic: from Ficino to Campanella*. State College: Pennsylvania State University Press, 2000.

Weinstein, Donald. *Savonarola and Florence*. Princeton: Princeton University Press, 1970.

———and Valerie R. Hotchkiss, eds. *Girolamo Savonarola: Piety, Prophecy, and Politics*. Dallas: Bridwell Library, 1994.

White, Michael. *The Pope and the Heretic*. New York: William Morrow, 2002.

Weiss, Roberto. *Renaissance Discovery of Classical Antiquity*. Oxford: Blackwell, 1969.

Wightman, W.P.D. *Science in a Renaissance Society*. London: Hutchinson & Co., 1972.

Wilcox, Donald J. *The Development of Florentine Humanist Historiography in the Fifteenth Century*. Cambridge: Belknap Press, 1969.

Wilkins, E.H. *Studies in the Life and Works of Petrarch*. Cambridge, Mass.: Medieval Academy of America, 1955.

Wind, Edgar. *The Religious Symbolism of Michelangelo: The Sistine Ceiling*. Oxford: Oxford University Press, 2000.

Witt, Ronald. *Coluccio Salutati and His Public Letters*. Geneva: Librairie Droz, 1976.

Wittkower, Rudolf. *Architectural Principles in the Age of Humanism*. New York: W.W. Norton, 1971.

Woodward, W.H. *Vittorino da Feltre and Other Humanist Educators*. Rept. Toronto: University of Toronto Press, 1996.

Yates, Frances. *Giordano Bruno and the Hermetic Tradition*. Chicago: University of Chicago Press, 1964.

Acknowledgments

"Culture" by Gene A. Brucker. From *Renaissance Florence* by Gene A. Brucker: 213–255. © 1969 by John Wiley & Sons, Inc. supplements © 1983 by the Regents of the University of California. Reprinted by permission.

"Giannotti and Contarini: Venice as Concept and as Myth" by J.G.A. Pocock. From *The Machiavellian Moment: Florentine Political Thought and the Atlantic Republican Tradition* by J.G.A. Pocock: 272–330. © 1975 by Princeton University Press. Reprinted by permission of Princeton University Press.

"Interpretations of the Renaissance" by Eugenio Garin. From *Science and Civic Life in the Italian Renaissance* by Eugenio Garin, translated by Peter Munz: 1–20. © 1969 by Doubleday & Company, Inc. Reprinted by permission.

"Humanism and Scholasticism in the Italian Renaissance" by Paul Oskar Kristeller. From *Renaissance Thought and its Sources* by Paul Oskar Kristeller, edited by Michael Mooney: 85–105. © 1979 by Paul Oskar Kristeller. Reprinted by permission.

"Did Women Have a Renaissance" by Joan Kelly. From *Becoming Visible: Women in European History*, edited by Renate Bridenthal and Claudia Koonz. © 1977 by Hougton Mifflin Company. Used by permission.

"Worldviews: Some Dominant Traits" by Peter Burke. From *The Italian Renaissance: Culture and Society in Italy* by Peter Burke: 181–208. ©

1986, 1999 by Peter Burke. Published by Princeton University Press. Reprinted by permission of Princeton University Press.

"The Italian View of Renaissance Italy" by Denys Hay. From *Renaissance Essays* by Denys Hay: 375–388. © 1988 by Denys Hay. Published by Hambledon Press, 1988. Reprinted by permission.

"Politics and Aesthetics in Castiglione's II Cortegiano: Book III and the Discourse of Women" by Carla Freccero. From *Creative Imitation: New Essays on Renaissance Literature In Honor of Thomas M. Greene*, edited by David Quint, Margaret W. Ferguson, G.W. Pigman III, and Wayne A. Rebhorn, *MRTS* vol. 95 (Binhamton, NY, 1992): 259–279. © 1992 by the Center for Medieval and Early Renaissance Studies, State University of New York at Binghampton.

"*Virtù* and the Example of Agathocles in Machiavelli's *Prince*" by Victoria Kahn. From *Representations* 13 (Winter 1986). © 1986 by the Regents of the University of California. Reprinted by permission.

"From Pen to Print: Writers and Their Use of the Press" by Brian Richardson. From *Printing, Writers and Readers in Renaissance Italy* by Brian Richardson: 77–104. © 1999 by Brian Richardson. Reprinted with the permission of Cambridge University Press.

"Image and Text: The Paragone" by Francis Ames-Lewis. From *The Intellectual Life of the Early Renaissance Artist* by Francis Ames-Lewis: 145–161. © 2000 by Francis Ames-Lewis. Reprinted with the permission of Yale Univesity Press.

"Civic Humanism and Florentine Politics" by John M. Najemy. From *Renaissance Civic Humanism: Reappraisals and Reflections*, edited by James Hankins: 75–104. © 2000 by Cambridge University Press. Reprinted with the permission of Cambridge University Press.

"The Debate Between Arms and Letters in the *Gerusalemme Liberata*" by David Quint. From *Sparks and Seeds: Medieval Literature and Its Afterlife: Essays in Honor of John Freccero*, edited by Dana E. Stewart and Alison Cornish with an Introduction by Guiseppe Mazzotta: 241–266. © 2000 by Brepols. Reprinted by permission.

"The History of the Furioso" by Alberto Casadei. From *Ariosto Today: Contemporary Perspectives*, edited by Donald Beecher, Massimo Ciavolella, and Robert Fedi: 55–70. © 2003 by University of Toronto Press Incorporated. Reprinted by permission.

Index

YA945.05   Italian renaissance
ITALIAN

Wallingford Public Library
Wallingford, CT 06492

A2170 524657 5

WALLINGFORD PUBLIC LIBRARY
WALLINGFORD, CT 06492

DEMCO